Major Problems
in
Mexican American History

MAJOR PROBLEMS IN AMERICAN HISTORY SERIES

GENERAL EDITOR
THOMAS G. PATERSON

Major Problems
in
Mexican American History

DOCUMENTS AND ESSAYS

EDITED BY
ZARAGOSA VARGAS
UNIVERSITY OF CALIFORNIA, SANTA BARBARA

WADSWORTH
CENGAGE Learning

Australia • Brazil • Japan • Korea • Mexico • Singapore • Spain • United Kingdom • United States

WADSWORTH
CENGAGE Learning™

Major Problems in Mexican American History: Documents and Essays
Edited by Zaragosa Vargas

Editor-in-Chief: Jean Woy

Senior Associate Editor: Frances Gay

Senior Project Editor: Kathryn Dinovo

Associate Production/Design Coordinator: Jodi O'Rourke

Assistant Manufacturing Coordinator: Andrea Wagner

Marketing Manager: Sandra McGuire

Cover Design: Sarah Melhado

Cover Image: *Tamalada*, a painting by Carmen Lomas Garza

For product information and technology assistance, contact us at **Cengage Learning Customer & Sales Support, 1-800-354-9706**

For permission to use material from this text or product, submit all requests online at **www.cengage.com/permissions** Further permissions questions can be emailed to **permissionrequest@cengage.com**

Library of Congress Control Number: 98-72090

ISBN-13: 978-0-395-84555-4

ISBN-10: 0-395-84555-6

Wadsworth
20 Davis Drive
Belmont, CA 94002
USA

Cengage Learning is a leading provider of customized learning solutions with office locations around the globe, including Singapore, the United Kingdom, Australia, Mexico, Brazil, and Japan. Locate your local office at **www.cengage.com/global**

Cengage Learning products are represented in Canada by Nelson Education, Ltd.

To learn more about Wadsworth, visit **www.cengage.com/wadsworth**

Purchase any of our products at your local college store or at our preferred online store **www.cengagebrain.com**

Printed in the United States of America
3 4 5 6 7   19 18 17 16 15

To Zaneta

Contents

Preface

Nearly two-thirds of Latinos in the United States are of Mexican descent, or Chicanos*—a term of self-definition that emerged during the 1960s and early 1970s civil rights movement. Chicanos reside mainly in the Southwest, the Pacific Northwest, and the Midwest. Their history begins in the precolonial Spanish era, and they share a rich mestizo cultural heritage of Spanish, Indian, and African origins. The Chicanos' past is underscored by conquest of the present-day American Southwest first by the Spanish and then by the United States following the Mexican American War.

Constant migration from Mexico facilitated by United States immigration policy is also part of this chronicle. The story is laced with both triumph and travail. The voluntary and forced repatriations and deportations of Mexicans and Mexican Americans during the Great Depression and in the mid-1950s, and the current anti-immigrant prejudice that has sparked violations of the rights of Mexican immigrants and of Chicano citizens alike, are examples of tragedy. Notwithstanding their diverse political, social, and cultural backgrounds, the majority of Chicanos have become united through their relation to American society as a racial and ethnic minority group. As this book illustrates, racial discrimination and nativism have been persistent obstacles for Chicanos throughout their history in the United States. At the same time, the struggle of Chicanos to gain equal rights and full participation as citizens in American society has provided an ennobling experience.

Major Problems in Mexican American History documents the presence of the largest Spanish-speaking Latino subgroup in the United States while it marks its contributions to the nation's life. The primary aim of this volume is to illustrate the Chicano experience from as many vantage points as possible, and with as many Chicano views as possible. The documents and essays gathered here invite readers to see Chicanos in their everyday life and in their organizational life. Other themes include the interactions among Chicanos, Native Americans, and European Americans involved in the forging of the early Chicano experience; the challenges of settlement of the American Southwest and the Chicano response to American westward expansion; the particularities of the Chicano family, community formation, and the role of Chicana women; migration from Mexico and relations with the United States government; and the persistence and flexibility of Chicano ethnic identity and of sustaining a sense of community.

---

*In this book I use *Mexican, Texas Mexican, Mexican American,* and *Chicano* as terms of self and group reference. In the chapters covering the twentieth century, *Mexican American* and *Chicano* emphasize United States citizenship, while the term *Mexican* refers to both Mexican nationals and Mexican Americans.

Major Problems in Mexican American History follows the general format of other volumes in the series. Each chapter addresses a central issue in the subject area. Chapter 1 is a general opening and presents different approaches to the study of Chicano history. A brief introduction begins each chapter to help set questions and provide context. Headnotes introduce the documents, identifying key issues concerning the experience and feelings of the Chicano men and women. The balance of documentary selections was determined by the accessibility of materials in English. Many early period documents were in the original Spanish language and form part of collected translations produced by scholars and specialists in the respective fields. Some documents are given in full while others have been excerpted without changing their meaning. Organized chronologically and varying thematically, the documents include letters, diaries, speeches, manifestos, political platforms, songs, journals, newspaper editorials, magazine articles, and congressional debates. The documents proceed from the history of Chicanos in the United States in the precolonial Spanish era, to the early Mexican settlements in Texas, New Mexico, and California, through the history of Chicanos in the Southwest and Midwest to the present.

The essays in each chapter by specialists in the field offer a variety of perspectives. Like the documents, the essays are intended to provoke discussion. Each chapter's group of essays is introduced by a headnote that situates the readings in historical perspective. The purpose is to stimulate critical thinking and appreciation of the subject by encouraging readers to judge the evidence presented, evaluate the different interpretations, and form their own conclusions. At the end of each chapter is a Further Reading section comprised of books and articles so that students can read more about the richness and diversity of Chicano history.

I would like to thank the editors, colleagues, and students who provided me gracious and indispensable assistance with this book project. I want to thank Professor Thomas G. Paterson, general editor of the Major Problems in American History series, for extending me an invitation to compile this book and for providing valuable insights and suggestions. I want to acknowledge the help and guidance provided by Frances Gay, senior associate editor, at each stage of the book's development, and Kathryn Dinovo, senior project editor, who supervised the book's production. I appreciate the help of the following colleagues who provided syllabi and important advice: John R. Chávez at Southern Methodist University, Erasmo Gamboa at the University of Washington, Matthew García at the University of Illinois, Gabriel Gutiérrez at Loyola Marymount University, Lorena Oropeza at the University of California, Davis, and Francisco A. Rosales at Arizona State University. I am also grateful to the following reviewers who provided extremely helpful comments on the contents: Albert Camarillo at Stanford University, Sarah Deutsch at Clark University, Richard Griswold del Castillo at San Diego State University, and Susan M. Yohn at Hofstra University. For their suggestions, encouragement, and friendship I would also like to extend a warm thanks to my colleagues Luis L. Arroyo at California State University, Long Beach, Neal Foley at the University of Texas, Austin, Deena J. Gonzáles at Pomona College, Margaret Rose at the University of California, Santa Barbara, and Vicki L. Ruiz at Arizona State University. At the University of California at Santa Barbara, I would like to thank Patrick

Dawson and Raquel Quiroz-González for their assistance in acquiring documents. I continue to learn from my undergraduate students how to teach Chicano history. Alberto Herrera gave timely assistance to my research efforts, helping locate some of the documents that appear in this book. Christine Marín at Arizona State University also helped me locate documents that appear in this book. Finally, I dedicate this volume to Zaneta Kosiba-Vargas, my wife and best friend and an excellent teacher and scholar.

Z.V.

Major Problems
in
Mexican American History

Interpreting the Chicano Past

Mexican Americans are a large and fast-growing ethnic group within the United States, and they have a long and rich heritage that dates back to precolonial Spanish days. Until relatively recently the history of Latinos of Mexican descent in the United States had not been well developed as a separate field of study, but during the civil rights movement of the 1960s and 1970s Mexican Americans became more conscious of their own group identity. During this time Chicano became a popular term to express their heightened sense of self and group identity. The term Chicano encouraged Mexican Americans to take increased pride and interest in their history of struggle in America. Chicano historians are beginning to provide a framework for understanding the Chicano experience. Influenced by methods adopted from other disciplines, the new studies by Chicano historians are bringing other perspectives to issues, raising different questions, and leading to a better understanding of the Chicano people.

Through the introduction of new methods and concepts, Chicano scholars are providing unique historical insight on Chicanos. These fascinating and richly textured studies reveal that Chicanos, both men and women, have been active agents in their individual histories. Other research focuses on exploring the processes by which Mexican immigrants became Chicanos as well as examining the political tradition of the Chicano community. Chicano and Chicana historians are making important contributions to the growing body of research on gender and on the social construction of race in the United States. The latter work is of special value to historians interested in the social and cultural history of the multiracial Southwest as well as to scholars engaged in the current debate over racial identity formation. Insights are being provided into how such categories as race, class, and gender have intersected.

More important, Chicano historians relate these histories to other events and issues that confront the larger American society. The many dimensions of Chicano history, much of which remains unexplored, illustrate that along with common differences of race, ethnicity, and gender, there are also common patterns of historical experience. What is the focus of the essays in this chapter? How do they provide insight into new directions of historical research by Chicano/a historians? Is Chicano history an ongoing process of historical revision of scholarly work?

In developing alternative approaches to interpreting Chicano history, Chicano scholars agree that a complex intersection of racial and class oppression underlines the Chicano experience. Chicana historians have added gender to their scholarship, and the issues of ethnicity and identity are likewise a focus of historical study.

In the first essay, Gilbert G. González and Raúl Fernández, both professors of comparative culture at the University of California, Irvine, note that much of Chicano historiography uses cultural conflict and racism as models for historical explanation. According to González and Fernández, two other themes in Chicano historiography are the significance of the events of the nineteenth century and urban history. The weaknesses of these paradigms are elaborated on by the authors, who instead posit that economic factors, Chicano rural experiences, and a comparative approach are pertinent to Chicano history.

The general shift in Chicano history has been from the "them-versus-us" essentialism to an emphasis on agency. Alex M. Saragoza, an associate professor of Chicano Studies at the University of California, Berkeley, highlights key historical sources in the field. Saragoza states that Chicano history must be reevaluated in light of the diversity of the Chicano experience as well as the ongoing changes in the larger field of American history, particularly social history. He calls for historical writing on Chicanos that illuminates particularly the post-Depression era, Chicano self-identification, and the impacts of immigration from Mexico.

The significance of Chicano history to the larger history of the American West is the subject of the last essay by prize-winning historian David G. Gutiérrez, associate professor of history at the University of California, San Diego. Gutiérrez describes how the early historical interpretations of Chicanos, linked to the nineteenth-century ideology of American expansionism and romantic myth-making, were made at the expense of Chicanos. Gutiérrez next traces the efforts of Chicano scholars to represent Chicano history accurately by dispelling stereotypes of Mexicans. He focuses on the scholarship of George I. Sánchez and of the generation of scholars who emerged from the Chicano movement. The author concludes that Chicano historical scholarship has recently undergone a significant transformation through the use of interdisciplinary methods that examine questions of power and knowledge.

Alternative Approaches to Chicano History

GILBERT G. GONZÁLEZ AND RAÚL FERNÁNDEZ

Much Chicano historiography has built upon cultural and culture-conflict models focusing on race and nationality as the basis for social relations and, ultimately, for historical explanation. Clearly, in the post-1848 years in the newly acquired southwestern frontier, Anglo settlers frequently treated the Hispanic population much like they dealt with the native Indian population: as people without rights who were merely obstacles to the acquisition and exploitation of natural resources and land. And, to be sure, the violence of the conquerors was often met with the resistance of the conquered. But these cultural struggles and racial conflicts have be-

"Chicano History: Transcending Cultural Models" by Gilbert G. González and Raúl Fernández, *Pacific Historical Review* 63, no. 4 (November 1994): 469–497. Copyright © 1994 by American Historical Association, Pacific Coast Branch. Reprinted by permission.

come for many Chicano historians the principal basis for understanding Chicano history.

Culture-based explanations tend to minimize the role of economic factors, which are crucial in shaping social and cultural forms and very useful in drawing regional comparisons. Innovative scholarship by Rosalinda González, David Montejano, and Douglas Monroy moves away from culture-based models and toward an emphasis on economic power and processes. The goal here is to advance and elaborate on some of these ideas about socioeconomic forms in a more systematic manner.

We begin by critically analyzing approaches that describe the history of Chicano-Anglo relations as a story of cultural conflict and racism. . . . We seek to emphasize the *systemic* roots of conflict between pre-1848 Spanish-Mexican society and post-1848 Anglo-imposed social economy. . . .

Historians who subscribe to the culture-based paradigm ground their perspectives in particular characterizations of pre-Anglo Spanish and subsequent Mexican societies in the Southwest. Some . . . describe those societies as pastoral, communal, peasant, traditional, frontier, or hacienda. Other historians who place more emphasis on economic factors . . . characterize this era as "early capitalist." All, however, agree that Anglo-American society is capitalist and all use their own characterizations of the period as points of departure for their inquiries. . . .

If the period that began in 1848 is viewed as one in which two distinct socioeconomic formations, one largely precapitalist and quasifeudal and the other predominantly capitalist, collide, the situation looks akin to the North-South conflict in the eastern United States. More than just a "rough and tumble," racially conscious Anglo society conquering and subduing quaint Mexican pastoralists, the conquest can be viewed also as one step in the economic . . . transformation of the United States from east to west. In other words, . . . the Anglo conquest was also a capitalist conquest. Economic change took place on a par with cultural transformation.

. . . A perspective grounded in economic power and processes can also be applied to two other themes in Chicano history. The first is the significance of the nineteenth century for Chicano historiography. Some scholars . . . find the Anglo conquest of 1848 and the ensuing Spanish, Mexican, and Anglo conflict to be a historical watershed that initiated a continuous nineteenth- and twentieth-century Chicano experience. . . . The second theme . . . is an emphasis on a common Chicano urban experience. Chicanos have been predominantly urban dwellers only since the 1940s, but scholars too often disregard the origins of socioeconomic structures that underlie the contemporary urban experience. . . .

The Character of Southwestern Spanish and Mexican Society

The transition from Spanish and Mexican rule to U.S. governance in the nineteenth century is critical to Chicano historiography. Most Chicano history scholars argue that the evolving relations between the Spanish-speaking and English-speaking peoples in the post-1848 era can be understood by studying the particular characteristics of these peoples, but they disagree about the characteristics themselves. Two definitions of Spanish/Mexican society have been offered most often. Albert

Camarillo provides a succinct example of the first: "Once the subdivision of rancho and public lands had begun, the dominance of the emerging economic system of American capitalism in the once-Mexican region was a foregone conclusion. The process of land loss and displacement of the Mexican *pastoral economy* was fairly complete throughout the Southwest by the 1880s." In a second view, which also emphasizes economic elements, Spanish/Mexican societies are seen as "early capitalist." Juan Gómez-Quiñones contends, for example, that the essence of Mexican society was an emerging capitalist order, a transition away from a formal, feudal social order. . . .

Historians utilizing the first approach characterize Spanish/Mexican society less specifically than Anglo-American society. Vague terms—for example, traditional or pastoral—define the former; a more analytic one—namely, capitalism—the latter. The invading society is distinctly described as capitalist in economy, culture, institutions, and behavior. We would expect it either to conflict with opposing social forms or to merge with similar ones. However, the existing categorizations describe Spanish/Mexican society without regard to specific economic structure. We cannot examine a conflict between a society whose economy remains vaguely described (pastoral or traditional) and one with a specifically described (capitalist) economy. . . .

Historians using the second approach . . . cite as evidence the existence of wage labor and the "capitalist" character of the hacienda or rancho. The problem with this evidence is that it is not altogether convincing. Several studies, for example, demonstrate the widespread presence of debt-peonage, hardly the stuff of free labor. Gilberto Hinojosa's study of Laredo, Texas, reveals that "the indebted poor fled Laredo rather than submit to a peonage system which amounted to slavery. The frequency of calls for assistance in returning runaways suggests both the widespread use of peonage and the extensive escape from it." Conversely, solid documentation for the prevalence of wage labor does not appear in the relevant literature. There is, for example, no entry for "wage labor" in the index of David J. Weber's *Mexican Frontier,* the most thorough study of the 1821–1848 period.

The descriptions of life in the Southwest prior to the Anglo conquest strongly suggest precapitalist . . . relations. California Indians, working as servants or laborers, were greatly exploited by the landowners and lived at the bottom of the class hierarchy. New Mexico consisted primarily of . . . farming communities in which poverty-stricken subsistence villagers were forced into sharecropping and servitude by . . . the dominant economic, political, and social actors. . . .

The idea that a Mexican "working class" existed before 1848 may arise from the appearance of monetary compensation for labor services. However, the existence of money payment does not, in itself, create a capitalist, free wage-labor system. . . .

. . . Generally, ranches and villages in California, New Mexico, and Texas provided for most of the needs of the residents, both laborers and landowners. They functioned largely as self-subsistence units. Although some of the products of the hacienda—primarily hides and tallow and, later, livestock—were exported, landholders used the proceeds to satisfy their taste for luxury, not to accumulate capital. In New Mexico, small landowners and communal village farmers performed their own labor, had no servants, and often sharecropped for the larger owners.

Within the large, small, and communal landholding system, labor remained relatively unspecialized. On the large landholdings, owners extracted wealth through the labor of their *peones*; in the communal villages, families eked out a marginal existence by their own labor and generally relied on payment in kind for labor services outside the village. . . .

. . . Admittedly, every work in Chicano history cannot be wholly arranged into our scheme. A very important example is Ramón Gutiérrez's award-winning work on Spanish-Pueblo and gender relations in colonial New Mexico which we cannot neatly place in the two groups above. While Gutiérrez mentions the prevalence and, in fact, the increase of servile forms of labor in New Mexico towards the end of the eighteenth century, he focuses on gender systems and sexual practices as indicative of relations of domination and key to the construction, mediation, and defense of cultural identity. In his view, the Hispano-Anglo conflict can be seen primarily as a form of culture clash that can be explained without significant reference to systemic economic conflict.

We now turn to drawing on currents present in some of these works to suggest what we think would be a stronger analytic framework for examining Chicano economic and social history.

On Relationships of Production

. . . The social heritage of the southwestern Spanish/Mexican era derived from hierarchical and inherited class relations characteristic of the Spanish social order. This is not to say, however, that the pre-1848 New World social formations replicated Spanish social relations exactly and had no history of their own. The New World manifested numerous variations due to climate, topography, demography, and so forth. . . .

After the conquest of New Mexico, first the *encomiendas* and later the *repartimientos* formed the basis of colonial production. . . . Through the encomiendas, the Pueblo villages contributed an annual tribute in kind to the leading colonists, usually consisting of maize and cotton blankets. In New Mexico, the tribute accruing from the encomienda did not amount to much. The repartimiento—or apportionment of coerced labor required from the Indian population living near an encomienda—was utilized to the fullest extent by the settlers living on ranches.

. . . California missionaries confronted a different situation than those in New Mexico. In New Mexico, as in large parts of Mexico and South America, the Indian population was concentrated in relatively large native towns and villages where the missionaries took the faith to the residents. In California, where the Indians were scattered in hundreds of small hamlets, the Spaniards brought many of them into specially created mission settlements and, despite some examples of "benevolence," subjected them to forced labor that resembled slavery in all but name. That system came to an end in the 1830s with secularization and the rapid transformation of mission and other lands into privately held ranchos. The size and number of these ranchos and the social relations they engendered predominated for several decades. . . . Although there were exports of hides and tallow, those exports satisfied the luxury needs of the rancheros. . . .

The absence of capitalism is also apparent in Arizona and Texas. Arizona was settled as early as 1696, when Father Eusebio Kino founded a number of missions . . . near present-day Tucson. By the end of his work, around 1712, twenty-five years of quiet were shattered by the discovery of silver in Arizona. After this brief mining boom, Arizona's economy was dominated by livestock production at the missions and the few haciendas. From the mid-eighteenth century onward, warring Indians made maintenance of this frontier next to impossible. With Mexican independence and the disappearance of the presidios, the area was abandoned from 1822 to 1862.

The case of Texas was at once different and similar. The settlements were small and dispersed mostly around San Antonio, La Bahia, and Nacogdoches. The recent work by Gerald Poyo and Gilberto Hinojosa . . . provides what seems like a check list for the lack of capitalist characteristics: absence of laborers, lack of markets for products, backward agricultural technology, and local "elites" concentrating on raising cattle in an extensive manner, much like the Californios. . . . The population of Texas barely reached 4,000 at the end of the eighteenth century. In the lower Rio Grande Valley (where the way of life was quite similar to that of early California), a "few large Mexican landowners lived an idle and lordly existence based on a system of peonage." Already by 1830, Anglo-Americans outnumbered Mexicans by ten to one. They included some farmers, the harbingers of a new social system; many held slaves, planted cotton, and sold it. In Texas, then, two sets of relations—precapitalist and slavery—existed side-by-side.

On Relations of Exchange

Commodity production—that is, organized production of goods for sale in the marketplace . . . —was nearly absent in the Mexican Southwest. To be sure, there were trade contacts with the outside. Despite centuries of isolation, the Spanish/ Mexican Southwest maintained an array of commercial ties with surrounding economies, but this trade cannot be considered capitalistic. . . .

. . . The intensification of commerce in the Southwest from 1831 to 1848 was not conducive to the development of local industry and manufacturing or to the growth of towns and handicraft industries. . . . Much of the revenue gained through trade was used to purchase luxury goods, manufactured items, and land. Consequently, the influx of revenue had little appreciable impact on the redistribution of land, division of labor, and technology in production. In fact, during the Mexican era, when trade expanded in New Mexico and California, class distinctions hardened, large land grants multiplied, and peonage increased. Moreover, by 1846, foreigners dominated in artisan production. . . .

Periodization: The Key in the Nineteenth Century?

. . . The notion that Chicano history begins with the conquest of 1848 is a common thread running through a majority of works in Chicano history. Moreover, Chicano historians nearly unanimously emphasize a continuity of Chicano history from that point to the present, with cultural conflict between Anglos and Mexicans being the explanatory center of the discourse. Typically these same historians apply concepts that inadequately identify significant differences between nineteenth- and twentieth-century Chicano history, just as they tend to leave vague the nature of the economic conflict between conqueror and conquered in the mid-nineteenth century. On the other hand, a shared "cultural" trait—for example, being Spanish-surnamed or Spanish-speaking—provides prima facie evidence for continuity between the nineteenth and twentieth centuries.

The conquest of 1848 appears to be the key event that subordinated Mexicans and thus represents the beginning of Chicanos as a discrete population in the United States. . . . Later immigrants entered a society that had institutionalized the separate and subordinated status of Mexicans. This view is most clearly advanced by Albert Camarillo: "The history of the Chicano people as an ethnic minority in the United States was forged primarily from a set of nineteenth-century experiences." "The key to reconstructing the history of Chicano society in Southern California," he continues, "is understanding the major developments of the half-century after the Mexican War. . . . In sum, the nineteenth- and twentieth-century Chicano experience seems fundamentally more continuous than discontinuous. The "importance of the nineteenth century for understanding the twentieth-century Chicano experience" has emerged as "self-evident to historians," according to David J. Weber. We question that assumption. The argument can be made for northern New Mexico, where twentieth-century Mexican immigration played a less significant role, and it may perhaps be extended to other subregions, but not persuasively to the region as a whole. . . .

The conventional view that the contemporary Chicano experience derives from social relations established after the 1848 conquest and that the nineteenth century is thus "key" to understanding Chicano history rests upon the assumption that today's Chicanos share certain characteristics with those of the past: possessors of a distinct culture and victims of racial prejudice that has led to life in segregated barrios, stereotyped behavior, violence, and subordinate social and occupational status. . . . Thus, the Chicanos' "conquered" legacy distinguishes them from other minorities such as the Chinese and Japanese . . . and parallels the involuntary origins of African-Americans and American Indians.

If one focuses on issues of economic development, however, important differences emerge between the nineteenth and twentieth centuries. Our examination of the record suggests the existence of two separate epochs and populations in the history of Spanish-speakers in the Southwest. . . . Of primary importance is the fact that, with the exception of New Mexico and southern Colorado, the small number of Mexicans annexed as a result of the conquest was inconsequential when compared to the much larger number of late nineteenth- and twentieth-century Mexican migrants to the region. Second, the parallels between the nineteenth-century Chicano experience and the experiences of other nonwhite minorities are striking. Mexicans suffered segregation, violence (such as lynching), and exploitation, but so too did the "non-conquered" Chinese, Japanese, Filipinos, and Asian Indians, among others. Third, the massive economic transformations of the Southwest created a great demand for cheap, unskilled labor, which was met by unprecedented migration from Mexico beginning around the turn of the century.

Certainly, the pattern of regional development in the United States greatly affected Chicano history. The growth of southern California in particular became intimately related with demographic shifts in the Chicano population. The extraordinary development of the western half of the Southwest region—a result of mass migration—came with the growth of California agriculture and southern California industry, both of which would have been impossible without massive water projects. Carey McWilliams noted economist Paul S. Taylor's trenchant 1927 observation: "Irrigation equals Mexicans." Additionally, the recent regional development of the Southwest has depended on massive east-to-west U.S. migration and on migrants from Asia, many of whom shared a common experience with those Mexican immigrants laboring for agribusiness.

There were frequent violent struggles between precapitalist Mexican and capitalist Anglo societies after 1848, but by 1900 they had faded as a new, integrated economic order arose. The 15,000 Mexican citizens living outside of New Mexico at the time of the conquest either accommodated to the new society or were overwhelmed by Mexican migrants. The conquered group lacked sufficient numbers to have a significant impact in the Anglo era. Moreover, once they had lost their lands by the late nineteenth century, they suffered further significant cultural disintegration. Except in New Mexico and southern Colorado, Mexican migrants introduced a completely new period in the history of the Spanish-speaking people in the Southwest, including Texas where the break with Mexico had come earlier in 1836.

Migration in the twentieth century altered the character of the southwestern Mexican community. By the 1920s, the Spanish-speaking population had grown dramatically, older settlements had expanded and many new ones had appeared, and Mexican labor had become of fundamental importance in economic development. There were other changes as well. Earlier Anglo-Mexican social relations had turned on the conflict between two distinct socioeconomic formations, while twentieth-century social relations centered upon the internal class conflicts inherent to corporate capitalism. The economic issues affecting Anglo-Mexican social relations had shifted from conflicting systems of production to class relations within the same system. Likewise, the political conflicts shifted from land issues in the nineteenth century to working-class concerns in the twentieth. . . . These conflictive relations are expressed in the racial and ethnic dimensions of the contemporary Southwest. The Mexican community, as we know it today, developed in this new atmosphere of corporate capitalism, a twentieth-century phenomenon. . . .

The Urban Emphasis: A Reappraisal

Besides calling for a rethinking of the periodization of Chicano history, we also suggest a reappraisal of the emphasis on the urban experiences of Chicanos. In a review of three major books in Chicano history by Albert Camarillo, Mario García, and Richard Griswold del Castillo, David J. Weber notes that "all three try to link their work to the mainstream of social and urban history while still focusing on the particularity of the Mexican American experience." Moreover, these scholars have "established the importance of the city as the crucible of change in Chicano society and culture, and have provided a valuable corrective to the notion of Chicanos as an essentially rural people. Ricardo Romo, while acknowledging that "Chicanos have not always lived in urban areas," nonetheless contends that "since 1609, at least, when their Spanish-Mexican ancestors founded the pueblo of Santa Fe, they have contributed to and have been a part of the urbanization process in the Southwest." Griswold del Castillo concurs, adding that "[d]uring Spanish colonial times probably a larger proportion of the region's population lived in pueblos, towns, and cities than did the population in other areas of the United States." Thus, historians have tended to view Chicano history since the Spanish era as a branch of urban history. An immediate problem with this view is that it labels as "urban" even small population centers, such as Tucson in 1850. Such practice blurs the distinction between "urban" and "rural" to the point where it virtually disappears.

Another consideration here is that pre-1848 southwestern towns and pueblos can hardly be classed with contemporary industrial urban centers on the East Coast, . . . because precapitalist population centers differ significantly from cities and towns in a capitalistic social economy. Moreover, fully seventy percent of the southwestern population lived in rural areas at the turn of the century. It is doubtful that Chicanos were more urbanized at that time than the general population. As late as the 1930s, urban Chicanos made up only half of the Chicano population. . . .

As a consequence of the emphasis upon so-called "urban" life, Chicano historiography has focused primarily on industrial, blue-collar labor and neglected rural and semiurban Chicano communities like the citrus picker villages of southern California. Carey McWilliams, one of the few historians to recognize the rural character of such communities, has observed: "This citrus belt complex of peoples, institutions, and relationships has no parallel in rural life in America and nothing quite like it exists elsewhere in California. It is neither town nor country, neither rural nor urban. It is a world of its own."

Attention to the economic developments that engendered these communities would reveal, especially by the early 1900s when commodity production in large-scale agriculture, mining, and transportation was assuming economic predominance, a variety of community forms shaped by the industries that fostered them. Labor camps reflected the needs of railroad, mining, agricultural, stock-raising, lumbering, and other industrial enterprises. For example, Arizona mining towns, which employed considerable Mexican labor beginning in the late nineteenth century, differed in character from sharecropping communities of Texas, and from cities with a large commercial/industrial character like Los Angeles. Many communities existed only briefly, disappearing when a mine was exhausted, a track completed, or orchards subdivided. The Mexican community, affected by the demand for its labor power, settled according to the pattern of economic activity.

Rural citrus communities in southern California, as revealed in recent research by Gilbert G. González, tended to be permanent, remaining as barrios today in spite of the suburban sprawl that has engulfed them. . . . Thus, some labor camps were clearly defined, permanent, stable, and well-structured Mexican villages. Such camps existed not only in the southern California citrus belt, but also in migrant agricultural areas (especially in sugar beet fields), and in mining, railroad, and construction regions as well. On the other hand, those camps consisting of laborers under the contract system, which structured family labor in agriculture, were transitory and labor was unorganized (except in beet work).

Some camps were essentially company towns, owing their existence to a single company or grower association. *Colonias,* or barrios, in the copper towns of

Arizona, the Goodyear cotton-town of Litchfield, Arizona, the beet-fields of California and Colorado, the steel mills of Indiana, and the citrus-grower association camps of southern California were part of a larger pattern of company towns in the West, the Midwest, and the South. There were significant variations among these communities. For example, the sugar beet company towns in Ventura County, California, had a decidedly different atmosphere than the towns of the South Platte Valley, Colorado. Even within southern California, the citrus company towns varied, some experiencing heavy-handed paternalistic intervention into daily life, others a hands-off policy by growers, and still others something in between.

The great variety among camps led to significant differences in gender and family relations. For example, employment and/or educational opportunities available to women and children varied with the organization of labor in particular enterprises. These, in turn, affected family, culture, and, ultimately, community. In the regions where family labor was widespread, the independence of women as economic actors was sharply curtailed in comparison to their urban counterparts. Where family labor was largely absent, as in the citrus industry, it was because such labor was of little significance in maintaining production. In the citrus industry, this permitted women to be widely employed in the packinghouses where they earned wages equal to those of their male counterparts, the pickers. This distinguished female employment in citrus from that of migrant family labor in such activities as cotton production. Women packers developed a sense of self-worth based upon their individual labor and talents that was all but impossible for women who worked as part of a family unit. In the latter system, the male head of household nearly always received the wages directly from the employer or labor contractor. Thus, women engaged in family cotton picking rarely received individual compensation for their labor. This pattern decidedly affected gender relations. . . .

Educational opportunities also varied among the communities. In urban settings they were much greater than in the rural migrant settlements. Rural migrants were far less likely to attend school, or if attending at all, to attend only a portion of the school year. Statistics for Texas in 1945 indicate that only half of the Mexican children were enrolled in school. In part, this was due to a deliberate policy by boards of education to bar Mexican children, especially migrant children, from enrolling in school. In citrus towns, however, opportunities for education were greater due to the absence of family labor, and they were greater still in urban areas where fewer families were engaged in migratory work.

Differences between rural and urban communities can also be detected in other areas, including the civil rights activities of the 1940s and as recently as the 1970s. César Chávez, for example, left the Community Service Organization in the mid-1950s because the latter focused upon urban issues. Chávez had dedicated himself to resolving the problems of rural Mexican communities, a decision with far-reaching and well-known effects on the history of farmworker unions and California agriculture. That urban and rural settlements differ is further underscored by their contrasting emphases on school reform during the 1960s and 1970s. Rural activists generally demanded integration, while urban activists turned toward separatism, community control of neighborhood schools, and bilingual education.

Fortunately, the urban emphasis in Chicano historiography may be waning. For example, Sarah Deutsch's analysis of the transition from rural to urban life,

Vicki Ruiz's incorporation of gender issues in her examination of women's organizations in the agriculture-based food-processing industry, Richard Griswold del Castillo and Richard García's . . . biographical study of César Chávez, Robert Alvarez's study of Baja California migrating families, and Arnoldo De León's several works demonstrate that some communities do not fall into the urban pattern emphasized in the earlier literature. Still, much remains to be done before we will have an adequate understanding of the complexity and enduring significance of Chicano community life.

We hope that the preceding pages have caused readers to think more deeply about the conventional wisdom that passes for much of Chicano history. Close attention to economic transformations questions the standard periodization of Chicano history and suggests that the nineteenth- and twentieth-century Spanish-speaking populations of the Southwest should be viewed as largely two different populations. And even within those populations, the nature of economic development has produced communities that vary significantly. Behind our approach lies the conviction that culture and economic life should not be kept in separate historical compartments. Moreover, our findings suggest that Chicano history should be viewed as something more than the distinct experience and contribution of one particular regional, ethnic group. Perhaps Chicano historians will also find value in the work of those southern historians who focus on capitalist development as a way of integrating the history of the South into the history of the entire nation. Chicano scholars might then take the first step in demonstrating that Chicano history is an integral component of American history. They might also be encouraged to advance efforts toward a multicultural history by distilling the common as well as the different experiences of cultural, ethnic, and gender groups. To paraphrase Cornell West, keen attention to economic structures can assist historians to contextualize cultural history.

Recent Approaches to Chicano History

ALEX M. SARAGOZA

Introduction

The intent of this essay is to assess Chicano historiography over the last decade as a means of interpreting the Chicano past. . . . I . . . argue that past formulations of Chicano historical experiences have been inadequate and require a critical reevaluation. . . . The conceptual moorings of Chicano history have been affected by recent shifts and debates in the broader field of American history, particularly the area of social history. Combined with other factors, this . . . holds important consequences for Chicano historiography and its direction. . . .

"Recent Chicano Historiography: An Interpretive Essay" by Alex M. Saragoza, *Aztlán* 19, no. 1 (Spring 1988–1990): 1–52. Reprinted by permission.

. . . Basic questions of interpretation, analysis, and methodology continue to vex students of the Chicano past. In this light, Chicano history . . . confronts an important . . . point in its development. This turn in Chicano historical writing consists of several elements, and they merit brief mention.

The first issue is generally underestimated: the very small number of new scholars entering the field. . . . The motivation of a group of academics in the wake of the Chicano movement of the 1960s contributed importantly to the conceptual origins and early production of Chicano history. With relatively few exceptions, . . . the overwhelming majority of Chicano graduate students in the last decade have avoided academic careers generally, and specifically in history.

. . . Furthermore, . . . with notable exceptions, . . . non-Chicano historians have generally not entered the field. Hence, even a cursory review of published articles and books on Chicano history finds sparse results. . . .

Second, it is clear that the place of Chicano history in the profession continues to be neglected. . . . The relative insignificance of Chicanos as subjects in the writing of American history raises several questions, and the issue is not related simply to professional visibility, or to the number of titles of books and articles on Chicanos in the bibliographies of standard United States history texts. . . . Chicanos and other peoples of color continue to be subordinated to and/or subsumed in the historical trajectory of Blacks. Questions of race, ethnicity, and even class and gender in American history remain often bounded by references to Blacks. The history of African Americans continues to be the essential reference point in the acknowledgment of race in United States history. Only a casual glance at the textbook indices or tables of contents and survey materials is necessary to underscore the point. . . .

Third, intrinsic to this problem was the propensity of social history . . . to focus its interpretive lens on geographic areas other than the West. Thus, many of the main currents of American historical writing, especially those spawned by the "new social history," essentially left out Chicanos. . . . Given the bias . . . of practitioners of the new social history to locate their research in the East or Midwest, Chicano were subsumed in the application of ideas and concepts generated by research on Blacks or European immigrants, or both. . . .

The combination of the scarcity of Chicano historians, the relative unimportance accorded to Chicanos in United States history, and the tendency of the "new history" to slight the West has made the field of Chicano history largely dependent . . . on the interpretive aspects that undergirded the spate of books that appeared roughly from 1979 to 1984. . . . That initial generation of "Chicano" historical works reflected to a large extent the reigning questions of . . . the "new social history." . . . The debates and discussion engendered by the approach of the "new historians" resonated in the writing of Chicano scholars and their interpretive outlook. The monographs on Chicanos that began to appear in the 1970s marked a sharpening of the debate over interpretation among Chicano scholars. . . .

Central to this debate is the issue of labor, or workers, of the so-called new labor history, perhaps the most vibrant subfield encompassed by the new social history. . . . Understandably, such a view engendered a perspective amenable to "Chicano" history as opposed to the history of working-class Chicanos. Or, as I will discuss below, the new social history facilitated a "them-versus-us" notion of the Chicano past.

Such an approach is no longer tenable. . . .

. . . The assumptions of Chicano history, particularly the tendency to suggest a collective experience, require rethinking. . . . Class tensions and social rifts have marked the history of people of Mexican origin from the beginning. . . . If American racism lessened such differences among Chicanos, it did not erase them. A sense of nationalism or group grievance may have attenuated class distinctions, but class cleavages endured. The implications of a basic bifurcation within the "Chicano community" over time clearly undermine the initial premises of Chicano historiography.

In this respect, the issue of gender also challenges the notion of a collective experience as a core element in the interpretation of the history of Chicanos. . . . The incorporation of gender suggests more than mentioning Chicanas, regardless of the criteria. . . . Gender implies a major challenge to the writing of Chicano history. . . .

. . . Recent Chicano historical scholarship represents a departure from the conceptual origins of the field. . . . Recent works point to the fundamental diversity and complexity of the Chicano experience. . . . Students of Chicano history have illuminated . . . the sources of differentiation within the Chicano community, past and present. More important, recent research confirms that issues of class, as well as race, represent critical factors in the interpretation of Chicano history. And . . . gender questions clearly form a crucial dimension for the conceptualization of the Chicano past.

Them-versus-Us History

. . . During the 1970s, the conjunction of the civil rights movement and fresh trends in American historiography, particularly the rise of the "new social history," moved historians to depict the evolution of American society "from the bottom up." . . . The intellectual roots of Chicano history were nourished by the profession's enthusiasm for labor, urban, family, and related historical fields that fell under the rubric of social history. Furthermore, the orientation of the practitioners of the new social history tended to be revisionist, critical of previous treatments of minorities, workers, and women.

This view within the profession facilitated . . . the emergence of Chicano history and its intrinsic disapproval of an assimilationist perspective on ethnic/race relations in American history. . . . The nationalist currents among various minority groups paralleled the development of the new social history. . . .

This nationalistic bent formed an essential element in the underpinnings of much Chicano scholarship through the 1970s. The concept of racial conflict, or racism, complemented this premise and prompted a generalized acceptance of a Chicano-Anglo dichotomy, i.e., a "them-versus-us" approach. . . . The consequences were . . . significant. First, this approach tended to emphasize the separation and conflict that existed between the two groups by the very nature of the dichotomy. Second, and related to the latter point, the "them-versus-us" perspective minimized internal stratification and gender differences in the historical experience of Chicanos. Third, the conceptualization of Chicano history in such terms exaggerated the continuities in Chicano/*mexicano* culture and obscured its discontinuities and variation. Fourth, a tendency toward local community studies inhibited a geographically comparative view.

As a consequence, the theme of victimization ran through much of the historical literature on Chicanos. Not surprisingly, occupational charts revealed the historic downward mobility of most Chicanos in the face of Anglo ascendancy. For those Mexicans who held property, landholding patterns after 1848 exposed frequent dispossession at the hands of venal Anglo lawyers, a racist judicial system, and corrupt politicians. To complete the picture, many stressed the resistance offered by Chicanos to their historical subjugation. The publication of Rodolfo Acuña's first edition of *Occupied America* culminated this trend through its use of the internal colonial "model." . . . Published originally in 1972, Acuña's landmark book greatly popularized the application of the concept of internal colonialism as an interpretive framework for a synthesis of the Chicano experience. . . .

. . . The internal colonial model was found inadequate by several Chicano scholars by the time of the publication of the second edition of *Occupied America* (1981). . . . Yet . . . the colonial framework fails to explain adequately the experience of Chicanos in the nineteenth century. . . . For instance, the colonial framework did not explain satisfactorily the discrepancies in timing and character of Chicano resistance. Why the rise of the *gorras blancas* [white caps] in the late nineteenth century in New Mexico as opposed to the solitary social banditry of Murrieta in California half a century earlier? . . .

Between 1979 and 1984 over a half dozen publications appeared that . . . surpassed Acuña's popular text. The majority of these efforts . . . reflected the imprint of the currents generated by the new social history. . . . Urban history figured prominently in these works. Southern California, specifically Los Angeles, received deserved attention. Richard Griswold del Castillo, Albert Camarillo, and Ricardo Romo provided an excellent foundation to which historians of the City of Angels and its environs will remain indebted for years to come. Mario T. García's fine account of El Paso complemented Oscar Martínez's study of Ciudad Juárez. Arnoldo De León offered much valuable information with his works on Texas. . . . David Weber produced an important book on the Mexican era of the Southwest, an accomplishment supplemented by Oakah Jones's contribution on northern Mexico in the colonial period. . . .

. . . Other examples may be cited, but the conclusion was clear: the conceptualization of Chicano history had to take into account the diversity of the Chicano experience from its beginnings. . . .

. . . In brief, as a whole these works constituted a transition away from mere chronicles of victimization to a perspective open to nuance, subtlety, and complexity.

This shift, however, also made for certain dilemmas. Notably, there arose the problem of reconciling two distinctive yet interrelated dimensions over time *and* space: first, the apparent inequities of intergroup relations (Chicano and Anglo); second, the differences in intragroup relations (among Chicanos themselves). . . . And, equally important, in what ways was gender to be taken into account to deepen our understanding of both intergroup and intragroup relations? Thus, the surge of published monographs from 1979 to 1984 served to underscore the need for, and contributed to the question of, the conceptualization of Chicano history. . . .

Structural Origins of Chicano Diversity. Capitalist development in the United States occurred in a series of fits and starts that leapfrogged certain areas and engulfed others at the same time. And the consequences, when analyzed carefully, failed to meet the easy generalizations of "them-versus-us" history. . . .

Thus, . . . careful scrutiny found contrasting outcomes in the timing of capitalist penetration dominated by the new, non-Spanish-speaking population. Population distribution and growth in Texas, California, and New Mexico varied greatly and had significant implications for the Spanish-speaking communities of those areas. New Mexico, for example, held approximately two-thirds of the Mexican population of the Southwest at the time of the Mexican War. The majority of New Mexico's *hispanos* were concentrated in the northern region of the province. In contrast, the Spanish-speaking population of California hugged the coast so that the land boom of the 1840s led to American immigrants being "geographically isolated from the Californios" in the Central Valley. The substantial size and density of the New Mexican population conditioned the gradual entry of Americans *into the same area* as opposed to the initial geographic distance between the American and Mexican populations in California. The location, size, and density of the Mexican population in the two areas distinguished the impact of the "Anglo invasion": for New Mexico it meant a longer period of adjustment to, and defense against, American encroachment; for California, it facilitated the victory of the American immigrants.

As Weber's account of the Mexican frontier illustrates, demography and geography in Texas also figured prominently in the transition away from Mexican control. *"Tejano* oligarchs saw the economic growth in Texas . . . , and their fortunes," Weber observes, "as inextricably linked to the well-being of the Anglo newcomers and their slave-based, cotton growing economy." On the eve of the Texas revolt, *tejanos* were outnumbered ten to one, due in part to efforts of *tejanos* of the upper class to promote American immigration. . . .

In this light, Weber's account of the northern Mexican frontier provides an indispensable reference point to assess the repercussions of the early interaction between the capitalist penetration of the United States and the Southwest's Spanish-speaking population. The similarities *and the variation* in that process make works concerning the period *before* United States-Mexican hostilities important to understanding the specific consequences of annexation. . . .

Responses to Subordination. Despite the diversity that marked the experience of Mexicans in the post-1848 era, the process of subordination touched the lives of most Spanish-speaking people. . . . Erosion or loss of landholdings, reduction in opportunities, or the effects of institutional racism held consequences for even the upper crust of Mexican rancheros, merchants, and artisans. In certain areas such as California, the process of subjugation took place rapidly in the wake of the tremendous influx of Americans that overwhelmed the small coastal settlements of the Spanish-speaking population. In other regions, the shift in power, numerical superiority, and/or American geographic expansion differed, such as in New Mexico. Consequently, the responses by Mexicans varied given their status, resources, and ability (or time) to respond to the seemingly unavoidable confrontation with American domination and its consequences.

Most Mexicans, nonetheless, were or became laborers, ranch hands, farm workers, railroad crewmen, and the like. While regional variations occurred, the vast majority of Mexican workers generally faced various forms of economic discrimination: dual wage structures, job segregation, and racist labor practices. Organized protest to these conditions took place, yet the work on Chicano labor history prior to the 1920s suggests a rather paltry record of strikes, unionization efforts, and overt labor actions. Further research on Chicano workers in the 1848 to 1900 period may alter this impression. Still, this apparent lack of labor activism demands explanation.

The answer appears complex and seems further complicated by the arrival of Mexican immigrant workers. Mario T. García . . . emphasized that the "Mexicans' response to their conditions must be seen in light of their motives for having left Mexico." In García's view, "Mexicans tolerated their economic subordination" because a job in the United States made for a "significant improvement over their previous lower paying or unemployed positions in Mexico."

This does not mean, as García went on to stress, "that Mexicans were not incapable of struggling against exploitative conditions." Clearly, there were forces that limited overt resistance, but one must also appreciate the specific circumstances of the Mexican, particularly the immigrant, worker. . . .

The historical rendering of Chicano workers . . . remains incomplete when reduced to obvious, organized forms of resistance. . . . Chicano labor history must also take into account more subtle expressions of protestation. Particularly for Mexican labor between 1848 and the 1880s (when immigration accelerated substantially from Mexico), one must take into consideration the structures of power, authority, and economic necessity that forced many Mexican workers to avoid explicit confrontations with their employers (Anglo or Mexican). Instead, the seeming "passivity" of Mexican workers reflected a pervasive and often effective system of repression, compelling Mexican workers to indirect forms of protestation, e.g., leaving their jobs, returning to Mexico or moving elsewhere, slowdowns, workplace "sabotage," and other forms of resistance. And the labor movement in the United States into the late nineteenth century held scant hope for Mexican workers for a number of reasons, not the least of which was the general racism that characterized early labor organizations. In sum, the responses of Mexicans to American domination in the post-conquest era contained an essential diversity, including among Mexican workers, whose protests ranged widely in form and magnitude.

In light of the above, the conceptualization of the Chicano experience must be anchored in the extension and penetration of capitalist development in the West. Furthermore, . . . several factors mediated the specific outcomes of the interaction between Mexicans and an expanding American economy: local economic structures, geographic location, proximity to the border, ethnic composition of the population, and the presence of Mexicans in the area as merchants, landholders, or

political figures. In brief, the interface between Mexicans and the westward movement of American capitalism and its intrinsic racism reflected a variegated, complex process. . . .

. . . Mexicans in the United States . . . responded in various forms to their encounters with an essentially racist economy and its socializing institutions. *This
process was cumulative, complex, and subject to the conditions in which it took
place.* . . . Male-female relations, gender roles, childhood and adolescence, religion, popular culture, social network, i.e., the inner lives of *mexicanos,* have escaped the concerted focus of the historical writings of the last ten years.

Periodization and Conquest. . . . "Chicano history" begins before 1836, and
certainly prior to 1848. . . . The actual "conquest" commenced with the Texas
revolt of 1836 and culminated with the signing of the Treaty of Guadalupe
Hidalgo. In this respect, a full understanding of this period must extend beyond an
emphasis on the sources of American imperialism. The underlying causes of
Mexico's inability to defend its borders must also be examined, as well as the role
of other foreign powers . . . in conceding United States territorial expansionism.

The post-conquest era reflected the consolidation of American domination and
the structural incorporation of the Southwest into the United States economy, signaled by the completion of the transcontinental railroad (1869). This process took
place with wide variations in timing and specific consequences given the context of
the locality involved. . . . The years from the 1880s to the 1920s mark a distinctive
period in the post-conquest era owing to two key elements. First, the period witnessed the hardening of the structures of subordination that eclipsed the remnants of
the "Spanish" population, symbolized by the virtual disappearance of the landed
elite of pre-conquest society. Second, the four decades following the railway linking
of the East and West accelerated dramatically the absorption of the Southwest into
the rapid spread of industrial capitalism. Hence, the general economic development
of the West intensified the demand for cheap labor, generating an increasing migration of Mexicans to the region. This latter trend was furthered by the particular conditions in Mexico that induced migration to the United States. . . .

These two elements formed the basis of the distinction between immigrants
and the Spanish-speaking population that derived from the pre-conquest era. More
important, this basic bifurcation in the Mexican/Spanish-speaking communities of
the Southwest occurred despite the similar treatment accorded to both groups by
American rule. . . . Nevertheless, stratification and social hierarchies . . . persisted
within chicano communities. Moreover, in social and cultural terms the arrival of
increasing numbers of immigrants changed in many respects the ethos of Spanish-
speaking communities in the United States. . . .

As noted earlier, it seems that for most Chicano historians the years from 1836
to the 1920s create the foundations of Chicano inequality. Thus, recent Chicano
historiography suggests, if only indirectly, that the depression years represent a
pivotal time, as they precipitated a sharp intensification of anti-Mexican sentiment
and the dissipation of a thirty-year surge in Mexican immigration. The question remains, however, whether the period after the New Deal . . . marks a distinct stage
in the Chicano experience.

Modern Chicano History: Problems and Issues

. . . World War II represented a rare moment where the social distance between Anglos and Mexicans diminished before the exigencies of an external threat. . . . Wartime meant an enormous common experience which touched virtually the entire spectrum of the Chicano community. Nonetheless, this common experience failed to stem the growing differentiation among Chicanos. Rather, it served to reveal its fragmentation and to crystallize a singular group, i.e., the so-called Mexican American generation. "These 'new' Mexican Americans . . . increasingly saw themselves as closer to United States conditions," Mario T. García has concluded, and "specially the more middle class members of this generation sought full integration and achievement of the 'American Dream.' " In this respect, the variation of the Mexican population apparently continued and multiplied in the post-World War II era with important consequences. . . .

. . . The American economy underwent a momentous period of growth . . . during and following World War II, especially in the Southwest where most of the Chicano population was concentrated. The flux created by wartime meant job openings, . . . which had been difficult if not impossible to acquire before 1940. The postwar boom sustained this greater degree of opportunity for Chicanos. . . .

As the 1960s wore on, however, signs of change in the structure of the United States economy appeared that held adverse consequences for most Chicanos. . . . First, the now well-recognized process of de-industrialization began to take effect. . . . Second, the cumulative effects of decades of discrimination and institutional racism meant that most Chicanos were ill-prepared for an economy where higher skills were required. . . . Thus, the mobility of the two decades after World War II waned for working-class Chicanos in the 1970s. . . . Third, the number of secondary labor market jobs (the so-called service sector) accelerated through the 1970s and into the 1980s. . . .

Fourth, these shifts in the economy took place with particular force (and volatility) in the so-called Sun Belt, including the Southwest. . . . Fifth, the combination of a declining American economy and the fiscal conservatism of the 1980s had especially negative consequences for cities. . . . The level of urbanization of the Chicano population spelled an intensification of the problems faced by inner city, poor Chicanos. . . .

. . . The historical basis of this phenomenon . . . continues [to be] unexplored. The recent work of Martín Sánchez-Jankowski, Joan Moore, Ruth Horowitz, and James Diego Vigil documents primarily the contemporary outcomes of a historical process for significant segments of the Mexican origin population. . . .

The Impact of Immigration.   Immigration represents a fundamental source of the continuing differentiation within the Chicano community. . . .

Immigrants generally differ upon arrival from their American-born counterparts; and the *recién llegado* should remind historians of the different ways of "seeing" self and society in the Chicano experience in specific times and places. . . . Yet, the historian's analysis of the meaning of immigration must be construed carefully, especially regarding questions of culture, identity, and ideology. . . .

As a whole, the Mexican immigrant experience of the last forty years or so remains largely unexamined. . . .

This post-1940 generation of *mexicanos* and their experience of adjustment, including the process of cultural change, continue to be slighted by historians. . . . The historical rendering of the immigrant—who came with the bracero program, who overcame "operation wetback," and the termination of the bracero program in 1964, and who continued to arrive thereafter—awaits an author. Significantly, this neglect suggests a persistent flaw in Chicano scholarship: the tendency to underestimate the importance of continuing immigration, including the complexities of Chicano-*mexicano* relations in the formation of Chicano communities since World War II. And, though the controversy over contemporary immigration has fueled prodigious amounts of research, it sustains a preoccupation with economic considerations and an aversion for understanding the Chicano-*mexicano* dimensions of Mexican immigration. . . .

New Directions for Historical Research.   Recent Chicano historiography, in spite of its strengths, reveals certain shortcomings that must be addressed by students of the Chicano past. Four key areas of need can be identified. First, . . . there is an urgent need for research on Chicanas. Most of the studies under review include women in their examination of occupational patterns, labor relations, and other areas related to employment. Still, the deeper questions of male-female relations, family, child-rearing, and the like remain often unexplored. . . .

Clearly, historians must begin to explore this dimension of the Chicano experience in a way that is sensitive to the critical place of women in the formation of the Chicano community without losing sight of the differentiation that apparently occurred among women themselves. . . .

. . . The lack of research on Chicanas and of an adequate approach to the complexity of their lives hinders substantially a full understanding of the Chicano experience. . . .

. . . The relationships between new immigrants and previous generations of immigrants represent an important focus of analysis. . . . Chicano historians must acknowledge . . . the continuing significance of immigration for a full understanding of the Chicano experience. . . .

Immigration suggests a third area of concern for Chicano history, i.e., the impact of American culture and ideology on the Mexican origin community. On this point, the current discussion among historians of the influence of advertising, the mass media, fashion, consumerism, and related issues holds important possibilities for examining the sources, as well as the consequences, of the ideological variation among Chicanos, particularly after 1940. . . . Furthermore, . . . historians must not lose sight of the manifestations of "counter ideology" among Chicanos, without falling prey to romanticizing such expressions.

This last point underscores the necessity of taking into account the specific texture of American society, a fourth area of need in Chicano history. The recent wave of Chicano historical scholarship has tended to concentrate on certain geographic areas or cities. As a result, the interface between Chicanos and broad trends in the United States economy, polity, and culture possesses a disparate quality, given the diversity of the Chicano community. . . .

. . . Chicano history would be enormously improved by work that compares different geographic areas in the context of political, economic, and social currents in American history.

Summary and Conclusion

. . . This essay has emphasized the fundamental diversity of the Chicano experience, a diversity complicated by an expanding American capitalism and its attendant cultural forces, including its pervasive racism. I have argued that the post-depression era witnessed an acceleration of an antecedent differentiation because of a widening class structure in the Mexican-origin community. . . . This . . . has exacerbated if not created sources of divisiveness over time. It appears . . . that the presence of a persistent racist ideology and the spread of a consumer culture have extended and deepened the cleavages among Chicanos with diverse consequences, including a wide range of self-identification.

The resultant variation in self-perceptions has implied political distinctions as well as social and cultural diversity. And this process of differentiation has been furthered by the recurring and varying impacts of immigration from Mexico. Consequently, these rifts in the Chicano community have intensified with time. . . . Given the diversity of the Mexican-origin population in the United States and their specific circumstances, the history of their responses has understandably lacked uniformity.

The contemporary Chicano community and its differences reflect, therefore, the diverse ways in which people of Mexican descent have responded to their conditions over time. . . .

. . . The commonalities in the Chicano experience have waned. . . .

. . . The historical literature of the last few years suggests the complexity of the Chicano experience. To press history to yield essentially an epic of heroes, victories, gallant resistance, and labor militancy blurs the everyday struggles of working Mexican men and women to sustain their dignity in a world that has taken a great deal, including, at times, their sense of self. The outcomes of those struggles, it seems, represent the basis of the Chicano past and present.

Chicano/a Historians and the Revision of Western History

DAVID G. GUTIÉRREZ

In considering Mexican American history one might argue that the debate about the significance or importance of ethnic Mexican people in the West has reflected the central themes of the social and political history of the region. Whether one considers initial Mexican resistance to American exploration of the Mexican Northwest (a territory now encompassing the five southwestern states plus Nevada and Utah); Mexicans' active resistance to American imperialism during the Mexican American War; or ethnic Mexicans' subsequent campaigns to achieve the full rights of citizenship; we might argue that on one fundamental level, ethnic Mexican residents of the American West have been involved in a protracted struggle to prove their importance, to prove themselves significant in American society.

One might argue more generally that . . . a substantial portion of the ethnic conflict that has occurred historically in the American West has involved subject peoples' efforts to contest and resist efforts to impose ascriptive social judgments on them, particularly by interpreting and representing their histories in certain ways. Much of the most compelling recent theoretical work in social history, cultural criticism, and feminist studies relies on this as one of its central premises: military conquest or absorption of one society by another usually represents only the first step of the process by which one society imposes itself on another. Ultimately, however, the most crucial development as a result of expansion and domination is the subsequent construction of elaborate sets of rationales which are designed to explain why one group has conquered another and to establish and perpetuate histories that help "set . . . and enforce . . . priorities, [repress] some subjects in the name of the greater importance of others, [naturalize] certain categories, and [disqualify] others."

Myth and Myopia

The salience of applying such a perspective to historical analysis of ethnic Mexicans in the American West is clear, for any such exploration must begin with an acknowledgement of how American ideologies of expansion have powerfully influenced historical representations of and about "Mexicans" (and other subject groups) after the United States acquired the region. Of course, this process was well under way even before the actual annexation of the West. Indeed, Americans had developed a rather detailed demonology about Mexicans (and about Spaniards before them) even before they had established regular contact with Spanish-speaking people in the region in the 1820s. . . . With the advent of the cluster of racist and nationalist ideas collectively known as Manifest Destiny in the early 1840s, these stereotypes assumed a more virulent form. Although the specific ideas that contributed to the notion of Manifest Destiny seemed diverse and complex, virtually all derived from Americans' belief in the superiority of the United States' civilization, culture, and political institutions. . . .

Acceptance of these fundamental premises in turn enabled Americans to demean, and ultimately to dismiss, the people they had incorporated into their society. This process was speeded along by the segregation of ethnic Mexicans that occurred in varying degrees throughout the region. As Mexican Americans were slowly forced by population pressures and discrimination to withdraw into shrinking urban barrios and isolated rural *colonias,* they seemed to gradually disappear from the landscape, thereby fulfilling the prophesies of those proponents of Manifest Destiny who had predicted that the West's indigenous peoples would "recede" or "fade away" before the advance of American civilization. By the turn of the century, Mexican Americans had become, to use the words of one well known historian, America's "forgotten people."

To assert, however, that America forgot this ethnic group oversimplifies a far more complicated story. What actually occurred was a rather peculiar reenvisioning of the role Mexicans played in the region's past. Gradually released from the necessity of viewing Mexicans as any kind of political or military threat, Americans were able to indulge themselves in romantic reveries about what the landscape must have looked like before the war. In a process no doubt similar to the one that allowed Americans to construct the notion of the noble savage after Indians had been effectively removed from lands they coveted, the consolidation of American control over former Mexican domains allowed westerners to construct what Carey McWilliams aptly called "the Spanish fantasy heritage." With historians and history buffs, artists, travel and fiction writers, amateur ethnographers, and eventually, local chambers of commerce and real estate boosters all contributing, Anglo American residents of the region helped to construct a benign history of the not-so-distant past where gracious Spanish grandees, beautiful señoritas, and gentle Catholic friars oversaw an abundant pastoral empire worked by contented mission Indians. . . . This creation not only fit nicely with the images that Americans held of themselves; it also allowed them the freedom to extol and selectively appropriate for their own use those aspects of the region's culture that amused them. . . . By the early decades of this century, it was rare to find a town of any size in the "Old Spanish Southwest" that did not celebrate its illustrious past by restoring missions, erecting historical markers, and holding what seemed to be a nearly endless round of annual Spanish fiestas, replete with dons and doñas (usually Anglos) in full "Spanish" regalia astride matched palominos.

Resistance, Excavation, and Recovery

While some may persist in arguing that the elaborate historical and popular reimaginings constituting "the Spanish fantasy heritage" were harmless examples of romantic myth-making, Mexican Americans have long been aware of the ways such myths have helped to obscure, and thus to diminish, the actual historical producers of the culture that Anglos ostensibly celebrated. It was one thing to suffer the humiliation of conquest and the subsequent indignity of relegation to an inferior caste status in the emerging social order of the American-dominated West, but it was quite another to sit idly by and watch the Americans appropriate for their own amusement aspects of Mexican culture they found quaint and picturesque reminders of the past. Moreover, many Mexican Americans knew, to a painful degree, that the seemingly harmless celebration of Spanish fiestas masked the disdain so many Americans felt about the actual remaining representatives of Hispanic culture in the West. One can easily imagine Mexican Americans' bewilderment and anger as they watched gringos celebrate appropriated cultural events knowing that the very term "Mexican" had already become deeply embedded in the vocabulary of the region as a label of derision and stigma.

In many ways, ethnic Mexicans' awareness that they had been rendered insignificant as human beings in this manner has provided one of the major forces driving both their efforts to achieve full political rights in American society, and their attempts to recapture and rewrite their own history. In fact, these two objectives have worked hand in hand since the 1850s, even if the resultant efforts went largely unheeded until very recently. But even a cursory knowledge of the region's ethnic history reveals that Mexican Americans have long considered the struggle to represent their own history and, to be represented accurately in the West's history generally, to be crucial components of their ongoing campaign to achieve their full rights as American citizens and as human beings.

The dual nature of this struggle is readily apparent in the work of the first generation of scholars who began publishing research on the West's ethnic Mexican population in the years following World War I. Most of this generation of Mexican Americans were either descendants of the Spanish-speaking people whose presence predated that of the conquest or, more commonly, were the children of the huge numbers of Mexican immigrants who settled in the United States after 1910, so they had first-hand knowledge of what it meant to grow up with the stigma of being Mexican in the American West. Thus, when reviewing the work of pioneering intellectuals such as George I. Sánchez, Arthur L. Campa, Carlos Castañeda, Ernesto Galarza, Jovita González, or Américo Paredes, it is immediately clear that these individuals were driven by more than a merely dispassionate pursuit of knowledge for knowledge's sake. . . . They recognized that before they could ever hope to gain a fair reading of their work it would be necessary to break through the deeply entrenched, dehumanizing stereotypes about Mexicans that Americans had come to accept since the early nineteenth century. This first generation of intellectuals also faced the burden of having come of age during an era of heavy immigration from Mexico. Forced to do their work in an atmosphere of intensifying anti-Mexican sentiment, this generation of Mexican American scholars had to be even more careful in the way they framed their research questions and in the language they used to represent the subjects of that research.

. . . When viewed in hindsight, . . . the body of work produced by these individuals is unified in several important respects. The most important theme unifying this research was these scholars' obvious concern to represent ordinary working-class Mexican Americans and Mexican immigrants as complex, fully-formed, and fully-functional human beings. While this might not seem to be a significant point, when viewed in the context of the times, this work should be seen as the first stage of a bold—and inherently political—project of excavation and recovery that was designed, at least partially, to upset the prevailing regional social order by demonstrating the extent to which stereotypes about Mexicans were the products of Americans' active, and truly powerful, imaginations.

A brief discussion of George I. Sánchez's research helps illustrate some of the ways Mexican American scholars of this period used their work both to advance objective knowledge and to alter what had become the master discourse used to describe Mexicans in the United States. Superficially, the work of the longtime University of Texas history and education professor appears to be an example of fairly straightforward academic research. But a closer analysis of his work reveals that Sánchez pursued a self-consciously political agenda throughout his long career. But this was not politics in the sense that most Americans associate with the word. . . . In some ways his attempts to get the readers of his research simply to recognize Mexican Americans as human beings represented the most radical political position he could have advanced in the 1930s and 1940s. From the time he wrote his earliest work on general issues concerning education, Mexican American bilingualism, and intelligence testing, Sánchez focused intently on destroying prevailing notions of Mexican Americans as a culturally monolithic, socially unstratified population by demonstrating the complexity and utility of the Southwest's syncretic Mexican American culture. . . .

. . . Sánchez sought to illustrate, in a subdued and scholarly way, that because Mexican Americans disagreed about politics and were divided, among other things, by class, religion, customs, and language preference, their community was as internally complex and functionally cohesive as any other. Building on this basic premise, Sánchez systematically dissected theories that attributed Mexican American poverty and low educational achievement to putative flaws inherent in Mexican culture or biology. . . .

. . . On the most fundamental level, Sánchez's arguments, and those made by other Mexican American scholars and activists of this generation, undermined an ideological edifice that had long maintained notions of American superiority and Mexican inferiority as fact. . . . In the context of their own times, these individuals' efforts represented a serious and inherently subversive assault on the entire system of meanings that Americans had constructed about the annexation of the West, and perhaps more importantly, about the significance of the ethnic Mexican people living there. By attacking Americans' common assumptions of racial, cultural, and political superiority—using scientific and objective research methods that could not be faulted by mainstream scholars—Sánchez and his generation issued a crucial first challenge to the very core of the ethnically stratified social order in the American West.

The Chicano Moment

. . . Sánchez's generation of scholar-activists in many ways anticipated the research agenda, modes of analysis, and political rhetoric of the generation of intellectuals and social activists . . . of the Chicano movement. This second generation of intellectuals and social critics, however, were in a much better position than their predecessors to take the project of humanization begun earlier several crucial steps further. Coming of age during a period of social ferment symbolized by the civil rights movement, inner-city revolts, and the intensifying protests over the war in Vietnam, by the mid-1960s young Mexican Americans in scattered locales across the Southwest had embarked on a series of political campaigns that became known collectively as the Chicano movement. . . . One of the least noticed, yet most important effects of the Chicano movement was the extent that it helped force open the doors of colleges and universities to Mexican American students. The opening of such previously restricted institutions not only allowed unprecedented numbers of students the opportunity to pursue a higher education; it also helped fuel a renewed drive among Mexican Americans to recapture and rewrite their own history. . . .

From the point of view of many Chicano militants, history would play a central role in the project to reconstruct Chicano identity. Indeed, from the very outset of the movement, Chicano activists argued that ethnic Mexicans must learn their true history before they could even hope to develop a strong sense of community and solidarity. . . .

. . . At its worst, the history produced during this period helped to create a different totalizing discourse that in some ways was as distorting, essentialistic, and exclusionary as the one activists were attempting to transform. . . . Some Chicano activist-scholars showed a tendency to reify "Chicano culture" into a set of codes and symbols designed to offset what they argued was the inherent acquisitiveness, materialism, chauvinism, and rapaciousness of Anglo culture. . . . Few seemed to realize that much of the rhetoric of the Chicano movement—and the scholarship that drew inspiration from that rhetoric—slid perilously close to replicating the same kind of exclusionary, hierarchical, and dehumanizing ideologies that Anglo Americans had used so effectively for so long to suppress minority peoples.

At their best, however, scholars writing during this period broadened and deepened comprehension of the social history of the West by pulling Mexican Americans and Mexican immigrants out of obscurity, by rendering them visible and significant in regional history. And perhaps more importantly, the best of this generation of historians gave new life to the humanizing project their predecessors had initiated nearly fifty years earlier. At the level of the academic production of history, scholars such as Rodolfo Acuña, Tomás Almaguer, Mario Barrera, Arnoldo De León, Mario T. García, Richard Griswold del Castillo, Juan Gómez-Quiñones, Ricardo Romo, David Weber, and others published important works that compelled scholars—and at least some of the general public—to replace the traditional, stereotypical representations of ethnic Mexicans that had long dominated regional history with more complex and subtle renderings of individual Mexicans and Mexican culture. Employing the same sophistication in conceptualization, methodology, and argument that other so-called new social historians were developing at this time, Mexican American scholars publishing in the 1970s and early 1980s produced work that gained increasing notice, respectability, and legitimacy in mainstream academic circles. . . .

The Changing Significance of Difference in Western History

Though some would argue that the project of humanization pursued by historians of the ethnic Mexican experience since early in this century continues in the present period, the character of this enterprise has recently undergone a significant transformation. In fact, the present generation of ethnic Mexican and other Latino intellectuals . . . seem intent on pushing their demands for recognition and inclusion even further than the militants of the 1960s and 1970s. Moving well beyond the rhetoric of mere inclusion, many in the present intellectual . . . generation are insisting on developing a fundamental reconfiguration in the ways minority peoples are conceived of, categorized, and analyzed in history and contemporary American society. . . .

The effect of this political sea change on historical scholarship has been no less profound. The widespread challenges to established authority issued on the streets and in the universities during the 1960s contributed to a sharpening of debate about the politics of representation of minority peoples and, more broadly, about the nature of historical authority itself. . . .

Although it is impossible in this limited space to assess the full impact of this revolution on questions such as those concerning the historical significance of minority populations in the West, . . . the emergence of three interrelated trends in recent regional historical interpretation is particularly relevant to this discussion.

First, consider the dramatic increase in the number of scholars who are bringing interdisciplinary or transdisciplinary approaches to their study of the history of ethnic Mexican peoples in the West. Drawing theoretical, methodological, and critical insights and research questions from what used to be much more discreetly demarcated disciplines, the recent "blurring of genres" . . . so evident in western historiography has brought a variety of new perspectives to the study of minority populations. It is also contributing to a rapid dismantling of the kind of victor's history that has dominated regional historiography since the Mexican Cession. Whether one considers the recent explorations in autobiography and literary theory by scholars such as Hector Calderón, Angie Chabram, Clara Lomas, Genaro Padilla, José David Saldívar, Ramón Saldívar, or Rosaura Sánchez; the musings of anthropologist Renato Rosaldo; the historical investigations of folklorists such as María Herrera-Sobek, José Limón, or Manuel Peña; the ruminations on regional history of sociologists such as Tomás Almaguer or David Montejano; or the work of formally trained interdisciplinary social historians such as Deena J. González, Ramón A. Gutiérrez, Douglas Monroy, or George J. Sánchez, one cannot help but be struck by the extent that old "us versus them" interpretations of interethnic relations have given way to extremely subtle analyses in which Mexicans, Anglos, Indians, and others emerge as complex, multifaceted, sometimes cooperative, and often contradictory actors on the regional stage. For example, it is impossible to read the work of González, Padilla, or Gutiérrez on New Mexico, Montejano or Peña on Texas, or Monroy or Almaguer on California, and not come away with the understanding that the conquest of the Mexican Northwest in the 1840s involved more than the abject subjugation of ethnic Mexicans and Indians. . . . In short, work of this type shows the extent to which Mexicans were simultaneously objects of subordination and active agents of political and cultural opposition and resistance.

While the move toward interdisciplinary analyses represented by such work has accelerated the project of humanization initiated by pioneering ethnic Mexican activists and intellectuals, an even more fundamental challenge to "business as usual" in regional history has been issued by western historians of women, gender, and sexuality. Spurred by developments similar to those that stimulated women in the civil rights, antiwar, and New Left movements to reassess their relationships to male activists in the 1960s and 1970s, the recent florescence of Chicana history grew out of Mexican American and Mexican immigrant women's experiences in the Chicano movement. Ethnic Mexican women played central roles in the myriad organizations that made up the Chicano civil rights struggle, but like their counterparts in the other social movements of the times, they quickly discovered that they were expected to conform to traditional subordinate gender roles within their culture.

Exposed through their political activities to the raw dynamics of continuing gender subjugation within a movement ostensibly dedicated to their liberation, Chicana and Mexicana activists soon began asking more comprehensive questions about the actual nature of their oppression in society. Logically, the answers to these questions initially tended to focus almost exclusively on the dynamics of male/female relationships within contemporary Mexican American and Mexican culture. However, as increasing numbers of women activists gained access to higher education along with their male counterparts in the Chicano movement, such inquiries inevitably began to influence the production of regional historical scholarship and interpretation.

The work of a new generation of women scholars influenced by these political and intellectual developments began to appear in the 1980s. Led by women's historians such as Vicki L. Ruiz, Rosalinda González, Sarah Deutsch, Deena J. González, Antonia Castañeda, Peggy Pascoe, Susan Johnson, and others, this generation of scholar/activists immediately transformed the research agenda in the West by systematically including, often for the first time, women as primary subjects of analysis in regional, social, and cultural history. Perhaps just as important, from the time they first entered graduate school, women scholars made it a fundamental part of their business to insist that male historians rethink the ways they framed and pursued their own research.

While this insistence played a crucial role in reducing the glaring distortions resulting from traditional research methods that had obliterated at least half of the putative subjects of social history, it proved to be just the first step in a series of logical steps that led women's historians and feminist theorists to ask deeper questions about the nature of gendered systems more generally construed. The importance of the critique that arose from such a realization extended far beyond its proximate concentration on women, per se. On the most basic level, scholars who sought to analyze gender—that is, the complex systems of social and cultural meanings assigned to sexual difference—played at least as powerful a role in ordering and stratifying men *and* women in society as do race or class. Using this basic premise as a point of departure, women's historians and feminist theorists explicitly and implicitly raised important theoretical questions about the production and reproduction of all kinds of subjective identities, including those based on race, ethnicity, and class. . . . Just as importantly, such a line of inquiry eventually led feminist scholars to reject notions of unified naturalized identity categories in favor of those that treat identity as "a contested terrain, the site of multiple and conflicting claims. . . .

The third, and potentially greatest contribution of the present generation of critical scholars to the project to render significant the ethnic Mexican population of the West is its unwavering commitment to explore and illuminate the intrinsic relationship between power and knowledge in scholarship and in society at large. Although many academics refuse to acknowledge that the production of *any* historical knowledge is an inherently political act, it is clear that many (if not most) scholars of the ethnic Mexican experience in the West have accepted the view, as Peter Novick notes of those who believe this, that "postures of disinterestedness and neutrality [in historical scholarship are] outmoded and illusory."

The production of knowledge based on acceptance of such a premise has not occurred without cost to those actively engaged in it. On the contrary, . . . scholars pursuing this type of innovative, nontraditional research will continue to face charges that the inherently political nature of their work renders their project an exercise in polemics rather than rigorous, objective historical scholarship. . . . Clearly, practitioners of this kind of research . . . will inevitably continue to attract the ire of those in society who feel personally threatened by the implicit and explicit challenges to the social status quo (or who have a vested interest in *pre-serving* the status quo).

. . . By drawing from and building on theoretical and methodological insights developed by those involved in interdisciplinary cultural studies, and more recently, by women historians and feminist theorists, historians interested in analyzing other kinds of socially constructed systems of difference and power seem committed to struggle to transform the ways we conceive of and understand the histories of subordinated peoples in the region. This exceedingly diverse and complex work should not be thought of as a monolithic project, or as some magical device that will provide historians the means to bridge the gap between the lived experiences and historians' representations of ethnic Mexicans' (or, for that matter any group's) social history. . . .

Taken together, however, research of this type suggests a number of innovative ways to reconceptualize historical inquiry that perhaps will help us to challenge more effectively the racist, sexist, and culturally chauvinistic stereotypes and structures that have for so long permeated thought and discourse about the significance of different peoples in the American West. By exposing and painstakingly analyzing the constructed, manipulated nature of social hierarchies of all types, scholars and social critics working from this point of view might help change the terms of debate about the historical and contemporary significance of ethnic Mexicans and other minority peoples. . . . If these trends continue, to paraphrase the recent musings of two scholars of the emergence of multiculturalism, we may be witnessing "the development of a new definition of what comprises 'mainstream' culture." If such hopeful prognostications turn out to be true, then the question of who is, and who is not, considered significant in this society will itself take on an entirely new significance.

FURTHER READING

Rodolfo Acuña, *Occupied America* (1988)

Tómas Almaguer, "Ideological Distortions in Recent Chicano Historiography: The Internal Model and Chicano Historical Interpretation," *Aztlán* 18 (Spring 1987), 7–28

Rudolfo A. Anaya and Francisco A. Lomelí, *Aztlán: Essays on the Chicano Homeland* (1989)

María Linda Apodaca, "The Chicana Woman: An Historical Materialist Perspective," in *Latin American Perspectives: Women in Latin America* (1979)

John R. Chávez, *The Lost Land* (1984)

Teresa Córdova et al., eds., *Chicana Voices* (1993)

Adela de la Torre and Beatríz M. Pesquera, eds., *Building with Our Hands* (1993)

Adelaida R. Del Castillo, ed., *Between Borders* (1990)

Juan Goméz-Quiñones and Luis Leobardo Arroyo, "On the State of Chicano History: Observations on Its Development, Interpretations, and Theory, 1970–1974," *Western Historical Quarterly* 7 (1976), 155–185

Leo Grebler, Joan W. Moore, and Ralph C. Guzmán, *The Mexican-American People* (1970)

Richard Griswold del Castillo, *North to Aztlán* (1996)

Richard Griswold del Castillo, "Chicano Historical Discourse in the 1980s," *Perspectives in Mexican American Studies/Emerging Themes in Mexican American Research* 4 (1993), 1–25

Ramón A. Gutiérrez, "Community, Patriarchy and Individualism: The Politics of Chicano History and the Dream of Equality," *American Quarterly* 45 (March 1993), 44–72

Gilberto López y Rivas, *The Chicanos* (1973)

Cary McWilliams, *North from Mexico* (1990)

Matt S. Meier and Feliciano Ribera, *Mexican Americans, American Mexicans* (1993)

Alfredo Mirandé and Evangelina Enríquez, *La Chicana* (1979)

Joan W. Moore and Harry Pachon, *Mexican Americans* (1976)

Wayne Moquin, ed., *A Documentary History of the Mexican Americans* (1972)

Cynthia E. Orozco, "Getting Started in Chicana Studies," *Women's Studies Quarterly* 1–2 (1990), 46–69.

Vicki L. Ruiz, *From Out of the Shadows* (1997)

———, "Teaching Chicano/American History: Goals and Methods," *History Teacher* 20 (February 1987), 167–177

Julian Samora and Patricia Vandel Simon, *A History of the Mexican-American People* (1993)

The Precolonial Period

About 145 million Indians lived in North and South America before the coming of the Spanish in 1492, but by the close of the sixteenth century, between 60 and 80 million were dead from both the cruel treatment and disease brought by the Spanish. In northern Mexico the Indian population fell from 2,500,000 to less than 320,000. From 1546 onward, disease preceded the Spanish into the present-day southwestern United States, as mining activity in northern Mexico created routes of infection that killed from 30 to 40 percent of the Indian population even prior to Spanish contact.

By 1600 most of the territory in the Southwest eventually controlled by Spain had been explored, and over three hundred towns had been established. The main goals shaping Spanish colonial policy were to maintain and expand political control and to convert Indians to Christianity. There was little interest in long-term development of the area. As a result, this northern frontier was more fluid and less subject to official Spanish control. Through both flight and armed revolt, the Indians of the Southwest resisted forced labor in the mines and ranches as well as the exorbitant demands for supplies imposed upon them by the Spaniards. The Pueblo Revolt of 1680 in the New Mexico territory, for example, which ended one hundred years of Spanish colonization efforts in the region, was a response to the Spanish oppression in the form of forced labor and the imposed routine of mission life. By the end of the eighteenth century, however, the Spaniards had overcome Indian resistance. The two thousand Spanish inhabitants in the Southwest were an important link in Spain's northern defense against the Indians and the French, who were moving westward from the lower Mississippi Valley and present-day Illinois. The nomadic Indians who owned guns and horses provided the greatest opposition to the emerging Spanish colonial culture and in fact would alter Spanish policy toward them.

Although most Indians of California had no concept of conquest and invasion nor experience in organizing and conducting wars, they would carry out such revolts as the one that occurred in 1734. Other acts of resistance, such as the Yuma Indian Revolt of 1781, would continue in present-day Arizona. Given the fact that the Lipan Apache were driven south and east by the Spaniards in New Mexico, why did Spain fail to settle Texas? Why were the Spaniards unable to contain the Apache and the Comanche, who by the late eighteenth century were already raiding present-day Mexico? Although the Mexicans after gaining independence from Spain would wage a war to exterminate the Indians, why was Mexico unable to end Indian resistance? Did border warfare continue because the early Chicano set-

tlers exerted pressure on the area Indians, such as the Navajo and Apache, in their competition for land? Would the United States inherit the Apache and Comanche Wars from the Mexicans?

❧ D O C U M E N T S

Historians of the Southwest have characterized the Spanish colonial period as a romantic time that served as the basis for the spread of European civilization in the area. The following documents, however, indicate that all was not so idyllic. Document 1 is a description of the land and people of New Mexico in 1541 by a Franciscan friar who accompanied the Coronado expedition into the Southwest. Document 2 is a royal order issued by the king of Spain on May 26, 1570, commanding the Spanish in Mexico to control the Indians, convert them, and use them as labor. The Indians, however, did not passively accept the Christianizing efforts of the Spanish. Document 3 offers an Indian version of the Pueblo Indian Revolt of 1680. Continued Indian resistance along with failed Spanish policy in governing its northern frontier led to the reorganization of the region by the Spanish crown. Document 4 is a selection from the 1781 progress report of Teodoro de Croix, the commandant general of New Spain's Indian provinces, which included present-day Texas, New Mexico, Arizona, and California. Partly because of continued Indian hostilities, including the wars waged by the Apache, in 1776 Spain began an eighteen-year campaign to pacify the Indians. Document 5 is an excerpt from the notes of Colonel Don Antonio Cordero, dated 1796. Cordero had firsthand experience with the Apache; for many years he had fought them, learned their language, and had various other dealings with them. In his writing he offers reasons for the Apache prowess and success in their wars of resistance.

1. A Franciscan Friar Describes the Land and People of New Mexico, 1541

This Is the Latest Account of Cíbola, and of More Than Four Hundred Leagues.

It is more than three hundred leagues from Culiacán to Cíbola, and little of the way is inhabited. There are very few people, the land is sterile, and the roads are wretched. The people go about entirely naked, except the women, who, from the waist down, wear white dressed deerskins which reach to their feet like skirts. Their houses are built of reed mats, and are round and small, a man being hardly able to stand up inside. The place where they are settled and where they have their planted fields has sandy soil. They grow maize, although not much, and beans and calabashes; they also live on game: rabbits, hares, and deer. They do not offer sacrifices. This is true from Culhuacán to Cíbola.

Cíbola is a pueblo of about two hundred houses, which are two, three, four, and five stories high. Their walls are a span thick. The timbers used in their construction are round, as thick as a wrist; the roofs are built of small reeds with the

From George P. Hammond and Agapito Rey, eds. and trans., *Narratives of the Coronado Expedition, 1540–1542* (Albuquerque: University of New Mexico Press, 1940), pp. 308–312. Used with permission from the publisher.

leaves on, on top of which they add well-packed dirt; the walls are built of dirt and mud; the house doors are like the scuttles of ships. The houses are built compact and adjoining one another. In front of them there are some estufas built of adobe, in which the natives shelter themselves from cold in winter, for it is extremely cold; it snows six months of the year.

Some of the people wear cotton and maguey blankets, and dressed deerskins. They wear boots made of these skins that come to above their knees. They also make blankets of hare and rabbit skins, with which they keep warm. The women wear maguey blankets reaching to their feet and wear their clothes tight around the waist. They have their hair rolled above their ears like small wheels. These natives grow maize, beans, and calabashes, which is all they need for subsistence, as they are not very numerous. The land they cultivate is all sandy. The water is brackish; the land is very dry. They possess some chickens, although not many. They have no knowledge of fish.

In this province of Cíbola there are seven pueblos within a distance of five leagues. The largest one must have 200 houses; two others have 200, and the rest sixty, fifty, and thirty houses.

It is sixty leagues from Cíbola to the river and province of Tibex [Tiguex]. The first pueblo is forty leagues from Cíbola, and it is called Acuco. This pueblo is situated on the top of a very strong rock. It must contain about 200 houses, built similar to Cíbola, which has a different language. It is twenty leagues from there to the Tiguex river. This river is almost as wide as the one at Seville, although not so deep. It flows through level lands; its water is fine; it has some fish; it rises in the north.

The one who makes the foregoing statement saw twelve pueblos within a certain region of the river; others claim to have seen more up the river. Down the river the pueblos are all small, except two which must have about 200 houses. These houses have very strong walls made of mud and sand. The walls are a span thick. The houses are two and three stories high. Their woodwork is like that of the houses of Cíbola. The natives have their estufas as at Cíbola. The land is extremely cold, and the river freezes so hard that laden animals cross over it, and carts could cross also. The natives plant maize, beans, and calabashes, enough for their needs, and they possess some chickens, which they keep to make blankets with their feathers. They grow some cotton, although not much. They wear cotton blankets and shoes of hides as at Cíbola. They are people who know how to defend themselves from their very houses, and they are not inclined to leave them. The land is all sandy.

Four days journey from the province and river of Tiguex the Spaniards found four pueblos. The first must have thirty houses; the second was a large pueblo destroyed by war; the third had about thirty-five houses, all inhabited. These three pueblos are similar in every respect to those on the river. The fourth is a large pueblo situated between mountains, and is called Cicuic. It had some fifty houses with terraces like those of Cíbola, and the walls are of dirt and mud like those of Cíbola. The inhabitants have abundant maize, beans, calabashes, and some chickens.

At a distance of four days' travel from this pueblo, the Spaniards came to some land as level as the sea. In these plains there is such a multitude of cattle that they are beyond counting. These cattle are like those of Castile, and some larger. They have small humps on their backs, and are more reddish in color, blending into black. Their hair, over a span long, hangs down between their horns, ears, and chin, and from the neck and shoulders like a mane, and down from the knees. The rest of their bodies is covered with short wool like sheep. Their meat is fine and tender and very fat.

Traveling many days over these plains the Spaniards came to an inhabited ranchería with about two hundred houses. The houses were made of tanned cattle skins, white, and built like pavilions or tents. These Indians live or sustain themselves entirely from the cattle, for they neither grow nor harvest maize. With the skins they build their houses; with the skins they clothe and shoe themselves; from the skins they make ropes and also obtain wool. With the sinews they make thread, with which they sew their clothes and also their tents. From the bones they shape awls. The dung they use for firewood, since there is no other fuel in that land. The bladders they use as jugs and drinking containers. They sustain themselves on their meat, eating it slightly roasted and heated over the dung. Some they eat raw; taking it in their teeth, they pull with one hand, and in the other they hold a large flint knife and cut off mouthfuls. Thus they swallow it, half chewed, like birds. They eat raw fat without warming it. They drink the blood just as it comes out of the cattle. Sometimes they drink it later, raw and cold. They have no other food.

These people have dogs similar to those of this land, except that they are somewhat larger. They load these dogs like beasts of burden and make light pack-saddles for them like our pack-saddles, cinching them with leather straps. The dogs go about with sores on their backs like pack animals. When the Indians go hunting they load them with provisions. When these Indians move—for they have no permanent residence anywhere, since they follow the cattle to find food—these dogs carry their homes for them. In addition to what they carry on their backs, they carry the poles for the tents, dragging them fastened to their saddles. The load may be from thirty-five to fifty pounds, depending on the dog.

From Cíbola to these plains where the Spaniards came it must be thirty leagues, and perhaps more. The plains extend ahead—we do not know how far. Captain Francisco Vázquez traveled ahead over these plains with thirty mounted men, and Fray Juan de Padilla accompanied him. The rest of the people went back to the settlement by the river to await Francisco Vázquez, for so he had commanded. It is not known whether he has returned.

The land is so level that the men get lost when they draw half a league away. This happened to a man on horseback who got lost and never returned, and also to two horses, with harnesses and bridles, that were never again found. No tracks are left over the places which are traveled. On account of this they must leave land marks of cow dung along the way they follow in order to find their way back, for there are no stones or anything else.

2. Spain Asserts Control over the Indians of Nueva Galicia, Mexico, 1570

The King to our *oidores, alcaldes mayores* of the Audiencia of the province of Nueva Galicia:

As found in Charles W. Hackett, ed., *Historical Documents Relating to New Mexico, Nueva Vizcaya, and Approaches Thereto, to 1773,* collected by Adolph F. A. Bandelier and Fanny R. Bandelier (Washington, D.C., 1923), 1:101–103.

Juan de la Peña, in the name of the council of justice and government of the city of Guadalajara, has made a report to me saying that because the Indian inhabitants of the province are not gathered into towns where they may have political government, much harm is done and many difficulties arise in their conversion and indoctrination, and they are not taught to live under the control and ordered system conducive to their salvation and welfare. For, scattered as they are over the mountains and deserts, the religious are unable to go everywhere to visit them; moreover, the Indians began to flee for the purpose of preventing interference with their manner and custom of life, and of securing better opportunities to assault, rob, and kill both Spaniards and peaceful Indians on the highways as they had repeatedly done. De la Peña supplicated me to order as a remedy for this that the Indians of that province who are wandering about in the mountains should be gathered together and made to live in established towns where they might have political organization for their better instruction in the things of the faith, and not be allowed to live as they do in the mountains and out-of-the-way places, because of the difficulties which would result. The plan suggested has been discussed by the members of our Council of the Indies, who considered how much benefit to the Indians would accrue from it; I have therefore approved it, and do now command you to issue orders and instructions for gathering the Indians of that province who are wandering in the mountains into towns where they may live in a civilized manner and have their organized government, that they may better communicate with each other, have order and system in their living, be more advantageously converted and indoctrinated, and escape the dangers and difficulties which may attend the opposite mode of living in the mountains and deserts. Whatever you may do in this matter above your ordinary obligation we shall accept as service to us, and you will report to us how this order is complied with and executed.

3. The Pueblo Indians Call for War, 1680

Declaration of Pedro Naranjo of the Queres Nation [*Place of the Rio del Norte, December 19, 1681*]

In the said plaza de armas on the said day, month, and year, for the prosecution of the judicial proceedings of this case his lordship caused to appear before him an Indian prisoner named Pedro Naranjo, a native of the pueblo of San Felipe, of the Queres nation, who was captured in the advance and attack upon the pueblo of La Isleta. He makes himself understood very well in the Castilian language and speaks his mother tongue and the Tegua.

Asked whether he knows the reason or motives which the Indians of this kingdom had for rebelling, forsaking the law of God and obedience to his Majesty, and committing such grave and atrocious crimes, and who were the leaders and principal movers, and by whom and how it was ordered; and why they burned the images, temples, crosses, rosaries, and things of divine worship, committing such atrocities as killing priests, Spaniards, women, and children, and the

As found in Charles W. Hackett, "Revolt of the Pueblo Indians of New Mexico in 1680," *Quarterly of the Texas State Historical Association* 25, no. 2 (October 1911).

rest that he might know touching the question, he said that since the government of Señor General Hernando Ugarte y la Concha they have planned to rebel on various occasions through conspiracies of the Indian sorcerers, and that although in some pueblos the messages were accepted, in other parts they would not agree to it; and that it is true that during the government of the said señor general seven or eight Indians were hanged for this same cause, whereupon the unrest subsided. . . . Finally, in the past years, at the summons of an Indian named Popé who is said to have communication with the devil, it happened that in an estufa of the pueblo of Los Taos there appeared to the said Popé three figures of Indians who never came out of the estufa . . . and these three beings spoke of the said Popé. . . . They told him to make a cord of maguey fiber and tie some knots in it which would signify the number of days that they must wait before the rebellion. . . . The said cord was taken from pueblo to pueblo by the swiftest youths under the penalty of death if they revealed the secret. Everything being thus arranged, two days before the time set for its execution, because his lordship had learned of it and had imprisoned two Indian accomplices from the pueblo of Tesuque, it was carried out prematurely that night, because it seemed to them that they were now discovered; and they killed religious [*sic*], Spaniards, women, and children. . . . Finally the señor governor and those who were with him escaped from the siege, and later this declarant saw that as soon as the Spaniards had left the kingdom an order came from the said Indian, Popé, in which he commanded all the Indians to break the lands and enlarge their cultivated fields, saying that now they were as they had been in ancient times, free from the labor they had performed for the religious and the Spaniards, who could not now be alive. He said that this is the legitimate cause and the reason they had for rebelling, because they had always desired to live as they had when they came out of the lake of Copala. Thus he replies to the question. . . .

. . . Asked what arrangements and plans they had made for the contingency of the Spaniards' return, he said that what he knows concerning the question is that they were always saying they would have to fight to the death, for they do not wish to live in any other way than they are living at present; and the demons in the estufa of Taos had given them to understand that as soon as the Spaniards began to move toward this kingdom they would warn them so that they might unite, and none of them would be caught. He having been questioned further and repeatedly touching the case, he said that he has nothing more to say except that they should be always on the alert, because the said Indians were continually planning to follow the Spaniards and fight with them by night, in order to drive off the horses and catch them afoot, although they might have to follow them for many leagues. What he has said is the truth, and what happened, on the word of a Christian who confesses his guilt. He said that he has come to the pueblos through fear to lead in idolatrous dances, in which he greatly fears in his heart that he may have offended God, and that now having been absolved and returned to the fold of the church, he has spoken the truth in everything he has been asked. His declaration being read to him, he affirmed and ratified all of it. He declared himself to be eighty years of age, and he signed it with his lordship and the interpreters and assisting witnesses, before me, the secretary. . . . Before me, Francisco Xavier, secretary of government and war.

4. Teodoro de Croix Reports on Pacifying the Indians in California, 1781

It appears to me, most excellent señor, that my measures with relation to California have been efficacious and diligent, and that from them ought to be expected the increase of its population, the security of its defenses, the union and free communication of the old possession and the new ones by the important establishment of the presidio of the Santa Bárbara Canal, its three inchoate missions, and pueblos of Guadalupe and Porciuncula. These successes have been achieved with a minimum of expense, and those promised by a regulation, made up of methodical points of easy and simple practice, will lessen some part of the expenditures of the annual allotments. . . . It is increasing the number of officers, troops, and settlers; sets up for them the observance of the particular good rules of government and discipline; assures the pure management of their interest; redeems the royal treasury in this region from bankruptcies, losses, damages, and waste; facilitates, though in small amount, the circulating of money; and creates the pleasing prospect of permanency and increase of the military and colonizing establishment. Finally, with the most minute points clarified, the door is opened wide to the erection of new missions for propagating the voice of the gospel and reducing docilely the numerous small bands of barbarians that are vagrant in the territory and on the coasts of California as far as the boundaries of the province of Sonora and New Mexico. . . .

Most excellent señor, may all the provinces have the happy aspect of that of the Californias! However, Your Excellency already sees that Texas is surrounded by a numerous heathenism that it cannot resist without uniting its weak forces, dispersed settlements, and few and dissident settlers; that Coahuila, experiencing the sufferings of Texas, produces its own because of its friendship with the Lipan Apache whom it protects in its bosom without being able to protect itself from their devastation of a territory that would be opulent in agricultural resources, mineral riches, and advantageous sites for settlement. The well-known riches of New Vizcaya would be destroyed shortly by the incessant hostility of all Apache that it resists, were not the Apache forestalled by my efficient measures of covering the extensive frontiers of the province with the number of troops that I have at my orders, by increasing the provincials, and by operations which make possible its defense and conservation. New Mexico, because of its distance and because of the proximity of all the barbarous enemy nations, will always offer grave cares. The unfortunate province of Sonora, afflicted notably with the cruel plagues of war, pestilence, and hunger, is beginning to breathe in alleviation from its sorrows and in the hope of their remedy. I am devoting myself to all, aiding, succoring them as far as forces and resources reach, and maintaining vigilance by seeking all exact means for establishing the zeal that animates me in my profound loyalty to the king and my humble gratitude to Your Excellency.

From Alfred B. Thomas, ed., *Teodoro de Croix and the Northern Frontier of New Spain, 1776–1783* (Norman: University of Oklahoma Press, 1941), pp. 241–243. Used with permission from the University of Oklahoma Press.

5. Colonel Don Antonio Cordero
Discusses the Apaches, 1796

The Apache Nation is one of the savage [nations] of North America bordering on the interior provinces of New Spain. . . .

Having been born and raised in the open country and strengthened by simple foods, the Apache is endowed with an extraordinary robustness which makes him almost insensible to the rigors of the seasons. The continuous movement in which he lives, moving his camp from one to the other location for the purpose of obtaining new game and the fruits which are indispensible for his subsistence, makes him agile and nimble in such a degree that he is not inferior in speed and endurance to horses, and certainly is superior to them when in rugged and rocky territory. The vigilance and care with which he watches out for his health and preservation likewise stimulates him to change camps frequently in order to breathe new air, and so that the place he evacuates may be cleansed, his care for the health of his camp even goes to such an extreme that he will abandon those who are gravely ill when he judges that they may infect the rest. . . .

In general [the Apache] choose for dwelling places the most rugged and mountainous ranges. In these they find water and wood in abundance, the wild produce necessary, and natural fortifications where they can defend themselves from their enemies. Their hovels or huts are circular, made of branches of trees, covered with skins of horses, cows or bison, and many likewise use tents of this type. In the canyons of these mountain ranges the men seek large and small game, going as far as the contiguous plains; and when they have obtained what was necessary, they bring it to their camp, where it is the work of the women, not only to prepare the foods, but also to tan the skins which are then used for various purposes, particularly for their clothing. . . .

Much destruction is caused by four or six Indians who decide to carry out a short campaign by themselves, it being much more difficult to avoid the destruction caused by them, just as it is easier for them to cover their trail and penetrate without being detected into the most distant territories, for which reason they always make such a trip through the brush and rocky slopes of the mountains, which they leave for the populated places, committing the attack with the greatest rapidity and then retiring precipitately to occupy the same rough territory, and to continue their march through it, it being almost impossible to find them, even though they are sought with the greatest diligence.

The occasion in which the valor or temerity of these barbarians is best recognized, is when they are attacked by their enemies. They are never lacking in calm, even though they be surprised and have no chance for defense. They fight to the last breath and usually they prefer to die rather than surrender.

They proceed with the same intrepidity when they attack, but with the difference that if they do not obtain the upper hand immediately and see that luck is against them, they do not hesitate to flee and desist from their project, and with this

Daniel S. Matson and Albert S. Schroeder, eds. and trans., "Cordero's Description of the Apache—1796," *New Mexico Historical Review* 32 (October 1957). Reprinted with permission of Regents of University of New Mexico and the New Mexico Historical Review.

in view they provide for their retreat ahead of time and determine the direction to take for safety.

A camp no matter how cumbersome and how numerous its occupants, makes forced marches on foot or on horseback, which in a few hours frees them from their pursuers. It is impossible to measure the speed with which they break camp when they have perceived hostile superior forces in their vicinity. If they have animals, in a moment they are laden with their belongings and children; the mothers with their infants suspended from their heads in a hand basket of willow in which they place them with much security and ease; the men armed and mounted on their best horses; and everything in order to start out for country which they judge properly safe.

If they are lacking in horses the women carry the equipage, as well as the children. The men cover the vanguard, rearguard, and sides of the party, and choosing the most difficult and inconvenient terrain, they make their journey like wild beasts, through the most impenetrable rough places.

Only by surprise and by capturing all their places of retreat is it possible to succeed in punishing these savages, because since they detect the presence of their enemies before action commences, they succeed in placing themselves in safety with very little footwork. If it is determined, however, to fight them, this is with great risk, because of the extreme agility of the barbarians and the impregnable rocks where they take up their station.

In spite of the continuous movement in which these people live, and of the great deserts of their country, they find each other easily when they desire to communicate, even though it should have been a long time since they have seen each other, and have no news of recent events. Aside from the fact that all know more or less the territories in which such and such leaders are probably living by the character of the mountain ranges, valleys and watering courses which they recognize, smoke is the most efficient means by which they communicate. Understanding it is a science; but is so well known by all of them, that they are never mistaken in the meaning of its messages. . . .

It is not our business here to investigate the origin of the cruel and bloody war which the Apaches have been carrying on for many years in the Spanish possessions. Perhaps it was originated in former times by the trespasses, excesses and avarice of the colonists themselves who lived on the frontier exercising a subordinate authority. At present, the wise provisions of a just, active and pious government are bringing it to a close, and it should be noted that this system not only does not aspire to the destruction or slavery of these savages, but that it seeks their happiness by the most efficacious means, allowing them to possess their homes in peace precisely because being well aware of our justice and our power to sustain it, they respect our populations and do not disturb them.

❦ *E S S A Y S*

Spanish exploration and colonization of the Southwest took place between 1530 and 1800. Prior to the arrival of the Spanish, the Indian nations of the Southwest were a very heterogeneous people, ranging from hunter-gatherer societies to those like the

Anasazi (the Ancient Ones) with advanced agriculture. In A.D. 500 the Anasazi civilization was centered in Chaco Canyon, the four-corner area of present-day Arizona, Utah, Colorado, and New Mexico. The Anasazi later migrated southeast to the Indian settlements of the upper Río Grande Valley—the Hopi, Zuni, and Pueblo peoples that the Spanish encountered in the mid-sixteenth century. Russian and English interests in California spurred Spanish colonization as a defensive measure in the late eighteenth century. Shortly thereafter, a mission system was established along with presidios and towns from southern to northern California.

In the first essay, Carlos G. Vélez-Ibáñez, professor of anthropology and dean of the College of Humanities, Arts, and Social Sciences at the University of California, Riverside, describes and analyzes the pre-Columbian history of the Southwest. He traces the cultural interactions among the Meso-American populations of Mexico and the U.S.—Mexico border region, focusing on the Hohokam, Mogollon, and Anasazi. Vélez-Ibáñez demonstrates that the Southwest region was a culturally vibrant and highly populated region well before the Spanish arrived in the sixteenth century.

The next essay, by Carroll L. Riley, a specialist in southwestern Native American history, provides an overview of the cultural life of Pueblo Indian tribes in the Río Grande Valley in 1492, on the eve of Columbus's voyage to America. Riley notes that the rich bottomlands of the Río Grande Valley were ideal for the irrigation agriculture that supported large numbers of towns with sizable Indian populations with a complex social, political and religious life that still exists today. An extensive trading system based on foods and medicinal plants also flourished among the Indians of the region. Riley concludes that many generations of the descendants of Pueblo Indians born in 1492 would live to see the very different world that was formed after the Spaniards invaded and conquered the Southwest.

Antonia I. Castañeda, associate professor of history at Saint Mary's University, San Antonio, Texas, has written extensively on women of color in the West. In her essay, she looks closely at the causes and consequences of the sexual assaults against California Indian women that began as soon as the Spanish presidios and missions were established. These assaults in turn spurred Indian rebellions that impeded pacification and missionization efforts by causing the Indians to make peace with one another and join forces against the Spaniards. In her view, rape was an act of domination and power emerging from patriarchal Spanish colonial ideas about sex, gender, race, and the role of conquest. These ideas affected relationships between the sexes and races on the southwestern frontier, all of which worked to insure the Indians' subordination and compliance. Castañeda argues that historians have failed to focus on the impact of sexual violence against Indian women in examining Spanish policy on the California frontier.

Cultural Roots of Ancient Southwest Indians

CARLOS G. VÉLEZ-IBÁÑEZ

It is highly likely that major parts of the Northern Greater Southwest were well populated at the time of Spanish expansion in the sixteenth century. It is also probable that Indian populations were concentrated in urban agricultural pueblos and/or in small dispersed agricultural settlements (*rancherías*) along riverine systems. Uto-Aztecan speakers came out of the south from the Mesoamerican region carrying maize and squash and "bumped" into recipient populations from as early as 300 B.C. From A.D. 1 on, peripheral Mesoamerican groups may have introduced pottery to the region and inspired the adoption of certain practices, such as the construction and use of ball courts (ideas which may have emerged from the south as early as A.D. 500–700). . . .

Although there is some controversy as to whether early peoples such as the Hohokam, Mogollon, or Anasazi were direct ancestors of the concentrated populations the Spanish bumped into in the sixteenth century, there is no doubt that these groups had developed complex social and economic systems. The Opata of northern Sonora alone numbered 60,000 persons and inhabited hierarchically stratified systems of rancherías, villages, and towns containing public monuments at the time they were encountered by Spanish explorers and missionaries. The notion that this region was only sparsely settled prior to the arrival of the Spanish is not borne out by recent work demonstrating that the region of the northwestern borderlands was inhabited by Pueblos, Opata, and Pimas Altos who numbered 220,000 prior to the Spanish expansion, but who were decimated by pathogens perhaps even before the actual physical encounter so that by 1764 only 32,000 of that number remained. Between the early contacts of explorers in the sixteenth century who described "kingdoms" with well-populated complex urbanized settlements and later descriptions by Jesuits who described only remnants of decayed centers and dispersed rancherías, an ahistorical "gap" was created that later supported the stereotype of the region as an empty physical and cultural space. Only recently has significant attention been paid to the impact of disease on settlements in this region during the fifteenth and sixteenth centuries.

It is probable that prior to the Spanish influx the region was composed of permanent villages and urbanized towns with platform mounds, ball courts, irrigation systems, altars, and earth pyramids. The agricultural techniques common to the area included floodwater farming, canal irrigation, and wetland agriculture. A surplus, sufficient to support craft production and long-distance trade between adjoining populations and those stretching from and into central Mexico, was created. . . . One example of this type of political and economic creation in Mesoamerica is that of the Southern Mogollon of Casas Grandes in Northern Chihuahua. . . .

Even though many of the highly complex social and economic systems, such as that of the Hohokam, had all but disappeared by the mid-1400s, intensive and extensive trading and slaving had already been established. By the 1500s, Apaches . . . marketed not only hides and meat to the Pueblos of Northern New Mexico but human beings as well. Thus, at the time of conquest, the region was not an empty physical space bereft of human populations but an area with . . . a lively interactive system of "chiefdom"-like centers or rancherías, each with its own *cazadores* (hunters), material inventions, and exchange systems.

It was only in the aftermath of the introduction of European pathogens, which virtually decimated indigenous populations, that the region actually came to be defined in European terms as an empty vessel to be filled with colonizers. The survivors among the local populations became sources of cheap labor; and in their weakened condition, entire communities of the physically exploited were also made spiritually captive by an enforced religious ideology. The actual physical demise, with its attendant created "space," was reinforced by . . . the notion of political and cultural superiority.

Los Primeros Pobladores: The Development of Early Southwestern Cultural Centers

Anthropologist Henry Dobyns posed an interesting question on the 501st anniversary of the incipient European inundation of the indigenous worlds of the American continents, "What was here . . . in 1492?" Dobyns answered his own question by stating that unlike the way most North American newcomers arrived in this region in the nineteenth century from the East, most major human trails of the region ran from south to north. He stated that such trails were a result of the economic links within the urban population of almost 2 million in the various cities of the Valley of Mexico. Although there is a great deal of controversy among different archaeological authorities concerning this theory, compelling evidence does exist to support Dobyns's point of view. We can divide the issue into two basic questions: what were the processes that enabled these 2,000-mile links to develop, and how were these links to which Dobyns refers established?

The answer to the first proposition begins with the idea that the south to north movement is an old one. [Emil W.] Haury (1986, 443) placed the movement of populations carrying maize from the northwestern frontier of Mesoamerican "high cultures" to central Arizona at about 300 B.C. Especially pertinent to this view is the triad of complex agriculturally based societies that includes the Hohokam of Southern Arizona and Sonora, perhaps the Mogollon of Casas Grandes, Chihuahua, Mexico, and the mountain Mogollon of Southwestern New Mexico, and to a lesser extent the Anasazi of Chaco Canyon and Mesa Verde who inhabited the Four Corners area of New Mexico, Arizona, Utah, and Colorado.

Over a period of sixty years as a preeminent authority on Southwestern peoples, Haury concluded that "the richness of the oldest Hohokam ceramic tradition, their lithic technology, irrigation capability from the start, and echoes of Mesoamerican beginnings persuade me to hold fast" to the idea that an immigrant group from Mexico carried with them the technological hardware and cultural "funds of knowledge" to establish themselves in the aridity of the Sonoran desert region. For Haury, the Hohokam complex began with the migration of agriculturally sophisticated peoples into the Gila River Valley somewhat south of present-day Florence, Arizona. There they not only pursued complex irrigation agriculture, the knowledge of which they had brought with them, but they also developed hybrids of maize adapted to an arid environment.

These populations of the Greater Southwest . . . eventually inhabited and developed a technologically complex agricultural geographic area of 45,000 square miles . . . over a period of almost 2,500 years. The Hohokam, it was proposed, were more than likely direct migrants from Mesoamerica who bumped into the hunting and gathering peoples who were already present at their arrival. By the twelfth century, they had developed a "core" area of the Phoenix basin and eight peripheral areas.

From their very origin in 300 B.C. the Hohokam were a "frontier, spacially displaced Mesoamerican society" . . . (Haury 1976, 351). This interpretation hypothesizes that the Hohokam came from Mexico and after settling to the north maintained contact and were stimulated to develop culturally by periodic "infusions" from Mesoamerica. For a thousand years the Hohokam developed complex cultural forms and peaked both politically and economically about A.D. 700–900 with a final decline in A.D. 1450 only shortly before the intrusion by the Spanish (Haury 1976, 352).

There is, however, an opposite point of view that does not automatically deny influence from the south but denies that the Hohokam complex originated in Mesoamerica or its perpheries. Most recently, scholars have suggested that the complex Hohokam development occurred incrementally and that by the time of Christ, numerous groups in the region had already developed incipient agricultural "archaic" production patterns. Thus local groups after A.D. 700 had already developed a number of distinctive regional traditions and created interactive trade networks, major agricultural systems of production, social stratification, and other complex political and organizational forms. However, even those scholars that emphasize this point of view do not deny that by A.D. 1100 imported Mesoamerican ideas, practices, objects, and more than likely peoples were present among the Hohokam. [Paul R.] Fish (1989, 21), who is less predisposed to the Mesoamerican origination thesis, states unequivocally that what especially differentiates Hohokam public architecture such as platform mounds and ball courts from Pueblan complexes is their "Mesoamerican antecedents."

The resolution to the debate between origination and the influence of Mesoamerican traditions in the Southwest, I would suggest, is not an either/or matter. Rather it should be understood that the origination of complex production forms by early peoples in the region occurred differentially, and different complexes like the Hohokam, Mogollon, and Anasazi developed local systems and to different degrees were influenced by Mesoamerican traditions, ideas, and peoples.

For the Hohokam, influences probably originated out of northern Michoacán, Guanajuato, Aguascalientes, southern Zacatecas, and western Mexico and probably followed a coastal route, given the fact that the maize of the early Hohokam type more than likely was diffused from western Mexico. Once established, the Hohokam/Mesoamerican connection is best exemplified by (1) direct imports and (2) ideas and practices that led to their replication and adoption.

. . . The various cultural items and influences transmitted from Mesoamerica before A.D. 1 (according to the Haury thesis), . . . range from complex irrigation agriculture to pottery making itself, although there is evidence the Hohokam themselves developed an incipient form of agriculture after A.D. 1 and developed pottery as well. . . . The latest work on the Hohokam indicates that the development of an advanced agricultural way of life occurred more probably after A.D. 200, so that the Hohokam complex is much later than Haury originally estimated. Therefore, agriculture among the Hohokam was probably locally developed but also influenced by practices introduced by another source from the south. This "bumping" must have been a dramatic and intrusive process in the lives of the hunters and gatherers and original small-scale agricultural villages. Some types of pottery, stone sculptures, turquoise mosaics, censors, anthropomorphic figures, as well as the triad of Mesoamerican foods, kidney beans, squash, and new varieties of corn, were to different degrees influences from the south.

The major influences from the south included representative ceramics such as a Chac Mool–like figure, crematory and funerary practices, and artifacts, such as handled incense burners. In addition, the appearance of the macaw seems to indicate a greater and greater expansion of ceremonialism, and simultaneously of art styles and pottery painting with motifs similar to that of the "Quetzalcoatl cross." . . . The introduction in this period or perhaps earlier of human and bird effigy jars and of cotton shows an increasing complexity of ritual and ceremony, in which the former were used, and of important productive and economic infusions, in the case of the latter.

The importance of the imported ideas and practices should not be underestimated, for they may have influenced social complexity, environmental change, and cultural experimentation in the region. The use of irrigation systems alone required labor organization, knowledge of planting, crop tilling, harvesting, and plant rotation (all undertaken at appropriate times of the year). Undoubtedly, this information was integrated into a wider "fund of knowledge" concerning summer and winter solstices, ceremonial preparations, and sacrifice expressed in cosmological terms by priest specialists. Thus, it can be seen that influences from the south combined with technologies already present in the region, if the origination thesis is tempered to focus upon southern influences from A.D. 300 on. In the period A.D. 300–700 ceramic figures are similar to those from Mexico and tend to portray especially the idea of fertility and procreation. It is at the beginning of this period that a shift to agriculture from a reliance on hunting takes place, and the link between fertility and crop production rather than hunting also evolves. The belief in death and rebirth, perhaps associated with cremation practices and new crops, probably became part of the ancient world views that bind the present-day Pima and Tohono O'odham to their past. In fact, . . . before the European inundation ceremonial ball games were conducted by their Hohokam ancestors to celebrate ancient versions of what are today known as Green Corn maturation ceremonies.

The period of greatest Mesoamerican influence in the region occurred between A.D. 800 and 1200, even though Haury's estimate is some two hundred years earlier. Platform mounds and ball courts are two examples of that influence. The artificial elevated platforms, which were widely diffused to the southeastern United States from Mesoamerica in an earlier as well as contemporary period to that of the Hohokam, serve as symbols of an important architectural and ritual shift within this group. . . . Platform mounds of the Hohokam became central locations for ritual. Constructed in a layered manner, with the use of steps not unlike Mesoamerican models, the Hohokam platform mound imitated its southern model by shifting its geographical center as changes in the calendric cycle occurred. In the last period of their existence in the Classic period (1450), massive mounds were built with houses on top at various sites in the Salt River Valley of Arizona.

The eventual construction of some 200 ball courts . . . , the game itself, in which a rubber ball was used, and the attendant cultural practices are among the most obvious expressions of the influence of the Mesoamerican belief system and public ceremonial architecture, despite the views of some who would depict the structures as dance plazas rather than ball courts. . . . Other ideas related to macro-Indian cosmology that were imported and developed in the region and are associated with the ritual ball game would include "shamanism, vision quests, cosmologies of Earth Mother and Sky Father, moiety divisions and the conception of a cosmic whole formed from the relations of an underworld and an upperworld" ([David R.] Wilcox 1991, 101–2). In this vein, the game was traditionally an important part of the Mesoamerican cult of Quetzalcoatl/Tezcatlipoca and in its play articulated symbolically the struggle between good and evil represented respectively by the mythic brothers Quetzalcoatl and Tezcatlipoca—God of Life and Light and God of Death and Darkness. There is as well an indication that fertility-associated bone implements excavated at Snaketown, Arizona, may have been used as part of bloodletting ceremonies congruent with Mesoamerican and Maya practices.

Entire sets of ideas concerning the manner in which the world works were diffused at the same time as other sorts of ideas; and the ball court "way" was not merely a sport played as a competitive game between individuals and their teams, but was, as has been stated, a reflection of fundamental beliefs about the world. Much like the martial arts of pre-modern Asia in which there was a great difference in the combat between groups representing the corporate interests of communities and combat between lineages and their ancestors, ball court "ways" might have functioned and expressed the corporate interests of communities, their lineages and moieties, and their spiritual corporate ancestors. The ball game as a possible predictive device may have been played to reduce the uncertainty of life in a desert environment in which a combination of scarce rainfall, constructed irrigation works, and fragile water wells made a lack of resources an overriding probability. The ball game may have functioned psychologically to reduce the anxiety of the likelihood of failure by testing possible outcomes with one team representing success in predicting rainfall, crop success, favorable trading exchange, and the outcome of conflicts with neighbors. In addition, the ball game might have tested man's relations with the supernatural because the outcome of the game was in the province of the gods alone, and their beneficence would be expressed if the winning side represented a successful agricultural year.

Mesoamerican influence extended beyond the areas of architecture, agricultural technology, ceremonial practices, and beliefs already discussed. Artifacts from the period of contact provide evidence of some unspecific exchange between the cultures. About two hundred copper bells (spectrographic analyses have identified them as originating in the Mexican states of Jalisco and Nayarit), approximately one hundred highly reflective mosaic mirrors, pottery shapes like three-legged vessels, and stone sculptures are all indicative of the types of trade goods imported from distances to the south. In only probing these materials of the mirrors and the bells, it is clear that both are Mexican. Identical mosaic mirrors have been recovered from archaeological sites in Jalisco, Mexico, and as far as Guatemala among Mayan ruins. The mirrors found among the Hohokam are of Mexican derivation in both style and technique, and they are associated with death and cremation and anthropomorphized just as those in Guatemala are. However, more important is the strong association with the Quetzalcoatl-Tezcatlipoca cult: the mirrors were found primarily at Hohokam cremation sites, and among Mesoamericans such identical mirrors were sacrificed yearly to their warriors. Even today the Quetzalcoatl plumed snake seems to continue as "Corua," or water snake, in the myths and folk beliefs of U.S. Mexicans in the Southwest.

At the representational level . . . of the important Mesoamerican influences, one . . . is the bird-snake combination. . . . The bird-snake motif often served as a covert form of Quetzalcoatl, the plumed serpent, the mythic god-man who was related to the sea and wind, and had journeyed and reached the central plateau of Mexico and established himself at Teotihuacán. After his destruction in A.D. 650, the mythic personality reappeared at Tula where he rose again and with him the great Toltec center of Tula. The god-man was then exiled from Tula in A.D. 987, later to appear in a number of Mesoamerican and Northwestern Mexican cultural areas such as Tenayuca, Chulhuacan, Cholula, Cempoala, and finally to the desert. Reminiscent of the death and rebirth myth common to the Amerindian world of the Southwest, Quetzalcoatl as myth, together with his mythic journey, is of ancient origin. . . .

The Hohokam were not merely passive recipients of Mesoamerican influences; they created extensive commercial exchange systems, especially between A.D. 800 and 1100, maintaining "core" or middleman exchange relations with a number of other groups in other directions. For example, the Hohokam acquired shell on the California coast (both on the Baja Peninsula and northward) from which they produced bracelets that were exchanged for Cerillos turquoise in the Chaco Mogollon area. Other Hohokam derived, produced, or transferred goods, sent through their trade networks, included cotton, salt, lac, ground-stone tools such as metates, and finished pottery. After 1200, Mesoamerican influence in the region seemed to wane, possibly as an aftereffect of other than local environmental processes or ecological imbalances. . . .

The Hohokam as a regional system did shrink in this period; settlements became more concentrated in the Gila and Salt basins, architecturally adobe rooms above ground replaced pithouses, and even administrative centers like Casa Grande outside of Coolidge, Arizona, arose and traded with Casas Grandes of Chihuahua. By 1450 or so, most of the population centers had been abandoned; environmental causes such as water logging and salt concentration in the irrigation fields were partially to blame, but more than likely this collapse was also associated with the interruption of regional trading patterns with other cultural complexes such as the Mogollon, Anasazi, and Patayan. By the time of the Spanish inundation, the Hohokam population had been reduced to a tenth of its preconquest level; but at the same time a number of highly mobile, culturally diverse groups created less concentrated population centers with little reliance on large-scale irrigation-based agriculture. Despite the decline of the Hohokam, new forms of . . . relations emerged that permitted contact and extensive trade between groups in the same region.

With regard to the Mogollan complex, the second of the triad of complex Southwestern and Northern Mexican societies, Haury (1986, 455) suggested that the Mogollan north of the present Mexican border were in reality no more than technologically well developed populations from a "heartland centered in the Sierra Madre Occidental of Mexico." Casas Grandes in Chihuahua was thought to have served as a major trading and manufacturing center on the northern frontier within Mesoamerica, and northwestern peoples were agents of cultural exchange and trade between Mesoamerica and complexes further north. . . . Casas Grandes was not developmentally contemporaneous with the Anasazi but instead with their later survivors in the fourteenth century and with the Hohokam in the early 1300s.

The Chaco Anasazi and the Eastern Anasazi provide the strongest case for a slowly developing complex that was not directly derived from Mesoamerica but which, nevertheless, may have been strongly influenced by long-distance trade relations with Mesoamerica especially through groups that influenced local Anasazi culture. . . . A convincing argument is made by others who state that Mesoamerican goods like macaws, copper bells, and Mesoamerican cloisonné items were more than likely high-value commodities used as the basis of economic exchange between elites of Chaco and other elites of the Southwest and West Mexico. In addition, the compelling "astroarchaeological" analysis by [Jonathan E.] Reyman (1971, 283), who focused on the impact of Mexican influences on Anasazi ceremonialism, concludes that "Chaco Canyon appears to have been a central receiving and distribution area for Mexican trade in the 11th and 12th centuries." How that occurred prior to the emergence of Casas Grandes is difficult to discern considering that Casas Grandes would have been the most likely trade transfer point; however, the Chaco core dissolved almost at the advent of Casas Grandes in 1150. In terms of Mesoamerican connections there is overriding evidence that appears to be solely an importation from tropical Mexico (Oaxaca and southern Tamaulipas): the Scarlet Macaw (*Ara macao*), which was found in the ruins of Pueblo Bonito, the largest Chaco site of the tenth century. One doubts a "flying saucer connection."

. . . Mesoamerican trade items were highly valued and served as symbols of elite status. However, it is probable that Southwestern ceremonialism at Chaco was significantly influenced by Mexican sources. What has to be sorted out is whether all three cultural complexes either originated in Mesoamerica, were recipients of Mesoamerican cultural influence but did not play an important role in economic or political relations, or played a crucial role in the Southwestern-Mesoamerican connection.

First, . . . the Hohokam, Mogollon, and Anasazi rose and fell in different periods and were more than likely connected one to the other by trade and exchange relations at different times. During the historical existence of these cultural centers, each served as a core area of an "interaction sphere" expanding its trade and communication networks and routes throughout the Greater Southwest and beyond. In some cases (Hohokam and Chaco), they interacted one with the other and were to varying degrees trading partners and cultural bearers and borrowers. . . . They were never isolated from either each other or other groups and certainly not from Mesoamerica. Second, it is probable that their connections to Mesoamerica were generally not direct (except perhaps for the Hohokam) and that complexes in Northern and Western Mexico served as transit and transfer points for goods and populations.

María Teresa Cabrero [García] (1989, 49–50) states that the Chalchihuites cultural center of Zacatecas was a transfer point because it had the closest connections with the Greater Southwest. Even though it was an extension of Mesoamerican centers, it also developed its own original complex cultural system. Its province eventually extended north to Durango and to the south strongly influenced the Malpaso and Bolanos-Julchilpa cultures. During the Pre-Classic period of Teotihuacán ca. A.D. 200, Chalchihuites served primarily as an autonomous transfer point, but by A.D. 350 (during the Classic period) it had become a core periphery. The interest in the center was probably increased because of the availability of turquoise in the Greater Southwest (particularly in New Mexico); in addition, Chalchihuites served as a major mining center for the mineral chalchihuite so that after A.D. 350 exploitation of the area increased. . . .

It has been suggested that with the fall of Teotihuacán, Tula became the main trade center for minerals in Mesoamerica, and Casas Grandes, situated in the middle of Chihuahua and La Quemada in central Zacatecas, was thought to have been the principal commercial center on the trade route to Tula. However, . . . recent findings . . . date the advent of Casas Grandes much too late for it to have served as a commercial center on the route from Tula to La Quemada and then on to Durango with commercial exchange taking place in Zape until it was transferred to Casas Grandes from where it continued on to the Hohokam and Mogollan. However, it is certain that Chalchihuites served as a transfer site for New Mexican turquoise, which was more than likely carried there beginning in A.D. 350 and continuing perhaps until the twelfth century. At El Vesuvio and Cerro de Moctezuma, two Chalchihuites culture areas located near each other, X-ray diffraction techniques have identified eighty turquoise artifacts as having come from turquoise mines in New Mexico, probably from the Cerrillos mines near Santa Fe, New Mexico, during that area's formative development (Basketmaker Period). It is also possible that expeditions formed in Chalchihuites were organized to exploit this resource in the early phases of New Mexican turquoise export.

There was a probable connection between Casas Grandes and the Durango area, but at a later period in time and through the trade center of Cañon de Molino in the early fourteenth to late fifteenth century. In addition, it is more than likely that Casas Grandes would have established exchange relations with coastal Sinaloa and Guasave and would have interacted with Sonora statelets and the Hohokam.

To return, however, to the period 350–1100, turquoise did become the mineral of choice for the various elites of the Greater Southwestern centers, their Northwestern Mexican counterparts, and for the Toltec lords of Tula. As late as 1492 turquoise was the most important item to be traded to the south, and the trade routes followed what Dobyns (1993, 5) has termed "Mesoamerica's Western Turquoise Trail," by means of which Mesoamericans imported turquoise from Los Cerrillos in New Mexico, the Gleason deposit in Southwestern Arizona, and from the Cerbat Mountains in the Mojave, California, area. They also imported green hyaline opals from the upper Rio Grande in the same period.

Some scholars have suggested that the Greater Southwest maintained peripheral trade relations with Mesoamerica from at least A.D. 1050 to 1350. However, this position is difficult to maintain since there would be little if any political authority, physical force, or conviction to coerce such distant peripheral centers. Rather, they were probably relatively equal "core" trading partners one with the other; in the case of Casas Grandes, it probably was part of a peripheral trade system into the late fifteenth century.

Thus, at the time of conquest, the Northern Greater Southwest region was not an empty physical space bereft of human populations even after the demise of great urban centers, but more than likely was a lively interactive system of "chiefdom"-like centers, *rancherías,* and *cazadores* (hunters) with their material inventions and exchange systems. Elaborate trade systems in the protohistorical period may have been in operation and goods, traders, ideas, and innovations continued to flow up to the time of the Spanish inundation and perhaps afterwards to a much more limited degree.

Certainly, by A.D. 300 people and ideas may have moved from the south, as was the case with the Hohokam, and influenced the technological and productive ways of organizing natural resources, labor, and agricultural activity. The impact of ideology ebbed and flowed as some compact cultural centers like the Mogollan rose and fell because of environmental reasons, as was the case for Casas Grandes, razed by invasion and fire. Even when such a grand center as the Chaco Canyon complex deteriorated to the degree that the human inventors abandoned it, others slipped in behind or traveled further north and south to form even more complex systems, or much more compact systems in the south known as Pueblos in the various provinces described.

. . . All of these populations of the Greater Southwest did in fact interact directly in some cases or indirectly in others with complex systems further into what is known as Mesoamerica. There is little evidence to lead one to think that by some means Teotihuacán, Tula, Tarasca, or Tenochtitlán, considering the great distances involved, maintained coercive relationships with other populations, inducing them into a politically subservient position to be controlled economically without the use of force. However, there is sufficient evidence to conclude that for at least 1,696 years the pre-Hispanic Greater Southwest was part of a series of exchange systems made up of centers of production, trade, and redistribution that functioned according to the availability of food and its acquisition. When this process was made impossible because of drought, flooding, wars, and/or pestilence, the centers died out and others eventually took their place. What can be concluded is that the environmental, social, and economic dynamics of the Greater Southwest demanded that its populations be amazingly adaptable, which at times meant learning from or becoming amalgamated with other groups. Simultaneously, they created rituals—ceremonial, artistic, and physical expressions—that reflected ancient ideas from the south but included as well their own versions that tended to better fit the existing conditions in which they found themselves.

The Indians of the Southwest in 1492

CARROLL L. RILEY

For the Pueblo Indian tribes in the Rio Grande valley, 1492 was relatively uneventful except for one troublesome incident at the end of the year. In the Pueblo world, proper ceremonies were necessary to keep crops growing and the universe in harmony. In turn, fixing the planting calendar and setting the great annual ceremonies demanded painstaking measurements of the winter solstice. Measurements were made over a number of days by carefully observing the morning sun as it broke the

"1492 on the Rio Grande," in Carroll L. Riley, *Rio del Norte: People of the Upper Rio Grande from Earliest Times to the Pueblo Revolt* (Salt Lake City: University of Utah Press, 1995). Reprinted by permission of the publisher.

plane of the eastern horizon. For six months, each sunrise had seen the sun inch slightly southward. Now, around December 20 or 21, there would be two or three days in which the sun seemed to rise in the same spot. The solstice was reached, and the sun's disk over the following days and weeks would slowly track northward along the horizon.

The solstice was fully dependable, but the weather-control priests also considered it important that the solstice coincide with a full moon. Every year they attempted to match these two events, and sometimes they succeeded. At other times, because of the nature of celestial mechanics—not fully understood by the Indians—the attempt would fail, and the solstice would come at or near a new moon. In 1492 the attempt failed miserably, for the solstice fell nearer the time of the new moon. Perhaps it was an omen!

Other aspects of the natural and cultural world, however, were reasonably satisfactory in 1492. Rainfall had been adequate for the past two or three years. A decade of extreme drought, reaching its peak in 1420, had taken a toll, but even folk memory of this grim time faded as the century wore on. Struggles over land, trade routes, and valuable resources were no greater this year than usual. Of late, Apachean nomads who lived to the east and north of the Pueblos had begun to press harder on the settled towns, but plains Indians would not become really threatening for another thirty years.

At the time of Columbus the names by which Pueblo peoples knew themselves and each other were probably about what they would be when Coronado entered the area in 1540. Spanish usage of Pueblo and other native names generally depended on their first source or sources of information. The Zuni towns were collectively called Cíbola by the earliest Spanish explorers. Cíbola is most likely a variation of *shiwana,* the Zuni name for the Zuni area (though it may possibly have been a misunderstanding of the Zuni word for bison, *si:wolo*). This term was picked up by Marcos de Niza from Indians in Sonora who were acquainted with the Zunis. The name Zuni itself was introduced in the 1580s by the two Spanish expeditions of that decade. These expeditions came into Zuni from the east rather than from the south and simply borrowed the tribal name used by the Keresan-speaking Acomas.

Spaniards of the Coronado expedition called the Hopi region Tusayán, which may possibly derive from a Navajo term, *tasaun,* meaning "country of isolated buttes." Such an identification might indicate that Apachean speakers were in the Hopi area by Coronado's time. However, Spaniards do not mention nomadic Indians at Hopi until the early 1580s. By that time Spaniards had started using an Acoma word for Hopi, rendering it *Mohose,* a term still current in the nineteenth century under its shortened form, *Moqui.* In recent times, however, outsiders have switched to *Hopi,* meaning "peaceful," "wise," or "good" people—the word used by the Hopi Indians to designate themselves. . . .

The Rio Grande valley, with its great potential for irrigation agriculture and its rich bottomlands, was home in 1492 to a large number of towns, many of them quite sizable. People continued to aggregate in towns in certain portions of the northern Rio Grande basin, although population had shrunk some from its peak in the mid-fifteenth century. By 1492 the large Arroyo Hondo Pueblo south of Santa Fe had been deserted for thirty or forty years, and some marginal regions like Tijeras Canyon west of modern Albuquerque lost population during the fifteenth century.

Still, the Tiguex region, the Galisteo basin, the middle and lower Jemez valley, the east flank of the Pajarito Plateau, and the lower Chama valley continued to be heavily occupied, as did the Piro and Tompiro areas. Towns were built of sandstone blocks or river cobbles set in mud mortar or simply of coursed adobe. In some towns, houseblocks were three or more stories high. These "apartment houses" caught the imagination of Indians farther to the south, who, a few decades later, described them to the earliest Spanish explorers. Houseblocks might be separated by streets or lanes and generally were built around plazas in which the kivas were often located.

The political organization of the Pueblo Indians in the late fifteenth century is still a matter of some argument. . . .

Certainly, the priests held ample power, as did quasi-religious political figures such as the war chiefs. Still, the Pueblos seem basically to have been egalitarian, with large social groups such as clans or moieties and the nonelitist societies handling matters of ceremonialism, war, social control, curing, and redistribution of surplus through trade. Nor does there seem to have been any domination of surrounding pueblos by a major primate town. . . .

This is not to say that cooperation among pueblos was completely lacking. At Zuni and Hopi in the west and at Tiguex in the Rio Grande valley there are signs of loose federations whose individual towns were tied by linguistic bonds and most likely ceremonial and familial bonds as well. The kachina cult and the war and other societies also helped cement ties between villages. . . . Pueblo people could act together, but such action depended on decisions made by individual towns. They could and did unite for specific purposes, but it was an ad hoc sort of unity. . . .

Rio Grande Indian economies in 1492 were based on production of basic foodstuffs: maize, beans, squash, and domesticated dogs and turkeys. . . . Cotton was probably being grown in the southern and central part of the area, perhaps as far north as the Keresan, or even the Chama River Tewa, towns. Large amounts of cotton and cotton goods, however, continued to be imported from the Hopi towns. Tobacco seeds . . . have been found . . . , and ceremonial use of the domesticated plant continued among the Pueblo Indians into modern times. . . .

A variety of wild plants were collected for eating and for medical purposes. . . . Important plants included goosefoot . . . , the seeds of which were ground and treated much like maize flour. The garden green purslane was cooked with meat as a flavoring or was boiled and eaten as a separate dish. The Rocky Mountain bee plant . . . was collected both for seeds and for its leaves, which were cooked as greens. Wild potatoes were eaten, as were the seeds of the wild sunflower; there is even a possibility that the sunflower was domesticated in pre-Spanish times. Piñon nuts and the fruit of the yucca plant were also eaten. Mormon tea . . . produces tannin and a certain amount of an ephedrine-related alkaloid and was taken for respiratory problems and as a diuretic. . . .

The datura or jimsonweed plant . . . was also used in medicine, its ground seeds or roots being rubbed on wounds for quicker healing and its seeds, leaves, and roots boiled to make a drink to control pain. . . . It seems certain that the datura plant was both important and widespread, used both medicinally and as a hallucinogen in religious ceremonies in the Pueblo world of 1492.

Dogbane, or black hemp . . . , was also collected from early times. The plant . . . has the medical properties of a stimulant and diuretic. . . .

. . . The Pueblos ate rabbits, both cottontail and jackrabbit, as well as deer, antelope, and a number of smaller animals and birds, including the domestic turkey. Larger animals were hunted with bows and arrows, but rabbits were literally harvested by means of communal rabbit drives in which the animals were surrounded and killed with clubs or sticks—sometimes with the ubiquitous digging stick used in cultivation. Rabbit drives . . . represent a way of life thousands of years old.

Agriculture provided the staples of life, even though a considerable percentage of the food resources came from gathering and hunting. . . . Maize was generally planted as soon as the frost season ended. For people on or near the main river, this was April or early May, with harvest time in September or early October. The Pecos area had a shorter growing season, as did Taos and the Tompiro country. Beans and squash tended to be planted in or around the cornfields. . . .

. . . The Rio Grande inhabitants often grew enough foodstuffs, especially maize, for trade. Plains nomads were particularly eager to trade bison meat, bison skins, and other items for dried or parched corn or cornmeal, and these commodities were important in the trade going eastward. It remained a very important exchange item into the nineteenth century.

The costume à la mode in 1492 was about the same as that of half a century later when the first Spanish explorers wrote down what they saw. Women wore a blanketlike garment usually woven of cotton but sometimes of yucca fiber or strands of apocynum, tied with a sash at the waist. Both breasts might be bare, or the garment might be fastened over one shoulder with the other shoulder and breast exposed. In cold weather a second blanket of cotton or skin would be draped over the first. Men wore loincloths, often decorated with tassels, or short, kiltlike skirts, and in cold weather covered their upper bodies with a draped blanket. Children went nude. According to one Spanish account . . . , mature women also went nude until marriage—but if true at all, this probably held only for the summer months.

Costume jewelry included turquoise, garnets, peridots, and other semiprecious stones, along with shell, bone, and jet, all worn as pins, bracelets, finger rings, earrings, pendants, and brooches. Among the western Pueblos, one of the earliest chroniclers described the traditional squash-blossom hairdo in which the hair is put up in two large whorls, one on each side of the head. We are not certain whether this was the general custom in the Rio Grande.

The sociopolitical life of Rio Grande peoples in 1492 was closely intertwined with religion and ceremony. Even today, after four centuries of Spanish, Mexican, and American control, Pueblo religion still deeply influences every aspect of life. . . .

. . . Three kinds of sociopolitical organizations are usually described for Rio Grande Pueblos today. The first . . . is, collectively, the various societies and kiva groups that share social and religious functions. Second is the moiety, the division of a society into two halves. A third type of organizational group is the clan. Now, the proper meaning of the word *clan* to anthropologists is "descent group"; classically, it meant *matrilineal* descent, that is, descent in which ancestors are traced primarily in the mother's line. . . . Among strongly clan-oriented societies, both father's and mother's families are important, but kinship titles and attitudes toward the father's relatives and the mother's relatives may differ considerably. . . .

Important in all the Rio Grande pueblos was the war chief, who took over from the peace-associated cacique in times of conflict. The functions of the war chief and associated war societies have become somewhat blurred by the fact that Spanish authorities in the seventeenth and eighteenth centuries encouraged the office of war captain (*capitán de la guerra*), winking at the Pueblo habit of collecting scalps from Apache or Navajo enemies. . . . There is some reason to believe that they arose about the same time as the kachina cult, and like that cult served as an integrating mechanism for the pueblos.

The supernatural underpinnings for such societies were the Twin War Gods, or elder and younger twins, a mythological concept spread throughout much of Mesoamerica. At a guess, the situation of the warrior societies and officials in the Rio Grande pueblos in 1492 was somewhat like the historic Zuni situation, with an elder and younger bow priest representing the Twin War Gods. At any rate, scalp taking was an important part of socioreligious life in the pueblos. . . . If traditional Pueblo stories are to be believed, head taking was also practiced in the prehistoric past.

It should be stressed that individual offices such as war chief or bow priest, as well as social divisions such as moieties and clans, always had religious significance. . . .

Archaeologist Marc Thompson has traced the divine twin motif in Mesoamerica, where it appears as far south and east as the Maya country. The twins represent the sun and the moon, as do two totem animals, deer (sun) and rabbit (moon). In the course of their adventurers the twins undergo death and are resurrected as fish or fish men. Not only are the divine twins part of the religious and political hierarchy, as at Zuni, but folktales and graphic depictions of these twins in various stages of their adventures are widespread in the Southwest. . . .

Somewhere in the course of their travels the divine twins picked up a Quetzalcoatl association, but originally they seem to have been part of a separate religious complex. In prehistoric times it seems likely that a Quetzalcoatl identification with the war deities was part of the Pueblo ceremonial structure. . . .

The cult of the kachinas—the ancestor gods who bring rain and harmony to Pueblo life—was everywhere focused on the kivas in 1492, as had surely been the case since its inception in the fourteenth century. The ceremonial house, or kiva, among modern Rio Grande Pueblo Indians varies from group to group. Tewas tend to have one very large ceremonial house shared by the two moieties, and this seems also to be true of at least the southern Tiwas. There are also rectangular moiety houses and society houses in the Tewa houseblocks, used for storing ceremonial equipment. The same situation holds among the Towas, whereas the Keresans normally have two large kivas for the two moiety groups, plus society houses. Modern Rio Grande kivas can be either round or rectangular, as was true in 1492 and, indeed, throughout the golden age.

To sum up, at the time of Columbus's first journey, both the sociopolitical and the religious structures of the Rio Grande pueblos possessed many of the same elements found today. But in many cases the organization of these elements was quite different. The kachina cult, so rich in the fifteenth century, barely survived the on-slaughts of Christianity among the Tiwas and suffered much change among the Tewas and Keresans. Rio Grande Pueblo religion generally has been drastically af-fected by Christian dogma, ritual, and iconography. Social organization may not seem much altered in basic structure, but the introduction of Spanish secular offi-cers has confused the old lines of command and diluted the once overpoweringly religious nature of social control.

By 1492 the far-reaching trading system had been in place for a century and a half, and the Rio Grande Pueblos received goods that originated as far away as central and eastern Kansas, Oklahoma, and Texas, the Pacific coast of California, and western Mexico. In addition, the Southwestern Pueblos were involved in an extremely important and rich internal trade.

If we were visiting one of the towns of the Tiguex region in 1492, we would see ample evidence of this trade. Tiguex parties were sent out both east and west, certainly as far as Zuni to the west and probably to Hopi. Such parties may occa-sionally have reached the Sonoran statelets, the Gulf of California, the lower Col-orado River, or even the Pacific coast. . . . Fifty or more men would be involved in a trading expedition, and they could be from more than one pueblo and even from more than one language group. . . . It is likely that the heads of the war societies handled trade in pre-Spanish times. Travel to potentially hostile areas, especially out of the immediate Pueblo realm, meant that traders must also be equipped on a war footing.

. . . Goods from those far-flung places were mostly transshipped, with Cíbola-Zuni acting as a major redistribution center. The same was true for trade going east. Though indications are that Tiguex and other Rio Grande Indians, es-pecially the Galisteo groups, sent parties out to the High Plains, many of the goods from the central plains came through Pecos Pueblo, and those from the southern plains, through the Tompiro towns. . . . Some of this trade was in the hands of Pecos Pueblo Indians, but part of it was carried out by Querecho-Apache and Teya Indians. . . .

An observer at one of the Tiguex towns in the year of Columbus's first voyage would see a great deal of plains Indian goods, including bison hides, meat, bois d'arc, eastern river shell, and fibrolite, some of it already shaped and polished in the form of axes. From the west came shells, feathers, pottery, and other luxury goods. . . .

All in all, life in the upper Rio Grande valley in 1492 was relatively uneventful and satisfying, with rich trade and beautiful and complex ceremonials to break up the drudgery of the agricultural round. Selected Pueblo traders were able to travel, sometimes great distances. Threats from neighboring nomads, the Querecho and Teya Indians, would trouble the Puebloan future, but in the year of Columbus's sailing there was no great indication that these nomads were a serious menace. Even the most indirect effects of the Spanish invasion of the New World would not seep into the Southwest for another two or three decades. Still, some of the babies born in the fateful year 1492 would live to see the invaders, and those babies' grandchildren would face a very different world indeed.

Sexual Violence and the Politics of Conquest in Alta California

ANTONIA I. CASTAÑEDA

The father president of the California missions, Junipero Serra, described the depredations of the soldiers against Indian women in his reports and letters to Viceroy Antonio María Bucareli and the father guardian of the College of San Fernando, Rafaél Verger. Sexual assaults against native women began shortly after the founding of the presidio and mission at Monterey in June 1770, wrote Serra, and continued throughout the length of California. The founding of each new mission and presidio brought new reports of sexual violence.

The despicable actions of the soldiers, Serra told Bucareli in 1773, were severely retarding the spiritual and material conquest of California. The native people were resisting missionization. Some were becoming warlike and hostile because of the soldiers' repeated outrages against the women. The assaults resulted in Amerindian attacks, which the soldiers countered with unauthorized reprisals, thereby further straining the capacity of the small military force to staff the presidios and guard the missions. Instead of pacification and order, the soldiers provoked greater conflict and thus jeopardized the position of the church in this region.

Serra was particularly alarmed about occurrences at Mission San Gabriel. . . . He wrote to Father Verger, "this mission gives me the greatest cause for anxiety; the secular arm down there was guilty of the most heinous crimes, killing the men to take their wives." Father Serra related that on October 10, 1771, within a month of its having been founded, a large group of Indians suddenly attacked two soldiers who were on horseback and tried to kill the one who had outraged a woman. . . . "A few days later," Serra continued, "as he went out to gather the herd of cattle . . . and [it] seems more likely to get himself a woman, a soldier, along with some others, killed the principal Chief of the gentiles; they cut off his head and brought it in triumph back to the mission."

The incident prompted the Amerindians of the coast and the sierra, mortal enemies until that time, to convene a council to make peace with each other and join forces to eliminate the Spaniards. The council planned to attack the mission on October 16 but changed the plan after a new contingent of troops arrived at the mission. Despite this narrowly averted disaster, the soldiers assigned to Mission San Gabriel continued their outrages.

The soldiers' behavior not only generated violence on the part of the native people as well as resistance to missionization, argued Serra; it also took its toll on the missionaries, some of whom refused to remain at their mission sites. In his 1773 memorial to Bucareli, Serra lamented the loss of one of the missionaries, who could not cope with the soldiers' disorders at San Gabriel. The priest was sick at heart, Serra stated: "He took to his bed, when he saw with his own eyes a soldier actually committing deeds of shame with an Indian who had come to the mission, and even the children who came to the mission were not safe from their baseness."

Conditions at other missions were no better. Mission San Luis Obispo also lost a priest because of the assaults on Indian women. After spending two years as the sole missionary at San Luis, Father Domingo Juncosa asked for and received permission to return to Mexico because he was "shocked at the scandalous conduct of the soldiers" and could not work under such abominable conditions. Even before San Luis Obispo was founded in the early fall of 1772, Tichos women had cause to fear. The most notorious molesters of non-Christian women were among the thirteen soldiers sent on a bear hunt to this area during the previous winter of starvation at Monterey.

The establishment of new missions subjected the women of each new area to sexual assaults. Referring to the founding of the mission at San Juan Capistrano, Serra wrote that "it seems all the sad experiences that we went through at the beginning have come to life again. The soldiers, without any restraint or shame, have behaved like brutes toward the Indian women." From this mission also, the priests reported to Serra that the soldier-guards went at night to the nearby villages to assault the women and that hiding the women did not restrain the brutes, who beat the men to force them to reveal where the women were hidden. Non-Christian Indians in the vicinity of the missions were simply not safe. They were at the mercy of soldiers with horses and guns.

In 1773, a case of rape was reported at San Luis Rey, one at San Diego, and two cases at Monterey the following year. Serra expressed his fears and concern to Governor Felipe de Neve, who was considering establishing a new presidio in the channel of Santa Barbara. Serra told Neve that he took it for granted that the insulting and scandalous conduct of the soldiers "would be the same as we had experienced in other places which were connected with presidios. Perhaps this one would be worse."

Native women and their communities were profoundly affected by the sexual attacks and attendant violence. California Amerindians were peaceable, nonaggressive people who highly valued harmonious relationships. Physical violence and the infliction of bodily harm on one another were virtually unknown. Women did not fear men. Rape rarely, if ever, occurred. If someone stole from another or caused another's death, societal norms required that the offending party make reparations to the individual and/or the family. Appropriate channels to rectify a wrong without resorting to violence existed.

Animosity, when it did surface, was often worked out ritualistically—for example, through verbal battles in the form of war songs, or song fights that lasted eight days, or encounters in which the adversaries threw stones across a river at each other with no intent actually to hit or physically injure the other party. Even among farming groups such as the Colorado River people, who practiced warfare and took women and children captive, female captives were never sexually molested. The Yumas believed that intimate contact with enemy women caused sickness.

Thus, neither the women nor their people were prepared for the onslaught of aggression and violence the soldiers unleashed against them. They were horrified and terrified. One source reported that women of the San Gabriel and other southern missions raped by the soldiers were considered contaminated and obliged to undergo an extensive purification, which included a long course of sweating, the drinking of herbs, and other forms of purging. This practice was consistent with the people's belief that sickness was caused by enemies. "But their disgust and abhorrence," states the same source, "never left them till many years after." Moreover, any child born as a result of these rapes, and apparently every child was white blood born among them for a very long time, was strangled and buried.

Father Pedro Font, traveling overland from Tubac to Monterey with the Anza expedition between September 1775 and May 1776, recorded the impact of the violence on the native people he encountered. Font's diary verifies the terror in which native Californians, especially the women, now lived. Everybody scattered and fled at the sight of Spaniards. The women hid. They no longer moved about with freedom and ease. The people were suspicious and hostile. The priests were no longer welcome in the living quarters.

The Quabajay people of the Santa Barbara Channel, Font wrote, "appear to us to be gentle and friendly, not war-like. But it will not be easy to reduce them for they are displeased with the Spaniards for what they have done to them, now taking their fish and their food . . . now stealing their women and abusing them." Upon encountering several unarmed Indians on Friday, February 23, Font commented that "the women were very cautious and hardly one left their huts, because the soldiers of Monterey . . . had offended them with various excesses."

At one village, Font noted, he was unable to see the women close at hand because as soon as the Indians saw his party, "they all hastily hid in their huts, especially the girls, the men remaining outside blocking the door and taking care that nobody should go inside." Font attempted to become acquainted with the people of another village on the channel. He went to the door, but "they shut the inner door on me . . . this is the result of the extortions and outrages which the soldiers have perpetrated when in their journeys they have passed along the Channel, especially at the beginning." Font echoed Serra's concern that the sexual assaults and other outrages had severely retarded missionization in California. . . .

Few historians have recognized that the sexual extortion and abuse of native women gravely affected the political, military, religious, and social developments on this frontier. In 1943, Sherburne F. Cook commented that "the entire problem of sexual relations between whites and the natives . . . has apparently escaped detailed consideration by later historians." Cook tackled the issue in demographic terms and wrote about the catastrophic decline in the Indian population as a result of alien diseases, including venereal diseases, brought in by Europeans, as well as other maladies of the conquest.

Almost thirty years later, Edwin A. Beilharz wrote that "the major causes of friction between Spaniard and Indian were the abuse of Indian women and the forced labor of Indian men. . . . Of the two, the problem of restraining the soldiers from assaulting Indian women was the more serious." . . .

Since the 1970s, . . . the development of gender as a category of analysis has enabled us to reexamine Spanish expansion to Alta California with new questions about sex and gender. Cook, Beilharz, and other scholars initiated but did not develop the discussion about the centrality of sex/gender issues to the politics and policies of conquest.

It is clear that the sexual exploitation of native women and related violence seriously threatened the political and military objectives of the colonial enterprise in California. Repeated attacks against women . . . undermined the efforts of the priests to attract Amerindians to the missions and to Christianity. They also thwarted whatever attempts the military authorities might make to elicit political or military allegiance from the native peoples. . . .

. . . Fundamentally, the assaults against women were unwarranted, unprovoked, hostile acts that established conditions of war on this frontier. Although the native peoples by and large did not practice warfare, they were neither docile nor passive in the face of repeated assaults. The people of the South were especially aggressive. The country between San Diego and San Gabriel remained under Indian control for a long time. It was in this region that the Indians marshaled their strongest forces and retaliated against the Spaniards. Some of the engagements, such as the one at San Gabriel in 1771, were minor skirmishes. Others were full-fledged attacks. In 1775 at Mission San Diego, for example, a force of eight hundred razed the mission, killed one priest and two artisans, and seriously wounded two soldiers. Women participated and sometimes even planned and/or led the attacks. In October 1785, Amerindians from eight *rancherías* united under the leadership of one woman and three men and launched an attack on Mission San Gabriel for the purpose of killing all the Spaniards. Toypurina, the twenty-four-year-old medicine woman of the Japchivit *ranchería,* used her considerable influence as a medicine woman to persuade six of the eight villages to join the rebellion. The attack was thwarted. Toypurina was captured and punished along with the other three leaders. . . .

. . . In any event, despite laws and prosecutions, the sexual exploitation of Indian women did not cease. The missionaries continuously reported that soldiers "go by night to nearby villages for the purpose of raping Indian women." And while some cases were recorded, many more must surely have gone unreported. Nevertheless, it is clear that the commandants and the governors did prosecute and take disciplinary action when charges were filed against individual soldiers. Contrary to Serra's charges of laxity and complicity, [Commander Pedro] Fages, [Commander Fernando de] Rivera [y Moncada], and Neve did exert the full measure of their authority in . . . other reported cases of sexual violence or abuse. Abundant evidence details the dual policy of prevention and punishment implemented by the three seasoned frontier administrators in their ongoing effort to check the soldiers' excesses.

Ever concerned that Amerindians would discover the real weakness of the Spanish position in California, Neve sought to prevent the sexual attacks, and thereby to defuse the military and political conflicts they gave rise to, by forbidding all troops, including sergeants and corporals, from entering Indian villages. Only soldiers escorting the priests on sick calls were exempt from this order, and then the soldier was not to leave the missionary's side. Escort guards were strictly admonished against misconduct and were severely punished if they disobeyed.

In the same vein, he prohibited soldiers of the mission guard from spending the night away from the mission—even if the priests demanded it. Neve emphatically repeated this same order in the instructions he left to Pedro Fages, who succeeded him as governor in September of 1782. "It is advisable," Neve further instructed Fages, "that we muzzle ourselves and not exasperate the numerous heathendom which surround us, conducting ourselves with politeness and respect. . . . It is highly useful to the service of the King and the public welfare that the heathen of these establishments do not learn to kill soldiers."

Governor Fages was equally emphatic when he issued the following order in 1785: "Observing that the officers and men of these presidios are comporting and behaving themselves in the missions with a vicious license which is very prejudicial because of the scandalous disorders which they incite among the gentile and Christian women, I command you, in order to prevent the continuation of such abuses, that you circulate a prohibitory edict imposing severe penalties upon those who commit them."

A decade later, Viceroy Branciforte followed up Neve's earlier order with his own decree prohibiting troops from remaining overnight away from the presidios, because among other reasons this practice was "prejudicial to good discipline and Christian morals." Governor Diego de Borica, who succeeded Fages in 1794, issued a similar order the following year. These edicts had little effect.

Soldiers and civilian settlers alike disregarded the civil laws against rape as well as military orders against contact with Amerindian women outside of narrowly proscribed channels. The records verify that sexual attacks continued in areas adjacent to missions, presidios, and pueblos throughout the colonial period. Amerindian women were never free from the threat of rapacious assaults.

Why, despite strenuous efforts by officials of both church and state, did the sexual attacks persist unabated? Why, despite the obviously serious political and military conflicts the assaults ignited, did they continue? In view of extensive legislation, royal decrees, and moral prohibitions against sexual and other violence, what, in the experience of the men who came here, permitted them to objectify and dehumanize Indian women to the degree that chasing and lassoing them from mounted horses and then raping them reveals?

Until recently, scholars attributed sexual violence and other concurrent social disorders in early California to the race and culture of the mixed-blood soldier-settler population recruited or banished to this frontier. Institutional historians concluded, with [Hubert Howe] Bancroft, that the "original settlers, most of them half-breeds of the least energetic classes . . . , were of a worthless character." Institutional studies generally concurred with Serra's view that the soldiers were recruited from the scum of the society. Serra had repeatedly beseeched Bucareli to send "sturdy, industrious Spanish families" and asked him to advise the governor of the Californias "not to use exile to these missions as punishment for the soldier whom he may detest as insolent or perverse."

In the last two decades, the conditions that shaped institutional development on this frontier have been reexamined. In addition, studies of the social history of the people recruited to Alta California have been undertaken. As a result, the earlier interpretations have been rejected. Scholars now conclude that the slow development of colonial institutions in California was attributable to limited resources, lack of uniform military codes, and other structural problems—and not to the racial or social-class origins of the soldier-settler population. . . .

But these revisionists do not address sex/gender issues. The informality of disciplinary codes does not explain the origins or the continuation of sexual violence against native women. Moreover, as the documents for Alta California clearly reveal, Spanish officials enforced colonial criminal statutes and punished sexual crimes to the extent of their authority. However, neither the highly regulatory Laws of the Indies (the extensive legislation enacted to protect the rights of Amerindians), which mandated nonexploitive relations with Amerindians, nor punishment for breaking the laws arrested the violence.

To begin to understand the soldier-settler violence toward native women, we must examine the stratified, patriarchal colonial society that conditioned relationships between the sexes and races in New Spain; the contemporary ideologies of sex/gender and race; and the relations and structures of conquest imposed on this frontier. While rape and other acts of sexual brutality did not represent official policy on this or any other Spanish frontier, these acts were nevertheless firmly fixed in the history and politics of expansion, war, and conquest. In the history of Western civilization writ large, rape is an act of domination, an act of power. As such, it is a violent political act committed through sexual aggression against women.

"The practice of raping the women of a conquered group," writes historian Gerda Lerner, "has remained a feature of war and conquest from the second millennium to the present." Under conditions of war or conquest, rape is a form of national terrorism, subjugation, and humiliation, wherein the sexual violation of women represents both the physical domination of women and the symbolic castration of the men of the conquered group. These concepts and symbolic meanings of rape, as discussed by Lerner, Susan Brownmiller, Anne Edwards, and others, are rooted in patriarchal Western society—in the ideology that devalues women in relation to men while it privatizes and reifies women as the symbolic capital (property) of men. In this ideology, rape has historically been defined as a crime against property and thus against "territory." Therefore, in the context of war and conquest, rape has been considered a legitimate form of aggression against the opposing army—a legitimate expression of superiority that carries with it no civil penalty. In nonmilitary situations, punishment for rape and other crimes of sexual violence against women in Western civilization has, until very recently, generally been determined by the social condition or status of the women violated and by the status of the violator.

In eighteenth-century California, the status of Amerindian women—as members of non-Christian, indigenous groups under military conquest on Spain's northernmost outpost of empire—made them twice subject to assault with impunity: they were the spoils of conquest, and they were Indian. In the mentality of the age, these two conditions firmly established the inferiority of the Amerindian woman and became the basis for devaluing her person beyond the devaluation based on sex that accrued to all women irrespective of their sociopolitical (race, class) status. The ferocity and longevity of the sexual assaults against the Amerindian woman are rooted in the devaluation of her person conditioned by the weaving together of the strands of the same ideological thread that demeaned her on interrelated counts: her sociopolitical status, her sex, and her gender.

From their earliest contact with Amerindian peoples, Europeans established categories of opposition, or otherness, within which they defined themselves as superior and Amerindians as inferior. These categories were derived from the Aristotelian theory that some beings are inferior by nature, and therefore should be dominated by their superiors for their own welfare, and from the medieval Spanish concept of "purity of blood," which was based on religion and which informed the sense of national unity forged during the reconquest. These ideas . . . prevailed during the era of first contact with Amerindians and the early conquests of the Americas.

By the late eighteenth century, a different political concept—racial origin— defined place and social value in the stratified social order of colonial New Spain. Race was inextricably linked to social origin and had long been a symbol for significant cleavages in society; it was one primary basis for valuation—and devaluation—of human beings. In the contemporary ideology and society, Amerindian women were thus devalued on the basis of their social and racial origins, which placed them at the bottom of the social scale, and as members of a conquered group.

Two aspects of the devaluation of Amerindian women are especially noteworthy. First and foremost, it is a political devaluation. That is, it is rooted in and driven by political considerations and acts: by war, conquest, and the imposition of alien sociopolitical and economic structures of one group over another. Second, the devaluation rationalized by conquest cuts across sex. At this level, women and men of the conquered group are equally devalued and objectified by the conquering group. Amerindian women and men were both regarded as inferior social beings, whose inferiority justified the original conquest and continued to make them justifiably exploitable and expandable in the eyes of the conqueror. The obverse, of course, also holds in this equation: women and men of the conquering group share the characterization and privileges of their group. In this instance, the primary opposition is defined by sociopolitical status, not sex. . . .

The soldiers, priests, and settlers who effected the conquest and colonization of Alta California in the last third of the eighteenth century perceived and acted toward Amerindians in a manner consistent with the ideology and history of conquest—regarding them as inferior, devalued, disposable beings against whom violence was not only permissible but often necessary. For, despite the Laws of the Indies, the contradictions in the ideology and corresponding historical relations of conquest were great from the very beginning. These contradictions were generally exacerbated, rather than resolved, across time, space, and expansion to new frontiers. . . .

Finally, perhaps the greatest contradictions were those of the greatest champion of Amerindian rights—the Catholic church. On the one hand, Catholic clergy sought to remove Amerindians from contact with Spaniards, in order to protect them from the exploitation and violence of conquistadores, soldiers, and colonists; on the other hand, Jesuits, Franciscans, and other religious orders relied heavily on corporal punishment in their programs to Christianize and Hispanicize native people. While proclaiming the humanity of Amerindians, missionaries on the frontier daily acted upon a fundamental belief in the inferiority of the Indian. Their actions belied their words.

Accordingly, in his lengthy memorial of June 19, 1801, refuting the charges of excessive cruelty to Amerindians leveled against the Franciscans by one of their own, Father President Fermín Francisco de Lasuén disputed the use of extreme cruelty in the missions of the New California. Force was used only when absolutely necessary, stated Lasuén; and it was at times necessary because the native peoples of California were "untamed savages . . . people of vicious and ferocious habits who know no law but force, no superior but their own free will, and no reason but their own caprice." Of the use of force against neophyte women, Lasuén wrote that women in the mission were flogged, placed in the stocks, or shackled only because they deserved it. But, he quickly added, their right to privacy was always respected—they were flogged inside the women's dormitory, called the *monjero* (nunnery). Flogging the women in private, he further argued, was part of the civilizing process because it "instilled into them the modesty, delicacy, and virtue belonging to their sex."

A key element in the missionaries' program of conversion to Christianity included the restructuring of relations between the sexes to reflect gender stratification and the corollary values and structures of the patriarchal family: subservience of women to men, monogamy, marriage without divorce, and a severely repressive code of sexual norms.

In view of the fact that the ideologies, structures, and institutions of conquest imposed here were rooted in two and a half centuries of colonial rule, the sexual and other violence toward Amerindian women in California can best be understood as ideologically justified violence institutionalized in the structures and relations of conquest initiated in the fifteenth century. In California as elsewhere, sexual violence functioned as an institutionalized mechanism for ensuring subordination and compliance. It was one instrument of sociopolitical terrorism and control—first of women and then of the group under conquest.

FURTHER READING

L. R. Bailey, *Indian Slave Trade in the Southwest* (1966)
Gordon C. Baldwin, *The Warrior Apaches* (1965)
Herbert E. Bolton, *Coronado on the Turquoise Trail* (1949)
José María Cortes y de Olarte, *Views from the Apache Frontier* (1989)
Rupert Costo, *Natives of the Golden State* (1995)
Alfred W. Crosby, *The Columbian Exchange* (1973)
Brian M. Fagan, *The Great Journey* (1987)
Jack D. Forbes, *Apache, Navaho, and Spaniard* (1994)
Robert F. Heizer and Albert A. Elsasser, *The Natural World of the California Indians* (1980)
Rick Hendricks and John P. Wilson, eds., *The Navajos in 1705: Roque Madrid's Campaign Journal* (1996)
Paul Horgan, *The Heroic Triad* (1994)
Elizabeth A. H. John, *Storms Brewed in Other Men's Worlds* (1996)
Oakah L. Jones, *Pueblo Warriors and Spanish Conquest* (1966)
Philip Wayne Powell, *Soldiers, Indians, and Silver* (1952)
Daniel T. Reff, *Disease, Depopulation, and Culture Change in Northwestern New Spain, 1518–1764* (1991)
Thomas E. Sheridan and Nancy J. Parezo, eds., *Paths of Life* (1996)
Marc Simmons, *Border Comanches* (1967)
C. L. Sonnichsen, *The Mescalero Apaches* (1972)
Edward Holland Spicer, *Cycles of Conquest* (1962)
Alfred B. Thomas, *Forgotten Frontiers* (1932)
Alfred B. Thomas, *The Plains Indians and New Mexico, 1751–1778* (1940)
David Hurst Thomas, ed., *Columbian Consequences*, 3 vols. (1991)

CHAPTER
3

Early Mexicano Communities on the Northern Frontier, the Spanish Colonial Period to 1821

The formation of the Spanish frontier settlements in the Southwest in eighteenth and early nineteenth centuries was determined by Spanish royal ordinances, town planning, restrictions on movement, and the reluctance of Spanish subjects to emigrate north. Geographic isolation and conflicts with Apache, Comanche, and other Native American tribes not only shaped the various Spanish-speaking frontier societies being formed but also made their everyday life both challenging and difficult.

Because of the shortage of Spanish women, Mestizaje, the product of racial interbreeding with Indian, black, and mixed-blood women, was a prominent characteristic of life on the northern frontier. One's status in the social and legal hierarchy was ultimately determined by one's skin color. The number of different castas, or social and ethnic categories, was in the hundreds. By the eighteenth century mestizos were the fastest growing segment of Mexico's population, and emerged as a distinct social and cultural group as marriages among mestizos became more and more common.

An important element affecting community formation was the mission system. The missions, the military garrison, and the civilian town residents were interdependent both economically and socially. Ultimately the missions' drive for autonomy failed. The total subjugation of Indians as forced labor for economic gain was countered by desertions, lack of population growth, and resistance to recruitment among the native peoples. There were also repeated challenges to the mission system by town residents and the government. With time local interests and objectives came to take precedence over Spanish crown rulings on the northern frontier.

The mission economies established by the Franciscans in California, the Chihuahua Trail that linked New Mexico first to the Mexican interior and then to the United States, and the ranching and cattle economies of Texas all profoundly affected life on Mexico's northern frontier. The distinct frontier identity that arose was sustained by a strong penchant for autonomy that was both adaptive and resilient to change and underscored by a diverse range of experiences. The beginning *and development of many colonial communities were shaped chiefly by the soldiers and their families who had voluntarily moved to the northern frontier. How successfully were members of the various Indian populations incorporated into the social and economic life of the emerging multiracial frontier communities? How would Indian as well as early Chicano life be eventually altered by the influx of non-Spanish European colonists?*

❧ D O C U M E N T S

Document 1 is from the diary of Bishop Pedro Tamarón y Romeral who visited El Paso, Tomé, Albuquerque, and Santa Fe, the main settlements of the colony of New Mexico, in 1760. Tamarón's description of these settlements reveals a diverse population of Spanish, mestizo, and Indian peoples. Document 2 is from the account of the French captain Pierre Marie François de Pagès, whose journey around the world in 1767 took him across Spanish Texas, still an unknown country. His writings are among the first descriptions of the territory. Pagès's route took him up the Red River to Natchitoches, overland to Los Adeas, and then past Saint Augustine to Nacogdoches. From there he traveled southwest to San Antonio and then to Laredo before crossing the Río Grande. Throughout his sojourn, Pagès documented everyday conditions among the Spanish-speaking settlers and the different Indian tribes, and described the geography of Texas.

Yuma was a link in the chain of missions established by Teodoro de Croix on the Colorado River on the overland route to California (see Chapter 2, Document 4). An account of the Indian uprising there in 1781 appears here as Document 3. It was written by one of the survivors, María Ana Montielo, whose husband, a commander of the Colorado settlement, was killed in the hostilities. Document 4 is an excerpt from Jean François La Pérouse's description of the Indians of Carmel, California, in 1786. Among his observations are the punishment of Indians inside the missions, their daily routines, and their paternalistic treatment by the priests.

Communal land grants in the Southwest were made by the government of Mexico. The acquisition of these lands by the United States in 1848 altered their status, and various claims to their ownership and boundaries had to be adjudicated. Document 5 presents a response to a petition regarding the Conejos Land Grant in southern Colorado in 1842, which was then part of the New Mexico territory.

1. Bishop Pedro Tamarón y Romeral Visits New Mexico, 1760

El Paso

This town's population is made up of Spaniards, Europeanized mixtures, and Indians. Its patron saints are Our Lady of the Pillar [of Saragossa] and St. Joseph. There is a royal presidio with a captain and fifty soldiers in the pay of the king.

The [care] of souls is in charge of the Franciscan friars of the Province of the Holy Gospel of Mexico. Two friars are serving there. One is the Custos, who is

From Eleanor B. Adams, ed., "Bishop Tamarón's Visitation of New Mexico, 1760," *Publications in History,* Historical Society of New Mexico, Vol. 15. Reprinted with permission.

prelate of all the New Mexico missionaries. The other, who has the title of guardian, is the parish priest of that large town. Two secular priests also reside there. . . .

El Paso has 354 families of Spanish and Europeanized citizens, with 2,479 persons. There are 72 Indian families with 249 persons.

They gave me a solemn reception here, for not only did the captain of the presidio, Don Manuel de San Juan, who is also the chief magistrate, the Father Custos, and the vicar come out to the Río de Santa María, but when I entered El Paso, everyone came marching out in fine order and display. This cost me a night's sojourn in the country three leagues from El Paso, which I did not like at all, because it is a very dangerous region, even though I had been in the same situation for the six preceding nights from the time I left Janos since there are no settlements en route. But this last night was at their request so that they might make better preparations for my reception. . . .

El Paso is in latitude 32°9′, longitude 261°40′. There is a large irrigation ditch with which they bleed the Río del Norte. It is large enough to receive half its waters. This ditch is subdivided into others which run through broad plains, irrigating them. By this means they maintain a large number of vineyards, from which they make *generoso* wines even better than those from Parras, and also brandy, but not as much. They grow wheat, maize, and other grains of the region, as well as fruit trees, apples, pears, peaches, figs. It is delightful country in summer.

Tomé

This is a new settlement of Spanish citizens which could become the best in the kingdom because of its extensive lands and the ease of running an irrigation ditch from the river, which keeps flowing there. A decent church has already been built. It is thirty-three varas long by eight wide, with a transept and three altars. It is dedicated to the Immaculate Conception. There is a house for the parish priest, who is the one of the villa of Albuquerque. I confirmed 402 persons that afternoon. The population of this settlement is not recorded here because it was included in the census of the town to which it is subordinate (Albuquerque). The Father Custos was charged to assign a friar to Tomé, separate from Albuquerque, and I believe that he has already done so.

Albuquerque

This villa is composed of Spanish citizens and Europeanized mixtures. Their parish priest and missionary is a Franciscan friar. It is ten leagues north of Tomé. There are 270 families and 1,814 persons.

On the following day, May 21, I celebrated the announcement of my visitation. The edict concerning public sins was read, and then the commands of the Roman ritual were executed. The parish books were examined. Various faculties were conferred on the parish priest, and the title of vicar and ecclesiastical judge of this villa was issued to him because of the distance from Santa Fe, for there had never been one there. . . .

Santa Fe

This villa is the capital of New Mexico. It is four leagues east of the house of El Alamo, which I left the afternoon of the same day. And a half a league before we reached Santa Fe, the governor came forth with a numerous and brilliant retinue. He dismounted from his horse and joined me in the coach. This reception was very noteworthy. We proceeded to the villa among a crowd of people, and my entrance to Santa Fe was made with the same solemnity that the Roman ceremonial prescribes for cathedrals. After this function the governor himself lodged me in the very casas reales, and he moved to another house. And he provided food during my sojourn there. I accepted this, and the same from the captain at El Paso, because there was no other way of obtaining it; and they conformed, according to what I heard, to the practice of their predecessors with my predecessors, as likewise with regard to providing mules and horses.

On May 25 . . . the visitation was made with all possible solemnity in the principal church, which serves as the parish church. It is large, with a spacious nave and a transept adorned by altars and altarscreens, all of which, as well as the baptismal font and the other things mentioned in the Roman ritual, were inspected after the edict concerning public sins had been read and a sermon on the aims of the visitation given.

Two Franciscan friars serve continually in this villa, one with the title of Vice-Custos and the other as parish priest, with the status of missionary. To each of these friars, and to all who serve in New Mexico, the King contributes 300 pesos annually; and in addition to this, they receive their obventions in accordance with a fixed schedule. A secular priest also serves in that villa as vicar. He is paid 300 pesos a year from the tithes. This was the only vicar in the kingdom, and for that reason I decided to add the vicarship of Albuquerque and that of the Villa de la Cañada, so that decisions might be handed down with greater ease.

This villa of Santa Fe has 379 families of citizens of Spanish and mixed blood, with 1,285 persons. Since I have confirmed 1,532 persons in the said villa, I am convinced that the census they gave me is very much on the low side, and I do not doubt that the number of persons must be at least twice that given in the census.

2. Captain Pierre Marie François de Pagès Reports on Early Settlements in Texas, 1767

We arrived at the river Guadeloupe [Guadalupe], the last of any consequence on the road to San Antonio; and here the same tedious and irksome method of passing on rafts was repeated. In four days more we came to plantations of Indian corn, from the appearance of which I could easily perceive that the inhabitants of this settlement are not so miserably idle as those of Adaés. The crops are large and beautiful, and interspersed with meadow ground, upon which are reared herds and

From Marilyn McAdams Sibley, ed., "Across Texas in 1767: The Travels of Captain Pagès," *Southwestern Historical Quarterly* (April 1967), pp. 613–619. Reprinted courtesy The Texas State Historical Association, Austin.

flocks of almost every denomination. We began to observe the Barbary fig-tree and wild burnet; and I was shewn a root resembling the turnip, a thin slice of which purges severely, but I was told its operation is counteracted by swallowing a small quantity of ground Indian corn. Our animals, as well as ourselves, were now greatly fatigued, and therefore it was thought expedient to make a short rest. I bought a third mule, and we found ourselves under the necessity of appointing a guard to our mules and horses.

The reader is possibly surprised to find us attended by so numerous a train of animals; but if he only considers the difficulties of our march, the wild and rugged surface of the country, and the occasion we had for a fresh supply of horses each day, he will easily perceive the propriety of our conduct. In short, on the last day of November, we arrived in safety at the settlement of San Antonio.

At this post, the second in the same direction belonging to the Spaniards, I met with the new governor of the province, whom I had just seen at Adaés. . . . In the countries bordering on those rivers reside the savage tribes named Tegas and Apaches, the last of which entertain an implacable enmity against the Spaniards. The Apaches, after driving them from a settlement in those parts, called San Xavier, were repelled in their turn, and obliged to seek habitations in more northern regions. Although the population of savage nations is not expected to be very considerable, yet from the province of Louisiana to San Pedro we passed their villages at intervals of twenty-five and thirty leagues, and sometimes at a shorter distance. But that vast country situated on this side of the San Pedro villages, and which stretches all the way to Rio Grande, is totally destitute of inhabitants. It is true, those regions are still frequented by savages; but they have no other object in view than to make war upon the Spaniards, to drive off their cattle, to hunt the buffalo, and to gather *plaquemines* [persimmons] and chestnuts, with which they retire to their villages in the north. Owing to their very frequent incursions, however, they have been improperly represented as wandering tribes.

Whilst I remained at this settlement, the savages through whose boundaries we had passed at San Pedro, incensed against the governor on account of his prohibition of their trade with the French of [Nacogdoches], made an irruption into the country, and carried off four hundred horses from San Antonio. The alarm being given, the garrison beat to arms, and mounting their horses, pursued to the distance of a hundred leagues, without being able to come up with the enemy. The Spaniards were on their return home, and had reached the river Guadeloupe, when another party of the same nation rushed from the woods, and made a smart fire upon them. The garrison, after making a vigorous resistance for the space of three hours, at last yielded to superior numbers, and lost on this occasion, besides other property, a hundred and fifty horses. A few days after the garrison was insulted again by a detachment of the same tribe; and the governor began to see the necessity of putting the fort in a better state of defense. . . .

Fort San Antonio stands in a valley of an oblong form, one side of which fronts an angle of a small river in its vicinity. The different avenues leading to the settlement are defended by large pallisadoes, while the houses built upon its circumference serve the purpose of walls: but being of very considerable extent, and as many of the houses are in ruins, it is but weakly fortified, and has much occasion for a stronger garrison. It is besides much incumbered from without by several miserable villages, which give encouragement to the incursions of the enemy. The space too inclosed by the angle of the river is crowded by a multitude of huts, which are occupied by a number of emigrants from the Canary Isles. In other respects the settlement is pleasantly situated, on a small peninsula sloping gently towards the river; and commands an agreeable prospect over the opposite grounds. . . . The houses of the settlement may perhaps amount to two hundred, two-thirds of which are built of stone. Upon the roof is a kind of earthen terrace, which, on account of the small quantity of rain, and the temperate nature of the climate, are found abundantly lasting. . . . I am told, however, that the climate of Red River, Natchitoches, and Adaés, are wet, cold, and unwholesome; but the rains of Natchitoches and Adaés never extend so far as this settlement, which stands in the middle of a plain, and is only surrounded by thick woods of the mesquitte. If we except a few clumps of large trees which are found on the banks of the Guadeloupe, the noble forests of massy timber on this route totally disappear in the neighborhood of Red River or Colorado.

This military station is the most important of four, comprehended within the bounds of this province: to wit, Adaés, at seven leagues distance from Natchitoches; Acoquissas [Orcoquisac], a hundred leagues south-west from Adaés; Labadie de Spiritu Sancto [La Bahía del Espiritu Santo], two hundred to the west-south-west; and Fort San Antonio, two hundred and fifty leagues west and west-south-west from the same point of Adaés: west and a quarter north-west from San Antonio, there is also a station of San Saba. On the banks of that river, and at the distance of a hundred leagues from San Antonio, stands, the post of Rio Grande [San Juan Bautista del Rio Grande]; and nearly in the same direction, at the distance of two hundred and fifty leagues from the same point, are Passe de Nord [El Paso] and Santa Fé, in the province of New Mexico. . . .

In the settlement of San Antonio we find a Spanish colony from the Canary Isles; whilst all their other stations consist merely of soldiers, and a few Indians who have been seduced from the innocence of savage life. Their principal employment is to rear horses, mules, cows, and sheep. Their cattle, commonly allowed to roam at large in the woods, are once in two months driven into fields adjoining to the houses of their owners, where every means is used to render them tame and tractable. After having been subjected to hunger and confinement, they receive their liberty, and are succeeded by others, which experience in their turn a similar course of discipline. Such of the inhabitants as are at pains to prevent their herds from running entirely wild, are found to possess five or six thousand head of cattle.

The inhabitants of San Antonio are excellent horsemen, and particularly fond of hunting or *lacing* [lassoing] their wild animals. Having entered the field, and started an animal they mean to take alive, they give him chace [*sic*] at full speed from wood to valley, till his fatigue enables them to come within a certain distance of him. Here the hunter, holding the running noose of a strong lash or thong coiled around his arm in his right hand, throws it with such dexterity, that he seldom fails to catch him round the neck or horns; and in the same instant, by pulling up his horse, or turning him abruptly from the line of his career, he checks his prey, and obliges him to stand still. A custom very similar to this is described in Anson's Voyages, and represented by the author as peculiar to the coast of Patagonia.

They have likewise the use of tame animals, which, besides being serviceable to them in milk, supply them with fat and dried flesh for their extensive peregrinations. Their horses and mules are no sooner a little broken in, than they are offered to sale; but here the market price is so extremely low, as indeed may be imagined, that I have seen a good horse sold for a pair of shoes. Having only one or two keepers for all the cattle of the settlement, even their domestic animals run day and night in the woods.

The keen eye which the habit of close and minute attention has bestowed on those people is truly surprising. Discovering in the morning that one of their cattle has disappeared in the course of the night, they are at much pains to examine the inclination of the grass over which he must have passed, when they can distinguish by the prints of his feet whether he is a horse or mule, and whether he quitted his pasture grazing or in flight: nor do they despair of finding him before they have gone fifteen perhaps twenty leagues from home. In their wars with the savages this extreme nicety of fight is still of greater consequence; but as each party are on their guard against the discernment of the other, and both have the same motives to conceal the direction of their flight, it is usual to set fire to the sward as they retreat, leaving three or four leagues of black desert behind them.

They are often in danger of losing their way in the meadows, but in order to secure themselves against this inconvenience they are accustomed to give much attention to particular trees, and the position of the adjacent woods, which serve to assist their recollection, and answer the purpose of conducting posts in civilized countries. In their excursions through the woods they discover the quarter of the north by observing the side of the tree which, being hidden from the solar rays, acquires a coat of greenish moss, whilst that exposed to the south retains a neat clean skin of a whitish colour. In the neighborhood of this settlement, and situated on the river, at the distance of two or three leagues from one another, are four missions, consisting of a couple of Franciscans each. In the houses of those missionaries savages who have been captivated in war, and on whom the reverend fathers have conferred marriage and baptism, receive their maintenance and education. In this manner each house entertains seven or eight men, with their wives and children, who are employed, under the direction of these monks, in certain articles of industry, the profits of which are applied to the emolument of the mission. The rules of those missions, as to temporal affairs, are nearly the same with those observed by the Jesuits in their settlements in Paraguay; but they are applied by the disciples of St. Ignatius in a manner much more liberal and conciliating to the minds of their savage proselytes, than they are here by the followers of St. Francis.

The savages of Tegas are the last who have taken to the use of the firelock, and maintain any intercourse with the French. Those of Apaches, living about fifty leagues northward from San Antonio, as well as all the maritime tribes between the stations of Acoquissas and Labadie de Spiritu Sancto, still use the bow and arrow. Certain Europeans have represented the latter, named Coumaches, as a race of cannibals; but according to the Spaniards, who are probably better acquainted with their manners, they are merely a cruel dastardly kind of savages, who only escape the yoke of slavery by taking refuge among the rocks, bays, and fastnesses of the sea-coast.

The Spaniards made war upon those miserable tribes, which still retain the bow and arrow, almost in impunity. In case of engagement, the Spaniards, covering their heads with a sort of shield, and their bodies with a great coat, consisting of three or four folds of deer-skin, quilted with cotton, are in condition to set the darts of the enemy at defiance. If the savages happen to be few in number, and the Spanish cavalry think themselves ensured of an easy victory, reserving their fire for situations of greater necessity, they use the thong, and lace them like wild horses. As soon as a savage has been caught in the noose, he is bound hand and foot, and carried to the residence of a missionary, who makes it his business by threats, persuasion, severe fasting, gentleness, and last of all by marriage, to tame and civilize the manners of his prisoner. Having been instructed in the existence of a Supreme Being, providence, and the more peculiar doctrines of Christianity, he is admitted to the privilege of baptism.

3. Survivor María Ana Montielo Recounts the Indian Uprising at Yuma, Arizona, 1781

Altar.
December 21, 1785.

To Father Francisco Antonio Barbastro.

In your much appreciated letter, Your Reverence asked me to comment on, as you phrased it, "the events surrounding the death of the missionaries on the Colorado River."

Father Juan Barreneche celebrated the first mass that morning [July 17, 1781], which I myself attended. Father Francisco Garcés had the second mass. His mass-server was Ensign Santiago Islas, my deceased husband. As my husband was moving the missal from one side of the altar to the other for the gospel of the mass, the war whoops of the Indians began.

Corporal Pascual Baylón was the first to fall into their hands. As they were putting him to death with their war clubs, Father Juan Barreneche rushed out just in time to force his way through the yelling Indians and witness the corporal's last act of life as he squeezed the good padre's hand. Though battered by war clubs, Father Barreneche was able to regain the sanctuary of the church. My husband had observed a few armed Indians arriving in the village before he left for the service. As commander of the Colorado settlements, he took the precaution of placing Baylón on temporary guard, never dreaming that a full rebellion of the Yuma nation was about to break out. Though the mass was already begun, Father Garcés cut it short when the battle started.

Realizing that the whole Yuma nation had risen up against us, I gathered the women together and we fled for our lives to the church. There we found more

From Kieran McCarty, comp., *Desert Documentary: The Spanish Years, 1767–1821* (Tucson: Arizona Historical Society, 1976), Historical Monograph No. 4, pp. 35–40. Reprinted by permission.

refugee Spaniards arguing with Father Garcés about who should be blamed for the uprising. "Let's forget now whose fault it is," Father Garcés replied, "and simply consider it God's punishment for our sins." His voice was compassionate, though his face was an ashen gray.

That night the Yumas began to burn our houses and belongings and kill as many of our people as they could. That was the night my heart was broken, when my beloved husband was clubbed to death before my very eyes.

As day dawned on the 18th of July, Father Barreneche encouraged those of us who were still alive with the words: "The devil is on the side of the enemy, but God is on ours. Let us sing a hymn to Mary, most holy, that she favor us with her help, and let us praise God for sending us these trials." . . . All during the night, he and Father Garcés had moved stealthily about the village, administering the sacraments to the wounded and dying, consoling them in their hour of death.

When the hymn was finished, Father Barreneche offered mass for all of us, as we awaited death at any moment. After mass, he occupied himself by pulling out arrows and spears from the walls of the church and the houses and climbing up onto the roofs to review the movements of the enemy.

About three o'clock in the afternoon, when the Indians had finished killing Captain Rivera and his party on the other side of the river, Father Barreneche arrived from ministering to the last of the dying and told us that each of us should try to escape as best we could. He picked up his breviary and crucifix and, together with Father Garcés, the women, and the rest of the people, started out of the settlement, leaving behind forever the new mission of La Purísima Concepción and its property and possessions. He asked Father Garcés if they should perhaps try to reach our other settlement. Father Garcés assured him that it was completely destroyed and its inhabitants killed.

Father Barreneche was following the trail of blood of a wounded man named Pedro Burgues, who had sent for him to come and hear his confession. The trail led across a seemingly shallow lagoon. The priest waded in, armed with crucifix and breviary. Before he knew it, he was in over his head. Though he did not know how to swim, he thrashed about till he was able to grasp a log and some roots. By pulling himself along the roots, he was able to reach the other bank. Though he miraculously escaped drowning, he lost his breviary and crucifix.

From here, the two fathers went on alone. We women stayed beside the lagoon. Father Garcés warned us: "Stay together, do not resist capture, and the Yumas will not harm you." With this, he plunged into the lagoon to join Father Barreneche on the other side. This was the last we saw of the two fathers as we sat huddled together awaiting death at any moment.

Through another Spanish woman captive, who was not with my group, I later learned that Fathers Garcés and Barreneche were not killed until three days later [July 21, 1781]. After leaving the lagoon, the fathers were discovered by a friendly Yuma whose wife was a fervent Christian. He hurried the fathers to his own ranchería, where his wife was waiting.

The enemy fell upon them as they sat in the Yuma's dwelling, drinking chocolate. The rebel leader shouted: "Stop drinking that and come outside. We're going to kill you."

"We'd like to finish our chocolate first," Father Garcés replied.

"Just leave it!" the leader shouted. The two fathers obediently stood up and followed him.

The Indians tell the story that at the first attack of the executioners, Father Garcés disappeared from their sight, and they were left clubbing the air. Word had spread among the Yuma nation that he was more powerful than their own witch-doctors. Time and again I heard that many of the Yumas did not want to see the fathers killed. Nevertheless, their blood was spilled, and the woman who told me of this was close enough to hear their pitiful moans as they lay dying. The husband of the pious woman recovered their lifeless bodies and buried them.

The woman who told me this was Gertrudis Cantud, wife of the wounded man that Father Barreneche was following to hear his confession when the fathers crossed the lagoon.

This is all I can remember to tell Your Reverence concerning the ill-fated settlement of the Colorado River, Mission La Purísima Concepción, and the rest of the territory we traveled until the fathers left us beside the lagoon.

Maria Ana Montielo

4. Jean François La Pérouse Describes the Mission Indians of Carmel, California, 1786

The color of these Indians, which is that of Negroes; the house of the missionaries; their storehouses; . . . the appearance of the ground on which the grain is trodden out; the cattle, the horses—everything in short—brought to our recollection a plantation at Santo Domingo or any other West Indian island. The men and women are collected by the sound of a bell; a missionary leads them to work, to the church, and to all their exercises. We observed with concern that the resemblance is so perfect that we have seen both men and women in irons, and others in the stocks. Lastly, the noise of the whip might have struck our ears, this punishment also being administered. . . .

Corporal punishment is inflicted on the Indians of both sexes who neglect the exercises of piety, and many sins, which in Europe are left to Divine justice, are here punished by irons and the stocks. And lastly, . . . it must be observed that the moment an Indian is baptized, the effect is the same as if he had pronounced a vow for life. If he escapes to reside with his relations in the independent villages, he is summoned three times to return; if he refuses, the missionaries apply to the governor, who sends soldiers to seize him in the midst of his family and conduct him to the mission, where he is condemned to receive a certain number of lashes with the whip. . . . They have so little courage that they never make any resistance to the three or four soldiers who so evidently violate the rights of men in their persons. This custom . . . is kept up because theologians have decided that they could not in conscience administer baptism to men so inconstant unless the government would in some measure serve as their sponsor and answer for their perseverance in the faith. . . .

The Indians as well as the missionaries rise with the sun, and immediately go to prayers and mass, which last for an hour. During this time three large boilers are set on the fire for cooking a kind of soup, made of barley meal, the grain of which has been roasted previous to its being ground. This sort of food, of which the Indians are extremely fond, is called *atole*. They eat it without either butter or salt, and it would certainly to us be a most insipid mess.

Each hut sends for the allowance of all its inhabitants in a vessel made of the bark of a tree. There is neither confusion nor disorder in the distribution, and when the boilers are nearly emptied, the thicker portion at the bottom is distributed to those children who have said their catechism the best.

The time of repast is three quarters of an hour, after which they all go to work, some to till the ground with oxen, some to dig in the garden, while others are employed in domestic occupations, all under the eye of one or two missionaries. . . .

At noon the bells give notice of the time of dinner. The Indians then quit their work, and send for their allowance in the same vessel as at breakfast. But this second soup is thicker than the former, and contains a mixture of wheat, maize, peas, and beans; the Indians call it *pozole*.

They return to work from two to four or five o'clock, when they repair to evening prayer, which lasts nearly an hour and is followed by a distribution of *atole*, the same as at breakfast. These three distributions are sufficient for the subsistence of the greater number of these Indians. . . .

. . . Punishments are adjudged by Indian magistrates, called *caciques*. There are three in each mission. . . . These *caciques* are like the overseers of a plantation: passive beings, blind performers of the will of their superiors. Their principal function . . . [is] to maintain order and the appearance of attention.

Women are never whipped in public, but in an enclosed and somewhat distant place that their cries may not excite a too lively compassion, which might cause the men to revolt. The latter, on the contrary, are exposed to the view of all their fellow citizens, that their punishment may serve as an example. They usually ask pardon for their fault, in which case the executioner diminishes the force of his lashes, but the number is always irrevocable. . . .

. . . An hour after supper, they take care to secure all the women whose husbands are absent, as well as the young girls above the age of nine years, by locking them up, and during the day they entrust them to the care of elderly women. All these precautions are still inadequate, and we have seen men in the stocks and women in irons for having eluded the vigilance. . . .

These Indians have no knowledge of a God or of a future state. . . .

The missionaries, persuaded from their prejudices and perhaps from their experience that the reason of these men is scarcely ever developed, consider this a just motive for treating them like children, and admit only a very small number to the communion. . . .

This government is a true theocracy for the Indians, who believe that their superiors have immediate and continual communication with God, and that they cause him to descend every day on the altar. By virtue of this opinion, the holy fathers live in the midst of the villages with the greatest security. Their doors are not shut, even in the night.

5. Justice of the Peace Cornelio Vigil Restores a Land Grant to New Mexican Citizens, 1842

It appears that in 1833 some citizens of New Mexico petitioned for and were granted lands on the Conejos River, present Colorado. War with the Navajo Indians intervened and prevented the occupation of the tract. . . . Jose Maria Martinez, Antonio Martinez, Julian Gallegos and Seledon Valdez, for themselves and in behalf of other named persons, petitioned the prefect for a renewal of the decree of possession. . . .

The prefect, Archuleta, responded to the petition despite the fact that the "petitioners had certainly lost their right under the law, having abandoned the land granted to them," and ordered the justice of the peace again to place them in possession. . . .

"In company with the two witnesses in my attendance, who were the citizens Santiago Martinez and Eugenio Navanjo, and eighty-three heads of families being present, . . . I produced and explained to them their petition, and informed them that to obtain said land they would have to respect and comply in due legal form with the following conditions:

"That the tract aforesaid shall be cultivated and never abandoned; and he that shall not cultivate his land within twelve years or that shall not reside upon it will forfeit his right, and the land that had been assigned to him will be given to another person—that the pastures and watering places shall be in common for all the inhabitants—that said land is donated to the grantees to be well cultivated and for the pasturing of all kinds of live stock and therefore, owing to the exposed frontier situation of the place, the grantees must keep themselves equipped with firearms and bows and arrows . . . that the towns they may build shall be well walled around and fortified—and in the meantime the settlers must move upon said tract and build their shanties there for the protection of their families.

"And all, and each for himself, having heard and accepted the conditions hereinbefore prescribed, they accordingly all unanimously replied that they accepted and comprehended what was required of them; whereupon I gook them by the hand, and declared in a loud and intelligible voice, that, in the name of the sovereign constituent Congress of the Union, and without prejudice to the national interest or to those of any third party, I led them over the tract and granted to them the land; and they plucked up grass, cast stones, and exclaimed in voices of gladness, saying, Long live the sovereignty of our Mexican nation! taking possession of said tract quietly and peaceably without any opposition, the boundaries designated to them being: On the north the Garrita Hill, on the south the San Antonio Mountain, on the east the Rio del Norte and on the west the timbered mountain embraced by the tract, and measuring off to them the planting lots from the Plato Bend, there fell to each one of the settlers two hundred varas in a straight line from the San Antonio river and its adjoining hills and its margins to the Iarra [La Jara] river inclusive,

From Leroy R. Hafen, "Mexican Land Grants in Colorado," *The Colorado Magazine* 4, no. 3 (May 1927): 81–93. Reprinted with permission.

there being eighty-four families, a surplus in the upper portion towards the canon of said river remaining for the settlement of others from where the two separate upwards, and in the lower portion from the Bend aforesaid to the Del Norte river, notifying the colonists that the pastures and watering places remain in common as stated, and the roads for entering and leaving the town shall remain open and free wherever they may be, without any one being authorized to obstruct them; and be it known henceforth that Messrs. Antonio Martinez and Julian Gallegos are the privileged individuals, they having obtained the said grant to this land on the Conejos, and they should be treated as they merit.

"And in order that all the foregoing may in all time appear, I signed this grant with the witnesses in my attendance, with whom I act by appointment, for want of a public or national notary, there being none in this department of New Mexico, to all of which I certify."

Attending,

Santiago Martinez   Cornelio Vigil
Eugenio Navanjo

E S S A Y S

Much of the history written about early California was racially derogatory, because scholars like Hubert Howe Bancroft wrote biased accounts. These scholars, for example, made distinctions between Spanish and Mexican women, although the vast majority of California women were mestiza, mulatta, other mixed bloods, or Mexican. This is the subject of the first essay, by Antonia I. Castañeda, an associate professor of history at Saint Mary's University, San Antonio, Texas. As Castañeda explains, the worst of these stereotypes of Mexican women were written during the Pre-American conquest period and served an ulterior purpose. Other accounts expressed similar stereotypes of Spanish-speaking women that were perpetuated in newspapers, novels, and in nonprofessional histories. Castañeda argues that by focusing on Spanish frontier institutions, Southwest borderlands historians omitted Mexicans in general and notably women in particular from their work. She believes that even recent scholarship by social and feminist historians, despite its revisionist outlook, fails to include frontier Spanish-Mexican women, although there now are some sources for the study of this population.

Over 350 years of Spanish colonial history are missing from most accounts of Chicano history. In the next essay, Gerald E. Poyo, a professor of history at Saint Mary's University, San Antonio, and Gilberto M. Hinojosa, an associate professor of history at the University of Texas, San Antonio, argue for a reexamination of the history of the Spanish borderlands. They note the general omission of this region from U.S. survey textbooks as well as from Texas histories, which not only neglect the important connections between the Spanish period and subsequent eras but also provide a racist view of Spanish activities in the borderlands. During the late nineteenth century historians began to study this region in accounts that emphasized the development of its institutions and its defensive character. Later, historians tied the Spanish borderlands to a larger Mexican and Caribbean context. According to the authors, new interpretations, including regional links, agricultural studies, demographics, and a consideration of the complexities of race and politics, are leading to a better understanding of colonial Texas. Poyo and Hinojosa claim that the focus should be on the internal socioeconomic development of the area, although local and regional approaches are necessary to recognize the borderlands' significance to the formation of the United States.

Gender, Race, and Culture in the History of the California Frontier

ANTONIA I. CASTAÑEDA

The Popular Histories of the Late Nineteenth Century

Written by lawyers, bankers, and other prominent men who came to California in the aftermath of the Mexican War and the gold rush, the multivolume popular histories of the late nineteenth century provide the first composite description and interpretation of Spanish-Mexican California. These histories fundamentally reflect the political and socioracial ideology that informed both the war with Mexico and the subsequent sociopolitical and economic marginalization of Mexicans in California. With respect to women, they reaffirm the contradictory but stereotypic images found in the travel journals and other documents written by entrepreneurs, merchants, adventurers, and other members of the advance guard of Euro-American expansion between the 1820s and 1840s.

In the tradition of the patrician historians whose romantic literary style set the standards and popular patterns from the end of the nineteenth century until well into the twentieth, [Hubert Howe] Bancroft, [Theodore H.] Hittell, and other popularizers intersperse their voluminous histories of California with musings about race, religion, national character, savagery, and civilization. Riddled with the nationalistic fervor of the post–Civil War decades and with an unquestioning belief in Nordic racial superiority, these historians predictably conclude that the Anglo-Saxon race and civilization are far superior to the Latin race and Spanish-Mexican civilization that had produced in California, according to Bancroft, "a race halfway between the proud Castillian and the lowly root digger," existing "halfway between savagery and civilization." Only Amerindians ranked lower than the minions of Spain.

In the works on early colonial development, the discussion of women is only incidental to the larger consideration of specific institutions—the mission, *presidio,* and *pueblo*— or of great men—the governors. Thus, for example, a brief discussion of the maltreatment of Amerindian women in the mission system has no importance beyond its illustration of institutional development and Spanish brutality. . . . Similarly, Bancroft treats sexual and other violence against native women primarily in relation to the bitter conflict between the institutions of church and state, and attributes it to the moral degeneration of the racially mixed soldier-settler population. . . .

In general, the popular historical accounts of the Spanish period (1769–1821) are notable for their absence of pejorative gender-specific sexual stereotypes. Instead,

From Antonia I. Castañeda's article, "Gender, Race and Culture and the History of the California Frontier," in *Frontiers: A Journal of Women's Studies,* Vol. XI, No. 1 (1990), pp. 8–20. Reprinted by permission.

pejorative stereotypes are generalized to the entire group and focus on race. In accounts of Mexican California (1822–1846), the popular historians divide women into two classes: "Spanish" and "Mexican." Although the vast majority of Californians, including the elite, were *mestizo* or *mulato* and Mexican, not Spanish, in nationality, women from long-time Californian elite, land-owning families, some of whom married Europeans or Euro-Americans, were called "Spanish." Women from more recently arrived or non-elite families were called "Mexican." "Spanish" women were morally, sexually, and racially pure; "Mexican" women were immoral and sexually and racially impure. These sexual stereotypes not only reveal the convergence of contemporary political and social ideological currents but also underscore the centrality of the politics of sex to the ideological justification of expansion, war, and conquest. The dominant social Darwinism of the late nineteenth century . . . also held that a society's degree of civilization could be judged by the status and character of its women. The Victorian True Woman . . . represented the most advanced stage of civilized society. Physically and mentally inferior to men but possessed of the cardinal female virtues—piety, purity, submissiveness, and domesticity—she was confined to the home, where she could neither threaten nor challenge the existing order. She was the norm by which historians judged Mexican women, individually and collectively, and thus one of the norms by which they judged Mexican society. Like other reductionist representations of Mexicans in the literature that treats the Mexican period as a "backdrop to the coming of Old Glory," pejorative stereotypes of *Mexicanas* thus served a political purpose. The worst stereotypes of women appeared in the histories of the Mexican rather than the Spanish period not just because the primary sources were written largely by white men who visited and/or lived in Mexican, not Spanish, California, but because the war was fought with Mexico.

The most extensive treatment of Mexican women appears in Bancroft's interpretative social history, *California Pastoral,* in which he devotes an entire chapter to "Woman and Her Sphere." By virtue of publishing the earliest work of this genre, Bancroft became the main source for the stereotypes of women in Mexican California in subsequent histories. . . .

Bancroft's Mexican women are dunces and drudges. They work laboriously and continuously; bear twelve, fifteen, and twenty children; and are subject to being prostituted by their husbands, who "wink at the familiarity of a wealthy neighbor who pays handsomely for his entertainment." Women have no recourse to laws, which men make and women obey. At the same time, however, Bancroft quotes earlier writers to the effect that "the women are pretty, but vain, frivolous, bad managers, and extravagant. They are passionately fond of fine, showy dresses and jewelry . . . their morality is none of the purest; and the coarse and lascivious dances show the degraded tone of manners that exist." Nevertheless, infidelity is rare because *Californianas* fear the swift and deadly revenge exacted by jealous husbands.

Bancroft based his negative images of Mexican women on the accounts of Richard Henry Dana and others who visited California in the 1840s, on the eve of the war with Mexico. But he also recorded a positive image derived from the writings of Alfred Robinson and other Euro-Americans who traveled to California in the 1820s and 1830s to ply the hide and tallow trade and who married elite *Californianas* and settled there.

Robinson's accounts expressed similar negative stereotypes of men but presented positive portrayals of "Spanish" or "*Californio*" women. Robinson, who married María Teresa de la Guerra y Noriega, wrote that "the men are generally indolent and addicted to many vices . . . yet . . . in few places of the world . . . can be found more chastity, industrious habits and correct deportment than among the women." Similar images appeared in literary pieces written on the eve of the Mexican War by individuals who had no firsthand experience of California. In this literature, Spanish-speaking women invited the advances of Euro-American men whom they anxiously awaited as their saviors from Mexican men. . . .

. . . The chaste, industrious Spanish beauty who forsook her inferior man and nation in favor of the superior Euro-American became embedded in the literature. The negative image that Bancroft et al. picked up from the English-language primary sources was reserved for Mexican women: *fandango*-dancing, *monte*-dealing prostitutes, the consorts of Mexican bandits. These dual stereotypes became the prototypic images of Spanish-speaking women in California. They were the grist of popular fiction and contemporary newspapers throughout the latter part of the nineteenth and early twentieth centuries, and they resurfaced in the popular historical literature of the twentieth century, including the few works that focused specifically on women of Spanish California.

The Makers of Modern Historiography: The Teutonic Historians

While Bancroft, Hittell, and other popularizers stereotyped women in their sweeping general histories of California, their scholarly contemporaries, the Teutonic historians, barely mentioned women at all. As professional historical scholarship took root in the post–Civil War era, the question of gender became a nonissue. . . .

While imbued with the more objective scientific approach to historical research being taught at Johns Hopkins and other graduate schools, scholarly studies were nevertheless informed by the racist attitudes that saturated the primary sources and popular histories, particularly those of the Mexican War era, and by the colonial legacy of the Black Legend [the long-held unfavorable image of Spain as an oppressor nation]. In explaining the Spanish presence and institutions in the region ceded to the United States, the Teutonic historians concluded that Spain had failed to implant permanent institutions in this area, for two reasons. First, Spanish political institutions were not free. Second, Spanish cohabitation with inferior Amerindian and Negroid races in the Americas had produced an even more inferior, mongrelized population incapable of self-government. The low level of population across New Spain's vast northern region, its inability to pacify Amerindian groups fully, and its lack of strong agricultural, commercial, or industrial development were offered as proof positive that Spanish institutions had been a dismal failure. Spain's colonizing institutions, the missions, *presidios,* and *pueblos,* were not adequate to develop the region, nor did they leave a lasting influence on the people or landscape. . . .

Since women were not a formal part of institutional life, the Teutonic historians did not discuss them. Frank W. Blackmar, for example, who relies heavily on Bancroft for his description of colonial California, makes only passing reference to women in his discussion of the institution of the mission and the social and political life of the Spanish colonies. But popular and amateur historians of the time continued to include women in their works, stereotyping Mexican women on the basis of both sex and race, as we have seen. . . .

Turner's Frontier Hypothesis and the Fantasy Spanish Heritage

As the mission revival movement and the rediscovery of California's "Spanish" past gained force toward the end of the nineteenth century, Frederick Jackson Turner's presidential address to the American Historical Association in 1893 redefined Euro-American history and civilization. By the early twentieth century, Turner's concept, the "frontier" hypothesis," had supplanted the Teutonic germ theory of history and American institutions. . . .

While on the one hand Turner conceived of Euro-American history as discontinuous from European origins, on the other hand his reinterpretation merely shifted the emphasis on institutional origins from the Old to the New World—from the German forest to the American wilderness—and stressed the impact of the new environment on diverse groups of Caucasian males. It left intact the Teutonics' basic assumptions about representative government, democratic institutions, race, culture, gender, and economics. In both interpretations, neither women nor non-Caucasian men were active participants in the creation of democratic institutions. That both were legally prohibited from direct participation in such institutions was not an issue; rather, their exclusion was consistent with theories of biological and social evolution.

Joan Jensen and Darlis Miller have identified four major stereotypes of Euro-American women in the Turnerian literature of the western frontier; gentle tamers, sunbonneted helpmeets, hell raisers, and bad women. The first two types were extolled as bastions of the pioneer family; the second two were condemned as libertines, created by the same frontier influence that liberated men. But in the Turnerian studies that extol and stereotype Euro-American women, Spanish-Mexican women were entirely absent—a fact hardly surprising in view of the school's racist attitudes toward non-Caucasian peoples and its ignoring of what Richard Hofstadter called "the shameful aspects of Western development, including the arrogance of American expansion, the pathetic tale of the Indians, anti-Mexican [and] anti-Chinese nativism.". . .

The majority of Anglo Californians seeking to understand their past probably did not read the scholarly studies of the frontier historians. The newspapers, novels, and nonprofessional histories that they did read continued the romanticized "Spanish" stereotypes first applied to *mestizas* in the primary sources and in Bancroft. In these works, women were featured prominently, and even males were now romanticized. . . .

Dispossessed of their lands and politically disenfranchised, the former rancheros represented no threat to Euro-American supremacy and thus could be safely romanticized. The new popular histories converted Mexican rancheros into "the California Dons," dashing, silver-saddled *caballeros* who roamed baronial estates from dawn to dusk in a remote Spanish past. The new Dons, however, continued to be inept; incapable of hard work, they lacked the genius or moral strength to develop California's lush, fertile land. . . .

The women of Spanish California, however, according to these novels and histories, surpassed the men. Like the primary sources of the 1840s, the new popularizers concluded that women were men's superiors in "modesty, moral character, and sound common sense." California's "Spanish" (read Caucasian) daughters were industrious, chaste, and morally as well as racially pure. In short, they could be claimed as the pure-blooded "Spanish" grandmothers of many a Euro-American frontier family. But Mexican women fared less well. While the literature seldom specifically discusses Mexican women, a designation that included non-elite *Californianas* and *Mexicanas* who came during the gold rush, it implies that they were licentious women—common prostitutes who, like their male counterparts, deserved to be wiped out. Thus popular historical interpretations of California's Spanish-Mexican past essentially dichotomized *Californianas* the same way the scholarly frontier historians dichotomized and stereotyped Anglo-American women—as good and bad women. For *Californianas,* however, the values of good and bad were explicitly related to their race and culture or class. . . .

The Spanish Borderlands School

In the 1930s Turner's frontier thesis came under increasing scrutiny and attack. A new generation of revisionist historians argued that national development resulted not from a single cause but from many, from economic and class forces as well as from ideas rooted in East Coast intellectualism rather than western individualism. . . .

. . . At the University of California at Berkeley, Herbert Eugene Bolton and his students developed a new revisionist school, the Spanish borderlands school of historiography. The new school revised the Teutonics' original theory of Spanish institutional failures by turning it on its head. . . .

Rejecting both the Hispanophobia of the Teutonics and the strident nationalism of the Turnerians, the borderlands school effectively refuted the allegation of Spain's institutional failure. Nevertheless, Bolton and his students retained their predecessors' definitions of the makers and nature of history. Caucasian males engaged in exploration and in the development of religious, political, military, and economic institutions make history. But the Spaniards whom the Teutonics had disparaged as a cruel, greedy, bigoted nonwhite lot of miscreants the Boltonians lauded as valiant, daring, heroic Europeans. Where the Teutonics had seen institutional failure, the Boltonians saw a seedbed for Spanish civilization.

In either view, however, women and nonwhite males do not contribute to history. . . . The early Spanish borderlands studies rarely mention racially mixed soldiers and settlers. When Bolton does briefly discuss California's *mestizo* and *mulato* colonists, he reaffirms Bancroft's views of their idle but kindly, hospitable, and happy character: and, like the contemporary popular historians, he makes a racial distinction between Californians and Mexicans: "Californians were superior to other Spanish colonists in America, including Mexicans," a superiority that he attributes to "the greater degree of independence, social at least if not political," caused by their isolation from Mexico and to their "good Castillian blood." Women, who (to the historians) were neither intrepid explorers, barefooted black-robed missionaries, nor valiant lancers for the king, do not figure in Spanish borderlands studies. Until very recently, mention of women was limited to scattered references to intermarriage in the Americas, to women's relationship to the men who founded Spanish institutions, or, in the case of Amerindian women, to the institution of the mission itself. . . .

Just as the early Boltonians dismissed the common soldier, so they dismissed the racially mixed wives of the artisans, soldiers, settlers, and convicts—women who endured difficult ocean voyages or who trekked over desert wastelands to settle Alta California. The only women systematically included are the wives of the governors, principally Eulalia Callis, with her marital strife, her "scandalous behavior," and the problems that she caused the missionaries.

Although the borderlands school studies end with the close of the Spanish colonial era. Bolton makes brief reference to Mexican women in connection with Euro-American expansion into the old Spanish borderlands in the 1820s and 1830s. Though he shows an awareness of the importance of intermarriage and miscegenation to frontier development, and of the significance of Mexican women's economic roles as property owners and consumers on the borderlands, he joins the popular historians in his uncritical acceptance of Euro-American males' claims that Mexican women preferred them to Mexican males. While noting that James Ohio Pattie was a notorious braggart, Bolton nevertheless paraphrases Pattie's report that "at a *fandango* in Taos, the gateway to New Mexico, the American beaux captured not only all the señoritas, but the señoras as well. The jealous *caballeros* drew their knives." And "in California, long before the Mexican War," wrote Bolton, "it was a customary boast of a señorita that she would marry a blue-eyed man." Thus Bolton accepts the distorted view that equated California women with the land that promised "freedom-loving, adventure-loving, land-hungry Americans" romance, exoticism, and adventure.

Reinterpreting Spanish-Mexican Women in Frontier California

Within the last two decades, social historians and feminist historians have illuminated nineteenth-century U.S. social, women's, Chicano, borderlands, and family history; and recent studies on colonial women in Mexico and Latin America have yielded information and analysis pertinent to women in Spanish-Mexican California. Yet even this new body of literature fails to deal directly with Spanish-Mexican women on the remote outposts of empire. There are no published book-length scholarly studies of *Mexicanas* on nineteenth-century frontiers, and the periodical literature is sketchy and impressionistic rather than grounded in substantive primary research. . . .

In many respects, however, these initial efforts continue to mirror the larger problems of the earlier historiography. That is, the new scholarship lacks a clear framework to examine the historical experience of women whose race and culture are not Anglo North American. Moreover, it often reflects the underlying assumptions and race and class biases of the earlier historiography. Historians of women in the frontier West, for example, have not yet grappled with defining the term *frontier* from a non-Anglo perspective, nor have they yet tackled the roles of English-speaking women in the imposition of Anglo hegemony. The new scholarship has indeed focused on gender, but its concept of gender ignores nonwhite, non-middle-class experiences on the frontier. And the lack of an integrative conceptual framework particularly hampers attempts to address the question of race and the nature of interracial contact, including interracial marriage. . . .

Earlier studies of nineteenth-century Chicano history include general discussions of Chicanas, particularly in relation to labor and the family, but they do not incorporate gender as a category of analysis. Those of Albert Camarillo, Richard Griswold del Castillo, and Ricardo Romo begin on the eve of the Mexican-American War and center on the development of Chicano communities in California's urban centers during the latter half of the nineteenth and early twentieth centuries. Griswold del Castillo's more recent study on the Chicano family also begins after the U.S. war with Mexico, as does the earliest social history of the *Californios;* and Roberto Alvarez's anthropological examination of family migration in Baja and Alta California focuses mainly on the period after 1880. Recent social and frontier histories of Spanish and Mexican California and the Southwest, whether they derive from the Spanish borderlands school or from Mexican historical studies, either ignore women entirely or discuss them in very general terms. . . .

But there is new scholarship in colonial Mexican and Latin American women's and family history that is invaluable to the study of Spanish-speaking women in eighteenth- and nineteenth-century California. Ramón Gutiérrez's *When Jesus Came the Corn Mothers Went Away* offers a singularly important point of departure for an examination of gender and marriage in colonial New Mexico. . . . The new scholarship revises earlier interpretations of *Mexicanas* as passive, male-dominated, and powerless. While most of these studies do not focus on frontier women, they provide a well-defined sociocultural and political context for such discussion by illuminating gender-specific Spanish colonial and Mexican laws and policies.

And there are rich sources for the study of frontier Spanish-Mexican women. Though the standard archival sources for the Spanish colonial period are official reports, correspondence, diaries, and journals written by male missionaries and military authorities, they yield factual information about women's work and life in the missions and *presidios,* as well as insights into the gender ideology of the era. And although few Spanish-speaking women were literate, they did have petitions and letters penned for them. There are also quantifiable sources: censuses, court records, and mission registers of baptisms, marriages, and deaths. The marriage registers reveal the extent of interracial marriage between Amerindian women and Spanish-*mestizo* men. Both ecclesiastical and military records document the violence that soldiers committed against Amerindian women.

For the Mexican period, civil, criminal, and ecclesiastical court records reveal that women sued and were sued for divorce (legal separation), for land, and for custody of children and godchildren, as well as for numerous social transgressions. Court records document a significant increase in domestic violence against women; they also document violence by women. Court records, official reports, and correspondence yield information about race relations. *Libros de solares* (books of lots) record women's ownership of town lots, and there are also documents proving women's receipt and ownership of Mexican land grants. Before secularization in 1836, interracial marriages—now of Mexican women with European and Euro-American men—may be traced through mission registers.

For the era just before and after the American conquest, there are further quantifiable sources, in addition to the journals and correspondence of Anglo men and women, contemporary newspapers, and the literature of the gold rush. The records of the Land Grant Commission detail Mexican women's loss and retention of land grants. Extant *Ayuntamiento* (later City Council) records and Sole Trader records permit examination of Mexican women's economic life, as do the federal manuscript censuses. Women's wills and probate court records reveal the nature and disposition of women's property. Justice of the peace and parish records document interracial marriage. Justice of the peace and superior court records document crimes with which women were charged, crimes of which women were the victims, and indentures of children. Hubert Howe Bancroft's collection includes narratives from eleven Mexican women that provide significant information and insight into women's lives, work, family, race relations, and politics up to the 1870s, when the women were interviewed. Finally, family collections and papers in various repositories throughout the state contain women's correspondence, diaries, and journals of elite, literate *Californianas* and, in some cases, middle-class Mexican women who came to California in the latter half of the nineteenth century.

The threads of Spanish-Mexican women's history run throughout these sources. What is missing is an approach to the history of the frontier that integrates gender, race, and culture or class as categories of historical analysis. An integrative ethnohistorical approach would enable us to examine women's roles and lives in their societies of origin, as well as to describe and interpret how conquest changed their lives and restructured economic and social relationships not only between the sexes but also among persons of the same sex. . . . Nor have historians compared gender stratification and patriarchy in Spanish-Mexican and Euro-American frontier California. . . .

For three centuries, American frontiers were bloody battlegrounds of European and Euro-American expansion and conquest and of Amerindian resistance. Impoverished Spanish-speaking *mestiza, mulata,* and other *casta* women who migrated to Alta California in the eighteenth century came as part of soldier-settler families recruited and subsidized to populate the military forts in imperial Spain's most remote outpost. These women began the process of reproducing Hispanic culture and society on this frontier. Their daughters and granddaughters continued it as the region changed from Spanish to Mexican political control. A developing agropastoral economy built on trade and Amerindian labor gave rise to greater social stratification and the beginning of class distinctions. By the mid 1840s the great-granddaughters of the first generation of women, then in the midst of their own childbearing years, themselves experienced war, conquest, and displacement. Many of them became part of the menial wage labor force of a new, expanding, capitalist economy and society that bought their labor as cheaply as possible while it devalued their persons racially, culturally, and sexually. It is time to reexamine the history of these women within a conceptual framework that acknowledges the sex-gender, race, and culture or class issues that inhered in the politics and policies of frontier expansion, and to reinterpret the terms that define our changing reality on this frontier—presidarias, pobladoras, Californianas, Chicanas.

Spanish Texas and Borderlands Historiography

GERALD E. POYO AND GILBERTO M. HINOJOSA

United States Historians and the Spanish Borderlands

Examination of the survey textbooks used in colleges and universities across the nation reveals the lack of interest in the Spanish Borderlands displayed by historians of the United States. Characteristically, one very important classroom text treats the entire Spanish enterprise in the Americas in less than eight pages. A cursory discussion of Christopher Columbus's voyages of exploration is followed by an even briefer review of the conquest. Then, in two paragraphs, the volume describes Spain's establishment of settlements in the Borderlands, from Florida to California. The book notes that "during the seventeenth century Spain sowed missions in Texas and during the eighteenth in California." "But," the commentary concludes, "long before this, the force of the Spanish thrust had spent itself, and other countries were ready to make use of the vast and lonely North American continent." The text does not mention the territories colonized by Spain again until after their incorporation into the United States. A second textbook is more generous but also superficial and disappointing. Readers are told that "the Spanish gradually established the present-day economic structure of the Southwest" through the introduction of "techniques of mining, stock raising, and irrigated farming," but the textbook does not elaborate in any significant detail. Neither textbook traces the development of enduring Spanish communities with clear continuities to their nineteenth- and twentieth-century formation and development.

Texas histories also neglect continuities between the Spanish period and subsequent eras. While such textbooks dedicate more space to the Spanish period than do national survey texts, they usually treat colonial Texas as a colorful, but for the most part irrelevant, prelude to the rest of the state's history. One popular history of the state, *Lone Star,* by T. R. Fehrenbach, proclaims that "the first successful Hispanic colonization of Texas was not to come until much later, in the 20th century." Most of the textbook writers have difficulty transcending established ethnocentric perspectives legitimized by the anti-Spanish attitudes of the Black Legend. Generally they follow the long tradition in Texas historiography of dismissing the Spanish era as irrelevant. . . .

The earliest historians of the state purposefully set out to depict Spain as contributing little of enduring value. Many Texas writers dismissed Spain's deeprooted past as insignificant and undeserving of study except . . . to demonstrate how Anglo-Americans rescued the area from the "ignorance and despotism" that "hung like a dark cloud over her noble and luxuriant pastures." Frank W. Blackmar's disparaging study of Spain's institutions, written in 1891, projected a similar interpretation for the entire Southwest. Recognizing that the Spanish heritage "represents a part of our colonial life," Blackmar pointed to the necessity of studying

Gerald E. Poyo and Gilbert M. Hinojosa, "Spanish Texas and Borderlands Historiography in Transition: Implications for United States History," *Journal of American History* 75 (September 1988): 393–416. Reprinted with permission.

the period, but he premised his entire work on the inevitable decline of Spain's North American empire, which came about "on account of inherent[ly inferior] characteristics and peculiar conditions." Blackmar exulted that "the United States [is] now slowly crushing the last remnants of the institutions of this romance people." In time, the cultural and racial stereotypes basic to such negative historical assessment contributed to the popular conviction that the Spanish colonial system was pervasively backward, irrational, inferior to advanced Anglo-American processes, and therefore destined to fade away or be replaced.

The Spanish Borderlands Historians and the Case of Texas

Fortunately not all North American scholars accepted a fundamentally racist view of Hispanic activities in Texas and the Borderlands. During the late nineteenth and early twentieth centuries some historians offered a competing historical tradition designed to include those regions in United States history. Hubert Howe Bancroft's studies of Mexico and its northern frontier called attention to Spain's role in the entire North American Southwest and sparked the interest of other scholars. Among them the most prominent was Herbert Eugene Bolton, who in 1911 wrote that "one of the greatest needs in the field of American history is the publication of a comprehensive body of historical materials relating to Spanish activities within the present limits of the United States." The nation's history, Bolton lamented, was written "solely from the standpoint of the East and the English colonies."

Responding to Bolton's challenge, Carlos E. Castañeda, Charles W. Hackett, Charles E. Chapman, Lawrence Kinnaird, Alfred Barnaby Thomas, Arthur Preston Whitaker, Abraham P. Nasatir, and a score of others meticulously described the exploration and settlement of the former Spanish possessions, determined to counter the derogatory historical accounts colored by anti-Hispanic prejudices and the ever-present Black Legend. These scholars created a substantial and important literature that evaluated Spanish civilization in a generally admiring tone and argued explicitly the value and importance of Spain's past in the Borderlands regions. Their research and teaching activities led to the emergence of a formal field of study known as the Spanish Borderlands, which they hoped would be included in United States history.

Although Borderlands scholars argued convincingly against the Black Legend, they did not make an effective case for the incorporation of the region's history into that of the United States. Indeed, historians of the Borderlands focused on themes and utilized methodologies that made such integration difficult. In particular, their emphasis on the Spanish Empire and its geopolitical concerns led Borderlands historians to neglect the socioeconomic development of regions and communities. Thus the local factors that shaped settlers' daily lives and their emerging communities escaped the historians' notice. That unintended result is apparent in the general literature on the region and in the specific works on colonial Texas. . . .

The Spanish Borderlands and Texas Historiography in Transition

A focus on the settlers and towns eventually emerged from a border perspective of the field itself. As new essential narrative information on the Borderlands came to light, historians noted that the similarities of the frontier institutional structures were not unique to the northernmost provinces, but were, in fact, shared with the heartland. Bolton had often noted as much, particularly in reference to missions, and [John Francis] Bannon wrote that "there are not a few historians who broaden the concept of the Borderlands so as to encompass the north Mexican provinces [from Nuevo Santander to Baja California]." Bannon had agreed that "the broadest concept has its merits," but he and most other Borderlands scholars had maintained their focus on the provinces that became part of the United States. They perceived those regions as only loosely attached to the heartland of New Spain and therefore as a logical unit of study.

As research continued, other historians increasingly expanded the Borderlands framework and examined what Bolton and his students had often acknowledged but had failed to emphasize: the northern provinces were tied to a broader political and socioeconomic network. While the basic assumptions regarding the unity of those provinces remained unchallenged, researchers focused on the origins of frontier institutions and settlement patterns, linking them to their larger Mexican and Caribbean context. In the case of New Spain, they traced the origins, evolution, and northward movement of institutions. They effectively demonstrated that the northernmost provinces were an extension of the core and its surroundings, and not an insular appendage.

As they extended the territorial definition, Borderlands historians also broadened their methodological treatment. Incorporating the perspectives and work of scholars in disciplines such as archaeology, anthropology, and sociology, researchers went beyond studying explorations and institutions and focused on the cultural and socioeconomic underpinnings of Hispanic communities. Such scholars also adopted the methods of the new social history and increasingly recognized the relevance and importance of local and regional Latin American colonial historiography to the Spanish Borderlands. Indeed, they began to suggest that the inherent significance of the Borderlands was not to be found in institutions or imperial policies, but in the people and their communities, which lived on after the incorporation of these areas into the United States. The communities could be understood through specific attention to socioeconomic themes, including demographics, migration, land and water, class and race. For example, a 1979 work on New Spain's northern frontier, edited by David J. Weber, brought together studies of cultural, social, and demographic topics written during the previous decade. Oakah L. Jones, Jr.'s work on settlers on the northern frontier, published in the same year, surveyed census material for the civilian (non-mission, non-presidio) population, exemplifying the interest in issues beyond institutions and geopolitical concerns. Others used demographic data in their research on settlers in Tucson, Santa Fe, Albuquerque, San Francisco, Nacogdoches, Laredo, and Saltillo and examined the complexities of land, water, labor, marriage, acculturation, and social interaction in the northern communities.

The recent literature adds an entirely new dimension to Borderlands history. The studies point to the complex nature of the frontier communities by going beyond narratives of Crown institutions to describe the social and economic growth and development of the settlements. The studies rest on a basic assumption that social structures, environmental factors, and technological limitations influenced community developments as much as, if not more than, geopolitical considerations. These studies acknowledge the influence of the Crown in local communities, but unlike Bannon's work, they suggest that settlers also pursued individual strategies for survival and security based on local and regional considerations.

Scholars working on Texas history are now using approaches and methodologies suggested by social and economic history. Valuable work continues to be done from a traditional perspective, but historians are increasingly researching regional links, agriculture, ranching, commerce, demographics, race and class issues, the dynamics of local politics, and group interactions. This research is already suggesting new interpretative approaches that will provide a clearer understanding of colonial Texas and perhaps of all the northern provinces.

Recent investigations have highlighted, though not thoroughly explored, the regional links connecting Texas to Louisiana and Coahuila, an implicit departure from the traditional Borderlands framework that imputed to Texas a special affinity with Florida, New Mexico, and California. Interestingly, the focus on the colonial ties between Texas and its immediate neighbors first surfaced in the work of Mexican scholars who, free of the perspective adopted by North American historians, studied the development of settlements in the north in the context of expansion from the central heartland. . . .

Another unexplored but significant theme in the history of colonial Texas is agricultural development. Most studies note, but do not explain, the absence of farming endeavors. Some have suggested that agriculture did not prosper because the inhabitants were lazy or because their poverty precluded substantial investment in farming. Those explanations are unsatisfactory because they do not consider the region's economic dynamics. In fact, farmers in eighteenth-century Texas faced a variety of obstacles. The civilian population lacked markets for farm products and often had to compete with the missions or with the presidios themselves in providing foodstuffs to the soldiers. Moreover, the scarcity of laborers and the limitations to expansion imposed by Indian attacks impeded rapid agricultural growth. The high cost of building irrigation systems and the lack of adequate farming technology on the frontier prevented significant increases in agricultural productivity. Finally, agriculture had to compete with ranching, which had markets, needed relatively few hands, could often evade the Indians, and required little capital. Given the circumstances, the local elites quite understandably chose to concentrate on ranching and commerce. Ultimately, the lack of agricultural surpluses worked against demographic growth, limiting the life-span and dissuading immigration. That lack helps explain why the population in Texas amounted to only about four thousand at the end of the eighteenth century. . . .

Historians have assumed that a vibrant demographic growth did not occur on the Texas frontier because local institutions could not effectively pacify the Indians and secure the region for Spain. As one historian has noted, "From 1765 to 1810 Spanish officials in Mexico had struggled continually with the problem of the Apache menace that had blunted the northward thrust of the missionary effort and made the borderlands untenable for settlers." At first glance the assumption seems reasonable, given the ongoing conflicts between Spaniards and Indians, but recent researchers have suggested greater complexities. Although Apaches and Comanches posed problems for the Spanish communities, Elizabeth A. H. John has demonstrated that peaceful interaction between Indians and Spaniards may have been as frequent as conflict. "By painful trial and error," John notes, "Indian and Spanish communities evolved toward peaceful coexistence in eighteenth-century New Mexico and Texas." "Santa Fe and San Antonio were seats of lively interaction among Indian allies come to trade and to talk, and to nourish the bonds of brotherhood." John demonstrates Indian motivations and strategies for dealing with the Spanish that call into question the idea that the Indian "threat" decisively hindered demographic growth. Indeed, an argument can be made that the economy, living conditions, and social structure in Texas affected the area's eighteenth-century demographic experience more than the limitations imposed by Indians.

In addition to the scarce employment opportunities inherent in the ranching economy, social factors also obstructed demographic growth. In her landmark demographic study of Texas, Alicia V. Tjarks suggested that short life-spans, a generally hostile environment, and epidemics all kept the population down. A recent work on the San Antonio missions reveals that natural population increase was minuscule. In all but five years between 1718 and 1821 for which records are available, deaths outnumbered births. Under ordinary circumstances (that is, in the absence of epidemics), the average mortality rate was high. That and a low birth rate precluded a natural increase in the mission population. Similar research in baptismal and burial records and census data for the broader society may provide a more sophisticated understanding of overall demographic experience in Texas. The frontier environment apparently limited natural population growth, leaving immigration as the primary means of demographic expansion. . . .

Demographic issues aside, the complexities of racial dynamics in New Spain, and indeed all of Latin America, suggest the need for further research into the significance of race in Texas. Indians, blacks, and Caucasians constituted the original population groups of colonial Mexico, but they mixed relatively freely, creating a miscegenated population known collectively as *castas*. A detailed categorization emerged that defined the various racial groups according to their mixtures. A certain status was attached to each designation, with the *español* (Spaniard) holding the highest social rank. Thus an important historiographic issue in Latin American colonial studies is the relative significance of race in the various regions.

With regard to Texas, an analysis of marriage patterns for [San Antonio de] Béxar from the 1730s through the 1760s reveals that intermarriage between the early Canary Islands settlers who had established the formal town and mixed-blood members of the presidial community was frequent, creating a mestizo elite by the late eighteenth century. However, a systematic examination of marriage records for the late colonial period may demonstrate that elite marriages were heavily influenced by racial considerations, a pattern suggested in other records. In numerous land records, for example, petitioners base their claim to privileges on their marital connections with Canary Islander families. Perhaps racial distinctions between *españoles* and (Spanish-Indian) mestizos were blurred in the northern provinces, whereas sharp distinctions marked off Spaniards and mestizos on the one hand and all other *castas* (for example, white-black, Indian-black, or mestizo-black) on the other. A scarcity of Spaniards, rather than a lack of racial concern, may explain the concurrent phenomena of exogamy and racial bias. As a recent article on marriage patterns in the northern Mexican town of Parral concluded, "A *sistema de castas* [caste system] was very much in evidence in this mining town toward the end of the colonial period . . . *calidad* [race] seems to have been at least as important as *clase* [class] in marital pairings." In Texas too, that seems to have been the case, suggesting that racial attitudes may have been more restrictive than Tjarks argued. . . .

Socioeconomic themes will also suggest new perspectives on political development in colonial Texas. To view provincial politics as defined primarily by geopolitical considerations or institutional conflicts is to ignore much of Texan political life. Political studies ought to examine factors related to the province's social and economic development. The search for social status and control over limited economic resources within a constantly changing socioeconomic environment naturally produced interest groups that competed for political influence. The challenge is to identify the competing groups and to define the determinants of political conflict, a task that will be facilitated by understanding social and economic developments. Research may well show that politics in Texas were influenced as much by internal social and economic developments as by the imperial goals of the Crown.

The research for a new political history has already begun. A few historians are examining the emergence of a ranching and commercial elite in Béxar. They note a clear relationship between kinship, ranching connections, and participation in the San Fernando cabildo or city council. Initially, immigrants from the Canary Islands who founded the town controlled the city council. For some time they dominated the body absolutely because councils elected their successors annually. Within twenty years, however, a process of intermarriage and the emergence of a ranching economy in which most inhabitants of Béxar participated provided non-Canary Islanders the means to gain sufficient social or economic status to be elected to the cabildo. The cabildo became a heterogeneous body and politics came to reflect communitywide competition for land, water, and commerce. The competing political interests need to be identified and studied. For example, members of the Arocha and Travieso families struggled for control of the cabildo during the 1780s and 1790s. Earlier in the century, the heads of those families had been allies, working together to promote Canary Islander political and socioeconomic dominance in Béxar. That divergence of interests of the two important islander clans is an unexplored but crucial theme in the town's political development. Simply examining the cabildo's legal structure and identifying its prominent personalities outside the context of their social and economic relationships is insufficient to obtain an understanding of colonial politics in Texas. . . .

Implications for Borderlands and United States History

This reevaluation of the Texas colonial experience from a socioeconomic perspective has implications for Borderlands history in general. To begin with, communities did exist in Texas and in the other northern provinces that cannot be dismissed as "failures" simply because Spanish-American civilization was unable to resist Anglo-American intrusion. Béxar exhibited a noteworthy and sophisticated political and socioeconomic system. Furthermore, Texas communities such as Béxar, Nacogdoches, and La Bahía were not committed exclusively to Crown or institutional objectives. Indeed, provincial elites in Texas often ignored the Crown's political desires. Communities and elites in other provinces may have done the same. Researchers must go beyond the formative literature's concern for the region's "inadequacy" in the face of United States expansion and focus on the internal development of the colonial societies themselves. And finally, Texas did not have more affinity with Florida, New Mexico, and California than with other Spanish provinces. Indeed, the political, economic, and social development of Texas is more effectively examined in the context of developments in the adjacent areas of Louisiana and Coahuila and those in the heartland of New Spain than as part of the history of a conceptual unit known as the Spanish Borderlands. Such a local and regional approach to Spain's northernmost frontiers will clarify their internal development and deemphasize the traditional preoccupation with their eventual fate as part of the United States. The conventional framework is perhaps no longer the most effective conceptual tool for understanding the Spanish Borderlands.

Finally, and paradoxically, it is the regional and local framework, and the consequent focus on socioeconomic development, that will prompt scholars to reconsider the colonial Borderlands' significance to the United States. By studying the dynamics of communities that came under North American control, historians will identify continuities across sovereignties. Commercial ties, migration patterns, class structures, racial attitudes, economic pursuits, and cross-cultural relationships are significant themes in the nineteenth and twentieth centuries that need to be traced from their origins.

Scholars in Mexico-American history have recognized the importance of those topics. A decade and a half ago, Chicano historian Juan Gómez-Quiñones noted the need for a critical evaluation of pre-1900 socioeconomic forces to better understand the contemporary Mexican-American community. Researchers responded with numerous significant social and demographic studies for the nineteenth century. Similarly, it may now be said that to understand the nineteenth-century communities fully there is need for research on their Spanish and Mexican antecedents. In fact, some historians have already produced works that not only examine the eighteenth-century origins of United States communities, but also trace them across sovereignties. Ultimately, research that examines the development of communities will integrate the Spanish and Mexican periods into United States history. Important as it might be, the study of Spanish institutions and imperial strategies has not succeeded in fulfilling Bolton's dream of integrating Spain's past in the northern frontier into the history of the United States. Only when historians of the United States perceive the socioeconomic forces that endured will they be persuaded that the history of the Borderlands is in fact part of this nation's formation.

❧ *F U R T H E R   R E A D I N G*

John Francis Bannon, *The Spanish Borderlands Frontier, 1513–1821* (1974)

Herbert Eugene Bolton, *The Spanish Borderlands* (1996)

Victoria Brady, Sarah Crome, and Lyn Reese, "Resist!: Survival Tactics of Indian Women," *California History* 63 (Spring 1984), 140–151

Antonia I. Castañeda, "*Presidarias y Pobladoras:* The Journey North and Life in Frontier California," in Norma Alarcon et al., eds., *Chicana Critical Issues* (1993)

Fray Angelico Chávez, *Origins of New Mexico Families* (1992)

Harry W. Crosby, *Antigua California* (1994)

Jesús de la Teja, "Building a Frontier Community," in Jesús de la Teja, *San Antonio de Bexar* (1995)

Franklin Folsom, *Indian Uprising on the Río Grande* (1996)

Ramón A. Gutiérrez, *When Jesus Came, the Corn Mothers Went Away* (1991)

Thomas D. Hall, *Social Change in the Southwest, 1350–1880* (1989)

Solamé Hernández, "*Nueva Mxicanas* as Refugees and Reconquest Settlers 1680–1696," in Joan M. Jensen and Darlis A. Miller, eds., *New Mexico Women* (1996)

Gilberto M. Hinojosa, *A Borderlands Town in Transition* (1983)

Alan Hutchinson, *Frontier Settlement in Mexican California* (1969)

Jack Jackson, *Los Mesteños* (1986)

Oakah L. Jones, *Los Paisanos* (1979)

John L. Kessell, *Friars, Soldiers, and Reformers* (1976)

John L. Kessell, *Kiva, Cross, and Crown* (1979)

Andrew L. Knaut, *The Pueblo Revolt of 1680* (1995)

Manuel P. Servín, "The Beginnings of California's Anti-Mexican Prejudice," in Manuel P. Servín, ed., *The Mexican Americans: An Awakening Minority* (1974)

Marc Simmons, *Coronado's Land* (1991)

Angelina Veyna, "A View of the Past: Women in Colonial New Mexico, 1744–1767," in Adela de la Torre and Beatríz Pesquera, eds., *Building with Our Own Hands* (1993)

David J. Weber, ed., *New Spain's Far Northern Frontier* (1979)

David J. Weber, *The Spanish Frontier in North America* (1992)

CHAPTER 4

Early Mexicano Life and Society in the Southwest, 1821–1846

Texas, particularly the Spanish-speaking villages of the New Mexico region be-tween the Nueces River and the Río Grande, was transformed from a Mexican hacienda and ranching economy to an Anglo capitalist system based on agricul-ture and trade between 1821 and 1846. This change had a negative impact on the region's Chicano populations. Property and wealth were assumed by Anglos after Texas independence and annexation, although there was apparent accom-modation between the wealthy and privileged Mexicans and the new Anglo elites. In the transfer of land from Mexican to Anglo, a semifeudal pastoral economy was replaced by a commercial cattle industry that relied heavily on Mexican labor. How would the loss of economic dominance that led to the politi-cal subordination and eventual proletarianization of Texas Mexicans set the context from which Mexican and Anglo relations would evolve along the Texas border region?

The small population of settlers faced conflict with area Indian nations like the Navajo, who, after 1800, raided the villages of New Mexico for their sheep and horses and for captives who were either traded or kept. Meanwhile, before annexation American and Spanish-speaking New Mexicans paved the way for the American conquest of New Mexico, for a quarter century before annexation was dependent economically on the United States. This trade enriched the ricos of New Mexico, who functioned as feudal lords and perpetuated feudal like so-cial relations with New Mexico's masses. To the majority of Americans, however, the native New Mexicans, like all Mexicans, were regarded as inferior beings and as obstacles to the acquisition and consolidation of a continental empire. How did such attitudes make life for the native New Mexicans both challenging and difficult?

In California, as the Spanish crown pursued its double goal of Christianiza-tion and Hispanicization, the world of the Indian was systematically destroyed through a sustained policy of military campaigns and forced labor; disease and malnutrition would also take their toll on the native populations. The Spanish, through a reign of violence, imposed their religious, military, and civil institu-tions on the California Indians. By 1800, the mission system, four presidios, three towns, and two dozen ranchos that the Spanish had established along the California coast had all been built by and were dependent upon compulsory Indian labor. Control of the economy shifted to the large estates owned by the Spanish-speaking Californios, who appropriated the mission lands for themselves and their relatives. Family alliances achieved through marriage solidified and strengthened mutual interests. Was the period between secularization of the missions in 1833 and cession to the United States in 1848 truly the heyday of Californio ranch life?

❦ D O C U M E N T S

Indian labor, both skilled and unskilled, formed the basis of the highly productive and self-sufficient mission system of California. As Eulalia Pérez, who worked as a cook and housekeeper at Mission San Diego in the early nineteenth century, describes in Document 1, the contributions of women were integral to the survival of these settlements. She recalls, for example, that her many duties included making clothes for the soldiers and delivering supplies.

During this period nations such as Britain and the United States were expressing interest in the Pacific Northwest as a site for ports for the Asian trade. In Document 2, dated 1826, Captain Frederick W. Beechy of the British Royal Navy, who commanded the ship *Blossom,* details the weaknesses of the San Francisco presidio and describes how the mission system operated.

Mexican officials were fearful of the growing American presence in Texas, for Mexico's hold on California was weak, as Spain's had been. In the fall of 1827, General Manuel Mier y Terán was sent by the Mexican government as head of a special commission to inspect the Texas–U.S. boundary. Document 3 is an excerpt from the letter Mier y Terán wrote to the president of Mexico on June 30, 1828, to report on the extent of American influence in East Texas. In 1829, Mier y Terán, now commander of Mexico's northeastern provinces, sent a letter to the Mexican minister of war expressing his concern over the spread of the Americans in the area. This resulted in Mexico's passage of the Law of April 6, 1830, which closed the Mexican border to further American immigration. In Document 4, Texas Mexican Eulalia Yorba recalls her experience in San Antonio during the siege of the Alamo as well as the final assault on the mission in 1836, during which she attended to the wounded Mexican soldiers. She had vivid memories of this famous battle, including seeing the body of Colonel Davy Crockett. Olibama López's reminiscences of life in the early settlements of the San Luis Valley in Colorado are reproduced in Document 5, which details living conditions, the self-sufficiency of the settlers, women's tasks, leisure activities, and religious holidays.

The impressions of the Spanish-speaking residents of the Southwest recorded by the first American visitors to the region have profoundly shaped American perceptions of these inhabitants. This was especially true for Mexican women, who were often romanticized and stereotyped. In Document 6, written in 1843, the American Joshua Gregg gives his view of one of the more infamous New Mexican women, Gertrudes Barceló, popularly known as "La Tules." Gentleman historian Ralph Emerson Twitchell, in Document 7, also from 1843, uses Gregg's account to perpetuate the stereotype of La Tules as a notable, albeit notorious, gambler. Such inaccurate pictures illustrate the importance of reading these early histories of the Southwest critically.

1. Eulalia Pérez Remembers Early California, 1823

I, Eulalia Pérez, was born in the Presidio of Loreto in Baja California.

My father's name was Diego Pérez, and he was employed in the Navy Department of said presidio; my mother's name was Antonia Rosalia Cota. Both were pure white.

I do not remember the date of my birth, but I do know that I was fifteen years old when I married Miguel Antonio Guillén, a soldier of the garrison at Loreto Presidio. During the time of my stay at Loreto I had three children—two boys, who died there in infancy, one girl, Petra, who was eleven years old when we moved to San Diego, and another boy, Isidoro, who came with us to this [Alta] California.

I lived eight years in San Diego with my husband, who continued his service in the garrison of the presidio, and I attended women in childbirth. . . .

In 1812 I was in San Juan Capistrano attending Mass in church when a big earthquake occurred, and the tower fell down. I dashed through the sacristy, and in the doorway the people knocked me down and stepped over me. I was pregnant and could not move. Soon afterwards I returned to San Diego and almost immediately gave birth to my daughter María Antonia. . . .

After being in San Diego eight years, we came to the Mission of San Gabriel, where my husband had been serving in the guard. In 1814, on the first of October, my daughter María del Rosario was born, the one who is the wife of Michael White and in whose home I am now living. . . .

My last trip to San Diego would have been in the year 1818, when my daughter María del Rosario was four years old. I seem to remember that I was there when the [anti-Spanish] revolutionaries came to California. . . .

Some three years later I came back to San Gabriel. The reason for my return was that the missionary at San Gabriel, Father José Sánchez, wrote to Father Fernando at San Diego . . . asking him to speak to the commandant of the presidio at San Diego requesting him to give my son Isidoro Guillén a guard to escort me here with all my family. The commandant agreed.

When we arrived here Father José Sánchez lodged me and my family temporarily in a small house until work could be found for me. There I was with my five daughters—my son Isidoro Guillén was taken into service as a soldier in the mission guard. . . .

When I came to San Gabriel the last time, there were only two women in this part of California who knew how to cook [well]. One was María Luisa Cota, wife of Claudio López, superintendent of the mission; the other was María Ignacia Amador, wife of Francisco Javier Alvarado. She knew how to cook, sew, read and write and take care of the sick. She was a good healer. She did needlework and took care of the church vestments. She taught a few children to read and write in her home, but did not conduct a formal school. . . .

From *Three Memoirs of Mexican California* by Carlos N. Hijar, Eulalia Pérez and Agustín Escobar, 1877, from The Friends of the Bancroft Library, University of California at Berkeley, 1988. Reprinted by permission.

The priests wanted to help me out because I was a widow burdened with a family. They looked for some way to give me work without offending the other women. Fathers Sánchez and [José María] Zalvidea conferred and decided that they would have first one woman, then the other and finally me, do the cooking, in order to determine who did it best, with the aim of putting the one who surpassed the others in charge of the Indian cooks so as to teach them how to cook. . . .

. . . No one told me anything regarding what it was all about, until one day Father Sánchez called me and said, "Look, Eulalia, tomorrow it is your turn to prepare dinner–because María Ignacia and Luisa have already done so. We shall see what kind of a dinner you will give us tomorrow."

The next day I went to prepare the food. I made several kinds of soup, a variety of meat dishes and whatever else happened to pop into my head that I knew how to prepare. . . .

Because of all this, employment was provided for me at the mission. At first they assigned me two Indians so that I could show them how to cook, the one named Tomás and the other called "The Gentile.". . .

The missionaries were very satisfied; this made them think more highly of me. I spent about a year teaching those two Indians. I did not have to do the work, only direct them, because they already had learned a few of the fundamentals.

After this, the missionaries conferred among themselves and agreed to hand over the mission keys to me. This was in 1821, if I remember correctly. . . .

The duties of the housekeeper were many. In the first place, every day she handed out the rations for the mess hut. To do this she had to count the unmarried women, bachelors, day-laborers, vaqueros. . . . Besides that, she had to hand out daily rations to the heads of households. In short, she was responsible for the distribution of supplies to the Indian population and to the missionaries' kitchen. She was in charge of the key to the clothing storehouse where materials were given out for dresses for the unmarried and married women and children. Then she also had to take care of cutting and making clothes for the men.

Furthermore, she was in charge of cutting and making the vaqueros' outfits, from head to foot—that is, for the vaqueros who rode in saddles. Those who rode bareback received nothing more than their cotton blanket and loin-cloth, while those who rode in saddles were dressed the same way as the Spanish-speaking inhabitants; that is, they were given shirt, vest, jacket, trousers, hat, cowboy boots, shoes and spurs; and a saddle, bridle and lariat for the horse. Besides, each vaquero was given a big silk or cotton handkerchief, and a sash of Chinese silk or Canton crepe, or whatever there happened to be in the storehouse.

They put under my charge everything having to do with clothing. I cut and fitted, and my five daughters sewed up the pieces. When they could not handle everything, the father was told, and then women from the town of Los Angeles were employed, and the father paid them.

Besides this, I had to attend to the soap-house, . . . to the wine-presses, and to the olive-crushers that produced oil, which I worked in myself. . . .

I handled the distribution of leather, calf-skin, chamois, sheepskin, Morocco leather, fine scarlet cloth, nails, thread, silk, etc.—everything having to do with the making of saddles, shoes and what was needed for the belt- and shoe-making shops.

Every week I delivered supplies for the troops and Spanish-speaking servants. These consisted of beans, corn, garbanzos, lentils, candles, soap and lard. To carry out this distribution, they placed at my disposal an Indian servant named Lucio, who was trusted completely by the missionaries.

When it was necessary, some of my daughters did what I could not find the time to do. . . .

I served as housekeeper of the mission for twelve or fourteen years, until about two years after the death of Father José Sánchez, which occurred in this same mission. . . .

. . . I think it was, of 1833. In that month there was a great flood.

2. Captain Frederick W. Beechy Describes the California Missions, 1826

The object of the missions is to convert as many of the wild Indians as possible, and to train them up within the walls of the establishment in the exercise of a good life, and of some trade, so that they may in time be able to provide for themselves and become useful members of civilized society. As to the various methods employed for the purpose of bringing proselytes to the mission, there are several reports, of which some were not very creditable to the institution: nevertheless, on the whole I am of opinion that the priests are innocent, from a conviction that they are ignorant of the means employed by those who are under them. . . .

Immediately the Indians are brought to the mission they are placed under the tuition of some of the most enlightened of their countrymen, who teach them to repeat in Spanish the Lord's Prayer and certain passages in the Romish litany; and also to cross themselves properly on entering the church. In a few days a willing Indian becomes a proficient in these mysteries, and suffers himself to be baptized, and duly initiated into the church. If, however, as it not unfrequently happens, any of the captured Indians show a repugnance to conversion, it is the practice to imprison them for a few days, and then to allow them to breathe a little fresh air in a walk round the mission, to observe the happy mode of life of their converted countrymen; after which they are again shut up, and thus continue to be incarcerated until they declare their readiness to renounce the religion of their forefathers. . . .

. . . The Indians are so averse to confinement that they very soon become impressed with the manifestly superior and more comfortable mode of life of those who are at liberty, and in a very few days declare their readiness to have the new religion explained to them. A person acquainted with the language of the parties, of which there are sometimes several dialects in the same mission, is then selected to train them, and having duly prepared them takes his pupils to the padre to be baptized, and to receive the sacrament. Having become Christians they are put to trades, or if they have good voices they are taught music, and form part of the choir of the church. Thus there are in almost every mission weavers, tanners, shoemakers, bricklayers, carpenters, blacksmiths, and other artificers. Others again are

---

As found in Captain F. W. Beechy, *Narratives of a Voyage to the Pacific and Bering's Strait* (London, 1831), 3:1–23.

taught husbandry, to rear cattle and horses; and some to cook for the mission: while the females card, clean, and spin wool, weave, and sew; and those who are married attend to their domestic concerns.

In requital of these benefits, the services of the Indians, for life, belong to the mission, and if any neophyte should repent of his apostasy from the religion of his ancestors and desert, an armed force is sent in pursuit of him, and drags him back to punishment apportioned to the degree of aggravation attached to his crime. It does not often happen that a voluntary convert succeeds in his attempt to escape, as the wild Indians have a great contempt and dislike for those who have entered the missions, and they will frequently not only refuse to re-admit them to their tribe, but will sometimes even discover their retreat to their pursuers. This animosity between the wild and converted Indians is of great importance to the missions, as it checks desertion, and is at the same time a powerful defense against the wild tribes, who consider their territory invaded, and have other just causes of complaint. The Indians, besides, from political motives, are, I fear, frequently encouraged in a contemptuous feeling towards their unconverted countrymen, by hearing them constantly held up to them in the degrading light of *bestias!* [beasts] and in hearing the Spaniards distinguished by the appellation of *génte de razón* [people of reason]. . . .

The children and adults of both sexes, in all the missions, are carefully locked up every night in separate apartments, and the keys are delivered into the possession of the padre; and as, in the daytime, their occupations lead to distinct places, unless they form a matrimonial alliance, they enjoy very little of each other's society. It, however, sometimes happens that they endeavor to evade the vigilance of their keepers, and are locked up with the opposite sex; but severe corporeal punishment, inflicted . . . with a whip . . . , is sure to ensue if they are discovered. Though there may be occasional acts of tyranny, yet the general character of the padres is kind and benevolent. . . . It is greatly to be regretted that, with the influence these men have over their pupils, . . . the priests do not interest themselves a little more in the education of their converts, the first step to which would be in making themselves acquainted with the Indian language. Many of the Indians surpass their pastors in this respect, and can speak the Spanish language, while scarcely one of the padres can make themselves understood by the Indians. They have besides, in general, a lamentable contempt for the intellect of these simple people, and think them incapable of improvement beyond a certain point. Notwithstanding this, the Indians are . . . clothed and fed; they have houses of their own . . . ; their meals are given to them three times a day, and consist of thick gruel made of wheat, Indian corn, and sometimes acorns, to which at noon is generally added meat. . . .

Having served ten years in the mission, an Indian may claim his liberty. . . . A piece of ground is then allotted for his support, but he is never wholly free from the establishment, as part of his earnings must still be given to them. We heard of very few to whom this reward for servitude and good conduct had been granted; and it is not improbable that the padres are averse to it. . . . When these establishments were first founded, the Indians flocked to them in great numbers for the clothing with which the neophytes were supplied; but after they became acquainted with the nature of the institution, and felt themselves under restraint, many absconded. Even now, notwithstanding the difficulty of escaping, desertions are of frequent occurrence, owing probably, in some cases, to the fear of punishment—in others to the deserters having been originally inveigled into the mission by the converted Indians or the neophytes, as they are called by the way of distinction . . . the wild Indians.

3. General Manuel Mier y Terán Reports on the Texas-Coahuila Territory, 1828–1829

As one covers the distance from Béjar to this town, he will note that Mexican influence is proportionately diminished until on arriving in this place he will see that it is almost nothing. And indeed, whence could such influence come? Hardly from superior numbers in population, since the ratio of Mexicans to foreigners is one to ten; certainly not from the superior character of the Mexican population, for exactly the opposite is true, the Mexicans of this town comprising what in all countries is called the lowest class—the very poor and very ignorant. . . . It would cause you the same chagrin that it has caused me to see the opinion that is held of our nation by these foreign colonists, since, with the exception of some few who have journeyed to our capital, they know no other Mexicans than the inhabitants about here, and excepting the authorities necessary to any form of society, the said inhabitants are the most ignorant of negroes and Indians. . . . Thus, I tell myself that it could not be otherwise than that from such a state of affairs should arise an antagonism between the Mexicans and foreigners. . . . Therefore, I am warning you to take timely measures. Texas could throw the whole nation into revolution.

The colonists murmur against the political disorganization of the frontier, and the Mexicans complain of the superiority and better education of the colonists: the colonists find it unendurable that they must go three hundred leagues to lodge a complaint against the petty pickpocketing that they suffer from a venal and ignorant *alcalde* [mayor], and the Mexicans with no knowledge of the laws of their own country, nor those regulating colonization, set themselves against the foreigners, deliberately setting nets to deprive them of the right of franchise. . . . Meanwhile, the incoming stream of new settlers is unceasing; the first news of these comes by discovering them on land already under cultivation, where they have been located for many months; the old inhabitants set up a claim to the property . . . for which there are no records. . . .

In spite of the enmity that usually exists between the Mexicans and the foreigners, there is a most evident uniformity of opinion on one point, namely the separation of Texas from Coahuila and its organization into a territory of the federal government. This idea, which was conceived by some of the colonists who are above the average, has become general among the people and does not fail to cause considerable discussion. In explaining the reasons assigned by them for this demand, I shall do no more than relate what I have heard with no addition of my own conclusions, and I frankly state that I have been commissioned by some of the colonists to explain to you their motives, notwithstanding the fact that I should have done so anyway in the fulfillment of my duty.

Mier y Terán to Pablo Viejo, Mexican Minister of War, 14 November 1829. As found in Ohland Morton, *Terán and Texas: A Chapter in Texas-Mexican Relations* (Austin: University of Texas Press, 1948), pp. 99–101. Reprinted courtesy The Texas State Historical Association, Austin.

They claim that Texas in its present condition of a colony is an expense, since it is not a sufficiently prosperous section to contribute to the revenues of the state administration; and since it is such a charge it ought not to be imposed upon a state as poor as Coahuila, which has not the means of defraying the expenses of the corps of political and judicial officers necessary for the maintenance of peace and order. Furthermore, it is impracticable that recourse in all matters should be had to a state capital so distant and separated from this section by deserts infected by hostile savages. Again, their interests are very different from those of the other sections, and because of this they should be governed by a separate territorial government, having learned by experience that the mixing of their affairs with those of Coahuila brings about friction. The native inhabitants of Texas add to the above other reasons which indicate an aversion for the inhabitants of Coahuila; also the authority of the *comandante* and the collection of taxes is disputed. . . .

. . . The whole population here is a mixture of strange and incoherent parts without parallel in our federation: numerous tribes of Indians, now at peace, but armed and at any moment ready for war, whose steps toward civilization should be taken under the close supervision of a strong and intelligent government; colonists of another people, more progressive and better informed than the Mexican inhabitants, but also more shrewd and unruly; among these foreigners are fugitives from justice, honest laborers, vagabonds and criminals, but honorable and dishonorable alike travel with their political constitution in their pockets, demanding the privileges, authority and officers which such a constitution guarantees.

1829

The department of Texas is contiguous to the most avid nation in the world. The North Americans have conquered whatever territory adjoins them. In less than half a century, they have become masters of extensive colonies which formerly belonged to Spain and France, and of even more spacious territories from which have disappeared the former owners, the Indian tribes. There is no Power like that to the north, which by silent means, has made conquests of momentous importance. Such dexterity, such constancy in their designs, such uniformity of means of execution which always are completely successful, arouses admiration. Instead of armies, battles, or invasions, which make a great noise and for the most part are unsuccessful, these men lay hands on means, which, if considered one by one, would be rejected as slow, ineffective, and at times palpably absurd. They begin by assuming rights, as in Texas, which it is impossible to sustain in a serious discussion, making ridiculous pretensions based on historical incidents which no one admits—such as the voyage of La Salle, which was an absurd fiasco, but serves as a basis for their claim to Texas. Such extravagant claims as these are now being presented for the first time to the public by dissembling writers; the efforts that others make to submit proofs and reasons are by these men employed in reiterations and in enlarging upon matters of administration in order to attract the attention of their fellow-countrymen, not to the justice of the claim, but to the profit to be gained from admitting it. At this stage it is alleged that there is a national demand for the step which the government mediates. In the meantime, the territory against which these machinations are directed, and which has usually remained unsettled, begins to be visited by adventurers and *empresarios;* some of these take up their residence in the country, pretending that their location has no bearing upon the question of their government's claim or the boundary disputes; shortly, some of these forerunners develop an interest which complicates the political administration of the coveted territory; complaints, even threats, begin to be heard, working on the loyalty of the legitimate settlers, discrediting the efficiency of the existing authority and administration; and the matter having arrived at this stage—which is precisely that of Texas at this moment—diplomatic maneuvers begin: They incite uprisings in the territory in question and usually manifest a deep concern for the rights of the inhabitants.

4. Eulalia Yorba Gives an Eyewitness Account of the Siege of the Alamo, 1836

I well remember when Santa Anna and his two thousand soldiers on horses and with shining muskets and bayonets marched into the little pueblo of San Antonio. The news ran from mouth to mouth that Colonel Travis, Davy Crockett and Colonel Bowie and the 160 or so other Texans who had held that locality against the Mexicans for several weeks had taken refuge in and had barricaded themselves in that old stone mission, which had been used as a crude fort or garrison long before I came to the country. It belonged to Mexico and a few stands of muskets and three or four cannons were kept there. When Santa Anna's army came they camped on the plains about the pueblo and a guard was put about the Alamo fort. That was from the last day of February to March 4. Of course, I kept at home with my little boys and never stirred out once, for we women were all terribly frightened. Every eatable in the house, all the cows, lumber and hay about the place were taken by the troops, but we were assured that if we remained in the house no personal harm would come to us.

Of course, we were hourly informed of the news. We knew that the Texans in the Alamo were surrounded by over five hundred soldiers constantly, while fifteen hundred more soldiers were in camp out on the plains. We learned that four days had been given the Texans to surrender. We heard from the soldiers that not one of the imprisoned men had so much as returned a reply to the demand for surrender and that on the morning of the 6th of March 1836, Santa Anna was going to bring matters to a crisis with the beleaguered rebels. I never can tell the anxiety that we people on the outside felt for that mere handful of men in the old fort, when we saw around hostile troops as far as we could see and not a particle of help for the Texans, for whom we few residents of the town had previously formed a liking.

The morning of Sunday—the 6th of March—ah! indeed, I could never forget that, even if I lived many years more—was clear and balmy. . . . The shooting began at six in the morning. It seemed as if there were myriads of soldiers and guns about the stone building. There was volley after volley fired into the barred and bolted windows. Then the volleys came in quick succession. Occasionally we heard muffled volleys and saw puffs of smoke from within the Alamo, and when we saw, too, Mexican soldiers fall in the roadway or stagger back we knew the Texans were fighting as best they could for their lives.

It seemed as if ten thousand guns were shot off indiscriminately as firecrackers snap when whole bundles of them are set off at one time. The smoke grew thick and heavy and we could not see clearly down at the Alamo, while the din of musketry, screams of crazy, exultant Mexicans increased every moment. I have never heard human beings scream so fiercely and powerfully as the Mexican soldiers that day. . . .

Next several companies of soldiers came running down the street with great heavy bridge timbers. These were quickly brought to bear as battering rams on the mission doors, but several volleys from within the Alamo, as nearly as we could see, laid low the men at the timbers and stopped the battering for a short time. Three or four brass cannons were loaded with what seemed to us very long delay and were placed directly in front of the main doors of the mission. They did serious work. Meanwhile, bullets from several thousand muskets incessantly rained like hail upon the building and went through the apertures that had been made in the wood barricades at the windows and doors. The din was indescribable. It did not seem as if a mouse could live in a building so shot at and riddled as the Alamo was that morning.

Next we saw ladders brought and in a trice the low roof of the church was crowded with a screaming, maddened throng of men armed with guns and sabers. Of course we knew then that it was all up with the little band of men in the Alamo. . . .

Along about nine o'clock, . . . the shooting and swearing and yelling had ceased, but the air was thick and heavy with blue powder smoke. A Mexican colonel came running to the priest's residence and asked that we go down to the Alamo to do what we could for the dying men.

Such a dreadful sight. The roadway was thronged with Mexican soldiers with smoke and dirt begrimed faces, haggard eyes and wild, insane expression. There were twelve or fifteen bodies of Mexicans lying dead and bleeding here and there and others were being carried to an adobe house across the way. The stones in the church wall were spotted with blood, the doors were splintered and battered in. Pools of thick blood were so frequent on the sun-baked earth about the stone building that we had to be careful to avoid stepping in them. There was a din of excited voices along the street and the officers were marshaling their men for moving to camp.

But no one could even tell you the horror of the scene that met our gaze when we were led by the sympathetic little colonel into the old Alamo to bandage up the wounds of several young men there. I used to try when I was younger to describe that awful sight, but I never could find sufficient language. There were only a few Mexicans in there when we came and they were all officers who had ordered the common soldiers away from the scene of death and—yes—slaughter, for that was what it was. The floor was literally crimson with blood. The woodwork all about us was riddled and splintered by lead balls and what was left of the old alter at the rear of the church was cut and slashed by cannon ball and bullets. The air was dark with powder smoke and was hot and heavy. The odor was oppressive and sickening and the simply horrible scene nerved us as nothing else could.

The dead Texans lay singly and in heaps of three or four, or in irregular rows here and there all about the floor of the Alamo, just as they had fallen when a ball reached a vital part or they had dropped to their death from loss of blood. Of course we went to work as soon as we got to the mission at helping the bleeding and moaning men, who had only a few hours at most more of life. . . .

So thick were the bodies of the dead that we had to step over them to get [near] a man in whom there was still life. Close to my feet was a young man who had been shot through the forehead. He had dropped dead with his eyes staring wildly open and, as he lay there, seemingly gazed up into my face.

I remember seeing poor old Colonel Davy Crockett as he lay dead by the side of a dying man, whose bloody and powder-stained face I was washing. Colonel Crockett was about fifty years old at that time. His coat and rough woolen shirt were soaked with blood so that the original color was hidden, for the eccentric hero must have died of some ball in the chest or a bayonet thrust.

5. Olibama López Recalls Pioneer Life in Colorado's San Luis Valley in the Early Nineteenth Century

Invariably the first houses built by the Spanish settlers in the San Luis Valley were *jacales,* or log cabins made by setting cottonwood posts upright in the ground and filling the crevices with mud. After a colony became established, adobe houses were built because they offered better protection from both the weather and the Indians. . . .

There was but little furniture, the main piece being the bed, which was only a thick, wool-filled mattress. During the day the mattress was placed on a *tarima,* or bench made of adobe along the wall. At night the mattress was unrolled and placed on the floor. Rough benches were used almost exclusively, although there were some home-made chairs. There were but few tables.

The early settlers were almost entirely self-dependent in the matter of clothing. They carded, spun, and wove the wool from their own sheep; they tanned and worked the hides of deer and buffalo which they hunted.

The men wore either deerskin suits, copied from those of the Indians; or else trousers of *jerga,* a coarsely woven heavy woolen cloth, and a shirt of *sabanilla,* also of wool but finer in weave and lighter in weight. They wore the *tilma,* a short version of the sarape, as an overcoat.

Women's clothes were also of *sabanilla,* very simply made. Their millinery consisted of the *rebozo,* or silk scarf, and the *tapalo,* a shawl made of light wool or silk for summer wear, and of heavy wool for winter. It served admirably as both overcoat and hat. Moccasins were almost universally worn by both men and women, supplemented in winter by moccasin-shaped overshoes of sheepskin with the wool next to the feet.

The men carried on the work of farming, hunting, and fighting, and later served as freighters or traders.

Olibama López, "Pioneer Life in the San Luis Valley," *Colorado Magazine* 19, no. 5 (September 1942): 161–167. Reprinted with permission.

Cultivation of the virgin soil was extremely difficult, for the settlers had only a few implements and these were of the most primitive kind. A plow was often nothing more than a crooked stick, or at best was a hand-made affair of pine with a plowshare of oak, or in a few cases of iron, shaped by the local blacksmith, and lashed in place with leather thongs. Home-made wooden hoes and spades were in general use because those of steel were very scarce and equally expensive. Oxen were the draft animals used for farm work and for hauling, their only vehicles being crudely-fashioned, handmade, two-wheeled carts. . . . The grain was harvested with a scythe and hand rake and threshed by running the stock around and around on the piled-up grain.

To the women fell the inevitable task of feeding and clothing the family under conditions which proved their courage and adaptability. Even the preparation of a simple meal involved a great deal of previous work. For instance, before they could make the *tortilla,* or *atole,* . . . they had to grind blue corn on the *metate.* After mills were constructed, this was not necessary, except on occasions when it was impossible to go to the mill. Even then they had to prepare the corn to be ground, since the process was different for each dish. The women made their own candles and soap. They spun the wool and wove all the cloth used in the making of clothing or for other purposes. They also plastered the walls of the home, in addition to attending to the usual spring and fall cleaning.

Since during the summer and early fall everyone worked early and late, there was little opportunity for leisure activities. But during the winter the men had but little to do, outside of a few chores. . . . The older men gathered somewhere daily to chat; while the younger men amused themselves with horse races, foot races, wrestling, cockfights and games. The most popular games were: *la pelota,* a game similar to field hockey; *las cazulejas,* a game similar to baseball; *las tejas,* much like horseshoe pitching, in which a stone was used instead of a horseshoe; *pitarilla,* a checker game played on the ground; and most popular of all, *el cañute,* a gambling game.

. . . Even in the midst of the work of colonization the settlers should give to the *fiesta* an important place in the life of the community. The holidays that were celebrated were for the most part saints' days, and are treated here chronologically rather than in the order of their importance.

On New Year's Eve almost the entire community would attend midnight mass. Next morning a group of men . . . would go to the homes of the various *Manueles* [residents] and there, accompanied by violin and guitar, would serenade the particular Manuel with versus either composed for him or else adapted from the most current ones.

Some years on January sixth, *Los Reyes Magos* [The Three Wise Men], a play or *auto* depicting the story of the coming of the Magi to worship the Christ child, was performed. The performance of the play took place in the afternoon in the courtyard of the plaza, because the church, the only large building, was too small to accommodate the audience. . . .

Sometimes the play *El Nino Perdido,* The Lost Child, was produced in February.

During Holy Week the *Penitentes* performed their rites. Many of the settlers in Colorado naturally belonged to the order of *Penitentes,* since they came from New

Mexico. Some years members of the community reenacted the entire story of the capture, trial and crucifixion of Christ. Any person who wished to sponsor this ceremony paid a certain fee—*el paso*—to the church, and was given the most important role, that of *el centurión.*

Each community had its own particular patron saint's day, which was celebrated with special masses, a procession, large family dinners, a *corrida de gallo*—a cock-race in which several men mounted on horses tried to be the first to succeed in lifting a cock buried in the ground—and a dance at night.

On Christmas Eve the biblical story of the birth of Christ was usually dramatized in *Los Pastores* [The Pastors], another of the popular *autos.* . . .

Weddings were occasions of festivity, and served to break the monotony of village life. A wedding was a very formal affair. The first step was the *pedimento,* or the ceremony of asking for the girl's hand. When a young man fell in love and wished to marry a certain girl, he would tell his parents, who, if they approved, would go to her parents to ask for her hand. Sometimes the "asking" was done by letter, and in either case the young man must wait eight or ten days for an answer. If it were in the affirmative, the banns were read on the following three Sundays and arrangements were made for the wedding.

The next step was the *prendario,* which took place the day before the wedding. On this occasion the groom and his parents and relatives were invited to the bride's home to a *fiesta,* or banquet, which usually was followed by a dance. The object of the ceremony . . . was to present the bride and groom to the respective families. Gifts were presented to the bride by the relatives of both, and the groom also presented her with a new trunk which contained the *donas,* or trousseau. . . .

The wedding itself took place in the church. The *padrino,* or best man, gave the bride away, and the *madrina,* or bride's maid, accompanied the groom to the altar. After the ceremony, the newlyweds returned to the girl's home for the dinner. A dance at night followed, to which the bride wore her wedding gown for a while so that those who had not been invited to the wedding but who could attend the dance without an invitation, might see her.

When the wedding dance was ended, the bride and groom, their families, the guests, and the musicians returned to the bride's home, where refreshments were served. Then followed the *entrega,* or the ceremony of returning the wedded couple to their parents once more. . . .

After communication with New Mexico became easier, the monotony of village life was relieved by the appearance of a troupe of *maromeros,* or tumblers, which was usually accompanied by the *payazo,* or clown and the slight-of-hand artist.

Perhaps a group of performers presented *Titeres,* or puppet shows, whose skits, bordering on slap-stick, were a source of unending delight as some members of the audience quickly memorized the cleverest parts and told them over and over.

Not infrequently the villagers themselves gave a performance of the *Matachines,* the dance drama which depicts the story of the conquest of Mexico.

For the most part, however, the only other amusements were the social gatherings, which were usually no more than a meeting of friends around the open fireplace in some home during the long winter evenings. Here they gossiped and recounted their experiences, real and fancied; they related tales of fabulous hidden treasures, of former *campanas* against the Indians, of witches and goblins. Here, too, was read aloud that classic beloved of all Spaniards, *Don Quijote*. . . . Sometimes the evening was spent in guessing riddles. These could be simple enough for a child to guess, or so difficult or complicated that it required a great deal of thought to solve them. Sometimes two persons alone would carry on a contest. In this case one would make up a riddle in verse form and the other would answer also with a verse.

6. Joshua Gregg Paints a Picture of La Tules

The following will not only serve to show the light in which gambling is held by all classes of society, but to illustrate the purifying effects of wealth upon character. Some twelve or fifteen years ago there lived (or rather roamed) in Taos a certain female of very loose habits, known as *La Tules*. Finding it difficult to obtain the means of living in that district, she finally extended her wanderings to the capital. She there became a constant attendant on one of those pandemoniums where the favorite game of *monte* was dealt *pro bono publico*. Fortune, at first, did not seem inclined to smile upon her efforts, and for some years she spent her days in lowliness and misery. At last her luck turned, as gamblers would say, and on one occasion she left the bank with a spoil of several hundred dollars! This enabled her to open a bank of her own, and being favored by a continuous run of good fortune, she gradually rose higher and higher in the scale of affluence, until she found herself in possession of a very handsome fortune. In 1843, she sent to the United States some ten thousand dollars to be invested in goods. She still continues her favorite "amusement," being now considered the most expert "monte dealer" in all Santa Fé. She is openly received in the first circles of society: I doubt . . . whether there is to be found in the city a lady of more fashionable reputation than this same Tules, now known as Señora Doña Gertrudes Barceló.

7. Ralph Emerson Twitchell Offers an Opinion on La Tules

In Spanish and Mexican times women of the better class were frequent visitors at gambling houses and lost and won at *mónte* and other games with all the *sang froid* of their masculine escorts and companions. Gradually, however, the gentler sex withdrew from this sort of amusement, until finally only women of the lowest classes and habitues would be met in gambling houses or in dance halls where gambling was also carried on.

In Mexican times the most notable or notorious of the women monte-bank dealers and proprietors was Gertrudes Barcélo, familiarly known as "La Tules." She was a native of Taos and came to Santa Fé in search of "fame and fortune," where she found both. Her resort was located on the corner of San Francisco street and Burro alley and extended through to Palace avenue on the north. She was con-

Document 6: As found in Joshua Gregg, *Commerce of the Prairies,* ed. by Max L. Moorhead (Norman: University of Oklahoma Press, 1954), pp. 168–169.

Document 7: As found in Ralph Emerson Twitchell, *Old Santa Fe: The Story of New Mexico's Ancient Capital* (Santa Fe: The Santa Fe New Mexican Publishing Corporation, 1925), pp. 338–339.

sidered the most expert *mónte* dealer of her time. Fair to look upon, of a distinctly Spanish type of beauty, she became a great favorite in official Mexican circles. Her private card rooms and the principal hall were patronized by the elite. Magnificent pier-glass mirrors adorned the walls, brussels carpets, brought from the "states," covered the *adóbe* floors, while large homemade chandeliers accommodated an unusual number of candles for lighting purposes. In a long *sala, bailes* were given, where the officers attached to the Mexican garrison disported themselves as inclination demanded; these entertainments, however, being by invitation only. Hundreds of thousands of dollars were won and lost in this "sporting emporium" where this goddess of chance ruled supreme. Her wealth procured recognition in social circles and she became very prominent in business and political affairs. During the military occupation régime she was a great favorite among the American officers, and it was she, having received information as to the conspiracy of December, 1846, through a mulatto servant, who gave the warning to the civil and military authorities. She died about 1851, and was buried with the highest honors of the church, at an expense of upward of sixteen hundred dollars for spiritual services in the interment ceremonies alone.

E S S A Y S

David J. Weber, professor of history at Southern Methodist University, Dallas, Texas, and one of the foremost scholars of the Spanish-speaking Southwest, presents in the first essay a discussion of the origins and evolution of the myth of the Alamo, especially in Texas writing. According to Weber, Texas history has romanticized the Battle of the Alamo and the Texas Revolution of 1835. But Weber identifies the key people in Mexico and the United States who participated in these events. Discounting cultural conflict as a cause of the Texas rebellion by outlining the contributions of Texas Mexicans to the resistance against Santa Ana's forces, he argues that politics as well as personal gain were more important factors that led to the fighting. To the annoyance of Americans in Texas, their government was controlled by the Mexican state of Coahuila. Friendly relations between Coahuila and Texas quickly soured because of continuing conflicts over issues of slavery, tariffs, and efforts by the United States to annex Texas. By focusing on the importance of the construction and manipulation of the myth of the Alamo, Weber demonstrates how ordinary events are often sensationalized and glorified. Americans, he concludes, see themselves in events and heroes they venerate.

The Battle of the Alamo was the key moment in the foundation of the Republic of Texas. Its legacy remains firmly embodied in the annual commemorative ceremonies held each year in San Antonio. Perhaps most importantly, the Alamo myth exemplifies how the victors control the writing of history. This is the subject of the essay by Holly Beachley Brear, an assistant professor of anthropology at George Mason University, Fairfax, Virginia. Through a careful reading of various history texts, she analyzes how historical details have been selected to present distorted versions of the persons and events in Texas history. These inaccuracies have had consequences for both the Mexican and the Anglo heritage of the Alamo.

The rise of commercial traffic in New Mexico 1848, after the end of the Mexican American War significantly altered the political and economic growth of the region. Social factors were changing as well. Americans' firsthand accounts that described the local Mexican men and women as undependable, treacherous, dishonest, and addicted to gambling, promiscuity, and other vices promulgated negative attitudes about the Spanish-speaking residents, which is the focus of the essay by Deena J. González, associate professor of history at Pomona College, Clairmont, California. In particular she examines the life of Doña Gertrudis Barceló, or La Tules, who has been the object of numerous exaggerations that follow the larger stereotypes of Mexicans that helped to legitimize the conquest of the Southwest. These distortions obscured the reality of the process of accommodation and resistance by the people of New Mexico to growing American encroachment. For example, La Tules's contributions to the new economy and society unfolding in New Mexico were denied, even though this enterprising woman embraced the same values of acquisitiveness cherished by Americans. Her legend is representative of key themes in Chicana women's lives currently being researched and attests to a changing conception of these women in the postconquest Southwest.

Mythmaking and the Texas Revolution

DAVID J. WEBER

If we had some way to measure it, I think that it might be proved that more ink than blood has been spilled over the Texas Revolution in general, and the Alamo in particular. And with much less effect, for although the war has ended, the ink continues to flow. . . .

Perhaps this is as it should be. Not only does each generation have a need to rewrite history, but major events in particular invite frequent reinterpretation to make them meaningful to the sensibilities and concerns of new generations. And the Texas rebellion *was* a major event, representing a turning point for Mexico and the United States, as well as for Texas. For Mexico it seems to mark the beginning of a series of dismal setbacks that culminated with the United States invasion of 1846 and that resulted in the loss of half of Mexico to the United States. For the United States, which would annex Texas nine years after its successful rebellion, the Texas Revolution marked a turning point in the Americans' long and unsuccessful efforts to purchase Texas from Mexico and another large step in the fulfillment of what Americans perceived to be their manifest destiny—a continental nation with harbors on the Pacific. . . .

As *fact,* then, the Texas struggle for independence was, and has been regarded as, an event of sufficient importance for Texas and for two nations to merit the spilling of considerable ink. Nonetheless, much of the Texas writing about the events of 1836, and about the Alamo in particular, seems designed to magnify and romanticize this significant series of events. . . .

First, it was not just "upstart Anglos" in Texas who defeated Mexican forces, but those Anglos had the help of Texas Mexicans, too. Second, Santa Anna may have been a "sometimes brilliant general," but most writers find him rather consistently flawed. . . . Third, although the roots of Spanish colonialism in Mexico run a

From David J. Weber, "Refighting the Alamo: Mythmaking and the Texas Revolution," in *Myth and the History of the Hispanic Southwest: Essays by David J. Weber* (Albuquerque: University of New Mexico Press, 1988), pp. 133–150. Used with permission from the publisher.

century deeper than the roots of English colonialism in North America, we should remember that when Mexico achieved its independence in 1821, the United States had already been a nation for forty years. Two generations of political stability gave the Americans a tremendous advantage over a chaotic young Mexico, whose economy and politics were in shambles at the time of the Texas revolt. Fourth, Mexico was not the equivalent of the United States in size and in strength. . . . A ruinous decade of warfare against Spain had brought Mexico into nationhood in 1821 with her population literally decimated (a tenth of the population, mostly young men of fighting age, had lost their lives). Mexico's population in 1821 was some 6,200,000, and remained at that level for decades. In contrast, at nearly 9,600,000, the population of the United States was half again as large as Mexico's in 1821. . . . Finally, it is important to remember that much of the Mexican population consisted of Indians who did not identify themselves with the nation, or even speak the national language. . . .

On March 6, 1986, 150 years after the carnage ended, a number of Texas history buffs from across America gathered in San Antonio to remember the fall of the Alamo. In commemoration of the battle that raged in and around the walls of the former Spanish mission compound, participants reenacted the famous scene in which Colonel William Barret Travis supposedly traced a line in the dirt and said: "Those of you who are willing to stay with me and die with me, cross this line."

Although reenactment of this dramatic moment brought tears to the eyes of some onlookers, there is no convincing evidence that Travis uttered his famous speech or that he drew such a line. Historians have repeatedly made this point. Nor is there convincing evidence to support the common notion that the defenders of the Alamo knew *from the first* that their situation was hopeless. To the contrary, they prepared for the battle with remarkable indecision and lassitude. . . . Although Colonial Travis's slogan was "Victory or Death," in the early stages of the siege he clearly expected victory. From his first call for help on February 24 through March 3, just three days before the Alamo fell, Travis believed that the Alamo could be defended if, as he expected, additional support arrived. Nor were the defenders of the Alamo—nearly 200 men—hopelessly outnumbered by Mexican troops. At the beginning of the siege Santa Anna's army numbered about 1,500. By the time of the assault, some 2,600 Mexican soldiers had arrived, not the 5,000 to 6,000 that is often suggested. Many of the Mexican soldiers were bewildered Indian conscripts who did not even speak Spanish. Woefully ill-equipped, they were no match for superior Texas artillery and long rifles. Travis, then, had reason to remain confident of victory until toward the end, when it became clear that no help from fellow Texans would be forthcoming.

Finally, let us remember that it is by no means certain that all of the defenders died in an heroic fight to the finish. Strong evidence suggests that Mexican troops captured Davy Crockett and a half a dozen others (they may even have surrendered), and Santa Anna ordered them executed. The evidence for this comes from Mexican sources. . . . The idea that Mexican sources indicate that Crockett died at the hands of an executioner rather than fighting to his last breath, has . . . not won widespread acceptance for it seems to tarnish a hero. In 1978 historian Dan Kilgore received scorching mail when he stirred the embers of that controversy in a book entitled *How Did Davy Die?* One newspaper called it "a commie plot to trash our heroes." More recently, Paul Hutton won similar opprobrium when . . . he, too, suggested that Davy might not have died fighting. One angry Texan associated Hutton with Communists, while another unappreciative reader . . . questioned his manhood and described him as a "gutless wonder." If doubts about Hutton's politics and masculinity were not enough, another critic accused him of committing "blasphemy." Arguing that students need heroes, a Texas history teacher told Hutton: "I will *never* teach my students what you wrote. A real Texan would not. . . . You wrote that the evidence of Crockett's surrender came from a Mexican diary. Well that isn't good enough." . . .

The lore surrounding the battle of the Alamo provides the clearest examples of how the Texas rebellion, like so many major events, has been romanticized to take on meanings that transcend the event itself and its principal characters reduced to caricature—to heroes and villains. In certain kinds of history, and in American popular culture, the Texas fight for independence has come to represent a triumph of Protestantism over Catholicism, of democracy over despotism, of a superior white race over a degenerate people of mixed blood, of the future over the past, of good over evil. Heroes of the Texas revolt are portrayed as committed republicans fighting for the noblest of motives. . . . The conflict over Texas has been reduced to nothing more than a conflict of two incompatible cultures. And the rebellion itself . . . has been elevated to the status of a "revolution"—a designation that few, if any, modern social scientists would apply to a revolt that did not seek a profound restructuring of society.

What are the sources of these exaggerated notions about the Texas rebellion? Certainly one source was wartime propaganda—myths invented to stir people to action during conflict. Writing just after the fighting ended, for example, Stephen Austin explained the conflict as "a war of barbarism and of despotic principles, waged by the mongrel Spanish-Indian and Negro race, against civilization and the Anglo American race." That refrain echoed in nineteenth-century Romantic historiography. . . .

Still another source of distorted versions of the events of the Texas rebellion is almost certainly the well-known proclivity of Texans to embellish upon a story— to stretch the truth. . . .

. . . I do not think I would find much argument about Texans' tendency to exaggerate, and that may explain in part why we have such grandiloquent versions of the events of 1836. Ironically, the reverse is also true. The Texas war for independence may also explain why Texans exaggerate. Historian Joe Frantz of the University of Texas has argued that the "real genesis [of Texas tendency toward braggadocio] lies in the Texas Revolution" itself, and his argument seems plausible. The simple fact that Texas became an independent nation as a result of the rebellion has given Texans enormous pride—perhaps too much pride. . . .

Rather than trying to read our present-day concerns into the past, let us try to reconstruct the past and look briefly at the coming of the Texas rebellion as contemporaries might have seen it. What did it mean to them? Certainly there was less heroism, less altruism, less patriotism, less clarity of purpose, and less unity than most of us might imagine. Instead, much as today, events moved along more quickly than contemporaries could grasp them and most Anglo Americans and

Mexicans in Texas pursued their private lives, wishing that the entire affair would go away.

Let us look first at the proposition that the Texas rebellion represented a clash of cultures, rendering it nearly inevitable. . . .

Certainly it is easy to view the revolt as an "ethnic" conflict, for in some respects it was. Between 1821, when Mexico became independent, and 1836 when the armed struggle between Mexico and Texas began, perhaps 35,000 Anglo Americans had flocked across the border and into Mexican Texas, outnumbering the Mexican Texans, or tejanos, by a ratio of ten to one. The Anglo Americans, so the argument goes, could not adapt to Mexican culture. Historians have identified a number of sources of cultural friction.

First, Anglo Americans were required to become Catholics, and were not permitted to hold Protestant services.

Second, Anglo Americans, some 75 percent of whom were southerners, were shocked when Mexico prohibited slavery in 1829. Mexicans seemed to have little respect for private property.

Third, Anglo Americans could not tolerate the lack of a jury system and deplored the Mexican system of justice in which alcaldes made decisions on the merits of a case.

Fourth, Anglo Americans could not abide the lack of local autonomy in Texas—of home rule. Since 1824 Texas had been subservient to a larger and more populous state, Coahuila. Both Coahuila and Texas had been joined together as the single state of Coahuila y Texas. Control of state government rested squarely in the hands of officials in the distant state capital at Saltillo. . . .

Fifth, many Anglo Americans could not abide Mexicans themselves. Stephen Austin, on visiting Mexico City in 1822–23, wrote in private correspondence that "the people are bigoted and superstitious to an extreem [sic], and indolence appears to be the order of the day." "To be candid the majority of the people of that whole nation as far as I have seen them want nothing but tails to be more brutes than apes." Many years after the bloody days at the Alamo and San Jacinto, one pioneer who had settled in Texas in 1827, Noah Smithwick, echoed Austin's sentiments. "I looked upon the Mexicans as scarce more than apes," Smithwick recalled.

Anglo Americans made no attempt to conceal their sense of superiority from Mexicans. In 1819, two years before Mexico won her independence from Spain, the Spanish minister who was negotiating with John Q. Adams what became the transcontinental treaty, characterized Americans as an "arrogant and audacious" people who believed themselves "superior to all the nations of Europe," and who were convinced "that their dominion is destined to extend . . . to the isthmus of Panama, and hereafter, over all the regions of the New World." . . .

. . . Indeed, there seems little reason to doubt that profound cultural differences, including American racism, contributed to the Texas rebellion and gave it a special virulence.

Nonetheless, it would be easy to exaggerate the importance of cultural differences, incorrectly identifying them as the principal cause of the rebellion. *Within* Texas itself, relations between Mexicans from Texas and the Anglo-American newcomers were generally amicable. A few Anglo Americans had settled in the

Mexican communities of San Antonio and Goliad, where they became assimilated. In the main, however, the two groups lived essentially apart, separated by considerable distance. Most Anglo Americans lived in East Texas and most Mexicans in the area of San Antonio and Goliad. As a result, Anglo Americans enjoyed a good deal of autonomy. Differences in religion, philosophy, or what we have come to call "lifestyles," did not become major irritants.

The alleged "religious conflict" offers a case in point. Some writers have argued that Anglo Americans chaffed at the lack of religious freedom in Texas. In practice, the law requiring immigrants to become Catholics was never enforced. The Mexican government failed to send priests to minister to the Anglo-American colonists, as the Colonization Law of 1824 required, so the colonists were not obliged to practice Catholicism. . . .

Put simply, the Mexican government never forced Catholicism on the Anglo-American colonists in Texas. To the contrary, in 1834, two years before the revolt broke out, the state of Coahuila y Texas went so far as to guarantee that "no person shall be molested for political and religious opinions provided the public order is not disturbed." Freedom of worship never became as important issue among the foreigners in Mexican Texas and, notwithstanding Anglo-Texan wartime propaganda, the issue of freedom of worship did not directly cause the Texas revolt in 1836.

The idea that cultural conflict caused the Texas rebellion has contributed to the notion that the struggle itself was fought along ethnic lines, pitting *all* Mexicans against *all* Americans in Texas. This was decidedly not the case. Tejanos, for example, contributed substantially to the resistance against centralist forces in the fall of 1835, in the wave of hostilities that preceded Santa Anna's march into Texas. The Texas forces that laid siege to . . . San Antonio in the fall of 1835 included as many as 160 *tejanos*. . . . The next spring, seven tejanos died inside the Alamo, fighting alongside Anglo Americans *against* Santa Anna. Colonel Seguín and the Second Company of Texas Volunteers, which he raised, performed valuable scouting services prior to the fall of the Alamo and contributed to the defeat of Santa Anna at San Jacinto. . . . Tejanos also participated in the famous "Consultation" at San Felipe on November 7 of 1835, which endorsed a conditional declaration of Texas independence. Four months later José Antonio Navarro and Francisco Ruiz, both Texas-born, signed the declaration of Texas independence at Washington-on-the-Brazos.

Thus, the sides did not divide up uniformly along ethnic lines. The issues that caused men to take to arms in 1835–36 may have had to do more with the culture of politics than with the politics of culture. And both tejanos and Anglos *within* Texas found much about politics with which they could agree. Let us look at some areas of agreement.

Elites in the predominantly *tejano* communities of San Antonio and Goliad had apparently *shared* Anglo-American concerns about the need to improve the system of justice and to achieve greater autonomy by separating Texas from Coahuila. . . . Nor, it would appear, did the large influx of Anglo Americans into Texas trouble the tejanos as much as it did the Mexican government. For the tejano *elite,* Anglo-American immigrants meant economic growth. . . .

. . . Francisco Ruiz of San Antonio put it squarely when he wrote in 1830: "I cannot help seeing advantages which, to my way of thinking, would result if we admitted honest, hard-working people, regardless of what country they come from . . . even hell itself.

. . . No matter how much mutual interests might tie them together, however, once the fighting began it must have been agonizing for tejanos to decide whether to remain loyal to Mexico or to join forces with Americans and take up arms against fellow Mexicans. Although they might agree with Anglo Texans on certain issues, the idea of separation from Coahuila, much less independence from Mexico came to hold less attraction for tejanos in the mid-1830s than it had in the 1820s. Anglo Americans, who vastly outnumbered tejanos by the early 1830s, would surely dominate the state and tejanos would become, to paraphrase Juan Seguín, "foreigners in their native land." When, however, Coahuila fell into anarchy in the mid-1830s and Santa Anna's centralist dictatorship replaced Mexico's federalist Republic, tejano leaders must have wrung their hands over their unhappy alternatives—domination by Anglo Americans or domination by the centralist dictatorship. . . .

The same may also be said for most Anglo Texans, who had no desire to fight over political issues until Mexican forces threatened their lives and property. Until autumn of 1835, Anglo Americans in Texas were divided between groups that had come to be called the "war party" and the "peace party." Both parties sought greater political autonomy for Texas in order to enable Texans to adopt measures that would make Texas more attractive to immigrants from the U.S.—measures such as more favorable tariffs, an improved judicial system, and the maintenance of slavery. While they agreed on the goals, the peace and war parties disagreed about the means to achieve them. The "peace party," of which the *empresario* Stephen Austin was the most influential representative, wanted Mexico to grant Texas a divorce from its unhappy and unequal marriage with Coahuila. The radical war party, led by ambitious and sometimes angry young men such as William Barret Travis . . . , sought independence from Mexico itself.

Until the autumn of 1835, the "war party" remained a decided minority. . . . Then, Mexico committed the blunder of sending troops into Texas under the direction of Santa Anna's brother-in-law, Martín Perfecto de Cos. In part, Mexico had been provoked into that action by the attack on a small Mexican garrison at Anahuac in June of 1835, led by Travis and thirty-some radicals. At first, Anglo-American communities throughout Texas repudiated that attack and professed loyalty to the government, but when Anglo Americans learned that Mexican troops would be sent to Texas, public opinion swung away from the "Tories," as Travis called the peace party, and over to the "war party." Even the foremost Texas "Tory," Stephen Austin, became convinced of the necessity of armed resistance. . . .

Clearly, then, the Texas struggle for independence was not a simple conflict of Mexicans versus Anglos, of Mexican culture versus American culture, of democracy versus despotism, or of good versus evil. It was not a conflict in which issues were so clearly drawn that men of good will united readily to fight for principles greater than themselves. That such men existed, I have no reason to doubt, but it should be remembered that many Anglo Americans who came to Texas had more interest in fleeing the law than in changing the law; that they came to Texas for personal gain. Pragmatism rather than principle, self interest rather than political democracy, had driven a disproportionate share of Anglo Americans to Texas in search of opportunity. And the unbridled pursuit of self-interest on the part of some Anglo Americans, rather than the quest for liberty, may have helped to bring on the Texas rebellion. . . . Land speculation by certain Anglo Americans, and their manipulation of the state government in Saltillo, helped win the wrath of the federal government, bring Mexican troops into Texas, and provoke the Texas revolt.

If cheap land and opportunity attracted to Texas some unscrupulous men . . . , so, too, did the fear of the debt collector and the sheriff in the United States push a good many American lawbreakers and criminals toward Texas—James Bowie and William Barret Travis among them. Early travelers to Texas often commented on the high number of murderers and thieves in Texas. Indeed, Texas enjoyed . . . a reputation as a refuge for criminals from the United States. . . .

. . . I hope that I have at least succeeded in suggesting that in a historical event as complicated as the Texas struggle for independence, there are few heroes or villains, but rather men and women much like us, looking after their day-to-day interests and responding to a variety of impulses. . . .

Many of the giants of yesteryear—both heroes and villains—are, of course, creatures of our own making, invented to serve salutory ends. First, they provide us with a way to avoid abstractions and complicated issues and to focus instead on the personal, the concrete, the easily understood. . . . Second, by conjuring heroes of mythic proportions and keeping their memories alive, we hope to offer lessons in morality to the young, or to inspire the young with patriotism and pride. And such lessons have been well learned. . . .

. . . The mythology surrounding the Alamo has served as rationalization for aggressive behavior toward Mexico and Mexicans that runs counter to our finest national ideals. In the immediate aftermath of the Texas revolt, the enshrinement of the Alamo as a holy place and the popular sanctification of its defenders as martyrs helped reinforce and intensity two complimentary articles of faith among Anglo Americans: belief in the moral superiority of Anglos and the degeneracy of Mexicans. From those antipodal myths, which ran strongest among Anglo residents of Texas, it followed that Mexico's conquest by its morally superior neighbor might redeem her benighted citizenry. Their faith affirmed by the windy rhetoric of their elders, young American men of the mid-1840s swallowed the myth of a holy war against Mexico. Entering a fantasy world of promised glory and heroism against a foe they believed to be inferior, many young Americans marched to the Halls of Montezuma. . . .

. . . This is not to say that we cannot draw lessons from the past, and use the past to inform our judgment about the present and future, but to do so realistically, we must be realistic and clearheaded about the past. We must see historical figures and events as they *were* and not magnify them or romanticize them into something that we *wish* they had been. The Texas rebellion is no exception.

Creating the Myth of the Alamo

HOLLY BEACHLEY BREAR

Annual Alamo ceremonies occurring on March 6 and during Fiesta proclaim the creation of Texas. But in the annual cycle, the time between March 6 and April 21 is the gestational period for Texas. On March 6 Texas is engendered at the Battle of

From *Inherit the Alamo: Myth and Ritual at an American Shrine* by Holly Beachley Brear, copyright © 1995. By permission of the author and the University of Texas Press.

the Alamo, and she has her epiphany on April 21 when, after Sam Houston's victory at San Jacinto, the rest of the world recognizes Texas as an independent nation. During annual performances held in front of or inside the Alamo church, speakers recount the 1836 events from March 6 to April 21 as a unified narrative with the sacrificial fall of the Alamo and the victory at San Jacinto as the inseparable alpha and omega of the Texas creation mythology.

No group is more convinced of the interconnectedness of the battles than the Daughters of the Republic of Texas [DRT], the state-appointed custodians of the Alamo. In the introduction of speakers at the 1989 Pilgrimage to the Alamo (held on Monday of Fiesta week), one DRT member justified celebrating Fiesta in San Antonio by connecting the fall of the Alamo to the victory at San Jacinto:

> We celebrate the San Jacinto victory here at the Alamo because the two . . . events are forever linked together. There was no real army in Texas in 1835 and '36, and given the developments in Texas at that time, it became necessary for William Barret Travis to devise a strategy at the Alamo, and that strategy was to keep Santa Anna occupied until General Houston could muster an army for the east. Travis was buying time for Houston, and that time was bought with the lives of the Alamo heroes. Had it not been for the delay here at the Alamo, the story would have been undoubtedly much different.

According to this account of the Texas Revolution, the death of the Alamo defenders is a strategic and well-executed military move; as a successful sacrifice, the Alamo story ends with victory rather than defeat. Travis's decision to stay appears as a redeemed investment rather than a needless waste of human lives, the inception of a painful birth rather than of death. Within the mythology the Alamo harbors the metaphorical altar on which the Alamo defenders—led by the trinity of Travis, Bowie, and Crockett—offer their lives to allow this birth of Texas liberty. The old mission itself becomes part of the birthing process as it is reborn as a Texas shrine from its former fallen self, never again to be in the same family as its sister missions. In the words of one account of the battle, the Alamo was baptized in the fire of battle and the blood of heroes.

The sacred character of the Texas creation myth is portrayed in ceremonies performed in front of the Alamo by various groups. To understand the significance of details offered by these groups and the rituals performed, we must look at the entire myth. I offer the following compilation of favored details.

The Texas Creation Myth

In December 1835, the city of San Antonio de Bexar was in the hands of the Mexican army under Gen. Martín Perfecto de Cos. Texan forces, camped outside of San Antonio, had been anxiously waiting for the command to attack for two months. But on December 3, to their disappointment, the Texan commander Gen. Edward Burleson ordered retreat. Ben Milam, a crusty old soldier serving under Burleson, despised the thought of retreating; on December 4 he stormed out of Burleson's tent, shouting, "Who will go with old Ben Milam to San Antonio?" Over two hundred cheering men rushed to join him. The next morning Milam led his men in house-to-house fighting with the Mexican army. One by one the enemy succumbed to the superior fighting skill of the Texans. On December 10, General Cos surrendered; the Texans had taken San Antonio.

But the victory had its price, for on December 7 the Texans' leader Ben Milam, hit by a bullet at the entrance to the governor's palace, became a sacrifice to the Texan cause. The Texans buried Milam in the courtyard of the house where his blood has hallowed the ground.

General Cos and his surviving troops were ordered to leave Texas and never to return. The Texans then began to prepare San Antonio's defense. The old mission compound of San Antonio de Valero, known as the Alamo, became the focus of the military strategists.

But Gen. Sam Houston, the commander of the entire Texas army, wanted the Texans in San Antonio to fall back and reinforce him and Col. James Fannin. So Houston sent James Bowie to San Antonio to destroy the Alamo. Bowie, however, could not bring himself to destroy the crumbling old mission. Perhaps he felt the power in the stones, perhaps he was simply considering his own landholdings, which lay near the city. Whatever the reason, he spared the Alamo. He declared that he would rather "die in these ditches" than leave San Antonio, and he worked with the Texans to transform the old Spanish mission into a Texan fortress.

Bowie was but the first Texan to feel drawn to the Alamo. William Barret Travis, upon his arrival on February 3, agreed with Bowie and the new commander of the Texans in San Antonio, Colonel Neill, that the Alamo would serve as a fortress and that San Antonio must be kept out of the Mexican army's hands.

Although Bowie and Travis agreed on where to make a military stand, they did not initially agree on who should be the garrison's commander after Colonel Neill was called away. Bowie, being almost twice Travis's age and well known for his fighting ability, felt he should hold the reins of authority. He had come to Texas long before Travis arrived there and had converted to Mexican citizenry and Catholicism as required by the Mexican government; he knew the people and the culture of San Antonio and Texas and had survived along with them in this frontier community. His prowess with the famed Bowie knife had made him a living legend.

Despite his triumphs of the past, however, Bowie was not at this time the powerful man he once had been. Sorrow over the deaths of his beautiful Mexican wife, Ursula Verimendi Bowie, and their children had led him to seek solace in the bottle. Now as he struggled with Travis to be commander, Bowie leaned heavily on alcohol. The young, headstrong Travis had no patience with Bowie's drunkenness and felt he was the more capable leader for the Texans. Travis knew in his heart that they were fighting for Texas' independence from Mexico, not to continue under the mother country's rule; the burden of taxes and the required Catholicism had made the yoke of Mexican citizenry unbearable. This fiery young South Carolinian withdrew from the drunken rampages being conducted by Bowie and his men throughout the city and moved his men into the Alamo compound. Bowie at last realized the damage he was doing to the Texan force and sent his apologies to young Travis. The two men settled on a joint command.

A man of great spirit soon joined Travis and Bowie in their desire to defend the Alamo: David Crockett. With his rifle Old Betsy in his arms and his Tennessee volunteers by his side, he rode into San Antonio a few days after Travis's arrival there. A veteran of the Creek Indian wars, Crockett accepted Texas as his next mission in the settling of America's western frontier. . . .

But even as the Texans worked to ready the Alamo for her stand against the Mexican army, Gen. Antonio López de Santa Anna, the self-styled Napoleon of the West, marched toward Texas. If not the most brilliant of military strategists in history, Santa Anna was perhaps the most vain. The general's uniform contained enough silver on the epaulets and frogging for an entire set of dinner spoons; he rode on a saddle with gold-plated trim; and at his side hung a seven-thousand-dollar sword. He rode on toward Texas with the confidence that his massive army, drilled in European military maneuvers, would quickly bring the rebellious Texans to their knees.

Upon his arrival in San Antonio, Santa Anna had his men raise a blood-red banner above the San Fernando Cathedral bell tower signifying no quarter for the Alamo defenders. Travis boldly fired a cannon shot in response; he had made his decision to stay with the Alamo and defend her to the death. He then sent out his first appeal for aid from his fellow Americans. Through the ensuing days, he continued to appeal for help, and in his letter of February 24 Travis vowed, "I shall never surrender or retreat. . . . Victory or death."

But there was to be no help for the American heroes, save thirty-two men from Gonzales who, determined to stand beside their countrymen, rushed through the Mexican lines and into the Alamo. Travis's appeals to the men at the Goliad garrison had failed; Goliad's woefully inept commander, Colonel Fannin, had decided, after a feeble attempt to march his men toward San Antonio, that he would not aid the Alamo defenders. And Sam Houston, despite his grave concern for the fate of the Alamo defenders, was in the eastern part of Texas trying to organize the major force of the Texas army; he needed every moment Travis and the Alamo defenders could buy him in their stalling of Santa Anna.

On March 3, James Bonham, Travis's messenger to Fannin, braved the run through enemy lines to report that Fannin would not come to their aid. Travis now faced the absolute desperation of their position. Two days later, Travis called his men before him and offered each man a choice: he could stay with Travis and defend the Alamo, selling his life dearly by destroying as many of the enemy as possible; or he could scale the Alamo's walls and try to slip through the Mexican lines. Travis then unsheathed his sword, drew its tip through the dirt in front of his men, and said, "Those prepared to give their lives in freedom's cause come over to me." Each Texan then made his choice, sealing his fate as he crossed over to Travis's side. Bowie, bedridden by a mysterious disease, called to the men to come and carry him across.

Only one man chose not to cross Travis's line: Louis (Moses) Rose. Rose, a Jewish Frenchman and veteran of the Napoleonic wars, declared that he had survived too many military encounters to lay down his life at the Alamo. He took his leave of the other men, scaled the Alamo wall, and disappeared into the darkness of the night.

That night, the twelfth one of the siege, Travis and his men slept peacefully for the first time since the siege had begun, for there was no gunfire from the Mexican lines. All was strangely quiet. But in the darkness, the Mexican soldiers crept into position, and lay waiting for the command to begin the final assault. As dawn streaked the sky with red, the battle cry "Viva Santa Anna" broke the peace, and out of the darkness wailed the trumpet notes of the dread *deguello,* whose title means "to slit the throat." Travis leapt from his bed and called his men to arms. He raced to meet the Mexican charge at the north wall. He spun around, a single bullet in his forehead, and slid dazed and dying against the embankment.

On the south side of the compound, David Crockett fired his rifle as long as he was able to reload her, and then swung Old Betsy as a war club, piling up the bodies at his feet before a saber cut him across the brow. He fell, Old Betsy in his arms.

In the Long Barracks Bowie lay ready in his sickbed to meet his final challenge. The door to his sickroom burst open, and Bowie fired his pistols, killing the first onslaught of Mexicans. Then with all his remaining strength he wielded his famed knife against those daring to come within arm's reach. At last the Mexicans crowding into the room pierced him with their bayonets and jubilantly lifted his body high above their heads.

Huddled in a front room of the Alamo church was Susanna Dickinson and her fourteen-month-old daughter, Angelina. One of the panicked defenders ran into the room pursued by Mexican soldiers. At Susanna's side he pleaded for his life, but was stabbed by several bayonets. The bloodthirsty Mexican soldiers lifted him up in the air on their bayonets and tossed his body like fodder, the man screaming in agony until he expired.

At last the Alamo compound fell silent; the 189 defenders lay dead. Santa Anna paraded on his horse through the battle site. One of his officers congratulated him on his great victory, and Santa Anna replied, "It was but a small affair."

But this was no small affair. Travis and his men had indeed sold their lives dearly. More than one thousand Mexican soldiers had fallen as casualties to the Texans' guns; so many that the Mexican officers were unable to carry out Santa Anna's order that all Mexican soldiers be given a Christian burial. Many bodies were simply thrown into the San Antonio River, where downstream they choked the waters and fouled the air with their stench. For days the sky was blackened with buzzards come to feed on the flesh.

By Santa Anna's command, the Alamo heroes received no Christian burial. Their bodies were stacked between layers of wood and burned. The flame from the funeral pyre rose high into the sky of early evening. The defenders had offered their lives as sacrifice on Freedom's alter; they had paid the ultimate price.

Though the Alamo heroes could not have known it, they had fought for what Travis had known would be the final goal of the Texas Revolution: an independent Republic of Texas. On March 2 the convention held at Washington-on-the-Brazos had voted to declare independence from Mexico. The duty of Travis and his men at the Alamo had become clear to the men at that historic convention.

Twelve days after the fall of the Alamo, the Mexican troops under General Urrea besieged the Texans at Goliad under Col. James Fannin. On March 20 Fannin decided that his situation was hopeless and surrendered his four hundred men, placing them "at the disposal of the Supreme Mexican government" and hoping for mercy. The men were forced into small, hot rooms and given tiny amounts of water and raw beef while Urrea awaited Santa Anna's sentence on the prisoners. Despite their desperate situation, many of the imprisoned Texans still hoped that they would be freed and allowed to go home. But on Palm Sunday, March 27, the four hundred prisoners were marched out on the open prairie and shot at point-blank range. The Mexican guards then stripped the bodies, stacked them, and burned them.

These were indeed dark days for Texas. Santa Anna's cruelty at the Alamo and Goliad spawned a reign of terror, and fear whipped across the young republic. Some soldiers abandoned the newly formed Texas army and raced home to gather loved ones and belongings. They then joined in the Runaway Scrape, a flood of people trying to outrun Santa Anna's army.

And it must have seemed at first glance that even Sam Houston was running away as he ordered his men to retreat. He knew he must still find more time to organize his military force and strategy if he were to end the tyranny of Santa Anna. His men cried out against what they felt was cowardice in the call to retreat. People along the way laughed at Sam Houston as he moved eastward. One old woman screamed scornfully, "Run, run, Santa Anna is behind you!". . .

Only Houston could know the importance of his moves as he pulled his men farther into east Texas. When they arrived at the San Jacinto River, Houston carefully chose his campsite where he would allow Santa Anna to think that he had "trapped" the Texans. There he waited.

On April 20 Santa Anna sent his infantry to try the Texan lines, but the Texans repelled the infantry with the deadly fire of the Twin Sisters, two cannon sent by the citizens of Cincinnati to accompany Sam Houston into battle. Santa Anna then decided to pull his men back to camp, less than a mile from the Texan camp.

On April 21 both armies appeared ready for battle. But the Mexican army, even though it was much larger than Houston's, seemed to be waiting for even more troops to arrive. At half past three in the afternoon, Houston, after hearing that the Mexican soldiers had stacked their arms for *siesta,* decided the moment had arrived; he gave the command for Texans to advance on the Mexican lines.

Quietly they came, these angry men, resolved to avenge the unjust deaths of their countrymen. In the clear, bright afternoon sun, they advanced on the sleeping Mexicans without being seen even to within two hundred yards of the enemy.

Then from the enemy barricade a shot rang out, and the fighting began. "Fight for your lives!" cried the Texas officers. Sam Houston's voice roared commands, the Twin Sisters boomed, as the Texans charged the Mexican soldiers with wild whoops and screams: "Remember the Alamo! Remember Goliad!" The enraged Texans, though greatly outnumbered, fought with a fury deep within them.

In only eighteen minutes the battle was over. Knowing that all was lost for them, the Mexican soldiers broke and ran. Forlorn Mexican soldiers fell down before the vengeful Texans pleading "Me no Alamo. Me no Goliad." But there would be no excuses taken that day, no mercy given. The anger building in the six weeks since the Alamo had fallen raged inside the Texans; now the real killing began. With a score to settle, they took prisoners the way Santa Anna had done, dispatching them with Bowie knives, bullets, and gun butts.

Finally, at sundown, the killing subsided. The Texans, their anger spent, were finally able to follow Houston's orders to take prisoners instead of lives. Then the Texans began to count the losses: the Mexican army had killed 9 Texans; the Texans had killed 630 Mexicans.

But the victory was not complete, for Santa Anna had slipped away. Around noon the next day, Texans searching for stragglers found a man crawling through the grass near a destroyed bridge. He was dressed in common clothes and was wet and dirty. As the Texans brought this man into their camp, the other Mexican prisoners began calling out "El Presidente," pointing to this new prisoner. It was indeed Santa Anna, and the Texans took him immediately to Sam Houston. Houston, who had been wounded during the battle the day before, lay under an oak tree resting when the men brought Santa Anna before him. Santa Anna announced, "I am General Antonio López de Santa Anna, and a prisoner of war at your disposition." He then congratulated Houston, saying, "You have conquered the Napoleon of the West." As Santa Anna stood before Sam Houston, many of the Texans cried out for his execution. But Houston knew that he was not the authority within the new republic, and declared that the Texas Congress must decide the fate of Santa Anna. Furthermore, Sam Houston knew that Santa Anna was worth more alive than he would be dead, and so he wisely held on to the Texans' prize prisoner.

The justice dispensed by Sam Houston marked the reign of a new law in Texas. But the sovereignty of this new law would not have been possible without the sacrifice at the Alamo. Travis and his men paid the price of freedom; with their blood they bought time, vital time for Houston to organize. But more important, they gave the Texans the spirit to fight and the battle cry that drove the Texans forward and that made the Mexicans abandon all hope: "Remember the Alamo!" From the Alamo heroes' funeral pyre rose the spirit of sacrifice, freed from the flesh to embolden the hearts of the Texans at San Jacinto. And this spirit, present in every man who crossed Travis's line, engendered within that old mission, the newly born fortress—Texas liberty. . . .

Table 1 shows the frequency with which certain details of the myth appear in various types of history texts. [They are] divided . . . into [six] categories. The section labeled "Juvenile" contains those written for (and, in one case, by) schoolchildren. The "Historians" section contains texts written for a general audience but with an academic intent (education as opposed to entertainment). But the tone of these texts is often difficult to distinguish from that of texts appearing in popular journals, particularly the tone in Lon Tinkle's work; thus the distinction between this category and that of "Popular" is somewhat arbitrary, the main distinction being that the "Popular" are those appearing in popular magazines or guidebooks. The "Local" section contains those aimed at Texans and appearing in Texas newspapers and other Texas publications. Many local versions use expected background knowledge of the battle to make their effects felt, especially Mike Kelley's "Edited for Length: Alamo Cut from Epic to Mini-Miniseries." The dates on most of these histories are significant (i.e., they are published during the liminal period or on the anniversary of one battle or the other). The section "Debunkers" contains two attempts to debunk the Texas creation myth, especially the success imagery of the Alamo battle. The final section, "Films," contains two popular film versions of the Alamo story, John Wayne's *The Alamo*, produced in 1960, and *Alamo: . . . The Price of Freedom*, produced in 1988.

The texts within each section are merely a sampling of such texts. . . . I have tried to draw the texts examined from a wide time frame (1874–1990). Within each section the texts appear in chronological order, with the earliest text first.

The Texas creation myth depicts the violent birth of a new nation, Texas; the Alamo is the cradle of this nation and source of her liberty. On the metaphorical al-

Table 1. Occurrence of Details in Various History Texts

				JUVENILE				
	PENNYBACKER 1907	DAFFAN 1908	SMITH 1924	LOWMAN 1942	MOFFITT 1953	JAKES 1986	PEARSON 1987	ALAMO TOUR 1990
Initial sacrifice of Ben Milam	*	*	*	*	*		*	
Santa Anna as Napoleon/corrupt	*	*	*			*	*	
Blood-red banner		*		*			*	*
Cannon-shot response	*	*	*	*	*	*		*
Travis's appeals for help	*			*	*	*		*
Help denied							*	
Travis's line	*	*g					*g	*g
Deguello played							*	*
Darkness at fall of Alamo	*	*		*	*	*	*	*
Travis's death	*			*		*	*	*
Crockett's death		*		*	*		*	*
Bowie's death		*				*	*	*
Santa Anna's comment		*					*	
Number slain	*	*		*	*	*	*	*
Funeral pyre	*	*						
Cruelty at Goliad	*	*					*	
Runaway scrape	*	*				*	*	
Houston's retreat	*	*				*	*	
Sleeping Mexican army	*	*	*			*	*	
Savagery of Texans	*	*	*			*	*	
Excuses offered	*	*	*			*	*	
Capture of Santa Anna	*	*	*			*	*	
Houston's justice	*	*	*					
Positive effects	*	*	*	*	*	*	*	*
Battle cry	*	*	*	*	*		*	*
Thermopylae saying	*her							*

g, ground.

Continues

Table 1. Occurrence of Details in Various History Texts (continued)

	HISTORIANS				POPULAR						
	TITHERINGTON 1874	TINKLE 1953	LORD 1961	PROCTOR 1986	GOULD 1883	HUMBLE 1936	MULLER 1940	BANKS 1952	RAY 1955	WARREN 1958	DOBIE 1959
Initial sacrifice of Ben Milam											
Santa Anna as Napoleon/corrupt	*	*	*	*	*	*			*	*	
Blood-red banner		*	*	*	*				*	*	
Cannon-shot response	*	*	*	*	*		*		*	*	
Travis's appeals for help		*	*	*	*	*	*	*	*	*	
Help denied		*	*	*	*		*		*	*	
Travis's line	*	*nr	*nr	*g	*nr	*g	*ds	*f	*e	*ds	
Deguello played	*	*	*	*	*	*		*		*	
Darkness at fall of Alamo			*		*				*	*	
Travis's death	*	*	*	*	*	*	*		*		
Crockett's death	*	*	*	*	*	*	*		*		
Bowie's death	*	*	*		*	*	*		*		
Santa Anna's comment			*	*	*						
Number slain	*	*	*	*	*	*			*	*	
Funeral pyre	*	*	*	*	*					*	
Cruelty at Goliad		*	*			*					
Runaway scrape			*								
Houston's retreat			*							*	
Sleeping Mexican army		*	*		*	*	*			*	
Savagery of Texans		*	*			*				*	
Excuses offered		*	*		*						
Capture of Santa Anna			*		*					*	
Houston's justice			*	*	*	*	*	*			
Positive effects		*	*			*	*	*	*		
Battle cry	*	*	*		*				*	*	
Thermopylae saying	*three		*her						*her		

	POPULAR		GOOD ROADS 1914	LOCAL			DEBUNKERS		FILMS	
	PARADE 1987	MCALISTER 1988		S. A. LIGHT 1936	PUGH 1986	KELLEY 1990	MCWILLIAMS 1978	LONG 1990	WAYNE 1960	MERRILL 1988
Initial sacrifice of Ben Milam	*	*	*					*		
Santa Anna as Napoleon/corrupt	*	*	*					*	*	*
Blood-red banner		*		*	*			*		*
Cannon-shot response	*	*	*		*			*	*	*
Travis's appeals for help	*	*	*	*	*	*		*	*	*
Help denied	*	*	*					*	*	*
Travis's line	*ds	*dr	*nr	*nr	*dr	*nr	*s	*dr	*	*
Deguello played	*	*		*		*		*		*
Darkness at fall of Alamo	*	*							*	*
Travis's death		*	*		*		*	*	*	*
Crockett's death		*	*		*		*	*	*	*
Bowie's death		*	*				*	*		*
Santa Anna's comment	*	*						*		*
Number slain	*	*	*		*			*		*
Funeral pyre								*		*
Cruelty at Goliad								*		
Runaway scrape								*		
Houston's retreat								*		
Sleeping Mexican army								*		
Savagery of Texans								*		
Excuses offered								*		
Capture of Santa Anna								*		
Houston's justice						*		*		
Positive effects	*	*			*		*	*		
Battle cry	*	*			*			*		*
Thermopylae saying			*her							

dr, dirt; ds, dust; e, earth; f, floor; nr, nothing referenced; s, sand.

tar within the Alamo walls the Alamo heroes offer their lives. Through their violent deaths, the Alamo is born to a new life, "with almost every stone baptized in human blood, shed in the defence of liberty" [Steven Gould, 1883]. The mythic baptismal font flows with the blood of the Alamo heroes, the life-giving fluid from which Texas liberty is born. Their blood waters the ground where Travis has sown the seed of the new nation, and she arises, "springing forth from the flow of the martyrs' blood." . . . [Good Roads 1914].

Within the mythology, the Alamo defenders' blood is the baptizing current for the Alamo and nourishment for the seed of Texas liberty. But a close look at the exchange metaphors offered in several versions of the Alamo story reveals that the heroes' blood also serves as currency with which Travis and the rest of the defenders purchase (1) time and (2) land. The heroes "pay" for Texas' independence from Mexico with their lives. . . . In the speech by the DRT member quoted earlier in this [essay], she states: "Travis was buying time for Houston, and that time was bought with the lives of the Alamo heroes." According to the mythology, time is a quantitative commodity, and Travis and his men purchase thirteen days' worth.

The land obtained in the exchange is also quantifiable in the number of acres that make up Texas. The image of defined land purchased with blood appears in the poem by Marvin Davis Winsett recited at the 1990 DRT March 6 memorial service; in this poem Winsett declares Travis, Crockett, Bowie, and Bonham to be men who paid for "this plot of earth with their own blood." The "plot of earth" gives the impression of defined farmland with individual ownership.

Within the mythology, the heroes' blood simultaneously purchases the land and waters the fertile earth where they have sown the seed of Texas liberty. Travis, as director of this purchase, appears as an astute businessman, wisely investing his life and those of his men to "buy" time and finally land. . . . But if we look carefully at the entire Texas creation myth, we see that Texas is already rightfully in the hands of the Texans at the time of the Alamo battle. Ben Milam has already paid the price with his blood, or at least he has given a down payment on the land with his life. The popular inclusion of Ben Milam's death is vital to making Travis and his men "defenders" of the Alamo. Rather than the Texans appearing as invaders who simply usurp power, they rightfully possess Texas, according to the myth, at the time of the Alamo battle because of Ben Milam's sacrifice. Within this script, Santa Anna and the Mexican army are the invaders coming in to destroy order and steal what rightfully belongs to the Texans.

The men inside the Alamo are also "defenders" in the concept of "Manifest Destiny" supported in the nineteenth century: Texas was destined to be part of the United States. Perhaps as Manifest Destiny has retreated as a means of justifying the taking of Texas and the rest of what is now the American Southwest, the sacrifice of Ben Milam has become a more popular means of making Travis and the others defenders.

The death of the Alamo defenders (in terms of both Manifest Destiny and initial sacrifice) at the hands of the Mexican army marks an inversion of the proper order, one that is righted only after the Battle of San Jacinto. . . . With the entrance of Santa Anna, order, the cultural influence brought by the Texans, is lost, and chaotic fear pervades the land.

In the mythology, the chaos that Santa Anna brings is corruption—Old World corruption—as revealed in his association with Napoleon. He is European culture gone bad, dripping and rotting with excess, which becomes the perversion of culture. Santa Anna is death incarnate, as revealed in his order that the "blood-red banner" of no quarter be flown. But, according to the mythology, death has no power over Travis, as is apparent in his defiant cannon-shot response; he is committed to standing against death.

Once Travis has committed himself to this task, he becomes similar to Christ in the Garden of Gethsemane: although Travis calls out for help, there is no one to "take this cup" from him. He realizes that his sacrifice must be carried out; he has already crossed the line separating the living and the dead. He then asks his men to cross that line as well.

The defenders as a group become, mythologically, the divine sacrifice for the Texas cause, and in crossing Travis's line they have agreed to be sacrificed on "the altar of Liberty." . . . As in ancient fertility rites, Travis has plowed a furrow with his sword in the dirt and has planted the seed of Texas liberty with his words. The sacrificial blood will then water this seed, it will emerge from the martyrs' blood, and it will bear fruit at the Battle of San Jacinto.

It is important to note that in the texts [discussed] above words denoting fertile land—dirt, earth, ground—are used in reference to the substance in which Travis draws his sword more than twice as frequently as words suggesting a soil lacking fertility—dust and sand. The mythology declares that in the hands of Travis and the Texans this land will produce rather than lie as a crumbling wasteland.

But the planting of the seed of Texas liberty and the new nation offers only potential; nourishment by blood is essential if it is to emerge. In the mythology, Travis and his men understand this need and prepare for the sacrificial death that brings new life. To this end, the Texans *allow* the Mexican army to carry out this sacrifice; it is the Texans' choice to die rather than the Mexicans' choice to defeat them.

There is an unnatural quiet as this intended inversion of order begins. Santa Anna and the Mexican army prepare for the final role of high priest of the sacrifice. Darkness, broken only by streaks of red, foretelling the blood to flow, surrounds the fall of the heavenly rulers. The Mexican army rides on the wave of fear, swelling with the notes of the *deguello* and the cries in Spanish praising this Mexican prince of darkness. According to the mythology, cruelty is the norm as the Mexican soldiers ghoulishly carry out their role. Death and chaos reign. After the fall of the Alamo, the normally clear water and air become fouled by death, and carrion seekers darken the skies.

Inversion in the mythology continues during the period between March 6 and April 21: Fannin and the Texans with him surrender rather than fight; soldiers who have willingly surrendered receive cruel treatment and execution rather than mercy; would-be brave Texans abandon home and army, joining in the Runaway Scrape; Houston, who deserves the respect and obedience of his men, is mocked for his seeming cowardice; and the Mexican soldiers enjoy the abandoned goods of the Anglo settlers, elements of culture the Texans rightfully own.

The finale of inversion in the mythology comes in the savagery of the Texans as they overrun the Mexicans during their *siesta*. In this reversal, the Texans are the purveyors of death, cruelty, and terror. They run without order, creating chaos throughout the battlefield; they utter "wild" screams and refuse the pleading prisoners mercy; and they ignore the orders of their commanders. Inversion stops only after anger is spent. Then they begin to follow the orders of their commanders and act in a humane fashion toward the Mexican prisoners.

This return to order in the mythology brings a return of rightful status with the Texans as captors and guards and the Mexicans as prisoners. Santa Anna's cultural veneer is stripped away, and he shrinks in the shadow of the Texans' charge. He is stripped of his finery, save his slippers and underwear; he becomes a foolish figure rather than an embodiment of terror, a laughable varmint rather than a fearsome monster. He flees from the battle, and later crawls like a serpent through grass in an attempt to escape.

When Santa Anna is brought to face the victor (Sam Houston), he expects to be murdered by the men who hold him or upon the order of Houston. But, as proper order has returned, Houston recognizes that justice lies not in an individual's hands but in the legislative body; he sends his prisoner to face the higher power of this civilized land, the Texas Congress. A new culture reigns.

According to the mythology, this transition to a new order is due in part to a fatal flaw within the old culture: *siesta* in the middle of the day. The Mexican soldiers have stacked their arms when they should be ready to use them. This cultural deficiency stands in contrast to the high productivity of the Texans expressed in the number of Mexicans they kill. Several versions of the Texas creation myth state with pride the number of Mexicans killed versus the number of Texans killed. This juxtaposing of the war dead creates a scoring technique which allows the Texans to "win" both at the Alamo and at San Jacinto. . . .

The favorite score within the mythology is that of the San Jacinto encounter; what a rout! The Texans are obviously superior on the field. . . . The scoring approach is particularly significant when we consider that the Texas public school system indoctrinates its students in Texas history during seventh grade, about the same age level that football competition becomes heated in the schools; scoring is all-important. . . .

But the leaders of such warriors, Travis and Houston, do not measure their value in the number of men they kill. Houston is the implementor of the new law, one in which justice is determined by the state rather than by an individual. Although Houston is ridiculed during the liminal period, he knows that he is the rightful commander within Texas and that the new order as embodied within him will ultimately rule Texas. Mythologically, it is for this new order of justice and government that Travis has laid down his life; he is the fate-ordained sacrifice for the new law of the land.

Within the mythology, all Texans are united in their quest for this justice; to this end there are no dissenters within the ranks, even among the Alamo defenders. For that reason, some historians interpret the saying "Thermopylae had her messenger of defeat; the Alamo had none" to mean that no one at the Alamo turned traitor to lend aid to Santa Anna in defeating the Texans. But a more common interpretation of this saying is that the Alamo defenders "did Thermopylae one better"; the Texans lost *all* their men in the battle. But at least one DRT representative has protested the saying on the grounds that the Alamo *did* have a messenger of defeat: Susanna Dickinson. However, her status as messenger is not recognized because women are not significant within the battle imagery of this story line.

In the mythology, the Texans possess the cultural and technological wisdom necessary to clear Texas of barriers to productivity; reproductivity must wait. Sacrifice is the order of the hour. With sacrifice as goal, the Alamo again does Thermopylae one better, because according to this mythology, it is not a defeat but a successful sacrifice; there can be no messenger of defeat if there is no defeat. . . .

In the mythology surrounding the Alamo the ancient past combines with the puritan of the western frontier and with the cavalier of the South to create Texas. Texas' past civilization, the western frontier, and the American South have corresponding figures who form a revered trinity. The Alamo trinity's structure parallels that of the Christian Trinity, which consists of the Father (the ancient ancestor), who engenders the second figure (the Son), who brings the new order to the world and who is engendered through the third figure (the Spirit) within a platonic woman. In the Alamo trinity James Bowie corresponds to the ancient father, Travis the son (the young sacrifice who brings the civilizing law), and David Crockett the ageless spirit.

The ancient father image explains the old order within Texas and why it must surrender its command to the new. James Bowie is the embodiment of ancient warfare and the past. At the time of the Texas Revolution, Bowie was already a legendary warrior. His hand-to-hand combat with a knife represents the savagery needed to survive in the primeval darkness of the Louisiana swamps, an ability he carries with him to the Texas frontier. Knife fighting requires a close contact with one's adversary, allowing a more intimate relationship between the combatants than does the frontier rifle. . . .

Even in the early histories of the Alamo, Bowie is the ancient past. He is the most untamed man in the Alamo: "[H]e was a typical product of the wild Southwest in its wildest days . . . a man who had slain a hundred enemies, . . . who feared absolutely nothing, and who was as reckless in his anger as he could be in his generosity." . . . Bowie's image is that of the ancient hero. He must use primitive means to survive desperate times. Of the men in the Alamo trinity, Bowie is the most closely related to the distant past and its *wilder*ness.

Bowie's connection to the ancestral past pervades all his mythologized stages of life. When he moves to Texas, he associates with the established order within the region; he becomes part of Old San Antonio living in colorful antiquity. According to record, he became a Mexican citizen, converted to Catholicism, and married a Canary Island descendant; that is, he married into one of the established families in San Antonio. As the Texas Revolution nears, Bowie's "Mexican ways," according to historian Lon Tinkle, become a point of departure between him and other Texas colonists who favor independence from Mexico. . . . Bowie is thus married to a culture and a time more than to an individual. . . .

This "marriage" to the land during Mexican rule in Texas is significant, for Mexico is often referred to as the "mother country" prior to Texas' independence; Bowie, as father figure, is still married to the mother country. Both become part of the ancestral past once the move for independence begins. Part of Bowie's father image, however, departs from the image of God the Father: Bowie, as a mortal, succumbs to the aging process, appearing frail in comparison to the youthful Travis. Bowie takes on the characteristics of the ailing father who, though past his prime, struggles to maintain his position of authority. Certainly at the time of the Alamo battle, Bowie appears as one no longer able to provide leadership. He at first wrestles with Travis for authority, then agrees to a joint command. He is finally confined to his bed and forced by illness to "surrender" full command to Travis.

Bowie will ultimately accept Travis's offer of salvation by crossing his line in the dirt. *It is important to note that Bowie must be carried across by the other men.* He is the past, married to the mother country, and is unable to cross the line on his own.

But at least Bowie makes it across the line to the new order. Moses Rose does not. Rose is the old order, being both Jewish and European. In the mythology, he is similar to Judas in the Gospels who, though initially part of Christ's inner circle, abandons Christ and his disciples in their darkest hour.

Bowie's image as the dying commander is juxtaposed to the youthful Travis, the second figure in our trinity. Whereas Bowie's time of love, family, and fortune has passed, Travis's life lies ahead of him. Bowie has nothing left to lose; Travis has everything and is thus the most fitting member of the trinity to serve as sacrificial victim. He is the "paladin extraordinary" who, according to George McAlister, "favored clothes for his legal practice and social occasions instead of the usual rough boots and other frontier garb worn by most of the local men." . . . Travis is the "red-haired stranger". . . ; that is, he is different from the others in Texas at the time, and he comes in from the outside to bring a new order to Texas.

As mentioned previously, Travis takes on a Christ-like aura in his decision to die at the Alamo and in his ability to extract the same commitment from the men of the garrison; all gain immortality in following Travis. This "transformative power of war," apparent in the Texas creation mythology, is part of a widely held view of battle sites as places of such transformation. . . .

The mythologized transformation of the Alamo trinity figures, especially Travis's transformation, is a particularly poignant example of such power. He, more than any of the other men within the Alamo, becomes the sacrifice necessary to bring life to an independent Texas. Birth is, according to the nineteenth-century mind-set in which these legends arose, an extremely dangerous yet productive process. In some births, the mother dies (sacrifices herself) to produce a child. Similarly, Travis dies in the process of birthing Texas.

If Travis is the right man at the right place for a sacrificial beginning of the Southwest, it is the westward movement embodied in the third trinity figure which brings him there. David Crockett is the spirit of the West who fills the men of the garrison with the conviction that they are right and that they should go ahead. Formed of the same Puritan ideology that immortalized Daniel Boone, Crockett is the frontiersman who must work hard at surviving as well as at clearing the way for future colonists.

Even though Crockett displays ferocity in battle, he is not the wilderness spirit James Bowie is. A model frontier hero, Crockett serves as a mediator between the old older and the new and between savagery and civilization. He shares the frontiersman image with Bowie; but he respects the ordered world of military ranks, and offers to submit, as a private, to the new order as embodied in Colonel Travis.

As the model frontier hero, Crockett must quantitatively assess his worth in numbers of bears, Indians, and Mexicans he can kill. This productivity appears in Lon Tinkle's description of Crockett's successes:

Davy was the champion sharpshooter; in one season back in Tennessee he killed 109 bears. Some of these, of course, may have been in hand-to-hand combat, but Davy Crockett had already staked his claim to number-one marksmanship. He had picked off the first Mexican on the first day. He didn't imagine the Texans would find enough guns to take care of all the notches he was going to cut. *The scoring was just starting* [emphasis added]. He intended to surpass himself. . . .

Crockett is the high scorer in this war tally. Tinkle's inclusion of bears and Mexicans within the same paragraph reveals a mythological equation of the two as proper targets of Crockett's frontier rifle and as numbers to be counted in assessing Crockett's worth.

Crockett, as high scorer in the battle, adds to the sacrifice image of Travis: not only are the Alamo heroes the sacrificial victims; they are also the sacrificers, surrounded by the bodies of enemy soldiers sacrificed at their deaths. In this sacrifice/sacrificer duality, Travis exemplifies the successful, life-giving sacrifice, and Crockett exemplifies the sacrificer who exacts a heavy toll from those who would kill these Texas heroes.

Thus sacrifice in the Texas creation mythology both confirms the transformation of Travis and the other defenders to the realm of the sacred . . . and serves as recompense for the wrong done in inverting the proper order of the universe. Although Texans play both roles of sacrificer and sacrifice in the Alamo battle, Texans fill only the sacrificer role at the Battle of San Jacinto. Folklorist Sylvia Grider refers to the "score" at San Jacinto as the legends' means of portraying the Texans as "exacting almost divine retribution upon the Mexicans for what they did to the Texans at the Alamo and Goliad." . . . In the depictions of this battle, the concept of righting wrongs serves to justify the killing of so many unarmed Mexican soldiers.

With the roles of spirit, sacrificial son, and father filled by Crockett, Travis, and Bowie, respectively, the issue remains of platonic female vessel with whom the spirit conjoins to allow the birth of the new order. McAlister's description of Crockett's arrival on the scene best reveals the woman in this role: "In his foxskin [*sic*] cap . . . with old Betsy cradled in his arms, he appeared bigger than life itself. He was just the tonic needed at the right time." . . . In actuality, Crockett had left his famous rifle in Tennessee. *Old Betsy was not at the Alamo at the time of the 1836 battle.* But she's there now, entombed in a glass case dedicated to David Crockett. And she's there in the narratives, the ever faithful wilderness companion to Crockett. As part of the violent birth, she stands in opposition to reproductive women, as she is an instrument of death meant to rid the West of barriers so that productivity can flourish. She is paralleled in the Battle of San Jacinto by the two cannon sent from Cincinnati, the Twin Sisters, who accompany Sam Houston into battle.

These Texas "women" of cold metal are asensual beings who allow the Texas men to become masters of the field. Within the Texas creation myth, real men hold steel women. By giving guns women's names, men portray their perceived ability to control the power of life (and death) that is the "nature" of biological women.

In the Texas creation mythology, it is specifically Anglo men who control this power of women. It is interesting to note that the Texans' cannon which the Mexican soldiers turn upon the Texans in their storming of the Alamo have no names. The *named* steel women—Old Betsy and the Twin Sisters—remain in the hands of the Texans at all times. These "women" are technological rather than biological, and the Anglos . . . possess the better women.

In possessing these women, the Anglo men control life and death via technological superiority. This possession of steel women ideologically mirrors men's possession of biological women, a presumption which is very much alive at the end of the twentieth century. . . . In declaring male possession of women, the reproductivity of women—a power which men do not possess in and of themselves—comes under male control, thus suggesting that men have both productivity and reproductivity as their dominion.

The Anglo men, that is. Social boundaries within the Texas creation mythology declare that both types of women (technological and biological) owe their fealty to Anglo men. When Hispanic men attempt to control biological women by engaging them (or trying to engage them) in sexual relationships, women bring about the downfall of these men. In its portrayal of the Hispanic male's inability to control the power of women, the Texas creation mythology dictates who is superior—technologically, biologically, and socially.

La Tules of Image and Reality

DEENA J. GONZÁLEZ

In the summer of 1846, Doña Gertrudis [*sic*] Barceló stood at an important crossroad. Exempted from the hardships and tribulations endured by the women around her, Barceló had profited enormously from the "gringo" merchants and itinerant retailers who had arrived in Santa Fé after the conquest. The town's leading businesswoman, owner of a gambling house and saloon, and its most unusual character, Barceló exemplified an ingenious turnaround in the way she and others in her community began resolving the problem of the Euro-American. . . . Barceló also epitomized the growing dilemma of dealing with newcomers whose culture and orientation differed from hers.

Since 1821, people like Barceló had seen traders enter their town and change it. But local shopkeepers and vendors had done more than observe the developing marketplace. They had forged ahead, establishing a partnership with the adventurers who brought manufactured items and textiles to Santa Fé while exporting the products of Nuevo México, including gold, silver, and equally valuable goods. . . .

Barceló's life and activities were indisputably anchored in a community shaped by a changing economy, as well as by other political, social, and cultural demands. . . . Moreover, by 1846, she would become the female object of the . . . most exaggerated misunderstandings bred by such complicated frontier situations. The exaggerations have been examined from several perspectives; but standard works have failed to assess the role that sex and gender played in discussions of Barceló's business and personality. The outcome has been the creation of a legend

Deena J. González, "La Tules of Image and Reality: Euro-American Attitudes and Legend Formation on a Spanish-Mexican Frontier," in Adela de la Torre and Beatriz M. Pesquera, eds., *Building with Our Hands: New Directions in Chicana Studies,* University of California Press, 1993. Copyright © 1993 The Regents of the University of California. Reprinted with permission. The full version of this article appeared in *Building with Our Hands: New Directions in Chicana Studies,* edited by Adela de la Torre and Beatriz Pesquera and in *Unequal Sisters,* second edition, edited by E. DuBois and V. Ruiz.

around her, one directly shaped by the disruptions experienced by her generation and focused on her business and her sex.

Gertrudis Barceló was said to have controlled men and to have dabbled in local politics, but these insinuations do not form the core of her legend. Rather, reporters of her time, professional historians today, and novelists have debated her morals, arguing about her influence over political leaders and speculating about whether she was operating a brothel. . . . The negative images and anti-Mexican stereotypes in these works not only stigmatized Barceló but also helped legitimize the Euro-Americans' conquest of the region. Absorbed and reiterated by succeeding generations of professional historians and novelists, the legend of Barceló has obscured the complex reality of cultural accommodation and ongoing resistance.

Moreover, the legend evolving around Barceló affected the lives of other Spanish-Mexican women. Her supposed moral laxity and outrageous dress were generalized to include all the women of Santa Fé. Susan Shelby Magoffin, the first Euro-American woman to travel down the Santa Fé Trail, observed in 1846 that "These were dressed in the Mexican style; large sleeves, short waists, ruffled skirts, and no bustles. . . . All danced and smoked cigarittos, from the old woman with false hair and teeth [Doña Tula], to the little child."

This was not the first account of La Tules, as Barceló was affectionately called. . . . Josiah Gregg [see document 6], a trader during the 1830s, said that La Tules was a woman of "loose habits," who "roamed" in Taos before she came to Santa Fé. In his widely read *Commerce of the Prairies,* Gregg linked local customs—smoking, gambling, and dancing—to social and moral disintegration. La Tules embodied, for him and others, the extent of Spanish-Mexican decadence.

La Tules's dilemmas predated 1846 and, at a social and economic level, portended a community's difficulties, which were not long in developing. . . . In this period, Barceló and other Spanish-Mexicans experienced the tightening grip of the Mexican state, which was bent on rooting out uncontrolled trading; but they gained a reprieve accidentally. . . . The United States chose to invade, hurling General Stephen Kearny and his troops toward the capital city.

Barceló's activities and business acumen demonstrated, despite these pressures, the *vecinos'* (residents') proven resilience and the town's characteristic adaptability. But in the 1840s Barceló also became the object of intense Euro-American scrutiny and harsh ridicule. She was an expert dealer at monte, a card game named after the *monte* (mountain) of cards that accumulated with each hand. She drew hundreds of dollars out of merchants and soldiers alike; it was the former who embellished her name and reputation, imbuing her facetiously with characteristics of superiority and eccentricity.

Josiah Gregg, the trader, first brought Barceló notoriety because his book described her as a loose woman. But Gregg also argued that money from gambling eventually helped elevate her moral character. . . . During her lifetime, she became extraordinarily wealthy, and for that reason as well, Gregg and others would simultaneously admire and disdain her.

In the face of such contradictory attitudes toward her, Barceló ventured down a trail of her own choosing. . . . As early as 1825, she was at the mining camp outside of Santa Fé, Real del Oro, doing a brisk business at monte. By the 1830s, the card dealer was back in town, enticing Euro-Americans to gamble under terms she prescribed. At her saloon, she served the men alcohol as she dealt rounds of cards. Controlling consumption as well as the games, Barceló accommodated the new-comers, but on her own terms. "Shrewd," Susan Shelby Magoffin, wife of the trader Samuel Magoffin, called Barceló in 1846. . . .

When Barceló died in 1852, she was worth over ten thousand dollars, a sum twice as high as most wealthy Spanish-Mexican men possessed and larger than the average worth of Euro-Americans in Santa Fé. Her properties were extensive: she owned the saloon, a long building with large rooms, and she had an even larger home not far from the plaza. She made enough money to give generously to the church and to her relatives, supporting families and adopting children. Military officers claimed that she entertained lavishly and frequently.

Dinners, dances, gambling, and assistance to the poverty-stricken elevated Barceló to a special place in New Mexican society, where she remained throughout her life. The community respected her. . . . Even her scornful critics were struck by how well received and openly admired the woman with the "red hair and heavy jewelry" was among Santa Fé's "best society." . . .

Barceló's gambling and drinking violated the rigid codes organizing appropriate female behavior, but such behavior was not the key to her distinctiveness. Rather, her success as a businesswoman and gambler gave her a unique independence ordinarily denied women. . . .

. . . Barceló cleverly crossed social and sexual barriers to gamble, make money, buy property, and influence politicians, but she avoided marginality. She did not regard herself as a marginal woman, nor was she necessarily marginalized, except by Euro-Americans. She was unusual and she was mocked for it, but not by her own people. In fact, her life and legend are interesting precisely because, in the eyes of observers, she came to represent the worst in Spanish-Mexican culture while, as a Spanish-Mexican, she mastered the strategies and methods of the Americanizers; she achieved what they had professed in speeches and reports originally to want for all New Mexicans.

Barceló's life and her legend contradict . . . notions of marginality in a situation of conquest. In their writings, conquerors maligned and ostracized her. The opinions they expressed and the images they drew of her sealed her legend in the popular imagination, because their works were distributed throughout the United States. Translated into several languages, Gregg's *Commerce of the Prairies* was reprinted three times between 1844, when it first appeared, and 1857. Thousands of readers learned through him of the "certain female of very loose habits, known as La Tules." . . . Dancing, drinking, and gambling—the order was often changed according to how much the writer wanted to emphasize licentious behavior—gave these Protestant travelers pause, and they quickly made use of the observations to fictionalize Barceló's, and all women's, lives. . . .

. . . Yet Barceló was hardly the excessive woman the travelers depicted. Instead, she became pivotal in the achievement of their conquest. Worth thousands of dollars, supportive of the army, friendly to accommodating politicians, Barceló was in the right place to win over Spanish-Mexicans for the intruders. Using business and political skills, she made the saloon the hub of the town's social and economic life, and at the hall she kept abreast of the latest political developments. Politicians and military officers alike went there seeking her opinion, or involved her in their discussions about trade or the army. As adviser and confidante, she took on a role few other women could have filled. If she existed on the fringes of a society, it was because she chose to place herself there. . . .

Such caricatures denied her contributions to the economy and the society. Had she not been a gambler, a keeper of a saloon, or a woman, she might have been praised for her industry and resourcefulness, traits that antebellum Americans valued in their own people. But from the point of view of the writers, the admirable qualities of a woman who lived by gambling and who was her own proprietor would have been lost on Protestant, middle-class readers. . . . It became easier to reaffirm their guiding values . . . by making La Tules a symbol of Spanish-Mexican degeneracy or an outcast altogether. . . .

. . . The aspersions heaped on Barceló . . . created an image that fit the Euro-Americans' preconceptions about Spanish-Mexicans. Thus described to the readers, the image of Barceló in the travel documents merely confirmed older, pernicious stereotypes. . . . Historians and others have traced a . . . critical stage in the development of anti-Mexican fervor to the antebellum period, when expansionist dreams and sentiments . . . gave rise to a continued confusion about Spanish-Mexican culture. Not only travelers from the United States but residents in general harbored deep prejudices toward Spanish-Mexicans. . . .

Racial slurs and derogatory comments about Mexicans appeared regularly in the *Congressional Record,* in newspapers, and . . . in travel accounts. Speeches and statements consistently equated brown skin with promiscuity, immorality, and decay. Albert Pike, who arrived in New Mexico from New England in 1831, called the area around Santa Fé "bleak, black, and barren." . . . The chronicler of a military expedition to New Mexico in the 1840s, Frank Edwards, said that all Mexicans were "debased in all moral sense" and amounted to little more than "swarthy thieves and liars." The same judgments were made later, long after the war had ended, and reflect the persistence of the same thinking. The historian Francis Parkman argued that people in the West could be "separated into three divisions, arranged in order of their merits; white men, Indians, and Mexicans; to the latter of whom the honorable title of 'whites' is by no means conceded." In the same period, William H. Emory of the boundary commission declared that the "darker colored" races were inevitably "inferior and syphilitic." . . .

To the Protestant mind, nothing short of the complete elimination of gambling would lift New Mexicans out of their servility and make them worthy of United States citizenship. . . . Yet initial misgivings about Barceló and the games passed after many entertaining evenings at the gambling house. Once soldiers and others began going there, they lingered, and returned often. Deep-seated anti-Mexican feelings and moralistic judgments gave way to the profits that awaited them if they won at monte, or the pleasures to be savored each evening in Santa Fé even if they lost.

At the numerous tables that lined Barceló's establishment, men who could not speak Spanish and people who did not understand English learned a new language. Card games required the deciphering of gestures and facial expressions but did not depend on any verbal communication. Soldiers and travelers new to Santa Fé understood easily enough what was important at the gaming table. Over cards, the men and women exchanged gold or currency in a ritual that emblazoned their meetings with new intentions. Drinking, cursing, and smoking, the soldiers and others unloaded their money at the table; if Barceló profited, they lost. . . . The stakes grew larger at every turn, and many dropped away from the table to stand at the bar. Barceló's saloon took care of those who did not gamble as well as those who lost. Sometimes a group of musicians arrived and began playing. Sometimes women—who, if not gambling, had been observing the scene—cleared a space in the long room, and dancing began.

Barceló did more than accommodate men by inviting them to gamble. She furthered their adjustment to Santa Fé by bringing them into a setting that required their presence and money. At the saloon, the men were introduced to Spanish-Mexican music, habits, and humor. They could judge the locals firsthand, and could observe a community's values and habits through this single activity. After they had a few drinks, their initial fears and prejudices gradually yielded to the re-laxed, sociable atmosphere of the gambling hall.

In the spring of 1847, Lieutenant Alexander Dyer first visited the saloon. By June, his journal listed attendance at no fewer than forty fandangos and described numerous visits to La Tules' saloon. . . . Dyer's "Mexican War Journal" leaves the distinct impression that a soldier's life, for those of his stripe, involved a constant round of entertainment; visits and parties at Barceló's hall were part of an officer's busy social life.

Thus, rhetoric about gambling or cavorting lessened with time. If visitors did not entirely accept the sociable atmosphere, they were sufficiently lonely for Euro-American women and companionship to go to Barceló's saloon and attend other events to which they were invited. . . .

Court cases offer other impressions of how sojourning Euro-Americans changed their organizing concepts and values. . . .

Investigations in these records delineate the onset of the newcomers' accommodation. Barceló was not the only one practicing accommodation; it worked in two directions. Whether obeying the community's laws or breaking them, new men were adjusting to life away from home. Santa Fé modified the settling Euro-Americans, at times even the sojourning ones, and Barceló had begun to social-ize them in the traditions of an older settlement. The people of the Dancing Ground continued their practice of accepting newcomers, particularly those who seemed able to tolerate, if not embrace, the community's religious and secular values.

At the same time, the conquering soldiers were armed . . . with purpose and commitment. Military men brought plans and realized them: a fort above the town was begun the day after Kearny marched into Santa Fé. Soldiers built a two-story-high flagstaff, and the imposing structure on the plaza attracted visitors from the Dancing Ground, who came supposedly to admire it, but probably also were there to assess the military's strength. . . . Soldiers hailed these crowning achievements as signs of blessings from God to a nation destined to control the hemisphere, but locals were not so pleased.

A new wave of resistance derailed Barceló's efforts to help resettle Euro-Americans in Santa Fé. Nevertheless, even after her death in 1852, Barceló's leg-end continued to indicate that her role extended beyond the immediate helping hand she had lent Euro-Americans. No documents written by her, except a will, have survived to tell whether she even recognized her accomplishment. . . . Her wealth would suggest that she might have harbored an understanding of her influential status in the process of colonization. One fact remains . . . : beginning with her, the accommodation of Euro-Americans proceeded on several levels. Barceló had inaugurated the first, at the gambling hall, and she set the stage . . . for the second, when women began marrying the newcomers.

But as one retraces the original surrounding tensions—deriving from the steady and continuing presence of traders, merchants, and soldiers—and juxtaposes them against Barceló's achievement as an architect of a plan that reconciled the Euro-American to Santa Fé, the realities of displacement and encroachment must not be forgotten. Lieutenant Dyer reported problems as he observed them, and he commented a year after his arrival in Santa Fé: "Still it began to be apparent that the people generally were dissatisfied with the change." In January 1847, resisters in Taos caught and scalped Governor Charles Bent, leaving him to die. In the spring, a lieutenant who had been pursuing horse thieves was murdered, and forty-three Spanish-Mexicans were brought to Santa Fé to stand trial for the crime. In October of the same year, some months after several revolts had been suppressed and their instigators hanged, Dyer reported "a large meeting of citizens at the Palace," where speakers expressed "disaffection at the course of the commissioned officers."

Local dissatisfaction and political troubles had not subsided, in spite of Barceló's work. In the late 1840s, . . . Dyer reported that "a Mexican was unfortunately shot last night by the sentinel at my store house. Tonight we have a rumor that the Mexicans are to rise and attack us." The government in Santa Fé was being forced again to come to terms with each new case of racial and cultural conflict. . . . Problems no longer brewed outside; they had been brought home by accommodated Euro-Americans.

But Barceló should not be blamed here, as she has been by some, for so many problems. She symbolized the transformations plaguing her people. She symbolized as well how an older community had handled the arrival of men from a new, young nation still seeking to tap markets and find a route to the Pacific. . . . The political and social constraints within which she existed had not disappeared as a community contemplated what to do with the strangers among them.

. . . Surrounding the Dancing Ground, stories and legends of other people resisting Americanization were about to begin, and these no longer emphasized accommodation. . . .

Yet, in New Mexico and throughout the West, resistance was giving way to Euro-American encroachment. Richard Henry Dana, traveling in California during the 1830s, mourned the seemingly wasted opportunity presented by land still in the possession of Spanish-Mexicans: "In the hands of an enterprising people, what a country this might be!" His fellow sojourners to New Mexico concurred. What Dana and the other Euro-Americans failed to see was that the land and its communities were already in the hands of such enterprising persons as Barceló. But rather than acknowledge the truth, they disparaged her; their conquerors' minds could not comprehend her intellect, enterprise, and success. Barceló, they believed, had erred. Yet in giving herself to the conquest, but not the conquerors, she survived and succeeded. She drew betting clients to her saloon; they played but lost, she gambled and won.

❧ *FURTHER READING*

Ray Allen Billington, *The Far Western Frontier, 1830–1860* (1995)

Gene M. Brack, "Mexican Opinion, American Racism, and the War of 1846," *Western Historical Quarterly* 1 (1970), 161–174

Carlos E. Castañeda, *The Mexican Side of the Texas Revolution* (1970)

Angelico Chávez, *But Time and Chance* (1981)

Seymour V. Connor, *Adventure in Glory, 1836–1849* (1965)

Rebecca M. Craver, *The Impact of Intimacy* (1982)

Jesús F. de la Teja, ed., *A Revolution Remembered* (1991)

Jane Dysart, "Mexican Women of Texas, 1830–1860: The Assimilation Process," *Western Historical Quarterly* 7 (October 1976), 365–375

Richard Griswold del Castillo, "The Del Valle Family and the Fantasy Heritage," *California History* 49 (Spring 1980), 3–15

Charles L. Kenner, *The Comanchero Frontier* (1994)

David J. Langum, *Law and Community on the Mexican California Frontier* (1987)

Jeff Long, *Duel of Eagles* (1990)

Samuel H. Lowrie, *Culture Conflict in Texas, 1821–1835* (1967)

William M. Mason, "Alta California's Colonial and Early Mexican Era Population, 1769–1846," In Antonio Rios-Bustamante, ed., *Regions of La Raza* (1993)

Jill Mocho, *Murder and Justice in Frontier New Mexico, 1821–1846* (1997)

Douglas Monroy, "They Didn't Call Them 'Padre' for Nothing: Patriarchy in Hispanic California," in Adelaida R. Del Castillo, ed., *Between Borders: Essays on Mexican/Chicana History* (1990)

Joseph M. Nance, *After San Jacinto* (1963)

Frances L. Swadesh, *Los Primeros Pobladores* (1974)

Andres Tijerina, *Tejanos and Texas Under the Mexican Flag, 1821–1836* (1994)

David J. Weber, *The Mexican Frontier, 1821–1846* (1982)

CHAPTER 5

Mexican Americans After the Mexican War, 1848–1860

The mid-nineteenth-century American ideals of Manifest Destiny and national mission were interwoven with expansionist goals that eventually led to war with Mexico. An equally powerful belief was the migrating Anglos' nativism, which contributed to the persecution suffered by the early Chicano community after war.

With the signing of the Treaty of Guadalupe Hidalgo in 1848, which brought the Mexican American War to a close, the United States gained possession of over 529,189 square miles of land at the cost of some $18 million. The acquired territory included all of Texas north of the Río Grande, New Mexico, Arizona, Utah, Nevada, parts of Colorado, and Alta (Upper) California. This meant that the United States also extended its jurisdiction over both American Indian populations and Mexicans living in this area. However, by establishing the civil and land rights of the Spanish-speaking inhabitants of this area, the treaty was the first formal acknowledgment of their legal and economic status. The cession of California to the United States, as well as the gold discoveries there and the ongoing sectional conflict, also had major consequences for Chicanos. While American rule brought increased opportunities to upper-class Chicanos, who often colluded with the Anglos in the ensuing land grabs, the majority of Chicanos were less fortunate. Why did Mexican Americans remain preoccupied with the question of civil rights and especially land titles, when these issues had been guaranteed by the Treaty of Guadalupe Hidalgo? Were local conditions, economic competition, and racial conflict the major causes of anti-Mexican sentiment? Why did the maintaining of their former land holdings, social standing, and prosperity remain tenuous for Mexican Americans?

DOCUMENTS

On February 2, 1848, the signing of the Treaty of Guadalupe Hidalgo ended the Mexican American War. Document 1 is a copy of that treaty, which is essential for understanding the future events that unfolded for the Mexicans of the Southwest. Articles VIII and IX concern the rights and privileges of the Spanish-speaking inhabitants of the area. Document 2, an excerpt from a letter Secretary of State James Buchanan wrote to the Mexican Minister of Foreign Relations, addresses disputed articles related to issues of citizenship and land. Unfortunately, the new American residents of Mexican descent experienced considerable violence and discrimination following the signing of the Treaty of Guadalupe Hidalgo. Individuals like Joaquín Murieta and Juan Cortina defended their own rights as well as those of the wider Mexican community. In Document 3 John Rollin Ridge examines the problems that led Murieta into a life of banditry. Other Mexicans protested the injustices committed against their compatriots, including murder and the loss of lands guaranteed them by the treaty. In Document 4, dated 1856, the editor of the Los Angeles Spanish-language newspaper *El Clamor Público* protests such acts of discrimination as the land seizure and lynchings suffered by Mexicans. Among the many Americans who recorded their observations and experiences in the newly acquired areas was William W. H. Davis, U.S. attorney for the New Mexico territory. An excerpt from his book *El Gringo; or, New Mexico and Her People,* is reproduced as Document 5, in which the author recounts a visit with a wealthy New Mexican family in Santa Fe in the 1850s.

The inability to verify Mexican ownership of land ruled public property by the California state legislature in 1851 opened up Californio ranchero lands to squatters. In Document 6 California lawyer John Hittell discusses the litigation over the boundaries of land grants in northern California that arose after the 1851 law was passed. Document 7 is the 1859 proclamation by Juan Cortina, in which he calls on his fellow Texas Mexicans to defend themselves against the Anglo violence that was especially widespread in the Río Grande Valley.

1. The Treaty of Guadalupe Hidalgo Establishes Borders, 1848

Article I

There shall be firm and universal peace between the United States of America and the Mexican Republic, and between their respective countries, territories, cities, towns and people, without exception of places or persons.

Article II

Immediately upon the signature of this Treaty, a convention shall be entered into between a Commissioner or Commissioners appointed by the General in Chief of the forces of the United States, and such as may be appointed by the Mexican Government, to the end that a provisional suspension of hostilities shall take place, and that, in the places occupied by the said forces, constitutional order may be reestablished, as regards the political, administrative, and judicial branches, so far as this shall be permitted by the circumstances of military occupation. . . .

Article V

The Boundary line between the two Republics shall commence in the Gulf of Mexico, three leagues from land, opposite the mouth of the Rio Grande, otherwise

Treaty of Guadalupe Hidalgo, U.S. Congress, Senate Executive Documents, 30th Cong., 1st Sess., 1847, no. 52.

called Rio Bravo del Norte, or opposite the mouth of it's deepest branch, if it should have more than one branch emptying directly into the sea; from thence, up the middle of that river, following the deepest channel, where it has more than one, to the point where it strikes the southern boundary of New Mexico; thence, westwardly, along the whole southern boundary of New Mexico (which runs north of the town called *Paso*) to its western termination; thence, northward, along the western line of New Mexico, until it intersects the first branch of the river Gila; (or if it should not intersect any branch of that river, then, to the point on the said line nearest to such branch, and thence in a direct line to the same;) thence down the middle of the said branch and of the said river, until it empties into the Rio Colorado; thence, across the Rio Colorado, following the division line between Upper and Lower California, to the Pacific Ocean.

The southern and western limits of New Mexico, mentioned in this Article, are those laid down in the Map, entitled *"Map of the United Mexican States, as organized and defined by various acts of the Congress of said Republic, and constructed according to the best Authorities. Revised Edition. Published at New York in 1847 by J. Disturnell:"* of which Map a Copy is added to this treaty, bearing the signatures and seals of the Undersigned Plenipotentiaries. And, in order to preclude all difficulty in tracing upon the ground the limit separating Upper from Lower California, it is agreed that the said limit shall consist of a straight line, drawn from the middle of the Rio Gila, where it unites with the Colorado, to a point on the coast of the Pacific Ocean, distant one marine league due south of the southernmost point of the Port of San Diego, according to the plan of said port, made in the year 1782 by Don Juan Pantoja, second sailing master of the Spanish fleet, and published at Madrid in the year 1802, in the Atlas to the voyage of the schooners *Sutil* and *Mexicana:* of which plan a copy is hereunto added, signed and sealed by the respective plenipotentiaries.

In order to designate the Boundary line with due precision, upon authoritative maps, and to establish upon the ground landmarks which shall allow the limits of both Republics, as described in the present Article, the two Governments shall each appoint a Commissioner and a Surveyor, who, before the expiration of one year from the date of the exchange of ratifications of this treaty, shall meet at the Port of San Diego, and proceed to run and mark the said boundary in its whole course, to the Mouth of the Rio Bravo del Norte. They shall keep journals and make out plans of their operations; and the result, agreed upon by them, shall be deemed a part of this Treaty, and shall have the same force as if it were inserted therein. The two Governments will amicably agree regarding what may be necessary to these persons, and also as to their respective escorts, should such be necessary.

The Boundary line established by this Article shall be religiously respected by each of the two Republics, and no change shall ever be made therein, except by the express and free consent of both nations, lawfully given by the General Governments of each, in conformity with its own constitution.

Article VI

The Vessels and citizens of the United States shall, in all time, have a free and uninterrupted passage by the Gulf of California, and by the River Colorado below its confluence with the Gila, to and from their possessions situated north of the Boundary line defined in the preceding Article: it being understood, that this passage is to be by navigating the Gulf of California and the River Colorado, and not by land, without the express consent of the Mexican Government.

If, by the examinations which may be made, it should be ascertained to be practicable and advantageous to construct a road, canal or railway, which should, in whole or in part, run upon the river Gila, or upon its right or its left bank, within the space of one marine league from either margin of the river, the Governments of both Republics will form an agreement regarding its construction, in order that it may serve equally for the use and advantage of both countries.

Article VII

The river Gila, and the part of the Rio Bravo del Norte lying below the southern boundary of New Mexico, being, agreeably to the fifth Article, divided in the middle between the two Republics, the navigation of the Gila and of the Bravo below said boundary shall be free and common to the vessels and citizens of both countries; and neither shall, without the consent of the other, construct any work that may impede or interrupt, in whole or in part, the exercise of this right: not even for the purpose of favouring new methods of navigation. Nor shall any tax or contribution, under any denomination or title, be levied upon vessels or persons navigating the same, or upon merchandise or effects transported thereon, except in the case of landing upon one of their shores. If for the purpose of making the said rivers navigable, or for maintaining them in such state, it should be necessary or advantageous to establish any tax or contribution, this shall not be done without the consent of both Governments.

The stipulations contained in the present Article shall not impair the territorial rights of either Republic, within its established limits.

Article VIII

Mexicans now established in territories previously belonging to Mexico, and which remain for the future within the limits of the United States, as defined by the present treaty, shall be free to continue where they now reside, or to remove at any time to the Mexican Republic, retaining the property which they possess in the said territories, or disposing thereof, and removing the proceeds wherever they please; without their being subjected, on this account, to any contribution, tax or charge whatever.

Those who shall prefer to remain in the said territories, may either retain the title and rights of Mexican citizens, or acquire those of citizens of the United States. But they shall be under the obligation to make their election within one year from the date of the exchange of ratifications of this treaty: and those who shall remain in the said territories, after the expiration of that year, without having declared their intention to retain the character of Mexicans, shall be considered to have elected to become citizens of the United States.

In the said territories, property of every kind, now belonging to Mexicans, not established there, shall be inviolably respected. The present owners, the heirs of these, and all Mexicans who may hereafter acquire said property by contract, shall enjoy with respect to it, guaranties equally ample as if the same belonged to citizens of the United States.

Article IX

The Mexicans who, in the territories aforesaid, shall not preserve the character of citizens of the Mexican Republic, conformably with what is stipulated in the preceding article, shall be incorporated into the Union of the United States and be admitted, at the proper time (to be judged of by the Congress of the United States) to the enjoyment of all the rights of citizens of the United States according to the principles of the Constitution; and in the mean time shall be maintained and protected in the free enjoyment of their liberty and property, and secured in the free exercise of their religion without restriction.

[One of the amendments of the Senate struck out Article X.]

Article XI

Considering that a great part of the territories which, by the present Treaty, are to be comprehended for the future within the limits of the United States, is now occupied by savage tribes, who will hereafter be under the exclusive control of the Government of the United States, and whose incursions within the territory of Mexico would be prejudicial in the extreme; it is solemnly agreed that all such incursions shall be forcibly restrained by the Government of the United States, whensoever this may be necessary; and that when they cannot be prevented, they shall be punished by the said Government, and satisfaction for the same shall be exacted: all in the same way, and with equal diligence and energy, as if the same incursions were meditated or committed within its own territory against its own citizens.

It shall not be lawful, under any pretext whatever, for any inhabitant of the United States, to purchase or acquire any Mexican or any foreigner residing in Mexico, who may have been captured by Indians inhabiting the territory of either of the two Republics, nor to purchase or acquire horses, mules, cattle or property of any kind, stolen within Mexican territory by such Indians.

And, in the event of any person or persons, captured within Mexican Territory by Indians, being carried into the territory of the United States, the Government of the latter engages and binds itself in the most solemn manner, so soon as it shall know of such captives being within its territory, and shall be able so to do, through the faithful exercise of its influence and power, to rescue them and return them to their country, or deliver them to the agent or representative of the Mexican Government. The Mexican Authorities will, as far as practicable, give to the Government of the United States notice of such captures; and its agent shall pay the expenses incurred in the maintenance and transmission of the rescued captives; who, in the mean time, shall be treated with the utmost hospitality by the American authorities at the place where they may be. But if the Government of the United States, before receiving such notice from Mexico, should obtain intelligence through any other channel, of the existence of Mexican captives within its territory, it will proceed forthwith to effect their release and delivery to the Mexican agent, as above stipulated.

For the purpose of giving to these stipulations the fullest possible efficacy, thereby affording the security and redress demanded by their true spirit and intent, the Government of the United States will now and hereafter pass, without unnecessary delay, and always vigilantly enforce, such laws as the nature of the subject may require. And finally, the sacredness of this obligation shall never be lost sight of by the said Government, when providing for the removal of the Indians from any portion of the said territories, or for its being settled by citizens of the United States; but on the contrary special care shall then be taken not to place its Indian occupants under the necessity of seeking new homes, by committing those invasions which the United States have solemnly obliged themselves to restrain.

Article XII

In consideration of the extension acquired by the boundaries of the United States, as defined in the fifth Article of the present Treaty, the Government of the United States engages to pay to that of the Mexican Republic the sum of fifteen Millions of Dollars.

2. Secretary of State James Buchanan Reacts to the Treaty of Guadalupe Hidalgo, 1848

To His Excellency, the Minister of Foreign Relations of the Mexican Republic.

Sir: Two years have nearly passed away since our Republics have been engaged in war. Causes which it would now be vain if not hurtful to recapitulate, have produced this calamity. Under the blessing of a kind Providence, this war, I trust, is about to terminate, and, hereafter, instead of the two nations doing each other all the harm they can, their mutual energies will be devoted to promote each other's welfare by the pursuits of peace and of commerce. I most cordially congratulate you on the cheering prospect. This will become a reality as soon as the Mexican Government shall approve the treaty of peace between the two nations concluded at Gaudalupe Hidalgo on the 2nd February, last, with the amendments thereto which have been adopted by the Senate of the United States.

The President, in the exercise of his constitutional discretion, a few days after this treaty was received, submitted it to the Senate for their consideration and advice as to its ratification. Your Excellency is doubtless aware that under the Constitution of the United States, "the advice and consent of the Senate" is necessary to the validity of all treaties and that this must be given by a majority of two thirds of the Senators present. Every Treaty must receive the sanction of this august Executive Council in the manner prescribed by the Constitution, before it can be binding on the United States.

The Senate commenced their deliberations on this Treaty on the 23rd February, last, and continued to discuss its provisions until the 10th instant (March)

From *Treaties and Other International Acts of the United States of America,* vol. 5 (Washington, D.C.: Government Printing Office, 1937), 253–257.

when they finally advised and consented to its ratification by a majority of 38 to 14. Your Excellency will perceive that a change of 4 votes taken from the majority and added to the minority would have defeated the Treaty.

I have now the honor to transmit you a printed copy of the Treaty with a copy, in manuscript, of the amendments and final proceedings of the Senate upon it. This is done to hasten with as little delay as practicable the blessed consummation of peace by placing in the possession of the Mexican Government at as early a period as possible all the information which they may require to guide their deliberations.

In recurring to the amendments adopted by the Senate, it affords me sincere satisfaction to observe that none of the leading features of the Treaty have been changed. Neither the delineation of the boundaries between the two Republics— nor the consideration to be paid to Mexico for the extension of the boundaries of the United States—nor the obligation of the latter to restrain the Indians within their limits from committing hostilities on the territories of Mexico nor, indeed, any other stipulation of national importance to either of the parties, has been stricken out from the Treaty by the Senate. In all its important features, it remains substantially as it was when it came from the hands of the negotiators.

The first amendment adopted by the Senate is to insert in Article 3 after the words "Mexican Republic" where they first occur, the words, *"and the Ratifications exchanged."*

Under this article, as it originally stood, the blockades were to cease and the troops of the United States were to commence the evacuation of the Mexican territory immediately upon the ratification of the Treaty by both Governments. The amendment requires in addition that these ratifications shall have been first exchanged.

The object of this amendment doubtless was to provide against the possibility that the American Senate and the Mexican Congress might ratify the Treaty, the first in its amended and the latter in its original form: in which event peace would not thereby be concluded. Besides, it was known that this amendment could produce no delay, as under the amendment of the Senate to the 23rd article, the ratification of the Treaty may be exchanged at the seat of Government of Mexico the moment after the Mexican Government and Congress shall have accepted the Treaty as amended by the Senate of the United States.

The second amendment of the Senate is to strike out the 9th Article and insert the following in lieu thereof.

[Here follows the English version of Article 9]

This article is substantially the same with the original 9th article; but it avoids unnecessary prolixity and accords with the former safe precedents of this Government in the Treaties by which we acquired Louisiana from France and Florida from Spain.

The Louisiana Treaty of the 30th April, 1803 . . . contains the following article.

ARTICLE 3

The inhabitants of the ceded territory shall be incorporated in the union of the United States, and admitted as soon as possible, according to the principles of the Federal Constitution, to the enjoyment of all the rights, advantages and immunities of citizens of the United States, and in the mean time they shall be maintained and protected in the free enjoyment of their liberty, property, and the religion which they profess.

Again, in the Florida Treaty of 22nd February, 1819, . . . the following articles are contained.

ARTICLE 5

The inhabitants of the ceded Territories shall be secured in the free exercise of their religion, without any restriction; and all those who may desire to remove to the Spanish Dominions, shall be permitted to sell or export their effects, at any time whatever, without being subject, in either case, to duties.

ARTICLE 6

The inhabitants of the territories which His Catholic Majesty cedes to the United States, by his Treaty, shall be incorporated in the Union of the United States, as soon as may be consistent with the principles of the Federal Constitution, and admitted to the enjoyment of all the privileges, rights and immunities of the citizens of the United States.

Under these Treaties with France and Spain, the free and flourishing States of Louisiana, Missouri, Arkansas, Iowa and Florida have been admitted into the Union; and no complaint has ever been made by the original or other inhabitants that their civil or religious rights have not been amply protected. The property belonging to the different churches in the United States is held as sacred by our Constitution and laws as the property of individuals; and every individual enjoys the inalienable right of worshipping his God according to the dictates of his own conscience. The Catholic Church in this country would not, if they could, change their position in this particular.

After the successful experience of nearly half a century, the Senate did not deem it advisable to adopt any new form for the 9th Article of the Treaty; and surely the Mexican Government ought to be content with an article similar to those which have proved satisfactory to the Governments of France and Spain and to all the inhabitants of Louisiana and Florida, both of which were Catholic provinces.

I ought perhaps here to note a modification in the 9th article, as adopted by the Senate, of the analogous articles of the Louisiana and Florida Treaties. Under this modification, the inhabitants of the ceded territories are to be admitted into the Union, "at the proper time (to be judged of by the Congress of the United States)" &c.

Congress, under all circumstances and under all Treaties are the sole judges of this proper time, because they and they alone, under the Federal Constitution, have power to admit new States into the Union. That they will always exercise this power as soon as the condition of the inhabitants of any acquired territory may render it proper, cannot be doubted. By this means the Federal Treasury can alone be relieved from the expense of supporting territorial Governments. Besides, Congress will never lend a deaf ear to a people anxious to enjoy the privilege of self government. Their application to become a State or States of the Union will be granted the moment this can be done with safety.

The third amendment of the Senate strikes from the Treaty the 10th Article.

It is truly unaccountable how this article should have found a place in the Treaty. That portion of it in regard to lands in Texas did not receive a single vote in the Senate. If it were adopted, it would be a mere nullity on the face of the Treaty, and the Judges of our Courts would be compelled to disregard it. It is our glory that no human power exists in this country which can deprive one individual of his property without his consent and transfer it to another. If grantees of lands in Texas, under the Mexican Government, possess valid titles, they can maintain their claims before our Courts of Justice. If they have forfeited their grants by not complying with the conditions on which they were made, it is beyond the power of this Government, in any mode of action, to render these titles valid either against Texas or any individual proprietor. To resuscitate such grants and to allow the grantees the same period after the exchange of the ratifications of this Treaty to which they were originally entitled for the purpose of performing the conditions on which these grants had been made, even if this could be accomplished by the power of the government of the United States, would work manifold injustice.

These Mexican grants, it is understood, cover nearly the whole sea coast and a large portion of the interior of Texas. They embrace thriving villages and a great number of cultivated farms, the proprietors of which have acquired them honestly by purchase from the State of Texas. These proprietors are now dwelling in peace and security. To revive dead titles and suffer the inhabitants of Texas to be ejected under them from their possessions, would be an act of flagrant injustice of not wanton cruelty. Fortunately this Government possesses no power to adopt such a proceeding.

The same observations equally apply to such grantees in New Mexico and Upper California.

The present Treaty provides amply and specifically in its 8th and 9th Articles for the security of property of every kind belonging to Mexicans, whether acquired under Mexican grants or otherwise in the acquired territory. The property of foreigners under our Constitution and laws, will be equally secure without any Treaty stipulation. The tenth article could have no effect upon such grantees as had forfeited their claims, but that of involving them in endless litigation under the vain hope that a Treaty might cure the defects in their titles against honest purchasers and owners of the soil.

And here it may be worthy of observation that if no stipulation whatever were contained in the Treaty to secure to the Mexican inhabitants and all others protection in the free enjoyment of their liberty, property and the religion which they profess, these would be amply guarantied by the Constitution and laws of the United States. These invaluable blessings, under our form of Government, do not result from Treaty stipulations, but from the very nature and character of our institutions. . . .

James Buchanan,
Department of State,
Washington, 18th March, 1848.

3. John Rollin Ridge Reflects on the Life of Joaquín Murieta, 1850

He had been brought in contact with many of the natives of the United States during the war between that nation and his own, and had become favorably impressed

As found in John Rollin Ridge, *Life of Joaquín Murieta, The Brigand Chief of California. Being a Complete History of His Life from the Age of Sixteen to the Time of his Capture and Death at the Hands of Capt. Harry Love in the Year 1853* (San Francisco: California Police Gazette, 1859).

with the American character, and thoroughly disgusted with the imbecility of his own countrymen; so much so that he often wished he had been born on the soil of freedom. The sluggishness and cowardice of the Mexicans he compared with the energy, activity, and bravery of the Americans, and their undying love of liberty; and were it not for that happy and peaceful little home in one of the most charming valleys of Sonora, he would have relinquished at once all claim to nativity, and have become, what he already was at heart, an American.

His meditations were suddenly cut short by the wild shouting and yelling of hundreds of miners in the streets, intermixed with cries of "hang 'em!" "hang 'em!" "string 'em up and try 'em afterwards!" "the infernal Mexican thieves!" Joaquín rushed out, and was just in time to see his brother and Flores hauled up by their necks to the limb of a tree. They had been accused of horse-stealing by the two Americans from San Francisco, who claimed the animals as their own, and had succeeded in exciting the fury of the crowd to such an extent that the doomed men were allowed no opportunity to justify themselves, and all their attempts to explain the matter and to prove that the horses were honestly obtained, were drowned by the fierce hooting and screaming of the mob. Struck dumb with surprise and horror, Joaquín could at first only gaze upon the swinging corpse of Carlos, and the crowds of demoniac wretches around him, and wonder if the scene were real; but tears at length came to his relief and saved his brain from madness, and then with a heart full of desire for revenge, he obtained a mule and returned with all speed to Sacramento. Here he took the boat for San Francisco, from whence he proceeded to the Mission, sought the house of Sepulveda and acquainted his wife with the murder of his brother. Although Carmela shuddered with horror at the recital of the facts by Joaquín, yet with true womanly feeling, she begged him to seek not for revenge and thus endanger his own life, but to leave the perpetrators to that punishment which their guilty conscience would mete out to them sooner or later. She assured him that all Americans were not as depraved and bloodthirsty as those who composed that mob of murderers, and with all the strength of a loving heart, implored him to yield to no criminal temptation.

With tears and entreaties, and words of love and consolation, a change was wrought in the heart of Joaquín, and his spirit imbued with a feeling of forgiveness.

"Well," said he, rising from the feet of his beloved partner, where he had been reclining, and listening with deep devotion, "Well, it is all past; let us be cheerful and happy, and when I have collected some of this golden sand, we will return." A few days afterwards, Joaquín, accompanied by his wife, reached the mines on the Stanislaus River, where he built a comfortable cabin, and commenced washing the glittering particles from the earth. The country was then full of lawless and desperate men, calling themselves Americans, who looked with hatred upon all Mexicans, and considered them as a conquered race, without rights or privileges, and only fitted for serfdom or slavery. The prejudice of color, the antipathy of races, which are always stronger and bitterer with the ignorant, they could not overcome, or would not, because it afforded them an excuse for their unmanly oppression. A band of these men, possessing the brute power to do as they pleased, went to Joaquín's cabin and ordered him to leave his claim, as they would not permit any of his kind to dig gold in that region. Upon his refusing to leave a place where he was amassing a fortune, they knocked him senseless with the butts of their pistols, and while he was in that condition, ravished and murdered his faithful bosom-friend, his wife.

The soul of Joaquín now became shadowed with despair and deadly passion; but still, although he thirsted for revenge, he felt himself as yet unable to accomplish anything, and would not endanger his freedom and his life in attempting to destroy single-handed, the fiendish murderers of his wife and brother. He determined to wait and suffer in silence, until a fitting opportunity occurred for the carrying out of his plans. Accordingly he went (in April, 1850) to mining at "Murphy's Diggings" in Calaveras County; but meeting with very little success, he abandoned the business, and sought to improve his fortune by dealing "monte," a game very common in Mexico, and considered by all classes in that country as an honorable occupation. For a time, fortune smiled upon him and furnished him with a golden evidence of her good will; but then came a change, suddenly and heavily, and Joaquín was at once hurled into the deep and dark abyss of crime. He had gone a short distance from camp to see a friend by the name of Valenzuelo, and returned to Murphy's with a horse which his friend had lent him. The animal, it was proved by certain individuals in town, had been stolen some time previously, and a great excitement was immediately raised. Joaquín found himself surrounded by a furious mob and charged with the theft. He informed them when and where he had borrowed the horse, and endeavored to convince them of Valenzuelo's honesty. They would hear no explanation, but tied him to a tree and disgraced him publicly with the lash. They then went to the residence of Valenzuelo and hung him without allowing him a moment to speak. Immediately there came a terrible change in Joaquín's character, suddenly and irrevocably. His soul swelled beyond its former boundaries, and the barriers of honor, rocked into atoms by the strong passion which shook his heart like an earthquake, crumbled and fell. Then it was that he resolved to live henceforth only for revenge, and that his path should be marked with blood.

On a pleasant evening, not long after this unfortunate occurrence, an American was wending his way along a trail at a short distance from the town. Upon descending into a ravine, through which ran the narrow pathway, he was suddenly confronted by Joaquín, whose eyes glared with the fury of an enraged tiger, and whose whole form seemed to quiver with excitement. For an instant each gazed upon the other, and then with a fierce yell Joaquín sprang upon the traveler and buried in his breast a long two-edged dagger.

"What—what means this?" gasped the victim as he sank to the ground, "why do you murder me? oh! mercy—spare my life."

"You showed no mercy to me," replied Joaquín, "when you assisted in tying and lashing me in the presence of a multitude of people. When, in the proud consciousness of your strength, and supported by the brute force of some of your own countrymen, you seized upon an innocent man—a *man*—with heart and soul, and with all the noble attributes received from his Maker—a man possessed of more truth and honor than could have been found among those who helped to torture him; when you seized him and bound him, and scored his back with the ignominious lash, you did not then think of *mercy*. When your countrymen hung my brother by the neck like a dog, was there any mercy shown him? When they cruelly murdered my heart's dearest treasure, in my own presence and almost before my eyes; and when she must, with her silvery voice, have faintly appealed for mercy, was that appeal heeded by the inhuman wretches? Ah! my brain is on fire!" he added, pressing his left hand to his forehead, while with the other he inflicted another wound.

"Murder?" muttered the damned man, raising himself upon his elbow and staring with wild, glassy eyes upon the savage features of the desperado. "The mercy—mer—," but the steel had now entered his heart—and he fell back a corpse. . . .

Fear and consternation spread among the individuals who had been leaders in that mob and they were afraid to go as far as the outskirt of the town. Whenever any of them strolled out of sight of the camp, or ventured to travel on the highway, they were suddenly and mysteriously killed. Reports came in from time to time that the dead bodies of Americans had been found on the roads and trails, and it was always discovered that the murdered men belonged to the mob who had whipped Joaquín. He had now made himself amenable to the law by the commission of these bloody deeds, and his only safety lay in a continuance of the unlawful course which he had begun. For the furtherance of his plans he found it necessary to have horses and money, which he could not obtain except by adding robbery to murder, and thus he became a bandit and an outlaw before his twentieth year.

It became generally known, in 1851, that an organized banditti was ranging the country, and that Joaquín was the leader. Travelers were stopped on the roads and invited to "stand and deliver"; men riding alone in wild and lonesome regions, were dragged from their saddles by means of the lasso, and murdered in the adjacent chaparral. Horses were stolen from the ranches, and depredations were being committed in all parts of the State, almost at the same time.

Joaquín's superior intelligence and education gave him the respect of his comrades, and appealing to the prejudice against the "Yankees," which the disastrous results of the Mexican war had not tended to lessen in their minds, he soon assembled around him a powerful band of his countrymen, who daily increased, as he ran his career of almost magical success.

4. A California Newspaper Condemns Violence Against Mexicans, 1856

El Clamor Público, **July 26, 1856**

. . . We do not wish to excuse or justify the disorders that occurred on the unforgettable night of Tuesday. The behavior of the people that fomented that meeting is quite mistaken. Their thinking is bad—if they wanted to attack the Americans who have entrenched themselves in the walls of the city. They can never accomplish this with security, because at the same time they take on grave responsibilities, endangering the life of their families and causing hardships to their properties. The death of Don Antonio Ruiz has exasperated the feelings of all Mexicans. It is be-

---

As found in *El Clamor Público,* Los Angeles, July 26, 1856, and August 2, 1856.

coming a very common custom to murder and abuse the Mexicans with impunity. And the Mexicans are growing tired of being run over and having injustices committed against them: but to take up arms to redress their grievances, this is an act without reason. We desire to re-establish peace: those misguided Mexicans should return as before to their homes and we hope for an immediate reform to take place.

El Clamor Público, August 2, 1856

The first occupants of this sort were of Spanish descent and when California came to be an integral part of the Northern Republic, many citizens remained to enjoy their properties that they had just obtained from Mexico via cession, sale, etc. These people from the mere fact of having remained obtained the same rights and privileges of American citizens. But no sooner had order been re-established when the National Congress dictated a law that established a commission to revise land titles. This measure cost uncountable expenses for the property owners and many had spent all their fortune to defend their property. Before their titles were approved, they had to make two or three trips to Washington and finally their labors and watchfulness yielded them nothing. After three years of continuous litigation most of the landowners are ruined. At the end, not satisfied with having uprooted from the hands of the Californians and Mexicans their possessions, the last session of the Legislature passed a law whose object was to declare as public property all California land, except that which had a government title.

This latest blow has extinguished forever the hopes that they had in the new government that had just been inaugurated on the Pacific beaches. But this isn't all, for not content with having plundered their properties under the shadow of the law, they have subjected all Hispano-Americans to a treatment that has no model in the history of any nation conquered by savages or by civilized peoples.

All are convinced that California is lost for all Hispano-Americans and here in Los Angeles because of the latest revolution if before they asked for favors, now they will ask for justice on their knees and for freedom to pursue their jobs.

Almost all of the newspapers of the North are continually full of lynchings that happened in the mines. And, oh fate! Mexicans alone have been victims of the insane furor of the people! Mexicans alone have been sacrificed on ignominious gallows which are erected to hurl their poor souls to eternity. Is this the freedom and equality of the country that we have adopted?

5. William W. H. Davis Comments on the Customs of the Spanish-speaking New Mexicans, 1857

We next call upon a Mexican family, in order to obtain some knowledge of the manners and customs of the people in their social intercourse. A few steps bring us to the house of a friend, and we stand before the large door that leads into the *patio,* knocking for admittance. While the old *portero* is coming to inquire who is there and to let us in, I will say a few words more about the houses and their mode of

---

As found in William W. H. Davis, *El Gringo; or, New Mexico and Her People* (New York, 1857), chap. 7.

construction. It will be borne in mind that the material is simple earth in its raw state, and that all, whether in town or country, are built in the form of a square, with a courtyard in the centre. The style of building was borrowed from the East, and is as ancient as the time of Moses, and was essential here in early time because of the hostility of the Indians. The roof is called *azotea la puerta del zaguan* [porch roof]. An *adobe* is about six times the size of an ordinary brick, and they cost, delivered, from eight to ten dollars the thousand. Neither skill nor practice are required in order to make them. A piece of ground is selected for the purpose, upon which water can be turned from an acequia, and the earth is dug up and mixed until about the consistency of mortar. Each adobe maker has a frame the proper size, which he fills with the soft mud, strikes off the top evenly, when he empties it out upon the ground to dry in the sun. The adobes are very seldom laid in lime and sand, but with the same kind of mud they are made of. In time the walls become quite solid, and houses are in use, built in this manner, which have stood for nearly two hundred years; but they would not last long in the States, amid the great storms that prevail there.

By this time the porter has made his appearance at the door, where we have been standing some two or three minutes. There is great dread of robbers among the people, and they will not always admit you before you are known. The porter, therefore, as a matter of precaution, salutes us in the first place with *Quien es?* (Who is it?) to which we respond, *Amigos* (friends), when he opens the door sufficiently wide to see who we are, and permits us to enter. Being now assured that we are not robbers, he conducts us across the patio, and ushers us into the *sala,* or reception-hall, where we remain seated until the family come in to welcome us. While they are making their appearance—which may be some minutes, if the hour is afternoon, and they have not arisen from their *siesta* (afternoon nap)—we will, in imagination, make an excursion around the house to notice the *locus in quo,* as a lawyer would say, or, to speak more familiarly, to observe the manner in which it is furnished and the style thereof. The internal arrangement of a Mexican house is as different from that of an American as the building itself. The style is essentially Spanish, blended with which are observed many traces of the Moors, their early ancestors. As has been remarked before, all the rooms open into the patio, except some which communicate directly with the sala and with each other. It is a very rare thing to see a board floor in a Mexican house, the substitute being earth, cheaper in the first place, and more easily repaired. A coating of soft mud is carefully spread over the earth, which, when dry, makes a firm and comfortable floor. The common covering for the floors, when they are covered at all, is a coarse article of domestic woolen manufacture, called *gerga,* which answers the purpose of a carpet. The inside walls are whitened with calcined *yezo* or gypsum, which is used instead of lime, but it does not adhere to the walls with the same tenacity, and comes off upon every article that touches it. To prevent this, the rooms are lined with calico to the height of four feet, generally of bright colors. The coating of mud and yezo on the inside of the house is generally put on by females, who make use of their hands and a piece of sheep-skin with the wool on for that purpose, instead of brushes and plasterers' tools.

The ceiling is never plastered, but in those of the wealthier classes the beams that support the roof are planed and painted in various colors, and sometimes an artificial ceiling is made by tacking bleached muslin to them. In some sections of the country, small round sticks are laid from beam to beam in herring-bone style, and painted red, blue, or green; but it is only a choice room that is ornamented in this manner. The fire-place is built in one corner of the room, and occupies a small space. The mouth is somewhat in the shape of a horseshoe, not generally more than eighteen inches or two feet in height, and the same in width at the bottom. The back is slightly concave instead of being a plane surface, and the little circular hearth in front is raised a few inches above the level of the floor. The use of andirons is unknown, the wood being placed on end against the back of the fire-place. These small fire-places appear to give out more heat than the larger ones in use in American houses, and, being in a corner of the apartment, they occupy less space. I do not remember to have ever seen shovels or tongs in a Mexican house. When the house becomes dingy, if outside, they besmear it with a new coating of soft mud; or if inside, the walls are again daubed with yezo, followed by a coat of fresh mud on the floor. This renovation suffices instead of the semi-annual house-cleaning which causes American housewives so much annoyance.

The furniture, as well as the manner of arranging the same, differs materially from the style in the States. Few chairs or wooden seats of any kind are used, but in their stead mattresses are folded up and placed around the room, next to the wall, which, being covered with blankets, make a pleasant seat and serve the place of so-fas. This is an Eastern custom, and was undoubtedly borrowed from the Moors. At night they are unrolled and spread out for beds; and it is customary for the whole family to sleep in the same room at night that they sit in during the day. Bedsteads are almost unknown, and if the mattress is raised at all above the floor, it is placed on a low wooden frame. Bureaus and other furniture of that description, in such common use in American houses to contain the clothing of the family, are seldom seen among the Mexicans, their place being supplied by an increased number of trunks and antiquated chests. In the houses of the wealthier classes a few chairs and cumbrous settees are found, generally made of pine, but among the peasantry such articles of luxury are unknown. This economy in articles of furniture was an absolute necessity in early times, caused by the almost entire absence of mechanics in the country; and such as they possessed were handed down from generation to generation as heir-looms in the family. At the present day, although there are American mechanics, but few of the people have adopted our style of furniture, but cling to that of olden times. Every article of this description sells at a price enormously high, and ordinary pine furniture costs more than that made of mahogany in the Atlantic States. The females in particular, prefer the easy *colchon*—folded mattress—to the straight and stiff-backed chairs and settees; and frequently they spread a single blanket in the middle of the floor, upon which they sit at work and receive visitors.

The kitchen utensils are equally meagre in their appointment. They cook almost universally in earthen vessels, which bear the general name of *tinaja,* and it is a rare thing to see any other description of culinary articles. I have never seen a stove in a Mexican house. The *sala* is the largest room about the establishment, and in the colder parts of the country it is only used during warm weather, when, for the time being, the family literally live there, lounge among the *colchons* during the day, receive their visitors, sleep at night, and hold the *baile.* The family room is adorned with a number of rude engravings of saints, among which the Virgin of Guadalupe is always conspicuous.

It has been stated elsewhere that the *tortilla,* a thin cake made of corn, is one of the principal articles of food among all classes of the people. The duty of making them has devolved upon the women from the earliest times, and they pride themselves upon the skill and rapidity with which they can prepare them. While we are in the kitchen, should we extend our adventures in that direction, we will see the manner in which the tortilla is made. The corn is boiled in water with a little lime, to soften the skin so that it can be peeled off, when they grind it into a paste upon an oblong hollowed stone, called a *metate.* The operator kneels down behind it, and takes in both hands another long round stone like an ordinary rolling-pin, between which and the *metate* she mashes the corn. To bake, the *tortilla* is spread upon thin sheets of tin or copper, and in a few minutes they are ready for use. They are quite palatable when warm, but when cold are almost as tasteless as so much shoeleather. This, with the bean called *frijole,* makes the staff of life of all classes of the population. In Southern Mexico it is the custom for women, with small portable furnaces on their backs or strapped to a burro, to travel the streets of the large towns making and vending *tortillas* and *frijoles* to the passers-by.

By this time the siesta of *La Senora* has come to an end, and she makes her entrance into the sala where we have awaited her coming. The people of all classes receive their friends with much genuine affection, and it is customary to embrace each other when they meet. Our hostess upon this occasion, if perchance I am on intimate terms with herself and family, will encircle me with her fair arms, or, in common parlance, salute me with what is vulgarly called a *hug,* while you, who are a stranger, must be content with a shake of the hand. To make this distinction between a person and his friends is certainly aggravating to him who falls in the vocative, but a short acquaintance will place the outsiders upon an equally pleasant footing. If all the family should make their appearance, each one in turn will embrace you, which is by no means an unpleasant performance when the pretty daughters are a party to the operation, but it is much less agreeable to be hugged in the brawny arms of the father and brothers. This custom is universal among all classes, and even the filthy beggars in the streets meet and embrace each other with an affection truly laughable.

The Mexicans are distinguished for their politeness and suavity, and the *lepero,* covered with abominations, often exhibits a refinement of manners and address that would well become a prince, and which they as well practice toward each other as toward strangers. In their houses they are particularly courteous, and in appearance even outdo the most refined code of politeness. It is customary for them to assure you that you are in your own house the moment you cross their threshold, or to place themselves entirely at your disposal. If you admire an article, the owner immediately says to you, *"Tomele Vmd., Señor, es suyo"* (Take it, sir, it is yours). But in these flattering expressions the stranger must bear in mind that the owner has not the most remote idea that he will take him at his word—that he will either command his household, lay his personal services under contribution, or carry off whatever pleases his fancy.

We have already gone through with the hugging and kissing, and are now seated in the presence of our fair hostess. One of the first acts of courtesy of the mistress of the house is to invite you to smoke. She carries about her person a small silver tobacco-box, in which she keeps the noxious weed, and also has at hand a little package of corn-husks, one of which she fills with the fine-cut tobacco, rolls it up into a *cigarrito,* lights it, and hands it to you to smoke. The American cigar is rarely used by the men, and never by the females, both substituting the article here named. The *cigarrito* is made by each person as he requires them, who always has on hand for that purpose his box of tobacco and package of husks. [Joshua] Gregg, in his "Commerce of the Prairies," says upon this subject, "The mounted vaquero will take out his *guagito* (his little tobacco-flask), his packet of *hojas* (or prepared husks), and his flint, steel, etc., make his cigarrito, strike his fire, and commence smoking in a minute's time, all the while at full speed; and the next minute will perhaps lazo the wildest bull without interrupting his smoke." Smoking is habitual with all classes, not excepting the most lovely and refined females in the country. The habit is bad enough in men, but intolerable in women. The *cigarrito* seems to be an abiding presence, being handed round at the dinner-table as a refreshment, and served up in the ballroom; and it is common to see ladies smoking while they are engaged in waltzing and dancing, and some even indulge the luxury while they lie in bed. In Southern Mexico the ladies use a pair of golden tongs to hold the *cigarrito* while they light it, and the coal of fire is brought by a servant on a small silver salver.

In the more southern cities of Mexico, next to providing the guest with the means of smoking, chocolate and sweet bread are served up, the former being a delicious article of domestic manufacture, and the latter a superior quality of sponge-cake. During our stay, the mistress of the establishment and her daughters will endeavor to make the time pass as agreeably as possible. They are great talkers, and we will have enough to do to maintain the negative side of the question, now and then throwing in a word, in order to draw out the colloquial powers of our fair companions. When we come to take leave, the same ceremony is used as at the arrival, and you are passed around the family circle to receive an embrace from each member. This custom is as much a matter of course as that of shaking hands among the Americans, touching noses among the Chinese, or grunting among the North American Indians; and the most modest lady in the land has no scruples about giving and receiving such salutation. The whole family accompany us to the door, and wait there until we have fairly made our exit, instead of turning us over to an impudent lackey, as has become the *fashion* in the States.

6. John Hittell Reviews Mexican Land Claims in California, 1857

The establishment of the American dominion in California made it necessary that the titles to land owned in the state under grants from Mexico should be recognised and protected in accordance with the principles of American law. Protection was due to the landowners under the general principles of equity and the laws of nations, and had been expressly provided in the Treaty of Guadalupe Hidalgo. It was

As found in *Hutching's California Magazine,* July 1857.

necessary that the protection should be in accordance with the principles of American law, becuase the vast majority of the population soon came to be composed of Americans, who naturally introduced their own system of law—the only system suited to their method of conducting business.

But there was a question of much difficulty as to how this protection should be furnished. The Mexican titles were lacking in many of the conditions necessary to a perfect title under the American laws. The land systems of the two countries were constructed on entirely different principles and with different objects. The Mexican system was a good one for the purposes to be attained by it; it was suited to the wants of the natives of California. They were stock-growers; their only occupation and wealth and staple food was furnished by their herds. They owned immense numbers of horses and horned cattle, and to furnish them with pasture, each ranchero required a large tract of land, which might be used by his own stock exclusively. . . . These grants were usually made without any accurate description of the land; there never had been any government survey of any portion of the territory; there were no surveyors in the country to locate the boundaries; neither would the applicants have been willing in most cases to pay for surveys; nor was there any apparent need for them, land being very cheap and quarrels about boundaries very rare. Sometimes the land granted was described with certain fixed natural boundaries. In other cases, the grant might be described as lying in a narrow valley, between two ranges of mountains, and extending from a tree, rock, or clump of willows, up or down the valley far enough to include three, six, or ten square leagues. . . .

The grants made were not carefully registered. The law prescribed that the petitions for land should all be preserved, and a record of them kept, and that a registry should be made of all the lands granted; but the affairs of the governor's office were loosely conducted, and in many cases where the claimants have been in possession for twenty years, and have an undoubted title, there is nothing in the archives or records of the former government to show for it. In many respects the California governor had been very careless about granting lands. Sometimes they would grant the same lands to several persons. . . .

When the great immigration of 1849 filled the land with Americans, it became necessary to provide for the recognition and protection of the good Mexican titles by the American courts. But how was this to be done? By the ordinary state courts? The judges would not be sufficiently able, and would be ignorant of the laws under which the grants had been made; the juries would be composed of Americans whose interests would lead them to do injustice to the large landowners. Besides, the lawmakers and judges elected by a deeply interested populace could not be depended upon to do justice under such circumstances.

Or should the protection be rendered by the appointment of a commission, instructed to make a summary examination of all claims, declare all those valid which had been in possession previous to the conquest, and of which some record might be found in the archives, leaving the other claims to be tried in the U.S. courts? This was the policy which should have been pursued.

But that plan was not to prevail. Mr. Gwin's bill "to ascertain and settle the private land claims in the state of California," became a law, on the 30th of March, 1851. This act provides for the appointment of a special judicial committee (to be composed of three judges), before which all claimants to land in the state under Mexican titles, should bring suit against the federal government within two years after the date of the act, under penalty of forfeiting their land. It provided further, that a law agent should be appointed, who should "superintend the interests of the United States in every case." It provided further, that appeals might be taken in these land cases, from the judgments of the commission to the U.S. district court, and from the latter, to the Supreme Court of the United States. It provided further, that in the trial of these cases, the commission and the courts should "be governed by the Treaty of Guadalupe Hidalgo, the law of nations, the laws, usages, and customs of the country from which the claim is derived, the principles of equity, and the decisions of the Supreme Court of the United States.". . .

The land commission was opened in this city [San Francisco], January 1, 1852, and in the ensuing fourteen months, 812 suits were brought, and these were all decided previous to the 3rd of March, 1855, at which time the commission dissolved.

It was severe hardship for owners of land under grants from Mexico, that they should be required to sue the government of the United States (which ought to have protected, not persecuted them) or lose their land; but this hardship was rendered much more severe by the peculiar circumstances under which the suits had to be tried. The trials were to be had in San Francisco at a time when the expenses of traveling and of living in San Francisco were very great, and the fees of lawyers enormous. The prosecution of the suits required a study of the laws of Mexico, in regard to the disposition of the public lands, and this study had, of course, to be paid for by the clients. In many cases the claimants had to come to San Francisco from remote parts of the state; having 300 miles to travel, bringing their witnesses with them at their own expense. The witnesses were nearly all native Californians, and it was necessary to employ interpreters at high prices. . . .

. . . Many squatters were, no doubt, glad of a pretext under which they might take other people's land and use without paying rent, but the circumstances were often such that they were justified in refusing to buy. The number of settlers or squatters became large; they formed a decided majority of the voters in several of the counties; their political influence was great; politicians bowed down before them; all political parties courted them; and most of the U.S. land agents, and district attorneys, appointed under the influence of the California congressmen, became the representatives of the settler interest, and failed to represent the true interest of the United States. Every device known to the law was resorted to to defeat the claimant, or delay the confirmation of his grant, as though it were the interest of the federal government to defeat every claimant, or to postpone his success as long as possible. . . .

. . . This delay, which would have been disastrous in any country, was doubly so in California. . . . The consequence of the system was that a large portion of the most valuable farming land in the state was occupied by squatters. This occupation contributed greatly to injure the value of the property. The landowner could not sell his land, nor use it, and yet he was compelled to pay taxes. His ranch brought serious evils upon him. It was the seat of a multitude of squatters, who, as a necessary consequence of antagonistic pecuniary interest, were his bitter enemies. Cases we know, where they fenced in his best land; laid their claims between his house and his garden; threatened to shoot him if he should trespass on their inclosure; killed his cattle if they broke through the sham fences; cut down his valuable shade and fruit trees, and sold them for firewood; made no permanent improvements, and acted generally as though they were determined to make all the immediate profit possible out of the ranch. Such things were not rare: they are familiar to every person who knows the general course of events during the last five years in Sonoma, Napa, Solano, Contra Costa, Santa Clara, Santa Cruz, and Monterey counties. Blood was not unfrequently spilled in consequence of the feuds between the landholders and the squatters; the victims in nearly every case, belonging to the former class.

7. Juan Cortina Calls Texas Mexicans to Armed Resistance, 1859

An event of grave importance, in which it has fallen to my lot to figure as the principal actor since the morning of the twenty-eighth instant, doubtless keeps you in suspense with regard to the progess of its consequences. There is no need of fear. Orderly people and honest citizens are inviolable to us in their persons and interests. Our object, as you have seen, has been to chastise the villainy of our enemies, which heretofore has gone unpunished. These have connived with each other, and form, so to speak, a perfidious inquisitorial lodge to persecute and rob us, without any cause, and for no other crime on our part than that of being of Mexican origin, considering us, doubtless, destitute of those gifts which they themselves do not possess.

To defend ourselves, and making use of the sacred right of self-preservation, we have assembled in a popular meeting with a view of discussing a means by which to put an end to our misfortunes. . . .

Innocent persons shall not suffer—no. But, if necessary, we will lead a wandering life, awaiting our opportunity to purge society of men so base that they degrade it with their opprobrium. Our families have returned as strangers to their old country to beg for an asylum. Our lands, if they are to be sacrificed to the avaricious covetousness of our enemies, will be rather so on account of our own vicissitudes. As to land, Nature will always grant us sufficient to support our frames, and we accept the consequences that may arise. Further, *our personal enemies shall not possess our lands until they have fattened it with their own gore.* . . .

There are, doubtless, persons so overcome by strange prejudices, men without confidence or courage to face danger in an undertaking in sisterhood with the love of liberty, who, examining the merit of acts by a false light, and preferring that of the same opinion contrary to their own, prepare no other reward than that pronounced for the "bandit," for him who, with complete abnegation of self, dedicates himself to constant labor for the happiness of those who, suffering under the weight of misfortunes, eat their bread, mingled with tears, on the earth which they rated.

House Executive Documents, 36th Cong., 1st sess., H. Exec. Doc., no. 52, ser. 1050 (Washington, D.C.: Thomas H. Ford, Printer, 1860).

If, my dear compatriots, I am honored with that name, I am ready for the combat. . . .

Mexicans! When the State of Texas began to receive the new organization which its sovereignty required as an integrant part of the Union, flocks of vampires, in the guise of men, came and scattered themselves in the settlements, without any capital except the corrupt heart and the most perverse intentions. Some, brimful of laws, pledged to us their protection against the attacks of the rest; others assembled in shadowy councils, attempted and excited the robbery and burning of the houses of our relatives on the other side of the river Bravo; while others, to the abusing of our unlimited confidence, when we intrusted them with our titles, which secured the future of our families, refused to return them under false and frivolous pretexts; all, in short, with a smile on their faces, giving the lie to that which their black entrails were meditating. Many of you have been robbed of your property, incarcerated, chased, murdered, and hunted like wild beasts, because your labor was fruitful, and because your industry excited the vile avarice which led them. A voice infernal said, from the bottom of their soul, "kill them; the greater will be our gain!" Ah! this does not finish the sketch of your situation. It would appear that justice had fled from this world, leaving you to the caprice of your oppressors, who become each day more furious toward you; that, through witnesses and false charges, although the grounds may be insufficient, you may be interred in the penitentiaries, if you are not previously deprived of life by some keeper who covers himself from responsibility by the pretence of your flight. There are to be found criminals covered with frightful crimes, but they appear to have impunity until opportunity furnish them a victim; to these monsters indulgence is shown, because they are not of our race, which is unworthy, as they say, to belong to the human species. . . .

Mexicans! Is there no remedy for you? Inviolable laws, yet useless, serve, it is true, certain judges and hypocritical authorities, cemented in evil and injustice, to do whatever suits them, and to satisfy their vile avarice at the cost of your patience and suffering; rising in their frenzy, even to the taking of life, through the treacherous hands of their bailiffs. The wicked way in which many of you have been oftentimes involved in persecution, accompanied by circumstances making it the more bitter, is now well known; these crimes being hid from society under the shadow of a horrid night, those implacable people, with the haughty spirit which suggests impunity for a life of criminality, have pronounced, doubt ye not, your sentence, which is, with accustomed insensibility, as you have seen, on the point of execution.

Mexicans! My part is taken; the voice of revelation whispers to me that to me is entrusted the work of breaking the chains of your slavery, and that the Lord will enable me, with powerful arm, to fight against our enemies, in compliance with the requirements of that Sovereign Majesty, who, from this day forward, will hold us under His protection. On my part, I am ready to offer myself as a sacrifice for your happiness; and counting upon the means necessary for the discharge of my ministry, you may count upon my cooperation, should no cowardly attempt put an end to my days. This undertaking will be sustained on the following bases:

First: A society is organized in the State of Texas, which devotes itself sleeplessly until the work is crowned with success, to the improvement of the unhappy condition of those Mexicans resident therein; exterminating their tyrants, to which end those which compose it are ready to shed their blood and suffer the death of martyrs.

Second: As this society contains within itself the elements necessary to accomplish the great end of its labors, the veil of impenetrable secrecy covers "The Great Book" in which the articles of its constitution are written; while so delicate are the difficulties which must be overcome that no honorable man can have cause for alarm, if imperious exigencies require them to act without reserve.

Third: The Mexicans of Texas repose their lot under the good sentiments of the governor elect of the state, General Houston, and trust that upon his elevation to power he will begin with care to give us legal protection within the limits of his powers.

Mexicans! Peace be with you! Good inhabitants of the State of Texas, look on them as brothers, and keep in mind that which the Holy Spirit saith: "Though shalt not be the friend of the passionate man; nor join thyself to the madman, lest thou learn his mode of work and scandalize thy soul."

✎ E S S A Y S

The Spanish-speaking population of the Southwest constituted a new racial and ethnic population in the United States. Their civil, property, and religious rights as American citizens, although protected by the Treaty of Guadalupe Hidalgo, were not respected. Eventual loss of political power threatened the civil liberties of Mexican Americans, who experienced a double standard of justice and growing economic competition from the Anglos. Many of the landowning elites lost their lands, while the majority of the new American citizens of Mexican descent entered the ranks of wage labor. Conflict between Mexicans and Anglos was inevitable in such a climate of race hatred and violence in which resentment and animosity between the two groups grew.

Anti-Mexican sentiment among Americans had originated from the time of Spanish control of the Southwest, but it intensified between 1821 and in the years after the Treaty of Guadalupe Hidalgo as a result of increased contact between Mexicans and Americans. The origins of such bad feelings in the California gold rush is the subject of the first essay by Leonard Pitt, professor of history at California State University, Northridge. He argues that historians have failed to examine the relationship between the rise of nativism in California and the efforts to stabilize the state's economy, the strong opposition to exclusivism, and the anti-Mexican attitudes of California's middle class. In her essay, Antonia I. Castañeda, associate professor of history at Saint Mary's University, San Antonio, Texas, seeks to break the pattern of stereotypical thought toward Californianas by examining such stereotypes in the American literary works that served as primary sources for historical narratives and popular accounts of early California. She concludes that because these stereotyped images changed over time, according to the needs of the American capitalist and imperialist system, this literature has obscured the historical reality of Mexican women from the nineteenth century to the twentieth century. Castañeda confronts many of the questions now being raised by Chicana and feminist historians about the experiences of the early Mexican women of the Southwest.

In the last essay Arnoldo De Léon, professor of history at San Angelo State University, San Angelo, Texas, provides a historical overview of the Mexico-Tejano community after the Texas Revolution of 1836. He argues that although their culture remained the same, the social, economic, and political fortunes of the Spanish-speaking residents of Texas underwent considerable change. Because of deeply rooted Anglo racism, a reign of violence figured prominently in the transformation of life in Texas for the Mexicano-Tejanos, who now were outnumbered by Anglos. Despite clashes such as those that unfolded in south Texas between Juan Cortina and the Anglos, Tejanos were continuously victimized by racial conflict.

The Origins of Nativism in California

LEONARD PITT

[California] Nativism was born in the months of 1849 and early 1850 when mining enterprise was most individualistic, government most ineffectual, and immigration most rapid. Statistics suggest the problem: early in 1849, 4,000 or 5,000 men were in the mines, at the end of the year 40,000 or 50,000, and by 1852, 100,000. . . . Agencies to control such a vast, mobile, and individualistic population were limited. The army of occupation was too weak to impose its will upon California, and the Congress, which theoretically retained full constitutional authority over the public domain, was too preoccupied elsewhere to formulate consistent policy. *De facto* government receded into the mining camps and problems of order were handled piecemeal, according to the miners' good sense and nonsense. Even if foreign immigrants had never set foot in California, that territory would have suffered from an acute case of social disorganization brought on by rapid physical and social mobility.

For the Yankee, the normal discomforts of such a life were intensified immeasurably in 1849 by the sudden arrival of waves of Pacific immigrants—Mexicans, Chileans, Peruvians, Australians, and Pacific Islanders. By race and class this was an unusual immigration: except for the freebooting Australians, most were lowly bondsmen traveling in the company of their masters. These parties could swiftly set to work and outdig any couple of hundred independent prospectors. Sheer economic jealousy, therefore, brought on the first xenophobia and throughout 1849 the wildest rumors were circulated: organized "foreign capitalists" would pack off with four to nine million in gold and leave behind a scum of "degraded underlings" before the Yankees had a chance to get started; 10,000 Mexican miners "started up by the great capitalists and friends of Santa Anna" would seize California by force; 50,000 hungry, poor, and immoral wretches from Pacific countries would impoverish the state, for even now it had barely enough food to go around. . . .

The first attempt to cope with immigration was made by the army. In 1848 Oregon Yankees had clashed with naturalized native Californians but gold was still plentiful and after each side sustained a few bruises all ended well. Military Governor Richard B. Mason advised Washington that although some of the immigrants were obnoxious he saw no way to keep them out and was following an expedient policy of laissez-faire immigration. But his successor, General Persifor F. Smith, while traveling from Panama to California in January, 1849, was prevailed upon by a mass meeting of Yankees at the Isthmus port to discourage Pacific immigrants from crowding onto American ships. Smith issued a circular to all American consuls in Pacific ports declaring that in California he would "consider everyone, not a citizen of the United States who enters upon public land and digs for gold . . . a trespasser." Americans vowed solemnly to find the means of putting his policy into practice.

This was not an idle boast. . . . Although Smith's pronouncement had "but little effect" in cutting down immigration at its sources, and although the army was impotent to impose that or any other edict in the mines, "some Yankees who had arrived by water" called a meeting at Sutter's Mill in April and were able to put teeth into the "doctrine of trespass." The crowd purged the neighborhood of all Chileans, Mexicans, and Peruvians—on the grounds that they had "no right" to occupy any claim. Many were chased to other diggings. Some sought relief in San Francisco but were set upon by a "patriotic" company of veterans called "The Hounds.". . . In August and September the Hispanos were again systematically harrassed in the southern diggings (Mariposa, Stanislaus, and Tuolumne counties) and were forced to scamper to new mining sites, unless they could find employment with American protectors. . . .

. . . [In 1849 the first California legislature] immediately took up the problem of immigration. Their only hesitation was how exactly to draw the line against noncitizens and monopolists. The Assembly listened with greatest interest to a report submitted by Representative Tingley as he groped after words to express his contempt of the immigrants:

> Devoid of intelligence sufficient to appreciate the true principles of a free form of government; vicious, indolent, and dishonest, to an extent rendering them obnoxious to our citizens; with habits of life low and degraded; an intellect but one degree above the beast of the field, and not susceptible of elevation; all these things combined render such classes of human beings a curse to any enlightened community.

The legislature, voting on a series of joint resolutions to Congress, accepted Tingley's radical suggestion and voted to ask Congress to keep all persons of foreign birth out of the mines—even naturalized citizens. Later, however, this resolution became entangled with an antimonopoly resolution which was equally radical (it proposed to prohibit the sale or lease of mining claims) and was rejected along with it. Officially, Congress remained uninstructed.

In Washington Senator John C. Frémont read the early reports of the debate and hastily estimated the legislature's wants. He proposed a Gold Bill which would "bar monied capitalists" and all noncitizens as well. The Senate approved his bill, although it voted to allow European noncitizens into the mines. The House, however, tabled the measure. By this action Congress forfeited its prerogative concerning tenure and immigration on the public domain; it was never to regain the initiative.

Since Congress was so indecisive in enforcing its constitutional powers, declared State Senator Thomas Jefferson Green, California was compelled to fall back upon "universal laws . . . higher, greater, and stronger than the written constitution." He asked that the state impose upon the foreign miners a monthly tax of twenty dollars. Green had as much contempt for servile immigrants as had exclusionists and had once written that he could "maintain a better stomach at the killing of a Mexican than at the killing" of a louse, but he preferred not to expel them. He was chairman of the Senate Finance Committee and was sorely pressed to find revenue for a bankrupt treasury. . . . Green explained how California might secure a steady source of labor by issuing pass permits to foreigners: "Upon the arrival in our waters of shiploads of foreign operatives . . . [an American] can employ their services at a fair rate, and advance money for their license(s), which he holds until the labor is performed according to contract." The permits, he asserted, would pacify Americans while enriching the state by $200,000 each month. Thus the Foreign Miners' Tax of 1850 was not an exclusionist measure as has been assumed, but a system of taxation and indenture. Its object was to exploit alien caste laborers rather than expel them and to aid American mining capitalists by blocking foreign capitalists. Having found what seemed an easy solution to the problems of labor, tenure, and immigration, the legislature approved the bill overwhelmingly, by a vote of seven to four in the Senate and nineteen to four in the Assembly. . . .

Expulsionists had their day in the enforcement of the tax. A delegation representing 3,000 Frenchmen and Hispanos (out of a total of some 10,000 foreign-born in the neighborhood) declared to the collector of Tuolumne County that they could pay a tax of four or five dollars but were prepared to resist the "petty tyrants" who asked for twenty. The collector refused to compromise, and after obtaining the co-operation of the sheriff and local judge in prohibiting merchants from selling them any more goods, sent for a posse. From Mormon Gulch came 150 Mexican War veterans flourishing rifles and pistols, waving their old regimental colors, decked out in the remnants of their military uniforms and marching to the cadence of a battered bugle and drum. Sonora, normally a peaceful town, seethed with rumors of Mexican incendiarism, assassination, and massacre. In the hysteria one unfortunate Mexican who blundered into an argument with the sheriff was killed. By nightfall the town had "assumed the appearance of . . . martial law."

The following day, 400 troopers toured the diggings collecting the tax from the few miners who could afford it and chasing the others away.

> Alas! as we marched along [wrote a member of the posse], what a scene of confusion . . . marked out the way. Tents were being pulled down, houses and hovels gutted of their contents; mules, horses, and jackasses were being hastily packed, while crowds were already in full retreat. What could have been the object of our assembly, except as a demonstration of power and determination, I know not; but if intended as an engine of terror it certainly had the desired effect, for it could be seen painted upon every countenance, and impelling every movement of the affrighted population. . . .

Crimes committed by foreigners provided the pretext for a second wave of expulsions which coursed through the same diggings two months later. Clues from a score of heinous murders pointed darkly to a band of Mexican robbers (actually identified later as Mexicans, Australians, Americans, and Indians). Three suspected Hispanos narrowly escaped a lynching and were tried and acquitted in the presence of 400 surly spectators, including the Mormon Gulch battalion which again came to Sonora "bearing the American flag and marching a la militaire." Suspecting that the culprits were commanded by a "notorious Mexican chief," the troops herded all the men of a nearby Mexican camp into the town corral, but the local justice of the peace adjudged each suspect innocent and declared an official end to the "craze of murther against 110 Greesers." . . .

Burdened with compromises meant to satisfy all its dissident proponents, the foreign miners' tax broke down in practice. It succeeded in eliminating many foreigners from the mines, but failed to drive enough of the remaining bondsmen into the arms of American employers, and instead of reducing conflict in the mines it provided new pretexts for trouble. . . . Most significantly the tax failed to enrich the treasury. In its first year it yielded a paltry $30,000 instead of the expected $2,400,000. The brash collector of Tuolumne County was lucky enough to sell 525 permits in the first months after his show of force, but when the tax opponents enveloped him with litigation and destroyed his prestige, his sales declined and he quit in disgust. The governor, realizing that the collectors were reaping more resentment than revenue, cut the levy to twenty dollars for five months. . . .

Outright repeal of the tax, delayed temporarily by a decision of the California Supreme Court, was merely a few months away. Opponents had harried a collector all the way up through the court system arguing that the tax violated the state and federal constitutions and contravened various treaties with foreign powers. The court, however, jealously anxious to adopt a state rights philosophy in matters involving federal jurisdiction, interpreted the tax so as to sustain the collector. It held that California's power of taxation remained inviolate as long as Congress did not specifically proscribe it and that the state retained police powers against undesirables. Gratuitously it added that even if the law had contravened a treaty protecting foreigners—which it had not—the rights of the state might still take precedence. This was a key decision, subsequently providing support for many laws discriminating against foreigners and immediately encouraging the governor to send out new collectors to enforce the tax. . . .

In 1852 the legislature was again compelled to debate whether to curtail or utilize immigrants. . . .

Shock waves emanating from the debates in the state capital flowed into the diggings. . . . In mid-May miners at Columbia . . . expelled all Asiatics from their camp and the taboo ritual spread to seven nearby locations taking on local variations as it went. By a coincidence the nativist tremors reached the remotest camps in the north and south almost simultaneously. . . . The "Shirley Letters" graphically describe an incident at Indian Bar, a northern camp from which all foreigners had been exiled, where some Hispanos were flogged for homicide by a lively fraternity of viligantes.

At Mariposa Creek in the southern diggings a self-appointed ranger company, led by "Captain" Reynolds, arrested a Mexican operator and twenty menials in defiance of some 400 outraged Mexicans and Frenchmen. Reynolds auctioned off the operator's dirt and equipment, assigning $1,000 to the crowd of Americans in recompense for time lost in mining. A sheriff reported to the local newspaper that actually some vigilantes were unnaturalized Europeans while some of their victims were Californians who had become naturalized Americans.

Reynolds' rangers methodically scoured the hills exiling all "Spaniards, China-men, Manilamen and Mexicans." Summer dissipated nativist energies and en-couraged antinativists to rise in protest, but fall saw the miners at Jamestown and Sonora again resolved to expel the "countless hordes of low and servile Asiatics and Mexicans." In all the permutations of 1852 there was one constant element: the Foreign Miners' Tax had gone into effect without opposition and was bring-ing in money.

In the four years since the beginning of agitation, policy makers, searching for a way out of a difficult problem, had doubled back in their tracks several times. They had tried to keep foreigners out of the state, to expel them from the mines, to exploit them and to encourage them to come from abroad. It is clear, however, that the problem was significantly different in 1852 than it had been in 1849. Capitalist mining operations had matured and companies now profitably utilized cheap labor to build dams and flumes. Within a year foreign labor would be applied to a newly-mechanized quartz industry. Furthermore, foreign companies had been altogether eliminated and Mexican immigration had been cut to a minimum. And the official policy over the supply of labor had taken a new turn: the state was now sure of its authority to encourage modified exploitationism; it established a tax which was to remain on the books until 1870, constituting throughout that period the largest sin-gle source of state revenue.

The Chinese paid the bulk of the tax. But they were newcomers; the "Chinese Question" which was soon to loom so large in California history was a relatively late development. It was only in 1852 that the Asiatics began arriving in numbers sufficiently great—10,000 in that year—to replace the Hispanos as the leading mi-nority. But even in 1853 Yankees spilled more blood in quelling Mexican bandits than in ousting Chinese "coolies." . . .

As the nativist vanguard carried its banner to California it signified that its tac-tics and strategy were quite unlike that of its eastern counterparts. . . .

. . . The chief reason why California nativists moved on a tangent away from Anglo-Saxonism, anti-Catholicism and anti-radicalism was that their struggles arose from rural social traditions. Instead of modeling themselves after working-class rioters on the streets of Boston, California nativists drew on the techniques devised by rangers deploying on the Texas border to put down Indians and Mexi-cans, soldiers instituting martial law in Mexico, southern white planters checking Negro rebels, and earlier frontiersmen seeking to impose order where none yet ex-isted. . . .

. . . It is difficult to prove that the instigators of nativist policy in California were rabble or that the respectable, responsible class was derelict in its concern for order. . . . The evidence seems to suggest, on the contrary, that nativism arose among men spurred to action by an excessive zeal for order rather than among men lurching toward dissoluteness. Xenophobia had begun as a selfish economic de-fense but had broadened to a moralistic campaign. Notwithstanding the crudities of some of the men who participated in the clashes of 1849 or the working-class ori-gins of the men who responded to the agitation of Denis Kearney on the sand lots of San Francisco just thirty years later, the earliest nativism originated in the "re-spectable" middle class.

Anglo American Stereotypes of Californianas

ANTONIA I. CASTAÑEDA

Richard Henry Dana in *Two Years Before the Mast* (published anonymously in 1840), presented the first major image of Mexican women in California. Dana, the scion of a cultivated patrician family in Cambridge, Massachusetts, sailed to California on the *Pilgrim*, a ship belonging to Bryant, Sturgis, and Company, the major American firm engaged in the hide and tallow trade. In this work, Dana recorded his experiences as a sailor as well as his impressions of the country, the land and the people he saw on his journey during his two years aboard ship.

Dana has little to say of a positive nature about Mexican people in general. His views of Mexican women, which center on virtue, are moralistic and judgmental. According to Dana, "The fondness for dress among the women is excessive, and is sometimes their ruin. A present of a fine mantel, or a necklace or pair of earrings gains the favor of a greater part. Nothing is more common than to see a woman living in a house of only two rooms, with the ground for a floor, dressed in spangled satin shoes, silk gown, high comb, gilt if not gold, earrings and necklace. If their husbands do not dress them well enough, they will soon receive presents from others." Therefore, Dana points out, "the women have but little virtue," and "their morality is, of course, none of the best." Although the "instances of infidelity are much less frequent than one would at first suppose," Dana attributes this to "the extreme jealousy and deadly revenge of their husbands." To this Yankee patrician, Mexican women are profligate, without virtue and morals, whose excesses are only kept in check by a husband's vengeful wrath. In this narrative Mexican women are seen as purely sexual creatures.

Dana's work, which had immediate success in the United States and England, set the precedent for negative images of Mexican women in California. He created the image of Mexicanas as "bad" women. This condemnation of Mexican women's virtue appears again and again in subsequent works. The view of Mexicanas as women of easy virtue and latent infidelity easily led to the stereotype of the Mexicana as prostitute in the literature of the gold rush.

While Dana's writing attempted to convey the impression of an interested but rather detached objective observer of California's people and life, Thomas Jefferson Farnham's *Travels in California and Scenes in the Pacific Ocean*, published in 1844–45, was sensationalistic and vituperative. Farnham, a lawyer, came to California from Illinois by way of Oregon. He arrived in Monterey in 1841. . . . Farnham described his travels on the Pacific Coast. . . . Throughout his account Farnham consistently derided the Californianos. In his words, "the Californians are an imbecile, pusillanimous race of men, and unfit to control the destinies of that beautiful country." In clear, direct and hostile terms, Farnham echoed the same sentiment that Dana and others had expressed with more subtlety, replacing passionate partisanship for the previous pretense of objectivity.

Antonia I. Castañeda, "The Political Economy of Nineteenth Century Stereotypes of Californianas," in Adelaida R. Del Castillo, ed., *Between Borders: Essays on Mexicana/Chicana History* (Encino, Calif. Floricanto Press, 1990). Reprinted with permission by Floricanto Press: www.floricantopress.com.

The Californiano's mixed racial background is a constant theme in Farnham's narrative. It is also the focus of his blunt comment on women, of whom he states "The ladies, dear creatures, I wish they were whiter, and that their cheekbones did not in their great condescension assimilate their manners and customs so remarkably to their Indian neighbors." Unlike Dana, who was, at times, ambivalent about the racial characteristics and beauty of the elite Californianas, Farnham was clear about their racial origins and his own racial views.

Like Dana, Farnham was also concerned with the Californiana's dress and appearance. While Dana focused on the extravagance of dress, Farnham centered on the looseness of the clothing and the women's "indelicate" form. "A pity it is," notes Farnham, "that they have not stay and corset makers' signs among them, for they allow their waists to grow as God designed they should, like Venus de Medici, that ill-bred statue that had no kind mother to lash its vitals into delicate form." Since Californian women do not lash their own or their daughter's "vitals into delicate form," they obviously are neither proper themselves nor are raising proper daughters for California. Farnham would have women's dress hide their form in the multiple layers of clothing that simultaneously hid the bodies of middle-class women in the United States and severely limited their physical mobility. Although Farnham made few additional direct statements about women, he did relate the woeful tale of a Southern lad's romance with a Californiana. The young man, who was ready to bequeath her all his worldly goods, was left bereft by the infidelity of his Californiana sweetheart. For Farnham, whose work justified the fillibustering efforts of foreigners in California, Mexican women had no redeeming qualities.

Alfred Robinson, while no less concerned than Dana or Farnham with Californiana's virtue, morality, race and appearance, countered his countrymen's negative image by presenting the polar opposite view—albeit only of upper-class women—in his work, *Life in California,* published in 1846. Unlike Dana, who spent only a short time in California, or Farnham, who came in 1841, Robinson had been in California since 1829 and was on intimate terms with the Californianos. . . .

Robinson interspersed descriptions of women's physical appearance, dress, manners, conduct and spiritual qualities throughout his work. In this book, Californianas are universally chaste, modest, virtuous, beautiful, industrious, wellbred aristocratic Spanish ladies. "With vice so prevalent amongst the men," Robinson states in his most explicit passage, "the female portion of the community, it is worthy of remark, do not seem to have felt its influence, and perhaps there are few places in the world where, in proportion to the number of inhabitants, can be found more chastity, industrious habits, and correct deportment, than among the women of this place." Robinson defended the morals, virtue and racial purity of elite Californianas. By making racial and class distinctions among Californianas he transformed the image of immoral, bad and sexual women into the image of the sexually pure, good Californiana.

Dana and Farnham cast Mexican women into molds of the women of easy virtue, no morals and racial inferiority. Robinson cast elite Californianas into the stereotype of a genteel, well bred Spanish aristocrat with virtue and morals intact. Her European ancestry and aristocratic background, to say nothing of her economic value, made her worthy of marriage. Dana and Farnham, in their concern with the Californiana's race, virtue and morals set the parameters of the stereotype. Robinson accepted the parameters and addressed the same issues.

Recently, these nineteenth century narratives have attracted the attention of scholars and others working in Chicano, Women's, California and Southwestern history and culture. While Chicano historians and other scholars have noted the existence of contradictory stereotypes of women, few have examined the nature of these dual images. Generally, these scholars have attributed Mexicano stereotypes to historical Hispanophobia, anti-Catholicism, racial prejudice and to the economic and political issues involved in the Mexican-American War. . . .

My research leads me to concur with the conclusions of earlier studies that nineteenth century North American literature on California expressed an ideological perspective reflecting an economic interest in California, that the stereotypes of Mexicanos, including those of women, functioned as instruments of conquest, and thus served the political and economic interests of an expanding United States. However, . . . the stereotypes of women were not static; they changed across time—from the pre-War period, through the War, the gold rush and the late Victorian era. The changing images of Mexicanas in California, . . . were consistent with the economic and socio-political needs of a changing U.S. capitalist and imperialist system.

Initially, the pejorative images of Mexican people, which derived from the authors' firm belief in Anglo America's racial, moral, economic and political superiority, served to devalue the people occupying a land base the United States wanted to acquire—through purchase if possible, by war if necessary. The values of supremacy, including male supremacy, expressed in the creation of negative stereotypes and embedded in the notion of Manifest Destiny, were central to America's ideology—an ideology based on the exclusion of non-whites from the rights and privileges of American democratic principles and institutions. Thus, the early negative stereotypes of Mexican people focused on their racial characteristics and alleged debased condition. These stereotypes appeared regardless of class or circumstance of the writers. Their writings uniformly portrayed the same image of Mexicanos whether the latter were encountered in the Mexican interior or in Mexico's northernmost provinces. . . .

The changing image of Mexican women . . . derived from America's unfolding system of beliefs and ideas about sex and race, as well as about economic and political expansion. With reference to Mexicanas, these images functioned on two levels: first, as rationalization for war and conquest and, second, as rationalization for the subordination of women. . . .

Although the image of woman sheltered from the competition of the marketplace was generally appropriate only for middle-class women, by the mid-nineteenth century the notion of woman as the purveyor of a people's morality was being applied to all women in general. The American woman became the symbol of the country's innocence, morality, and virtue; she was held almost solely responsible for the morality and virtue of the nation. Thus, in the 1840s, women's value was not only determined by her newly defined gender-specific roles, but she represented the moral strength of her country. This view of women was part of the ideological framework within which North American authors, most of whom were from the middle class, perceived, interpreted and judged the Mexican female in California.

Anglo American male writers assigned to Mexican women the same social value based on gender specific norms and roles they assigned to white womanhood in the United States. However, for Mexican women, the dimension of race was also integral to the judgment of their virtue and morality. Nineteenth century Anglo Americans' views of Mexican people as racially inferior are well-documented and need not be elaborated here. What does need to be understood is that in terms of women, America's racial bias against Mexicanos coalesced with the moral judgment of women and hardened into a stereotype of Mexicanas as both racially and morally inferior, with one reinforcing the other in a most pernicious way. . . . The most salient stereotype of Mexicanas in the pre-War literature is that of the racially inferior sexual creature—the "bad" woman of easy virtue and no morality. In America's ideological framework, racially inferior people found wanting in moral strength deserved to lose their country. Stereotypes of Mexican women's morality not only encompassed both the sexual and racial dimensions, but were also the basis for moral judgments about Mexican people as a whole.

While Anglo women in industrializing North America were being economically displaced and entombed in the virtues of domesticity, Mexican women in agro-pastoral California were an economic asset. Hispanic law protected women's property rights and gave them equal inheritance rights with males. Mexicanas held an economic power their North American sisters were rapidly losing. Mexican women's economic significance did not escape the Anglos' perception or appropriation; and it clearly affected the creation of a new image—a counter to the pejorative stereotype of the "bad" woman.

From the mid 1820s to the end of Mexican rule, a number of intermarriages between elite Californianas and Anglo males were celebrated in California. Most of the Anglos who married Californianas prior to the North American occupation acquired land through their marriage. The land grants often became the basis for vast wealth.

Californiana-Anglo marriages were occurring at the moment that commercial capitalism of international proportions was penetrating the developing agro-pastoral economy of Alta California. The nascent economy, based on the rise of private property and the corollary rise of an elite *ranchero* class of large landowners, was tied through the hide and tallow trade to European, Latin American and North American markets. Manufactured goods and products from these markets were being rapidly introduced into this remote Mexican province. At the same time, Mexican women, particularly elite women, held significant economic power as large property owners in their own right, as conveyors of property to others, and as consumers in a nascent but expanding market. Most of the Anglos who married Californianas were merchants and traders who were directly related to the development of commerce in California. Marriage to an elite Californiana, in addition to landed wealth, also established family and kinship ties with the largest Californiano landowners. Marriage solidified class alliances between Anglo merchants and the Californiano elite, who were jointly establishing control of California's economy. The image of Californianas as "good" women emerged from these marriages and economic alliances on the eve of the Mexican-American War. . . .

As the United States consolidated its conquest of California and the Southwest in the post-War period, the negative and positive images of Mexicanas and

Californianas hardened into stereotypes of the Mexican prostitute and the romantic, but fading Spanish beauty that still plague us today. In the literature of the gold
rush the negative views of women's morality were generalized to Mexicanas and
Latinas who migrated to California during the period. These views found continued expression in the almost singular depiction of Mexicanas/Latinas as fandango
dancers, prostitutes and consorts of Mexican bandits. The pejorative stereotype of
Mexicanas as women of easy virtue was cemented into the image of the volatile,
sensuous, Mexican prostitute. It is significant that Juanita (Josefa) of Downieville,
the only woman hanged during the gold rush era, was Mexicana. For her, the image, the beliefs and the ideas that manufactured them, had dire consequences.

The commonly advanced notion that women, due to their scarcity in the
Mother Lode, were afforded moral, emotional and physical protection and respect
by Anglo miners, does not hold for Mexican women. Mexicanas, as part of the
conquered nation, and as part of the group of more knowledgeable, experienced
and initially successful miners competing with Anglos in the Placers, became one
object of the violence and lawlessness directed against Mexicanos/Latinos. Mexican women's gender did not protect them from the brutality of racism or the rapac-
ity attendant in the competition for gold. . . . For Mexicanas in the gold rush era,
the combined force of sexism, racism and economic interest resulted in a hardening of pejorative stereotypes which further impugned their sex and their race.

The image of the woman of easy virtue, firmly fixed in the literature in the
years preceeding the war, easily transformed into the Mexican prostitute. It further
helped to justify the exclusion of Mexicanos/Latinos from the mines and rationalized their subordination in California. With specific reference to women but also
inclusive of men, the literature of the post-War/gold rush era further cemented the
earlier shift that divided Mexican women along racial and class lines.

Negative stereotypes of women from the post-War period to the end of the
nineteenth century were specifically applied to Mexicanas and Latinas who migrated to California from Mexico and Latin America. Newspaper accounts make a
distinction between Mexicanas/Latinas and Californianas. Mexicanas are prostitutes and would remain so for the rest of the century—Californianas are not.

In the literature of the late nineteenth century, Robinson's positive image of
Californianas as aristocratic Spanish ladies was picked up, further elaborated and
generalized to women living in California prior to the Mexican-American War.
And in the pre-War period, now romanticized as the "splendid idle forties," and the
"halcyon days of long ago," Californianas are depicted as gentle reposing souls
sweetly attending to the sublime domestic duties of ministering to large households of family and Indian servants on their *caballero* husband's baronial estate. If
single, these gay and beautiful Spanish *senoritas* are in a constant flurry of girlish
activity and preparation for the next *fiesta* and the next beau—a dashing American,
of course.

The important point here is that this image not only negates Californianas'
mestizo racial origins, ignores or denies the existence of any kind of work and as-
signs them all the attributes of "True Womanhood," it also locates their existence
in a remote, bygone past. They were, but they no longer are. In this representation,
the Mexican prostitute and the Spanish Californiana are totally unrelated by race,
culture, class, history or circumstance. In the former there is immorality, racial im-

purity, degradation and contemporary presence. In the latter there is European racial origins, morality, cultural refinement and historical distance.

Irrespective of the view, the end result was the same. Mexicana or Californiana, both representations rended women in California ignorant, vacuous and powerless. In both cases, her Catholicism and culture made her priest-ridden, male dominated, superstitious and passive. Undemocratic Spanish and Mexican governance made her ignorant. If Mexicana, however, her immorality and racial impurity established her lack of value and exacerbated her ignorance. As part of the conquered Mexican nation, the War confirmed her powerlessness. If Californiana, on the other hand, her racial purity, morality and economic worth elevated her status, making her worthy of marrying an Anglo while dispossessing her of her racial, historical, cultural and class roots. With marriage and a husband's possession of her property, elite Californianas forfeited their economic power. Finally, the Californiana's presence was abstracted to an era long past, her person romanticized. In either case, Mexicana or Californiana, the conquest was complete. . . .

Finally, the early narratives which set the parameters for the dichotomous images of Mexican women were written during the brief Republican period of Mexican California. Yet, these dual images have become the standard view of Californianas for the entire nineteenth century in the historical, as well as the novelistic, poetic and popular literature. The dichotomous stereotypes cast in the 1840s have not only frozen Mexican women into a specific, exceedingly narrow time frame and effectively obscured her historical reality for the nineteenth century, they have also exacerbated the notion of discontinuity between nineteenth and twentieth century Mexican women and their history.

In view of the consistency of the stereotypes, Mexican women appear not to have an historical presence prior to the 1840s, and to exist only as romantic, but fading Spanish beauties after the Mexican-American War. By the turn of the century, Californianas, like their brethren, cease to exist historically. Within this perspective there is no continuity with women prior to the 1840s, nor any room for continuity between Mexicanas who were here during the 1840s and those who migrated from Mexico during the gold rush or who were part of the Mexican migration in the latter part of the century. In the literature, Mexican women's historical existence is defined out of all but a few short years of the nineteenth century. Her historical presence is confined to the 1840s and left to the assumptions, perceptions and interests of Anglo-American entrepreneurs and filibusters who wrote about California in a period of American continental imperialism that resulted in the Mexican-American War.

Life for Mexicans in Texas After the 1836 Revolution

ARNOLDO DE LEÓN

The Spanish-Mexican population [of Texas], excluding soldiers, numbered approximately 2,240 in 1821 and increased to over 4,000 by 1836. San Antonio, Goliad, and Nacogdoches (also Victoria, founded in 1824) remained the main

"Spaniards, Mexicans and Americans," from Arnoldo De León, *The Tejano Community, 1836–1900,* 1982, pp. 4–11, 13–22. Reprinted by permission.

Hispanic settlements, and society continued divided into two classes—the *ricos* and the *pobres*. The former descended from the Canary Islanders of the 1730s or from Spanish families that held government positions, while the latter derived from the mixed-blood *pobladores* and performed common labor. Frontierlike conditions persisted—fear of Indian attacks lingered, manufacturing of essential articles like blankets, shoes, and hats were lacking, and disease was ever-present. In the same period, Mexican Texas begin taking on Anglo features as white men from the United States commenced arriving by the hundreds.

Events in Mexico between 1821 and 1836 touched the lives of the Tejanos only peripherally. The substance and structure of local government remained the same after 1821. Political vicissitudes in Mexico City did little to alter those affairs, and the transition to the state government of Coahuila y Tejas did not disrupt the daily lives of Tejanos. They enjoyed a salutary rule over themselves and exercised some influence on issues at the state level.

No dramatic historical modifications disturbed the cultural structure of the Mexican-Tejano community. Traditions and institutions of the colonial era continued. . . . Towns retained standard forms. . . . Life for the common folks, who lived generally in jacales, centered around the *barrios* and *vecindarios* (neighboring populace). At this level, a resident *comisario* (or judge of the barrio) saw to the social welfare and administrative well-being of their respective neighborhoods.

In the countryside, the *rancherías* reflected the cultural patterns of town life, . . . many of the owners were the wealthier citizens of the urban communities. Ranches in the area between Béxar and Goliad, which had been almost deserted after Indian attacks in the 1810s, experienced a resurrection. . . . They dotted the entire stretch on both sides of the San Antonio River and its tributaries. . . .

The work force was poorer day laborers. With the United States now a potential market, ranch hands rode into the countryside, selected cattle from the huge herds, and drove the animals into makeshift *corrales*. They then separated, counted, branded or marked the cattle and prepared them for the *correduría* (drive) up the Camino Real from Béxar or Goliad to Nacogdoches. As many as 20,000 cattle . . . left Texas annually for the United States via this route. The entire operation borrowed from the ranch techniques perfected by mestizo ancestors in the days when the rancho functioned as a frontier institution. . . .

Only a limited number pursued nonagricultural work. Censuses of the period show only a small corps of artisans who earned their living as tailors, carpenters, blacksmiths, or masons. Many Tejanos engaged in the transportation of goods by using oxen to pull *carretas* (carts). The skill they displayed in training oxen or wild range bulls for their trade enabled them to dominate the carting industry until the 1850s.

Entertainment resembled that of previous years. Municipalities, reflecting the continuity of old communal traditions, took the lead in the preparations for social functions. . . . The *Junta Patriótica* (Patriotic Committee), . . . involved itself in the official celebration of such events as Constitution Day, the Feast of Corpus Cristi, Christmas, Good Thursday and Friday, the Feast of San Felipe de Jesús, the Feast of the Virgen de Guadalupe, and the newer holiday of *Diez y Seis de Septiembre* (Sixteenth of September). . . .

Fandangos held at dancing and gaming halls or in the plaza attracted a fair portion of the population. . . .

Other entertainment forms . . . included billiards, ball games, cockfights, and raffles. . . .

As for religion, Tejanos practiced a nominal frontier Catholicism. The Catholic Church had all but abandoned its work in Mexico's far northern frontier during this period. . . . The Catholic presence of old was an anachronism, and instruction from the top had ended in inaction. . . .

. . . Tejanos possessed a creative and regenerative folk tradition. Folklore provided an essential world view. . . . It . . . identified them with their environment, provided community solidarity, and gave them a dignified view of themselves and their life style. . . .

Tejanos also employed folklore to express intimate feelings about courtships, relations between relatives. . . .

The Anglo-Texan victory over the Mexican army in 1836 and the resulting independence from Mexico marked a major institutional change for Tejanos. The revolution introduced new ways of doing things, a new language and a new socioeconomic and political order. Rapidly, Tejanos became virtually foreigners in their native land. The future seemed to augur travail. . . .

. . . Offenses against Tejanos continued long after memories of the Alamo and Goliad abated. . . . Such transgressions sprang from deeply rooted Anglo American attitudes. American responses to the native Tejanos were shaped by feelings against Catholics and Spaniards and antipathy to Indians and Negroes. . . .

. . . Anglos brought with them racial views affected by the long frontier association with red men and black. . . . The great majority . . . hailed from west of the Appalachians and South of the Ohio River, with such areas as Louisiana, Alabama, Arkansas, Tennessee, Missouri, Mississippi, Georgia, and Kentucky strongly represented. Many were Eastern born but had been part of the frontier movement before settling in the state. Because of this Southern and frontier-oriented culture they imported a certain suspicion of dark-skinned people and an obstinate belief that the mores of their own . . . institutions . . . should apply in the new frontier.

The immigrants, then, did not arrive in Texas with open minds concerning the native Tejanos: their two-hundred-year experience with "different" peoples had so shaped their psyche that their immediate reaction was negative. . . . Most of the immigrants . . . , despite their honest, industrious habits, were racists. They had retained impressions acquired before their arrival in the state then reapplied and transposed those racial attitudes upon the native castas. White men had an inherent distaste for miscegenation, were acutely mindful of the significance of color, and assumed an aura of superiority and condescension toward the natives. Racial and ethnocentric feeling were evident from the very start. . . .

In the fifteen years before the Texas Revolution, the attitudes whites held toward Mexicans influenced their response to living under Mexican rule. Whites, who outnumbered the native Tejanos by ten to one in 1836, were not about to countenance being ruled . . . by a people who in their view resembled Negroes and Indians, were inclined toward lethargy and indolence, and who spent their days gambling and doing lascivious dances. And, while the Revolution erased that possibility, it did not set aside already hardened feelings against both the Mexicans of Mexico and those of Texas.

Such attitudes, combined with political and economic competition, governed the post-1836 relations between Anglos and Tejanos. From 1836 to 1846, the period between the Texas Revolution and the Mexican War, interaction between the two peoples restricted itself to the areas north of the Nueces River and east of San Antonio, but primarily to the old Tejano settlements of Goliad, Victoria, and Béxar. It was there that Tejanos held a firm grasp of the land base, dominated certain occupations such as that of ranch hands and *arrieros* (cartmen), retained an influence over politics, especially in San Antonio, and made up a substantial element in the society. It was in that region where Anglos were in closest proximity with Tejanos and where rivalry for supremacy first occurred.

In the aftermath of the revolution, Tejanos became the targets of attacks upon their holdings and their honor. Hundreds of Bexareños fled to the ranchos and finally to Coahuila. Those around Nacogdoches sought refuge in Louisiana. Families in the Goliad area sped to Tamaulipas, Nuevo Léon, and Louisiana. Throughout the new republic, many lost their lands through a number of subterfuges, including fictitious law suits, sheriff's sales, and dubious transfers of titles.

Those that remained or returned after a short absence incurred further depredations from individual Anglos acting outside the law. John Browne, an officer in the regular army of Texas, visiting Victoria in 1839

> found it filled with a set of men who [had] given themselves the title of a *band of Brothers*[.] I soon found that what they said was law[.] [T]hey are all in the cow stealing business and are scattered all over this frontier[.]. . . They drove off from Carlos Rancho a Caballarda belonging to Alderetta [José Miguel Aldrete] and [Juan N.] Seguín[,] that the owners know well where their property is but dare not to proceed to recover it.

Harassment and persecution appeared as daily occurrences. In Béxar in the early 1840s, citizens complained that a criminal Anglo element treated them worse than brutes simply because "they were Mexicans." Squatters moved into vacant property previously belonging to Tejanos. In 1842, the precarious situation deteriorated further following the capture of San Antonio by two well-organized expeditions from Mexico in the spring and fall. The second raid enraged the white population and prompted some to consider banishing Tejanos from the Republic. One editorialist proposed:

> there is no faith to be put in them; and until the war is ended, they should be compelled, every one of them, to retire either east or west from the frontier; or if they choose to remain, be subjected to the rigorous treatment due to enemies.

Others formed into vigilante groups and took the law into their own hands. Angry citizens from Victoria, for instance, visited nearby Carlos' Rancho and compelled the fifty or so Mexican families who had settled there to leave the country. In Béxar itself, volunteer soldiers

> acted very badly, having ventured to force the Mexican families from their homes, [causing them]to droop about in the woods and seek shelter wherever they could find it. Moreover to gratify their beastly lusts [they have]compelled the women and Girls to

yield to their hellish desires, which their victims did under the fear of punishment and death.

The rest of the decade did not improve things for the old Tejanos. The Mexican War served only to reinforce ill feelings toward these "sons of the enemy." Yet hostility did not result in a complete exodus. Fifteen hundred of the original Tejanos remained in the old Béxar-Goliad region during the period. By 1850, moreover, 600 Mexican born heads-of-households had entered the region since the revolution, while several hundreds of the émigrés had returned from their refuge to Nacogdoches, Victoria, and "New La Bahía."

New clashes emerged, though, ostensibly over the issue of slavery but based in economic rivalries. Whereas Anglos viewed slavery as essential to economic development in the state, Tejanos understood it as oppression and for years had extended aid to slaves and helped them escape to Mexico. But by 1854, whites had reached the limits of tolerance. The town of Seguín drafted resolutions prohibiting Mexican peons from entering the country and forbidding Mexicans to associate with blacks. In October, delegates from different counties convened in Gonzales and implemented stringent measures to stop the Mexican menace. In Austin, where a citizens' committee accused Mexican residents of horse theft and exiled twenty families from their homes in the spring of 1853, similar resolutions were passed.

Quickly thereafter, a "Cart War" broke out in 1857. While Anglos had wrested much of the economic foundation of the Central Texas region from Mexicanos by the 1850s, skilled arrieros continued monopolizing the freight business between San Antonio in the interior and the coast. White teamsters had sought strenuously to infiltrate the commerce, valued into the millions of dollars, but they had failed to undercut the lower rates charged by Tejano cartmen. During the summer, in the general area between San Antonio and the gulf, . . . they initiated an organized campaign of lawlessness, wanton injury, harassment, assassination, waylaying of carts, and pillaging and confiscating of valuable cargoes. The affair ultimately ended through a combination of pressure from the Mexican government, the American secretary of state, and volunteer companies organizing to bring about order. But many Tejano cartmen had perished in the episode.

On the eve of the Civil War, the old Tejanos of Central Texas were a distinct minority amid an Anglo and European immigrant population. Hispanos now lived along the Indianola-San Antonio road where many earned their livelihood as carters, packers, and drovers. To the west of this area, they lived in all Mexican communities like "New La Bahía" and Alamita, or apart in a particular section of a town, as in the case of San Antonio where they occupied the south and southwest sections of the city along the river and the Laredo road. . . . These early demographic patterns in Central Texas remained generally stable for the remainder of the century.

In the area between the Nueces River and the Rio Grande, the rivalry that appeared in Central Texas did not surface in the years immediately after the Texas Revolution for only a few Anglos penetrated the region which technically belonged to the northern Mexican state of Tamaulipas. . . . Direct competition for livelihood did not occur until later.

The Tamaulipecos owed their origin to the settlements founded by José de Escandón in the 1740s. . . . Approximately 350 rancherías existed in this region by

1835, among them San Diego, San Juan, Palo Blanco, Agua Dulce, El Sauz, Los Olmos, San Luis, Pansacol, Zapata, San Ignacio, and Los Saenz. It was into this area that some of the old Tejanos of the Béxar-Goliad area had fled in their attempts to escape the ire of Anglos in 1836.

Despite Tamaulipas' claim to the region, these Tamaulipecos became Tejanos when the Republic of Texas claimed the Rio Grande as its southern boundary. . . . They . . . became citizens of Texas by settling lands under the new headright program of the Republic. Despite their incorporation into Anglo-Texas, the area in general remained culturally Mexican during this period as only a few Americans ventured into the region. The 1850 census enumerated 1,665 Hispanic heads of households in the Rio Grande Valley. . . .

The ending of the Mexican War in 1848 effected an arrangement comparable to the one in the interior of the state, except that in south Texas the Tejano population remained an overwhelming majority. The birth of Anglo communities like Brownsville, Rio Grande City, Eagle Pass, Roma, and Nuecestown, plus the building of army establishments like Fort Brown, Ringgold Barracks, Fort McIntosh, Fort Inge, Fort Merill, Fort Ewell, and Fort Clark signaled the arrival of white men. The transformation brought with it war veterans and unscrupulous swindlers looking for the most opportune ways of acquiring land and fortune. In the Nueces County area, where all the land belonged to Mexicans at the time of the Texas Revolution, Anglos and Americanized Europeans had wrested it from Tejanos by the time of the Civil War. In the Lower Valley, land grabbers used their acquaintance with the legal system and their association with friends in high places to rob old Mexican grantees. Charles Stillman, for example, used both threat and influence to acquire the valuable *Espiritu Santo* grant. . . . By intermarrying with native Mexican women of the upper class, by developing ties with influential families, and employing political chicanery, the newcomers swiftly gained domination of the real estate and government of South Texas. They now executed the laws to their advantage.

The war also opened an era of disorder as border ruffians of both races preyed upon the property of settlers in the region, most of whom where Tejanos. Anglo American desperadoes treated the Mexicans with open disdain and called them "greasers." Others . . . dealt with them as if they did not count and took advantage of the presence of American authorities to harry them. Resentment against the Anglos finally reached its extreme when on July 13, 1859, an encounter between a local rancher named Juan "Cheno" Cortina [see Document 7] and the Brownsville city marshal left the lawman injured; the incident enraged the Anglo population in the city. For a while the initiative passed to Cortina and his followers as they lay seige to Brownsville and threatened "death to the *gringos*." For too long, Cheno proclaimed, whites had been despoiling Tejanos of their land and prosecuting and robbing them "for no other crime . . . than that of being of Mexican origin." His primary purpose . . . was to seek redress for those wrongs. . . . But by the time Texas Rangers and federal troops extinguished the "insurrection" in early 1860, the episode had left a number of people dead, much property destroyed, and ugly tensions between the two races.

By then, South Texas was divided into two zones—one Anglo, the other Tejano—but bicultural features were appearing as well. The region consisted of a line of new Anglo towns extending from Corpus Christi, to San Patricio, to Beeville, to Pleasanton, down to Uvalde. But a hundred miles of chaparral still separated the Nueces country from the settlements along the Rio Grande where Tejanos enjoyed numerical predominance. Despite the fact that Anglos controlled the major institutions, Mexican culture saturated the border area. . . . Indeed, many of the Anglo and European ranchers and merchants became Hispanicized white men.

During the decade and a half following the Cortina episode, Texas did not change much. . . .

Anglos continued victimizing Tejanos. Around San Marcos, noted a San Antonio newspaper . . . , the trees were "bearing a new kind of fruit," that is, Mexican cattle thieves hung by so-called vigilance committees organized for self-protection against the rustlers infesting that section. In Boerne, where suspicion touched Mexicanos for recent murders and depredations . . . , a party of volunteers from neighboring counties gathered to punish the unknown perpetrators of a wholesale murder that occurred five miles east of town. Upon finding weapons that seemed to fix the crime on the Mexicans, the vigilantes indiscriminately began executing them, slaying seven Mexicans. In Goliad County, a mob lynched Juan Moya and his two sons . . . for allegedly killing a white family. Some days later peace officers captured the real killers, but those who had murdered the Moyas escaped prosecution. These violent attacks were but an extreme form of the racism that frequently surfaced in everyday affairs.

Tejanos in South Texas faced equally violent times. Despite their numerical superiority . . . , the major institutions remained fundamentally in the hands of whites who seemed helpless in checking a veritable war of races between cattle thieves from Mexico and a motley array of Anglo ranchmen, rustlers, and cowboys encountering each other over "unbranded" mavericks. For crimes committed against them, white ranchers and citizens invariably sought vengeance by launching vendettas against local Tejanos. According to Texas Adjutant General William Steele, "a considerable element in the country bordering on the Nueces and west thought the killing of a Mexican no crime." Senator Joseph E. Dwyer similarly reported that terrible outrages were being committed upon citizens of Mexican origin. In Bee County, he continued, whites brutally murdered a Mexican who refused to go play the fiddle for them. Thomas F. Wilson, United States consul at Matamoros, likewise testified that white authorities disregarded aggressions upon Mexicanos and that no one made a great fuss over the hanging or killing of a Mexican in the neighborhood of Brownsville or along the frontier. . . . The San Antonio *Express* . . . remarked that along the border regions "Mexicans were no longer safe upon the highways, or outside of the towns; that they will be shot down as if they were savages," and that a number had already been murdered in cold blood "just because they were Mexicans." There is no telling how many Mexicanos fell victim to the reprisals. . . .

These border troubles subsided . . . as Porfirio Díaz's *rurales* suppressed bandits from Mexico and American troops succeeded in preventing American cattle thieves from penetrating into Mexican territory. The easing of tensions coincided with economic changes taking place throughout the state. Texas entered an incipient phase of modern industrialization as railroads now seemed to connect most points in the state. . . . Béxar County suddenly emerged among the leaders in manufacturing, and San Antonio as the largest city in the state. South Texas now gradually shifted from subsistence agriculture to commercial farming, concentrating on the production of cotton. . . . And for the first time, Anglos began penetrating West Texas en masse as the range cattle industry thrust westward and the sheep and goat industry found a home. Railroads followed, attracting farmers in their wake. Towns now made their appearance in an area where Mexicanos had lived somewhat apart from the Anglo masses for nearly a quarter century after the Mexican war.

In that western region, the Hispanic presence traced its beginnings to Spanish activity in the 1680s. In the nineteenth century, Tejano residents lived in the small communities of Socorro, Ysleta, San Elizario, and El Paso. Anglos had moved into this El Paso Valley in the 1850s, but . . . many assimilated themselves into Hispanic society and became Mexicanized gringos. West Texas settlements like Fort Davis, Fort Stockton, Alpine, and San Angelo grew out of the American westward movement following the Civil War. Mexicans came into those communities shortly thereafter searching for work as shepherds, vaqueros, and farm hands.

Racial friction and economic rivalry in West Texas resulted in the same pattern of violence found elsewhere in the state. In the El Paso Valley, a handful of Anglos in the early 1860s began monopolizing the nearby Guadalupe Salt Lakes upon which Mexican livelihood depended. Animosity slowly mounted and reached a violent peak . . . when the monopolizers closed the lakes to Tejanos and killed Don Luis Cardis, a Mexican sympathizer. . . . Suddenly, the world seemed turned upside down for the small Anglo community in the Valley (5,000 Tejanos, compared to less than 100 whites) as the Mexicans sought to avenge the death of Cardis and regain access to the salt lakes. Finally, help for the Anglos arrived in the form of a company of Ranger volunteers, who were adventurers and other lawless men. They committed wanton outrages, . . . riddling two Mexican prisoners with bullets "unnecessarily and unjustifiably," slaughtering a Mexican and wounding his wife . . . , and committing rapes. . . . This was the infamous "Salt War."

Similar violence typified the newer Anglo communities of West Texas. In the little town of Murphyville (modern Alpine), racial tensions had been increasing as each race talked of running the other out of town. When . . . a number of Mexicans reportedly raided the Cattle Exchange Saloon, gunning down a number of white patrons, armed Anglos swiftly responded, killing some of the Mexicans and driving the rest from town. In the San Angelo area, . . . indignant whites . . . lynched Jesús Salceda in nearby Knickerbocker. . . . Following a feud in Presidio County, white cowboys . . . considered exterminating the Mexican sheepherders.

Tejanos in the two other sections controlled by Hispanics prior to 1836 saw little relief from racism and oppression in the last twenty years of the century. In Cotulla, masked men . . . took Florentino Suaste from the jailer, lynched him from a mesquite limb, and riddled his body with bullets. . . . Whites near Senior, Texas, mutilated and burned Aureliano Castellón for paying romantic attention to a white woman. Fiendish cases of lynching in Eagle Pass and Brownsville in that era attested to the same pattern of violence in South Texas. Troubles plagued the Tejanos in other ways, as when . . . White Cappers in Hays, Wilson, Gonzales, and DeWitt counties called upon landlords to run off Mexican renters and to discharge their Mexican hired hands. . . .

Manifestly, tragedy had befallen the Tejanos after 1836. They had come to live in a world where just about everything from their skin color to their cultural ways evoked perverse racial responses. Anglos saw Tejanos as being the color of "niggers" or resembling the Indians in physiognomy, as being a "race of mongrels" set apart by their physical differences from white men. They imputed to Mexicans a childlike mentality and regarded them as unambitious, indolent and satisfied with grinding poverty. They thought Mexicanos were concerned only with frolic and pleasure, and the pursuit of gambling, dancing, and sleeping the *siesta*. To whites, Mexicanos were a sexually degenerate people lacking any morality. And as if this were not enough, they repeatedly questioned the Tejanos' Americanism, wondering if these people . . . , could have true American sentiments.

White men sought gallantly to keep Tejanos at a distance. . . . Hence, their every effort was directed at handicapping Mexicanos, to make sure that they remained subordinate and economically and politically defenseless. Among the mechanisms that maintained them in powerlessness was employing the Texas Rangers as a legal corps to keep them in their place. Oppression is what the 165,000 Spanish-surnamed Americans of Texas still knew in 1900.

FURTHER READING

María Amparo Ruiz de Burton, *The Squatter and the Don* (1992)

Pedro G. Castillo and Albert Camarillo, *Furia y muerte* (1973)

Robert Glass Cleland, *The Cattle on a Thousand Hills* (1975)

Mario T. García, "Merchants and Dons: San Diego's Attempt at Modernization, 1850–1860," *The Journal of San Diego History* 21 (Winter 1975), 52–80

Deena J. González, "The Widowed Women of Santa Fe: Assessments on the Lives of an Unmarried Population, 1850–80," in Vicki L. Ruiz and Ellen Carol DuBois, eds., *Unequal Sisters* (1990)

Richard Griswold del Castillo, *The Treaty of Guadalupe Hidalgo* (1990)

Charles Hughes, "The Decline of the Californios: The Case of San Diego, 1846–1856," *The Journal of San Diego History* 21 (Summer 1975), 1–31

David J. Langum, "Californios and the Image of Indolence," *Western Historical Quarterly* 9 (April 1978), 181–196

Jacqueline D. Meketa, *Legacy of Honor* (1986)

Douglas Monroy, *Thrown Among Strangers* (1990)

Pablo Neruda, *Splendor and Death of Joaquin Murieta* (1972)

Angustias de la Guerra Ord, *Occurrences in Hispanic California* (1956)

Raymund Paredes, "The Origins of Anti-Mexican Sentiment in the United States," *New Scholar* 6 (1977), 139–165

Richard H. Peterson, "Anti-Mexican Nativism in California, 1848–1853: A Study in Cultural Conflict," *Southern California Quarterly* 62 (Winter 1980), 309–327

Leonard Pitt, *The Decline of the Californios* (1966)

Alan Rosenus, *General M. G. Vallejo and the Advent of the Americans* (1995)

Marc Simmons, *The Little Lion of the Southwest* (1973)

Alvin R. Sunseri, *Seeds of Discord* (1979)

Jerry D. Thompson, ed., *Juan Cortina and the Texas-Mexico Frontier, 1859–1877* (1994)

Jerry D. Thompson, *Vaqueros in Blue and Grey* (1976)

CHAPTER
6

Conflict and Community Among Mexican Americans in the Southwest, Late Nineteenth and Early Twentieth Centuries

By the end of the nineteenth century Anglos has consolidated their economic and political power in the Southwest. In Texas Anglo merchants and lawyers figured prominently in this accumulation of land and resources, and, with ranchers and farmers, became the new elite. This displacement of the Spanish-speaking residents at first did not have a destructive effect on relations between Anglos and Texas Mexicans, but the plight of the latter changed with the influx of capital, the start of railroad construction, and the enclosure of the cattle range. An open border allowed tens of thousands of migrants from Mexico to move into the Río Grande Valley, thereby increasing the local labor force. In the light of the bitterly fought range wars in the drive by Texas Anglos to consolidate their landholdings, did Texas Mexicans became victims of heightened racial hostilities?

In the New Mexico territory, land titles became an issue of dispute for Mexicans following the end of the Civil War. Anglos backed by the U.S. government began to contest long-held titles and then to appropriate huge parcels of land. By 1880 Anglo dominance of the New Mexico economy had rendered a large part of the territory's Spanish-speaking population economically and politically powerless. Mexican Americans soon began to resist Anglo encroachment and challenge the further loss of their civil rights and the accompanying political disfranchisement. Some formed clandestine organizations that cut fences, destroyed railroad tracks, and harassed homesteaders. The most famous of the vigilante groups was the Gorras Blancas, or White Caps, who became embroiled in the Las Vegas Grant dispute. They were affiliated with the labor federation to Holy Order of the Knights of Labor and embraced a populist political agenda. Was the White Caps' struggle over the rightful ownership of communal lands a just cause? What would be the consequences of the loss of land for the next generation of Spanish-speaking New Mexicans?

176

By 1870 Anglos had become the dominant landowners and merchants in California. Increased Anglo emigration led to a rapid decline of the Mexican population in the urban centers. Overall, Mexican Americans comprised about one-fourth of the state's total population in 1880 and about one-tenth by 1890. In the rural areas, migrants from Mexico continued to arrive, and their number soon surpassed that of Mexican Americans.

Mexican Americans became the main source of low-wage labor on ranches, farms, and the railroads in the Southwest as dual labor markets based on race developed. Occupational and wage disparities, founded on the Anglo belief that Mexican Americans were racially unsuitable to perform the better jobs, underscored the region's distinct labor relations. What would cause Mexican American workers to repeatedly challenge the dual labor market? Why would such an inequitable system remain in place throughout most of the Southwest until World War II?

❥ D O C U M E N T S

Much of the violence against Mexicans in the 1870s occurred along the Texas-Mexico border. Robbery, land and cattle theft, and murder marked the region. Both the United States and Mexico authorized commissions to investigate this crime; Document 1 is an excerpt from the report filed in 1873 by Mexico's Comisión Pesquisadora (Investigative Committee). It discusses the Cart War of 1857 and other incidents of violence and reveals the desperate situation of the current Mexican population of southern Texas. In the New Mexico territory in the 1880s, Mexicans likewise were embroiled in conflict over the issues of land and Anglo encroachment. Document 2, dated 1880, is a selection from the autobiography of Miguel Antonio Otero, a former governor of New Mexico, in which he describes the activities of the Gorras Blancas, or White Caps, in San Miguel County, New Mexico. Document 3 is a proclamation the Gorras Blancas issued in 1890 concerning matters of land grants, race, law and justice, local politics, and voting.

The majority of California's elite Mexican American families, the Californios, lost their lands to the Anglos after the Mexican American War. Although their fame and prestige quickly faded, they did became part of a fantasized version of the region's Spanish heritage. Document 4 is from a review of the unique position of the Californios in the state's history written by Charles Howard Shinn of the University of California for *Century Magazine* in 1891. Many of the actions of Mexican Americans who fought for and defended their rights and those of their countrymen were recorded in *corridos,* or "ballads." One of the most popular—"The Ballad of Gregorio Cortez," which appeared in 1901—is included here as Document 5. The song celebrates how Cortez eluded capture by Texas law enforcement officers.

1. Mexico's Investigative Commission Reports on Violence and Theft Along the Texas-Mexico Border, 1873

The Commission has already referred to the condition of the Mexicans in Texas subsequent to the treaty of Guadalupe. Their lands were especially coveted. Their

From México, Comisión Pesquisadora de la Frontera del Norte (Report of the Mexican Commission on the Northern Frontier Question) (Mexico: Díaz de Leon y White, 1874).

title deeds presented the same confusion as did all the grants of land made by the Spanish government, and this became the fruitful source of litigation by which many families were ruined. The legislation, instead of being guided by a spirit of equity, on the contrary tended toward the same end; attempts were made to deprive the Mexicans of their lands, the slightest occurrence was made use of for this purpose, and the supposition is not a remote one, that the cause of such procedure may have been a well settled political principle, leading as far as possible to exclude from an ownership in the soil the Mexicans, whom they regarded as enemies and an inferior race.

At the commencement, and during the disorganization which was prolonged after the Treaty of Guadalupe, robberies and spoliations of lands were perpetrated by parties of armed Americans. It is not extraordinary to find some of them whose only titles consist of having taken possession of and settled upon lands belonging to Mexicans. After these spoliations there came the spoliations in legal forms, and all the resources of a complicated legislation.

At the time the Commission made its report it had not then received various documents to which reference will be made in the proper places by notes. Some of these show the insecurity under which the Mexican population in Texas had labored, and refer to the difficulties known as the cart question.

The residents of Uvalde county, Texas, in September, 1857, passed several resolutions, prohibiting all Mexicans from traveling through the country except under a passport granted by some American authority. At Goliad several Mexicans were killed because it was supposed that they had driven their carts on the public road.

On the 14th and 19th of October the Mexican Legation at Washington addressed the United States Government a statement of these facts, adding that it had been informed that in the vicinity of San Antonio, Bexar [County], Texas, parties of armed men had been organized for the exclusive purpose of pursuing the Mexicans upon the public roads, killing them and robbing their property, and that the number of victims was stated to have been seventy-five. That it was also informed that Mexican citizens by birth, residing peaceably at San Antonio, under the protection of the laws, had been expelled from the place, and finally that some of the families of the victims of these extraordinary persecutions had begun to arrive in Mexico on foot and without means, having been obliged to abandon all their property in order to save their lives.

The Secretary of State on the 24th of the same month addressed a communication to Mr. E. M. Pease, the Governor of the State of Texas, in which he says:

> These reports are not exclusively Mexican. The least among the outrages appear to be the violation of rights guaranteed by law, and under treaties, and I have no doubt that you will have adopted speedy and energetic measures to ascertain the truth and punish the aggressors.

Governor Pease on the 11th of November, 1857, sent a message to the Texas Legislature. In it he stated that during the month of September previous, the Executive had received authentic information that a train of carts had been attacked a short distance from Ellana, Carnes County, while peaceably traveling on the public highway, by a party of armed and masked men, who fired upon the cartmen, killing one and wounding three others. That at the same time he had also received notice of another attack which took place the latter part of July, upon a train in Goliad county. That the attack was made at night, and three of the cartmen were wounded. That the killed and wounded in both instances were Mexicans, with the exception of one who was an American. That with these same reports proof had also been received that a combination had been formed in several counties for the purpose of committing these same acts of violence against citizens of Mexican origin, so long as they continued to transport goods by those roads.

The Governor continues by stating the measures adopted by him for suppressing and punishing such outrages. He states that he proceeded to San Antonio for the purpose of ascertaining whether measures had been taken for the arrest of the aggressors and to prevent the repetition of such occurrences, to which end he had conferences with several citizens of Bexar. The result of these conferences convinced him that no measures had been taken or probably would be taken for the arrest of the guilty parties, or prevention of similar attacks. That in fact combinations of the kind mentioned did exist, and that they had been the origin of repeated assaults upon the persons and property of Mexicans who traveled over those roads. That in several of the border counties there prevailed a deep feeling of animosity towards the Mexicans, and that there was imminent danger of attacks and of retaliation being made by them, which if once begun would inevitably bring about a war of races.

The following paragraph of the same message shows how inexcusable these outrages were:

> We have a large Mexican population in our western counties, among which are very many who have been carefully educated, and who have rendered important services to the country in the days of her tribulation. There is no doubt but that there are some bad characters amongst this class of citizens, but the great mass of them are as orderly and law-abiding as any class in the State. They cheerfully perform the duties imposed upon them, and they are entitled to the protection of the laws in any honest calling which they may choose to select.

The condition of the Mexican population residing in Texas has changed but little since 1857. Governor Pease's message to the Texas Legislature that year exposes and explains the reason of revolts such as the one which occurred on the banks of the Rio Bravo under Cortina in 1859.

A large portion of the disturbances which occurred between the Bravo and Nueces rivers is attributable to the persecutions suffered by the Mexicans residing there; persecutions which have engendered the most profound hatred between the races.

Governor Pease, in the message referred to in the foregoing note, gives it to be understood that the Mexicans did not enjoy the protection of the courts and the authorities. He says our laws are adequate to the protection of life and property, but when the citizens and authorities of a county become indifferent to their execution, they are useless. Some remedy must be found for this condition of things, and the only means which suggests itself to me, is that jurisdiction be given to the grand jury, the officers and courts in any adjoining county where an impartial trial may be obtained, to arrest and try the offenders.

This passage shows that there was no justice for the Mexicans in Texas, and with regard to which the complaint has frequently been made.

The Texas Mexicans enjoyed no greater personal security than did their property, and what is remarkable, is that they were wronged and outraged with impunity, because as far as they were concerned, justice and oppression were synonymous. Here is what a Brownsville newspaper says upon the subject:

> We have had occasion frequently to deplore that want of the administration of the law in such manner as to render to all parties the justice to which they were entitled. According to our ideas, when an officer enters upon the discharge of his duties, he should mark out for himself such a line of conduct as would insure the impartial exercise of his duties, laying aside all distinctions of race and persons, and remove from his proceedings everything which would tend to give them the appearance of a farce. Our population is, as is well known, divided into two classes. Americans and Mexicans; the latter are unquestionably more exposed to wrong than the former; their natural timidity makes them inoffensive, and by reason of the difference of language they cannot well understand our laws or fully enjoy their rights. We have heard one of our highest officers state that it would be difficult to find a class of people more obedient to the laws. It is true that among them there are bad characters, and these should be severely punished, but this fact at times gives rise to their all being classed in the same category, and ill-used. We do not address any one in particular, our remarks are general. Americans have at times committed offenses which in them have been overlooked, but which, if committed by Mexicans would have been severely punished. But when election time comes, it is wonderful to behold the friendship existing for the Mexican voters, and the protection extended to them, the sympathy which until then had remained latent or concealed, suddenly reveals itself in all its plentitude, and many are astonished not to have found until then the amount of kindly feeling professed towards them by their whilom friends. Promises of all kinds are made to them, but scarcely are the promises made, when they are broken. An hour before the election they are fast friends, "—an hour after the election they are a 'crowd of greasers.' " The magistrates are not Pachas or absolute rulers; a certain respect is due to their position, and the consciousness of the responsibility resting upon them should make them feel their duties. . . .

The Mexicans, whether they be Texans or whether they preserve their original nationality, have been the victims both of their persons and property, and they have not been fully protected by the laws.

2. Miguel Antonio Otero Remembers New Mexico, 1880

The "Gorras Blanco," [*sic*] or White Caps, became very active in San Miguel County about this time, burning houses, cutting fences, and resorting to all kinds of intimidations. They stopped teams from hauling railroad ties, because the owners of the teams, usually the driver, were not charging the contractors enough money for the hauling. On these occasions the White Caps would unload the ties and either burn them or chop them up.

From Miguel Antonio Otero, *My Life on the Frontier, 1864–1882* (New York: Press of the Pioneers, 1935), pp. 248–251.

At night large parties on horseback, wearing white caps drawn over their faces, would ride through towns and settlements merely for the purpose of intimidating people. Once I saw more than a hundred pass my home at night, two abreast, and on this occasion they rode through both East and West Las Vegas. Numerous complaints had been filed with the county commissioners, asking them to hire detectives and "secret officers" to bring to the courts the perpetrators. . . .

Two nights before our return to Las Vegas it was reported that several haystacks had been burned, miles of fence wire had been cut, and many horses stolen, as well as milch cows, sheep, hogs, and even chickens. It was hard for the county commissioners to secure good and competent men to act as detectives because they were afraid the White Caps would take revenge. Still, a few men agreed to serve, provided their names were not mentioned and they were paid in cash. Very reliable information stated that everything had been properly arranged by S. E. Booth, chairman of the [commission] board, and Placido Sandoval, one of the members. In order that no leak should appear on the horizon, Booth took a fictitious name, "Joe Bowers," while Placido Sandoval assumed the fictitious name, "Baltazar Burmudez." These two county commissioners drew the warrants in their fictitious names, and received the cash which they were expected to pay to the detectives in a secret manner. . . .

. . . Matters were beginning to get hot for the White Caps, and, although no arrests were made, the organization decided to abandon their night rides and commit no further depredations in San Miguel County. They still retained their political organization until most of the leaders either died or left the county.

We had no sooner arrived in Las Vegas from . . . Mora . . . than we were again informed of the dastardly crimes committed by the "Gorras Blanco" or White Caps, under the leadership of two brothers, Juan Jose Herrera and Pablo Herrera. It was common talk that the White Caps had again organized, and that the present sheriff, Don Lorenzo Lopez, was very closely aligned with them. These rumors were evidently authentic, for, at the next general election, Pablo Herrera was nominated on the Lopez ticket for the House of Representatives from San Miguel County, and was duly elected.

Pablo Herrera spoke perfectly good English, was rather a large man, had dark hair, and always wore a heavy black mustache. Some years before he entered the House of Representatives, he had been convicted of murder and had served his time in the penitentiary.

Pablo was considered a labor agitator, and on his return to San Miguel County he reorganized the "Gorras Blanco," or White Caps, and started to run things. A warrant was soon issued for his arrest and given to Felipe Lopez, a brother of Sheriff Lorenzo Lopez, to serve. He met Pablo very close to the courthouse, pulled his pistol, and without a word shot him through the heart, killing him instantly. Pablo had a bad name, so nothing was ever done to Felipe Lopez.

This killing, however, had a salutary effect on the "Gorras Blanco," and, finding themselves without an aggressive leader, they soon went out of business as an organization, for Juan Jose Herrera was getting too old to take the leadership. Occasionally one would hear of small groups of White Caps cutting fences and burning burns, but nothing more on a large scale, and gradually the roughnecks disappeared, and quiet was restored throughout San Miguel County.

3. Las Gorras Blancas Announce Their
Platform, 1890

Not wishing to be misunderstood, we hereby make this our declaration.

Our purpose is to protect the rights and interests of the people in general; especially those of the helpless classes.

We want the Las Vegas Grant settled to the benefit of all concerned, and this we hold is the entire community within the grant.

We want no "land grabbers" or obstructionists of any sort to interfere. We will watch them.

We are not down on lawyers as a class, but the usual knavery and unfair treatment of the people must be stopped.

Our judiciary hereafter must understand that we will sustain it only when "Justice" is its watchword.

The practice of "double-dealing" must cease.

There is a wide difference between New Mexico's "law" and "justice." And justice is God's law, and that we must have at all hazards.

We are down on race issues, and will watch race agitators. We are all human brethren, under the same glorious flag.

We favor irrigation enterprises, but will fight any scheme that tends to monopolize the supply of water courses to the detriment of residents living on lands watered by the same streams.

We favor all enterprises, but object to corrupt methods to further the same.

We do not care how much you get so long as you do it fairly and honestly.

The People are suffering from the effects of partisan "bossism" and these bosses had better quietly hold their peace. The people have been persecuted and hacked about in every which way to satisfy their caprice. If they persist in their usual methods retribution will be their reward.

We are watching "political informers."

We have no grudge against any person in particular, but we are the enemies of bulldozers and tyrants.

We must have a free ballot and a fair count, and the will of the majority shall be respected.

Intimidation and the "indictment" plan have no further fears for us. If the old system should continue, death would be a relief to our sufferings. And for our rights our lives are the least we can pledge.

If the fact that we are law abiding citizens is questioned, come out to our homes and see the hunger and desolation we are suffering; and "this" is the result of the deceitful and corrupt methods of "bossism."

Be fair and just and we are with you, do otherwise and take the consequences.

The White Caps, 1,500 Strong and Growing Daily

Proclamation of Las Gorras Blancas, 1890, found in Prince Papers, New Mexico State Records Center and Archives.

4. The Californio "First Families" Are Recalled, 1891

The great families of the Spanish pioneer period have mostly representatives at the present day; some of them have retained wealth and influence, especially in the southern counties. Don Romualdo Pacheco, whose mother was Ramona Carrilo, became State senator, lieutenant-governor, and one of the leaders of the Republican party. The grandson of Captain Antonio del Valle, who came from Mexico to California in 1819, is now one of the most prominent politicians in the State. Don Juan B. Castro has held many offices of trust and profit in Monterey County. Don Ignacio Sepulveda, a thoroughly educated lawyer, married an American wife, and was long a superior judge in Los Angeles. A number of similar cases might be mentioned in which individuals of the conquered race have found their opportunity in the material development of the Pacific coast. Still, these were but exceptions; most of the old families sank into obscurity, and it is now difficult to trace their connections. Only about thirty Spanish families of California have retained any wealth or influence.

Among the families of the first rank as regards wealth, influence, dignity, and pride of birth were the Castros, Picos, Arguellos, Bandinis, Carrillos, Alvarados, Vallejos, Avilas, Ortegas, Noriegas, Peraltas, Sepulvedas, Pachecos, Yorbas, and their numerous connections. The Estradas, for instance, were relatives of the Alvarados, and Don José Abrego, of Monterey, treasurer of the province from 1839 to 1846, married in Estrada. This made the Abregos allies of the Alvarados. Don José's son married a daughter of Jacob P. Leese, the American, son-in-law of General Vallejo; his daughter married Judge Webb of Salinas: the Alvarado-Vallejo connection had drawn the Abregos towards the Americans. The founder of the Alvarado family was Juan B., a settler of 1769, whose son José was sergeant at Monterey, and whose grandson was the governor. The mother of the governor was Maria Josefa Vallejo; his wife was Martina Castro. The founder of the Arguello family was Don José Dario, who arrived in 1781; his wife was a daughter of the Moragas, and their children intermarried with the best families of the province. One daughter was the famous Maria de la Concepcion Marcela, born in 1790, and remembered because of her romance, of which Bret Harte has told the story. There is little to add to the outlines of the poem, except that the tale of the lady Concepcion Arguello is familiar to all the Spanish families, and one often hears it used to illustrate the "simple faith of the ancient days." One of the ladies of the Vallejo family retired to a convent. The lady Apolinaria Lorenzana, of Santa Barbara and San Diego, whose lover died, devoted her life to teaching and to charity, and was known for half a century as *"La Beata,"* to whom all doors were open and all sorrows brought. She planted the famous grapevine of Montecito, long known as the largest in the world, and bearing six thousand clusters in a single season. There were other women as worthy of saintship, of whom the elders still speak.

The well-known family of Pico was founded in 1782, by Don José Maria, the father of the governor. The northern branch of this family sprang from Don José

A Review of California's "First" California Familes from *Century Magazine*, January 1981.

Dolores, who arrived in 1790. The first of the Sotos was Don Ignacio, a pioneer of 1776; and the Moraga family date from the same year, their founder being Comandante José Joaquin, of San Francisco Presidio and San José Pueblo. A large and prominent Los Angeles family, that of the Avilas, was founded by Cornelio Avila in 1783. Alcade Avila was killed in the revolution of 1836. Several daughters married Americans. The Lugos are often spoken of in histories. They descend from a Mexican soldier, Francisco Lugo, who arrived in 1769, the date which ranks among Spanish Californians as 1849 does among American pioneers. His four daughters married into the four prominent families of Ruiz, Cota, Vallejo, and Carrillo. The town of Martinez, near Monte Diablo, takes its name from the Martinez family, whose founder was an early alcalde of San Francisco, and three of whose daughters married Americans. A far later arrival was the Jimeno family, one of whom was Governor Alvarado's Secretary of State, whose widow became the wife of Dr. Ord, and whose two sons were taken to the Atlantic States by Lieutenant Sherman in 1850 to be educated. An intimate friend of this famous secretary was Don José M. Romero, the most widely known teacher and author of the province, who wrote and printed the "Catecismo de Ortologia" at Monterey in 1836, and established an advanced school, the best in California until the days of Enrique Cambuston and José Maria Campina, whom Governor Alvarado brought from Mexico.

The Bandinis descended from an Andalusian family of high rank, and were in California by 1771. Old Captain José Bandini was the first to raise the Mexican flag, which he did on the ship *Reina,* at San Blas, in 1821. His son Juan married Dolores Estudillo, and, after her death, Refugio Arguello, and was very prominent in the province from 1825 to 1845. The extensive Carrillo family and also the great Ortega family date their Californian record from 1769. The Ortegas founded Santa Barbara. The Carrillos in the second generation married into the Vallejos, Castros, Pachecos, and many other proud families. At the time of the conquest they had connections in every part of the province. The late Judge Covarrubias, of Santa Barbara, one of the most prominent jurists of Southern California, was connected by marriage with the Carrillos. Captain Noriega, of Santa Barbara, also married a Carrillo, and when he died, in 1858, he left more than a hundred descendants. There were large families in those days of simple, healthy outdoor life; one often reads in the old documents of from twelve to twenty sons and daughters of the same parents. Don Cristobal Dominguez, who owned the Las Virgenes ranch, left fourteen living children, and one hundred and ten living descendants.

The founders of the early families came from all parts of the Spanish dominions. The Castros were from Sinaloa, and so were the Lugos. Old Don Aguirre, a wealthy ship-owner and merchant who first came in his vessel the *Guipuscuana,* was a Basque, and his family is still represented in San Diego and Santa Barbara. Another Basque pioneer was Don José Amesti, a rough, honest fellow, alcalde of Monterey, and afterwards the governor's secretary, who married Prudencia Vallejo. General Castro once told me that Don José "would even say 'carajo' before his children," a thing which "astonished all his friends," for it was not seemly; no other Californian did so. The officer who founded Branciforte, Colonel Pedro Albertia, was a Catalan. The first of the Alvisos, the Valencias, and the Peraltas were from Sonora. José Mariano Bonilla, from the city of Mexico, was one of the first lawyers in the province. The Vacas, descendants of the famous *conquistadore*

Captain Vaca, who was under Cortez, came from New Mexico. Don Manuel Requena of Los Angeles came to California from Yucatan. The Suñols, who owned one of the most beautiful of valleys, were from Spain, and the sons were sent to Paris to be educated. Lieutenant Valdez, who was in the Malaspina expedition of 1791, returned to Europe and was killed at Trafalgar. This noted expedition, under Alejandro Malaspina, consisted of two royal corvettes of Spain, which left Cadiz in 1789, reached California in 1791, and went around the world. In ways like these, and from a thousand channels of commerce and adventure, every province of Spain and Mexico became represented among the pioneer families of California.

The Vallejo family traces its descent from soldiers and nobles of the heroic days of Spain, and is as well known in the mother country as in California. A copy of the genealogical record of the family, which has been kept with great precision, was filed in 1806 in the Spanish archives of Alta California. It states that Don Alonzo Vallejo commanded the Spanish troops on board the vessel which brought the royal commissioner Bobadilla to America with orders to carry Columbus a prisoner to Spain. Another famous Vallejo was a captain under Cortez, followed that illustrious cutthroat to the complete conquest of Mexico, and became governor of the province of Panuco, lord of great silver mines, and master of peons innumerable.

Bilbao, the ancient capital of Burgos, Spain, was the place from which the branch of the Vallejos that is known in California started for the New World. Of this branch came Don Ignacio Vicente Vallejo, born in 1748, in the city of Guadalaxara, Mexico, and designed, as were many of the family before him, for holy orders and the service of the Church. The young man rebelled, volunteered under Captain Rivera y Moncada in Padre Junipero Serra's famous expedition, landing at San Diego in 1769, and thus became a pioneer among the Spanish pioneers themselves. He soon became prominent in the colony, and was not only made military commander of various towns, but was long the only civil engineer in the province, laying out most of the greater irrigation works of the Missions and pueblos, and becoming the owner of extensive and valuable estates. . . .

The link between the old and the new, between the quiet and happy pastoral age of the beginning of the century and the age of American growth and change that followed fast on the conquest, was that remarkable man, General Mariano Guadalupe Vallejo, whose children, as he once told me, "were born under three administrations—Spanish, Mexican, and American." One of his daughters said, "Two of us, when we were small, were called by our brothers and sisters 'the little Yankees.' " General Vallejo, the eighth of the thirteen children of Don Ignacio, was born in 1808, in the old seaport town of Monterey, long the capital of the province, and died January 18, 1890, in Sonoma, once the northern fortress of the province and guarded by the . . . general's soldiers. . . .

One has to go back to the days of the famous Spanish "marches," or frontier towns built and defended in Spain's heroic age by her proudest knights, to find a fit parallel in history to the position held by General Vallejo during the closing years of the Mexican rule in California. He had absolute sway for a hundred miles or more, and he "kept the border." His men rode on horseback to Monterey and to Captain Sutter's fort on the Sacramento, bringing him news and carrying his letters. Spanish families colonized the fertile valleys under his protection, and

Indians came and built in the shadows of the Sonoma Mission. He owned, as he believed by unassailable title, the largest and finest ranch in the province, and he dispensed a hospitality so generous and universal that it was admired and extolled even among the old Spanish families. J. Quinn Thornton, who visited the coast in 1848 and published his experiences, says: "Governor-General Vallejo owns 1000 horses that are broken to the saddle and bridle, and 9000 that are not broken. Broken horses readily bring one hundred dollars apiece, but the unbroken ones can be purchased for a trivial sum." More and more in the closing years of the epoch and the days of the conquest General Vallejo became the representative man of his people, and so he has received, among many of the old families, the reproachful name of a traitor to California and to his nation. The quiet intensity of this bitterness, even to-day, is a startling thing. I have seen men of pure blood, famous in provincial history, leave the room at the name of Vallejo. . . .

In his younger days General Vallejo not only knew almost every one of the five thousand Spanish Californians in the province, the greater part of the Mission Indians, and the chiefs of the wild tribes, but he gathered up, even in his youth, the traditions of the pioneers, and tested their accuracy by every possible documentary and other evidence. His journals are full of variety, and form a complete picture of the entire Spanish period. . . .

Everywhere, in the most picturesque portions of California, are the old adobes that once were social centers of the stately life of nearly a century ago. Most of them are merely ruins, but many are still the homes of the descendants of the first families of the province. The years that brought such change and wreck to the old days have now carried them so far back into the mists of tradition that they seem centuries away. Vallejo's fortress on the frontier is now a town, as dull and unromantic as Yonkers. About the ancient pueblo of Los Angeles has sprung up an intensely modern city. A railroad extends through the very graveyard of San Miguel Mission. Much needs to be done by Californians to preserve the memorials of the past that was so fair and so fruitful a beginning of the story of the commonwealth. The agency through which this is to be accomplished is likely to be the association known as the Native Sons of the Golden West, under whose public-spirited direction was conducted the recent successful celebration of the admission of California.

5. Gregorio Cortez Is Immortalized in Song, 1901

In the county of El Carmen, look what has happened;
  the Major Sheriff is dead, leaving Román badly wounded.

In the county of El Carmen such a tragedy took place:
  the Major Sheriff is dead; no one knows who killed him.

They went around asking questions about half an hour afterward;
  they found out that the wrongdoer had been Gregorio Cortez.

From *With His Pistol in His Hand: A Border Ballad and Its Hero* by Americo Paredes, pp. 158–161, Copyright © 1958, renewed 1986. By permission of the author and the University of Texas Press.

Now they have outlawed Cortez throughout the whole of the state;
    let him be taken, dead or alive, for he has killed several men.

Then said Gregorio Cortez, with his pistol in his hand,
    "I don't regret having killed him; what I regret is my brother's death."

Then said Gregorio Cortez, with his soul aflame,
    "I don't regret having killed him; self-defense is permitted."

The Americans were coming; they were whiter than a poppy
    from the fear that they had of Cortez and his pistol.

Then the Americans said, and they said it fearfully,
    "Come, let us follow the trail, for the wrongdoer is Cortez."

They let loose the bloodhounds so they could follow the trail,
    but trying to overtake Cortez was like following a star.

He struck out for Gonzales, without showing any fear:
    "Follow me, cowardly *rinches;* I am Gregorio Cortez."

From Belmont he went to the ranch, where they succeeded in surrounding him,
    quite a few more than three hundred, but he jumped out of their corral.

When he jumped out of their corral, according to what is said here,
    they got into a gunfight, and he killed them another sheriff.

Then said Gregorio Cortez, with his pistol in his hand,
    "Don't run, you cowardly *rinches,* from a single Mexican."

Gregorio Cortez went out, he went out toward Laredo;
    they would not follow him because they were afraid of him.

Then said Gregorio Cortez, "What is the use of your scheming?
    You cannot catch me, even with those bloodhounds."

Then said the Americans, "If we catch up with him, what shall we do?
    If we fight him man to man, very few of us will return."

Way over near El Encinal, according to what is said here,
    they made him a corral, and he killed them another sheriff.

Then said Gregorio Cortez, shooting out a lot of bullets,
    "I have weathered thunderstorms; this little mist doesn't bother me."

Now he has met a Mexican; he says to him haughtily,
    "Tel me the news; I am Gregorio Cortez.

"They say that because of me many people have been killed;
    so now I will surrender, because such things are not right."

Cortez says to Jesús, "At last you are going to see it;
    go and tell the *rinches* that they can come and arrest me."

All the *rinches* were coming, so fast that they almost flew,
    because they were going to get the ten thousand dollars that were offered.

When they surrounded the house, Cortez appeared before them:
    "You will take me if I'm willing but not any other way."

Then said the Major Sheriff, as if he was going to cry,
"Cortez, hand over your weapons; we do not want to kill you."

Then said Gregorio Cortez, shouting to them in a loud voice,
"I won't surrender my weapons until I am in a cell."

Then said Gregorio Cortez, speaking in his godlike voice,
"I won't surrender my weapons until I'm inside a jail."

Now they have taken Cortez, and now the matter is ended;
his poor family are keeping him in their hearts.

Now with this I say farewell in the shade of a cypress;
this is the end of the ballad of Don Gregorio Cortez.

❦ E S S A Y S

The overland trade from Independence, Missouri, to Santa Fe, New Mexico, prepared the way for the American conquest of New Mexico. When New Mexico was annexed to the United States and made a territory, many American traders and their enterprising New Mexico counterparts became commercial as well as political leaders. In contrast, the masses of New Mexicans became impoverished. How New Mexican women were affected by these economic and social changes is the subject of the essay by Deena J. González, associate professor of history at Pomona College, Claremont, California, who utilizes U.S. Census records to examine the status of Spanish-speaking widows living in Santa Fe between 1850 and 1880. With the economic displacement of Mexicans after the conquest, New Mexican women could not compete economically with the Americans and thus did not benefit from the improved standard of living the Anglos brought. According to González, the Santa Fe widows survived by embracing both continuity and change in traditional economic practices.

In the second essay, Sarah Deutsch, associate professor of history at Clark University, Worcester, Massachusetts, describes the regional community of the Hispanic villages of New Mexico's upper Río Grande Valley, southern Colorado mining towns, and northern Colorado's beet-growing areas that developed between 1880 and 1914. She focuses on Anglo and Hispanic interaction by discussing communal Hispanic village life on the eve of the beginning of Anglo economic activity and the strategies the villagers devised in response to their changing circumstances. While these events had both positive and negative ramifications for the Hispanic villagers, Deutsch concludes that continuity and adaptation rather than change were characteristic of their expanding communities.

The Unmarried Women of Santa Fe, 1850–1880

DEENA J. GONZÁLEZ

When the United States-Mexican War ended in 1848, all women in Santa Fe faced generally dismal economic circumstances. Only two years earlier, they had

From *On Their Own: Widows and Widowhood in the American Southwest, 1848–1939,* edited by Arlene Scadron. Copyright © 1988 by the Board of Trustees of the University of Illinois. Used with the permission of the University of Illinois Press. The full version of this 1985 article appears in A. Scadron, *On Their Own: Widows and Widowhood in the American Southwest, 1848–1939,* and in *Unequal Sisters,* first edition, edited by E. DuBois and V. Ruiz.

heard General Stephen Watts Kearny proclaim peace and promise prosperity. His army, Kearny declared, had come "as friends, to better your condition." When people first watched the soldiers occupy the area peacefully, perhaps they anticipated better times. Since 1820 they had witnessed traders trek to Santa Fe, introduce manufactured items, and alter the town's character. Now they stood on the verge of another conquest, neither military nor economic, but a mixture of both. . . .

. . . By 1850 a new stream of merchants began pouring in from the East and Europe. They arrived eager to make a quick fortune in a town teeming with visitors. Most retailers barely kept pace with the rising needs of investors, soldiers, and federal agents. One result was a Spanish-Mexican community gradually oriented toward an evolving market economy and increasingly removed from the slower exchange-barter practices of earlier eras.

The economy experienced ups and downs while newcomers tugged at tradition. Politics also changed. Four years after Kearny's successful march into town, New Mexico became a territory of the United States. Legislators then launched a long, optimistic battle for statehood. Ultimately, national acceptance was postponed because of concerns like slavery. Proponents of statehood meanwhile prepared the region by electing a legislature. . . .

Newcomers looking for territorial status envisioned an improving expanding economy. "Our business is with the future," proclaimed the first territorial governor. Still, controversy occurred at every juncture. In contrast to the Spanish-Mexican leaders, most federal appointees in the new government, including military officers, came to Santa Fe without experience. But they carried one great advantage: like the vendors in town, they brought cash. . . .

The immigrants, whether merchants or appointees, envisioned making over Santa Fe. Previous traders had bemoaned the town's overwhelming insularity and provincialism. . . . During the war changes began. The incentives for improvement, American style, lay everywhere. . . .

. . . In the mountains outside Santa Fe [they] staked claims and scoured the hills for copper and silver. They bought up land as rapidly as possible, filing deeds in a court system that was also undergoing Americanization. Retailers quickly built shops and paid for liquor or gambling licenses in a town now bustling with commercial activities. Food carts gave way to stores stocked with the supplies soldiers and miners needed. And merchants constantly stressed advancement. The developing market and its endless possibilities engaged their interests, so much so that before long sellers . . . were firmly ensconced in town politics as well as in the economy. Politicians and merchants joined voices to declare that New Mexico was indeed approaching better times.

New establishments and a well-equipped fort gave these men reason to celebrate. Santa Fe had been transformed. . . .

Apparently, the town had taken dramatic turns for the better. Yet despite the appearance of growth and prosperity, fully one-half of the town's population, its Spanish-Mexican women, remained mired in poverty, living under the harshest conditions. They washed and sewed the Euro-Americans' clothes or served them as domestics. For the same work, they received significantly less in wages than others were paid. . . . Women's circumstances, particularly in the matter of paid employment, became governed by white men and their needs. Such growing dependency insured that the majority of women remained trapped by decisions emanating from church, legislature, and army. . . .

. . . Meanwhile, the price of food and goods rose steadily. When Kearny's soldiers first entered Santa Fe, corn cost $3.50 a bushel. Five years later the soldiers and other newcomers had strained supplies, and the price had risen another dollar per bushel. The cost of eggs doubled, and in less than a decade the value of mules quadrupled. Low and barely rising wages for domestic, laundering, and sewing jobs meant that working women had no protection against such spiraling costs. Even worse, shortages frequently developed. The same amount of crops and number of livestock continued to support the expanding population. The scarcity of commodities led Sister Blandina Segale of the Sisters of Charity to report in the late 1870s that many poor women came into the plaza on Sundays, begging for food while trying to exchange precious possessions like Indian blankets.

Spanish-Mexican women could do little against rising inflation. They had previously supplemented their incomes by raising hens for the eggs but never in sufficient quantity to compete with farmers from the outlying areas in the marketing of chickens. Now women began raising the animals. . . . Regardless, the locals could not compete with the newcomers who invested in the more lucrative commodities of cattle and hogs. . . .

Postwar Santa Fe was a town turned upside down. Ethnically, it had changed substantially with the arrival of U.S. soldiers and citizens. But the 1870s witnessed unprecedented migration—over 1,300 new men entered Santa Fe. . . . Their cash flowed in and around the territorial capital lining the pockets of retailers and politicians. . . . Yet the economy of the 1870s continued to fluctuate, and its instability affected Spanish-Mexican families. The burgeoning population once more induced food shortages and lowered buying power. The male migrants upset ethnic and sex balances as never before. Men with money in the 1870s increasingly forced locals into menial work. Women in particular struggled under the pressing challenge of changing markets, a new demography, and different occupations. In a matter of decades dual jobs marked their lot.

Social and economic inequalities were most glaring for unmarried women. . . . The term "unmarried" signifies all adult women who, when enumerated by the census, were living without men. Perhaps 10 percent of adult females had lived or would live with men but were never "legally married." As many as 20 percent outlived their male partners. Placing such women in the broadest possible category reflects accurately their common status—women without men.

Among all groups, women over 15 without husbands remained at the bottom of the hierarchy, in income and jobs. From 1850 to 1880, such women made up at least 10 percent of the adult population. Not just work or marital status determined their low position. The majority headed their own households. . . .

These and other figures were slightly inflated by the number of women whose husbands were away at the mines or, after 1870, laboring for the railroad farther south. The percentage of women "abandoned" will never be known. Additionally, the number legally married and subsequently separated went unrecorded. Nevertheless, other key features of these women's lives coupled with their large number in the population . . . suggest that they were the group most adversely affected by the changes in their community.

Despite the renewed growth of the town, single mothers prospered least of all. More headed households in these decades, and their average family size grew by almost one child. Once able to count on relatives or neighbors, such women now found their traditional supporters similarly constrained. The census graphically marked the pattern. . . . The most common occupations were laundress and seamstress, undertaken by mothers and daughters of all ages. Whereas the 1850 census had been peppered with such skilled and semi-skilled trades as "midwife," "confectioner," and "farmer," the next two enumerations (1860, 1870) rarely listed vocations that veered from domestic and cleaning services. The wages paid . . . suggest that women did not take these jobs in unprecedented numbers for the extra money but from necessity. . . .

In 50 percent of the families, children over the age of 15 also worked, thereby aiding the household economy. Mothers heading households with working children appeared slightly better off than either single women listed within a household or women who apparently had no children. But the same random sample yielded the pattern of larger numbers of women per household working as laundresses, seamstresses, and domestics. . . .

. . . The selection highlighted, however simplistically, the remoteness of temporary separation. It attested to an equally strong possibility that the majority of adult women who appeared to be unmarried lived permanently without male partners and might have been widows.

Within this group of women, widowhood became a distinguishing characteristic. Widowhood also affected how women survived the growing disparities of their time. Unfortunately, because the census did not list familial relationships, age, income, and residential arrangement, and ethnicity must also be correlated to marital status to determine how widows and other husbandless women survived inflation and intrusion. . . .

Residentially, it could be argued, Santa Fe remained a town of old habits. Women's living arrangements portrayed a community still clustering around neighborhoods, the barrios, with related persons forming the nucleus in most homes. Juxtaposing residence habits, customs, and marital condition depicts a population consistently relying on each other in years of unprecedented growth and change. . . . A woman in these decades heading a family sustained it. In a majority of cases she lived without a male partner; in all cases, she labored. Living among relatives, taking several jobs, or remaining unmarried as well as age combined in diverse patterns to insure the household's and the community's survival.

The unmarried Spanish-Mexican woman remained an integral part of her society. She lived and worked with relatives, sons or daughters, married or unmarried. Frequently, she adopted children or cared for children other than her own. These circumstances identify the extent of her incorporation and leadership in family and community life. The widow followed the same pattern. . . .

Work, disparate property and income distributions, and marital status suggest initially a deepening schism between unmarried women and affluent immigrating men. With so many unmarried women living on the verge of poverty, especially single mothers, widows might have proved most susceptible to the influx of strangers and their cash. In fact, although widows were generally at the bottom of the social and economic ladder in other parts of the Far West, such was not entirely the case in Santa Fe insofar as women's finances can be measured and their status assessed. Widows indeed emerged at the low end of the economy, but, in comparison to all women without male partners, appeared to be slightly more prosperous. . . .

These assessments are based on several sources. Few Spanish-Mexican women left written letters or diaries, but they wrote a significant number of wills and testaments. Women comprised about one-third of the authors of 220 wills listed in probate court journals after 1850 and before 1880. Of additional wills located in private family papers, widows wrote about thirty. . . .

In addition to will making, another distinguishing feature of widows sets them apart: they had maintained or had held a legally sanctioned relationship with a man, sanctioned by the courts and by the church. Their better financial position might have derived as well from their husbands. But Spanish-Mexican women traditionally held and owned property in their maiden names. They could dispose of it without a husband's signature, and the wills reflected the tendency to retain and pass on inherited property. . . . Marriage might have sustained the property for these women or made it unnecessary to sell it, but the land originally belonged to a parent or a wife's family. It was entrusted but not surrendered in marriage.

Many women maintained farms and property apart from their husbands. They rarely drew additional income from it, nor did ownership of farmland indicate general prosperity. New Mexicans had developed a regard for land and concept of ownership that differed markedly from that of the immigrants, even in 1850. . . . The land did not necessarily carry a peso or dollar value, but it was useful in the exchange market of families or friends. . . .

. . . The worth they assigned the land stayed well below its true value on the open market until 1870, when the entry of the railroad was being discussed.

. . . Unlike inhabitants of other parts of northern New Mexico, Santa Fe's people did manage to hold on to these inherited shares, at least a time. Land prices . . . had not yet skyrocketed, and much of the pasturage remained in Spanish-Mexican hands. With that in mind, widows who owned land or pastures could hardly be distinguished financially from those who did not. . . . One book in the court records has been lost, but the remaining materials indicate that the number of women writing their final testaments after 1877 and depositing them before a local magistrate, with two witnesses present, rose dramatically. The rising number owed something to the influx of new people and the havoc they created.

Not all of the women writing wills did so to counter the presence of strangers. Some had even married the newcomers. Some testaments had been framed by widows of mixed marriages. But mixed marriages were complicated by the prevailing social disruptions of the time. In the 1870s, more than ever, such relationships had become primarily a matter of class. . . .

By the 1870s intermarriage had become a custom with important ramifications for a community experiencing a Euro-American onslaught. It offered Spanish-Mexican women—women with few choices and limited means—a degree of stability. For men without women, entering a new and decidedly different community, marriage afforded opportunities for financial success. Most transplanted easterners left their relatives behind, but the women they married in Santa Fe were privy to an entire network of extended family contacts. A tailor or blacksmith thus had his job virtually secured by his wife's family and friends. Equally important for the woman, the eastern or European-born husband stepped into *her* world. Her contact with people of his race or culture required little of her except by association with him. Even then, she had family or neighbors who spoke her language and who could assist if she found herself lost or confused. Despite imbalances in culture, class, and sense of place, people continued to marry across racial and cultural lines. It remained an important option available to the enterprising woman.

But it was not the only option. The unmarried women who wrote wills pointed to another solution. The majority did not marry the immigrants; women displayed minimal interest in easing men's transition to life in a new society. Instead, they sought stability in their own worlds; they sought to impose order on a world increasingly changed by easterners and their ways. For more and more of these women, the act of writing a will offered a measure of control over their circumstances. Spanish-Mexican women had followed the custom for generations; worldly possessions, however meager, required proper care. The custom took on added significance in the postwar period. Its assumption of stability contrasted sharply with an enveloping sense of disorder; further, it promised children a continuity, a certainty, that their parents lacked. . . .

Unmarried women had become a fact of life in postwar Santa Fe. They had always been present in Spanish-Mexican communities, but never had their numbers soared as they did after the war. Not all of their troubles could be attributed solely to the military presence or to the politicians who attempted to bind Santa Fe to the Union. But the circumstances of this period encouraged dependence among unmarried women already exceedingly vulnerable either to politicians or to merchants.

On the other side of the political and economic spectrum were the numerous attorneys and federal appointees arriving in Santa Fe. Although federal appointments were not permanent, the individual wealth of each officer marked the steady march toward higher incomes and richer people. . . . Each of the highest government positions and most skilled trades saw escalating improvement—for men.

Meanwhile, unmarried women's finances declined. Their buying power fell, the percentage of those living without a male partner rose, their families grew, and they witnessed a declining net worth during decades of unprecedented transformation. Emphasizing their marital status and ignoring the context in which it occurred would be misleading. They did not live apart or immune from the general dislocations of the period. In that regard, even the widow was not alone. She stood in a very long line of women experiencing conquest in the most fundamental way, as it affected their economy and families.

In Spanish-Mexican communities throughout the Southwest, the role and position of widows and other unmarried women have long been understood but never discussed. Their position may raise many disquieting questions. In this case, however, widows and all unmarried women shed light on the entire frontier. Dislocation and disparity had become facts of life, and yet women subsisted. Barter and exchange practices continued to serve them well, and many probably survived because the old skills had not eroded entirely. Gardening continued in Santa Fe's barrios, and the products were given and traded to relatives and neighbors alike. Extended family networks provided the security needed to raise children, and no matter how difficult reliance on relatives could become, such new institutions as hospitals or orphanages did not yet replace such dependence.

Life for the unmarried woman, the widow included, also exhibited a certain fluidity. Some married, or remarried, the new men in their midst. Others made wills to provide for a future generation. In that manner they might have been like other southwesterners. But they remained Spanish-Mexican women speaking Spanish and not English, practicing Catholicism and not Protestantism, residing in neighborhoods several centuries old, with roots stretching far back. Their story differed fundamentally from the stories of women to whom they might be compared, including Mormon women, city women, or westering women. . . .

At the end of the 1870s, when the railroad tracks had nearly reached Santa Fe, unmarried women stood at another critical juncture. Families and the community were changing; no longer did many groups reside on the periphery, isolated from the government or its institutions. Rather, Spanish-Mexicans were at the center of continuing colonization, their ways irrevocably altered. As immigrants became residents, the unmarried women faced difficult choices. They had persevered, but as the iron horse pushed toward their community, even more pernicious forms of intrusion threatened. They had little choice but to accommodate.

Chicano/a Frontier and Regional Communities in the Southwest

SARAH DEUTSCH

When U.S. Colonel Stephen Watts Kearney marched into Mexican Santa Fe in 1846, his work was quick and nearly bloodless. He annexed New Mexico without firing a shot. But that was only the official victory. Achieving domination and cultural conquest took far longer. Even after the uprising of the following year failed, Hispanics had the advantage of numbers and an entrenched society and economy. And in the years following 1848 they thrived and even expanded their frontiers, settling new villages in southern Colorado and exploring new trade routes to gold fields. By 1880 the Hispanic frontier and the Anglo one interlocked rather than merely met. It was at this joint frontier that the Anglos arrived in force in the 1880s, with railroads, lumber mills, coal mines, and commercial agriculture and stock enterprises. This renewed Anglo assault posed an even greater challenge to the territory's Hispanics.

As they vied for survival and power, both Anglos and Hispanics formulated new strategies. The developments of these years, from 1880 to 1914, set for at least the next four decades the basic lines of contact and conflict in the region. They also exposed the enduring tensions between Anglo aims for both the land and its inhabitants, and Hispanic villagers' own visions. . . .

To encourage the settlement of their vast arid frontier and to buffer the empire against the depredations of Indians and other ambitious rival powers, the Spanish and later the Mexican government had bestowed communal grants on groups petitioning for land in northern New Mexico. . . . By the mid-nineteenth century, although the population seemed thinly scattered on the land, Hispanics filled the arable river beds and slopes and grazed their cattle on the grassy plateaus. Relatively short distances separated settlements, and the settlers exploited the land, through a mixed economy, to the maximum feasible extent.

Village size and society varied depending on access to grazing lands, ease of irrigation, and the proximity of trade routes, but the communal mountain villages had more in common than not. In most villages, each settler owned a small agricultural lot, a house, and the land immediately surrounding the house. The rest of the grant, the pasturage and water, was held and managed communally. . . .

As on most frontiers, also, the villagers' economy depended on the labor of each family member. Women's work, in particular, and the flexibility of the sexual division of labor were essential elements in allowing seasonal migration by men to herd or to trade. While the husband selected the crops for other fields, the wife had exclusive control over the garden plot which produced most of the food for the family table, and which she tended with the help of the entire family. When men were away on seasonal absences, women irrigated the land. If the garden was as large as the fields, both sexes helped plant and harvest each.

As a reflection of the crucial nature of women's contribution, daughters usually inherited land equally with sons, although in some villages they received livestock, furniture, and household goods in lieu of land. This inheritance custom, their position as heads of households during men's absences, and the tradition that a woman retained her right to whatever property she had when she entered marriage, as well as her right to "community property" (property she shared with her husband), gave women a degree of independence, an ability to act on their own which would prove significant as more and more men left the village for longer periods.

Status differences did exist, but the differences were greatest between generations. . . . Geography, climate, and village structure helped minimize differences between families. With small private plots and diversified land, large-scale mono-cropping was impossible. With communal grazing lands, none could monopolize this vital resource for his or her own cattle or sheep. And with fully occupied families, a rainfall inconsistent at best, and a communal ethos, there was not much room for a single family to gain a lasting dominant position by using village resources.

Still, it was a communal system with ambiguities. . . . Men and women held their private land individually while they also shared in the larger communal property. Private land played a key role in the membership of individuals in the community and in their sustenance and autonomy. No written law governed its disposal. . . . Village mores militated against selling the land to an outsider, and such a sale was likely to result in the ostracism of seller and buyer. Privately held land gave room to individualism within the community, but at the same time the community limited that room in the interests of its own survival. . . .

. . . The village was not self-sufficient, and trade played a crucial role in its economy. There were few barriers to trade, and most families owned the necessary team and wagon. The villagers produced small amounts of hay, wheat, onions, chilis, cabbage, sheep, and wool—products from the women's garden as often as from the men's fields—for sale in such regional centers as Española, Taos, and Santa Fe. Individual enterprise was more often channeled even farther outside the village. Villagers traded at first with the Utes to the northwest and with St. Louis and Mexico. After the Mexican-American War stifled the Mexican market for New Mexico sheep, New Mexicans shifted their trade targets to take advantage of new opportunities. They drove their sheep to the California and Colorado gold fields, to Denver, and occasionally to Kansas and Nevada. . . .

As families could not survive solely on the profits of such trade, when villages became crowded or grazing land depleted, small groups from the parent village would form a new settlement. . . . In the 1840s and 1850s, for example, families from Abiquiu in Rio Arriba County settled Guadalupe in southern Colorado, families from El Rito settled Rincones, and Taos families settled San Luis. . . .

Ironically, the United States conquest increased such expansion. Families set out to occupy new sites on their old grants, moved onto Indian grants or even to the California gold fields not only because of over-grazing and diminishing land at home, but also to seek better trade conditions and to escape the increasing Anglo influence. . . . Some of this expansion was, in fact, made possible only by the expanding Anglo frontier, by the protection that Anglo forts afforded to Hispanic settlers, and the trade opportunities Anglo settlements provided.

The Anglo conquest and control over land had still barely begun to impinge on Hispanic movement and livelihood in the 1870s. The railroad had not reached New Mexico and had only just reached southern Colorado. At this point, its Anglo towns provided new outlets for trade rather than threats to old ones. Anglos entered New Mexico and southern Colorado with improved livestock, but in small numbers. . . . The boom in sheep brought attractive if ephemeral profits and prosperity to the villagers. Land grants were finding their way into Anglo hands, but were seldom fenced or Anglo-colonized so the loss held little tangible threat. . . .

Ultimately, however, the same Anglo frontier that stimulated expansion became a major obstacle. While northern New Mexicans continued to homestead and settle on grants, and traders sometimes moved permanently to the Anglo enclaves where they traded, Anglo cattlemen, Mormon farmers, and Anglo railroadmen, land speculators, and merchants formed an increasingly complete circle around the expanding Hispanics.

In the 1880s the changing pattern became clear. For the first time, Hispanic migrants from New Mexico to Colorado were matched by Anglos migrating from Missouri, Pennsylvania, Ohio, and Illinois. With each succeeding decade, while the number from New Mexico stood roughly the same, more and more states sent more and more people. In the 1880s, also, the railroad arrived in New Mexico, and brought increasing numbers of Anglos there as well. Before the 1880s, because of their relatively small numbers, Anglos in the region had found it to their advantage to adopt Hispanic customs, language, and wives. Now their increasingly complete community in the West rendered superfluous earlier Anglo assimilation of Hispanic ways, and their increasing numbers enabled them to impose their desire for and attitude toward land and business more effectively on the local scene.

For Hispanics, barriers to trade rose on all sides. Licenses were required to trade with the Indians, and agents were inclined to favor Anglos over Hispanics.

They believed "the average Mexican is too much like the Indian," and therefore trade between them would not perform its designated function of transforming Indian culture; would not, in the parlance of the day, Americanize the Indians. Other trade moved away from Old Hispanic villages to new Anglo railroad towns, and Hispanic freighters who had carried the majority of business could not compete on hauls covered by railroads. . . .

The new Anglo threat went even beyond the loss of trading income. The communal village land itself was at stake as Anglo attitudes toward land and economy, so different from Hispanic villagers', triumphed. Anglo capitalists who came to New Mexico in this period took for granted private property, commercial use, and a monetary economy. . . . To the Anglo, land not visibly occupied or, worse, not producing a profit, was wasted and vacant. In line with this philosophy, most Hispanic land grants, as confirmed by Congress, included only the home lots and the irrigated fields. Much of what had been the villagers' common land went to the public domain and in turn to railroads, Anglo homesteaders, and national forests. Without pasture, the land remaining in villagers' hands was often insufficient to sustain their pastoral economy.

Hardly quiescent, Hispanics filed suit after suit, but theirs was not the legal system. After forty years of turmoil, Congress established the Court of Private Land Claims in 1891 to depoliticize the land issue. But the court only increased the loss of land by Hispanics. Of 35,491,020 acres at stake, the court confirmed to Hispanic claimants in New Mexico, Arizona, and Colorado 2,051,526 acres. The judges interpreted the law rigidly, rejecting even grants which were over one hundred years old and without previous dispute. And the procedure was not free. Hispanics who won their case could lose land to their lawyers. . . . As the villagers usually had no cash—even the payment of new Anglo taxes required selling essential land—lawyers accepted payment either in land or, if the decision was for partition and sale as the . . . proceeds from the land. Some lawyers received as much as half the grant. . . .

Even for Hispanic villagers who did not lose title to their land, Anglo "progress" could spell disaster. Mine operators at Torres, Colorado, acquired right-of-way across Madrid Plaza in 1901 and used the land as a refuse site for mine tailings. The dumping caused erosion, leading to decreased agricultural productivity and the eventual abandonment of the plaza town—incidentally, making labor available for the mine. In addition, the once free range was limited by the government's removal of over six million acres of New Mexico's land for national forests and by new homesteaders who, as early as 1900, claimed nearly one million acres in New Mexico.

By 1900 most Spanish American villagers both in Colorado and in New Mexico found available range limited by Anglo settlement and corporations, and the range to which they did have access—whether by leasing privately held land or buying grazing permits for national forests—now cost them hard cash, if they could afford it at all. This set of circumstances changed the structure of the sheep industry in this region in the same way the railroads changed the structure of trade, and thus changed the structure of the villages themselves.

. . . By opening new markets, the railroad had brought a boom in sheep. At first it might have seemed to Hispanics as though the increased income from the expanding market for sheep would make up for the loss of trade outlets, but by the 1880s those commercial sheep operators which had been glimpsed in the 1870s had poured into the Southwest with capital and improved livestock. . . .

As the number of Anglo-owned livestock companies increased and the market became more competitive, pressure on the land also increased. Land rose in value, and land transfers accelerated. Public domain became an object of exclusive control as stock growers acquired title, if not to large acreage, to essential watering places. By controlling access to water, stock growers controlled the utility of the surrounding range. Railroads in New Mexico, as elsewhere in the trans-Mississippi West, had received vast land grants of their own. In their own freighting interests, when granting leases they tended to favor Anglo commercial users over Hispanic small-scale operators. The Hispanic village system of stock farming based on ownership of sheep rather than land was rapidly becoming obsolete.

Both Hispanics and Anglos enlarged their herds, but gradually the balance of ownership shifted and not solely because of shifts in control of land. . . .

The lack of a money economy in the region made credit extension an essential part of the business. . . .

This extension of credit brought the villagers directly into the national economy and made them vulnerable to its convulsions. In the depression years of the 1890s and in 1907 when debts were recalled, or at other times when the sheep men could not meet their accounts because of grazing fees or other expenses, many of the sheep farmers lost their flocks. They became "partidarios," or sheep sharecroppers. . . .

Unlike the traditional "partido" agreement, wherein owner and renter had shared both profit and loss, in the new arrangement the renter alone bore all the loss. What had started as a way for sons to establish their own herds became a self-perpetuating system to provide pastoral labor for consolidated and rationalized sheep farming. . . .

By 1900, one-quarter to one-half of all New Mexico's sheep were under partido contracts. Many villages shared the experience of Tierra Amarilla, which . . . had gone from a village of farmers with a few ranch hands in 1880 to a village of workers for wages. . . .

. . . Moreover, as the growing commercial livestock industry, railroads, and national forests consumed more and more land, Hispanics, like Indians, found themselves on a land base increasingly inadequate to their needs. . . . Faced with a truncated frontier and an increasingly intrusive conquering economy and culture, the Hispanics could not retreat. They had to find new modes of expansion, had to choose how to adapt or to resist. They had to formulate new strategies in order to maintain the viability of their villages. . . .

. . . Socially as well as economically marginalized by the new order, the economic and social foundations of their culture threatened by new Anglo institutions of industry, government, and education, many Hispanics organized along ethnic lines to resist the onslaught, control it, or even turn it back. . . .

The best remembered of these organized resistance movements is the "Gorras Blancas," or "White Caps" of San Miguel County. At their peak, the secret organization claimed 1500 members, including respected officials of the villages; a good number of the local, largely Hispanic, Knights of Labor, including a district organizer; and a sprinkling of "quasi-bandits." They rode abroad, mainly at night, in groups of varying size, from 66 to 300 or more, and, for the most part, confined their activities to fence cutting and the defense of fence cutters. They cut the fences of Hispanics as well as of Anglos, and of the parish priest, and were not above using the general "disorder" to settle personal grudges. But they also attacked the railroads. They tore up tracks, burned bridges, ordered teamsters to strike, hacked nine thousand railroad ties in half, and tried to set standard prices for all wood cut and hauled. Their platform, which they nailed to the buildings of East Las Vegas one midnight in March 1890, claimed, "Our purpose is to protect the rights of the people in general and especially those of the helpless classes."

In their platform, the Gorras Blancas cried out against land grabbers and "knavish" lawyers, against monopolizers of water, against bossism, and even against agitation on racial issues. They covered, in short, the whole scope of the Anglo impact, and they enjoyed the support of almost the entire Hispanic, and for a time even some of the Anglo community. In December 1889, when alleged fence cutters were released from jail in Las Vegas, they paraded down the street led by women waving the American flag and singing, "John Brown's Body," and were followed by "a squad of little girls." "These people," a mystified local editor, Russel A. Kistler, wrote, "in some way regard themselves as martyrs." The Gorras Blancas and their supporters did not see a necessary connection between living under the American flag, enjoying the liberties it promised, and living under a particular economic system. . . .

The Gorras Blancas met with some success. . . . But in general, the tide could not be turned back, and for Hispanic villagers, organized violence required time, money for lawyers' fees, and great personal risk for questionable rewards. Most Hispanics turned to other means, both outside and within the Anglo system, to resist Anglo incursions and dominance. They turned to other strategies, both organized and individual.

In the more remote villages, even local Penitente societies shifted focus and became politically active, some evolving into political machines. Elsewhere, in villages suddenly surrounded by Anglo-controlled mining or railroad towns and among Hispanic trackworkers, "mutualistas" (mutual aid organizations) sprang up; seventeen formed in New Mexico between 1885 and 1912. . . . Sharing the newer aims of the Gorras Blancas, such organizations stood against bossism and political corruption, and for mutual protection and an active role in determining the new hierarchy. Like the more violent groups, they were part of a broadly based attempt to retain or achieve some control over the confrontation with Anglos, but unlike those organizations, they were adapted to a situation of daily coexistence.

Hispanics as a group did retain some leverage in electoral politics. The numerical superiority of Hispanics in New Mexico . . . and in parts of Colorado ensured that politicians of either ethnic group would ignore the accusation that courting the Hispanic vote was "fanning the race issue." The People's Party victories had proved the efficacy of the ethnic vote, and in New Mexico, Spanish Americans long had a majority in the House of Representatives.

Predictably, however, working through Anglo institutions brought only limited success. . . . Networks of patronage erected in territorial days, extending from Anglo politicos in the capital to Hispanic villagers, continued to foster division on party lines among Hispanics. . . . Hispanics never succeeded in attaining sufficient political unity . . . to dominate New Mexico's government. . . .

. . . Villagers had to seek other modes of subsistence and expansion, other strategies. Among the options offered, seasonal wage labor proved the most attractive. . . . Seasonal wage labor permitted them to perpetuate a multi-source income . . . , a flexible sexual division of labor, a communal village, and seasonal migration into a cash economy as an outlet for individual enterprise. In it they beheld a new mode of expansion, one that allowed increased density on the land, and one that kept them from poverty without requiring either a permanent departure from their own culture or a permanent entry into Anglo culture. . . .

The railroads provided some of the earliest and most convenient opportunities for Hispanic wage laborers. In 1880 tracks reached Albuquerque and Santa Fe. In the next two years, the Denver and Rio Grande built two narrow-gauge lines through the heart of Hispanic southern Colorado and northern New Mexico, and the growth of railroad mileage in New Mexico did not slow until 1912. Although Chicanos in the United States were confined to track maintenance or section work—usually under American or European foremen—and other full- or part-time unskilled labor, even the sectionman's wage of one dollar for a twelve-hour day or about $25 per month compared favorably to shepherd's wages. It attracted mountain villagers who lived twenty and more miles from the nearest tracks. . . .

Hand in hand with the railroad in the creation of both a new Anglo economic framework and new opportunities for Hispanic wage labor came the exploitation of the coal deposits in southern Colorado. The railroad needed coal to run and provided the means to market it or ship it to steel plants. As the railroad arrived in southern Colorado in the 1870s, the first mines opened at Engleville and Starkville and, like the railroads, they expanded rapidly in the first years of the new century. The coal mines, too, were conveniently close at hand for Hispanic villagers needing seasonal wage labor. . . . The number and proportion of Hispanic mine workers varied from camp to camp, but in 1905, 11.5 percent of all Colorado Fuel and Iron's mine workers were Hispanic. By 1914 the figure had risen to 17.37 percent, and 92.59 percent of its 540 lumber workers were also Hispanic. Piece rates were standard, but Hispanics did tend to receive poorer "rooms" in the mines, and so as in railroad work where there was wage as well as occupational discrimination. Hispanics made less money than Anglos. Even so, Hispanic miners could earn up to twice the monthly income of Hispanic track laborers.

Whether they lived near the mines or not, Hispanic miners integrated their forays into this Anglo enterprise with their own cultural economy, as they did with their railroad work. . . .

The turn of the century brought yet another seasonal wage occupation into being: sugar-beet labor. In the 1890s would-be sugar-beet growers had, with local capital, put companies together all over Colorado. By the end of 1901 at least four processing factories had been built, covering each of the areas that was to become a major producer: the Arkansas River in southern Colorado, the South Platte River in the north, and the Western Slope. . . . The Spanish Americans, who often juggled their new wage-earning jobs, began to abandon railroad work during rushed times in the beetfields, or to spend one season on the tracks, the next in the mines, and the next in beets. . . .

Beet labor, in particular beet labor where colonies had been built, though onerous and a departure in some ways from older patterns, afforded yet another mode
of physical expansion and cultural survival for the Hispanic villagers. As in the
folk expansion of the previous century, families often came north in clusters and
never severed their ties with their parent village. These pioneering Chicanos often
sent money back to relatives in their villages who, in turn, sometimes sent produce
north. In the northern cities, on the isolated northern farms, these extended kinship
links retained for the otherwise bereft migrants a sense of community.

The interplay of Anglo and Hispanic strategies had, by 1914, resulted in this
regional community, this extension of community links, village by village, like
runners from a plant, to encompass an entire region. No longer could the village
exist or be understood apart from its laboring migrants, and the migrants, too, had
inseparable and essential links to the village. The railroads, the mines, the beet-
fields were all in place, and the people were moving. . . . As Victor Clark explained
in 1908, "The New Mexican no longer is village shy, averse to leaving the neighborhood where he was born and where he can always find shelter and food among
his friends. He makes seasonal migrations to distant parts of the west in search of
work, often leaving his family behind him to attend to the crop in his absence." Migration had become an essential and integral part of life for the Hispanic
villagers. . . .

Migration and the form of community it created had become the dominant
Hispanic strategy on the intercultural frontier. This strategy of strictly limited entry
into the Anglo world carried vital implications for intercultural dynamics. For the
new strategy had arisen not merely as a result of economic necessity and opportunities offered. Anglo attitudes toward land, business, and work had placed under
siege not only Hispanic sources of livelihoods, but Hispanics' ability to define
their own culture and values. The resulting Hispanic strategy was not merely an
economic but a cultural choice. Hispanic and Anglo frontiers interlocked, and so
did their strategies. . . .

By 1914, Hispanics in Colorado and New Mexico had largely lost control over
developments affecting the region as a whole, but, through their strategy of work
and migration patterns, they retained their control over their own enclaves, retained for themselves a homeland—both a refuge and a base for expansion without
loss of cultural identity. . . .

. . . When the traditional pastorally based expansion of settlement was made
impossible through federal land appropriations and Anglo incursions, migration
for wage work was substituted as a new solution to the problem of increasing population density. Permanent migration did at times accompany wage work in a continuation of the expanding frontier, but Hispanics rarely migrated as farmowners,
and they always maintained close connections with the home village. That this
strategy of migration also served Anglo needs did not, as yet, render it less effective as a Hispanic strategy of cultural autonomy in the face of a hostile and powerful rival. Hispanics did not abandon other strategies. They continued to seek Anglo
education, to form organizations, and to enter politics. For the largest number,
however, migratory labor was the strategy best adapted to their aims and interests.

The regional community had arisen between 1880 and 1914 as a strategy of
autonomy and expansion interwoven with Anglo strategies and development. It

had arisen, in short, from the changing dynamics of the intercultural frontier. The tradition of a multi-source income, family economy, communal village, and seasonal absence of men was proving a highly adaptable system. The villages, with their "living links," were not isolated and static, however unchanged their structure may have seemed. That very seeming continuity paid tribute to the early success of their efforts to control and limit the impact of the Anglo confrontation while still expanding their community to embrace both Colorado and New Mexico.

FURTHER READING

Larry D. Ball, *Desert Lawmen* (1992)
Susan C. Boyle, *Los Capitalistas: Hispano Merchants on the Sante Fe Trail* (1997)
Victor S. Clark, *Mexican Labor in the United States* (1909)
Maurice G. Fulton, *History of the Lincoln County War* (1968)
Nasario García, *Comadres: Hispanic Women of the Río Puerco Valley* (1997)
Juan Goméz-Quiñones, *Sembradores* (1973)
Alfonso Griego, *Good-bye My Land of Enchantment* (1981)
Richard Griswold del Castillo, *The Los Angeles Barrio, 1850–1890* (1979)
Robert E. Ireland, "The Radical Community: Mexican and American Radicalism, 1900–1910," *Journal of Mexican American History* 1 (Fall 1971), 22–32
William A. Keleher, *Violence in Lincoln County, 1869–1881* (1982)
James R. Kluger, *The Clifton-Morenci Strike* (1970)
Howard Roberts Lamar, *The Far Southwest, 1846–1912* (1970)
Robert W. Larson, *New Mexico Populism* (1974)
J. Methvin, *Andele, The Mexican-Kiowa Captive* (1996)
Joseph F. Park, "The 1903 'Mexican Affair' at Clifton," *Journal of Arizona History* 18 (1977), 148–199
Phillip Rasch, "The People of the Territory of New Mexico Versus the Sante Fe Ring," *New Mexico Historical Review* 47 (April 1972), 185–202
Richard Rodríguez and Gloria L. Rodríguez, "Teresa Urrea, Her Life, as It Affected the Mexican-U.S. Frontier," *Voices from El Grito: A Journal of Contemporary Mexican American Thought* (1973), 179–199
Robert J. Rosenbaum, *Mexicano Resistance in the Southwest* (1981)
Eugene T. Sawyer, *The Life and Career of Tiburcio Vasquez, the California Stage Robber* (1944)
Andrew B. Schlesinger, "Las Gorras Blancas, 1889–1891," *Journal of Mexican American History* 1 (Spring 1971), 87–143
C. L. Sonnichsen, *The El Paso Salt War, 1877* (1961)
Eva Antonia Wilbur-Cruce, *A Beautiful, Cruel Country* (1987)

Struggle and Strife: Social Conditions of Mexican Americans, 1910–1917

Massive changes in demography, lifestyle, and migratory patterns among nineteenth-century Mexican Americans were produced by the economic development of the Southwest spurred by the rise of silver, copper, and coal mining; cotton and vegetable agriculture; railway construction; and the boom-like expansion of the region's cities. For instance, the growth of large-scale agriculture in the lower Río Grande Valley of Texas in the early twentieth century altered social relations between Anglos and Mexican Americans. Racism began to exclude Mexican Americans from participation in the social and political life of their communities, and once again conflict between Anglos and Mexican Americans ensued. This conflict often led to widespread violence against Mexican Americans at the hands of the notoriously brutal Texas Rangers. The large number of lynchings and killings of Mexican Americans by Anglos comprised the collective experience of inequality shared by Mexican Americans. In what ways did this become the basis for struggle and resistance by Texas?

In the late nineteenth and early twentieth centuries the upheavals caused by labor unrest, the influence of anarchists and socialists, and disputes over law and land would result in a flurry of political activism by Mexican Americans. How was the local Mexican Americans' struggle for equality affected by immigrants coming from Mexico in search of work? The increase in Mexican immigration after the Mexican Revolution of 1910 was the result of the declining economic situation in Mexico coinciding with the improving fortunes of the American Southwest. Soon many American firms became dependent on cheap Mexican labor. The U.S. government worked closely with these groups to help shape the pattern of Mexican immigration. What role did Mexican immigrant women play in this larger process of immigration to the United States?

❦ D O C U M E N T S

Scholars credit the Mexican immigrants who arrived in the years following the Mexican Revolution for much of the economic development of the Southwest. Document 1 is an excerpt from the extensive study of Mexican labor written by Victor S. Clark, an economist with the U.S. Bureau of Labor, in 1908, shortly before the major influx of immigrants began. To protect the Spanish-speaking community of the lower Río Grande Valley from discrimination, El Congreso Mexicanista was founded in Laredo, Texas, in 1911. The 400 Texas Mexicans who were members included journalists, schoolteachers, representatives from fraternal organizations, and religious leaders. Document 2 is from the Reverend Pedro Grado's address at the meeting of the group held in El Paso, Texas, in 1911. In Document 3, also dating from 1911, Flores de Andrade, a Mexican immigrant, remembers her involvement with revolutionary activities in El Paso.

When the Chinese Exclusion Act of 1882, along with restrictions on Japanese immigration to California, eliminated two important sources of cheap agricultural labor in the state, the American farmers turned to Mexico. Document 4 is a selection from Samuel Bryan's 1912 article on the increase in Mexican immigration, especially in southern California. The popular *corrido* "*Los Sediciosos* (The Seditionists)," commemorating the outbreak of Texas Mexican resistance in South Texas after the call to arms in the Plan of San Diego in 1915, is reproduced in Document 5. The Plan of San Diego was a formal declaration of armed struggle by Texas Mexican insurgents to reconquer lands lost during the U.S.–Mexico War (1846–1848).

1. Victor S. Clark Comments on Changes in Mexican Immigration to the United States, 1908

So long as the Mexican immigration is transient it is not likely to have much influence upon the United States, except as it regulates the labor market in a limited number of occupations and probably within a restricted area; for transient labor is not likely to be largely employed beyond a certain radius from El Paso and the Rio Grande, or to enter lines of employment in which it competes with citizen labor. But the Mexicans are making their homes in the United States in increasing numbers and, being assimilated by the Spanish-speaking population of the Southwest, are forming the civic substratum of our border states. The proportion of the immigrants who ultimately take up a permanent residence north of the border is entirely a matter of estimate. As this immigration has assumed importance since the census of 1900, figures derived from the census reports do not indicate present conditions and tendencies.

Up to 1900 very few Mexicans had emigrated beyond the border states and territories. For instance, Colorado, which now employs several hundred Old Mexicans transiently, had but 274 residents of that nationality in the last census year. Louisiana had 488. Colorado, however, had 10,222 residents, mostly in the mining counties around Trinidad, who had been born in New Mexico.

As found in Victor S. Clark, *Mexican Labor in the United States.* Bulletin #78, Bureau of Labor. Washington, D.C.: U.S. Government Printing Office, 1908.

Between 1880 and 1890, the Mexican-born population increased more slowly than the total population; but during the following decade it increased at a more rapid rate than the total population, both in the United States as a whole and in all the border districts except Arizona. In 1880, Mexicans comprised 1.01 percent of the total foreign-born population of the United States; in 1890, .9 percent; and in 1900, 1 percent, showing the same general tendency of variation as to the total population. Of the more than five thousand immigrants who passed through El Paso in September 1907, not one expressed the intention of becoming an American citizen. The only one of several score questioned at the immigration station who had this intention was a skilled mechanic, of quite a different class from the main body of immigrants. Nevertheless, Mexicans are settling permanently, especially in Texas and California. Two persons in a position to be unusually well informed upon the subject, one of them a general official of a railway carrying immigrants to the frontier, estimated that 50 percent of those who visited the United States finally made their home there. On the Mexican Central Railway, which moves more immigrants than any other single road in Mexico, the official estimate of third-class passengers (laborers) crossing the frontier northward during the twelve months ending with August 1907 was fifty thousand and the return traffic during the same period was estimated to be thirty-seven thousand. However, the proportion of those passing through El Paso who return is larger than of those crossing the lower Rio Grande, because so much of the former labor is employed on railways and in mines in the desert, where there is little temptation to make a permanent home. Immigrants through El Paso are seldom accompanied by their families, while many women and children cross at Laredo, especially to pick cotton. A prominent Mexican merchant in San Antonio, Texas, said, "Mexicans who have come to the United States seldom go back to stay, because conditions are better here, and because they are not kept down so much in this country." The superintendent of public instruction in Arizona stated that in the southern counties of that territory nearly one half the children enrolled in public schools have foreign-born parents, mostly Mexicans, but that very few of these children were born in Mexico. In California, Mexican laborers were said to be accompanied by their families, and to be settled in little colonies near a number of the larger towns; but in Colorado there was no evidence that the immigrant Mexicans have come to remain. An evidence of increasing settlement in Texas is the large number of excursionists that return to Mexico each year to attend the religious festivals in Aguascalientes and in Mexico City. These people, though Mexican-born, buy return tickets to Texas.

The transition in Texas from an immigration of temporary laborers to one of settlers was thus described by a railroad official who had observed it from the outset: "Ten years ago our Mexican immigrants were chiefly men. It was rare to see a woman among those who came through here from any distance down the line. About one thousand men who had been in the United States and returned to Mexico began to bring back their families with them. Usually they were also accompanied by a number of single men, or married men without their families, who had never before been in this country. Most of the men who had families with them did not go back the following season, but the men without their families did, and some of them in turn came back the next year with their families to remain permanently. So the process goes on, with, I believe, a larger proportion of women and children among the immigrants each year, and a larger proportion remaining in this country."

The Bishop of the Texas diocese (Roman Catholic) stated that many thousands of immigrants from Old Mexico were settling in his parishes, and that the increase of Mexican population was general throughout the southern part of the state.

Probably a conservative estimate of the proportion of immigrants remaining permanently in the United States would be from one fourth to one third. The number is probably in the neighborhood of twenty thousand per annum. With the lack of more definite data than is possessed at present, the number can only be estimated—and the estimate has possibly a wide margin of error—because this annual increment to the permanent Mexican population of the country settles over such a wide area that its presence is hardly perceptible except in large city colonies.

Americans of Mexican descent take an active part in local politics and have their bosses and machines like English-speaking Americans. In New Mexico they were said to make very fair citizens, though more apt to be loyal to personal leaders than to political parties. The immigrants, even if they make their home in this country, seldom become naturalized. The records at San Antonio show that before the federal naturalization law went into operation the number of persons with German names who became citizens was eight or nine times the number of those bearing Spanish names, though the Mexican population of Bexar County is over one third the total foreign-born residents. In the entire state in 1900, the Mexican population was 39.6 percent of the total foreign-born population, and doubtless has been increasing relatively since that year. Those Mexicans who become naturalized have usually resided in the United States for many years, sometimes for the greater part of their lives. It is not unusual for several persons of the same family name to acquire citizenship at the same time, probably to facilitate the settling of an estate or for some other legal purpose.

Spanish-speaking citizens consider themselves socially superior to the immigrants, and rather pride themselves on being Americans. There is for this reason less social intermingling than the identity of language, religion, and customs might lead one to expect. The "Americanization" of the Spanish-speaking population of the Southwest is proceeding much more rapidly at present than heretofore, partly because these people are themselves migrating temporarily or permanently to English-speaking sections of the country, and partly because of the large immigration from other parts of the union. The history of Las Vegas, New Mexico, indicates how this change affects civic ideals. The original Mexican town in the river valley antedates the advent of the American. When the railway was built, an American town grew up in its vicinity, possibly a mile from the center of the older village. Later the two places were incorporated as a single city. But this arrangement was unpopular with the Mexicans, used to more primitive political arrangements and averse to taxation, and through their influence the town was disincorporated. The American town then went ahead, incorporated separately, constructed public works, and built up an excellent system of public schools, including a high school, housed in fine buildings. After several years the Mexican town finally incorporated separately and now is following the example of its neighbor in the matter of improvements and school facilities. So the New Mexican and largely Spanish-speaking community is now taxing itself more heavily than many a town in the

East for public education, and has issued bonds and erected creditable school-houses. This case is fairly representative of what is taking place wherever the railway and American example are bringing the influence of other sections of the country to bear upon the native population. An educational officer, who himself spoke Spanish fluently, whose duties made him familiar with conditions in the southern part of Colorado, said that a marked language change had occurred within ten years, so that while formerly it was comparatively rare to meet a person of Mexican race who spoke English, it was now rare to meet a young "Mexican" who was not familiar with that language.

These changes to American habits of life in the home and to American civic ideals in the community, coupled with the gradual acquisition of English in the public schools, are all recent. The public-school system of New Mexico is but fifteen years old, and railways have been in the territory less than a generation. They have as yet influenced appreciably only that part of the so-called Mexican population that has been born in the United States. At present, the immigrant Mexican does not seem likely to be assimilated by our own people; that is, actual fusion of blood appears to be remote. But barring this, which may not be permanent, he may learn to understand our institutions and adopt our habits of thought and action in public affairs.

2. The Reverend Pedro Grado Addresses El Congreso Mexicanista, 1911

Mr. President:

Respectable Audience:

My turn has arrived in the progression of the program of the *Congreso Mexicanista* to step in the place from which have come forth words full of erudition; ideas that, although heterogeneous, demonstrated with few exceptions beloved unity in the objective that occupies our attention. . . . In this conversation, and it is nothing more, I will touch on some of the points or topics which are most interesting to review, and which may be most useful to us in placing the first bricks of the great social edifice that this Congreso Mexicanista proposes.

There are two black points that, with a prophetic threat, sprout forth and grow in the pure heaven of our liberty and which day by day, worry all good Mexicans, all true patriots, and all persons who shelter altruism and philanthropy in their souls.

The first of these points concerns the oppression and the abuses that the sons of Uncle Sam commit daily to our countrymen, especially in the State of Texas.

The second is the imprudent conduct of men and women, our fellow citizens, in the State of Texas.

The first point has the following classification: I. Bad application of the law when it deals with Mexicans. II. Unpunished molesting of Mexicans by particular Americans. III. The exclusion of Mexican children from the American schools.

El Congresso Mexicanista, 1911. In David J. Weber, ed., *Foreigners in Their Native Land: Historical Roots of the Mexican Americans* (Albuquerque: University of New Mexico Press, 1973).

Order demands that the bad application of the law in treating Mexicans be discussed. The disease has its remedy, and it is here that the utility of the Congreso Mexicanista is illustrated, inasmuch as experience teaches us that isolation causes weakness and that weakness produces failure. Reason tells us to make ourselves strong. . . .

The Congreso Mexicanista can and should enhance the Mexican press of Texas. The newspaper is the scourge of the unjust and the denouncer of the abusers of office. It is a powerful medium to carry complaints to the desks of officials and demonstrate by turns that we are not indolent, that we are concerned about the poverty of our countrymen, and that we are able to do all that is within the law for them.

The Congreso Mexicanista can and should embrace wealthy, influential men because of their morality, their knowledge, and their contracts. These are the ones who, in case of difficulty, will have access to elevated representatives of the law.

The Congreso will broaden itself admirably, and admirable will be the results, if it tries to attract to it all the secret societies of the Masonic type, or whose members might be our countrymen, or the lodges that might be of this kind. It should do the same with the mutual societies and those that simply have altruism as their ideal. How surprising will be the effect of a petition, or a request, or of a communication backed by thousands of individuals! What greater satisfaction for a needy person than the loving hand of thousands of his fellow citizens, ready to put to flight the terrible anxiety which poverty causes. Considering that this Congreso will come to be that which I suppose, with the elements now established, the oppressions of the authorities will stop. . . .

The unpunished vexations of particular Americans may continue. This problem is more difficult to solve. The Mexican braceros ["laborers"] . . . who work in a mill, on a hacienda, or in a plantation would do well to establish *Ligas Mexicanistas* ["Mexican Workers' Leagues"], and see that their neighbors form them. Thus, once united, with the help of the press, and with the valuable group of philanthropists of wealth or influence in some department, they will be able to strike back at the hatred of some bad sons of Uncle Sam who believe themselves better than the Mexicans because of the magic that surrounds the word *white*.

It remains for us to say something of the exclusion of Mexican children from the Anglo-Saxon schools in the majority of the counties of the State of Texas. We can say this is a difficult but not unsolvable problem.

What happens in Laredo, Texas, in San Diego of the same state, and in other river communities where the Mexican children have free access to the American schools and high schools? The purpose of this question is to go to the reasons, because if these reasons are transmissible, the problem is not far from resolving itself. . . . In the aforementioned towns, the Mexican element dominates and is intimately bound to the Anglo-Saxon by ties of commerce and other kinds. In these same towns there are respectable Mexicans with prominent positions in the court houses, so that we find in this one of the causes, or the reason, for the Mexican children's access to American schools. Would we be able to make these means transmissible, and make the influence of those men extend to many miles round about? Yes, it is possible when all in mass distinguish themselves as *mexicanistas* and take interest in their countrymen. Whatever may be the reasons they exclude

Mexicans from the schools, I do not find another solution than the influence and heterogeneous powers of *mexicanismo.*

3. Flores de Andrade Recalls Her Revolutionary Activity as an Immigrant in El Paso, Texas, 1911

I was born in Chihuahua, [Mexico,] and spent my infancy and youth on an estate in Coahuila which belonged to my grandparents. . . . As I was healthy and happy I would run over the estate. . . . I rode on a horse bareback and wasn't afraid of anything. I was thirteen years of age when my grandparents died, leaving me a good inheritance. . . .

The first thing that I did, in spite of the fact that my sister and my aunt advised me against it, was to give absolute liberty on my lands to all the peons. I declared free of debts all of those who worked on the lands which my grandparents had willed me and what there was on that fifth part, such as grain, agricultural implements and animals, I divided in equal parts among the peons. I also told them that they could go on living on those lands in absolute liberty without paying me anything. . . .

Because I divided my property . . . , my aunt and even my sister began to annoy me. . . .

They annoyed me so much that I decided to marry, marrying a man of German origin. I lived very happily with my husband until he died, leaving me a widow with six children. Twelve years had gone by in the mean time. I then decided to go to Chihuahua, . . . to the capital of the state, and there . . . I began to fight for liberal ideals, organizing a women's club which was called the "Daughters of Cuauhtemoc," a semi-secret organization which worked with the Liberal Party . . . in fighting the dictatorship of Don Porfirio Diaz.* . . .

My political activities caused greater anger among the members of my family. . . . Under these conditions I grew poorer and poorer until I reached extreme poverty. I passed four bitter years in Chihuahua suffering economic want on the one hand and fighting in defense of the ideals on the other. My relatives would tell me not to give myself in fighting for the people, because I wouldn't get anything from it. . . . I didn't care anything about that. . . . I would have gone on fighting for the cause which I considered to be just.

My economic situation in Chihuahua became serious, so that I had to accept donations of money which were given to me as charity by wealthy people . . . who knew me and my relatives. . . .

Finally after four years' stay in Chihuahua, I decided to come to El Paso, Texas. I came in the first place to see if I could better my economic condition and secondly to continue fighting in that region in favor of the Liberal ideals . . . to plot

Manuel Gamio, *The Mexican Immigrant: His Life Story* (Chicago: University of Chicago Press, 1931), pp. 29–35. Reprinted by permission of the University of Chicago.

*Porfirio Diaz led a successful coup in Mexico in 1876 and ruled as a dictator until 1911, when he was forced to resign in a revolt led by Francisco Madero. *Ed.*

against the dictatorship of Don Porfirio. I came to El Paso . . . together with my children and comrade Pedro Mendoza. . . .

With comrade Mendoza we soon began the campaign of Liberal propaganda. We lived in the same house . . . and as we went about together all day working in the Liberal campaign the American authorities forced us to marry. I am now trying to divorce myself from my husband for he hasn't treated me right. . . .

. . . A group of comrades founded in El Paso a Liberal women's club. They made me president of that group, and soon afterwards I began to carry on the propaganda work in El Paso and in Ciudad Juarez. . . . I took charge of collecting money, clothes, medicines and even ammunition and arms to begin to prepare for the revolutionary movement, for the uprisings were already starting in some places.

The American police and the Department of Justice began to suspect our activities and soon began to watch out for me, but they were never able to find either in my house or in the offices of the club documents or arms or anything. . . .

In 1910, when all those who were relatives of those who had taken up arms were arrested by order of the Mexican federal authorities, I had to come to Ciudad Juarez. . . . I was then put into prison, but soon was let out and I went back to El Paso to continue the fight. . . .

. . . Sr. Madero . . . came to El Paso, pursued by the Mexican and American authorities. He came to my house with some others. I couldn't hide them in my house, but got a little house . . . and put them there.* . . .

. . . One day Don Francisco Madero entrusted my husband to go to a Mexican farm on the shore of the Bravo river so as to bring two men who were coming to reach an agreement concerning the movement. My husband . . . didn't go. Then I offered my services to Sr. Madero and I went for the two men who were on this side of the border, . . . in Texan territory. . . . Two Texan rangers who had followed me asked me where I was going, and I told them to a festival and they asked me to invite them. I took them to the festival and there managed to get them drunk; then I took away the two men and brought them to Don Francisco. Then I went back to the farm and brought the Rangers to El Paso where I took them drunk to the City Hall and left them there.

Later when everything was ready for the revolutionary movement against the dictatorship, Don Francisco and all those who accompanied him decided to pass over to Mexican territory. I prepared an afternoon party so as to disguise the movement. They all dressed in masked costumes as if for a festival and then we went towards the border. The river was very high and it was necessary to cross over without hesitating for the American authorities were already following us. . . . Finally, mounting a horse barebacked, I took charge of taking those who were accompanying Don Francisco over two by two. They crossed over to a farm and there they remounted for the mountains.

---

*Madero was in exile in Texas, following his arrest by Diaz. Madero began a new revolution on November 20, 1910, and forced Diaz into exile and was elected president of Mexico. *Ed.*

A woman companion and I came back to the American side, for I received instructions to go on with the campaign. This happened the 18 of May, 1911. We slept there in the house of the owner of the ranch and on the next day when we were getting ready to leave, the Colonel came with a picket of soldiers. I told the owner of the ranch to tell him that he didn't know me. . . . When the authorities camp up . . . , the owner of the ranch said that he didn't know me and I said that I didn't know him. They then asked me for my name and I gave it to them. They asked me what I was doing there and I said that I had been hunting and showed them two rabbits that I had shot. They then took away my . . . rifle and my pistol and told me that they had orders to shoot me because I had been conspiring against Don Porfirio. I told them that was true and that they should shoot me right away because otherwise I was going to lose courage. The Colonel, however, sent for instructions from his general. . . . He sent orders that I should be shot at once.

This occurred almost on the shores of the Rio Grande and my family already had received a notice of what was happening to me and went to make pleas to the American authorities. . . . They were already making up the squad to shoot me when the American Consul arrived and asked me if I could show that I was an American citizen so that they couldn't shoot, but I didn't want to do that. I told them that I was a Mexican. . . .

The Colonel told me to make my will for they were going to execute me. I told him that I didn't have anything more than my six children whom I will to the Mexican people. . . .

The Colonel was trying to stave off my execution so that he could save me, he said. An officer then came and said that the General was approaching. The Colonel said that it would be well to wait until the chief came so that he could decide concerning my life, but a corporal told him that they should shoot me at once for if the general came and they had not executed me then they would be blamed. . . . The corporal who was interested in having me shot was going to fire when I took the Colonel's rifle away from him and menaced him; he then ordered the soldiers to throw their rifles at the feet of the Mexican woman . . . , for the troops of the General were already coming. I gathered up the rifles and crossed the river in my little buggy. There the American authorities arrested me and took me to Fort Bliss. . . . On the next day the authorities at Fort Bliss received a telegram from President Taft in which he ordered me to be put at liberty, and they sent me home, a negro military band accompanying me through the streets.

At the triumph of the cause of Sr. Madero we had some great festivities in Ciudad Juarez. . . .

Afterwards Sr. Madero sent for me and asked me what I wanted. I told him that I wanted the education of my six children and that all the promises which had been made to the Mexican people should be carried out. . . .

During the Huerta revolution I kept out of the struggle, . . . and little by little I have been separating myself from political affairs.* . . .

---

*In a revolt in 1923, General Adolfo de la Huerta overthrew Mexican president Alvaro Obregón. *Ed.*

4. Samuel Bryan Analyzes Increases in Mexican Immigration, 1912

Previous to 1900 the influx of Mexicans was comparatively unimportant. It was confined almost exclusively to those portions of Texas, New Mexico, Arizona and California which are near the boundary line between Mexico and the United States. Since these states were formerly Mexican territory and have always possessed a considerable Mexican population, a limited migration back and forth across the border was a perfectly natural result of the existing blood relationship. During the period from 1880 to 1900 the Mexican-born population of these border states increased from 66,312 to 99,969—a gain of 33,657 in twenty years. This increase was not sufficient to keep pace with the growth of the total population of the states. Since 1900, however, there has been a rapid increase in the volume of Mexican immigration, and also some change in its geographical distribution. . . .

. . . In 1908, it was estimated that from 60,000 to 100,000 Mexicans entered the United States each year. This estimate, however, should be modified by the well-known fact that each year a considerable number of Mexicans return to Mexico. Approximately 50 percent of those Mexicans who find employment as section hands upon the railroads claim the free transportation back to El Paso which is furnished by the railroad companies to those who have been in their employ six months or a year. Making allowance for this fact, it would be conservative to place the yearly accretion of population by Mexican immigration at from 35,000 to 70,000. It is probable, therefore, that the Mexican-born population of the United States has trebled since the census of 1900 was taken.

This rapid increase within the last decade has resulted from the expansion of industry both in Mexico and in the United States. In this country the industrial development of the Southwest has opened up wider fields of employment for unskilled laborers in transportation, agriculture, mining, and smelting. A similar expansion in northern Mexico has drawn many Mexican laborers from the farms of other sections of the country farther removed from the border, and it is an easy matter to go from the mines and section gangs of northern Mexico to the more remunerative employment to be had in similar industries of the southwestern United States. Thus the movement from the more remote districts of Mexico to the newly developed industries of the North has become largely a stage in a more general movement to the United States. Entrance into this country is not difficult, for employment agencies in normal times have stood ready to advance board, lodging, and transportation to a place where work was to be had, and the immigration officials have usually deemed no Mexican likely to become a public charge so long as this was the case. This was especially true before 1908. . . .

Most of the Mexican immigrants have at one time been employed as railroad laborers. At present they are used chiefly as section hands and as members of construction gangs, but a number are also to be found working as common laborers about the shops and powerhouses. Although a considerable number are employed

As found in Samuel Bryan, "Mexican Immigrants in the United States," *The Survey* 20, no. 23 (September 1912): 726 and 730.

as helpers, few have risen above unskilled labor in any branch of the railroad service. As section hands on the two more important systems they were paid a uniform wage of $1.00 per day from their first employment in 1902 until 1909, except for a period of about one year previous to the financial stringency of 1907, when they were paid $1.25 per day. In 1909 the wages of all Mexican section hands employed upon the Santa Fe lines were again raised to $1.25 per day. The significant feature is, however, that as a general rule they have earned less than the members of any other race similarly employed. For example, 2,455 Mexican section hands from whom data were secured by the Immigration Commission in 1908 and 1909, 2,111, or 85.9 percent, were earning less than $1.25 per day, while the majority of the Greeks, Italians, and Japanese earned more than $1.25 and a considerable number more than $1.50 per day.

In the arid regions of the border states where they have always been employed and where the majority of them still live, the Mexicans come into little direct competition with other races, and no problems of importance result from their presence. But within the last decade their area of employment has expanded greatly. They are now used as section hands as far east as Chicago and as far north as Wyoming. Moreover, they are now employed to a considerable extent in the coal mines of Colorado and New Mexico, in the ore mines of Colorado and Arizona, in the smelters of Arizona, in the cement factories of Colorado and California, in the beet sugar industry of the last mentioned states, and in fruit growing and canning in California. In these localities they have at many points come into direct competition with other races, and their low standards have acted as a check upon the progress of the more assertive of these.

Where they are employed in other industries, the same wage discrimination against them as was noted in the case of railroad employees is generally apparent where the work is done on an hour basis, but no discrimination exists in the matter of rates for piecework. As pieceworkers in the fruit canneries and in the sugar beet industry the proverbial sluggishness of the Mexicans prevents them from earning as much as the members of other races. In the citrus fruit industry their treatment varies with the locality. In some instances they are paid the same as the "whites"— in others the same as the Japanese, according to the class with which they share the field of employment. The data gathered by the Immigration Commission show that although the earnings of Mexicans employed in the other industries are somewhat higher than those of the Mexican section hands, they are with few exceptions noticeably lower than the earnings of Japanese, Italians, and members of the various Slavic races who are similarly employed. This is true in the case of smelting, ore mining, coal mining, and sugar refining. Specific instances of the use of Mexicans to curb the demands of other races are found in the sugar beet industry of central California, where they were introduced for the purpose of showing the Japanese laborers that they were not indispensable, and in the same industry in Colorado, where they were used in a similar way against the German-Russians. Moreover, Mexicans have been employed as strikebreakers in the coal mines of Colorado and New Mexico, and in one instance in the shops of one important railroad system.

Socially and politically the presence of large numbers of Mexicans in this country gives rise to serious problems. The reports of the Immigration Commissions show that they lack ambition, are to a very large extent illiterate in their native language, are slow to learn English, and most cases show no political interest. In some instances, however, they have been organized to serve the purposes of political bosses, as for example in Phoenix, Arizona. Although more of them are married and have their families with them than is the case among the south European immigrants, they are unsettled as a class, move readily from place to place, and do not acquire or lease land to any extent. But their most unfavorable characteristic is their inclination to form colonies and live in a clannish manner. Wherever a considerable group of Mexicans are employed, they live together, if possible, and associate very little with members of other races. In the mining towns and other small industrial communities they live ordinarily in rude adobe huts outside of the town limits. As section hands they of course live as the members of the other races have done, in freight cars fitted with windows and bunks, or in rough shacks along the line of the railroad. In the cities their colonization has become a menace.

. . . .

In Los Angeles the housing problem centers largely in the cleaning up or demolition of the Mexican "house courts," which have become the breeding ground of disease and crime, and which have now attracted a considerable population of immigrants of other races. It is estimated that approximately 2,000 Mexicans are living in these "house courts." Some 15,000 persons of this race are residents of Los Angeles and vicinity. Conditions of life among the immigrants of the city, which are molded to a certain extent by Mexican standards, have been materially improved by the work of the Los Angeles Housing Commission. . . . However, the Mexican quarter continues to offer a serious social problem to the community. . . .

In conclusion it should be recognized that although the Mexicans have proved to be efficient laborers in certain industries, and have afforded a cheap and elastic labor supply for the southwestern United States, the evils to the community at large which their presence in large numbers almost invariably brings may more than overbalance their desirable qualities. Their low standards of living and of morals, their illiteracy, their utter lack of proper political interest, the retarding effect of their employment upon the wage scale of the more progressive races, and finally their tendency to colonize in urban centers, with evil results, combine to stamp them as a rather undesirable class of residents.

5. *"Los Sediciosos"* (The Seditionists) Commemorates Mexican American Resistance in South Texas, 1915

In nineteen hundred fifteen, oh but the days were hot!
   I am going to sing these stanzas, stanzas about the seditionists.

With this it will be three times that remarkable things have happened;
   the first time was in Mercedes, then in Brownsville and San Benito.

In that well-known place called Norias, it really got hot for them;
   a great many bullets rained down on those cursed *rinches* [Texas Rangers].

Now the fuse is lit by the true-born Mexicans,
  and it will be the Texas-Mexicans who will have to pay the price.

Now the fuse is lit, in blue and red,
  and it will be those on this side who will have to pay the price.

Now the fuse is lit, very nice and red,
  and it will be those of us who are blameless who will have to pay the price.

Aniceto Pizaña said, singing as he rode along,
  "Where can I find the *rinches?* I'm here to pay them a visit.

"Those *rinches* from King Ranch say that they are very brave;
  the make the women cry, and they make the people run."

Then said Teodoro Fuentes, as he was tying his shoe,
  "We are going to give a hard time to those *rinches* from King Ranch."

Then said Vicente el Giro, sitting on his great big horse,
  "Let me at that big Gringo, so we can amble arm-in-arm."

The American replies, holding his hat in his hands,
  "I will be glad to go with you; you are very good Maxacans."

Then said Miguel Salinas, on his almond-colored mare,
  "Ah, how disagreeable are these Gringos! Why don't they wait for us?"

In that well-known place called Norias, you could hear the sound of firing,
  but from Señor Luis de la Rosa, all you could hear was his weeping.

Señor Luis de la Rosa considered himself a brave man,
  but at the hour of the shooting, he cried like a baby.

Then said Teodoro Fuentes, smiling his little smile,
  "Pour on the bullets, boys; what a beautiful fracas!

"Fire, fire away, my boys; fire, fire all at once,
  for Señor Luis de la Rosa has besmirched his colors."

Teodoro Fuentes shouted, "We have to go through Mercedes,
  so we can show the *rinches* that we are too much for them."

Luis de la Rosa tells them, "Boys, what are you going to do?
  We cannot go through Mercedes, and if you doubt it, you soon will see."

Teodoro Fuentes replies, in a very natural voice,
  "It's best that you not go with us, because all you will do is cry."

So they did go through Mercedes, and also through San Benito;
  they went to derail the train at the station of Olmito.

The seditionists are leaving, they have gone into retreat;
  they have left us a red swath to remember them by.

The seditionists are leaving, they said that they would return;
  but they didn't tell us when because they had no way of knowing.

I will not give you my farewell, because I did not bring it with me;
  Luis de la Rosa took it with him to San Luis Potosí.

❥ *E S S A Y S*

By the early twentieth century the Mexican American people of the Southwest had been reduced to the status of landless and dependent wage laborers, resulting in a dramatic change in Mexican-Anglo relations. Treated as an inferior race, Mexicans were segregated and faced widespread discrimination. Misunderstandings between Anglos and Mexicans erupted in conflict. Meanwhile, the first period of large-scale Mexican immigration had begun. Recruited by labor agents to work for the railroads, the mines, and the farmers, the immigrants found that passage to the United States was relatively easy because of the demand for labor and favorable immigration laws. Many of the immigrant males were accompanied by their wives, daughters, and female extended family members. One of their major destinations was El Paso, Texas. In the first essay, Mario T. García, professor of history at the University of California, Santa Barbara, describes the experiences of Mexican immigrant women as housewives, workers, and participants in the labor movement in El Paso, explaining the role of chain migration and the growing importance of women as breadwinners in a variety of occupations. The participation of these women in labor unions was noteworthy. For example, although the Mexican female laundry workers' strike of 1919 failed because of the surplus of Mexican labor in the area, these women gained union consciousness and ethnic solidarity from the experience.

The many mutual aid and fraternal organizations Mexicans established throughout the Southwest formed a focal point of their communities as well as centers for unionization. This is the topic of the essay by Emilio Zamora, associate professor of history at the University of Houston, who examines the voluntary societies Mexicans founded in South Texas in the early twentieth century. Zamora states that these groups, which promoted social and cultural activities, were the locus of a strong Mexican nationalism. By serving as advocates for workers' rights as well as for civil and legal rights, the societies united Mexican immigrants and Mexican Americans in the struggle for higher wages, better working conditions, and racial equality.

Mexican Immigrant Women in El Paso, Texas

MARIO T. GARCÍA

Women of Mexican descent appear early in the story of the Southwest. On the whole, most were wives and mothers, and their story has yet to be told. Wives accompanied their husbands on the long and perilous trek to the United States during the late nineteenth and early twentieth centuries. The family, of course, represented the most important institution transferred across the border by Mexican immigrants. The Dillingham Commission report of 1911 on the state of foreign immigration to the United States, authorized by the United States Senate, noted that a high percentage of Mexican laborers in western industries had brought their wives from nearby Mexico. According to the commission, some 58.2 percent of Mexican railroad workers in the survey reported that their wives were with them in the United States. This figure was much higher than that for other immigrant railroad

Mario T. García, "The Chicana in American History: The Mexican Women of El Paso, 1880–1920—A Case Study," *Pacific Historical Review* 49, no. 2 (May 1980): 315–337. Copyright © 1980 by American Historical Association, Pacific Coast Branch. Reprinted by permission.

workers in the West who had arrived from more distant lands, such as southern Europe and Asia. . . . One railroad line, the Santa Fe, by 1910 was encouraging the migration of Mexican families in order to stabilize working conditions. As a Santa Fe engineer put it, hiring married men resulted in better and more productive workers. Investigators for the Dillingham Commission also discovered a similar condition in urban-related work. Sixty percent of Mexicans employed as construction workers by street railways, for example, admitted they had their wives with them. . . .

. . . The majority of Mexican immigrant families, as revealed in a sample taken from a 1900 El Paso census, were either nuclear or extended. . . . Over half of the immigrant household units were nuclear families living by themselves or in an augmented relationship with nonrelated household residents, such as boarders. In addition, 13 percent were extended families. More Mexican immigrant families lived in nuclear households than did non-Spanish surname families. . . . Since the 1910 and 1920 manuscript cenuses are not yet available to scholars, no comparisons can be made, but it is possible that over this twenty-year period [between 1900 and 1920] a pattern of chain migration set in and extended-family households grew among Mexican immigrants as other relatives arrived, especially those from the northern Mexican states.

Although some Mexican women in El Paso and throughout the urban Southwest contributed to household incomes by taking in wash or lodgers, no disintegration took place in the traditional pattern of men being the chief wage-earners and women doing household work. The sample taken from the El Paso census of 1900 shows that no mothers and few daughters, most of the latter being too young, in an immigrant family headed by the father worked outside the home. As wife and mother the Mexican housewife was primarily responsible for caring for the Mexican male worker and her family. Under a division of labor which relegated nearly all of them to housework, Mexican women, like most women, had to maintain the male work force as well as reproduce it. Within the family, Mexican males not only found relief from their job alienation, but nourishment for another day's hard work. Consequently, the family, and the women's role in it, performed a significant economic task.

Too poor to afford their own domestics, Mexican women in the border city performed their housework under depressed living conditions. "Chihuahuita," the largest Mexican settlement in El Paso and adjacent to the Rio Grande River border, contained the city's worst and most congested housing. While no legal restrictions prohibited Mexicans from living in the better homes found in American neighborhoods, lack of occupational mobility, in addition to race and cultural prejudice, kept Mexicans segregated in *barrios* (slums). Mexicans adjusted to these conditions, however, because of acquaintance with poverty, plus the mistaken belief they would soon return to Mexico with ample savings. . . .

Under these conditions, Mexican housewives did the hard manual labor which allowed immigrant families to live on husband's and sometimes childrens' limited earnings. Mexican women had to haul water for washing and cooking from the river or public water pipes. To feed their families, they had to spend time marketing, often in Cuidad Juárez across the border, as well as long, hot hours cooking meals and coping with the burden of desert sand both inside and outside their homes. Besides the problem of raising children, unsanitary living conditions forced Mexican mothers to deal with disease and illness in their families. Diphtheria, tuberculosis, typhus, and influenza were never too far away. . . . As a result, Mexican mothers had to devote much energy caring for sick children, many of whom died. The *El Paso Times* commented later in 1909 that out of thirty-six deaths during the previous week, twenty involved children less than three years of age. Almost all were Mexicans. "Death seems to be a frequent and common visitor in the homes of the Mexican element," the newspaper remarked. Lack of sewers, water, paved sidewalks, and streets plus overcrowded homes made housework one of the most arduous jobs in the Mexican settlement.

The Mexican housewife, although oppressed under a sexual division of labor, helped sustain the family's male workers and indirectly El Paso's economy which grew and prospered from the labor of Mexicans. Without the woman's housework, Mexican men could not have adjusted so easily to an American urban environment. . . .

While housework formed the most important work activity for Mexican women, some in El Paso also found jobs outside the home. El Paso, for example, had one of the earliest concentrations of Mexican female wage workers in the United States. Mexican women, as other women, worked either to augment the earnings of male family members or due to the loss of the male breadwinner. . . . A sample of 393 El Paso households taken from the 1900 manuscript census reveals that almost a fifth . . . of Mexican households contained a working woman. . . . Mexican women who worked, according to the census, were either unmarried daughters, mothers with no husbands, or single women. Of the 31 Spanish surnamed households in the sample with a working female, 17 had daughters or other young relatives with jobs while the remaining 14 contained working mothers with no husbands or single women. On the other hand, married Mexican women, both foreign and native born, within a nuclear or extended family, did not work. The sample revealed no instance of a woman with an employed husband having a job. Age and fertility help explain this condition. In the 1900 sample, 41.08 percent of married Mexican immigrant women were between fifteen and thirty years of age, a period when women generally give birth. Moreover, 38.44 percent of married Mexican immigrant women were between thirty and forty, a period when most women had children at home. . . .

If age and fertility worked against Mexican women finding jobs outside the home, so too did Mexican cultural traditions. Mexican men resented women, especially wives, working or wanting to work for wages. Most males believed their work a man's duty and that woman's consisted of raising children and keeping house. As one working class newspaper in Mexico during the age of Porfirio Díaz emphasized: "To be a wife is to be a woman preferably selected amongst many other women, for her honesty, for her religiousness, for her amiability, . . . for her industriousness, [and] for her docility. . . ." Despite such attitudes, the Mexican family in the United States did not remain static. Over the years more Mexican women, especially daughters, became wage-workers to augment the family income. Also, as the economy expanded, . . . El Paso and southwestern industries and services began to recruit more Mexican women workers. . . .

The increase in Mexican female wage-workers in El Paso by 1920 can be seen in census figures for that year. The census reported that 3,474 foreign-born females, almost all Mexicans, ten years of age and older were engaged in a gainful occupation. Foreign-born female wage-workers represented half of all females ten years and over who held jobs in El Paso. Most female workers in El Paso . . . did "women's work." The two largest occupations were servants . . . and laundresses . . .—jobs familiar to women in Mexico—where the majority of Mexican working women could be found. Due to deficiencies in skills and schooling, as well as prejudice against them, few Mexican women, unlike their American counterparts, were in such skilled professional occupations as teaching, nursing, or office work. . . .

Mexican women, besides working as servants, found other employment opportunities. Many worked as washerwomen, either in American homes or in their own as well as in the various laundries of El Paso. In laundries, they learned such other skills as the use of sewing machines and received from $4 to $6 a week. In 1917 the El Paso Laundry, the largest in the city, employed 134 Spanish-surnamed workers out of a total of 166 employees, and Mexican women, mostly doing collar and flatwork, composed what appears to have been over half of the Mexican employees. That same year the Elite Laundry had 76 Spanish-surnamed female workers out of a total of 128 employees. Another of the larger laundries, the Acme, employed 75 Spanish-surnamed females out of 121 employees in 1917. The same pattern prevailed in the smaller laundries. For example, the Post Laundry had 33 Spanish-surnamed women in their work force of 49. While many of these laundresses lived in El Paso, some came from Ciudad Juárez. . . . The use of nonresident Mexican women limited already low wages.

In addition to service jobs, some Mexican women labored as production workers, especially in El Paso's early garment factories. In 1902 Bergman's factory, which turned out shirts and overalls, reported that it had three American women and a large number of Mexican females. . . . Several years later, in 1919, the El Paso Overall Company advertised in a Spanish-language newspaper that it needed Mexican women for sewing and for general work. Mexican women likewise worked in the Kohlberg cigar factory. Although the exact nature of their work cannot be determined, 22 Mexican women out of 113 employees labored in the plant in 1917. Some women also found jobs as clerks and sales personnel in the downtown stores. . . . Still other Mexicans worked as cooks or dishwashers in restaurants. In more unfortunate cases, Mexican women sold food on the streets of Chihuahuita.

Finally, as in other societies, some women inhabited the saloons and gambling halls of the red-light district. . . . When the city government enforced an ordinance in 1903 to move the district further from the center of El Paso, the *Times* reported that many of the prostitutes "propose to go across the river, among the number being the Mexicans, which include the dance hall girls. . . .

Specific attention to the wages of Mexican women in El Paso occurred as the result of hearings held in the border city . . . by the Texas Industrial Welfare Commission. During three days of testimony by employers as well as female employees, the commission discovered that Mexican workers in the laundries and factories of the city received less pay than American women in other industries. The Mexicans also obtained less than the salaries of laundry and factory workers in other Texas cities who performed similar work but did not face Mexican competition. According to the commission, these differences made it more difficult to set a minimum wage throughout the state. The reason for the problem, the commission stated, could be found in the Mexican's lower standard of living, "and that is a condition which, it seems, cannot be remedied." The members of the commission concluded, although without evidence, that "the Mexican workers find it possible to 'live comfortably' on a wage that Anglo workers would regard as 'starvation wages.' "

Despite the commission's conclusions, Mexican women who appeared before it refuted those who claimed that Mexicans did not need higher wages because they had a lower standard of living. One group of laundry workers who had gone on strike for higher wages testified that the laundries had paid them $4 to $5 a week. . . . María Valles testified that she worked at the Elite Laundry and received $4.50 a week. She lived with her family and supported a nine-year-old daughter. "I have to support her and myself," she stated, "but I have to make great sacrifices, some days going without food, for lack of means." She believed she could live well on $15 a week. Mexican women employed in the El Paso Overall Company also testified before the commission about their need for higher wages. The *El Paso Herald* described one of these workers, Daniela Morena, as "a woman along in years," who stated that she made $7 to $8 a week and supported her mother and two children. She believed that she required at least $15 a week, "but if alone might get along with $8 or $9 a week, as she 'dressed very humbly.' " Other garment workers gave similar testimonies. The Mexican women's arguments, unfortunately, had little impact. Low wages for Mexicans, both men and women, continued to characterize the El Paso economy.

In addition to their roles as housewives and wage workers, a third major activity of Mexican women in the United States was their participation in labor unions and labor strife. Though relatively few women were active in unions or labor protests, Mexican women nonetheless were involved in some of the largest and most important labor strikes in the Southwest. . . . In October 1919 some of the Mexican women, together with state and local American Federation of Labor organizers, established the Laundry Workers' Union. The Union then began to organize workers, almost all Mexican women, in the Acme Laundry of El Paso. When this plant refused to accept the union and fired two of the organizers, Isabel and Manuela Hernández, the rest of the almost two hundred workers went on strike demanding that the employers rehire their co-workers. . . . F. B. Fletcher, the president and manager of Acme, denied any knowledge of a union and claimed he had dismissed the two workers for other reasons. . . .

When three other laundries attempted to do the work of Acme, the Mexican women at those plants joined the strike. Owners of two more laundries at first agreed to recognize the union, but then changed their minds. The women at these places also struck. In a few days somewhere between 300 and 575 workers, including some men, had gone on strike against all of El Paso's laundries. At a meeting of the Central Labor Union where representatives of the A. F. of L. addressed the laundry workers, the Mexican women unanimously agreed to stand by the union.

"Truly this was a sight that would do the heart of any one good to see these girls and women," the *Labor Advocate,* the A. F. of L. organ in El Paso, reported. "[S]ome of them hardly in their teens and some of them bent with age, standing up and solemnly promising that no matter what may come or what may happen, they would stand together for the mutual good of their fellow workers."

Besides the workers' own solidarity, the A. F. of L.'s support proved important in maintaining the strike. The Central Labor Union not only endorsed the action, but various locals raised funds for the women strikers. . . . The A. F. of L.'s willingness to organize and assist the Mexicans, however, did not represent a departure from Samuel Gompers' policy of excluding alien workers. . . .

The laundry workers obtained further assistance from various Mexican social organizations in El Paso, composed of both Mexican Americans and Mexican nationals. *La Patria,* the city's major Spanish-language newspaper, expressed its support of the Mexican women and called upon other Mexican groups to do likewise. . . . A delegation of twelve women and four men from the laundry union also received the endorsement of the influential mutual society, the Círculo de Amigos, which had been organized by Mexican American city employees. In a letter to all Mexican societies, Círculo officials expressed their support of the strikers "who are giving an example of character, strength and racial solidarity." Believing it important not to abandon the women in their hour of need, the Círculo called on all other Mexican organizations and the Mexican community to attend an informational meeting on how best to "help our sisters." . . .

While hurt by unfavorable newspaper publicity, the laundry workers' main problem concerned the owners' ability to hire strikebreakers as well as retain some of their employees. F. Ravel, proprietor of the Excelsior Laundry, refused to sign a union contract because his operation had not been seriously hampered by the strike. "Some of my Mexicans quit," he told a reporter, "and I put Americans in their places. In a few weeks every workman in my shop will be American." Ravel contended that American labor proved to be more productive and efficient than Mexican. Besides hiring unemployed Americans, the laundries also found it easy to hire numerous Mexican workers both in El Paso and Ciudad Juárez. The *Advocate* pointed out that even though 486 women and men had gone on strike, hundreds of other Mexicans were asking for work in the laundries. . . . Frustrated, the strikers verbally attacked their replacements by calling them "scabs" and labor leaders demanded that the city government stop the laundries from employing other workers. The city attorney, however, ruled that no municipal ordinance prohibited employers from hiring whom they pleased. Unfortunately for organized labor and the Mexican women, the A.F. of L.'s own refusal to organize or support Mexican alien workers only added to the availability of Mexican strikebreakers.

To compound their problems, the laundry workers failed to maintain the laundry drivers' support, despite an initial endorsement by the Laundry Drivers' Union. . . . Unlike the laundry workers, all of the truck drivers were Anglo-Americans. The Mexican women received an additional setback when an ad appeared in the *Herald* signed by thirty-four workers, including twenty-seven Mexicans, who had remained on the job at the El Paso Laundry. Addressed "To the Public," the notice stated that the undesigned "old employees" of the laundry "have at all times been treated in a most considerate manner, and our welfare has never been neglected; . . . we are not in sympathy with the laundry workers' unfair strike and positively will not support it."

El Paso's laundry strike continued until the end of 1919, but it had been lost almost from the start. The existence of a large pool of surplus Mexican labor both in El Paso and across the border proved to be the decisive factor. Although no doubt irritated by the strike, and by the fear of class disturbances in the city, laundry owners simply hired other workers, both Mexican and American. Hampered by El Paso's large number of Mexican aliens, plus its refusal to organize or support them, the A.F. of L. assisted as best as possible the laundry workers, but could not overcome organized labor's liabilities along the border. As for the Mexican women who went on strike, it appears most never regained their jobs. Their struggle, however, represents one of the earliest displays of union consciousness and ethnic solidarity among Mexican female workers in the United States. The fact that many of the women apparently were Mexican Americans rather than Mexican nationals must also be seen as a major factor in the laundry workers' ability to organize. More permanent, knowledgeable, and secure in their rights as American citizens, unionization of Mexican American workers symbolized a process of acculturation to an industrial and urban culture. . . .

This case study of Mexican women in El Paso between 1880 and 1920 has attempted to demonstrate some of the major research themes on women that might be pursued in Chicano history. The general topics of Mexican women as housewives, as wage workers, and as participants in unionization and labor strife constitute the most important activities that have affected Mexican women in the United States. An investigation of them by historians of the Chicano experience will contribute not only to an understanding of the history of Mexican American women, but to the history of all Mexicans north of the border. The history of Chicanos, especially Chicano workers, is only half complete without an appreciation of the contributions Mexican women have made.

Mexican Voluntary Organizations of South Texas

EMILIO ZAMORA

The Mexican community [of South Texas in the early twentieth century] was by no means homogeneous in cultural identity or political outlook. Mutual aid, pacifist, Masonic, and union organizations . . . at times reflected broadly defined civic outlooks, highly specialized interests, or narrow instrumental views. . . . The impressive amount of collectivist political activity that evolved around mutual aid societies . . . points to a unifying cultural frame of reference that gave impetus and meaning to Mexican organizational life.

. . . Calls for unity openly adhered to a Mexicanist, or all-inclusive, nationalist sense of community and a popular ethic of mutuality. . . . Mutualism incorporated such values as fraternalism, reciprocity, and altruism into a moral prescription for

Reprinted from *The World of the Mexican Worker in South Texas* by Emilio Zamora, 1993, by permission of Texas A & M University Press.

human behavior, a cultural basis for moralistic and nationalistic political action that was intended to set things right. . . .

Voluntary organizations expressed the clearest visions of mutualism and a Mexicanist orientation in their conscious working-class endeavors. The fundamental concern among the members was to help each other survive the very difficult conditions under which they lived and worked. Mutualista organizations, however, did not always confine their attention to the immediate and pressing material interests of their largely working-class membership, nor did they simply embrace a narrow self-help outlook. Mutual aid societies also reinforced a collectivist spirit with resolute statements of purpose in support of nationalist principles and moral values, an active civic role, and strict rules that disciplined their members into conscious Mexicanist proponents of the ethic of mutuality. Intellectuals, in turn articulated these principles and values into different calls for unity and collective action, including unionism. Consequently, even different and at times opposing groups adhered to the same legitimating set of fundamentally unifying principles and values. . . .

Social Divisions

. . . Luis Recinos, a researcher assisting Manuel Gamio in the preparation of his highly acclaimed study of Mexican immigration, noted . . . divisions between the immigrant and U.S.-born Mexicans during the late 1920s. He was careful to point out . . . that voluntary organizations included everyone regardless of nativity. In other words, a Mexicanist identity and organizational style predominated at the same time that divisions and an incipient ethnic outlook began to emerge.

Underlying the class and generational divisions was a popular tendency in Anglo society to view Mexicans as a homogeneous group. Mexicans were, as Texas Congressman James Slayden stated, " 'Mexicans' just as all blacks are Negroes though they may have five generations of American ancestors." . . . Johnny Solís, one of the founders of the Hijos de América and the League of United Latin American Citizens (LUCAC), confirmed this racially-defined division and the negative meaning associated with the term Mexican: "The biggest drawback which the Texas-Mexicans face is that no matter how we behave or what we do or how long we have been here we are still 'Mexicans'." Solís inferred that racism was especially onerous because it denied U.S.-born Mexicans the opportunities ordinarily extended to other upwardly mobile citizens.

The issues of immigration and denial of occupational mobility accentuated tensions among Mexicans. Immigration intensified job competition and depressed wages while occupational discrimination denied the U.S.-born and older immigrants the chance to escape their condition. Class and generational differences were often expressed in cultural terms, with Mexican nationals accusing the U.S.-born of being *agringados* and ashamed of their Mexican identity, and the U.S.-born charging that the new arrivals depressed wages and encouraged further exploitation with their alleged backward customs of extreme deference and reserve. The erosion of a unified Mexicanist identity became more noticeable among upwardly mobile U.S.-born Mexicans who felt the pressure of competition from below and social discrimination from above. Many of them sought to disassociate themselves from the immigrant population, giving emphasis to their nativity and citizenship as a way to challenge discrimination, improve opportunities for mobility, and gain a measure of acceptance in the larger world. Such an ethnic strategy of incorporation also challenged discrimination, although its proponents increasingly saw their association with the Mexican nationals as a source of their problems and not as a point of unity or common cause. . . .

Homeland rather than ethnic politics reflected a more serious source of divisions during the early 1900s. Homeland politics included numerous exiled groups, pacifist organizations, and other community institutions whose interest in Mexico and its politics guided many of their community activities. A number of factors contributed to the ascendancy of homeland politics. Population growth in northern Mexico along with increasing immigration strengthened historical and cultural ties with the homeland throughout the last half of the nineteenth century and the beginning of the twentieth. . . . Another important factor was the proximity of Mexico. Also, the revolution [of 1910] encouraged numerous economic refugees and political exiles to join the immigrant stream. Political exiles, refugees, and consular offices played an especially important role in politicizing homeland ties. The result was the transfer of divisions from the Mexican revolution to the political world of the Mexican community of Texas. . . .

Homeland politics . . . produced mixed results. It introduced and reinforced divisions. It also cultivated a nationalist Mexican identity and communitarian ideals on both sides of the border. These influences were direct when mutual aid societies secretly or openly endorsed a particular exiled group in the area. On other occasions, mutualista organizations rejected an outright affiliation because of differences of opinion among the membership. . . . On the other hand, the revolution indirectly influenced political life in the Mexican community by increasing the numbers of immigrants who joined mutual aid societies or established new ones. Immigrants joined other more permanent residents who assisted them in adjusting to their new surroundings.

. . . The most important force that contributed to mutualism originated in the experiences that Mexicans shared in Texas. These included a condition of poverty that required the sharing of resources and efforts for survival and advancement, and the problem of discrimination and inequality that called for collective actions of defense and protest. . . . The spirit of mutualism engendered mutual aid societies in Texas in the first decades of the twentieth century.

Las Sociedades

An imported artisan tradition associated with guilds and mutual aid societies in Mexico during the late 1800s had combined with a similar, yet smaller-scale artisan past along the border, giving rise to some of the first such organizations in Texas. Industrialization in Mexico had caused the decline of handicraft trades, forcing artisans to seek self-organization in order to defend their social status and to protect their economic interests. Mutual aid societies soon proliferated. The formality and ritualism of these alliances as well as the upstanding and self-respecting behavior of its members also must have contributed to organizational life in Texas. Local needs and grievances, however, were the most important and immediate determinants in the establishment of mutualista organizations. While the subordinated position and status of Mexicans in the socio-economy created the need to give institutional expression to overarching historical and contemporary grievances, the most pressing need was for mutual support.

Mutual aid societies met the material needs of their members with emergency loans and other forms of financial assistance, job-seeking services, and death and illness insurance. They also offered their members leadership experiences in civic affairs, sponsored other institutions like newspapers and private schools, provided their communities with popular community events for entertainment and socializing, and offered public forums that addressed the important issues of the day. Mutualista organizations thus gave their members and communities a sense of belonging and refuge from an often alien and inhospitable environment. The community, in turn, accorded the members and especially the officers the highly respected status of responsible, civic-minded individuals. A lesser-known characteristic of mutualistas is that they served as a major point of organizational unity that spawned local and regional political struggles. . . .

Mexicanist organizing appeals and critiques thus drew a popular response, primarily because workers sought material support and cooperation to meet the economic uncertainties of the day. Widespread concern and discontent over the issues of inequality and discrimination also served as a common frame of reference in the formation and development of mutual aid societies. This thinking was not limited to U.S.-born Mexicans and older immigrants. Discontent was an important motivation among the immigrants. According to a report commissioned by the Mexican Consul from San Antonio, there were

> hundreds, we might say thousands of complaints of Mexican citizens against both private individuals and corporations as well as against public officials. These complaints have covered a wide range, from a single alleged infraction of a verbal contract relating to wages, up to claims for personal injuries, and for alleged gross miscarriage of justice when Mexicans were accused of a crime or were the accusers of others who were charged with committing a crime on their persons or property.

Journalists played an important role in encouraging a Mexicanist identity and collective political action to combat discrimination and inequality. The editors of *La Prensa* [San Antonio, Texas], for example, always urged their readers to join mutual aid societies and contribute to the resolution of problems in their communities. In 1915 when a reader from Marquez [Texas] complained that public school officials denied his son admission, *La Prensa* recommended that he join with other Mexican parents and organize mutual aid societies. *La Prensa* predicted that "From this redeeming movement will come unions of workers from the rural areas and from the cities, also Mexican schools of Mexicans, where the children will be able to learn to speak and write their mother tongue."

The allusion to a "redeeming movement" denoted a moralistic sense of determined and committed purpose to public service befitting the circumstances that Mexicans faced. The leadership of the numerous mutual aid and Masonic organizations also demonstrated a righteous sense of responsibility and commitment to an all-encompassing cause for change, improvement, and protest. The popular Laredo Mason and educator Simón G. Domínguez, for instance, described the organization Logia, Benito Juárez, in a letter to a journalist friend as an organization working for "the general improvement of our people in this state of the American Union." Domínguez may have been speaking for the entire Masonic network in the state. . . .

Organizations that under other circumstances would have confined their attention to offering insurance coverage to their members were also compelled to embrace a higher purpose in service to the entire population. In Kingsville, an officer for the all-women Woodmen of the World, No. 1003, Ignacio A. de la Peña, for instance, made it a point to describe her organization in terms of a lofty principle: "In our circle we not only work for group insurance, but for the uplifting of our people. . . ."

The pressing problems facing the community no doubt compelled Mexicans to seek change and improvements collectively. The need for mutual support, and discontent over the effects of discrimination and inequality alone, however, do not explain the spirit with which they gave themselves to a high-sounding cause of redemption. Additional motivations originated in the indignation that Mexicans felt against a racism that denied them their humanity and sense of self-worth. . . .

Among the many organizing calls made through *La Crónica* [Laredo, Texas], the one made by Clemente Idar in preparation for El Congreso Mexicanista [see Document 2] underscored the salient issues in the community and revealed the prevailing Mexicanist sense of unity and purpose that guided regional organizing efforts. Prior to the [1911] conference, Idar gave his attention to such issues as lynchings, unity, and discrimination in the schools and in the work place. Among his most consistently expressed concerns was the exploitation of Mexican workers, an issue that chafed nationalist sensibilities because the land that they worked at one time belonged to their ancestors: "Texas-Mexicans have produced with the sweat of their brow the bountiful agricultural wealth known throughout the country, and in recompense for this they have been put to work as peones on the land of their forefathers."

Idar affirmed a Mexicanist identity. Mexican nationals also suffered exploitation despite the guarantees of the Treaty of Guadalupe Hidalgo, while U.S.-born Mexicans were denied the protection and guarantees of the Constitution. He concluded that "we are in the same situation," as he urged his readers to assist the more recent arrivals adjust to their new life in Texas. After the conference he continued to encourage immigrant and U.S.-born alike to join as brothers in the redemptive cause against discrimination. . . .

Clemente Idar based his case for political unity primarily on the ensuing racial conflict and popular feelings of resentment: "The barbarous acts of cruelty and savagery committed against Mexicans, burning them alive, lynching them without just cause, excluding them from the public schools, robbing them infamously of their work, insulting them in a thousand ways, gives rise to feelings of compassion for the Mexican people and hatred and aversion for the American people." . . .

The delegates who attended the conference also imbued their Mexicanist appeals for unity with a sense of moral righteousness and responsibility. The speakers argued passionately in an oratorical style, recounting the continuing loss of land, the violated rights of Mexican workers, school discrimination and exclusion, the violence against Mexican youth in legal custody, and the need for class and national unification. These were the same issues that Clemente Idar had enumerated when he made his call for the conference, indicating a general consensus among the delegates and the memberships that they represented.

F. E. Rendón, Grand Chancellor of the Mexican Masonic network [in Texas], paid special tribute to the patriotism, altruism, and "sense of humanity and nobility," that guided the work of El Congreso Mexicanista. They were fulfilling a high and noble purpose in seeking the moral emancipation and material improvement of Mexican people. Masonic organizations, Rendón noted, shared the delegates' concerns especially for the immigrant who was drawn by false promises and subjected to extreme forms of exploitation. . . .

Youth and women also participated in the conference as official speakers. . . .

Señora Soledad Flores de Peña offered a women's perspective to the goals of unity and improvement. She first commended the delegates for their work as the "honest gladiators of Texas-Mexican rights," who had won the hearts of the people and had encouraged many to join their ranks. . . . "I, like you," Flores de Peña told the delegates, "think that the best means to achieve it [unity and progress] is to educate women, to instruct her, encourage her at the same time that you respect her." The delegates apparently agreed with the idea of supporting the educational and economic advancement of women. They provided for the establishment of a separate organization for women, La Liga Femenil. . . .

The high-sounding principles and statements of political resolve heard at El Congreso Mexicanista and in numerous public programs that voluntary organizations sponsored throughout the state suggest an enthusiastic and committed leadership. The impressive number of voluntary organizations that appeared throughout the state . . . indicates that Mexicans responded favorably to organizing appeals. . . .

Inside Las Sociedades

Mutual aid societies gave concrete and conscious manifestation to a Mexicanist identity and the unifying ethic of mutuality through highly responsible and civic-minded activities. Their code of morality and mutual support owed much to the membership's genuine devotion to such cultural values as fraternalism, reciprocity, and altruism. Guiding statements of purpose regarding proper moral behavior and mutualism reflected this devotion. Mutualista members also adhered to strict rules that disciplined them into "examples of true moral values" and that cemented a Mexicanist identity. . . .

Members of mutual aid organizations clearly saw themselves as important members of their communities. They viewed their decision to contribute to the moral uplift and material advancement of fellow Mexicans as the most responsible and honorable responsibility that anyone could assume. These twin goals began with their membership. They believed that by pooling their resources and establishing a death and illness insurance fund, for instance, they not only helped each other but instilled the unifying values of mutualism, which they saw as moral imperatives in their communities. They also spoke about extending their spirit of mutualism beyond the confines of the organization. La Sociedad Mutualista Protectora, Benito Juárez, of San Benito, for instance, declared that it sought "progress and unity among the entire Mexican working class in this country, as well as of the U.S.-born." The Alice [Texas] mutual aid society named Hidalgo y Juárez explained that "philanthropy and humanitarian sentiments" would guide their efforts to build unity among "all social classes."

Members adopted a number of specific objectives to promote mutualism within and outside the organization. All of them established an insurance fund which made disability payments to ill members for up to thirty days and paid funeral costs in case of death. They also contributed to an ad hoc widow's fund that provided a lump sum to the family of the deceased member. Other sources of mutual and community assistance included informal job-seeking services for their members, charity funds to help needy families in the community, and savings funds which extended emergency loans to members. In some cases, the organizations established libraries, newspapers, and private schools for children and adults in the community. In all cases, they sponsored celebrations during Mexico's national holidays and the organizations' anniversaries. All of these activities were central to their commitment to the concepts of moral uplift and material advancement.

The material benefits that insurance coverage, emergency loans, and job placement assistance brought to the members were obvious. Most of them were poor and often without a stable source of employment. Schools, libraries, and newspapers were also important contributions to the educational advancement of the membership and the community. These activities, however, also contributed to the moral regeneration of the members and the community that they served. The insurance and savings funds reinforced a measure of trust among members who contributed their meager resources with the expectation that their money would be handled honestly and that they would receive their due benefits. The regular and timely payment of the required monthly fees and contributions also fostered frugality and a sense of family responsibility.

The charity funds, schools, newspapers, and public celebrations broadened the organizations' sphere of influence as examples of disinterested and morally rejuvenating public service. In Laredo La Sociedad Unión de Jornaleros saw in the patriotic celebrations an opportunity to demonstrate their adherence to a Mexicanist identity. The organization agreed that it needed to sponsor the celebration of "national holidays with the necessary solemnity to insure that our members and our children do not lose the precepts of our nationality." The Sociedad Hijos de Juárez added that its members should seek to promote through the press or their own organ "ideas in support of the moral and material development of the social masses." In San Benito mutualistas made one of the most impressive gestures of community support when they decided to admit into their school children from families who could not afford to pay the required fees.

The strict internal rules that mutual aid societies adopted to define the responsibilities and proper "moral comportment" of their members contributed the most to the practice of the ethic of mutuality. First of all, persons who applied for admission had to be of sound moral character. The organization confirmed this by requiring recommendations from at least one member who acted as a sponsor; a committee formally investigated their local reputation as responsible family persons and law-abiding citizens. The membership was required to vote unanimously in favor of positive recommendations by the sponsor and the committee. Otherwise, the applicants were rejected.

Rules also prohibited behavior that, according to La Sociedad Hidalgo y Juárez, of Alice, was "unbecoming to honest men." Vagrancy, giving oneself to vices, irresponsible family behavior, slander, and defamation of the organization or their brethren were causes for depriving members of their rights, and in some cases for suspending them from the organization. Members were discouraged from informally accusing others of these failings. Instead, organizations instituted a formal grievance process that allowed the membership to render a judgment on the basis of a recommendation by a jury of between five and ten members who heard opposing arguments.

Mutual aid societies also observed strict rules during discussions and debates, in order to avoid unnecessary conflicts and to foster a sense of propriety and mutual respect. They placed time limits on the arguments or presentations that each member made before the body. They also strictly prohibited offensive language. The membership could suspend anyone who left a meeting in the middle of a dispute or who threatened to quit the organization because of a heated discussion. Moreover, they avoided conflicts by appointing a committee to review issues of a sensitive nature before the membership was given an opportunity to discuss the matter.

These efforts to control the nature of the internal discussions reflected a concern for maintaining fraternal relations among the members and for projecting an image of sobriety and mutual consideration. It did not necessarily mean, however, that they shunned controversial issues. For instance, although most of them declared a ban on discussions of a religious or political nature, they all endorsed the idea of political unity and, . . . the members participated in important political events in their communities. Their decided reluctance to treat controversial issues underscored the importance of unity on the basis of mutual respect over any particular belief or idea that anyone wished to advocate.

Mutualistas also promoted fraternalism by maintaining friendly relations with sister organizations. Members in good standing of sister organizations who visited or moved into the area were always welcomed and sometimes seated in a position of honor with the executive committee. Mutualistas encouraged members who moved to other areas to join sister organizations. They usually gave departing members letters of recommendation and other documents to facilitate their admission. Mutual aid societies also agreed to assume the responsibility of assisting groups in their areas to establish other organizations and to cooperate with them in civic affairs. . . .

The internal discipline of the mutualistas and their attendant reputation as responsible and civic-minded Mexicanist institutions gave importance and ideal meaning to the ethic of mutuality as a source of unity, identity, and civic pride. This ethic, however, generally remained tied to mutual aid societies until intellectuals defined and translated key cultural values into specific political objectives or strategies.

Defining and Translating the Ethic of Mutuality

One of the best sources for examining the manner in which intellectuals conducted these translations were the formal presentations that they made during public meetings sponsored by mutual aid societies. In some important instances, they utilized moralistic and nationalistic precepts in support of workers' unity. Intellectuals demonstrated that collectivist values could be used to justify specific strategies such as unionism alongside efforts of a purely mutualist character. . . . They often spoke about the need for moral rejuvenation and civic participation. Many of them, however, sought to promote the values of mutualism, fraternalism, and reciprocity within larger political struggles that sought to effectuate change in both Mexico and the United States. One of the most sought-after speakers in Laredo, one who contributed to this discourse on culture and politics, was Sara Estela Ramírez.

Ramírez, a teacher, poet, journalist, and early supporter of the PLM [Partido Liberal Mexicano, or Mexican Liberal Party], came to Laredo around 1895 from Saltillo, Coahuila, where she attended a teachers' school named Ateneo Fuentes. Like many other Mexicana teachers that arrived in South Texas during the turn of the century, she may have been recruited by one of the many mutual aid societies and groups of parents that established private schools, or *escuelitas*, in response to the experience of exclusion and segregation in the public schools. As a teacher, she joined numerous other young, usually single, women who, by virtue of their roles as educators, assumed highly respected roles as intellectuals and community leaders. . . .

. . . Ramírez added an impressive ethical outlook that condemned exploitation and oppression and that justified cooperative ideals as the foundation for struggles in Mexico as well as in the United States. She gave a full exposition of her views in a talk during the twenty-fourth anniversary celebration of La Sociedad de Obreros, Igualdad y Progreso.

Ramírez proposed the ideals of altruism and mutualism practiced by La Sociedad as moral guideposts for solidarity among workers seeking to build effective working-class unity throughout the world. . . . She used both altruism and mutualism synonymously to mean a sense of fraternal respect, and spiritual and material assistance, values that were within the reach of everyone. . . . This, according to Ramírez, was made evident by the exemplary behavior of the members to La Sociedad.

In the second part of her talk, she recounted the converse state of affairs among workers in general. They were alienated, divided, disorganized, and subject to failure as workers in struggle. They lacked both a spiritual sense of fraternity, reciprocity, and the knowledge that "their arms maintain the wealth and growth of industry." . . . Ramírez concluded by exhorting Mexican workers in the audience to unite. . . .

Ramírez reasoned that . . . only in total harmony among themselves could workers be complete human beings. As moral statements, their logic legitimated communitarian values as cornerstones in a workers' struggle and justified its continuance until an inevitable reconstructed end was achieved.

The writings of José María Mora, a socialist orator and labor leader from Laredo, also demonstrate support for the ethic of mutuality as the basis for local and international workers' struggles. History records little about Mora. He was actively involved in mutualista and unionist activities and may have been a member of Federal Labor Union, No. 11953, an AFL affiliate. He also published extensively in local newspapers on the need for political unity by Mexicans as workers. . . . In 1918, he once again achieved local prominence when he was elected president of a typographical union affiliated with the AFL.

Like Ramírez, Mora propagated political ideas with an explicit moral thrust that he associated with the work of mutual aid societies. . . . Mora also urged the moral revitalization of workers' consciousness within mutual aid societies and labor unions. Moreover, he argued that it was especially important for Mexican workers to establish a natural order of equality and fraternity. . . .

Mora believed that . . . it was necessary for workers to understand that they had common material interests. They also had a moral obligation to practice equality and fraternity. Once in harmony among themselves, within the organizations that practiced the basic laws of humanity, workers were further obligated to extend principles of cooperation and support beyond their organizational confines. This meant that workers should treat other poor people with equal respect. Mora reasoned: "If we are happy when we unite as brothers, inspired by a principle of mutual protection, with common rights, without causing each other harm, without offending or even mildly hurting our fellow workers, we will be happier when everyone refrains from abusing the weak and defenseless." Unity was sequential and directional. It began with workers in struggle. It involved mobilization and sought moral salvation. In Texas, Mexican workers were to fulfill the historical imperative of effective working class unity.

Mora's call for working class unity and struggle at El Congreso Mexicanista suggested popular support for the ethic of mutuality as an essential organizing element among Mexican workers. He reminded the delegates that "the issue that we are concerned with at this moment directs us to work for the unification of the Mexican worker and that united as one complete family we will be guided by the principle of fraternity." Fraternity, according to Mora, was an inherent predisposition among humans, who often denied it by contributing to the oppression of others. This was the reason why in the mutual aid and fraternal societies, "it is said 'one for all and all for one,' and the avaricious ones say everything for us and damn the people."

Conclusion

Feelings of indignation and concern over the effects of discrimination, inequality, and violence gave special importance to the working class ethic of mutuality as a source of Mexicanist unity and identity. In the face of divisions and difficult living and working conditions, Mexicans looked inward and reinforced an outlook that not only gave them a sense of importance, but also a meaningful recourse to address their myriad problems. Mutual aid societies reflected the popular ethic of mutuality and reinforced it when they assumed political responsibility for promoting its values of fraternalism, reciprocity, and altruism through self-discipline, internal services of mutual support, and civic involvement.

The leadership gave added meaning to collectivist and egalitarian ideals with a language of Mexicanist struggle and righteous cause. The members offered concrete examples of the proper moral behavior expected of truly responsible Mexicans in their communities. Intellectuals, in turn, provided refined philosophical formulations that translated moral precepts into specific political strategies and goals. . . .

Although other political groups like the PLM also made organizing appeals on the basis of a collective Mexican identity and unifying cultural values, Ramírez and Mora demonstrated that calls for Mexican workers' struggles also drew inspiration and meaning from the values of mutualism. These values may have originated in a working class culture, but they acquired a Mexicanist political meaning in a world that often was defined in racial and nationalist terms. The result was the elaboration of a moralistic and nationalistic political culture that served as a basis for promoting several kinds of labor organizations.

FURTHER READING

Evan Anders, *Boss Rule in South Texas* (1982)

Lowell L. Blaisdell, *The Desert Revolution* (1962)

Charles C. Cumberland, "Border Raids in the Lower Rio Grande Valley, 1915," *Southwestern Historical Quarterly* 57 (January 1954), 285–311

———, "Mexican Revolutionary Movements from Texas, 1906–1912," *Southwestern Historical Quarterly* 52 (January 1949), 301–324

Manuel Gamio, "Señora Flores de Andrade," in Magdalena Mora and Adelaida R. Del Castillo, eds., *Mexican Women in the United States* (1980)

Mario T. García, *Desert Immigrants* (1981)

Alan Gerlach, "Conditions Along the Border, 1915: The Plan de San Diego," *New Mexico Historical Review* 43 (July 1968), 195–212

José Amaro Hernández, *Mutual Aid for Survival* (1983)

José Limón, "El Primer Congreso Mexicanista de 1911: A Precursor to Contemporary Chicanismo," *Aztlán* 5 (Spring/Fall 1974), 85–118

Martha O. Loustaunau, "Hispanic Widows and Their Support Systems in the Mesilla Valley of Southern New Mexico, 1910–40," in Arlene Scadron, ed., *On Their Own: Widows and Widowhood in the American Southwest, 1843–1939* (1988)

Leonor Villegas de Magnón, *The Rebel* (1994)

Patricia Preciado Martin, *Songs My Mother Sang to Me* (1992)

Oscar J. Martínez, *Border Boom Town* (1978)

Philip J. Mellinger, *Race and Labor in Western Copper* (1995)

Américo Paredes, *With His Pistol in His Hand* (1958)

Herbert B. Peterson, "Twentieth-Century Search for Cíbola: Post World War I Mexican Labor Exploitation in Arizona," in Manuel P. Servín, ed., *The Mexican Americans: An Awakening Minority* (1974)

Dirk Raat, *Revoltosos: Mexico's Rebels in the United States, 1903–1923* (1981)

James A. Sandos, *Rebellion in the Borderlands* (1992)

Jay S. Stowell, *A Study of Mexicans and Spanish Americans in the United States* (1920)

Emilio Zamora, *The World of the Mexican Worker in Texas* (1995)

CHAPTER
8

The Mexican Immigrant Experience, 1917–1928

With the start of the Mexican Revolution in 1910, large numbers of Mexicans fled the ravages and chaos of the upheaval by crossing the border into the United States. Political refugees, intellectuals, and workers formed part of the resident population who settled temporarily or permanently in the cities of the Southwest.

Nearly a half-million Mexicans entered the United States between 1920 and 1929, comprising over 15 percent of total immigration during that period. The Mexicans were drawn to the Southwest region by the good-paying jobs in agriculture, mining, and the railroads. Similarly, tens of thousands were lured into the Midwest by the promise of factory jobs. Almost half the Mexican immigrants lived in cities, reflecting the shift of the U.S. population at this time to urban centers. How would everyday life in the cities shape and transform the individual and collective identities of the immigrants from Mexico?

Mexicans participated in the era's prosperity, but they also experienced discrimination in jobs and housing. They were seen as outsiders by most Americans, who did not distinguish between Mexicans who were long-time residents and citizens of the United States and those who had recently arrived from Mexico. Various programs and associations promoted the Americanization of both U.S.-born Mexicans and Mexican nationals. Americanization was also the goal of Protestant denominations, the Catholic Church, and the corporate world, which wanted a disciplined workforce. The League of United Latin American Citizens (LULAC), founded in 1929 in Corpus Christi, Texas, launched its own version of Americanization among the Spanish-speaking population of the Southwest. LULAC also sought to protect the rights of Mexicans. Did racial discrimination and nativism foster suspicion and cynicism among Mexicans and contribute to their sense of ambivalence about the rewards Americanization would bring them? In light of the fact that Mexican identity and culture were continually reinforced through immigration and return migration, how successful were the Americanization efforts to mold Mexicans into loyal Americans? What was the impact of popular and material culture on the Mexican immigrant woman?

❦ D O C U M E N T S

In the early twentieth century, Protestant denominations began to compete with the Catholic Church in converting and Americanizing Mexican immigrants, and Chicano historians continue to question the merits of these efforts. In Document 1, Robert N. McLean, the Assistant Secretary of the Presbyterian Board of Home Missions, describes Protestant religious work among Mexicans in Los Angeles and El Paso, which had large concentrations of Mexicans. Document 2 is McLean's survey of the Spanish-speaking population in Colorado, principally in the southern and southeastern part of the state. Ten percent of the half-million Mexicans in the United States lived in the Midwest. Because of its railroad terminals, steel mills, and packing houses, Chicago was an important center for these immigrants. In Document 3 Anita Edgar Jones describes the numerous colonies Mexicans established in that city. The problems related to the rapid increase of Mexican immigration in the 1920s were not missed by either restrictionists or those who favored an open border. But, argues Mexican American scholar and labor activist Ernesto Galarza, neither side had heard from the Mexican immigrants themselves. The economic difficulties that they faced are profiled in Document 4, which is based on Galarza's own experiences. The development of successful Americanization programs for Mexican immigrants continued in the Southwest, especially among employers who sought a disciplined workforce. Document 5 outlines one such effort in the citrus-growing areas of California's San Bernardino County. Urban life represented new experiences for both Mexican American and Mexican immigrant women, whose responses differed widely. Although they enjoyed the excitement and independence of city life, most of these women were cast in new roles as workers outside the home. In Document 6, Elisa Silva, a Mexican immigrant, remembers her work in a dance hall in Los Angeles in the 1920s.

1. The Reverend Robert N. McLean Assesses Protestant Religious Work Among the Mexicans, 1923

It was a new Home of Neighborly Service—the very newest, and I had gone to visit it on a Sunday morning. During the past winter, thousands of Mexicans have come to Los Angeles from Texas, Arizona and New Mexico, and have settled in groups, some large, some small. In one district adjacent to Los Angeles as many as eight hundred lots were sold to Mexicans in the space of six weeks. . . .

My new Home of Neighborly Service was located in one of these mushroom settlements. . . .

The little Sunday-school was already in session when I arrived. The room was small, and the children were huddled. . . . The crowded appearance was exaggerated because all were so alert and active. . . .

I was invited to speak. . . .

"Which shall it be children, English or Spanish?" I asked the children who gazed up at me through boring black eyes.

"English!" came back the cry in unison. "We don't know that stuff!"

As found in Robert McLean, "Getting God Counted Among the Mexicans," *Missionary Review of the World* (May 1923), pp. 359–363.

I was reminded of another time when I had put the same question in another way. "How many of you speak Spanish?" I asked in English, and most of them raised their hands. "How many of you speak English?" I countered in Spanish, and every hand was raised save that of a small boy on the first row. One ought to know better than to try to be facetious with young America, even if it is young America only in the making. But I fell.

"Aha!" I said, "here's a boy who speaks neither English nor Spanish. . . . What do you speak?" . . .

"I speak American!"

The fact is that the public schools are changing the language of the children. Spanish among the youngsters is only for home consumption. . . .

. . . What is a Home of Neighborly Service and what is its purpose? The Home of Neighborly Service is an honest effort to get God counted in the Mexican population. These people fill the old houses and tenements in the downtown districts, or line their "jacales" along both sides of new streets in settlements they build for themselves. They are all counted by the census takers. Social surveys are made. . . . The Chamber of Commerce can tell you its estimate of the number of Mexicans in a given place. But nearly always God is not counted. . . . For the Mexicans . . . are pouring themselves into the stream of our national life, and these currents must be cleansed and filtered by the power of God. In most Mexican communities, God is not counted. True He is mentioned, and . . . He is honored, but as far as having any vital bearing upon conduct is concerned, He is non-existent. . . .

. . . Sometimes the feeling of antipathy toward "the church" is inherited by Protestantism; sometimes the honest conviction that all Protestants have horns and tails makes it hard to get God counted. In such communities the Home of Neighborly Service offers a point of approach. The program varies in different places, but the commonest method is through the medium of English classes. The mothers frequently furnish a key to the situation, and often they are the ones first touched by the new enterprise. Mrs. Garcia resents it when a "home visitor" comes to her little house, and makes friendly observations, however kindly, upon the subjects of home-making, care of babies or personal hygiene! But Mrs. Garcia realizes her ignorance of the English language, and is eager and anxious to learn the meaning of the strange words which she constantly hears in this strange land. With Mrs. Rodriguez and Mrs. Lopez and Mrs. Sanchez and others of her neighbors, she visits the Home of Neighborly Service for her first lesson in English. . . .

A course in English is easily based upon the house, and the articles it contains; and in learning these words, the wife and mother is familiarizing herself with the vocabulary of the things which she sees and uses most often. The work may cover a whole year, or several years; but the teacher by taking her class from room to room, gives lessons in home-making, care of the house, care of the children, cooking, sewing, sanitation, and marketing. As the confidence of the mothers is won, the children can be invited to play in the yard while their mothers take their English lesson. Then comes the "story hour" on Sunday afternoon. This easily grows into a Sunday-school, and the Sunday-school eventually becomes a church.

As the work grows other features are added, such as night school, clinic, employment bureau, boys' and girls' clubs. In some places a Daily Vacation Bible School, with its craft work, its picnics and its Bible study fill the house and the yard with eager children; and through them a contact is made with the community. All this calls for the aid of volunteer workers. . . .

But the work is not merely a work of beginnings. All of the larger denominations have been busy at the task of getting God counted among the Mexicans for the past decade. . . . There are at the present time, about twelve thousand Protestant Mexican church members in the Southwest. . . .

The Church of the Divine Saviour, in El Paso, Texas, is a fine illustration of one of these Spanish-speaking congregations. The building is both adequate and churchly. . . . There are ample facilities for a departmentalized Sunday-school, together with an auditorium. . . . The church functions not only through its preaching and prayer services and its Sunday-school, but also through a night school, a Saturday morning school of religious education, a day nursery, a Boy Scout organization, a Girls' Reserve, and a Woman's Club. There is an employment bureau and ample opportunity for social life, especially on Friday nights. . . . El Paso is the chief entry port, and the distributing point for Mexican labor all over the Southwest. As a consequence, there is scarcely an evangelical Mexican church of any denomination which has not felt the pulsating life of the El Paso church. . . .

Nearly two million Mexicans in our American commonwealth present a complex problem. Diverse will be the methods attempted in its solution; but real success will come when we can get God counted in . . . every Mexican community.

2. The Reverend Robert N. McLean Reports on Colorado Mexicans, 1924

I. General Description

(B) Population

1. In Trinidad and Las Animas County

The evidence obtained points to a population of about 16,000 Spanish Americans in Las Animas County [in Colorado]. There are very few Mexicans, and those few are found in the mining camps. Mr. Vigil, clerk of the County Court, stated that 35 per cent of Las Animas County (pop. 45,000) is Spanish American. . . . Mr. McCartney, assistant county superintendent of schools, also estimated the Spanish American population as 35 per cent. Mr. J. M. Madrid, a real estate man . . . who has lived his whole life in the county, . . . stated that there are 17,000 or 18,000 Spanish Americans in the county. He estimates there are 35,000 in the entire state.

At the present time, more of the Spanish population is found up toward the mountains, that is in the western third of the county, than on the plains. Formerly the eastern part of the county was all Spanish, but within the last ten years many Americans have come in. One of the priests of the Catholic Rectory in Trinidad . . . estimates that in the agricultural valleys in that section there are seven Spanish Americans to every three Anglo-Americans or others.

As found in Robert McLean, *Spanish and Mexican in Colorado* (New York: Board of National Missions of the Presbyterian Church, 1924), pp. 1–61.

The mining camps are found in the western third of the county. The mines employ about 4,500 miners, who with their families represent a population of some 14,000 or 15,000. We find that in the Colorado Fuel and Iron Company mines in this county approximately one-third of the miners are Spanish Americans or Mexicans. . . .

. . . In January 1923, out of a total of 14,051 miners in all the coal mines of Colorado, 3,218, or 23 per cent were Mexicans and Spanish Americans. . . .

The Spanish American population in the city of Trinidad was estimated by Mr. Madrid, as 2,000 or 2,500. It is not localized in any one section, but is scattered in all parts of the city. However, there is perhaps a larger proportion in the southwestern section than in others.

2. In Huerfano County

As we said above the total population of Huerfano County is about 18,000. Estimates place the Spanish population anywhere from 35 per cent to 60 per cent, or between 6,000 and 12,000.

Mr. J. B. Guerrero, the assistant county assessor, . . . states . . . that sixty to sixty five per cent of the county is Spanish, or between ten and twelve thousand. . . .

As for distribution, the Spanish agriculturists and ranches are found largely in the valley of the Huerfano River, which runs north and west from Walsenburg. Gardner is a center for them. . . . The Catholic priest reported 500 "Mexican" families in and around Gardner.

The coal mines of Huerfano County are found in a broad band which runs north and south across the eastern half of the county. Walsenburg lies almost in the center of this band. There are 2,491 miners in the county. . . . We may safely assume that between 25 per cent and 30 per cent of these are Mexicans and Spanish Americans; and 600–800 miners will give us a Mexican and Spanish American population in the mining camps of 2,500 to 3,000.

The city of Walsenburg has at present about 4,000 people. Of these probably about one third are Spanish. . . . They are found in all parts of the town, though a greater number live on the west side, near the Walsen mine.

(C) Economic Conditions of the Spanish Americans.   In the cities of Trinidad and Walsenburg, the Spanish Americans are found in many occupations; there are lawyers, doctors, jewelers, masons, clerks, merchants, etc. . . . They also take a prominent part in politics. . . . One-third of the delegates to the Republican and one-half of the delegates to the Democratic County Convention in Las Animas County were Spanish Americans, and in both conventions an interpreter was employed.

. . . For the Spanish Americans as a whole . . . they are found in two occupations—agriculture and mining. . . .

(D) Social Conditions

1. Education

The Spanish American and Mexican children in the larger towns of Trinidad and Walsenburg, and in the mining camps are attending school with regularity, and are profiting from their educational advantages. As a rule they speak English with facility. In Walsenburg there is a large parochial school which has twelve grades. It enrolls 800 pupils, of which the priest estimates that 500 are Mexican or Spanish American. There is, also, a parochial school in Trinidad. . . .

. . . In the rural sections Spanish is still the language of the natives. The younger children, up to eight or nine years of age, do not know English. . . .

2. Health

"Is there more illness among the Spanish American than among other population groups?" . . . In large families, with more than five or six children, there is a high mortality rate; often more than half of the children have died. For instance, here is a family of thirteen children, of which eight have died; another of seven children, of which five have died. Here is another, however, of six, of which five are living. . . .

. . . [Eighty] per cent of applicants for family relief are Spanish Americans, and about 90 per cent of these applicants have tuberculosis in the family. . . .

3. Recreation

The Mexicans and Spanish Americans living in the towns of Walsenburg and Trinidad have at their disposal all of the amusements usually available in any town of from five to ten thousand population—moving pictures, good, bad, and indifferent, pool rooms, athletics, occasional dances and parties, and various school, church, lodge, and club affairs. Many families in the rural districts still live an isolated existence. . . .

In the mining camps, particularly those of the C.F.&I. [Colorado Fuel & Iron Company], the center of social life is the industrial Y.M.C.A. or company club. The buildings are relatively new, having been built within the last five or ten years. . . . They house a satisfactory equipment including a reading room, a good-sized lobby, an auditorium with stage where moving pictures are shown once or twice a week, and also occasional dances are held, a soda fountain, pool tables, bowling alleys, a barber shop, moving picture machine, and games and magazines. In Walsen, Lester, Valdez, Primero, Morley, Berwind, and Segundo these institutions are directly under the Y.M.C.A. management, and are known as Y.M.C.A.'s. . . . In the other camps of Ideal, Pictou, Tioga, Farr, and Sopris, they are company clubs. . . . Those of this second class are not staffed as well as the first. . . .

These buildings provide an attractive social center for the men and boys, and are extensively used. Through their movies and dances they serve also the women and girls. The Mexicans and Spanish Americans are generally reported to use these buildings extensively; and in some camps, such as Morley and Primero, they are seen about the building more than any other group.

(E) Assimilation. In the contact of Anglo-American culture with the older Spanish American culture of southern Colorado, we have a unique and very interesting case of assimilation. The Spanish Americans were the pioneers and original settlers in this section. They came in during the fifties and sixties and were well-established economically and socially before the American infiltration began.

With the coming of the Americans in increasing numbers into this territory, the cultural isolation of the Spanish Americans was largely destroyed. In the more secluded rural districts they have maintained and still do, a certain degree of geographical isolation. But economically they found themselves in both mining and agriculture, the two dominant industries of the section, thrown in company with the "gringos." Politically they have also mingled, for Spanish Americans are found in both Republican and Democratic parties. They play the game of politics with great enthusiasm and interest, and often with intense feeling. . . . The strongest group bonds of these people have been the Spanish language, the Catholic religion, and their heritage of Spanish culture.

. . . They look on themselves as real Americans, and cordially resent any accusation of lack of patriotism. Mr. J. M. Madrid, a leading Spanish American of Trinidad, told of starting out on April 17, 1917, only eleven days after the entrance of the United States into the World War, in company with two other men on a campaign of enlistment. "The first eighty-one men who enlisted," he said, "were Spanish Americans."

These people look not to Mexico . . . as their home land. They have been born in the United States and America is their country. But they do look with regret at the passing of their old Spanish culture. . . .

Socially, the racial line is still evident between the Spanish Americans and the Anglo-Americans. In the mining camps the "Mexicans" are reported to mix very well with the other national groups. . . . All the groups use the Y.M.C.A. or the company club, but when it comes to dances, the groups separate —Americans have their dances, the Italians theirs, the Spanish Americans theirs. . . .

Said one of the priests of Trinidad, "The two races (Anglo- and Spanish American) do not have an antipathy for each other. It is rather mistrust. . . . The American regards the 'Mexican' as inferior; the 'Mexican' is rather afraid of the American; he does not known what he will do to him." . . .

The Spanish Americans of course feel the condescending attitude of the Americans and heartily resent it. Said Mr. Guerrero of Walsenburg, "The Americans think we are no good; they class us with this trash that comes over from Mexico; we are greasers and nothing more. We have suffered much from these Mexicans, for the Americans lump us all together because we speak Spanish. . . ."

In Walsenburg, the Ku Klux Klan has been active, and has done much to drive the two groups apart. Last January the sheriff and the chief prohibition officer were shot, and shortly after that the Klan held a parade. As a result, feeling has been very bitter. Said a leading Spanish American, "The Klan has made the Spanish Americans a solid group again. We were drifting apart, away from the church, away from our old friends. But this has brought us all together again. . . ."

II. San Luis and San Juan Valleys

(A) San Luis Valley

1. Introduction

The six counties of Alamosa, Conejos, Costilla, Mineral, Rio Grande, and Saguache . . . comprise the San Luis Valley. . . . Rio Grande county is a leading potato growing district in the state and in September imports many Mexicans for the harvest. Rio Grande and Conejos counties are the two leading sheep producing counties of the state—an industry which provides employment for many Spanish Americans as herders. More field peas are grown in the San Luis valley than in all other sections of the state. . . . Mexican laborers are also imported for this crop. The 1920 census gave the six counties of this valley a population of 31,751.

2. *Spanish Americans in the Valley*

Rev. M. D. J. Sanchez, who has been in the valley all his life stated that it contains 5,000 Spanish Americans, the majority of whom are found in the two southern counties, Conejos and Costilla.

3. *Economic and Social Conditions*

The Spanish population of this section is maintained principally by agricultural activities. In Alamosa there are railroad shops and a newly established lumber mill, but otherwise the occupation of the people is dominantly agricultural. Many of the Spanish Americans own their farms, small holdings running 80 to 160 acres. . . . Many others are agricultural laborers. Housing, educational, and health conditions are largely similar to those among the rural population of Las Animas and Huerfano counties. . . .

(B) San Juan Valley. . . . The Spanish Americans in this section are found principally in the La Plata and Archuleta counties. . . . The total population is 3,590, and the Spanish probably not more than 1,000, and largely rural. In La Plata County, Durango with a population of 5,000 is the principal center. The county has a total population of about 15,000 . . . and of these there are 5,000 registered voters. It is commonly estimated there are 700 "Mexican" voters, which would give us a population of 2,000 to 2,500. . . .

The Durango smelter, owned by the American Smelting and Refining Company is the principal economic foundation for the Spanish American colony in Durango. It employs 177 men of that group. . . . The men work the eight hour day and the six day week. Their wage runs from three to five dollars per day. Their work is largely semi- and unskilled; for example, there is no "Mexican" mechanic and only one "Mexican" carpenter. Mr. Reynolds, the general manager, reports them as satisfactory workmen, and that the turnover is not excessive. . . .

Some of the Spanish Americans . . . are agriculturists. Their farms are not large, running from 160 to 320 acres. They are reported as especially skillful as sheep herders. . . .

Not many of the Spanish Americans are reported in the mines of this section. . . .

The Spanish Americans in Durango are found in the south part of town on the eastern side of the railroad in the section known as "Mexicans Flats," and on the west in the region known as the "bottoms." . . .

III. Industrial Centers

(A) Pueblo. . . . All the information obtained points to an estimate of about 5,000 Mexicans in Pueblo. The steel works of the Colorado Fuel and Iron Company now employ almost 1,200 Mexicans. A proportion of these are Spanish Americans. . . . About fifty are employed by the U. S. Zinc Co., and small groups by the city, the contractors, and the railroads, notably the Sante Fe, D.&R.G. [Denver & Rio Grande], and the Missouri Pacific.

. . . The steel works dominate the industrial situation for the Mexican.

The steel works normally employ between five and six thousand men, and their figures show that the percentage of Mexicans increased from 8.1 per cent in 1912 to over 20 per cent in 1917, and has continued at that proportion or greater ever since. In 1920 the Mexicans employed comprised 39.8 per cent of the total force. . . . Mr. Selleck, the personnel manager, stated that the Mexicans are satisfactory workmen, and their number is not likely to decrease and may increase in future years.

. . . On being asked about the turn-over among the Mexicans, Mr. Selleck answered: "The Mexican cannot be blamed for a large turn-over. He is a common laborer; he does the hardest work for the lowest pay, and the turn-over is always greatest in that kind of work. Naturally if a man thinks he can better himself he will quit that kind of a job for something better. The cause for the turn-over among the Mexicans is industrial rather than racial."

In the steel works, the Mexicans as a rule do the unskilled or semi-skilled work. A few are wire-drawers; one finds an occasional man working as a machinist or boiler-maker, but the great majority do common labor. . . . There is a minimum of $3.98 for eight hours, and this or a little more is the average wage of the Mexicans. . . .

(B) Denver.   Denver, the capital and largest city of Colorado, with a present population of about 275,000, has never had a large Mexican population. The 1920 census could find but 1,390 Mexicans. Since that date, however, the number has grown. Mr. José Esparza, the Mexican Consul . . . , states that Denver now has a permanent Mexican population of over two thousand, and that in the winter time, when the beet and other migratory workers come to the city, that number is doubled or tripled. The Mexicans live in all parts of the city, on the outskirts to the west and north. . . .

They are engaged largely in common labor, but their economic situation is not dominated by any one industry as in Pueblo. They work for the railroads, the street car company, the city, and various manufacturing concerns. . . .

IV. The Mexican on the Railroads

In the table below will be found listed all the railroads in Colorado which have a mileage exceeding 100 miles:

RAILROAD	MILEAGE
Denver and Rio Grande Western	1,504.33
Colorado and Southern	729.15
Union Pacific	852.51
Santa Fe	505.62
Chicago, Burlington & Quincy	395.39
Denver and Salt Lake	252.00
Rio Grande Southern	171.16
Rock Island	165.83
Missouri Pacific	152.11

(From "Colorado Year Book, 1924," *page 10*).

The Mexicans work chiefly on these roads as section men. . . . We can safely say that the Mexican on the sections and in the extra gangs represents a population of 5,000.

Denver and Rio Grande Western.   On this road, all the regular section men . . . are Mexican. They have 3,000 men working on the sections, and of these probably two-thirds are in Colorado. . . . There are 1,000 men on "extra gangs," in groups of about fifty men each. These "extra gangs" are shifted to different parts of the system, and they lay tracks, and roadbeds, and do all special work. . . . In these extra gangs . . . eighty per cent of them are Mexicans.

Sante Fe.   In the Colorado Division, . . . there are about forty sections, with about four Mexicans to a section, or a total of 160. The number has recently been reduced from six to a section. Eighty-five men are in extra gangs. . . .

Missouri Pacific.   From Pueblo east to the state line, they have about fifty Mexicans averaging two to a section. There are three to four men usually in a section. . . .

Colorado and Southern.   This railroad has its division office at Trinidad, but no information was obtained.

Rock Island.   Reported to have few Mexicans employed. . . .
    . . . The section men who work near the large towns usually live in or near the Mexican colony, and so have the contacts which that association affords. But those living in the smaller towns, in groups of from two to eight families, are cut off from those of their own language and race. And, of course, the extra gangs, shunted around the system from place to place, lead a nomadic kind of existence. . . .

V. The Mexican in the Beet Fields

(A) The Beet Sugar Industry.   . . . Colorado, in 1920, produced more than one fourth of all the sugar refined in the United States. . . .

Of course, this new industry has demanded new labor, and throughout the United States, the greater part of the rough work is done by Mexican hands. . . .

. . . From southern Colorado and New Mexico Spanish American labor was recruited, but this supply was not adequate to meet the demand. And so agents were sent to Texas and the border of Mexico. Now Fort Worth, El Paso, and San Antonio have become important recruiting centers for beet-field laborers, from which whole trainloads of Mexicans are shipped north, east and west to the beet fields. . . .

(B) Number and Location of Mexicans.
    1. In the Arkansas Valley
The Holly Sugar Company, with their factory at Swink estimated that a population of about 800 Mexicans passed the winter of 1923 in their territory, half of them in

Otero County, some on the farms but most of them at La Junta, and the balance divided between Pueblo and Prowers Counties. In 1923 they imported 540 fares, and in 1924, 800. Six hundred of these were brought in from El Paso and the balance from Albuquerque, and other parts of New Mexico. Of the 800, 500 were sent to Otero County, and most of the rest to Prowers. . . .

The American Beet Sugar Company, with its sugar factory at Rocky Ford in Otero County, is estimated to have brought in 1,200, of which probably 1,000 came from El Paso. . . .

2. In the South Platte Valley

The Great Western Sugar Company has as its total acreage almost nine times as large an area as the combined acreage of the Holly and American Sugar Companies. . . .

At the beginning of the 1924 season there were 1,026 resident Mexican families within its territory. It shipped in 10,500 Mexican fares for its whole territory, of whom 7,481 were sent to Colorado. Of the 10,500, 2,500 were sent from Denver, 2,500 from New Mexico, some from Kansas City, and four or five thousand from Texas. . . .

(C) The Mexican as a Laborer. The Mexicans were brought in to do the contract hand labor, and in that status they have so far remained. . . .

Mr. Kaspar, Manager of the Holly Sugar Company, on being asked what they would do without the Mexican, threw up his hands and said, "We would be out of luck. We'd have to close up our factory and the farmers would lose the crop. You can't get white labor to do this work. We are absolutely dependent on the Mexican."

An official of the American Beet Sugar Company, said, "The Mexican is a good worker, if treated right. . . ."

There is unquestionably much child labor in the beet fields, and it is more prevalent among the Russian-German and Mexicans than other groups. . . .

(D) Colonization Schemes.   . . . The companies are endeavoring to hold as many of the Mexicans as possible, especially the steadier and more dependable class, within easy distance of the beet fields, and are developing Mexican colonies of various classes and sizes.

The Holly and American companies are building the colonies at their own expense, and giving the houses rent free to the Mexicans. . . .

La Junta in the Arkansas Valley has a considerable Mexican population of 600 to 1,000. . . .

The Great Western Sugar Company . . . is following a different policy from the two companies already mentioned. It is encouraging the Mexican to buy and own his own house and lot. . . .

. . . The farmers themselves are beginning to give the Mexican better housing on the individual farm. Some families are given enough work to occupy them through the winter, feeding stock, etc. . . .

The Holly Company expects about one-fourth of the 800 they imported this year to remain over the winter.

3. Anita Edgar Jones Surveys
Mexican Life in Chicago, 1928

The Industrial Areas

The Mexicans in Chicago live for the most part either in railroad camps or in well defined colonies. . . . The most important colonies are those which may be described as the Hull House colony, the University of Chicago Settlement colony, the South Chicago colony. . . .

The largest of the colonies is the one on the West Side near Hull House. . . . Perhaps 2,500 Mexicans are living in the Hull House neighborhood. . . .

The population of the University of Chicago Settlement neighborhood comprises perhaps an eighth of the population. . . . The Mexican population of this section is between 1,250 and 1,500 people.

The Mexican Colony of South Chicago has been estimated at two thousand six hundred people. Practically all the men work in the steel mills, the machine shops, and for the railroads located in South Chicago. . . .

Besides these neighborhoods there are several smaller and less well defined neighborhoods. . . .

West from the Hull House neighborhood is a scattered group. They are now found as far west as Ashland Avenue. Many of these are the families who formerly lived close to Hull House. As they find employment, they move to better quarters. . . .

There is also a group of Mexicans on Chicago Avenue and Clark Street in the vicinity of Illinois and Wells Streets. These, for the most part, are single men and are employed in the large hotels in the loop as kitchen helpers or bus boys. . . .

In connection with the employment offices on Madison and Clark Streets there has developed a series of rooming and boarding houses which cater especially to the unemployed Mexican. . . .

In the vicinity of the Crane Company, from Thirty-Seventh to Thirty-Ninth Streets on Kedzie Avenue especially, . . . there is a community of Mexicans. These are largely the employees of Crane Company. . . .

In the blocks bounded by Western Avenue, Robey Street, Eighteenth Street and Twenty-second Street there is a group of Mexican homes. These are in the vicinity of Pickard, Froebel, and Whittier Schools. . . .

Near the corner of Grand Avenue and Western Avenue there is also a group of Mexicans. These, for the most part, are employed by the Chicago Northwestern Railroad Company. . . .

East of the Stock Yards there are two groups of Mexicans living; one in the neighborhood bounded by Wentworth, Halstead, Forty-first, and Forty-seventh Streets . . . ; the other, also between Halstead and Wentworth, from Archer Avenue

Anita Edgar Jones, "Mexican Colonies in Chicago," *Social Service Review* 2 (December 1928): 39–54. Reprinted by permission of the University of Chicago.

to Twenty-sixth Place. . . . These men work especially for the Omaha Packing Company, and the Peanut Specialty Company.

Near Eighteenth and Jefferson Streets there are Mexican homes scattered thru one or two blocks. These men are largely employed by the Burlington Railroad Company. . . .

On Ogden Avenue between Harrison and Van Buren, also on Winchester Avenue near Ogden Avenue there are a few scattered Mexican residences. These are largely single men. . . .

Housing

The housing for all in the Hull House neighborhood is very poor. The buildings are old, very crowded, and kept in poor repair. The Mexicans live in the poorest houses in the neighborhood. They are nearly always to be found in the rear houses, in the basement, or the most undesirable part of the buildings. . . . There is very little play space and the smoke keeps the sunshine from penetrating. Many of the young children are found to have rickets, especially if they live in the neighborhood long. . . . The hopeful thing about this neighborhood is that the Mexicans do not stay in it long. . . . As soon as the families become established, they move to better quarters in more desirable neighborhoods.

The University of Chicago Settlement neighborhood is much like the Hull House neighborhood, except that the housing is not so poor. . . .

In South Chicago there are some Mexicans living in poor homes but the majority live in quite comfortable quarters. . . . The presence of many single men leads to many boarding houses which seem . . . to be run by couples without children. . . .

. . . Since there are so few Mexican girls, some Mexicans have found wives among the Norwegian, Polish or German girls. . . .

Employment

A great many of the Mexicans who live in the Hull House neighborhood are recent arrivals and are unemployed except at the best season of employment. . . . Work is always scarce in the winter. The first winter here is a hard one. Those already established lend a neighborly hand and do all they can to alleviate the suffering. The cold weather adds to the suffering, for the supply of clothing, bedding and furniture is very meagre. . . . Most of those who have work are at the Illinois Central Freight House, the bedding factories on Roosevelt Road, at the Cracker Jack factory, other candy factories and at the hotels in the loop. All this work is irregular and during periods of depression many of the Mexicans lose their places.

In the University of Chicago Settlement district, the railroads, and the packing companies furnish work for the Mexicans. When any of these industries reduces labor, it is the Mexican who suffers most. They are the last to arrive and the first to be laid off. . . .

The South Chicago Mexicans are largely employed by the steel mills. . . .

. . . Generally the men do not bring their families until they have a regular job. . . .

Recreation

Recreation for the Hull House neighborhood is limited almost entirely [to] that provided by Hull House and Firman Settlement House. . . .

Recreation at Hull House consists of parties for the English classes, a club of neighborhood families which meets weekly, a club for small boys, a few little girls in the Doll Club, and a few children in the Friday afternoon play hour. . . . Other Mexican groups who meet elsewhere use the halls and theatre for special functions.

The Hull House branch of the Public Library reports Mexican children and adults drawing books from the library. . . .

The "Banda Mexicana de Chicago" has as its headquarters the neighborhood at 618 Blue Island. . . . It is uniformed. It has been organized for several months. . . .

There is also a Mexican orchestra with headquarters at 837 South Halstead Street. This orchestra makes records for the Brunswick and Vocalion Phonograph Company. . . .

The University of Chicago Settlement neighborhood is poorly organized for recreation. The settlement is trying very hard to be neighborly but they have no worker who can speak Spanish and they have been unable to reach many of the women and children. . . .

While this is a Catholic neighborhood, with eleven churches of that faith in the neighborhood, there is no Spanish speaking priest. The Mexicans from the neighborhood must go to St. Francis Church, 12th Street and Newberry Avenue, in order to find a Spanish speaking priest. . . .

The recreation of the South Chicago Colony is largely left to its own organization. . . . The Independence Day celebration of the South Chicago Mexicans at the park was so orderly an affair that the park authorities would be glad to have them use the park again for similar occasions. The auditorium at the Bessemer Field House had been reserved for a Spanish play. . . . The librarian reported that there were about fifty children and ten adult Mexicans drawing books from the library.

Russell Square, South Chicago, reported that . . . a few children have been seen on the playgrounds during the summer, but have taken no part in the organized activities.

South Chicago Community Center . . . made a census of the neighborhood between Eighty-sixth and Ninety-third Streets, . . . and in September, 1927, they found 847 Mexicans living within that region. The Mexicans take part in all the Settlement activities along with 30 other nationalities.

Neighborhood House . . . reported 18 Mexican children taking part in the Daily Vacation Bible School in the summer of 1927. . . .

Friendship Center, 9114 Houston Avenue, reported the use of the center by the Mexican Methodist Church. A few Mexican mothers bring their babies to the Child Welfare station at the center. The activities for the Mexicans are all associated with the church activities.

The Y.M.C.A. is doing nothing in a recreational way for the Mexicans in South Chicago. . . .

The Friendship center and the Y.M.C.A. conduct a joint English class for the Mexican men at the Y. building. . . .

Business Enterprises

There are in Hull House neighborhood, 14 restaurants, 5 pool halls, 5 grocery stores, one barber shop, one shoemaker, 4 bakeries, one meat market, one print shop, two sign painter shops, one photograph gallery, one tailor shop, and one music shop, owned and operated by Mexicans. . . . The other neighborhoods have also similar business enterprises but not so numerous as in the Hull House neighborhoods. South Chicago adds a drug store to the list of business activities. . . .

4. Ernesto Galarza Defends Mexican Immigrants, 1929

The chief interest in the Mexican immigrant in the United States at the present moment centers around the question of whether Mexico shall be placed on the quota basis. The delegates to this Conference have already heard and probably will continue to hear the arguments marshaled by the opposing forces, and in these arguments they will have noted the usual alignment of racial purists versus economic expansionists. The restrictionists have mustered the familiar artillery of racial dilution and the color flood, while those who seek to keep the gates open, as they have been for the last eighteen years, are once more pressing the equally old argument that the very economic structure of the United States rests on the brawn and sweat of the immigrant.

. . . One effect of the controversy has been to obscure the very fundamental proposition that something must be done in the way of social and economic amelioration for those Mexicans who have already settled in the United States and whose problem is that of finding adjustment. Thus far in the discussion the Mexicans who have settled more or less permanently here have been taken into account negatively. . . .

For the moment . . . everyone has presented his side of the case except the Mexican worker himself. . . .

I speak to you today as one of these immigrants. I have only a simple and . . . suggestive statement based on a knowledge of the community life of these people and of what goes on in their minds concerning the economic aspects of "the Mexican problem."

First, as to unemployment. The Mexican is the first to suffer from depression in industrial and agricultural enterprises. . . . I flatly disagree with those who

Ernesto Galarza, "Life in the United States for Mexican People: Out of the Experience of a Mexican" from *Proceedings of the National Conference of Social Work, 56th Annual Session,* University of Chicago Press, 1929.

maintain that there is enough work for these people but that they refuse to work, preferring to live on charity. On the contrary, it is widely felt by the Mexicans that there are more men than there are jobs. . . . The precariousness of the job in the face of so much competition has brought home to the Mexican time and again his absolute weakness as a bargainer for employment. . . .

He has also something to say as to the wage scale. . . . The Mexican . . . recognizes his absolute inability to force his wage upward and by dint of necessity he shuffles along with a standard of living which the American worker regards with contempt and alarm. . . .

The distribution of the labor supply is felt by the Mexican to be inadequate. At present he has to rely mainly on hearsay or on the information of unscrupulous contractors who overcharge him for transportation. . . .

To these three aspects of the question—unemployment, wage scales, and seasonal migration in search of work—should be added . . . the persistence of race prejudice. . . .

. . . The Mexican immigrant still feels the burden of old prejudices. Only when there are threats to limit immigration from Mexico is it that a few in America sing the praises of the peon. . . . At other times the sentiments which seem to be deeply rooted in the American mind are that he is unclean, improvident, indolent, and innately dull. Add to this the suspicion that he constitutes a peril to the American worker's wage scale and you have a situation with which no average Mexican can cope.

I have tried to suggest some of the things which the Mexican would say if he were articulate. If his native reticence could be pierced, I believe these are his opinions on unemployment, wage scales, standard of living, seasonal migrations, and racial prejudices. . . .

First, some order should be brought out of the chaos of the seasonal labor supply, preferably by state initiative. As long as the present haphazard arrangement continues, surplus of laborers will be needed to compensate for the lack of correlation between the supply and the demand for farm workers. Control by private organizations of this phase of the question is subject to too many abuses to be recommended.

Second, a bilateral accord with the Mexican government should be sought to iron out the immigration question. . . .

Third, whenever feasible social service agencies working with Mexican groups should use workers of Mexican extraction to make the firsthand contacts.

Fourth, there should be more real understanding of the adjustment which the Mexican is making to his American environment. . . . Something more should be known also about how the Mexican lives and why before the stigma of a low standard of living is fastened on him.

Last, I would ask for recognition of the Mexican's contribution to the agricultural and industrial expansion of western United States. . . . From Denver to Los Angeles and from the Imperial Valley to Portland, it is said, an empire has been created largely by the brawn of the humble Mexican, who laid the rails and topped the beets and poured the cubic miles of cement. . . . If it is true that the Mexican has brought to you arms that have fastened a civilization on the Pacific slope, then give him his due. If you give him his earned wage and he proves improvident, teach him otherwise; if he is tuberculous, cure him; if he falls into indigence, raise him. He has built you an empire!

5. Merton E. Hill Outlines a Program for Americanizing the Mexicans, 1931

The Problem

One of the most momentous problems confronting the great Southwest today, is the assimilation of the Spanish-speaking peoples that are coming in ever increasing numbers into that land formerly owned by Mexico and since 1848 owned by the United States. The problem of developing, setting up, and carrying out an educational program that will lead ultimately to the "Americanization" of all aliens coming into a typical union high school district [Chaffey Union High School District in San Bernardino County, California], is the subject of this thesis.

Definition

. . . Americanization is hereby defined as the securing through instruction such reactions on the part of non-Americans that they will accept and practice those ideals, customs, methods of living, skills and knowledge that have come to be accepted as representative of the best in American life. . . .

The Program

The program to be presented . . . sets up those activities that will bring about the acceptance by aliens of American ideals, customs, methods of living, skills, and knowledge that will make them Americans in fact. . . .

Historical Beginnings

. . . The problem of Americanization involves not only the adults, but their children; . . . any program neglecting a full consideration of the educational needs of the foreign children is destined to fall short of complete success. . . . These and other problems can be wholly or partially solved; special classrooms adapted to the needs of the foreign element must be provided in the high school plant, in the elementary school buildings, in Mexican camps, and in central buildings within certain camps; a travelling school room on a bus chassis has been provided; teachers must be trained for Americanization work; lessons must be prepared to meet the needs of both children and adults; budgetary provisions must secure sufficient amounts of money; . . . the public must be aroused to a realization of the great and immediate need of making provision for educational, vocational, and sanitation programs that will result in . . . promoting the use of the English language, the right American customs, and the best possible standards of American life. . . .

Merton E. Hill, "The Development of an Americanization Program," *The Survey* 66, no. 3 (May 1931). In Carlos E. Cortes, ed., *Aspects of the Mexican-American Experience* (New York: Arno Press, 1976), pp. 10, 102–111. Reprinted by permission.

Lesson Plans

The educators who are concerned with an Americanization program must set up clearly defined objectives as to what ought to be taught the Mexican. . . . The latter will be required to use the English language. To meet this need language lessons should be developed by teachers and by boards of education to be adaptable to children, to adolescents, and to adults. . . . As the average Mexican adult has had no training in the "home-owning virtues," it will be necessary to develop lessons regarding thrift, saving, and the value of keeping the money in the banks. As the Mexicans show considerable aptitude for hand work of any kind, courses should be developed that will aid them in becoming skilled workers with their hands. Girls should be trained to become domestic servants, and to do various kinds of hand-work for which they can be paid adequately after they leave school.

Teaching Procedures

Such illustrative teaching procedures as the following have been determined by experience and through study of the problem:

1. Teach to all only the fundamental processes in arithmetic. . . .
2. Make use of intensive drill in penmanship. . . . Teach thrift through successive copying of Poor Richard's sayings; teach both men and women to spend less than they earn.
3. Teach reading. Include such things as road signs, railroad signs, and advertisements; the buying and selling language of the stores; our best patriotic utterances. Teach the use of the newspaper, the magazine, and the Americanization text-books.
4. Teach every mother during the pre-natal period the care of babies; the preparation and use of clothing; the selection and preparation of wholesome food. . . .
5. Teach every boy how to make inexpensive furniture for the home. Plans should be drawn for cheap but strong chairs, tables, shelves and cabinets. . . .
6. Girls should be trained to become neat and efficient house servants.
7. The outstanding students, boys and girls alike, should be trained in leadership. . . . All will be trained in voting.
8. Teach boys and girls, men and women how to enjoy wholesome amusements; provide an extensive physical education program that will include health education; train the adolescents of both sexes in self-control. Above all, set up a program such that every Mexican boy and girl . . . and every Mexican adult shall be organized into classes, arranged by groups according to their abilities and needs, and . . . taught and re-taught until they show the required proficiency to meet the ordinary needs of community life.

Organization

In order to secure the objectives enumerated above it will be necessary to organize with the object of putting across the Americanization program. The city board of education and the union high school board, and the county school department should co-operate to develop the program. Under them, the superintendent and the principal should develop a group charged with the duty of putting across the program. This should be a department of Americanization with a head, assistant teachers, clerical aid, and an attendance officer. Committees of teachers, elementary, junior high and senior high should be set to work on courses. Community contacts should be made, so that . . . welfare organizations, employers, companies employing large numbers of contract laborers, churches, women's clubs, D.A.R. [Daughters of the American Revolution], and other patriotic organizations, [and] chambers of commerce . . . will be co-operating to insure the success of the Americanization program. . . .

Importance of Co-Operation with the Board of Supervisors

There is a great Americanization work that can be done by the Board of Supervisors. By ordinance they can clean up all the rural Mexican camps; by ordinance they can limit in the camps the number of persons living in single rooms; they can by ordinance require sanitary conditions that will insure a pure water supply and adequate sewage disposal; finally, the Board of Supervisors can establish a Bureau of Placement and Labor Investigation that will perform under the Supervisors' direction the following service:

1. Study labor conditions within the county.
2. Study the labor supply and demand.
3. Maintain monthly correspondence with the supervisors of other counties.
4. Publish monthly statements showing labor needs.
5. Advise restrictions of further influx of laborers when not needed.
6. Establish the closest possible co-operation with the County Department of Education in a continued study of the problems arising from the presence of so large a Mexican population.

A County Supervisor of Mexican Education

There should be established under the direction of the County Superintendent of Schools an assistant County Superintendent of Schools charged with the duty of studying the problems of the education of Mexicans and the supervision of teachers of Mexican children. . . . The Mexican children are not progressing satisfactorily through the schools of the county. To meet this situation a new course of study should be developed for the Mexican pupils. . . . The new course of study should consider only the academic fundamentals of the English language, reading, and the fundamental processes in arithmetic and citizenship. Greater emphasis in the new course of study should be put upon . . . various forms of hand work. . . . Finally, the investigations . . . show the rating of Mexican pupils in eight traits or qualities that make for general success. There should be added thrift to these qualities for it is a well-known fact . . . that the Mexican laborers are not possessed of thrift. . . .

A Program of Adult Education

Finally, there should be established in the county . . . an intensive program of adult education. Funds should be provided . . . to teach every Mexican the English language, to teach every mother the care of infants, cleanliness, house sanitation, and economical house management including lessons in sewing, cooking, and thrift. The men should be trained in thrift, in gardening, and in the principles of the American government. In order to bring all the Mexican groups up to a higher level, parents and other adults must be taught as well as their children. . . . Class instruction . . . must exist for everyone; none should be allowed to escape the educational campaign.

Equipment

. . . There has been established [in the school district] a new department to be known as the Department of Mexican Education. . . . The purpose of this department is to make a scientific study of the Mexican. This study should trace the ethnological evolution of the modern Mexican; it should involve a study of the history of the Mexican people. . . . The Department of Mexican Education should make a further study of the temperament of the race for this should be thoroughly understood in dealing with the people. There should be studied most carefully those qualities and abilities that are recognized as peculiar to the Mexican people. . . . Their capacities to perform different types of service should be set forth that their employers may utilize them to the best interests of both employer and employed. . . .

. . . Learning needful lessons by the Mexican learner is the goal.

In communities where there is sufficient Mexican population . . . there should be developed industrial high schools for Mexican pupils and for Mexican adults. . . .

This school will mark the culmination of educational effort for Mexican advancement in the Chaffey district. The school will be located on a ten-acre campus. . . . There will be home-making and citizenship rooms provided for adults of the Mexican race. These rooms will be comfortably but simply equipped for social as well as instructional use, the ideal being the evolution eventuating in the Americanization Mexican.

6. Elisa Silva Describes Mexican Immigrant Life in Los Angeles, 1920s

My father died. Then my mother, my two sisters and I decided to come to the United States. As we had been told that there were good opportunities for earning money in Los Angeles, working as extras in the movies and in other ways, we sold our belongings and with the little which our father had left us we came to this place. . . . From the time we entered I noticed a change in everything, in customs, and so forth. . . . When we got to Los Angeles we rented a furnished apartment. . . . My sisters and I decided to look for work at once. One of my sisters

"Elisa Silva," in Manuel Gamio, *The Life Story of the Mexican Immigrant,* 1971, pp. 159–161. Reprinted by permission of Dover Publications, Inc.

. . . found work at once in the house of a Mexican woman doing sewing. My mother then decided . . . that I should also work in order to help out with the household expenses. . . . I found it hard to find work, much as I looked. As we had to earn something, a girl friend of mine, . . . from Sonora, [Mexico,] advised me to go to a dance-hall. After consulting with my mother and my sisters I decided to come and work here every night dancing. My work consists of dancing as much as I can with everyone who comes. At the beginning I didn't like this work because I had to dance with anyone, but I have finally gotten used to it and now I don't care, because I do it in order to earn my living. Generally I manage to make from $20.00 to $30.00 a week, for we get half of what is charged for each dance. Each dance is worth ten cents so that if I dance, for example, fifty dances in a night I earn $2.50. Since the dances are short, ten cents being charged for just going around the ball-room, one can dance as many as a hundred. It all depends on how many men come who want to dance. Besides there are some who will give you a present of a dollar or two. This work is what suits me best for I don't need to know any English here. . . . At times I get a desire to look for another job, because I get very tired. One has to come at 7.30 in the evening and one goes at 12.30, and sometimes at 1 in the morning. One leaves almost dead on Saturdays because many Mexican people come from the nearby towns and they dance and dance with one all night. In Mexico this work might perhaps not be considered respectable, but I don't lose anything here by doing it. It is true that some men at times make propositions to me which are insulting, but everything is fixed by just telling them no. If they insist one can have them taken out of the hall by the police.

❧ E S S A Y S

The demand for labor during and after World War I, combined with the passage of immigration laws that stopped the flow of European labor and favored the Mexicans, facilitated Mexican migration to the Midwest. This was a process based on family and kinship networks. Zaragosa Vargas, an associate professor of history at the University of California, Santa Barbara, writes in the first essay that the expanding production of beet sugar in the Great Lakes region would extend Mexican migratory work patterns to the north. Repair and maintenance work for eastern railroads, along with jobs in meatpacking houses, steel mills, and automobile companies, brought thousands of Mexicans to the industrial heartland of the Midwest during the 1920s.

During this period, urbanization had a great impact on Mexican immigrants, who assimilated to American culture in varying degrees. Material acculturation among young Mexican American women, who were particularly influenced by the material culture that surrounded them, is the subject of the essay by Vicki L. Ruiz, professor of history at Arizona State University, Tempe. She notes that not only was this aspect of Americanization never fully achieved, but Mexican identity was never completely undermined by the material acculturation that did occur because the Mexican values of the immigrants remained dominant. Pageants, festivals, and music that dramatized their Mexican heritage further reinforced the immigrants' culture.

Mexican Immigrants in the Midwest

ZARAGOSA VARGAS

Throughout the 1920s, and continuing well into the post–World War II years, Texas was the greatest contributor of Mexican labor to other states. Indeed, the sheer numbers of the Mexican labor reserve in the Lone Star State made it "the hub on which the wheel of the Mexican population in the United States . . . revolved." Mexicans set out for work from the state's farms and railroad-section projects. The cities of El Paso, Laredo, San Antonio, and Fort Worth served as staging areas for this migration to the Midwest and as relay stations for returning immigrants. . . .

North from Texas

Thousands of Mexican immigrants, many accompanied by their families, entered Texas at Eagle Pass, Laredo, and Brownsville, at the turn of the century and spread into the three distinct farm zones that emerged in the state's southwestern region. . . . In the Winter Garden area they planted and harvested onions and spinach; they picked citrus fruits in the lower Río Grande Valley and cotton in the Gulf Coast cotton belt. . . .

. . . Mexican migratory labor made cotton king in Texas in these early years, and this achievement made Mexicans the agricultural laborers of choice. Farmers endlessly praised them as ideal laborers. Costing less and demanding less, effi-cient, and, more important, plentiful, Mexicans first replaced white sharecroppers and then blacks in Texas as the preferred workers. . . .

Cotton picking in Texas took place in three areas and seasons: in south Texas from early June to the end of August, in central Texas from August to mid-Septem-ber, and in north and west Texas from September to December. The cotton season thus afforded tens of thousands of Mexicans continuous, uninterrupted employ-ment over a seven-month period. Moreover, the cotton-picking season followed the end of the fruit and vegetable harvest in the Winter Garden area and the lower Río Grande Valley. This pattern had a cumulative effect on the size of the labor force following the cotton crop; with the end of the harvest season in each farm zone additional Mexicans joined the pool of cotton pickers. . . .

The now-heralded big swing of the enormous reserve of Mexican workers who followed the cotton crop through each of these three areas suggested an army on the move to journalist Carey McWilliams:

> From the lower valley, where the season starts, comes the initial vanguard of about 25,000 Mexican migratory workers. As the army marches through the Robstown–Cor-pus Christi area, an additional 25,000 recruits join the procession. By the time the army has reached central Texas, it has probably grown to about 250,000 to 300,000 workers. Recruits join the army, follow it through a county or two, and then drop out, to be re-placed with new families from the next county.

Zaragosa Vargas, "Mexican Migration to the Midwest" from *Proletarians of the North: A History of Mexican Industrial Workers in Detroit and the Midwest, 1917–1933,* University of California Press, 1993, pp. 13–53. Copyright © 1993 The Regents of the University of California. Reprinted with permission of the University of California Press.

Cotton picking in Texas had drawbacks. One was the result of utilizing the family as the center of production. The use of women and children as unpaid labor not only tended to lower wages but as a rule depressed labor standards. In addition, the demanding, backbreaking labor was performed in unrelenting heat, involuntary unemployment was caused by a rainy season, and many Mexicans suffered the blatant racial abuse of Anglo ranchers. Mexicans were isolated in rural areas and small towns and segregated by race from Anglos. Hatred of Mexicans was deeply ingrained in Texas culture, and in this climate of virulent contempt it was not uncommon for hostility to culminate in violence. . . . Violence, the threat of violence, and legal means regulated the movement of Mexicans; these became physical as well as ideological extensions of segregation necessary to control and maintain this labor force. The laborers were expected to accept their inferiority as part of the ostensibly rational separation of the Anglo and Mexican races in Texas. . . .

Mexicans migrating from Texas to the Midwest therefore made conscious choices to leave behind working and living conditions made doubly oppressive by racism. . . . In comparing working conditions in Texas with those in the Midwest, workers remarked that less supervision, interference, and subservience were required in industrial work. More important, the men gained dignity and respect, which they had not known in Texas. As a Mexican steelworker stated, in the North one was allowed to "talk with your hat on."

San Antonio became a favorite city of the sojourners passing through Texas. The Southwest metropolis and cultural center antedated Los Angeles as the capital of Mexicans living within the United States. An estimated 20,000 laborers left each year from San Antonio to work in Texan cotton fields and in northern beet fields and factories, with the tip of this migration wave reaching into the north as far as Detroit and Pittsburgh. . . .

Mexicans seeking work in San Antonio congregated at Milam Park. . . . a popular gathering place for the city's Spanish-speaking population. A cross-section of the Mexican working classes assembled there: itinerant railroad workers from Mexico and east Texas, Oklahoma, Kansas, and Nebraska, previously on extragangs ballasting, laying ties, and doing ordinary pick-and-shovel work; experienced miners from the Mexican silver mines of San Luis Potosí and coal mines in Bridgeport, Texas, and southeastern Oklahoma; seasonal farm laborers finished with the Texas and Oklahoma cotton harvests, ready to join the migration to the sugar-beet, wheat, and corn fields in Colorado, Illinois, and Michigan; packinghouse workers who had processed hogs and cattle in Kansas City, Omaha, and Chicago; and former foundry men from Indiana and Ohio who had returned to San Antonio until the next start-up of production.

Recruitment by northern employers helped break the virtual quarter-century monopoly on Mexican labor held by Southwest farmers, railroads, and mining companies. Lured north by the promise of higher wages and their rising expectations for economic betterment, immigrants in increasing numbers bypassed work in Texas. Mexicans who went north returned home and told their relatives and friends about what they had seen in their distant travels in search of work. Through word of mouth the opportunities available in the Midwest became widely known. Brothers, uncles, and cousins drew their kin into railroad work, foundries, steel mills, and auto factories. . . . Family and friendship networks thus not only influenced the paths of Mexican migration to the North and decisions about work but determined settlement patterns within the region and aided adjustment to the new urban, industrial environment.

In 1927, the Mexican population in the Midwest totaled 63,700; it increased to 80,000 in the summer months, with the influx of migrants into the farming regions. This group was relatively young (half were between eighteen and thirty) and had a vast array of life experiences and backgrounds. . . . Most came from the states of Michoacán, Guanajuato, and Jalisco in Mexico's overpopulated west central region. Nearly two-thirds of the immigrants admitted into the United States had been laborers in Mexico. . . .

Mexicans in the Midwest alternated between factory labor and work in agriculture and on the railroads. This tendency demonstrated the influence of the sugar-beet sector, the pull still exerted by previous work patterns and employment cycles, as well as the preferences and priorities of family and friends. The expanding domestic production of beet sugar in the Great Lakes region led to the active recruitment of Mexicans. Indeed, many of the men who entered factory employment in the region first worked on sugar-beet farms, family members working alongside the men, planting and harvesting this crop on a seasonal basis. Mexicans made sugar the agricultural queen in the North.

Sugar-Beet Work

. . . Contracting families [for sugar-beet work] was preferred because it was a profitable arrangement for farmers. To the Mexicans not only was family work familiar and customary, but declining wages demanded the effort of all who could work. Laboring together, a household could make sufficient money for the remainder of the year. . . . The labor-intensive nature of sugar-beet work required ten to twelve hours of work, six days a week, from each worker to get the harvested beets to the refineries quickly in order to limit depletion of sugar content. Children had to take part, despite efforts to curb the exploitive excesses of child labor. . . .

The use of Mexican labor in northern sugar-beet work was quite extensive and produced a silent invasion of the rural Midwest by a myriad of workers. With the promise of good wages and the enticements of free transportation and housing, the sugar companies contracted thousands of Mexicans to perform handwork on beet farms in Minnesota, Wisconsin, Ohio, Iowa, and Michigan. The Dominion and the Michigan sugar companies even sent Mexicans to work as far as Ontario. Michigan sugar companies brought Mexicans to the state beginning in 1915, when it shipped them from Texas under contract with the Osborn Employment Agency. This recruiting agency of the Michigan Sugar Company became the biggest employer of Mexican contract labor. As a result of steady recruitment and the seasonal migration patterns, Mexicans constituted 33 percent of Michigan's sugar-beet workers in 1922, and that figure more than doubled to 75 percent by 1927. In 1927 the Michigan, Isabella, Columbia, Great Lakes, Continental, and St. Louis sugar companies employed nearly 20,000 Mexicans across the state.

. . . The American Crystal Sugar Company first hired Mexicans to work in Minnesota in 1907 and steadily recruited them thereafter; by 1927, 5,000 Mexicans worked in this state and 7,000 by the following year. . . . Contracted in Texas and in Kansas by the Continental Sugar Company, Mexicans entered sugar-beet work in northwest Ohio in 1917. After the harvest season, Continental Sugar provided its employees with work at its sugar refinery in Toledo. Recruitment of Mexicans by this company reached a peak in 1926, when 2,697 were brought into Ohio. In the ensuing years the growing number of Mexicans present in the Toledo area, many men former sugar-beet workers who had found jobs with the railroads, furnished Continental Sugar with an ample labor supply, and it no longer needed to recruit outside the state.

In 1927, some 58,000 Mexicans were employed on 800,000 acres of sugar-beet farmlands extending from eastern Colorado to northwestern Ohio; of these, half worked in the Midwest. Related through networks of family and kin, they formed an army of industrious field hands that was the northern equivalent of the multitude that harvested Texas cotton. And like their Texas counterparts, the Mexican sugar-beet workers gained the praise of farmers who endowed them with such characteristics as being "reasonable, obliging, . . . capable, less demanding," and showing "a willingness to take orders." Working as late as November and early December, when winter snowfalls blanketed the beet fields and the days grew colder and shorter, Mexicans harvested 7.5 million tons of sugar beets valued at between $60 and $65 million. One can appreciate why the sugar-beet industry lauded their boom years as the "Mexican Harvest."

These workers were now part of a migratory labor force that left from San Antonio and the Río Grande Valley in Texas and entered the Midwest on a seasonal basis. . . . Accustomed to sugar-beet work—the intensive nature of planting, hoeing, cutting, and blocking performed in the chilly spring rains, the humidity of summer, and the first snows of late autumn—these itinerant laborers arrived each spring in a convoy of Model Ts and Reo trucks for the start of the planting season and left in late fall after the harvest. . . . The constant recruitment of Mexicans by the sugar companies produced a seasonal migration from Texas to the Midwest that became self-perpetuating. The migration routes, which passed through northern Texas, Arkansas, Missouri, and Illinois and which remained largely invisible to Americans, were followed by future generations of Mexicans coming to work on the fruit and vegetable farms of the midwestern region. Like their predecessors, they too left the migrant stream and settled in the cities in order to secure work in the local factories.

Mexican sugar-beet workers were not immune to the many abuses that were associated with the work and that often went unreported. The independence they enjoyed working on the farms came with bad housing conditions, health problems, and destitution. Dishonest farmers cheated the Mexicans out of their wages or were cruel to the workers. However, none of the misdeeds proved as threatening as the encounters in Texas, where hostile Anglo farmers commonly said they "would rather kill a [Mexican] worker than pay him." Beet workers did not passively accept bad treatment but applied lessons of resistance they had learned from agricultural labor in Texas. Complaints were filed with Mexican consuls about poor living and working conditions and wage discrimination, but sometimes the laborers simply walked out of the fields or staged work slowdowns to protest their objectionable treatment. . . .

A vast number of Mexicans did not return to Texas at the end of the sugar-beet harvest season. Instead the workers repeated the patterns of their European predecessors and left sugar-beet work for jobs in the cities. Some Mexicans who stayed wintered in migrant camps and lived on their savings, which they supplemented with part-time farm work, until the start of the next beet season. . . . Many more moved to small towns nearby or to industrial centers within the region like Milwaukee, Chicago, and Detroit. With the help of family members and friends they were channeled into employment on railroads, on city maintenance and construction projects, and in foundries and factories. . . .

As time passed, Mexicans in the northern cities resorted to beet work only during prolonged periods of factory unemployment and when alternative kinds of work were unavailable. This growing reluctance stemmed from their habituation to city life and the routine of industrial work, which, despite periodic shutdowns, brought a semblance of permanence to their lives. . . .

The desire to disassociate themselves from farm labor became widespread because midwestern Mexicans recognized its lowly rank in the emerging hierarchy of obtainable labor that was an integral part of the social order they created in the North. In the Mexican colonies factory workers enjoyed the highest status and prestige; these relatively well-paid men were employed in unskilled and semiskilled operations in steel mills and car factories. Next in the ranking came the railroad workers, the men who repaired and maintained the local rail lines. Belittled by factory workers because track work entailed a transient life-style for the men and their families as well as living in deplorable boxcar camps, the proud track laborers nonetheless considered themselves better than the beet workers at the bottom echelon. Farm work was viewed as a last resort, casual labor performed only by greenhorns or by Mexicans who constituted the permanent labor migration force from Texas.

By the middle of the 1920s Mexicans with relatives and friends working in the beet fields were encouraging them to leave the farms and seek factory employment. They argued that jobs in the foundries and factories, though beset by bad working conditions, were far superior to the hard handwork, low earnings, bad housing, and winter unemployment that characterized beet work. More important, their children were placed at a disadvantage by having to work when they should be enrolled in school, an indication that education figured prominently in their world. The constant prodding by relatives and friends already in the cities helped to reinforce cognizance of the contrasting experiences of beet work and factory work, between rural and urban life, and between poverty and material prosperity. . . .

. . . For thousands of sugar-beet workers, . . . city life eventually became irresistible and a viable alternative. They gathered their families and meager belongings and loaded them on buses or into family jalopies and left the farms for the urban centers.

Joining them in their trek to the city were Mexicans who came north to work for the railroads. Railroading, like agriculture, was an important frame of reference for Mexicans after their nearly fifty years of employment by this industry in the Southwest. Like the returning beet workers, track men relayed news about job possibilities in the region and established a parallel migration route that followed the network of eastern rail lines to and within the North.

Working for the Railroads

. . . Eastern railroad companies faced shortages of unskilled labor and began contracting Mexicans in Texas, where the lines had terminals. . . . At first most of the recruits got their jobs through private labor agencies or through railroad employment offices set up in Texas cities. The companies soon tapped their workers' networks of relatives and friends to reduce costly recruitment expenses. Careful not to jeopardize the reputation of the family name, the men would strive to be good workers.

One of the railroad companies expanding its recruitment of Mexicans for maintenance-of-way service in Chicago was the Chicago, Rock Island and Pacific Railway (referred to as Rock Island). This company had a terminal in El Paso, and the Mexicans recruited shipped out on its trains directly to the Chicago area. The Rock Island circulated announcements printed in Spanish among its Mexican employees so they could send them to their relatives and friends in Mexico. In this way the railroad circumvented the extra costs of direct recruitment. In turn, Mexican kinship and friendship networks assured a steady flow of dependable and reliable men into the work crews of the rail line.

In 1916, 206 Mexicans worked year-round in Chicago for sixteen railroads with terminals there, but within ten years 5,255 were performing track labor in the area for twenty rail companies. This significant rise in employment was noted by a field researcher who stated, "More Mexicans worked for railroads than for any one single industry, over 25 percent of them being thus employed." Between 1923 and 1928, the percentage of Mexicans engaged in track maintenance in the Chicago area doubled from 21 to 42 percent. . . .

After the 1920–1921 depression, as eastern railroads began employing large crews of Mexicans drawn from the labor pools emerging in Chicago, a familiar pattern began to emerge. Beet workers who migrated to Chicago during the winter from farms in Michigan, Indiana, and Ohio constituted a sizable number of the recruits during the track maintenance and construction season. These men supplemented a company's regular work crews of Mexican track men. In 1926, 650 Mexicans shipped out from Chicago to Detroit with the Palma Construction Company for work on the Michigan Central Railroad. Others hired on with the Detroit Railway Company as section hands. All these men were seasonal track laborers. Thus while some Mexicans were long-time employees, most hired on in the summer and later quit to seek jobs in the local factories. . . .

Notwithstanding the fact that a distinguishable labor sector within track work had been established with its own work ethic and culture, and based on family and friendship networks, Mexican track laborers in the North performed physically strenuous tasks, often in the ice and snow and in below-freezing weather where the frost line was a major obstacle. For example, men with the Burlington Northern in Minnesota worked in winter temperatures of twenty degrees below zero, which the wind chill reduced even more. Such amenities as housing, coal for heating . . . , water, and commissary food were accepted as adequate compensation by the hardworking men. . . . Once they were steadily employed, many men began bringing their families north. . . . As the pace of recruitment for northern railroad work accelerated, Mexican boxcar communities began to dot the landscape; they were the beginning of many of the Mexican colonies in the Midwest. . . .

Given the low wages, hard work, and seasonal nature of track employment, labor turnover was a persistent problem for the railroads. . . . In addition to the pull of jobs in the urban centers, which promised material well-being through higher wages, family members influenced the decision of track laborers to head for the cities because of the transient nature of track work and the isolation and rusticity of boxcar camp life. Women found it hard to make the transition to a nomadic, often secluded existence and were disconcerted by the long absences of the men. The expectations of women for a better life—for having running water and electricity, owning a refrigerator, shopping in stores, putting their children in school—went unfulfilled as they faithfully followed their men up and down miles of rail line. These working-class expectations shaped and ordered the social world of the Mexican women, as they did the social world of their male counterparts. They too wanted good wages and the satisfaction of success along with the corollary high status among their countrymen in the northern colonies.

Eastern railroads continuously replenished their supply of workers. Mexicans with families were encouraged to sign contracts so as to maintain a stable labor pool and offset the desertions. Along with the sugar companies, the railroads thus fostered Mexican migration from Texas to the Midwest and helped to increase the Mexican population in the region. As the rail lines began recruiting laborers from midwestern cities, they aided the distribution of Mexicans throughout the heartland. Once Mexicans established beachheads in the various railroad industries of the Midwest, networks of family and friends supported and sustained the influx into this sector. . . .

Employment in Steel Mills and Meat-Packing Plants

Likewise, the wages and bonus and benefit plans offered by some steel companies increased the number of Mexicans who decided to work in this labor sector. The industrial North became identified with steel work, and Mexicans' entry into this industry added to the differentiation of the Mexican working classes. . . . Their experiences in the mills altered their lives as workers as well as altering the general perceptions of Mexican proletarians in the United States in the 1920s.

Factory employment of Mexicans in the Midwest signaled their transformation into industrial workers and marked a major change in the work habits and lifestyles of these migrants. As the newest members of the factory workforce, they helped reshape the composition of the American working class. More important, as factory operatives they internalized the values and culture of the industrial workplace. . . . Diverse experiences in mills, foundries, and factories delineated this working-class culture. . . .

The steady entrance of Mexicans into steelwork resumed after the 1920–1921 depression as employers expanded their recruiting efforts. . . . Some steel companies distributed fliers printed in Spanish to Mexicans aboard trains of the Santa Fe Railroad, a tactic some rail lines had used to attract workers in Texas. The mill owners attempted to draw these contract laborers into steelwork as they headed to Iowa to work for the Santa Fe. The offer of higher wages and benefits persuaded dozens to desert. Steel plants in the Chicago area relied on local employment offices or labor sources for recruiting Mexican workers. Like the sugar and railroad companies, the mills utilized the family and friendship networks of Mexicans already on the payroll to secure additional workers and thereby reduce recruitment costs. This practice benefited Mexican workers.

The U.S. Steel Corporation became the largest employer of Mexicans in steel, hiring thousands to work in its plants in Wisconsin, Illinois, Indiana, Ohio, Pennsylvania, and New York. The Carnegie Steel Corporation employed far fewer Mexicans, but the company helped disperse them into the steel-mill regions in Pennsylvania and Ohio. By the early twenties, nearly 900 Mexicans were working in the mills of Carnegie Steel in Homestead, Braddock, Duquesne, and Clairton, Pennsylvania, and in Mingo Junction, Ohio. Bethlehem Steel brought Mexicans into Pennsylvania, as did Jones and Laughlin and National Tube, both subsidiaries of U.S. Steel.

Steel plants in Pennsylvania hired fewer Mexicans as steel production shifted to the Great Lakes region. . . . No attempt was made by Pennsylvania steel firms to replace Mexican workers who deserted by bringing in new shipments of these men. In May 1925, the Pennsylvania Bureau of Employment reported that only 1,135 Mexicans worked in the state's steel plants. . . . The use of Mexicans in the mills of western Pennsylvania was likely restricted by the presence in the region of second-generation European immigrants (37 percent of the workforce by 1930) who monopolized the unskilled jobs. Also, reliance on blacks (10 percent of the workforce by 1930) further limited job opportunities. Most Mexican steelworkers were found in the steel districts of the Chicago-Gary area and in Lorain, Ohio. If the Great Depression had not cut off migration from Texas, as did the short-lived 1920–1921 depression, Mexicans would have contributed far more than they did to the ethnic transformation of the region's steel labor force. In Ohio, the National Tube plant in Lorain had as many Mexican steelworkers on the payroll as did all the steel mills in the entire state of Pennsylvania.

Mexicans responded to the call by National Tube for steady work at good wages when 1,000 arrived from Texas at its Lorain, Ohio, steel plant in 1923. Turnover of Mexicans at National Tube remained low, about 13 percent, because this mill carefully screened its applicants and required the possession of immigration papers. The local company paid the transportation costs back to the border for workers who entered the country illegally so they could obtain visas. National Tube also contacted former employers to verify applicants' work records. The slow but careful selection process proved worthwhile; as a result of its selective hiring policies and its willingness to employ these migrants, this steel plant gained the allegiance of its new employees. . . .

Though subject to business cycles, the work patterns Mexican steelworkers established at National Tube in Lorain demonstrated that as a group they were actively entering industrial employment and rising above their newcomer status. More important, the desire to return to Mexico was waning as immigrants resolved not to go back to their homeland because of limited opportunities. Mexicans in the Midwest were being integrated into the American blue-collar world. Their assimilation into an industrial work culture, an uneven process of adaptation, was taking place through the creation of enclaves in ethnic, working-class neighborhoods and the networks established there, all of which were influenced by the pervasive factory environment.

However, everyday life was far from idyllic for the Mexican proletarians. Alternating bouts of work and unemployment were ever present and undeniably unsettling. The workers paid exorbitant rents for some of the worst housing in factory districts. Overcrowding made living unhealthful, and pollution was widespread in the neighborhoods located in the vicinity of the steel mills, stockyards, and foundries. . . . Notwithstanding, these ethnic working-class settlements in the North were home to the Mexican immigrants, and the hardships and sacrifices were considered worthwhile. . . .

Steel production helped transform Chicago into a mecca for Mexicans migrating to the Midwest and into a staging area for those heading to other sections of the region. Chicago's steel mills offered thousands of Mexicans employment. In 1925, over half the 8,000 to 10,000 Mexican steelworkers in the Midwest held jobs in Chicago mills, and they constituted 14 percent of the total local workforce in steel. Wisconsin Steel and Illinois Steel employed nearly a third of these workers. The proportion of Mexicans working in Chicago's steel industry remained relatively constant until the end of the decade, at which time 82 percent of the 19,362 Mexicans in the Windy City were industrial workers. They could be found at work in freight yards, steel mills and foundries, and packing houses. This was the case for all of the Chicago-Calumet region.

Northwest Indiana was another center of steel production. In the twenties, thousands of Mexicans traveled by electric tram and bus to Indiana Harbor and Gary, Indiana, located east of Chicago, to seek work in the local steel mills. Some left fruit farms in southwestern Michigan to take jobs there. The Department of Labor reported that in late fall 1924 approximately 4,000 Mexicans from Michigan orchards arrived at the local steel mills in Indiana Harbor and Gary and that applications for work averaged twenty to thirty per day.

The number of Mexicans at the Inland Steel Company in Indiana Harbor increased in 1923, when the company expanded production and changed to the eight-hour day, adding an extra shift. Over the next six years Inland Steel hired 3,600 Mexicans, the majority from Gary, Chicago, and Pennsylvania, though some had come up from Texas. Despite the labor turnover, with men quitting to seek work elsewhere, the 2,526 Mexicans Inland employed in 1926 were nearly a fourth of the company's total employees. Their numbers declined thereafter, reflecting overall reductions of the company's workforce. However, the 2,000 Mexicans on Inland's payroll in 1928 still constituted almost a third of its workers and its main ethnic group. On the eve of the Great Depression, Inland Steel had the second largest number of Mexican workers of all U.S. manufacturing industries. Only the Ford Motor Company employed more at its massive River Rouge plant.

Unquestionably, Inland Steel's Mexican workers played an essential part in Indiana Harbor's economy. This role was noted in an interview by Edson of steelworker F. M. Figueroa, who was also co-publisher of the local Spanish-language newspaper *El Amigo del Hogar.* The steelworker pointed out that the significant contributions of his industrious countrymen to local prosperity came with sacrifices. They were not appreciated, nor did their labor exempt them from discrimination, which was rampant in Indiana Harbor. This worker pointedly remarked:

> The Mexicans of Indiana Harbor earn pay amounting to $7,000,000 a year. Of this amount they [only] send to Mexico . . . $1,000,000. That means that they turn $6,000,000, which they earn by hard labor, back into the money drawers of the city. . . . For this wealth . . . they get little more than a miserable existence, snubbed by their neighbors, abused by the authorities, and exploited by everybody. . . .

In addition to finding railroad work and steelwork, Mexicans entered the northern meat-packing industry, and within a short time a sizable number were performing unskilled jobs in the packing plants of Wilson and Company, Swift and Company, Cudahy, and the Omaha Company in Nebraska, South Dakota, Kansas, Iowa, Minnesota, and Illinois. In 1928, Mexicans constituted 5.8 percent of the labor force in Chicago meat packing; they were concentrated primarily in entry-level positions, working alongside Polish and Lithuanian immigrants in the pickle, glue, lard, and fertilizer departments. . . .

. . . Mexican packing-house workers attempted to keep up with the dangerously fast work pace, which added to the high number of work-related accidents and injuries that marked the industry. Former packing-house workers chillingly recalled co-workers being killed because of the frenzied pace of the work in the plants. Along with these hazards, erratic schedules and seasonal layoffs were endemic to packing-house work. In Chicago, the meat companies usually hired men for only a day's work at the beginning of a mass slaughter and sent them home once the job was finished. . . . The relatively low number of Mexicans in meat packing was a result of the huge ethnic and black workforce in this industry. However, a considerable number of Mexicans were employed in meat-processing plants in Kansas City, and some were long-time packing-house workers. Their presence in this industry contributed to the diversity of the Mexican proletarian experience in the North.

Entrance into Automobile Employment

Michigan's automakers played a central role in the development of the emerging Mexican industrial working class. Large numbers of Mexicans migrated to southeast Michigan specifically to seek high-wage work in the car and truck plants. However, the auto industry (except for Buick Motors) neither recruited Mexicans, as had the sugar companies and the railroads, nor brought them north initially as strikebreakers, as had the steel mills. Rather, the car companies drew Mexicans into their factories mainly from the ranks of sugar-beet workers on area farms, though railroad workers, steelworkers, and a few coal miners also yielded to the lucrative lure of auto work. As early as 1917 Mexicans began working in automobile factories in Detroit, Saginaw, Flint, and Pontiac, Michigan. The majority had migrated to Detroit from other parts of the Midwest; less than 10 percent were direct arrivals from Mexico.

Once again, networks of family and friends helped spur the influx of Mexicans into the Motor City, providing information about work and how to obtain employment. . . .

By 1920, about 3,000 Mexicans were in Detroit. . . . Detroit was the world's biggest manufacturer of cars, trucks, and tractors, and the nation's fastest growing metropolitan area because of its high-wage industry. Ford Motors hired the greatest number of Mexicans, employing nearly 4,000 at its Highland Park, Fordson, and River Rouge plants in 1928. Over 200 young men carefully selected by their government from engineering and technical schools in Mexico enrolled as students in the Henry Ford Service School. They worked as apprentices on cars, trucks, and tractors in the Highland Park and Fordson plants as part of their training to become technicians for dealerships in Mexico and Latin America. Mexican colonies developed in the working-class districts near car plants in Saginaw, Flint, and Pontiac. By the end of the 1920s, General Motors and Dodge Motors employed approximately 800 Mexicans, Fisher Body had several hundred in its plants in Detroit and Pontiac, and nearly 1,000 worked at the Buick Motors plant in Flint and at Chevrolet's Detroit and Saginaw plants. Untold numbers of Mexicans also found jobs with auto-parts and accessory firms that did subcontract work for the major carmakers. Because of the high labor turnover that characterized the auto industry, it is quite likely that thousands of Mexicans passed through the gates of the car plants of southeast Michigan.

Mexicans found employment with all the car companies and worked in most plant departments, though their distribution within the industry was uneven. Where they worked depended on the hiring policies of each auto and auto-parts maker and of plant managers and foremen who, with their own racial and ethnic preferences, determined job assignments. At some car plants Mexicans formed a considerable percentage of the men in the shops and even won promotions to foreman and supervisor. "There were lots of Mexicans at Chrysler Motors," retired autoworker Ramón Huerta remembered. "In my department were Mexicans, Spaniards, and Polackos [Poles], but no blacks. Our superintendent was a Mexican from Jalisco." Fisher Body used few Mexicans because of hiring restrictions on foreign and black workers. . . .

Exposed to dangerous working environments, untold numbers of Mexican autoworkers were blinded by flying metal, lost their fingers and sometimes their hands in the whirling machinery, inhaled poisonous gases, and suffered burns from molten metal. Work-related stress was an additional problem. Many could not withstand the fast pace of production and the regimented working environment, where discipline was strictly enforced by shop foremen. Foremen baited the Mexicans, racially harassed them, and did not hesitate to beat or kick them for minor violations. Outweighing the hazards of mass-production work, the sporadic prejudice of white autoworkers, the unsafe factory conditions, and the repressive forms of control, the promise of employment continued to attract Mexicans to Detroit throughout the twenties. The hope of achieving a better life prompted Mexicans to migrate to the Motor City. Good-paying jobs with the Ford Motor Company were greatly prized. To wear the silver Ford badge and short ("white-walled") haircuts, which were the distinctive trademarks of the Ford autoworker, became the ambition of Mexicans in the climb for status.

. . . A job with the popular auto company was a means to a better life and a way to attain pride and gain respect as a worker. This social status was sought more and more in the Mexican colony of Detroit, for thousands of Mexicans endeavored to become part of the elite corps of Ford mass-production workers. These new Ford men were the embodiment of the Mexican industrial proletariat.

The opportunity for work on the railroads, in the steel mills and foundries, in the packing houses, and in the auto factories brought thousands of Mexicans into the industrial heartland of the Midwest during the 1920s. . . . Sizable numbers were recruited by northern sugar companies, which with several eastern railroads helped augment Mexican migration to the North. Earlier legislation restricting immigration from Europe also proved favorable. Mexicans toiled in factories alongside immigrant and black co-workers and were prone to the same work slowdowns owing to swings in production cycles. During boom years Mexicans enjoyed full-time employment, enabling them to participate in the prosperity of the period. When industrial production shut down, as during the 1927 recession, Mexican factory workers faced layoffs and bouts of unemployment. Without work, thousands left the Midwest, though itinerant employment was commonplace. The Mexican proletarians of the North adjusted to their new environs and embraced the style of work of the different labor sectors. . . .

The Acculturation of Young Mexican American Women

VICKI L. RUIZ

This essay discusses the forces of Americanization and the extent to which they influenced a generation of Mexican American women coming of age during the 1920s and 1930s. The adoption of new cultural forms, however, did not take place in a vacuum. The political and economic environment surrounding Mexican immigrants and their children would color their responses to mainstream U.S. society. The Spanish-speaking population in the United States soared between 1910 and 1930 as over one million Mexicanos migrated northward. Pushed by the economic and political chaos generated by the Mexican Revolution and lured by jobs in U.S. agribusiness and industry, they settled into existing barrios and forged new communities both in the Southwest and the Midwest, in small towns and cities. For example, in 1900 only 3,000 to 5,000 Mexicans lived in Los Angeles, but by 1930 approximately 150,000 persons of Mexican birth or heritage had settled into the city's expanding barrios. On a national level, by 1930 Mexicans, outnumbered only by Anglos and blacks, formed the "third largest 'racial' group."

Pioneering social scientists, particularly Manuel Gamio, Paul Taylor, and Emory Bogardus, examined the lives of these Mexican immigrants, but their materials on women are sprinkled here and there and at times are hidden in unpublished field notes. . . . To set the context, I will look at education, employment, and media as agents of Americanization and assess the ways in which Mexican American women incorporated their messages. Drawing on social science fieldwork and oral interviews, I will discuss also the sources of conflict between adolescent women and their parents as well as the contradictions between the promise of the American dream and the reality of restricted mobility and ethnic prejudice.

This study relies extensively on oral history. The memories of thirteen women serve as the basis for my reconstruction of adolescent aspirations and experiences. . . .

Education and employment were the most significant agents of Americanization. Educators generally relied on an immersion method in teaching the English language to their Mexican pupils. . . . Even on the playground, students were en-

Vicki L. Ruiz, "Star Struck: Acculturation, Adolescence, and the Mexican American Woman, 1920–1950" in Adela de la Torre and Beatriz M. Pesquera, eds., *Building with Our Hands: New Directions in Chicana Studies,* University of California Press, 1993. Copyright © 1993 The Regents of the University of California. Reprinted with permission.

joined from conversing in their native Spanish. Admonishments such as "Don't speak that ugly language, you are an American now," not only reflected a strong belief in Anglo conformity but denigrated the self-esteem of Mexican American children and dampened their enthusiasm for education. Ruby Estrada remembered that corporal punishment was a popular method for teaching English. "The teacher was mean and the kids got mean." At times children internalized these lessons, as Mary Luna reflected: "It was rough because I didn't know English. The teacher wouldn't let us talk Spanish. How can you talk to anybody? If you can't talk Spanish and you can't talk English, what are you going to do? . . . It wasn't until maybe the fourth or fifth grade that I started catching up. And all along that time I just felt I was stupid."

Students also became familiar with U.S. history and holidays (e.g., Thanksgiving). In recounting her childhood, Rosa Guerrero elaborated on how, in her own mind, she reconciled the history lessons at school with her own heritage. "The school system would teach everything about American history, the colonists and all of that," she explained. "Then I would do a comparison in my mind of where my grandparents came from, what they did, and wonder how I was to be evolved and educated."

Schools, in some instances, raised expectations. Imbued with the American dream, young women (and men) believed that hard work would bring material rewards and social acceptance. . . . Some teenage women aspired to college while others planned careers as secretaries. "I want to study science or be a stenographer," one Colorado adolescent informed Paul Taylor. "I thinned beets this spring, but I believe it is the last time. The girls who don't go to school will continue to top beets the rest of their lives."

Courses in typing and shorthand were popular among Mexican American women, even though few southwestern businesses hired Spanish-surnamed office workers. In 1930, only 2.6 percent of all Mexican women wage earners held clerical jobs. . . . Skin color . . . played a role in obtaining office work. As one typing teacher pointed out to young Julia Luna, " 'Who's going to hire you. You're so dark.' "

Many young Mexican women never attended high school but took industrial or service-sector jobs directly after the completion of the eighth grade. . . . Family obligations and economic necessity propelled Mexican women into the labor force. One government study appearing in . . . 1931 . . . revealed that in Los Angeles over 35 percent of the Mexican families surveyed had wage-earning children. By 1930, approximately one-quarter of Mexicana and Mexican American female wage earners in the Southwest obtained employment as industrial workers. In California, they labored principally in canneries and garment firms. Like many female factory workers in the United States, most Mexican operatives were young, unmarried daughters whose wage labor was essential to the economic survival of their families. As members of a "family wage economy," they relinquished all or part of their wages to their elders. . . .

At times working for wages gave women a feeling of independence. . . . Some young women went a step further and used their earnings to leave the family home. Facing family disapproval, even ostracism, they defied parental authority by sharing an apartment with female friends. Conversely, kin networks, particularly in canneries and packing houses, reinforced a sense of family. Working alongside female kin, adolescents found employment less than liberating. At the same time, the work environment did give women an opportunity to develop friendships with other Spanish-surnamed operatives and occasionally with their ethnic immigrant peers. They began to discuss with one another their problems and concerns, finding common ground both as factory workers and as second-generation ethnic women. Teenagers chatted about fads, fashions, and celebrities.

Along with outside employment, the media also influenced the acculturation of Mexican women. Movie and romance magazines enabled adolescents (and older women as well) to experience vicariously the middle-class and affluent life-styles heralded in these publications and thus could nurture a desire for consumer goods. Radios, motion pictures, and Madison Avenue advertising had a profound impact on America's cultural landscape. . . . The Mexican community was not immune to this orchestration of desire, and there appeared a propensity toward consumerism among second-generation women. . . . As members of a "consumer wage economy," daughters also worked in order to purchase items for their families' comfort, such as furniture, draperies, and area rugs. Other teenagers had more modest goals. After giving most of her wages to her mother, Rosa Guerrero reserved a portion to buy peanut butter and shampoo. "Shampoo to me was a luxury. I had to buy shampoo so I wouldn't have to wash my hair with the dirty old Oxydol. I used to wash my hair with the soap for the clothes."

. . . Movies, both Mexican and American, provided a popular form of entertainment for barrio residents. It was not uncommon on Saturday mornings to see children and young adults combing the streets for bottles, so that they could afford the price of admission—ten cents for the afternoon matinee. Preteens would frequently come home and act out what they had seen on the screen. "I was going to be Clara Bow," remembered Adele Hernández Milligan. Another woman recounted that she had definitely been "star struck" as a youngster and attempted to fulfill her fantasy in junior high by "acting in plays galore." The handful of Latina actresses appearing in Hollywood films, such as Dolores Del Rio and Lupe Velez, also whetted these aspirations. Older "star-struck" adolescents enjoyed afternoon outings to Hollywood, filled with the hope of being discovered as they strolled along Hollywood and Vine with their friends.

The influential Spanish-language newspaper *La Opinión* encouraged these fantasies, in part, by publishing gossipy stories about movie stars . . . as well as up-to-the-minute reports on the private lives and careers of Latino celebrities. It also carried reviews of Spanish-language films, concerts, and plays. . . . Furthermore, the Los Angeles–based newspaper directly capitalized on the dreams of youth by sponsoring a contest with Metro-Goldwyn-Mayer. "Day by day we see how a young man or woman, winner of some contest, becomes famous overnight," reminded *La Opinión* as it publicized its efforts to offer its readers a similar chance. Touted as "the unique opportunity for all young men and women who aspire to movie stardom," this promotion held out the promise of a screen test to one lucky contestant. . . .

Although enjoying the creature comforts afforded by life in the United States, Mexican immigrants retained their cultural traditions, and parents developed strategies to counteract the alarming acculturation of their young. Required to speak only English at school, Mexican youngsters were then instructed to speak only

Spanish at home. Even when they permitted the use of English, parents took steps to ensure the retention of Spanish among their children. . . . Proximity to Mexico also played an important role in maintaining cultural ties. Growing up in El Paso, Texas, Guerrero crossed the border into Ciudad Juárez every weekend with her family in order to attend traditional recreational events, such as the bull fights. Her family, moreover, made yearly treks to visit relatives in central Mexico. Those who lived substantial distances from the border resisted assimilation by building ethnic pride through nostalgic stories of life in Mexico. . . .

In bolstering cultural consciousness, parents found help through youth-oriented community organizations. Church, service, and political clubs reinforced ethnic awareness. Examples included the "Logia 'Juventud Latina' " of the Alianza Hispano Americana; the Mexican American Movement, initially sponsored by the YMCA; and the youth division of El Congreso de Pueblos Que Hablan Español. . . .

Interestingly, only two of the thirteen women mentioned Catholicism as an important early influence. The Catholic church played more of a social role; it organized youth clubs and dances, and it was the place for baptisms, marriages, and funerals. For others, Protestant churches offered a similar sense of community. Establishing small niches in Mexican barrios, Protestant missionaries envisioned themselves as the harbingers of salvation and Americanization. . . . Whether gathering for a Baptist picnic or a Catholic dance, teenagers seemed more attracted to the social rather than the spiritual side of their religion. . . . Blending new behavior with traditional ideals, young women also had to balance family expectations with their own need for individual expression.

Within families, young women, perhaps more than their brothers, were expected to uphold certain standards. . . . Parents . . . often assumed what they perceived as their unquestionable prerogative to regulate the actions and attitudes of their adolescent daughters. Teenagers . . . did not always acquiesce in the boundaries set down for them by their elders. Intergenerational tension flared along several fronts.

Generally, the first area of disagreement between a teenager and her family would be over her personal appearance. During the 1920s, a woman's decision "to bob or not bob" her hair assumed classic proportions in Mexican families. . . . Differing opinions over fashions often caused ill feelings. One Mexican American woman recalled that when she was a young girl, her mother dressed her "like a nun" and she could wear "no makeup, no cream, no nothing" on her face. Swimsuits, bloomers, and short skirts also became sources of controversy. . . .

Once again, bearing the banner of glamour and consumption, *La Opinión* featured sketches of the latest flapper fashions as well as cosmetic ads from both Latino and Anglo manufacturers. The most elaborate layouts were those of Max Factor. Using celebrity testimonials, one advertisement encouraged women to "FOLLOW THE STARS" and purchase "Max Factor's Society Make-up." Factor, through an exclusive arrangement with *La Opinión,* went even further in courting the Mexican market by answering beauty questions from readers in a special column—"Secretos de Belleza" (Beauty Secrets).

The use of cosmetics, however, cannot be blamed entirely on Madison Avenue ad campaigns. The innumerable barrio beauty pageants—sponsored by *mutualistas,* patriotic societies, churches, the Mexican Chamber of Commerce, newspapers, and even progressive labor unions—encouraged young women to accentuate their physical attributes. Carefully chaperoned, many teenagers did participate in community contests from La Reina de Cinco de Mayo to Orange Queen. They modeled evening gowns, rode on parade floats, and sold raffle tickets. . . .

The commercialization of personal grooming made additional inroads into the Mexican community with the appearance of barrio beauty parlors. Working as a beautician conferred a certain degree of status, "a nice, clean job," in comparison to factory or domestic work. As one woman related: "I always wanted to be a beauty operator. I loved makeup; I loved to dress up and fix up. I used to set my sisters' hair. . . . Neighborhood beauty shops reinforced women's networks and became places where they could relax, exchange *chisme* (gossip), and enjoy the company of other women. . . .

The most serious point of contention between an adolescent daughter and her parents, however, regarded her behavior toward young men. In both cities and rural towns, girls had to be closely chaperoned by a family member every time they attended a movie, a dance, or even church-related events. . . .

. . . Women in cities had a distinct advantage over their rural peers in that they could venture miles from their neighborhood into the anonymity of dance halls, amusement parks, and other forms of commercialized leisure. With carnival rides and the Cinderella Ballroom, the Nu-Pike amusement park of Long Beach proved a popular hangout for Mexican youth in Los Angeles. It was more difficult to abide by traditional norms when excitement loomed just on the other side of the streetcar line.

Some women openly rebelled. They moved out of their family homes and into apartments. Considering themselves free-wheeling single women, they could go out with men unsupervised, as was the practice among their Anglo peers. "This terrible freedom in the United States," one Mexicana lamented. "I do not have to worry because I have no daughters, but the poor *señoras* with many girls, they worry." Those Mexican American adolescents who did not wish to defy their parents openly would "sneak out" of the house in order to meet with their dates or to attend dances with female friends. A more subtle form of rebellion was early marriage. By marrying at fifteen or sixteen, these women sought to escape parental supervision; yet . . . many of these child brides exchanged one form of supervision for another, in addition to taking on the responsibilities of child rearing.

The third option sometimes involved quite a bit of creativity on the part of young women as they sought to circumvent traditional chaperonage. . . . The practice of "going out with the girls," though not accepted until the 1940s, was fairly common. Several Mexican American women, often related, would escort one another to an event (such as a dance), socialize with the men in attendance, and then walk home together. . . . Daughters negotiated their activities with their parents. Older siblings and extended kin appeared in the background as either chaperones or accomplices. Although unwed teenage mothers were not unknown in the Los Angeles barrios, families expected adolescent women to conform to strict standards of behavior. As can be expected, many teenage women knew little about sex other than what they picked up from friends, romance magazines, and the local theater. . . .

The image of loose sexual mores as distinctly American probably reinforced parents' fears as they watched their daughters apply cosmetics and adopt the apparel advertised in fashion magazines. In other words, "If she dresses like a flapper, will she then act like one?" Seeds of suspicion reaffirmed the penchant for traditional supervision. . . .

However, . . . the impact of Americanization was most keenly felt at the level of personal aspiration. "We felt if we worked hard, proved ourselves, we could become professional people," asserted Rose Escheverria Mulligan. Braced with such idealism, Mexican Americans faced prejudice, segregation, and economic segmentation. Though they considered themselves Americans, others perceived them as less than desirable foreigners. During the late 1920s, the *Saturday Evening Post,* exemplifying the nativist spirit of the times, featured inflammatory characterizations of Mexicans in the United States. For instance, one article portrayed Mexicano immigrants as an "illiterate, diseased, pauperized" people who bear children "with the reckless prodigality of rabbits." Racism was not limited to rhetoric; between 1931 and 1934, an estimated one-third of the Mexican population in the United States (over 500,000 people) were either deported or repatriated to Mexico, even though many were native U.S. citizens. Mexicans were the only immigrants targeted for removal. Proximity to the Mexican border, the physical distinctiveness of *mestizos,* and easily identifiable barrios influenced immigration and social welfare officials to focus their efforts solely on the Mexican people, people whom they viewed as foreign usurpers of American jobs and as unworthy burdens on relief rolls. From Los Angeles, California, to Gary, Indiana, Mexicans were either summarily deported by immigration agencies or persuaded to depart voluntarily by duplicitous social workers who greatly exaggerated the opportunities awaiting them south of the border. . . .

By 1935, the deportation and repatriation campaigns had diminished, but prejudice and segregation remained. . . . The proportion of Los Angeles–area municipalities with covenants prohibiting Mexicans and other minorities from purchasing residences in certain neighborhoods climbed from 20 percent in 1920 to 80 percent in 1946. Many restaurants, theaters, and public swimming pools discriminated against their Spanish-surnamed clientele. In southern California, for example, Mexicans could swim at the public plunges only one day out of the week just before they drained the pool). Small-town merchants frequently refused to admit Spanish-speaking people into their places of business. "White Trade Only" signs served as bitter reminders of their second-class citizenship. . . .

Considering these circumstances, it is no surprise that many teenagers developed a shining idealism as a type of psychological ballast. Some adolescents, such as the members of the Mexican American Movement, believed that education was the key to mobility, while others placed their faith in the application of Max Factor's bleaching cream. Whether they struggled to further their education or tried to lighten their skin color, Mexican Americans sought to protect themselves from the damaging effects of prejudice.

Despite economic and social stratification, many Mexicans believed that life in the United States offered hope and opportunity. . . . More common perhaps was the impact of material assimilation, the purchase of an automobile, a sewing machine, and other accouterments of U.S. consumer society. The accumulation of these goods signaled the realization of (or the potential for realizing) the American dream. . . .

In this essay, I have attempted to reconstruct the world of adolescent women, taking into account the broader cultural, political, and economic environment. I have given a sense of the contradictions in their lives: the lure of Hollywood and the threat of deportation. The discussion gives rise to an intriguing question. Can one equate the desire for material goods with the abandonment of Mexican values? I believe that the ideological impact of material acculturation has been overrated. For example, a young Mexican woman may have looked like a flapper as she boarded a streetcar on her way to work at a cannery; yet she went to work (at least in part) to help support her family, as part of her obligation as a daughter. The adoption of new cultural forms certainly frightened parents, but it did not of itself undermine Mexican identity. The experiences of Mexican American women coming of age between 1920 and 1950 reveal the blending of the old and the new, fashioning new expectations, making choices, and learning to live with those choices.

FURTHER READING

Louise Año Nuevo-Kerr, "Chicano Settlements in Chicago: A Brief History," *Journal of Ethnic Studies* 2 (Winter 1975), 22–32

Emory Stephen Bogardus, *The Mexican in the United States* (1934)

Lawrence A. Cardoso, *Mexican Emigration to the United States* (1980)

Ernesto Galarza, *Barrio Boy* (1972)

Manuel Gamio, *The Life Story of the Mexican Immigrant* (1971)

———, *Mexican Immigration to the United States* (1971)

Juan R. García, *Mexicans in the Midwest, 1900–1932* (1996)

Mario T. García, "Americanization and the Mexican Immigrant, 1880–1930," *Journal of Ethnic Studies* 6 (Summer 1978), 19–34

John R. Martínez, *Mexican Emigration to the United States, 1910–1930* (1972)

Douglas Monroy, "Like Swallows at the Old Mission: Mexicans and the Radical Politics of Growth in Los Angeles in the Interwar Period," *Western Historical Quarterly* 14 (October 1983), 435–458

———, " 'Our Children Get So Different Here': Film, Fashion, Popular Culture, and the Process of Cultural Syncretization in Mexican Los Angeles, 1900–1935," *Aztlán* 19 (Spring 1988–1990), 79–108

Mark Reisler, *By the Sweat of Their Brow* (1976)

Ricardo Romo, *East Los Angeles* (1983)

———, "Responses to Mexican Immigration, 1910–1930," *Aztlán* 6 (Summer 1975), 173–194

Francisco Arturo Rosales and Daniel T. Simon, "Mexican Immigrant Experience in the Urban Midwest: East Chicago, Indiana, 1919–1945," in James B. Lane and Edward J. Escobar, eds., *Forging a Community: The Latino Experience in Northwest Indiana, 1919–1975* (1987)

George J. Sánchez, " 'Go After the Women': Americanization and the Mexican Immigrant Woman, 1915–1929," in Vicki L. Ruiz and Ellen Carol DuBois, eds., *Unequal Sisters* (1994)

Paul S. Taylor, "Mexicans North of the Rio Grande," *The Survey* 66, 3 (May 1, 1931), 135–140

———, "Mexican Women in Los Angeles Industry in 1928," *Aztlán* 2, 1 (1980), 99–132

Zaragosa Vargas, *Proletarians of the North* (1993)

Douglas Weeks, "The L.U.L.A.C.," *Southwestern Political and Social Science Quarterly* 10 (1929), 257–278

C. C. Young, *Mexicans in California: Report of Governor C. C. Young's Mexican Fact-Finding Committee* (1930)

CHAPTER 9

Mexican Americans in the Great Depression, 1929–1941

The effects of the Great Depression soon overwhelmed Mexican Americans, who found themselves with few means to overcome the discrimination that threatened their personal security as well as the social order of their communities. Mexicans quickly became a scapegoat for the ills of the depression. City and county officials cut expanding relief costs by sending hundreds of thousands of Mexicans, including untold numbers who were U.S.-born, back to Mexico. The voluntary and forced repatriations and deportations that occurred throughout the 1930s eliminated over 10 percent of the 3 million Mexican Americans living in the Southwest and Midwest, and constantly reminded them that their basic rights in the United States were tenuous. Did the repercussions of the Great Depression mean that Mexican Americans faced a certain bleak future?

From this period of immense hardship and change emerged the first generation of Mexican Americans. In part because of their status as second-class citizens, this group increased its efforts to gain broader opportunities. Race and ethnicity were vital sources of Mexican American working-class formation and consciousness. Mexican Americans, for example, would contribute to the dramatic growth of unions in the 1930s. How did the union movement become a means by which Mexican Americans would attempt to break the yoke of political, economic, and racial subordination?

The Great Depression was a watershed for Mexican Americans. The optimism of the New Deal raised their hopes and expectations, and its legislation gave them much needed employment, a voice in improving workplace conditions, and the impetus for continuing their struggle for equality. The discrimination they faced, however, did not end. The Social Security Act (1935) systematically excluded Mexicans, as it did blacks, by exemptions for agriculture and domestic labor. The Farm Security Administration (FSA) field reports revealed that most housing in the Southwest still lacked refrigeration and indoor toilets. Diseases such as tuberculosis remained rampant, and infant mortality rates were high. The same FSA reports also disclosed that many Mexican Americans were dependent on New Deal relief work in greater numbers than any other racial or ethnic group. How successful was the push by Mexican Americans for larger participation in Roosevelt's New Deal programs as well as for racial equality in the years before World War II?

❥ *D O C U M E N T S*

Prior to the Great Depression, the American economy began showing signs of slowing down. In 1929, the U.S. Congress placed restrictions on immigration from Mexico because of growing job shortages. Document 1 is an excerpt from a 1931 report by the U.S. Commissioner General of Immigration that describes the reduction in Mexican immigration as a result of the Great Depression and the efforts, both formal and informal, to curb this immigration even further. Numerous voluntary repatriation programs to send Mexicans back to Mexico were implemented throughout the United States. In Document 2, the journalist Carey McWilliams, well known for his books and articles on Mexican Americans, explains why Los Angeles carried out such a program. He cites the ways public relief agencies and employers got rid of the Mexican immigrant, which they viewed as cost-saving measures. In the early 1930s, farmworkers in California launched more than three hundred strikes for higher wages and better working and living conditions. In most instances, these actions were led or organized by Mexicans. The events leading to mediation of the 1933 strike by thousands of Mexican cotton pickers in the San Joaquin Valley of California over the issues of low wages and bad working conditions are detailed in Document 3 by Frank C. McDonald, the State Labor Commissioner. During the Great Depression, New Deal job programs such as the Civilian Conservation Corps (CCC) and the Neighborhood Youth Administration (NYA) offered numerous employment opportunities for Mexican American men and women. The need for jobs was especially great in New Mexico, as is revealed in Document 4, a selection from an interview with a New Mexican woman whose relatives worked for the CCC. In Document 5, a woman from northern New Mexico, where the majority of the state's Spanish-speaking population lived, recalls working for these New Deal programs. As Document 6 demonstrates, such programs similarly brought opportunities to El Paso, Texas, a major center of the Mexican American population of the Southwest. Notwithstanding the relief and jobs available through the New Deal, the Great Depression continued, and so did labor activism by Mexican Americans in the Southwest and the Midwest during the 1930s. Unfortunately, local and state officials, working with the U.S. Bureau of Immigration, helped employers halt such organizing by deporting labor leaders like longtime New Mexico coal miner Jesús Pallares. His case is the subject of Document 7. During the Great Depression, women led many of the efforts by workers to gain labor and civil rights. In Document 8 Emma Tenayuca recalls her role in organizing the 1938 strike by Mexican pecan shellers in San Antonio, Texas, one of the largest U.S. labor actions by a racial minority that was also a struggle over civil rights.

1. U.S. Commissioner General of Immigration Reports on Mexican Immigration, 1931

During the year [1931] but 7,715 aliens were admitted at the various ports of entry on the southern border. . . . This will cover transactions in three immigration districts, San Antonio, El Paso, and Los Angeles. The number admitted as immigrants is a great decrease from the 12,122 so admitted in the preceding year. . . . Mexicans . . . comprise practically all these 7,715 aliens admitted over the southern land border. . . . During the same period 17,733 Mexican aliens were recorded as leav-

House Committee on Immigration and Naturalization, 71st Cong., 2d sess., *Annual Report of the Commissioner General of Immigration to the Secretary of Labor for the Fiscal Year Ended June 30, 1931*, pp. 24–25. Washington, D.C.

ing the United States, practically all going to Mexico. . . . The net decrease of this race to the alien population of the United States for the year just ended . . . was 11,769, as compared with an increase of 5,390 in the previous year. . . .

From numerous sources it has been reported that the departures of Mexicans to their own country in the past year . . . have reached large proportions. Communities in the Far West and Southwest have aided in this repatriation to relieve their charity burdens, but from many parts of the country Mexicans and their families have gone back because of continued lack of employment in this country, the attraction of home ties, and the belief that they can . . . obtain assistance from their relatives or others.

2. Carey McWilliams Assails Mexican Repatriation from California, 1933

In 1930 a fact-finding committee reported to the governor of California that . . . Mexicans were being used on a large scale in the Southwest to replace the . . . labor . . . formerly recruited in southeastern Europe. The report revealed a concentration of this new immigration in Texas, Arizona, and California, with an ever-increasing number of Mexicans giving California as the state of their "intended future permanent residence." . . .

For a long time Mexicans had regarded Southern California, more particularly Los Angeles, with favor. . . . From 1919 to 1929 . . . there was a scarcity of . . . labor in the region and Mexicans were made welcome. . . .

During this period, . . . teachers of sociology, social-service workers, and other . . . sympathizers were deeply concerned about [the Mexican immigrant's] welfare. Was he capable of assimilating? . . . What was the percentage of this and that disease, or this and that crime, in the Mexican population of Los Angeles? How many Mexican mothers fed their youngsters . . . American infant foods? In short, the do-gooders subjected the Mexican population to a relentless barrage of surveys, investigations, and clinical conferences.

But a marked change has occurred since 1930. When it became apparent last year that the program for the relief of the unemployed would assume huge proportions in the Mexican quarter, the community swung to a determination to oust the Mexican. . . . He had not been able to accumulate any savings. He was in default in his rent. He was a burden to the taxpayer. At this juncture, an ingenious social worker suggested . . . wholesale deportation. But . . . the federal authorities . . . could promise but slight assistance, since many of the younger Mexicans . . . were . . . the American-born children of immigrants. Moreover, . . . in cases of illegal entry, a public hearing and a formal order of deportation . . . could not be used . . . in ousting any large number.

A better scheme was soon devised. Social workers reported that many of the Mexicans . . . receiving charity had signified their "willingness" to return to Mexico. Negotiations were at once opened with the . . . officials of the Southern Pacific Railroad. . . . In wholesale lots, the Mexicans could be shipped to Mexico City for

Carey McWilliams, "Getting Rid of the Mexicans," *American Mercury* 28 (March 1933), found in Matt S. Meier and Feliciano Rivera, eds, *Readings on La Raza: The Twentieth Century* (New York: Hill and Wang, 1974).

$14.70 *per capita.* . . . And so, about February 1931, the first trainload was dispatched, and shipments at the rate of about one a month have continued. . . .

No one seems to know . . . how many Mexicans have been "repatriated" in this manner. . . . The Los Angeles *Times* . . . gave an estimate of eleven thousand for the year 1932. The monthly shipments . . . have ranged from thirteen hundred to six thousand. The *Times* reported . . . that . . . more than 200,000 *repatriados* had left the United States . . . , of which . . . fifty to seventy-five thousand were from California, and over thirty-five thousand from Los Angeles County. . . .

The repatriation program is regarded locally as a piece of consummate statescraft. The average per family cost . . . is $71.14, including food and transportation. It cost Los Angeles County $77,249.29 to repatriate one shipment of 6,024. It would have cost $424,933.70 to provide this number with such charitable assistance as they would have been entitled to had they remained—a saving of $347,684.41.

One wonders what has happened to all the Americanization programs of yesteryear. The Chamber of Commerce has been forced to issue a statement assuring the Mexican authorities that . . . repatriation is . . . designed solely for the relief of the destitute—even . . . where invalids are removed from the County Hospital in Los Angeles. . . .

What of the Mexican himself? . . . He never objected to exploitation while he was welcome, and now he acquiesces in repatriation. . . . He has cooperated . . . with the authorities. Thousands have departed of their own volition. In battered Fords, carrying two and three families and all their worldly possessions, they are drifting back. . . .

. . . The Mexican can be lured back, "whenever we need him." But I am not so sure of this. He may be placed on a quota basis . . . , or possibly he will no longer look north to Los Angeles as the goal of his dreams. At present he is probably delighted to abandon an empty paradise. But it is difficult for his children. A friend of mine . . . found a young Mexican girl on one of the southbound trains crying because she had had to leave Belmont High School. Such an abrupt severance of the Americanization program . . . the professors of sociology did not anticipate.

3. Frank C. McDonald Recounts Events Leading to Mediation of the California Cotton Pickers Strike, 1933

November 3, 1933

Honorable James Rolf, Jr.
Governor of California, State Capitol
Sacramento, California

My Dear Governor: On . . . Sunday, September 17, 1933, representatives of the cotton pickers in the San Joaquin Valley announced that the cotton pickers had decided that they would pick cotton for $1 per hundred pounds.

Paul S. Taylor and Clark Kerr, "Documentary History of the Strike of Cotton Pickers in California, 1933," U.S. Congress, Senate, Subcommittee of the Committee of Education and Labor, *Hearings on S. Res. 266, Violations of Free Speech and the Rights of Labor,* part 64, exhibits 8764, 19945–20036. As found in Matt S. Meier and Feliciano Rivera, eds., *Readings on La Raza: The Twentieth Century* (New York: Hill and Wang, 1974), pp. 99–105.

On September 19, 1933, a meeting of . . . the San Joaquin Valley Agricultural Labor Bureau was held in Fresno. At that meeting it was decided that cotton growers would pay 60 cents per hundred pounds for the picking of cotton. . . .

On Wednesday, October 4, 1933, an extensive strike in which some ten thousand cotton pickers were involved was declared. This strike affected the California cotton-growing area of Kern, Kings, Tulare, Fresno, Madera, and Merced Counties. The effect of the strike was most pronounced in Kings, Tulare, and Kern Counties. . . .

On Saturday, October 7, 1933, a brief physical encounter took place between the cotton growers and the strikers in Woodville, Tulare County. . . .

On the evening of October 10, 1933, press dispatches stated that two strikers had been killed and eight wounded in front of the cotton pickers' strike headquarters in Pixley, Tulare County. Subsequently, eight cotton growers were indicted by the Tulare County Grand Jury for the murder of the two striking cotton pickers. Press dispatches of the same date also stated that one striker had been killed and a number of strikers and cotton growers had been injured during a fight at the E. O. Mitchell Ranch in Kern County. As a result of this fight, seven strikers were arrested on a charge of rioting. . . .

Owing to the tense, dangerous situation . . . in the strike area, the deputy labor commissioners in the district and I, assisted by Mexican consuls E. Bravo and L. D. Acosta, redoubled our efforts to bring about the termination of the strike. We were informed by a large number of strikers and also by a number of cotton growers of their willingness to settle the strike by mediation or arbitration. I thereupon phoned . . . Mr. Edward Fitzgerald, Conciliator of the United States Department of Labor, . . . urging him to come immediately to Visalia to assist in bringing about a settlement of the strike. Commissioner Fitzgerald arrived in Visalia on Friday, October 13, 1933, and . . . we . . . met with a committee representing the cotton growers, the cotton-gin owners, . . . financial interests, and others . . . in Visalia. During the meeting Mexican consul Bravo stated that the Mexican strikers had informed him that they had four hundred guns and were prepared to die defending their rights. . . .

A fact-finding commission held public hearings in the Municipal Auditorium in Tulare on October 19, 1933, and October 20, 1933. . . . All interested parties, striking cotton pickers and cotton growers were accorded full opportunity to present all their evidence to the commission.

During the strike, the strikers had continuously used what is known as "mass-picketing tactics." On October 23, 1933, a large number of striking pickets, principally Mexican men and women, proceeded along the highway until they came to the Guiberson Ranch near Corcoran, where they found strikebreakers at work, picking cotton. The strikers invaded the ranch, and in the fight which ensued between the strikers and strikebreakers, a number of persons were struck with clubs and fists. It is also reported that the sacks containing cotton were slashed and ripped open.

On that same day, October 23, 1933, your Fact Finding Commission announced the following decision:

> . . . It is judgment of Commission that upon evidence presented growers can pay for picking at rate of seventy-five cents per hundred pounds and your Commission begs leave . . . to advise this rate of payment be established. Without question civil rights of

strikers have been violated. We appeal to constituted authorities to see that strikers are protected in rights conferred upon them by laws of State and by Federal and State Constitutions. . . .

Thereafter, on October 25, 1933, representatives of the cotton growers of Kern, Kings, Tulare, Fresno, Madera, and Merced Counties assembled in Fresno and . . . served public notice of their willingness to pay 75 cents per hundred pounds for the picking of cotton. . . .

Late that evening, October 25, 1933, I received information . . . that the strikers would not declare off the strike and that they would not pick cotton for 75 cents per hundred pounds. The next morning, . . . we proceeded to the strike headquarters in Tulare and to the Central Strike Encampment at Corcoran. We informed strike leaders and strikers that they were not acting in good faith. . . .

At about eleven o'clock a.m., October 26, 1933, W. V. Buckner, Sheriff of Tulare County, addressed the strikers at their camp in Corcoran and served notice that the strikers must evacuate the camp by three o'clock p.m. that day. Prior to addressing the strikers, a cordon of some thirty California state traffic officers, accompanied by a corps of deputy sheriffs, formed a line in front of the sheriff, armed with revolvers and . . . with gas bombs. . . .

The notification served by Sheriff W. V. Buckner . . . was met with angry hoots and jeers and cries of "We won't leave" by the assembled mass of strikers. A most critical and dangerous situation threatened.

The least overt act by any person would undoubtedly have precipitated a bloody battle. . . . Strike leaders . . . protested that the sheriff's ultimatum was illegal, that the strikers were legally occupying the campsite, that the state health authorities had not condemned the camp, and that therefore they had a lawful right to resist any attempt of the sheriff to evict them. They insisted that the sheriff had no lawful right to serve an evacuation notice until the matter had been passed upon by the courts and that any attempt upon his part to enforce his ultimatum by force would be resisted. . . .

During the afternoon the strikers massed their men at the entrance to their camp and informed the deputy labor commissioners that they would resist any attempt to force them and their women and children, which it was estimated at that time to be some twenty-five hundred persons, to leave the camp.

A large number of cotton growers and their sympathizers also assembled at the camp, and angry threats were made . . . that they would force the strikers to leave the camp. Unquestionably, had such an effort been made at that time, an entirely unnecessary and unjustifiable bloody battle would have been precipitated. The lives of many would have been taken, and numerous men, women, and children would have been injured, for . . . not only were the authorities armed but the Mexican strikers . . . had four hundred guns. The situation was gravely tense and dangerous. At a quarter to three o'clock, I caused an automobile truck to be driven . . . immediately in front of the striking cotton pickers, who were massed at the entrance to their camp. Standing on the platform of the truck, I then addressed the strikers and advised them of the request that had been made by the Central Strike Committee for an extension of time of evacuation of the camp and . . . that they would that day vote upon the question of accepting the 75 cents per hundred pounds for picking cotton. I urged the strikers . . . to accept the 75-cents decision of the Fact

Finding Commission and to declare the strike off. Mexican consular representative L. D. Acosta . . . translated my remarks into Spanish to the assembled strikers, the great majority of whom were Mexicans. Thereafter, at 3:30 p.m. on that day, October 26, 1933, the Central Strike Committee accepted the 75 cents per hundred pounds rate for cotton picking, subject to conditions that were not . . . agreed to at the time of their appearing before your Fact Finding Commission.

4. Elsie Chavez Chilton Recalls Relatives Working with the Civilian Conservation Corps Near Las Cruces, New Mexico, 1930s

At that time there was a lot of bartering. That was pre-depression and I was such a small child I don't remember too much about it, but I know they got along just fine. When the depression hit we were already living in town. We had no money to lose because we had no money in the bank. We did have hard times—especially the families whose fathers didn't have a steady income. I had uncles who had steady incomes. They were ditch riders. One was at Leasburg Dam and one at Mesilla Dam. . . . No matter how small it was, if it was a steady income it meant a lot. Since my father was self-employed that was worse. We managed somehow. Also there was the NYA [National Youth Administration] and the WPA [Works Progress Administration]. . . .

We had a lot of boys . . . working in the CCC camps around here. . . . We had a lot of work done by the CCC camp boys—Jornada Range was one area. . . . I would go over there and have dinner where the officials had dinner. My friend showed me all the fence that they had built. I don't know what they were fencing in but they built miles and miles of fence. I remember my brother went to Vista Viento in California. He got himself into a CCC camp and we were delighted. My folks got $25 a month that summer as a result of his working in the camp. . . . For a short time, my father worked as a "pusher" at a camp in Radium Springs. Can you image that! That's what the boys used to call him. In the camps they called the supervisors that because they used to push the boys to do the work. That was soon over and he had to resort to his other jobs.

5. Susana Archuleta Looks Back at Jobs with the Civilian Conservation Corps and the National Youth Administration in Northern New Mexico, 1930s

During the Depression, things got bad. My dad passed away when I was about twelve, leaving my mother with eight children and no means of support. . . . My mother took in washings to make a living, and our job was to pick up the washings on the way home from school. We'd pick up clothes from the schoolteachers, the

Document 4: As found in Rita Kasch Chegin, "As It Was in Chiva Town: Elsie Chavez Chilton," in Rita Kasch Chegin, *Survivors: Women of the Southwest* (Las Cruces, NM: Yucca Tree Press, 1991), pp. 30, 32.

Document 5: As found in Nan Elsasser, "Susana Archuleta," in Nan Elsasser, et al., *Las Mujeres: Conversations from a Hispanic Community* (New York: The Feminist Press, 1980), pp. 36–37.

attorney, and what-have-you. Then, at night, we'd help iron them and fold them. . . .

When I was a teenager, the Depression began to take a turn. Franklin Roosevelt was elected, and the works projects started. The boys and young men who'd been laid off at the mines went to the CCC camps, and the girls joined the NYA. . . .

They paid us about twenty-one dollars a month. Out of that we got five and the other sixteen was directly issued to our parents. The same was true of the boys working in the camps. They got about thirty dollars a month. They were allowed to keep five of it. The rest was sent to their families. All of us were hired according to our family income. If a man with a lot of children was unemployed, he was given preference over someone who had less children. . . . Those programs were great. Everybody got a chance to work.

6. Bert Corona Remembers the Civil Works Administration Camps in El Paso, Texas, 1934

I remember the 1929 crash. . . . I didn't understand what radio and newspaper accounts of the crisis meant for the daily life of people. But I recall that as 1930 came on, the layoffs began in El Paso. . . .

People's wages were cut. . . . Jobs became harder and harder to find; there were many unemployed. By the end of 1930 and the beginning of 1931, we saw all the manifestations of a severe economic crisis in El Paso. . . .

The election of FDR, however, changed the political climate. . . .

The New Deal opened up programs such as the CWA [Civil Works Administration] in El Paso. These work programs provided single men with dormitories and camps where they were housed and fed. The men kept the places clean. They worked if there was work. In the camps, they had recreational activities. They also had discussion groups.

Two or three of those camps were opened in El Paso not very far from where I lived, on Angie and Missouri streets above the second layer of railroad tracks. We lived adjacent to the tracks in a row of houses. This was between 1931 and 1935, the pit of the depression. Besides being close to one of the CWA camps, we were in close proximity to an NYA center that had been set up out of a large converted warehouse on Missouri Street.

7. Philip Stevenson Describes the Deportation of Jesús Pallares, 1936

On June 29, [1936,] Jesús was deported as an undesirable alien. Jesús Pallares is a skilled miner. . . . He has spent twenty-three of his thirty-nine years in the United

Document 6: As found in Bert Corona, "Border Depression," in Mario T. García, *Memories of Chicano History: The Life and Narrative of Bert Corona* (Berkeley and Los Angeles: University of California Press, 1994), pp. 56–58.

Document 7: "Deporting Jesus" by Philip Stevenson is reprinted with permission from the July 18, 1936, issue of *The Nation,* © 1936.

States. . . . Born in the state of Chihuahua, Mexico, Jesús joined the Madero revolution at the age of fifteen, fought four years, and mustered out in 1915 with part of his lower jaw missing. He entered the United States legally and obtained work as a miner. As miners' standards went, Jesús did well. He was an exceptional worker. There never was a time when he could not get a job. On the whole he got along with his bosses. . . .

The onset of the depression, 1930, found him working for the Gallup-American Coal Company, a subsidiary of the Guggenheim giant, Kennecott Copper. In 1930 Gallup was unorganized. So when Jesús found himself being paid . . . irregularly . . . , he kicked—as an individual—and like individual protestors in all depressed coal fields, was promptly fired.

Jobs were scarce now. . . . But after several months of unemployment he obtained work at Madrid, New Mexico. . . . The town is company-owned.

Jesús was elected local union organizer. . . . Jesús and his aides decided to ask the aid of the federal government in enforcing Section 7-a.* When the company prohibited all union meetings in Madrid, the unionists walked four miles to Cerrillos for meetings, passed resolutions, drew up petitions, framed protests, and sent them to the coal board, . . . to the state Labor Commissioner. From the coal board came a promise of a hearing—if the miners would withhold their strike and wait. And wait they did. . . . Not until . . . February, 1934 . . . did T. S. Hogan, chairman of the Denver District Coal Board, arrive in Madrid for an "impartial" hearing.

. . . Grievances went unredressed. Union meetings continued to be prohibited. A new coal code went into effect, only to be violated even more flagrantly by the company. . . . They struck. . . . The strike failed. Jesús was marked for riddance.

Under the NRA [National Recovery Administration] he could not be fired for union activity.† He finished work . . . in the mine and was assigned a new location. . . . He could make at best sixty-seven cents a day here—and the mine was then working only one day a week—while his rent alone amounted to $3 per week. Yet the boss refused him any better location. Then a fellow worker offered to share his place with Jesús. . . . Jesús asked the superintendent's permission to accept this offer.

"No. Take the place assigned you, or none." . . .

. . . Jesús refused. His fifth child was expected shortly. His savings went for food. Arrears on his rent to the company piled up. He was told to vacate his house or be evicted. He stayed put. The child arrived. . . .

. . . Jesús was charged with "forcible entry" of his house. The "court" was the company office, the justice of the peace a company employee. . . . Evicted, blacklisted as a miner, Jesús moved to Santa Fe and for the first time in his life went on relief. The family of seven lived in one room, on two cents per meal per person. . . .

. . . In the fall of 1934 Jesús began organizing for the Liga Obrera de Habla Española (Spanish-speaking Workers League) which concerned itself . . . with the problems of the Spanish-American rank and file. In November there had been a

*Section 7-A of the 1933 National Industrial Recovery Act (NIRA) guaranteed workers the right to organize and bargain collectively through representatives of their own choosing without interference by employers. *Ed.*

†The NRA was one of the two major recovery programs of the Roosevelt administration. Through the NRA, major public works projects were established to increase employment. *Ed.*

few hundred members. By February, 1935, the Liga had grown to some 8,000. . . . Jesús was elected organizer for the whole district, serving without pay and hitch-hiking to organize the most remote hamlets on his days off from FERA work.*

. . . Jesús . . . won the enmity . . . of the organized rulers of New Mexico. On April 23, 1935, he was arrested while at work on his FERA job and jailed on deportation charges. After three weeks' confinement, a secret hearing was held in an attempt to prove Jesús active in "communistic" organizations. . . .

. . . Jesús was held for deportation under $1,000 bond pending a review of the case. The bond was promptly furnished. . . .

He continued his task of organizing the Liga Obrera. . . .

As a leader in the Liga Obrera, Jesús often accompanied delegations to the local relief office presenting cases of discrimination. . . . Recently, a worker in that office has disclosed . . . the methods employed against Jesús "in an effort to create reasons for his deportation". . . :

> Attempts were made by my office to intimidate Pallares by withholding relief and by inventing reasons by which he could be removed from relief jobs which were the only types of employment open to him. He was repeatedly called into my office where threats were made to starve his family in order to involve him in an argument which the relief agency hoped would give rise to violence on his part, which in turn would give sufficient reason for a complaint to the Labor Department. Such violence never took place. . . . Nevertheless a complaint was made to Washington . . . that Pallares was a "troublemaker.". . .

At the hearing on his case before the Labor Department's Board of Review last spring Jesús was represented by an attorney for the American Committee for the Protection of Foreign Born. Among the papers on file . . . two remarkable documents came to light, the existence of which had hitherto been kept secret.

The first was a letter to Secretary of Labor Perkins from Governor Clyde Tingley of New Mexico, urging that Jesús's deportation be "expedited" on the . . . grounds that the Liga Obrera was "the New Mexico branch of the Communist organization.". . .

The second document was a telegram to the Immigration Bureau in Washington . . . :

> Having trouble with Jesús Pallares on strike in this county. I understand he is under bond on account of the strike at Gallup, New Mexico. . . . He is an alien from Old Mexico. We must act at once to save trouble and maybe lives in this county.
> Francisco P. Delgado, Sheriff [of San Miguel County].

In four sentences the telegram managed to utter five deliberate falsehoods. . . . 1. The sheriff's trouble was not with Jesús but with the strikers at the American Metals Company's mine at Terrero, New Mexico. . . . 2. Jesús was not on strike—did not even live in the sheriff's county. 3. Jesús was under bond for deportation, not for strike activity in Gallup or elsewhere. 4. At the time of the death of Gallup's sheriff, Jesús was living 230 miles away in Santa Fe. . . . 5. The deportation of

---

*The Federal Emergency Relief Administration (FERA), set up in 1933, provided funds for the unemployed in the form of jobs. *Ed.*

Jesús could not possibly save "trouble and maybe lives" so long as the sheriff insisted on breaking the strike by armed force and violence.

Curiously enough, two truths did creep into the sheriff's wire: first, that Jesús was indubitably "an alien from Old Mexico"; second that . . . New Mexico officials and the Bureau of Immigration . . . were acting in concert to railroad Jesús out of the country. And they have had their way. Jesús is deported.

8. Emma Tenayuca Reminisces About Labor Organizing in San Antonio, Texas, 1936–1938

Background and Influences

I was born in 1916 at the end of the year. If I look back on my life, I can't say there was one or two or three factors or influences. It was the entire situation here.

The attitudes of my grandparents, who raised me, and my mother, too, and my father were based on honesty. . . .

Then there was the plaza . . . on Milam Square. You could go there on Sundays. You could go there during the week. . . . I started going to the plaza and political rallies when I was . . . 6 or 7 years old. . . . You had the influence of Flores Magon brothers [anarcho-syndicalists active in the overthrow of Porfirio Diaz]. Then from our country we had the Wobblies [International Workers of the World]. And you had *enganchadores,* contractors who came in and took people out to the Valley. I was exposed to all that. . . .

After World War I we saw the beginning of the development of agriculture in the Southwest. Not only in Texas but in Arizona, Colorado. . . . You needed labor here. As long as there is a need for labor, Mexico will be the place where labor is most accessible. . . . These people were not coming to a foreign country. . . . They were coming to cities . . . very much like the cities they had left: Laredo, El Paso, Los Angeles. So you have the continuation and the development of a large section of Spanish speaking people here.

Also, remember the situation worldwide. Hitler came to power in 1933. . . . We stood by for quite a while before we did anything to join the fight against Hitler. . . . You had a world situation that was certainly bound to have some effect on anybody who was in school and was doing some type of thinking, was engaging in some kind of discussion. . . .

You Had to Act

In high school, I belonged to a group of students who selected and read books and gathered for discussion. . . . We started a newspaper. . . . All of us were affected by the Depression. We became aware that there were some aspects of the free enterprise system which were highly vulnerable. . . .

I saw my first strike activity during the Finck Cigar strike. It was not the first [such] strike. It was the second. It was 1934. I went down to the picket line. We had

Excerpted from an interview conducted by Geoffrey Rips, "Living History: Emma Tenayuca Tells Her Story," *Texas Observer* 75, no. 21 (October 28, 1983): 7–15. Reprinted by permission.

a sheriff here named Albert West. . . . He had a picture taken of himself with a brand new pair of boots. He said that was what was going to greet the strikers. They were mostly all women. That was the first time I went down and saw a police action. . . . I landed in jail and learned how difficult it would be to make this a union town. . . . I felt that the labor movement was the way: you organize the laborers and they'd change the situation.

The attitude of the establishment led me to activism. . . . Another thing was that the immigration authorities had always been used against strikers. A prominent San Antonio political leader made a statement that all he had to do was notify the immigration authorities and they would go to the picket line and that would break up the strike. . . .

I had a basic underlying faith in the American idea of freedom and fairness. I felt there was something that had to be done . . . , and I went out on the picket line. That was the first time I was arrested.

. . . I was 17 or 18, in my last year of high school. . . . I never thought that I would get that involved. . . .

After the Finck Cigar strike, I drifted into the Workers Alliance. I was very curious. I read everything that was given to me. . . . There were some cigar workers who lost their jobs, and I was going down to the unemployment offices with them. This was part of it. . . . Then, when I went to organizing meetings, I would always find members of the Workers Alliance. . . . We started a movement here. . . . There was never any factionalism in the Workers Alliance because the main issue was jobs. The ranks of the unemployed soared, and then so did the ranks of the Workers Alliance. . . .

There were meetings every Sunday in various places. There was pressure on the Administration for jobs. We didn't ask for relief; we asked for jobs. . . . There were a number of demonstrations. We had this demonstration for the Workers Alliance. . . . We went down to protest the layoff of WPA [Work Projects Administration] workers.* . . . The police came in and broke it up. There were five of us arrested. We were charged, and I was the first one who was tried. . . .

In dealing with the population at that time, you had to answer more than just the economic questions. Schooling: I had visions of a huge hall on the West Side, possibly maintained by several unions—pecan, laundry, ironworkers—which would become a center where you would help people become citizens, where you would have classes in English. The union had to serve as a social service organization because of the conditions of the people. You had to act. You had, perhaps, to take a very sick person to the hospital. The union had to do that. It had to. . . .

Among the very first issues at the Workers Alliance here was the right of workers to organize without fear of deportation. But the pressure of economic conditions moved faster in the direction of poverty. . . . The Workers Alliance gathered a tremendous momentum when the workers returned from the fields, not having worked, without money and without food.

The year 1938 proved to be a very disastrous year for the migratory workers. . . . I felt there was something that had to be done.

---

*The WPA (1935) was the largest of the New Deal relief agencies organized to provide jobs and income for the unemployed. *Ed.*

Pecan Shellers

The pecan shellers strike was the culmination of organizing. What I did was help
organize the Workers Alliance. . . . I was aware all along that any organization, especially of the Mexican laborers in San Antonio, would be a very difficult endeavor. To succeed you never rest. Pecan shelling was an industry where you had
subcontractors and you had hundreds of little shops. . . .

What happened here was a lot of the pecan shellers were members of the Workers Alliance. The Workers Alliance at its peak had more than 10,000 members. . . .
The Workers Alliance continued, carrying grievances, meeting on Sundays. For
anybody who'd been laid off, we'd go back to the WPA and back to the Relief Office here. At the same time we kept campaigns going for greater assistance.

I remember some members of the Workers Alliance coming by, saying, "We're
not going into the shops." So I went out with them. The workers just started marching
out. . . . The first thing was to prepare for a meeting and to keep the workers out [on
strike]. The person who was in charge was Donald Henderson, . . . the founder of the
United Cannery Workers [United Cannery and Agricultural Processors and Agricultural Workers of America—UCAPAWA]. It was one of the CIO left-wing unions. . . .

So the strike was on. But this had been preceded by many demonstrations, by a
continuous appeal, mass meetings, all kinds of activities in which people participated on all labor questions. . . .

There was tremendous pressure upon the CIO to remove me as the strike leader
because I was a Communist. Donald Henderson met with Homer Brooks [Emma
Tenayuca's husband at the time and former Communist Party candidate for Texas
governor]. . . . When he came in and already had the statement typed out to remove
me from the strike leadership, I did not buckle. . . . But, on the other hand, . . . I
knew that we had not developed the leadership to take care of the negotiations. . . .
So [veteran labor organizer and fellow Texan] George Landrum . . . took over. . . .
I continued to write all the circulars, met with all the picket captains. . . .

The pecan workers strike was the culmination of activity for jobs, for a much
broader program. As to whether it was an authorized strike [the CIO said it was
partially authorized]. . . .

I think there was a lot of support for the pecan workers. . . .

Remember this—so many people were scared. How many people would have
stepped out and helped? There were some ministers. There were a few others who
stuck their heads all the way out. . . . But others here, although their sympathies
were there, they would not stick their heads out. And perhaps I do deserve some
credit for sticking my head out. I have been asked if I had been afraid. I said, "No.
If I had been afraid I wouldn't have done it. I wouldn't have gone out." . . .

Ideas

. . . The Communist Party was semi-legal. . . . I think I joined the Party about
1937. . . . Your Communists were at the forefront of the struggles. . . . The idea of
sharing, of helping—this was brought into the Communist movement. You could
see it in the labor struggle—the sacrifices that were made, the number who went to
jail. . . .

These things everybody was feeling. But how many people got out there and did something about it? I think personally . . . I have contributed something. . . . I was arrested a number of times. I don't think that I felt exactly fearful. I never thought in terms of fear. I thought in terms of justice.

❧ E S S A Y S

The Mexican Americans of northern New Mexico were especially hard hit by the Great Depression. Regional migration in the traditional search for seasonal employment was no longer an option as economic conditions worsened. Spanish-speaking New Mexicans were forced to seek assistance from such federal agencies as the Civilian Conservation Corps, which provided much needed employment. In the labor actions that arose out of such conditions, Mexican American women joined the men and achieved prominence by addressing union rallies, joining picket lines, and going to jail. In the first essay, Devra Anne Weber, associate professor of history at the University of California, Riverside, explains that Mexican women were at the center of the 1933 San Joaquin Valley strike, which was one of the largest of its kind in American history. It grew out of the same aggravated conditions that had produced other farm labor troubles in California. Of the 18,000 farm workers harvesting cotton in the San Joaquin Valley, three-fourths were Mexican and Mexican American migrant families. Grower lawlessness and evictions occurred throughout the strike area. By focusing on the nature of gender consciousness and its relation to class, national, and ethnic identity as revealed through oral histories, Weber concludes that the 1933 San Joaquin strike led to transformations in consciousness and culture that were not limited to the Mexican women who participated.

Franklin D. Roosevelt's New Deal raised the expectations of a Spanish-speaking minority who no longer felt as powerless as they had during the earlier repatriation period. In her essay, María E. Montoya, assistant professor of history at the University of Michigan, Ann Arbor, examines the experiences of Spanish-speaking New Mexicans of Río Arriba County in the Civilian Conservation Corps. She demonstrates that the CCC aided these communities by providing job opportunities that momentarily delayed the need for Spanish-speaking residents to leave the area to seek work at the end of the Great Depression. Discrimination against Mexican Americans in the New Mexico CCC camps, however, was a problem, as it was elsewhere in the Southwest and Midwest. Nevertheless, Montoya concludes that the training received in the CCC provided New Mexicans with valuable experience that they used to obtain employment and to adapt to the regime of military life during World War II.

Oral History and Mexicana Farmworkers

DEVRA ANNE WEBER

Mexicana field workers, as agricultural laborers, have been remarkable for their absence in written agricultural history. Most studies have focused on the growth of capitalist agriculture and the related decline of the family farm. Concern about the

"Raiz Fuerte: Oral History and Mexicana Farmworkers," *Oral History Review* 17, no. 2 (Fall 1989). Copyright © 1989 by Oral History Association. Reprinted by permission.

implications of these changes for American culture, political economy, and the agrarian dream has generally shaped the questions asked about capitalist agriculture. If freeholding family farmers were the basis of a democratic society, capitalist and/or slave agriculture were its antitheses. Studies of capitalist agriculture have thus become enclosed within broader questions about American democracy, measuring change against a mythologized past of conflict-free small farming on a classless frontier.

When considered at all, agricultural wageworkers have usually been examined in terms of questions framed by these assumptions. Rather than being seen in their own right, they have usually been depicted as the degraded result of the family farm's demise. The most thoughtful studies have been exposés, written to sway public opinion, which revealed the complex arrangement of social, economic, and political power perpetuating the brutal conditions of farmworkers. As was the case with the history of unskilled workers in industry, the written history of farmworkers became molded by the pressing conditions of their lives. The wretchedness of conditions became confused with the social worlds of the workers. Pictured as victims of a brutal system, they emerged as faceless, powerless, passive, and, ultimately, outside the flow of history. Lurking racial, cultural, ethnic, and gender stereotypes reinforced this image. This was especially true for Mexican women.

These considerations make oral sources especially crucial for exploring the history of Mexican women. Oral histories enable us to challenge the common confusion between the dismal conditions of the agricultural labor system and the internal life of workers. They enable us to understand . . . the relationship for Mexicans between the economic system of agriculture and community, politics, familial and cultural life. Oral histories help answer . . . fundamental questions about class, gender, life and work, cultural change, values and perceptions neglected in traditional sources. They also provide an insight into consciousness.

In conducting a series of oral histories with men and women involved in a critical farmworker strike in the 1930s, I began to think about the nature of gender consciousness. How does it intersect with a sense of class? How does it intersect with national and ethnic identity? In the oral histories of Mexican women, their sense of themselves as workers and Mexicans frequently coincided with that of the men, and drew upon similar bonds of history, community, and commonality. Yet the women's perceptions of what it meant to be a Mexican or a worker were shaped by gender roles and consciousness that frequently differed from that of the men. . . .

This essay will explore how oral histories can help us understand the consciousness of a group of Mexican women cotton workers . . . who participated in the 1933 cotton strike in California's San Joaquin Valley. One was a woman I will call Mrs. Valdez.

Mrs. Valdez and the 1933 Cotton Strike

Mrs. Valdez came from Mexico, where her father had been a *sembrador,* a small farmer or sharecropper, eking out a livable but bleak existence. She had barely reached adolescence when the Mexican revolution broke out in 1910. . . . Her memories of the revolution were not of the opposing ideologies nor issues, but of hunger, fear, and death. Fleeing the revolution, the family crossed the border into the United States. By 1933, she was twenty-four, married with two children, and lived in a small San Joaquin Valley town.

The agricultural industry in which she worked was, by 1933, California's major industry. Cotton, the most rapidly expanding crop, depended on Mexican workers who migrated annually to the valley to work. Large cotton ranches of over three hundred acres dominated the industry. Here workers lived in private labor camps, the largest of which were rural versions of industrial company towns: workers lived in company housing, bought from (and remained in debt to) company stores, and sent their children to company schools. Work and daily lives were supervised by a racially structured hierarchy dominated by Anglo managers and foremen: below them were Mexican contractors who recruited the workers, supervised work, and acted as the intermediary between workers and their English-speaking employers.

With the depression, growers slashed wages. In response, farmworkers went on strike in crop after crop in California. The wave of strikes began in southern California and spread north into the San Joaquin Valley. While conducted under the banner of the Cannary and Agricultural Workers Industrial Union (CAWIU), the strikes were sustained largely by Mexican workers and Mexican organizers. The spread and success of the strikes depended on the familial and social networks of Mexican workers as much as, if not more than, the small but effective and ambitious union. The strike wave crested in the cotton fields of the San Joaquin Valley when eighteen thousand strikers brought picking to a standstill. Growers evicted strikers, who established ad hoc camps on empty land. The largest was near the town of Corcoran, where 3,500 workers congregated. The strikers formed mobile picket lines, to which growers retaliated by organizing armed vigilantes. The strikers held out for over a month before a negotiated settlement was reached with the growers and the California, United States, and Mexican governments.

Mexicanas were a vital part of the strike, and about half of the strikers at Corcoran were women. They ran the camp kitchen, cared for children, and marched on picket lines. They distributed food and clothing. Some attended strike meetings, and a few spoke at the meetings. And it was the women who confronted Mexican strikebreakers. In short, women were essential to this strike, though they have been largely obscured in accounts of its history. Mrs. Valdez went on strike and was on the picket lines. She was not a leader, but one of the many women who made the strike possible.

Voice and Community

Before examining her testimony, a word is in order about voice and tone as a dimension of oral histories. How information is conveyed is as important as what is said and can emphasize or contradict the verbal message. Conversation and social interaction are a major part of women's lives, and gesture and voice are thus particularly crucial to their communications. The verbal message, the "song" of a story, is especially important for people with a strong oral tradition which . . . has meaning as art form, drama, and literature. Oral histories or stories are often dramatic, moving with a grace and continuity that embody analytical reflections and communicate an understanding of social relations and the complexities of human existence.

Mrs. Valdez structured the telling of her oral history in stories or vignettes. Most sections of her oral history had distinct beginnings and endings. . . . She developed characters, villains and heroes, hardship and tragedy (but little comedy). How this story was constructed and its characters developed embodied her assessment of the conflict.

As she told her story, the characters developed voices of their own, each with separate and distinct tones and cadence, perhaps reflecting their personalities to an extent, but more generally expressing Mrs. Valdez's assessment of them and their role in the drama. Strikebreakers, for example, spoke in high-pitched and pleading voices: the listener understood them immediately as measly cowards. Her rendition of the strikers' voices offered a clear contrast: their words were given in sonorous, deep, and steady tones, in a voice of authority that seemed to represent a communal voice verbalizing what Mrs. Valdez considered to be community values.

Mrs. Valdez's sense of collective values, later embodied in collective action either by strikers as a whole or by women, was expressed in what I would call a collective voice. At times individuals spoke in her stories: the grower, Mr. Peterson; her contractor, "Chicho" Viduarri; and the woman leader "la Lourdes," but more often people spoke in one collective voice which transcended individuality. This sense of community as embodied in a collective voice became a central feature of her narrative, and permeated everything she said about the strike. This manner of telling underscored the sense of unanimity explicit in her analysis of solidarity and clear-cut divisions. How she told the story underlined, accentuated, and modified the meaning of the story itself.

Beyond her use of different voices, Mrs. Valdez's narrative contains substantial nonverbal analysis of the "facts" as she remembered them. Her voice, gestures, and inflections conveyed both implications and meanings. She gestured with her arms and hands—a flat palm hard down on the table to make a point, both hands held up as she began again. Her stories had clear beginnings and often ended with verbal punctuations such as "and that's the way it was." She switched tenses around as, in the heat of the story, the past became the present and then receded again into the past. Vocal inflections jumped, vibrated, climbed, and then descended, playing a tonal counterpoint to her words.

Mrs. Valdez's memories of the 1933 strike focused on two major concerns: providing and caring for her family, and her role as a striker. How she structured these memories says much about her perceptions and her consciousness as a woman, a Mexican, and a worker: it is striking to what extent her memories of the strike focused on the collectivity of Mexicans and, within this, the collectivity of Mexican women.

Mrs. Valdez's sense of national identity, an important underpinning to her narrative, reflects the importance of national cohesion against an historic background of Anglo-Mexican hostility. Mrs. Valdez vividly recounted the United States' appropriation of Mexican land in 1848 and the Treaty of Guadalupe Hidalgo which ceded the area to the United States. She drew from stories of Mexican rebellion against U.S. rule in California and the nineteenth-century California guerrillas, Tiburcio Vasquez and Joaquin Murieta: the knowledge that Mexicans were working on the land which once belonged to Mexico increased her antagonism towards Anglo bosses. Mrs. Valdez may well have felt like another interviewee, Mrs. Martinez, who upon arriving at the valley pointed out to her son and told him "Mira lo que nos arrebataron los bárbaros" ["Look at what those barbarians stole from us"].

Most of these workers had lived through the Mexican revolution of 1910 to 1920, and they utilized both the experience and legacy within the new context of a strike-torn California. The military experience was crucial in protecting the camp: often led by exmilitary officers, Mexican veterans at the Corcoran camp formed a formidable armed security system. Mrs. Valdez remembers that during the strike stories of the revolution were told, retold, and debated. The extent to which Mexicans employed the images and slogans of the revolution helped solidify a sense of community. Workers named the rough roads in the camp after revolutionary heroes and Mexican towns. Even Mrs. Valdez, whose individual memories of the revolution were primarily of the terror it held for her, shared in a collective memory of a national struggle and its symbols: she disdainfully compared strikebreakers with traitors who had "sold the head of Pancho Villa."

Mrs. Valdez expressed a sense of collectivity among Mexicans. There were, in fact, many divisions—between strikers and strikebreakers, contractors and workers, people from different areas of Mexico, and people who had fought with different factions of the revolution or Cristero movement. Yet conflict with Anglo bosses on what had been Mexican land emphasized an identification as Mexicans (as well as workers) that overshadowed other divisions.

The Community of Mexican Women

Mrs. Valdez remembered a collectivity of Mexican women. By 1933, Mexican women worked alongside men in the fields. Like the men, they were paid piece-rates and picked an average of two hundred pounds per ten-hour day. Picking required strength, skill, and stamina. As one woman recalled:

> But let me describe to you what we had to go through. I'd have a twelve foot sack. . . . I'd tie the sack around my waist and the sack would go between my legs and I'd go on the cotton row, picking cotton and just putting it in there. . . . So when we finally got it filled real good then we would pick up the [hundred pound] sack, toss [*sic!*] it up on our shoulders, and then I would walk, put it up there on the scale and have it weighed, put it back on my shoulder, climb up on a wagon and empty that sack in.

As Mrs. Valdez recounted, women faced hardships in caring for their families: houses without heat, which contributed to disease, preparing food without stoves, and cooking over fires in oil barrels. Food was central to her memory, reflecting a gender division of labor. Getting enough food, a problem at any time, was exacerbated by the Depression, which forced some women to forage for berries or feed their families flour and water. Food was an issue of survival. As in almost all societies, women were in charge of preparing the food, and Mrs. Valdez's concern about food was repeated in interviews with other women. Men remembered the strike in terms of wages and conditions: women remembered these events in terms of food. Men were not oblivious or unconcerned, but woman's role in preparing food made this a central aspect of their consciousness and shaped the way they perceived, remembered, and articulated the events of the strike.

Mrs. Valdez's memory of leadership reflects this sense of female community. After initially replying that there were no leaders . . . she named her labor contractor and then focused on a woman named Lourdes Castillo, an interesting choice for several leaders. Lourdes Castillo was an attractive, single woman who lived in Corcoran. She wore make up, bobbed her hair, and wore stylish dresses. Financially independent, she owned and ran the local bar. Lourdes became involved with the strike when union organizers asked her to store food for strikers. . . .

In some respects, Lourdes represented a transition many Mexican women were undergoing in response to capitalist expansion, revolution, and migration. When the revolution convulsively disrupted Mexican families, women left alone took over the work in rural areas, migrated, and sometimes became involved in the revolution. *Soldaderas,* camp followers in the revolution, cooked, nursed, and provided sexual and emotional comfort. Some fought and were even executed in the course of battle. This image of *la soldadera,* the woman fighting on behalf of the Mexican community, was praised as a national symbol of strength and resistance. Yet it was an ambivalent image: praised within the context of an often mythified revolution, the *soldaderas* were criticized for their relative . . . independence. . . .

Gender mores in the United States differed from rural Mexico. Some changes were cosmetic manifestations of deeper changes: women bobbed their hair, adopted new dress and make up. But these changes reflected changes in a gender division of labor. Women, usually younger and unmarried, began to work for wages in canneries or garment factories unobserved by watchful male relatives. Some women became financially independent, such as Lourdes, and ran bars. . . . Financial independence and a changing gender division of labor outside the house altered expectations of women's responsibilities and obligations. Yet these women still risked the approbation of segments of the community, male and female.

According to Mrs. Valdez, during the strike Lourdes was in charge of keeping the log of who entered and left the camp and spoke at meetings. She was also in charge of distributing food. Lourdes thus reflects women's traditional concern about food, while at the same time she epitomized the cultural transition of Mexican women and the changing gender roles from prerevolutionary Mexico to the more fluid wage society of California. It was precisely her financial independence that enabled her to store and distribute the food. Perhaps Mrs. Valdez's enthusiastic memories of Lourdes suggests Mrs. Valdez's changing values for women, even if not directly expressed in her own life.

While Mrs. Valdez described the abysmal conditions under which women labored, the women were active, not passive, participants in the strike. Women's networks that formed the lattice of mutual assistance in the workers' community were transformed during the strike. The networks helped form daily picket lines in front of the cotton fields. Older women still sporting the long hair and rebozos of rural Mexico, younger women who had adapted the flapper styles of the United States, and young girls barely into their teens rode together in trucks to the picket lines. They set up makeshift child-care centers and established a camp kitchen.

With the spread of the conflict, these networks expanded and the women's involvement escalated from verbal assaults on the strikebreakers to outright physical conflict. When, after three weeks, growers refused to settle, women organized and led confrontations with Mexican strikebreakers. According to Mrs. Valdez, the women decided that they, not the men, would enter the fields to confront the strikebreakers. They reasoned that strikebreakers would be less likely to physically hurt the women.

In organized groups, the women entered the field, appealing to strikebreakers on class and national grounds—as "poor people" and "Mexicanos"—to join the strike. Those from the same regions or villages in Mexico appealed to compatriots on the basis of local loyalties, denouncing as traitors those who refused.

Exhortations turned to threats and conflict. The women threatened to poison one man who had eaten at the camp kitchen—an indication again of the centrality (and their power over) food. But women had come prepared. Those armed with lead pipes and knives went after the strikebreakers. One ripped a cotton sack with a knife. Others hit strikebreakers with pipes, fists, or whatever was handy. Although strikers had felt that the women would not be hurt, the male strikebreakers retaliated, and at least one woman was brutally beaten:

> The same women who were in the trucks, who were in the . . . picket line. . . . These women went in and beat up all those that were inside [the fields] picking cotton. . . . They tore their clothes. They ripped their hats and the [picking] sacks. . . . And bad. Ohhh! It was ugly! It was an ugly sight. I was just looking and said "No. No." I watched the blood flowing from them.
>
> [She imitates the strikebreakers voice in a high pitched, pleading tone:] "Don't hit us. Leave them [other strikebreakers] alone. Don't hit them."
>
> [Her voice drops as the collective voice of the strikers speaks:] "Let them be set upon. . . . If we are going cold and hungry then they should too. They're cowards . . . sell outs. Scum."
>
> [Her voice rises as the strikebreakers continue their plea:] "Because we live far away, we come from Los Angeles. . . . We need to have money to leave. . . ."
>
> "Yes," she says [her voice lowers and slows as it again becomes the voice of the strikers]. "We also have to eat and we also have family," she says. "*But we are not sell outs!*"*

. . . The women went in because it was women's business, and they acted on behalf of the community. Mrs. Valdez implied that the men had little to do with the decision or even opposed it. "Because women take more chances. The men always hold back because they are men and all. But the women, no. The men couldn't make us do anything. They couldn't make us do anything [to prevent us from going] and so we all went off in a flash."

The issues of confrontation focused around food. This underlines a harsh reality—strikebreakers worked to feed their families, without food strikers would be forced back to work. Her memory reflects the reality of the confrontation but also her understanding of the central issue of the strike. Mrs. Valdez recalls the strikebreakers justifying themselves to the women in terms of the need to feed their families. But the striking women's ultimate rebuke was also expressed in terms of this need: "Yes . . . we also have to eat and we also have family. *But we are not sellouts!*" Food remained central in her memories. Discussions about the strike and strike negotiations were all couched in relation to food. Her interests as a Mexican worker were considered, weighed, and expressed within the context of her interests as a woman, mother, and wife.

As the strike wore on, conditions grew harsher in the Corcoran camp. Growers lobbed incendiaries over the fence at night. Food became hard to get, and at least one child died of malnutrition. In response to public concern following the murder of two strikers, the California Governor overrode federal regulations withholding relief from strikers under arbitration and, over the protestations of local boards of supervisors, sent in trucks of milk and food to the embattled camp. Mrs. Valdez remembers nothing of federal, state, or local government or agencies, but she remembered the food: ". . . rice, beans, milk, everything they sent in."

At a meeting where Lourdes addressed strikers, food, or lack of food, was juxtaposed against their stance in the strike:

> She [Lourdes] was telling them that they might have to go hungry for awhile.
> "But look," she said . . . "they are bringing us food. We'll each get just a little, but we're not going to starve," she says. "But don't leave. But don't ANYBODY go to work. Even if a rancher comes and tells you 'come on, let's go,' don't anybody go," she says.
> "Look, even if its a little bit, we're eating. But we aren't starving. They're bringing us food."
> [Mrs. Valdez interjected:]. They brought us milk and everything. Yes, everybody that was working [in the strikers camp] were told not to go with any rancher. They were told not to believe any rancher. But everyone had to stand together as one. Everyone had an equal vote [in what was decided] . . . equal.

Mrs. Valdez was clear about the effects of a united front on both sides, that if one grower broke with the others the rest would follow. [The collective voice speaks] "No. And no. [they said] No. No. If you play us this much, then we go. And if one [rancher] pays [the demand] then all the ranchers have to pay the same." They had to, you see.

Unity and the centrality of women was carried over into her recollection of the final negotiations:

> The Portuguese [a growers' representative] told [the strikers representative] that the ranchers . . . were going to have a meeting at [the strikers' camp] with "la Lourdes."
> "Yes," he says, . . . "We're going to pay you so much. All of us are going to sign so that then all of you can return to your camps to work."
> "Yes," said [the strikers' representative] "But not a cent less. No. We won't go until we have a set wage. Then all of us go. But if there is something more [if there is more trouble] NONE of us go. Not even ONE of us leave the camp."

The strike was settled, the ranchers had been beaten, and wages went up.

The Structure of Memory

Mrs. Valdez's account of the strike and women—how she structured her memories—tells us more about why Mexicans supported the strike than interviews with leaders might have. Without the perceptions of women such as Mrs. Valdez it would be more difficult to understand strike dynamics.

Of particular interest is the fact that she remembers (or recounts) a collectivity among Mexican strikers. In her telling, workers speak in a collective voice and act as a united group. She remembers little or no dissent. In her account, *all* the workers on the Peterson ranch walked out together to join the strike, *all* the women were on the picket lines, and *all* the strikers voted unanimously to stay on strike. Growers, also a united group, spoke with one voice as a collective opposition. The lines between worker and grower were clearly drawn. According to Mrs. Valdez it was this unity that accounted for the strikes success.

But within this collectivity of Mexicans was the collectivity of women. Mrs. Valdez focused on female themes and concerns about food, caring for their families and, by extension, the greater community. Women were the actors on the picket line, made decisions about the strike, and acted as a unit. It is perhaps this sense of female collectivity and the concern around the issue of food that accounts for why Lourdes was considered a leader, though she is never mentioned by men in their accounts. Mrs. Valdez stated flatly that the women were braver—men played little part in her narrative. She remembered female leadership, female participation, female concerns, and a largely female victory. While other interviews and sources may disagree (even among women), it does suggest Mrs. Valdez's reality of the strike of 1933.

What Mrs. Valdez did not say suggests the limitations of oral narratives. She either did not know, recall, or choose to recount several crucial aspects of the story: like many other strikers, she remembered nothing of the CAWIU [Cannery and Agricultural Workers Union, organized by the Communist party in 1931], nor Anglo strike leaders mentioned in other accounts. This was not uncommon. . . . The role of the New Deal and the negotiations of the governments—Mexican, United States, and Californian—play no part in her narrative. The visit by the Mexican consul to the camp; visits by government officials; threatens to deport strikers—she reconted nothing about the negotiations that led to the settlement of the strike.

Her memory of the strike thus is limited. But the fact that Mrs. Valdez's memories were so similar to those of other women indicates that hers is not an isolated perception. There are also many points at which the memories intersect with the men. We thus may be dealing with a community memory made up of two intersecting collective memories: the collective memory (history) of the group as a whole, and a collective memory of women as a part of this.

Conclusion

Oral narratives reflect peoples' memory of the past: they can be inaccurate, contradictory, altered with the passage of time and the effects of alienation. In terms of historical analysis, Mrs. Valdez's oral history used alone raises questions. Was there really such unity in face of such an intense conflict? There were, obviously, strikebreakers. Were there no doubts, arguments? In part she may have been making a point to me. But it may be also indicative of her consciousness, of the things important to her in the event. Mrs. Valdez also remembers a largely female collectivity. Certainly, from other sources, it is clear men played a crucial role as well.

Yet her focus on women provides information unavailable in other sources, and provides a point of view of women. It suggests which issues were important to the female collectivity, how and why women rallied to the strike, and how they used their networks within the strike.

So how may an oral history be used? Seen on its own it remains a fragment of the larger story. Oral narratives must also be read critically as texts in light of the problem. . . . Used uncritically, oral histories are open to misinterpretation and may reinforce rather than reduce the separation from a meaningful past. This is especially true of the narratives of those people usually ignored by written history. Readers may lack an historical framework within which to situate and understand such narratives. The filters of cultural and class differences and chauvinism may also be obstacles. Some may embrace these narratives as colorful and emotional personal statements, while ignoring the subjects as reflective and conscious participants in history.

In the case of the Mexican women farm laborers considered in this essay, oral testimonies are not a complete history. . . . Used with other material, and read carefully and critically, however, such narratives prove crucial to a reanalysis of the strike. They need to be interpreted and placed within an historical framework encompassing institutional and social relations, struggle, and change. But when this is done, testimonies like that of Mrs. Valdez become a uniquely invaluable source. Used critically, they reveal transformations in consciousness and culture; they suggest the place of self-conscious and reflective Mexican women—and farm laboring women in general—in the broader history of rural women in the United States.

The Civilian Conservation Corps in Northern New Mexico

MARÍA E. MONTOYA

. . . The economic, social, and cultural development caused by the intervention of the federal government in Rio Arriba County began during the New Deal era between 1933 and 1941. This first intrusion by the federal government into the affairs of northern New Mexico, ironically, sustained many of the communities in the upper Rio Grande Valley. The establishment of the Civilian Conservation Corps (CCC) camp at Bandelier National Monument in 1933 and the arrival of Los Alamos Laboratories almost a decade later forever changed the environmental, social, and political landscape of the valley. They also pulled many local inhabitants away from their rural lifestyle and into the industrial twentieth-century world. While at first glance the arrival of the federal government in the form of the CCC camp (and later the Los Alamos labs) appears to have been a disruptive force, in the long run these two federally sponsored and funded institutions helped support the communities within the Hispano villages. They forestalled migration to urban areas by infusing capital and cash into the stagnating economy.

While there were many New Deal and World War II projects in northern New Mexico, let us look particularly at the influence of the CCC. . . .

The Civilian Conservation Corps, founded in March 1933 under the Emergency Work Act, was part of President Franklin Roosevelt's "Hundred Days" legislation. The act sought to relieve the unemployment wave that had swept through the nation during the Depression. Male youth unemployment had become a particular concern in the early years of the Depression. . . . In 1932, one out of every four men age fifteen to twenty-four who was in the work force was unemployed, and another 29 percent was employed only part-time. . . .

In the Civilian Conservation Corps the Roosevelt administration believed it had found a partial solution for the two overwhelming problems of youth unemployment and environmental deterioration. The CCC enlisted the young men of the nation to fight a war against poverty, ecological waste, and idleness. . . .

The first CCC camp opened one month after Roosevelt signed the legislation into effect. By July of 1933, 1,300 camps operated across the nation, employing 275,000 enrollees. Two years later, 2,650 camps had employed or were employing 600,000 men. By the time the CCC disbanded in 1942, over 3 million men had worked in the program. Of those who worked for the CCC, more than half came from rural areas where jobs were difficult to find and cash was a scarce commodity. Only 13 percent had a high-school diploma and 45 percent of the enrollees had never held a job before. . . .

The Departments of Labor, Agriculture, and Interior, and the Army combined in a rare showing of interagency cooperation to administer the CCC. Through state and local relief agencies the Department of Labor enrolled healthy, unmarried men between the ages of eighteen and twenty-five. After acceptance, the War Department welcomed the recruits into induction camps. Here they went through a scaled down version of basic training, and within two weeks were shipped out to their work camps. The army ran the camps, but the men labored during the day for the Department of Agriculture or the Department of the Interior's National Park Service or U.S. Forest Service, depending on the kind of work done at specific camps. Each man received $30 a month ($25 was sent home) as well as room, board, equipment, and clothing, all supplied from army surplus.

New Mexico had always lagged far behind the nation and the western region in economic development. These economic problems were exacerbated by classism and racism, which had Anglos (and a few urban Hispanos) controlling the majority of the wealth in the state. Consequently, the ill effects of the state's downturned economy and the Depression fell on poor Hispanos and Native Americans who depended on wage labor to supplement their family farms. By 1930, New Mexico was one of the poorest areas in the United States. . . . The problems of poverty—infant mortality rates, illiteracy, disease—were not new to New Mexicans, but the Depression and the New Deal brought them to the forefront and forced state officials, under orders of the federal government, to come to terms with the deplorable condition of the majority of its citizens.

Nevertheless, the Hispanos of the northern New Mexican villages were not merely pawns in the economic games of Santa Fe politicians. The men in these communities also looked outward to the larger marketplace and sought wage labor in the mine fields, sugar-beet fields, and sheepherding areas of Utah, Colorado, and Wyoming. . . . The Depression, however, put an end to these migratory patterns: in the early 1930s, only two thousand men left to find work, and they returned having earned only one third of the wages that they had collected a decade earlier. . . . Clearly, the economic depression that devastated the rest of the nation had similar effects in even the most remote areas of New Mexico.

. . . A vicious circle began as the drought and the return of many villagers to their farms during the Depression exacerbated the problem of soil erosion; consequently, poverty increased as farming yields declined (and also because the village did not offer wage-labor alternatives). The upper Rio Grande valley was seemingly a perfect location to institute the idealistic policies of the New Deal and particularly to promote the philosophy behind the Civilian Conservation Corps. . . .

. . . The influx of dollars from the Federal Emergency Relief Administration (FERA), the Works Progress Administration (WPA), and particularly the CCC camps aided the northern New Mexican population. Benito Montoya, a CCC camp worker, remembered that . . . with the advent of many New Deal programs, people went back to work. "I had plenty to eat, I had clothes you know. I had brand new clothes when I went in the CCC camps."

Overall, the state operated 38 camps: 8 in the national forests, 15 in the Soil Conservation Service, 3 in state parks, 7 in the Division of Grazing, 4 in the Reclamation Service, and 1 in a national monument (Bandelier). The CCC camps alone employed 32,385 men during the CCC's tenure in New Mexico. . . . The CCC spent $63 million in the state, and almost $6 million of that went directly into the enrollees' family economy. . . .

Although the federal government billed the CCC as a relief measure, both administrators and enrollees believed the program provided legitimate employment, not merely a handout. Consequently, the enrollees felt a sense of accomplishment from working in the CCC and providing for their families. "In fact, I was not quite eighteen when I went in. But I wanted to go to work," said Benito Montoya. "Things were kind of hard at that time. . . . But things started picking up, like the WPA, my dad worked for the WPA, but I went to the CCC camp. I thought that was a real. I'd have a real steady job."

Though the perception of the CCC as a program of honest work rather than as a dole was correct, it often led state and local administrators to resort to illegal and hostile persuasion to get families off relief . . . and into the CCC programs. . . . By moving families onto the CCC roles, relief workers hoped to relieve the county's economic burden by forcing families to work for relief money. Despite the fact that the Civilian Conservation Corps was supposed to be an entirely voluntary program separate from any other form of relief available to suffering families, many local administrators felt that Hispanos and Native Americans did not deserve relief, and should work for every dollar given to them by the federal government.

The Bandelier National Monument CCC camp was by far one of the most popular and sought after locations in the Española Valley. Not only was it close to the workers' families, making it easy for the boys to go home on the weekends, but it also had a reputation as one of the best-run camps. . . . Furthermore, the Frijoles Canyon, site of the ruins of the pre-historic Anasazi, was . . . one of the most picturesque places in the area. . . .

When the Interior Department established the CCC camp on the rim of the canyon, there was much work to be done to make the monument a tourist attraction. The project's workers eventually completed five stone buildings made from hand-cut blocks and a two-mile road leading to the floor of the canyon. The buildings were filled with custom-made furniture, and tin ornamentation graced the insides of the beautiful buildings. Some conservation work was completed on the trails that led to the Ceremonial Kiva and Long House, but the majority of work centered on building a park headquarters. . . .

Although the CCC shipped in a few men from Texas and Oklahoma, the majority of Bandelier's enrollees were Hispanos from the northern half of New Mexico. . . . Although the state was under severe monetary constraints, the agency made an effort to visit the homes of all applicants before approving their request to join the CCC. After the home visit, the enrollee went for a physical examination. In New Mexico, the most common cause for not allowing men to enroll was insufficient weight. Amadeo Quintana remembered, "I couldn't make it [the weight limit of 125] so we went over to Kramer's Merchantile in San Juan, bought three pounds of bananas. I ate bananas and drank plenty of water and I made it.". . .

The agents assigned the men to various CCC camps around the state, and the ones sent to Bandelier quickly settled into the routine of the camp. Most of the young men worked on the rim of the canyon in the rock quarry. . . . First, the workers blasted the rock. Then they extracted the rock with hammers and chisels. Eventually, they loaded the stones onto trucks and hauled them to the bottom of the canyon. A second group of men unloaded the rock from the trucks. Finally, with only hammers and chisels, the enrollees shaped rectangular blocks to build the structures. Although this kind of work was labor intensive and unskilled, there were a few jobs in the camp . . . that were categorized as skilled labor. However, . . . Hispanos rarely worked at these jobs.

A typical day in the camp began at 6 A.M. with reveille. The men had an hour to make their beds, clean up the bunk house, and take showers. At 7 A.M. they went to role call, exercise, and breakfast. At 8 A.M. the camp commander turned over the enrollees to the Department of the Interior, which oversaw the construction of the facilities. The men worked straight through to lunch, with only a short coffee break. . . . Their workday ended at 4 P.M., at which time they returned to camp to shower and line up for roll call. Dinner was at 5 P.M., and after dinner they were free to read, talk, play games, go to classes, walk among the ruins, fish, or swim in Frijoles Creek. Lights went out at 10:30 P.M. On Saturday the men worked half days, and on Sunday they were free to go home or relax around the camp. . . .

Although free time was technically at the disposal of the enrollees, the camp directors encouraged, and in some cases compelled, the men to "improve" themselves. . . .

The education director of the camp offered courses in arithmetic, biology, English, geography, business law, current events, and typing. The small lending library had five hundred books and active subscriptions to the *Albuquerque Journal*, the *Denver Post, Life, Colliers,* and *Time.* Browsing over the list of classes, books, and subscriptions, one notes the emphasis on English, American politics, and good citizenship. The CCC offered courses three nights a week, and out of the 206 men in camp, 200 attended at least one course per week. . . .

. . . The CCC administrators believed that the enrollees could accomplish academic goals and industrial skills if given the right opportunities. Civilian Conservation Corps reformers pursued a technological solution to the plight of these villagers. The enrollees could use the skills learned in the CCC to leave the area, if necessary, and find other jobs. . . . In the end, it was the policies of the CCC, and not those of the WPA, that helped the village adapt to the post-Depression economy.

The enrollees' experience in the CCC was not only educational, it was also fun and entertaining. The National Youth Administration (NYA) recreational director planned group activities within the camp: "Inter-barrack competition is arranged weekly for basketball, softball, touch-football and volleyball. Tournaments for indoor games are arranged nightly." There were also non-athletic activities such as a camp orchestra and "Amateur Night" once a week in which the men would display their talents.

Enrollees especially enjoyed Saturday and Sunday, because they could either go home, or into Santa Fe, or into Española for the weekend. . . .

The men became quite close in their newly-created homes. The Hispano enrollees, despite, or perhaps because of, racial and social tensions with Anglo enrollees and administrators, created a strong bond among themselves. One indication of their closeness was the names they made-up for one another. . . . Naming was an endearing way of identifying those enrollees from their particular community and of creating a bond of shared culture and experience. For many of these boys—who were often homesick—the camp was their only community during some of the most formative years of their lives. "We had a lot of fun," said Tony Roybal, "we were mostly family. We looked like a family at the camp.". . .

While they had good experiences with one another, unfortunately, other relationships within the camp were often fraught with suspicion and discrimination. . . .

Although prejudice against Mexican Americans was not institutionalized, racist attitudes still permeated the ranks of the New Deal's administrators in New Mexico. One special investigator, M. L. Grant, was sent to report on the New Mexico camps. On 21 March 1934 he wrote . . . :

> The camp is almost 100% composed of Spanish-Americans, or Mexicans as they are known here, and about thirty Texans. . . .
> This camp [Bandelier] is unfortunate in that it has had three unrelated accidents in which four men were killed. One was caused by a truck turning over and killing two men; one man was killed by a delayed dynamite charge; and one by a burning snag which fell on him while he was fighting fire.
> I do not believe that racially these Latin Americans are as careful as they might be.

For investigators and reformers, who lived outside of the state, the racial dynamics of New Mexico were enigmatic: most found it difficult to fit the Hispanos of the villages into their preconceived notions of race and class and, like M. L. Grant, fumbled for the most useful racial name. They were often quick to find racial explanations for common occurrences such as poverty, illiteracy, and accident rates. These reformers believed that the source of New Mexico's economic and social problems stemmed not from the Depression, but from the unique racial make-up of the state.

Although bias and racism played a large part in the perceptions of these administrators, the real problem lay in their complete misunderstanding of the social and economic culture with which they were dealing. . . .

. . . All of the recruiting literature local agents received was printed in English, but the majority of the men who could potentially join the New Mexico corps did not read English. . . . Furthermore, there were virtually no Spanish-speaking recruiting agents: In 1939 only one of the thirty county directors in charge of enlisting recruits was Hispano. There was little chance that good communication occurred between the agency and the enrollees. Consequently, the problem was more complex than any of the outside reformers imagined. Hispanos, because of the language barrier, were unprepared for the realities of CCC life. . . .

One of the problems Hispano enrollees had to face and to adjust to was the overt and the hidden racism in the camps. In 1937, Neal Guy, an inspector for the CCC, observed the structure of the camps in New Mexico. Despite the fact that New Mexico had more than enough men willing to fill the state's quota, . . . the New Mexico camps imported 1,200 Texas and Oklahoma enrollees. Guy wrote, "The New Mexico selection officials admit that the New Mexico enrollees are mentally and physically inferior to the Texas and Oklahoma enrollees. The average New Mexico enrollee is of Spanish or Mexican descent, speaks little or no English, is small and not very well educated." Consequently, out-of-state enrollees were brought in to fill the more skilled jobs and the jobs that necessitated leadership skills. . . .

CCC officials at the local, state, and district level felt the New Mexico enrollees incapable of rising above their condition and taking up positions of leadership, which paid double the wages of the average enrollee. . . . In Bandelier, for example, during the camp's ten-year tenure, only one Hispano ever held a position higher than basic enrollee. . . . The administration of the CCC did nothing to alleviate the racism and discrimination that occurred both at the recruiting and job promotion levels. . . .

Racial tensions ran high within the camps. One particular incident, which attracted the attention of the camp and state administrators, arose in April 1936 when seventy-three Oklahomans arrived at Bandelier. By August of that year more than half of those enrollees had left the camp and returned to Oklahoma. . . .

. . . A petition had circulated among the Oklahomans asking that they be segregated from the "Mexicans" while working (there was de facto segregation already in the Barracks). Forty enrollees . . . had signed the petition and had written home asking their parents "to do all that they could" to get them transferred back to Oklahoma. The commanding officer at Bandelier did nothing regarding the request of the unhappy enrollees. . . .

Racial incidents between Anglos and Hispanos continued throughout the rest of the decade and the Hispano enrollees responded by retreating into their ethnic group and forging their own sense of community within the camp. Although almost fifty years have passed, most enrollees recall the de facto segregation and discrimination that occurred in the camp. Alex Salazar, who was in the camp the longest of all the enrollees, recalled that "Barracks 2 and 3, if I'm not mistaken was Spanish. The other barracks—all Anglos. That's the way it was when I went in the camp until we left." . . .

After the Depression subsided and outside wage labor again became available to these men from northern New Mexico, the villagers resumed their 1920s migration patterns—looking outside of the village for work. The difference, however, was that instead of looking to agricultural work (sheepherding, beet-picking, etc.) in Colorado and Utah, these young men, with their newly acquired skills, sought work in the western wartime industries of California and the Pacific Northwest. It was the first time that many of them had been outside New Mexico, and the war took them to such far away places as Long Beach, Burbank, Oakland, Seattle, and Anchorage, as well as to the Pacific and European theaters of war.

The CCC provided more than just relief to the residents of northern New Mexico. The program gave them job-skills training and prepared them for the rigors of day-to-day life in the non-agricultural world. Experiences in the CCC prepared the enrollees for the many changes that were to come about as a result of World War II, such as life in the armed forces and jobs in the war industries of California. . . . Just by being away from home and being responsible for themselves, the enrollees in the CCC were much better prepared for the rigors of army life and combat than if they had been drafted fresh from their rural hometowns.

More specifically, the actual experiences and tasks that they accomplished on the work site helped them find jobs in the wartime industries: many left the CCC to find work in the shipyards and airplane factors of California. CCC workers were considered good to hire because of the day-to-day rigors of camp and work life that they had endured. Amadeo Quintana remembered that because of his CCC experience he easily got a job at Vandenburg Air Force Base. That experience helped him get his next job as a welder in the shipyards of Oakland. Quintana spent most of the war years traveling around California and the Southwest working at the best-paying jobs he could find . . . because of the skills he acquired along the way. . . .

This story seems as if it should end with the stereotypical twentieth-century history of western migration from New Mexico's rural areas to the urbanized industrial centers of the American West, thereby leaving the villages financially and culturally devastated and unable to cope in a modern twentieth-century world. The emergence of Los Alamos National Laboratories, however, supplied some high-tech and many labor-intensive jobs that gave Hispanos and Pueblo Indians the means to persist in their agriculturally-based way of life. The outside income that many families attained by working directly for the labs or indirectly for the new Anglo arrivals injected much-needed cash into the agricultural economy.

The twenty years of the Depression, the New Deal, and World War II dramatically affected the lives of northern New Mexico Hispanos. The changes brought about by the New Deal programs, the rise of the military industrial complex and the accompanying migrations, both in and out of the area, continue to have their effects. . . .

❦ F U R T H E R   R E A D I N G

Louise Año-Nuevo Kerr, "Chicanas in the Great Depression," in Adelaida R. Del Castillo, ed., *Between Borders* (1990)
Francisco E. Balderrama, *In Defense of La Raza* (1982)

Francisco E. Balderrama and Raymond Rodríguez, *Decade of Betrayal* (1995)

Neil Betten and Raymond A. Mohl, "From Discrimination to Repatriation: Mexican Life in Gary, Indiana, During the Great Depression," in Norris Hundley, ed., *The Chicano* (1975)

Julia Kirk Blackwelder, *Women of the Depression* (1984)

Cletus E. Daniel, *Bitter Harvest* (1991)

Suzanne Forrest, *The Preservation of the Village* (1989)

Mario T. García, "Mexican-Americans and the Politics of Citizenship: The Case of El Paso, 1936," *New Mexico Historical Review* 59 (April 1984), 187–204

Richard A. García, *Rise of the Mexican American Middle Class* (1991)

Rosalinda M González, "Chicanas and Mexican Immigrant Families, 1920–1940: Women's Subordination and Family Exploitation," in Lois Scharf and Joan Jensen, eds., *Decades of Discontent* (1983)

Abraham Hoffman, *Unwanted Mexican Americans in the Great Depression* (1974)

Olaf L. Larson, *Beet Workers on Relief in Weld County, Colorado* (1937)

Carey McWilliams, *Factories in the Fields* (1969)

Richard Melzer, *Madrid Revisited* (1976)

Selden C. Menefee and Orin C. Cassmore, *The Pecan Shellers of San Antonio* (1940)

Alejandro Morales, *The Brick People* (1992)

Américo Paredes, *George Washington Goméz* (1990)

Harry R. Rubenstein, "The Great Gallup Coal Strike of 1933," *New Mexico Historical Review* 52 (April 1977), 173–192

Vicki L. Ruiz, *Cannery Women, Cannery Lives* (1987)

George I. Sánchez, *Forgotten People* (1996)

Daniel T. Simon, "Mexican Repatriation in East Chicago, Indiana," *Journal of Ethnic Studies* 2 (Summer 1974), 11–23

Devra Weber, *Dark Sweat, White Gold* (1994)

CHAPTER
10

Mexican Americans and
World War II, 1941–1945

On the eve of World War II racial minorities lived separate lives from the rest of
Americans politically, socially, and economically. Racial tensions in California
during the early World War II years were especially volatile following the surprise
attack on Pearl Harbor on December 7, 1941, as a result of which Japanese Americans on the West Coast were eventually sent to relocation centers. Migration and
personnel shortages in defense industries would also add to the racial tensions between whites and minorities, including Mexican Americans.

In Los Angeles, the Mexican American "zoot suiters" bore the brunt of this
racial animosity. They were the youth who defied mainstream society by wearing
the distinctive and loose-fitting dress clothes in vogue at the time. The city's newspapers contributed to the hostility by exaggerating crime and juvenile delinquency
among Mexican Americans. In the spring of 1943, police attacks on Mexican Americans culminated in the infamous "Zoot Suit Wars," with the federal government
intervening to quell the disturbances. Thereafter the once sensationalist newspaper
editorials instead urged public calm and a careful consideration of the underlying
causes of "zoot suit gangsterism." What factors led to the Zoot Suit Wars?

Notwithstanding such problems, social change for Mexican Americans was accelerated by World War II. Over 300,000 Mexican Americans volunteered or were
drafted into the military, serving with distinction in both the European and Pacific
theaters. Mexican American soldiers and marines won the most Congressional
Medals of Honor of all racial minorities. The community and political activities of
Mexican Americans in support of World War II were also numerous, as they organized war bond drives in their communities, were involved in keeping at bay the
Mexico-based fascist Sinarquista movement, which was attempting to establish a
base of support among Mexican Americans and worked with the President's Fair
Employment Practice Committee (FEPC) in advancing the rights of Mexican Americans. New Mexico Senator Dennis Chávez was instrumental in establishing the
FEPC, played an active role in the Senate subcommittee's FEPC hearings, and
helped place Mexican American workers in the war industries. At this time, the
League of United Latin American Citizens (LULAC) took up the issue of the employment discrimination faced by Mexican Americans. For example, LULAC
helped to enact New Mexico's Fair Employment Law. In the Midwest, the Spanish

Speaking People's Council of Chicago focused on fair employment in the defense industries. In what ways were Mexican American women active in the war effort?

During World War II, a solution to labor shortages in agriculture led to the Bracero Program. For the next twenty years, Mexican contract workers (braceros) were recruited by agricultural interests and the railroads in the Southwest and Midwest. At this time undocumented immigration from Mexico also reached new heights because U.S. policies were purposely ambiguous in order to favor American employers. Would the presence of large numbers of documented and undocumented Mexican nationals ultimately prove detrimental to the Mexican Americans' struggle for civil rights?

❧ D O C U M E N T S

Over a quarter-million Mexican Americans were either drafted or volunteered for military service during World War II. In many instances, this was the first time Mexican Americans and non-Mexicans had come in contact with one another, and these encounters were often less than friendly, as there was just as much discrimination in the military as in civilian life. Encountering such racial discrimination, argues Raúl Morín in Document 1, strengthened the quest for identity among Mexican Americans. Document 2, a government report issued in 1943, discusses the numerous contributions of Mexican American men and women at home and abroad toward the war effort. It observes that Mexican Americans fought on all fronts in the military campaigns, beginning with the defense of the Bataan Peninsula in the Philippines.

In 1943 racial disturbances erupted at war production centers throughout the United States. In Los Angeles, military personnel and Mexican American youth clashed in what became known as the Zoot Suit Wars. Sensationalist press coverage did not help matters. Document 3 is an *Los Angeles Times* editorial that attempts to quell the resulting unrest. In the Sleepy Lagoon incident, which contributed to the build-up of tensions that led to the Zoot Suit Wars, 17 young Mexican American men were indicted for murder and sent to prison. A passage from a report published by the Citizens' Committee for the Defense of Mexican American Youth appears as Document 4. During World War II, thousands of Mexican American women worked in war-related industries. However, the married women often found that their husbands objected if they took such jobs. In Document 5 one married Mexican American woman recalls her experiences at an airplane plant in 1944. The FEPC, established by President Franklin D. Roosevelt in 1941, investigated incidents of discrimination against minority workers throughout the United States. In Document 6, from the 1945 Senate hearings on a bill (later defeated) to prohibit discrimination because of race, color, and national origin, FEPC investigator Carlos E. Castañeda details the rampant discrimination encountered by Mexican American workers.

1. Raúl Morín Discusses Mexican Americans in Military Service, 1942

The first [Mexican American] volunteers were those who joined the regular army before World War II. They enlisted during peace time at military centers such as:

In Raúl Morín, "Draftees and Volunteers" in *Among the Valiant: Mexican Americans in World War II and Korea* (Los Angeles: Borden Publishing Company, 1963), pp. 25–33.

Fort Sam Houston, Fort Bliss, Fort McArthur, and the Presidio at San Francisco. . . .

On October 29, 1941, Pedro Aguilar Despart of Los Angeles was the holder of number 158 in the national draft lottery, . . . and thus became the first Angeleno to be drafted for selective service in World War II.

On December 8th of the same year, the National Guard was federalized. . . . Many civilian members who had signed up in the guard . . . suddenly found themselves in the role of real soldiers in many National Guard Divisions.

After the bombing of Pearl Harbor, the draft boards set up the machinery to send a steady stream of selectees into the Armed Forces. . . . Even alien non-citizens living in the United States were . . . drafted into the service. . . .

In June, 1942, Mexico . . . joined other Latin-America countries in declaring war on the Axis. Soon many young Mexican nationals crossed the border . . . to volunteer for service with the United States.

Other volunteers here in the States were . . . young high school students who, upon reaching the age of 18 (or 17 with their parents' permission), immediately signed up before being drafted . . . to . . . go into the Navy, Marines or Air Force. . . .

The draft boards in Los Angeles, Nogales, Albuquerque, San Antonio, El Paso, Corpus Christi, and the Lower Rio Grande Valley of Texas . . . were loaded with Spanish names on their files; and very few were ever exempted, reclassified, or found too essential to be drafted. Local rural youths were being drafted so fast . . . that . . . owners of large farms and ranches . . . voiced stern protests with the local draft boards.

Where They Came from

. . . They came from farms, from large cities, from small villages, from the backwoods, and from the hills—from all parts of the United States and from . . . Mexico.

They had been laborers, small businessmen, farmers, truck drivers, craftsmen, students. . . . While the majority of the Spanish-speaking recruits . . . were from the . . . cities of the . . . Southwest, the names most often-repeated . . . were . . . of the . . . small *barrios* (neighborhoods) . . . which many called "home.". . . Such places as *Maravilla, Chiques* (Oxnard), Simons, Jimtown, *Limonera,* . . . San Antonio's "Westside," *Calle Ancha* in Austin, "Magnolia" in Houston, Bessemer in Pueblo, "Larrimer" in Denver, *El Pachuco,* . . . *La Smelter,* Hollywood, . . . *El Ranchito,* Chinatown, and *El Hoyo* were well represented. They . . . had endearing nicknames for their hometowns . . . with which they identified[:] . . . "Sanjo,". . . "Corpos,". . . "Fresno," . . . "El Globo," "Jerome," "Tucson,". . . "Las Cruces," . . . "Conejos," "Trinidad,". . . *"Foré Wes,"* "Del Rio," "San Marcos,". . . "Los Dos Laredos,". . . and such.

Besides being from . . . towns in the Southwest, many of the Mexican-Americans . . . hailed from . . . North Platte, Nebraska; Garden City, Kansas; Cheyenne, Wyoming; . . . Chester, Pennsylvania; . . . Gary, Indiana; Detroit, Michigan; Lorain, Ohio; St. Louis, Missouri; and Oklahoma City, Oklahoma.

One could always tell where they came from by their manner of speech[:] . . . the fast-English-speaking Angelenos [or] the slow-Spanish-speaking Texan or

New Mexican. The *Caló* talk (slang words) of the . . . habitant from El Paso . . . was in contrast to the home-spun Spanish of the Coloradoan or Arizonan. Those that originated from far away localities . . . preferred the English language. . . .

A study of this particular group will give an idea of . . . the different kinds of "Mexicans" that were to be found in the Army.

First, we had the American-born of Mexican parents. . . . Born, raised, and educated in the United States, this type still clung to many of the Mexican customs and traditions. . . . Their speech was more Spanish than English, sometimes a mixture of both. . . .

Quite different were those born and raised in Mexico. Some had left there since early childhood, others more recently, although all had become naturalized citizens. . . .

Undoubtedly, the largest group were those born in the United States whose parental lineage ran back to the original settlers and the early immigrants of the Southwest. In this group were the Spanish-Americans from New Mexico and Colorado, the *Tejanos* from Texas, and the *Pochos* from California. Those belonging to this group were definitely more "American.". . . They enjoyed Spanish songs, Latin rhythms, and Mexican *mariachis,* but also were very "hep" to the latest American songs, dances, and the latest "craze" . . . of our modern-day youths. . . .

Among them were many . . . Mexican-Italians, Mexican-Filipinos, Mexican-Negroes, Spanish-Mexicans, French-Mexicans, Irish-Mexicans, Mexican-Germans, and English-Mexicans. . . .

. . . The GI's of Mexican descent were not too different. The only difference . . . was in what they called themselves, or . . . what they were accustomed to being called by the people back home.

The so-called "Spanish" were in many instances accused of being ashamed of the term "Mexican." Being native-born and raised Americans, they never felt any sentiment for Mexico . . . ; they had never lived there. . . .

Then came the "Spanish-Americans" or Hispanos. Most of these were from New Mexico or Southern Colorado. They had been told long ago that only the people from south of the border were Mexican. . . .

Next came the so-called "Latin-Americans." Most of these lived in Texas; a few came from the northern or middle-western states. They had struggled for many years to prove to everyone that they were from this country and not Mexicans from Mexico. . . .

Last, were . . . the proudest of all our groups, those boasting of being *"chicano,"* or *mejicano.* They had nothing but scorn for those who denied their racial ties or pretended not to understand Spanish. . . . Most had been raised in predominantly "Mexican" surroundings along the border towns and in southern Texas or southern Arizona. . . .

Native Californians were known as *Pochos;* New Mexicans as *Manitos.* Others were called just plain *Chicanos* or Tejanos. . . .

All the different terms to describe the Spanish-speaking people . . . have stemmed from the attempts by these groups to be set apart from the aliens. The futility . . . is noted by the small impression made on the other Americans. . . . We would always be referred to as "those Mexicans." . . .

For this reason we have made the term "Mexican-American" our choice. We then imply that we are proud to be Americans, and at the same time are not trying to deny our Mexican ancestry.

2. The Coordinator of Inter-American Affairs Applauds the Mexican American War Effort, 1943

War came, and all America changed—small town, big city, North and West. . . . The sons of the races and nations of the world, who came here to make this America, went off to fight for freedom the globe around.

The southwestern states gave their full complement, among them thousands of their Spanish speaking sons. One of them is . . . Ricardo Noyola. He was born . . . on a ranch "Los Potreros," in Texas near the Rio Grande. Like his father, Ricardo could speak no English. He had had no schooling, working as a farm hand growing cotton and wheat since he was 13. It took war . . . to bring about a change for Noyola. . . .

At Camp Robinson, Arkansas, . . . the U.S. Army . . . took Noyola and 54 other Spanish speaking boys . . . from Texas, . . . New Mexico, . . . California— and formed a special platoon. It gave them a leader who could teach them in their own language, share their troubles, advise and encourage. It sent them to Fort Benning, Georgia, and put them through 13 weeks of intensive training. . . . The result—a body of men who . . . received high commendation. . . .

. . . And today, . . . Noyola and his comrades are scattered throughout the 300th Infantry, 3 and 4 to a company. Reports the Army: "They have fallen in on an equal plane with the English speaking men and more than hold their own.". . . Spanish speaking Americans from the Southwest make topnotch soldiers. . . .

This is . . . one proof. There are others. . . .

. . . It was proved in blood at Bataan.

Bataan was a National Guard tragedy. The first soldiers ready, they were the first to go. . . . The Guards were home town units, local soldiers, local leaders. The threat of war was too great to allow time to regroup them. They went to the Philippines as they were. The 200th and 515th Coast Artillery of New Mexico were sent because they could talk Spanish and . . . because they were the crack anti-aircraft units the Filipino people needed.

On April 9th, it was over. The glory of Bataan is the nation's but the grief is in the homes of the small towns of America—from Harrodsburg, Kentucky to Salinas, California. . . . New Mexico gave the fullest measure of devotion—one quarter of the 9,000 men from the mainland lost.

Action was America's answer to Bataan.

America demanded fighters, workers, farmers. All these the Spanish speaking Americans gave to their country.

Along the U.S. side of the Rio Grande 1 out of every 2 Spanish speaking males between the ages of 15 and 65 is either in the armed forces or has left his home to farm, to mine, to build ships and planes.

In Coordinator of Inter-American Affairs, *Spanish-speaking Americans in the War: The Southwest* (Washington, D.C.: Coordinator of Inter-American Affairs and Office of War Information, 1943).

Food—in this global war we have learned the old lesson that the man who works the earth is basic to us all, soldiers, civilians and allies. . . .

The Spanish speaking Americans, heirs to the oldest agricultural tradition in America, are working with their hands and their machines to add the citrus fruits of California and Texas, the beet sugar of California and Colorado, the wheat of New Mexico and the cattle and sheep of the Rio Grande to the stores of the United Nations. . . .

With so many of our men in the armed forces and in war production plants, we needed help to grow and harvest the food we send our armies and our allies.

This our Mexican neighbours provided when they came into the Southwest to help us harvest our crops—and they came with full faith in the common cause. . . .

Machines and the skilled hands they require have changed life in the Southwest. To her copper mines war has added the airplane plants, and shipyards the length of the Pacific Coast. Through training courses many thousands of Spanish speaking Americans have found a place in these front line industries of modern war.

Todos—all of us are in this war.

Spanish speaking women are nurses and Red Cross aids, Spanish speaking girls are in the Waacs, the Marines, the Waves.

And Spanish speaking women have gone to work beside their men in the plants of the Southwest. One of many examples of the special contribution they make—at the Consolidated assembly plant at Tucson, Arizona the needle craft of the Spanish speaking women has proved the very skill necessary to complete the intricate cloth and leather fittings of the planes.

De Las Democracias

A young Spanish speaking boy put it this way: "I am the last of my family—my mother and my father are dead. My brother—I am very glad now—they thought he got killed out there some place; but now the War Department has sent me a telegram, saying that's not so—he's alive. I think I'm going out there, too, just where my brother is, then we can fight together. We got to fight—we got to win this war—maybe we die for liberty—maybe not—but we got to fight—we got to win."

3. *Los Angeles Times* Appeals for an End to the Zoot Suit Wars, 1943

If there was ever a time to avoid hysteria and wild accusations of whatever nature, it is in this so-called zoot suit war now going on in Los Angeles.

Instead there should be a concerted effort to solve a difficult situation as quickly and sanely as possible.

A far greater danger than the gangsterism and its attendant flare-up of retributive violence lies in the perverted purposes to which reports of the difficulties here are being, and will be, put both at home and in other countries.

"Time for Sanity," *Los Angeles Times*, June 11, 1943, p. 1 (editorial). Copyright © 1943 Los Angeles Times. Reprinted by permission.

Attempts by any group, faction or political philosophy to use the clashes for purposes of stirring up racial prejudice are unwarranted and are serving the aims of Axis propagandists.

There seems to be no simple or complete explanation for the growth of the grotesque gangs. Many reasons have been offered, some apparently valid, some farfetched.

But it does appear to be definitely established that any attempts at curbing the movement have had nothing whatever to do with race persecution, although some elements have loudly raised the cry of this very thing.

In fact, at the outset zoot suiters were limited to no specific race; they were Anglo-Saxon, Latin and Negro.

The fact that later on their numbers seemed to be predominantly Latin was in itself no indictment of that race at all, the American-born boy gangs merely came from certain districts where the Latin population was in the large majority.

No responsible person at any time condemned Latin Americans, as such, because some irresponsibles were causing trouble.

The present pressing problem, then, not only is to get to the bottom of the social causes which result in zoot suit gangsterism but also during that process to discourage as far as possible the loud and unthinking charges that the fault lies exclusively in racial prejudice, police brutality, or Fascist tendencies of the constituted authorities.

There can no more be justification for these unsupported assertions than there could be for a defense of unlimited mob violence. It would be as unfortunate on one hand to advocate cleaning up of the situation by military action alone as it would be to say that sailors and soldiers at the outset did not have the right to defend themselves from zoot suit attacks.

To prevent the disastrous consequences of further exaggerated and distorted reports being hurried to Latin America for purposes of creating disunity, it is absolutely essential that every pressure aim be subordinated to the sole objective of halting the disturbances and then endeavoring to apply the needed remedies at the source.

The Army and Navy have done their part in this specific program by forbidding soldiers and sailors from entering the trouble zone until quiet has been restored. The police and Sheriff's officers are laboring now to control the isolated and sporadic outbreaks which continue to occur.

Meanwhile, the State, county, city and interested citizens' groups are endeavoring to get to the bottom of the underlying causes and to begin the remedial measures at once. . . .

Experience has shown that gangsterism of this type marked by exaggerated dress usually is faddish and that it can be eradicated quickly.

Such undoubtedly can be the case here if we are careful to see that no unnecessary complications are injected into the situation by propagandists or anyone else.

These are the issues candidly stated.

There is no reason to underestimate their seriousness or to permit unfounded charges of racial strife to bring about an overemphasized reaction.

Common sense and restraint, plus a sincere effort at correction, can do the cleanup job.

4. The Citizens' Committee for Defense of Mexican American Youth Reports on the Sleepy Lagoon Case, 1943

I

On the night of August 2nd, 1942, one Jose Diaz left a . . . party at the Sleepy Lagoon ranch near Los Angeles, and sometime . . . that night he died. It seems clear that Diaz was drinking heavily and fell into a roadway and was run over by a car. Whether or not he was also in a brawl before he was run over is not clear.

On January 13th, fifteen American-born boys of Mexican descent and two boys born in Mexico stood up to hear the verdict of a Los Angeles court. Twelve of them were found guilty of having conspired to murder Diaz, five were convicted of assault. Their sentences ranged from a few months to life imprisonment.

The lawyers say there is good reason to believe the seventeen boys were innocent, and no evidence at all to show even that they were present at the time that Diaz was involved in a brawl, assuming that he actually was in a brawl, let alone that they "conspired" to murder Jose Diaz. Two other boys whose lawyers demanded a separate trial after the 17 had been convicted, were *acquitted* on the *same evidence*. . . .

What was the basis for this mass "prosecution?" Was it a necessary measure against a sudden, terrifying wave of juvenile delinquency? No. A report by Karl Holton of the Los Angeles Probation Department conclusively proves that "there is no wave of lawlessness among Mexican children.". . . Says Mr. Holton, we must not "lose our sense of proportion. The great majority of Mexican children are not involved in these delinquent activities." . . . He points out with factual clarity, the small war-time increase in delinquency among Mexican boys was *much less* than the increase in the total for all racial groups. . . .

"Seventeen for one!" thundered the Los Angeles District Attorney and the Los Angeles press. . . . It became clear that . . . the . . . boys were not standing alone at the bar of "justice."

It wasn't only seventeen boys who were on trial.

It was the whole Mexican people, and their children and their grandchildren. . . .

The weak evidence upon which the conviction was obtained consisted largely of statements given by these boys after they had been manhandled and threatened with beatings or been actually beaten . . . to give any statement desired by the police, in order to avoid further beating. The judge and the prosecuting attorneys worked as a . . . team to bring about the convictions. The newspapers continued to blast their stories about the "zoot suit gangsters" and with a jury with no Mexican member. . . .

It began to be that kind of a trial. . . . The Los Angeles papers started it by building for a "crime wave" even before there was a crime. "MEXICAN GOON SQUADS." "ZOOT SUIT GANGS." "PACHUCO KILLERS." "JUVENILE GANG WAR LAID TO

From Chapter 1 of *The Sleepy Lagoon Case,* prepared by the Citizens' Committee for the Defense of Mexican-American Youth, Los Angeles, CA, 1942.

YOUTHS' DESIRE TO THRILL." Those were . . . the headlines building for August 3rd.

On August 3rd the death of Jose Diaz was scarehead news. And the stories were of Mexican boys "prowling in wolf-packs," armed with clubs and knives and automobile tools and tire irons, invading peaceful homes. . . .

On August 3rd every Mexican kid in Los Angeles was under suspicion as a "zoot-suit" killer. Cops lined up outside of dance halls, armed with pokers to which sharp razor blades were attached, and they ripped the peg-top trousers and "zoot-suits" of the boys as they came out.

Mexican boys were beaten, jailed. "Zoot-suits" and "Pachuco" hair cuts were crimes. It was a crime to be born in the U.S.A.—of a Spanish-speaking father or mother. . . .

III

After the grand jury . . . returned an indictment and before the trial . . . began, Mr. Ed. Duran Ayres . . . of the Sheriff's Office, filed a statement.

That statement is the key to the Sleepy Lagoon case.

It isn't nice reading, but you will have to read . . . it to understand why Sleepy Lagoon challenges every victory-minded person in the United States, Jew or Protestant or Catholic, Spanish-speaking or Mayflower descendant, immigrant or native-born.

"The biological basis," said Mr. Ayres, "is the main basis to work from". . . :

When the Spaniards conquered Mexico they found an organized society composed of many tribes of Indians ruled over by the Aztecs who were given over to human sacrifice. Historians record that as many as 30,000 Indians were sacrificed . . . in one day, their bodies . . . opened by stone knives and their hearts torn out. . . . This total disregard for human life has always been universal throughout the Americas among the Indian population, which of course is well known to everyone. . . . This Mexican element . . . knows and feels . . . a desire to use a knife or some lethal weapon. . . . His desire is to kill, or at least let blood. . . .

IV

. . . Mr. Ayres again:

Representatives of the Mexican colony . . . may be loathe to admit that (this crime wave) is in any way biological—for reasons one can . . . understand, pride of race, nationality, etc., but the fact remains that the same factors, discrimination, lack of recreation facilities, economics, etc., have also always applied to the Chinese and Japanese in California, yet they have always been law abiding. . . .

Again let us repeat; the hoodlum element as a whole must be indicted as a whole. The time to rehabilitate them is both before and after the crime has been committed, as well as during his incarceration, but it appears useless to turn him loose without having served a sentence. . . . It is just as essential to incarcerate every member of a particular gang, whether there be 10 or 50, as it is to incarcerate one or two of the ringleaders. . . .

V

We are at war. We are at war not only with the armies of the Axis powers, but with
. . . Hitler and with his theories of race supremacy. . . .

We are at war with the premise on which seventeen boys were tried and convicted in Los Angeles, sentenced to . . . prison terms on January 13th. . . . We are at
war with the Nazi logic . . . set forth by Mr. Ed. Duran Ayres, the logic which
guided the judge and jury and dictated the verdict and the sentence.

And because this global war is everywhere a people's war, . . . all of us together take up the challenge of Sleepy Lagoon.

5. Beatrice Morales Clifton Recalls Her Experiences at a California Lockheed Airplane Factory, 1944

I'd never thought about working. My brother at that time had separated from his
wife, and he had an adopted girl. . . . He brought that girl to me and says, "I'll have
her stay with you and I'll give you some money every week." She was sixteen or
fifteen and she wanted a job.

They had these offices everywhere in Pasadena, of aircraft. I went in there to
try and get her something, but they said, ". . . She's too young." He says, "Why
don't you get it?" I said, "Me?" He said, "Yeah, why don't you get the job?" I said,
"Well, I don't know." But the more I kept thinking about it, the more I said, "That's
a good idea." So I took the forms and when I got home and told my husband, oh! he
hit the roof. He was one of those men that didn't believe in the wife ever working. . . . I said, "Well, I've made up my mind. I'm going to go to work regardless of
whether you like it or not.". . .

My family and everybody was surprised—his family. I said, "Well, yeah, I'm
going to work. . . . My mother didn't say nothing because I always told her,
"Mother, you live your life and I live mine." We had that understanding. When I
decided to go to work, I told her, "I'm going to go to work and maybe you can take
care of the children." She said, "Yeah.". . .

I filled out the papers . . . and I got the job. Why I took Lockheed, I don't
know. . . . Then they asked me, "Do you want to go to Burbank, to Los Angeles?" I
said, "I don't know where Burbank is." I didn't know my way around. . . . I said,
"Well, Los Angeles. The streetcar passes . . . close to where I live, and that drops
me off in front."

To me, everything was new. They were doing the P-38s at that time. I was at
Plant 2. . . . It was on the fifth floor. I went up there and saw the place, and I said,
"Gee———." See, so many parts and things that you've never seen. Me, I'd never
seen anything in may whole life. It was exciting and scary at the same time.

They put me way up in the back, putting little plate nuts and drilling holes.
They put me with some guy—he was . . . real mean. A lot of them guys at the time

resented women coming into jobs, and they let you know about it. He says, "Well, have you ever done any work like this?" I said, "No." I was feeling just horrible. Horrible. Because I never worked with men, to be with men alone other than my husband. So then he says "You know what you've got in your hand? That's a rivet gun." I said, "Oh." What could I answer? I was terrified. So then time went on and I made a mistake. I messed up something. . . . He got so irritable with me, he says, "You're not worth the money Lockheed pays you."

. . . When he said that, I dropped the gun and I went running downstairs to the restroom, with tears coming down. This girl from Texas saw me and she followed me. . . . She was one of these "toughies." . . . She asked me what was wrong. I told her what I had done and . . . she says, "Don't worry." She started cussing him. We came back up and she told them all off. . . .

At the end of that first day, I was so tired. I was riding the streetcar and I had to stand all the way from Los Angeles clear to Pasadena. When I got home, the kids . . . said, "Oh, Mom is here." My husband, he didn't have very much to say, 'cause he didn't approve. . . . As time went on, his attitude changed a little, but I don't think he ever really, really got used to the idea of me working. . . .

. . . They gave me a list of the stuff that I would be needing. At that time they used to sell you your tools and your toolboxes through Lockheed. So I bought a box. I bought the clothing at Sears. It was just a pair of pants and a blouse. . . . I felt kind of funny wearing pants. Then . . . I said, "Oh, what the heck." And those shoes! I wasn't used to low shoes. . . .

As time went on, I started getting a little bit better. . . . I learned my job so well that . . . they put me to the next operation. At . . . first, I just began putting little plate nuts. . . . Then afterwards I learned how to drill . . . and burr. . . . Later, . . . I learned to rivet and buck. I got to the point where I was very good.

I had a Mexican girl, . . . and she was as good a bucker as I was a riveter. She would be facing me and we'd just go right on through. We'd go one side and then we'd get up to the corner and I'd hand her the gun or the bucking bar . . . and then we'd come back. . . . We worked pretty hard all day until about 2:00. Then we would slack down.

I had a lot of friends there. . . . We'd sit in the smoking areas . . . in the aisle. Then, some of the girls—on the next corner there was a drugstore that served lunches. . . . We'd talk about our families. . . .

. . . I don't know why I got a chance to learn all the other jobs, but I learned the whole operation until I got up to the front, the last step. They used to put this little flap with a wire, with a hinge. . . . I used to go with a little hammer and a screwdriver and knock those little deals down so that it would be just right. That guy that I used to work with helped me, teached me how to do it, and I could do it just like him.

New people would come in, and they would say, "You teach them the job. You know all the jobs." Sometimes it would make me mad. . . ." But I would still show them.

Then, . . . they'd say, "Look at her now. You should have seen her a year ago when she first came in. You'd go boo and she'd start crying. . . ." I figured this is the only way you're going to survive, so I'm going to do it.

I was just a mother of four kids, that's all. But I felt proud of myself and felt good. . . . I felt good that I could do something, and being that it was war, I felt that I was doing my part.

6. Carlos E. Castañeda Testifies on Job Discrimination Against Mexican Americans in War Defense Industries, 1945

STATEMENT OF DR. CARLOS E. CASTAÑEDA, SPECIAL ASSISTANT ON LATIN-AMERICAN PROBLEMS TO THE CHAIRMAN OF THE PRESIDENT'S COMMITTEE ON FAIR EMPLOYMENT PRACTICE, BEFORE THE SENATE COMMITTEE ON LABOR AND EDUCATION IN THE HEARINGS HELD SEPTEMBER 8, 1944, ON S BILL 2048, TO PROHIBIT DISCRIMINATION BECAUSE OF RACE, CREED, COLOR, NATIONAL ORIGIN OR ANCESTRY.

Our Spanish-speaking population in the Southwest . . . are ill-dressed, ill-fed, ill-cared for medically, and ill-educated . . . because of the low economic standard to which they have been relegated as the result of . . . restricting their employment . . . to the lowest paid, least desirable, and most exacting jobs. . . . Not only have they been restricted to the lowest bracket jobs, but even in these jobs they have been paid wages below the minimum . . . in all the . . . industries in which they have been employed.

In the investigation of complaints filed with the President's Committee on Fair Employment Practice involving discrimination against Spanish-speaking . . . citizens . . . , I have visited the states of Arizona, California, Colorado, New Mexico, and Texas and I have had an opportunity to study conditions at first hand. I have gathered statistics that reveal the magnitude of the problem . . . as it affects . . . the largest underprivileged minority group in the Southwest.

In the State of Arizona, according to the 1940 census, there is a total population of 449,261, of which about 30% are persons of Mexican extraction. . . . The mining industry in Arizona . . . employs between 15,000 and 16,000 men. The percentage of . . . American citizens of Mexican extraction . . . is over 50% . . . and in many mining centers . . . as high as 80%. . . . There are between 8,000 and 10,000 persons of Mexican extraction employed in the mining industry in Arizona. Their employment is restricted, however, . . . to common labor and semi-skilled jobs and even the urgent need of Manpower as the result of the war has not broken down the prejudice which bars large numbers of skilled laborers from promotion. . . .

The total population of California, according to the 1940 census, is 6,907,387. The number of persons of Mexican extraction according to the same census is 457,900. . . . In the Los Angeles area with a population of 1,673,000, the persons of Mexican descent number about 315,000, or approximately 20%. . . .

Carlos E. Castañeda Testifies on Job Discrimination Against Mexican Americans in War Defense Industries, 1945.

. . . Out of the 315,000 persons of Mexican extraction, only 10,000 were being employed in the Southern California shipyards, 2,000 in the San Diego aircraft industry, and 7,500 in the Los Angeles aircraft industry, making a total of 19,500 employed in essential war industries in the area included between Los Angeles and San Diego. Much better utilization was being made of Mexican labor in the San Francisco area where, with a . . . population of . . . 30,000 persons of Mexican extraction, 8,000 were engaged in basic war industries. . . . 22% of the Mexican-Americans were being employed in San Francisco, while only 6% had found employment in basic war industries in the Los Angeles and San Diego area.

The failure to utilize . . . Mexican labor . . . in California, traceable in a good measure to prejudice, was not limited to essential . . . war industries. . . . Mr. Sid Panush, Personnel Examiner for the Los Angeles County Civil Service Commission, stated that . . . of 16,000 employees, about 400 were . . . Mexican . . . ; that is, . . . 2 1/2% of the total amount. Mr. John F. Fisher, Director for the Los Angeles Civil Service Commission explained . . . that . . . of the 16,500 civil service employees in the city government about 450 were . . . Mexican . . . , which makes the percentage the same as . . . in the County.

The population of Colorado, according to the 1940 census, is 1,123,296. . . . In the southern part of Colorado, . . . there are approximately some 50,000 Spanish-speaking . . . citizens. . . . In Denver, in Pueblo, and in Trinidad . . . these Mexican-Americans are restricted in their employment to common labor jobs. . . . The number of Mexican-Americans employed in the steel industry in Civil Service jobs, in military installations and in other war . . . industries, is less than 6%. . . . Mexican-Americans have been refused employment in clerical and office positions, and they have been denied promotion and upgrading . . . in private industry and by military installations in the area.

The State of New Mexico [has] a population of 531,818. . . . The number of Mexican-Americans is about 40% of the total population. In the . . . large mining area between Santa Rita and Silver City . . . from 40 to 60% of the men employed by the mining companies are . . . Mexican. . . . They are barred from promotion into certain departments and . . . they are refused upgrading into skilled jobs because of their national origin.

Texas, with a population of 6,414,824, has approximately 1,000,000 Mexican-Americans. . . . Less than 5% . . . are employed . . . in war . . . industries. Such industries . . . have restricted them to common or unskilled labor jobs . . . regardless of their ability, training, or qualifications. In the oil, aircraft and mining industries, in the numerous military installations, in the munitions factories and shipyards, and in the public utility corporations, . . . their employment has been limited and their opportunities for advancement restricted.

The prevalent . . . belief among employers for the various industries, personnel managers, officials of military installations, and . . . government agencies in the Southwest is that the Mexican-American is incapable of doing other than manual, physical labor; that he is unfit for the . . . skilled labor required by industry and the crafts. . . .

. . . The failure of the Mexican-American to enter the ranks of industry has been largely due to prejudice. . . .

The belief . . . that certain racial or national groups have different mechanical aptitudes, a conviction that is at the bottom of the prejudice held against Mexican-Americans, is completely unfounded in fact. . . .

The urgent need of manpower, in view of the increasing shortage of labor, forced industry to give the Mexican-American an opportunity, but not without the greatest reluctance and misgivings. Wherever he has been given an opportunity he has shown the ability to learn and produce with the same efficiency as members of any other group. . . .

Bill S 2048, being considered by your Committee to prohibit discrimination in employment based on race, creed, color, national origin or ancestry will enable three million Mexican-American citizens throughout this country . . . to secure equal economic opportunities in employment in the post-war era. The President's Committee on Fair Employment Practice is a war agency, designed to secure equal participation in the total war effort by all Americans regardless of race, creed, color or national origin. During its short period of operation it has done much to integrate Mexican-Americans in war and essential industries and in Government employ. Mexican-Americans have generously responded to their responsibility in the present world struggle for the victory of the democracies. They have unstintingly made the last sacrifice on a world-wide battle front in order that all peoples may enjoy the blessings of freedom and peace. Equal economic opportunities, the right to work and earn a decent living on a par with all other persons regardless of race, creed, color, national origin or ancestry, is a basic principle of American democracy.

❧ E S S A Y S

In the first essay, Stuart Cosgrove, an independent scholar from Perth, Scotland, argues that during World War II the zoot suit held social and political importance as an emblem of ethnicity and a way of negotiating identity for many Mexican American youth, or *pachucos*. The zoot suit riots of 1943 emerged at a time when American society was undergoing powerful structural change because of increased military recruitment and the entrance of women into the labor force, which in turn led to the erosion of parental control and authority. For Cosgrove, the hostilities that white servicemen expressed toward the zoot-suit-clad Mexican American youth, as the former tried to reestablish their status over the latter, revealed the polarization of wartime American society.

During the war Mexican Americans joined Americans' exodus to cities in search of jobs. By 1944, at the height of American war production, 16 percent of working women held jobs in war industries. In the Midwest over 5,000 Mexican American women were defense workers. They are the subject of the second essay, by Richard A. Santillán, professor of political science at California State Polytechnic University, Pomona, who observes that these Mexican American women held a broad range of jobs and, despite discrimination, interacted with their fellow African American and Anglo American women workers. He contends that because the Mexican American women's experiences working in war-related industries expanded the boundaries of their social worlds, they would play a larger role in the post–World War II struggle for equality.

An Interpretation of the Causes of the Zoot Suit Wars

STUART COSGROVE

The zoot-suit riots that erupted in the United States in the summer of 1943 had a profound effect on a whole generation of socially disadvantaged youths. It was during his period as a young zoot-suiter that the Chicano union activist Cesar Chavez first came into contact with community politics, and it was through the experiences of participating in zoot-suit riots in Harlem that the young pimp "Detroit Red" began a political education that transformed him into the Black radical leader Malcolm X. . . . During the summer months of 1943 "the killer-diller coat" was the uniform of young rioters and the symbol of a moral panic about juvenile delinquency that was to intensify in the post-war period.

At the height of the Los Angeles riots of June 1943, the *New York Times* carried a front page article which claimed without reservation that the first zoot-suit had been purchased by a black bus worker, Clyde Duncan, from a tailor's shop in Gainesville, Georgia. Allegedly, Duncan had been inspired by the film "Gone with the Wind" and had set out to look like Rhett Butler. This explanation clearly found favour throughout the USA. The national press forwarded countless others. Some reports claimed that the zoot-suit was an invention of Harlem night life, others suggested it grew out of jazz culture and the exhibitionist stage-costumes of the band leaders, and some argued that the zoot-suit was derived from military uniforms and imported from Britain. The alternative and independent press, particularly *Crisis* and *Negro Quarterly,* more convincingly argued that the zoot-suit was the product of a particular social context. They emphasized the importance of Mexican-American youths, or *pachucos,* in the emergence of zoot-suit style and, in tentative ways, tried to relate their appearance on the streets to the concept of *pachuquismo.*

In his pioneering book, *The Labyrinth of Solitude,* the Mexican poet and social commentator Octavio Paz throws imaginative light on *pachuco* style and indirectly establishes a framework within which the zoot-suit can be understood. Paz's study of the Mexican national consciousness examines the changes brought about by the movement of labour, particularly the generations of Mexicans who migrated northwards to the USA. This movement, and the new economic and social patterns it implies, has, according to Paz, forced young Mexican-Americans into an ambivalent experience between two cultures.

> . . . The pachucos are youths, for the most part of Mexican origin, who form gangs in southern cities; they can be identified by their language and behaviour as well as by the clothing they affect. They are instinctive rebels, and North American racism has vented its wrath on them more than once. But the pachucos do not attempt to vindicate their race or the nationality of their forebears. Their attitude reveals an obstinate, almost fanatical will-to-be, but this will affirms nothing specific except their determination . . . not to be like those around them.

From Stuart Cosgrove, "The Zoot-Suit and Style Warfare," *History Workshop Journal,* No. 18 (Autumn 1984), pp. 77–91. Reprinted with permission of Oxford University Press, Oxford, England.

Pachuco youth embodied all the characteristics of second generation working-class immigrants. In the most obvious ways they had been stripped of their customs, beliefs and language. The *pachucos* were a disinherited generation within a disadvantaged sector of North American society; and predictably their experiences in education, welfare and employment alienated them from the aspirations of their parents and the dominant assumptions of the society in which they lived. The *pachuco* subculture was defined not only by ostentatious fashion, but by petty crime, delinquency and drug-taking. Rather than disguise their alienation or efface their hostility to the dominant society, the *pachucos* adopted an arrogant posture. They flaunted their difference, and the zoot-suit became the means by which that difference was announced. Those "impassive and sinister clowns" whose purpose was "to cause terror instead of laughter," invited the kind of attention that led to both prestige and persecution. For Octavio Paz the *pachuco*'s appropriation of the zoot-suit was an admission of the ambivalent place he occupied. "It is the only way he can establish a more vital relationship with the society he is antagonising. As a victim he can occupy a place in the world that previously ignored him; as a delinquent, he can become one of its wicked heroes." The zoot-suit riots of 1943 encapsulated this paradox. They emerged out of the dialectics of delinquency and persecution, during a period in which American society was undergoing profound structural change.

The major social change brought about by the United States' involvement in the war was the recruitment to the armed forces of over four million civilians and the entrance of over five million women into the war-time labour force. The rapid increase in military recruitment and the radical shift in the composition of the labour force led in turn to changes in family life, particularly the erosion of parental control and authority. The large scale and prolonged separation of millions of families precipitated an unprecedented increase in the rate of juvenile crime and delinquency. By the summer of 1943 it was commonplace for teenagers to be left to their own initiatives whilst their parents were either on active military service or involved in war work. The increase in night work compounded the problem. With their parents or guardians working unsocial hours, it became possible for many more young people to gather late into the night at major urban centres or simply on the street corners.

The rate of social mobility intensified during the period of the zoot-suit riots. With over 15 million civilians and 12 million military personnel on the move throughout the country, there was a corresponding increase in vagrancy. Petty crimes became more difficult to detect and control; itinerants became increasingly common, and social transience put unforeseen pressure on housing and welfare. The new patterns of social mobility also led to congestion in military and industrial areas. Significantly, it was the overcrowded military towns along the Pacific coast and the industrial conurbations of Detroit, Pittsburgh and Los Angeles that witnessed the most violent outbreaks of zoot-suit rioting.

. . . The *pachucos* of the Los Angeles area were particularly vulnerable to the effects of war. Being neither Mexican nor American, the *pachucos*, like the black youths with whom they shared the zoot-suit style, simply did not fit. In their own terms they were "24-hour orphans," having rejected the ideologies of their migrant parents. As the war furthered the dislocation of family relationships, the *pachucos* gravitated away from the home to the only place where their status was visible, the streets . . . of the towns and cities. But if the *pachucos* laid themselves open to a life of delinquency and detention, they also asserted their distinct identity, with their own style of dress, their own way of life and a shared set of experiences.

The Zoot-Suit Riots: Liberty, Disorder and the Forbidden

The zoot-suit riots sharply revealed a polarization between two youth groups within wartime society: the gangs of predominantly black and Mexican youths who were at the forefront of the zoot-suit subculture, and the predominantly white American servicemen stationed along the Pacific coast. The riots invariably had racial and social resonances but the primary issue seems to have been patriotism and attitudes to the war. With the entry of the United States into the war in December 1941, the nation had to come to terms with the restrictions of rationing and the prospects of conscription. In March 1942, the War Production Board's first rationing act had a direct effect on the manufacture of suits and all clothing containing wool. In an attempt to institute a 26% cut-back in the use of fabrics, the War Production Board drew up regulations for the wartime manufacture of what Esquire magazine called, "streamlined suits by Uncle Sam." The regulations effectively forbade the manufacture of zoot-suits and most legitimate tailoring companies ceased to manufacture or advertise any suits that fell outside the War Production Board's guide lines. However, the demand for zoot-suits did not decline and a network of bootleg tailors based in Los Angeles and New York continued to manufacture the garments. Thus the polarization between servicemen and *pachucos* was immediately visible: the chino shirt and battledress were evidently uniforms of patriotism, whereas wearing a zoot-suit was a deliberate and public way of flouting the regulations of rationing. The zoot-suit was a moral and social scandal in the eyes of the authorities, not simply because it was associated with petty crime and violence, but because it openly snubbed the laws of rationing. . . .

The zoot-suit riots, which were initially confined to Los Angeles, began in the first few days of June 1943. During the first weekend of the month, over 60 zoot-suiters were arrested and charged at Los Angeles County jail, after violent and well publicized fights between servicemen on shore leave and gangs of Mexican-American youths. In order to prevent further outbreaks of fighting, the police patrolled the eastern sections of the city, as rumours spread from the military bases that servicemen were intending to form vigilante groups. The *Washington Post's* report of the incidents, on the morning of Wednesday 9 June 1943, clearly saw the events from the point of view of the servicemen.

> Disgusted with . . . the youthful hoodlums, the uniformed men passed the word quietly among themselves and opened their campaign in force on Friday night.
>   At central jail, where spectators jammed the sidewalks and police made no efforts to halt auto loads of servicemen openly cruising in search of zoot-suiters, the youths streamed gladly into the sanctity of the cells after being snatched from bar rooms, pool halls and theaters and stripped of their attire.

During the ensuing weeks of rioting, the ritualistic stripping of zoot-suiters became the major means by which the servicemen re-established their status over the *pachucos.* It became commonplace for gangs of marines to ambush zoot-suiters, strip them down to their underwear and leave them helpless in the streets. In one particularly vicious incident, a gang of drunken sailors rampaged through a cinema after discovering two zoot-suiters. They dragged the *pachucos* on to the stage as the film was being screened, stripped them in front of the audience and as a final insult, urinated on the suits.

The press coverage of these incidents ranged from the careful and cautionary liberalism of The *Los Angeles Times* to the more hysterical hate-mongering of William Randolph Hearst's west coast papers. Although the practice of stripping and publicly humiliating the zoot-suiters was not prompted by the press, several reports did little to discourage the attacks:

> . . . zoot-suits smouldered in the ashes of street bonfires where they had been tossed by grimly methodical tank forces of service men. . . . The zooters, who earlier in the day had spread boasts that they were organized to "kill every cop" they could find, showed no inclination to try to make good their boasts. . . . Searching parties of soldiers, sailors and Marines hunted them out and drove them out into the open like bird dogs flushing quail. Procedure was standard: grab a zooter. Take off his pants and frock coat and tear them up or burn them. Trim the "Argentine Ducktail" haircut that goes with the screwy costume.

The second week of June witnessed the worst incidents of rioting and public disorder. A sailor was slashed and disfigured by a pachuco gang; a policeman was run down when he tried to question a car load of zoot-suiters; a young Mexican was stabbed at a party by drunken Marines; a trainload of sailors were stoned by *pachucos* as their train approached Long Beach; streetfights broke out daily in San Bernardino; over 400 vigilantes toured the streets of San Diego looking for zoot-suiters, and many individuals from both factions were arrested. On 9 June, The *Los Angeles Times* published the first in a series of editorials designed to reduce the level of violence, but which also tried to allay the growing concern about the racial character of the riots.

> To preserve the peace and good name of the Los Angeles area, the strongest measures must be taken jointly by the police, the Sheriff's office and Army and Navy authorities, to prevent any further outbreaks of "zoot suit" rioting. While members of the armed forces received considerable provocation at the hands of the unidentified miscreants, such a situation cannot be cured by indiscriminate assault on every youth wearing a particular type of costume.
>
> It would not do, for a large number of reasons, to let the impression circulate in South America that persons of Spanish-American ancestry were being singled out for mistreatment in Southern California. And the incidents here were capable of being exaggerated to give that impression.

The Chief, the Black Widows and the Tomahawk Kid

The pleas for tolerance from civic authorities and representatives of the church and state had no immediate effect, and the riots became more frequent and more violent. A zoot-suited youth was shot by a special police officer in Azusa, a gang of *pachucos* were arrested for rioting and carrying weapons in the Lincoln Heights area; 25 black zoot-suiters were arrested for wrecking an electric railway train in

Watts, and 1000 additional police were drafted into East Los Angeles. The press coverage increasingly focused on the most "spectacular" incidents and began to identify leaders of zoot-suit style. On the morning of Thursday 10 June 1943, most newspapers carried photographs and reports on three "notorious" zoot-suit gang leaders. Of the thousands of *pachucos* that allegedly belonged to the hundreds of zoot-suit gangs in Los Angeles, the press singled out the arrests of Lewis D. English, a 23-year-old-black, charged with felony and carrying a "16-inch razor sharp butcher knife"; Frank H. Tellez, a 22-year-old Mexican held on vagrancy charges, and another Mexican, Luis "The Chief" Verdusco (27 years of age), allegedly the leader of the Los Angeles *pachucos.*

The arrests of English, Tellez and Verdusco seemed to confirm popular perceptions of the zoot-suiters widely expressed for weeks prior to the riots. Firstly, that the zoot-suit gangs were predominantly, but not exclusively, comprised of black and Mexican youths. Secondly, that many of the zoot-suiters were old enough to be in the armed forces but were either avoiding conscription or had been exempted on medical grounds. Finally, . . . that zoot-suit style was an expensive fashion often funded by theft and petty extortion. . . . What newspaper reports tended to suppress was information on the Marines who were arrested for inciting riots, the existence of gangs of white American zoot-suiters, and the opinions of Mexican-American servicemen stationed in California, who were part of the war-effort but who refused to take part in vigilante raids on *pachuco* hangouts.

As the zoot-suit riots spread throughout California, to cities in Texas and Arizona, a new dimension began to influence press coverage of the riots in Los Angeles. . . . The revelation that girls were active within *pachuco* subculture led to consistent press coverage of the activities of two female gangs: the Slick Chicks and the Black Widows. The latter gang took its name from the members' distinctive dress, black zoot-suit jackets, short black skirts and black fish-net stockings. In retrospect the Black Widows, and their active part in the subcultural violence of the zoot-suit riots, disturb conventional understandings of the concept of *pachuquismo.*

. . . What the zoot-suit riots brought to the surface was the complexity of *pachuco* style. The Black Widows and their aggressive image confounded the *pachuco* stereotype of the lazy male delinquent who avoided conscription for a life of dandyism and petty crime. . . . The Black Widows were a reminder that ethnic and generational alienation was a pressing social problem and an indication of the tensions that existed in minority, low-income communities.

. . . The appearance of female *pachucos* coincided with a dramatic rise in the delinquency rates amongst girls aged between 12 and 20 years old. The disintegration of traditional family relationships and the entry of young women into the labour force undoubtedly had an effect on the social roles and responsibilities of female adolescents. . . . There are many indications that the war years saw a remarkable increase in the numbers of young women who were taken into social care or referred to penal institutions, as a result of the specific social problems they had to encounter.

. . . The Black Widows and Slick Chicks were spectacular in a sub-cultural sense, but their black drape jackets, tight skirts, fish net stockings and heavily emphasised make-up, were ridiculed in the press. The Black Widows clearly existed outside the orthodoxies of war-time society: playing no part in the industrial war effort, and openly challenging conventional notions of feminine beauty and sexuality.

Towards the end of the second week of June, the riots in Los Angeles were dying out. Sporadic incidents broke out in other cities, particularly Detroit, New York and Philadelphia, . . . but these, like the residual events in Los Angeles, were not taken seriously. The authorities failed to read the inarticulate warning signs proffered . . . in California. The zoot-suit riots had become a public and spectacular enactment of social disaffection. The authorities in Detroit chose to dismiss a zoot-suit riot at the city's Cooley High School as an adolescent imitation of the Los Angeles disturbances. Within three weeks Detroit was in the midst of the worst race riot in its history. The United States was still involved in the war abroad when violent events on the home front signalled the beginnings of a new era in racial politics.

Official Fears of Fifth Column Fashion

Official reactions to the zoot-suit riots varied enormously. The most urgent problem that concerned California's State Senators was the adverse effect that the events might have on the relationship between the United States and Mexico. This concern stemmed partly from the wish to preserve good international relations, but rather more from the significance of relations with Mexico for the economy of Southern California, as an item in the *Los Angeles Times* made clear. "In San Francisco Senator Downey declared that the riots may have 'extremely grave consequences' in impairing relations between the United States and Mexico, and may endanger the program of importing Mexican labor to aid in harvesting California crops." These fears were compounded when the Mexican Embassy formally drew the zoot-suit riots to the attention of the State Department. It was the fear of an "international incident" that could only have an adverse effect on California's economy, rather than any real concern for the social conditions of the Mexican-American community, that motivated Governor Warren of California to order a public investigation into the causes of the riots. In an ambiguous press statement, the Governor hinted that the riots may have been instigated by outside or even foreign agitators:

> As we love our country and the boys we are sending overseas to defend it, we are all duty bound to suppress every discordant activity which is designed to stir up international strife or adversely affect our relationships with our allies in the United Nations.

The zoot-suit riots provoked two related investigations; a fact finding investigative committee headed by Attorney General Robert Kenny and an un-American activities investigation presided over by State Senator Jack B. Tenney. The un-American activities investigation was ordered "to determine whether the present zoot-suit riots were sponsored by Nazi agencies attempting to spread disunity between the United States and Latin-American countries." . . . The notion that the riots might have been initiated by outside agitators persisted throughout the month of June. . . .

. . . Examination of the social conditions of *pachuco* youths tended to be marginalized in favour of other more "newsworthy" angles. At no stage in the press coverage were the opinions of community workers or youth leaders sought, and so, ironically, the most progressive opinion to appear in the major newspapers was offered by the Deputy Chief of Police, E. W. Lester. In press releases and on radio he provided a short history of gang subcultures in the Los Angeles area and then tried, albeit briefly, to place the riots in a social context.

> The Deputy Chief said most of the youths came from overcrowded . . . homes that offered no opportunities for leisure-time activities. He said it is wrong to blame law enforcement agencies for the present situation, but that society as a whole must be charged with mishandling the problems.

On the morning of Friday, 11 June 1943, The *Los Angeles Times* broke with its regular practices and printed an editorial appeal, "Time for Sanity" [see Document 3] on its front page. The main purpose of the editorial was to dispel suggestions that the riots were racially motivated, and to challenge the growing opinion that white servicemen from the Southern States had actively colluded with the police in their vigilante campaign against the zoot-suiters.

> There seems to be no simple or complete explanation for the growth of the grotesque gangs. Many reasons have been offered, some apparently valid, some farfetched. But it does appear to be definitely established that any attempts at curbing the movement have had nothing whatever to do with race persecution, although some elements have loudly raised the cry of this very thing.

A month later, the editorial of July's issue of *Crisis* presented a diametrically opposed point of view:

> These riots would not occur—no matter what the instant provocation—if the vast majority of the population, including more often than not the law enforcement officers and machinery, did not share in varying degrees the belief that Negroes are and must be kept second-class citizens.

But this view got short shrift, particularly from the authorities, whose initial response to the riots was largely retributive. Emphasis was placed on arrest and punishment. The Los Angeles City Council considered a proposal from Councillor Norris Nelson, that "it be made a jail offense to wear zoot-suits with reat pleats within the city limits of LA," and a discussion ensued for over an hour before it was resolved that the laws pertaining to rioting and disorderly conduct were sufficient to contain the zoot-suit threat. . . . Only when Governor Warren's fact-finding commission made its public recommendations did the political analysis of the riots go beyond the first principles of punishment and proscription. The recommendations called for a more responsible co-operation from the press; a programme of special training for police officers working in multi-racial communities; additional detention centres; a juvenile forestry camp for youth under the age of 16; an increase in military and shore police; an increase in the youth facilities provided by the church; an increase in neighbourhood recreation facilities and an end to discrimination in the use of public facilities. In addition to these measures, the commission urged that arrests should be made without undue emphasis on members of minority groups and encouraged lawyers to protect the rights of youths arrested for participation in gang activity. The findings were a delicate balance of punishment and palliative; it made no significant mention of the social conditions of Mexican labourers and no recommendations about the kind of public spending that would be needed to alter the social experiences of *pachuco* youth. The outcome of the zoot-suit riots was an inadequate, highly localized and relatively ineffective body of short term public policies that provided no guidelines for the more serious riots in Detroit and Harlem later in the same summer. . . .

The zoot-suit was associated with a multiplicity of different traits and conditions. It was simultaneously the garb of the victim and the attacker, the persecutor and the persecuted, the "sinister clown" and the grotesque dandy. But the central opposition was between the style of the delinquent and that of the disinherited. To wear a zoot-suit was to risk the repressive intolerance of wartime society and to invite the attention of the police, the parent generation and the uniformed members of the armed forces. For many *pachucos* the zoot-suit riots were simply hightimes in Los Angeles when momentarily they had control of the streets; for others it was a realization that they were outcasts in a society that was not of their making.

The Contributions of Mexican American Women Workers in the Midwest to the War Effort

RICHARD A. SANTILLÁN

Thousands of Mexican American women made significant contributions to the industrial effort during World War II. . . . Mexican American women . . . labored as riveters, crane operators, welders, assemblers, railroad section workers, roundhouse mechanics, forklift operators, meatpackers, farmworkers, seamstresses, nurses, secretaries, and shipbuilders. They assisted in the critical production of aircraft, tanks, trucks, jeeps, ships, uniforms, tents, medical supplies, small arms, heavy artillery, ammunition, bombs, and communication equipment. The industrial work which they engaged in was extremely hazardous and physically strenuous. . . .

The wartime contribution of Mexican American women was not confined solely to work in defense industries, however. A handful of Mexican American women eventually enlisted in the military service, some of them even serving overseas prior to the conclusion of the war in 1945. . . . Meanwhile, thousands of other Mexican American women aided the war effort by assisting in homefront activities such as organizing war bond drives, working with the local Red Cross, cultivating victory gardens, and collecting scrap metal for armaments. Some women also formed social clubs, modeled after the USO, for Mexican American servicemen who were often barred from public establishments because of racial discrimination. . . .

. . . World War II triggered a new social period in the evolutionary development of the Mexican community in the Midwest, as both men and women . . . helped defeat fascism during the 1940s. . . .

From Richard A. Santillán, "Rosita the Riveter: Midwest Mexican American Women During World War II," *Perspectives in Mexican American Studies* 2 (1989): 115–147. Reprinted by permission of Mexican American Studies and Research Center.

. . . The Japanese bombing of Pearl Harbor on December 7, 1941, would . . . severely test . . . the endurance, courage, and strong sense of community and cultural pride of the Mexican people in the Midwest.

The Mexican American communities of the Midwest, along with the rest of the nation, anxiously sat in front of their Philco and RCA radios and listened as President Franklin D. Roosevelt asked for a declaration of war against Japan. Thousands of young Mexican-descent men . . . soon enlisted or were drafted into all the branches of the military. They registered in their local induction centers in Detroit, Chicago, Des Moines, St. Louis, Toledo, Gary, Milwaukee, Bethlehem, Kansas City, Omaha, St. Paul, and East Chicago. They also came from rural towns such as Sutherland and Hershey, Nebraska; Mason City and Davenport, Iowa; Albert Lea, Minnesota; Silvas, Illinois; Garden City and Emporia, Kansas; Holland, Michigan; Lorain, Ohio; and Kenosha, Wisconsin.

. . . Mexican Americans rushed to join the military service, despite the fact that most had experienced a great deal of discrimination during their lives. The majority enlisted out of a strong sense of patriotic obligation, most . . . feeling it was their civic duty:

> We believed, that by joining the service, we could lay to rest the idea that Mexicans were disloyal to the United States. We wanted to prove that . . . our home was here in this country. . . .

The majority of Mexican American recruits undertook their basic training in the southern states in 1942. What most of these former war veterans vividly remember . . . is . . . the terrible segregation and mistreatment of Black citizens in the states where the camps were located. Many Mexican American servicemen . . . sympathized with the Black population . . . because of their own personal experiences with discrimination in the Midwest.

Most Mexican American servicemen briefly returned home to visit their families and friends before being shipped overseas for combat duty. . . . Almost all of the homes of the Mexican communities in the Midwest had silver stars posted on their windows, indicating the number of men and women of that particular household serving in the armed forces. As the war dragged on, many of these silver stars were replaced by gold ones—indicating family members killed in action.

A Mexican American woman defense worker whose brothers saw combat action stated:

> We didn't understand the international politics that led to the war. We did know, however, that the Japanese had cowardly bombed Pearl Habor and had killed hundreds of young American boys—boys who were my brothers' ages. The Japanese had attacked our country. I say our country because I was born here. My generation went proudly to war because this country, despite the discrimination, had provided my family with a better life than my relatives (had) in Mexico. . . .

In the early months of the war, the United States government publicly predicted that labor shortages in war-related industries would not be a serious problem because of the high rate of volunteer recruitment. This optimistic forecast . . . changed by mid-1942, however, when the government announced severe labor shortages in several critical areas of war production. . . . Both the president and

Congress proposed in 1942 and 1943 the mandatory registration for all women between the ages of eighteen and fifty as a way to resolve this wartime problem. The policy was never implemented, however. . . . Women's groups lobbied against the proposed plan and eventually convinced the president and federal lawmakers that female volunteers were already doing their fair share . . . without the need for a mandatory civilian draft. In fact, by 1943, women had become an integral part of the wartime labor force, comprising nearly one-third of all workers and over fifty percent of the workers in the aircraft and munitions industries.

At the outbreak of the war, the vast majority of female workers in defense plants could be accurately characterized as young and single. This demographic profile changed dramatically by 1943 as married and divorced women, women with children, and elderly women swelled the ranks of defense workers.

There are no accurate records on the total numbers of Mexican American women who were employed in the Midwest during the war . . . in the defense industry, because Mexican American workers were simply categorized as "white" as opposed to "non-white" for company records . . . [An] estimate would be approximately five thousand Mexican American women. . . .

Mexican American defense workers were . . . composed of young single women, married and divorced women, including mothers, and women over fifty-five years of age. . . .

. . . The significant change . . . , however, was the number of married women working outside the home. Prior to the war, married women helped supplement the family income by taking in work at home, including washing, ironing, sewing, and taking care of children and boarders. . . . Mexican men strongly believed that their wives and daughters could help bring the war to a swift end by working in defense plants, thus increasing the chances that their sons would return alive from overseas.

Some women . . . sought outside employment as a way to keep themselves fully occupied in order to fight the loneliness of having their sons so far away. Finally, a minority of Mexican women between the ages of fifty and seventy-five . . . worked, mainly because they wanted to feel part of the community effort. A daughter of one such woman observed:

> It was simply amazing seeing our mothers and grandmothers outside the home working after watching them as housewives for all our lives. Almost none of these women spoke English and for many, it was the first real social contact with the Anglo world. Our mothers and grandmothers worked as cleaning women, carting material to the various shops, and sorting nuts, bolts, and screws. . . .

Most of these women walked to work, since their neighborhoods were often adjacent to the industrial sections of town. Each was issued her own personal locker in which she stored her work clothes and other necessities. . . . Almost all of these women had pictures posted inside their lockers . . . of their loved ones overseas. Some also confessed . . . to having pictures of Clark Gable or Rober Taylor taped inside their lockers.

Defense workers were often required to purchase their own work clothes and to pay to have their clothes cleaned. The work uniform generally consisted of overalls, slacks, shirt, steel-tip shoes, head covering, safety goggles, and work bib. . . .

For the Mexican American women who entered the labor force during World War II, the wartime experiences were very difficult, including the constant separation from loved ones, race and sex discrimination, and the physical demands required at work. . . .

The initial experience of being torn away from their families was a shattering feeling for women . . . accustomed to being an integral part of a close-knit unit:

> I knew women who hated coming to work because of the daily pain of leaving their children at someone's house as they worked in the factory. They couldn't wait for the war to be over so they could return to a normal family life. . . .

Notwithstanding steps by the federal government toward eliminating race and sex discrimination in the work place, . . . none of them were hired as clerical help in the front offices or promoted to supervisory positions on the factory floor, though they applied and were qualified. . . .

. . . There was a small segment of Anglo women who believed Mexican Americans were lazy, and initially balked at the idea of working with them. These Anglo women were persuaded by their supervisors to either work with Mexican American workers or face being fired. One woman told of an experience shared by many Mexican Americans at this time:

> This German man told me one day to go back to Mexico and I responded by telling him that I was more an American citizen than he was because my family just crossed a river to get to the U.S., whereas he had to cross several countries and a big ocean. No matter how much they taunted us, we would always have the last word.

Black women . . . were generally assigned to work with Mexican American women because many Anglos refused to work with Blacks in the defense plants. None of the Mexican American women . . . had any problems working with Black women and . . . many long-lasting friendships evolved from these partnerships during the war:

> Aircraft work generally required a team of two women for riveting—one person working outside the plane and the other person inside. At one particular plant, there were many white women from Missouri who refused to have anything to do with the Black workers. Our supervisor decided to pair several Black and Mexican women together. At first, there was some prejudice on both sides, but as time passed, we became good friends both in and out of the plant.

Another former defense worker recalled:

> I remember one day when some new Black workers came to our factory. From the start, some white workers absolutely refused to even say hello. The next day, some of us Mexican women invited the Black women over to our table for lunch. We did so because we knew what it was like to be discriminated against. By the end of the week, several white workers also joined us for lunch. We soon realized that we had to set aside our differences in order to win the war.

As the war went on, many Mexican American women developed good social relations with Anglo women . . . and often socialized together after working hours. The war had improved some race relations by dispelling a few of the stereotypes held by these various groups.

The majority of the women interviewed politely declined to speak about the twin issues of sex discrimination and sexual harassment in the work place during the war. One woman did recall . . . that:

Sex discrimination was much worse than racial prejudice . . . we were constantly harassed on the factory floor by male workers who told us that we should be home taking care of our children and that defense work was not for women. We often complained to our male supervisors . . . but nothing was ever done. Sometimes when we were working, one of the men would come by and grab us in a sexual way which made us very angry concerning this ugly treatment of women in the plant. Many women didn't formally complain, however, in fear of . . . losing their jobs. . . .

Defense work, . . . glamorized by the romantic image of Rosie the Riveter, was . . . physically exhausting and often hazardous. Women in the defense industry sometimes worked fifty to seventy hours a week. . . . Many former Mexican American defense workers recalled working several consecutive months of sixteen-hour days, with only one or two days of rest each month:

The company always encouraged—push is a better word—us to work two shifts because of the severe need for war materials. I remember so many days when I could barely stand up at work. . . . The companies . . . made us feel that if we did not work the extra hours, that somehow we were being unsympathetic to the war effort and letting our men down overseas. . . .

Mexican American women were employed in a variety of war-related occupations, especially in the areas of aircraft, munitions, railroads, steel, and meatpacking. The majority of Mexican American aircraft workers were employed in Missouri, Kansas, Michigan, Ohio, and Oklahoma. . . . Mexican American women worked for Cessna, North American Aviation, Boeing, Beech, Douglas, Pratt and Whitney, Ford, Gibson, Buick, Glen L. Martin, and the Goodyear Tire Company. Most worked as welders and riveters in the production of bombers, gliders, engines, instrument panels, fuel tanks, transport planes, fighters, and interceptors.

Some Mexican American women were successful in bringing their sisters and cousins . . . into the aircraft industry. Mexican American women were particularly in demand in this occupational field because of their small stature, which was an advantage when it came to working in cramped spaces aboard the aircraft. . . . One aircraft worker recalled:

We tended to be physically smaller and slender compared to both the Anglo and Black women. Some of us weighed only 90 pounds and stood around five feet. As a result of our small size, we were given the responsibility of welding and riveting in the hard-to-get places of the plane, including inside the wings, gun turrets, and both the nose and tail sections of the aircraft. We always did an excellent job despite the tight spaces we had to work with inside the planes. We prided ourselves because our work always passed inspection on the first check.

. . . Women comprised nearly forty percent of the labor force in the production of munitions. Mexican American women worked in many Midwest munitions plants including Kansas Ordinance, Savannah Ordinance, Green River Ordinance, J.I. Case Company, Elgin Watch Company, Hammond Ordinance, Kingsbury Ordinance, Standard Forge, Cushion Motors, Parsons Ordinance, Hastings Ammunition

Depot, and Lake City Ordinance. They helped produce bombs, fuses, timing devices, bullets, machine guns, shell casings, land mines, bomb caps, rifles, cartridge belts, grenades, light and heavy artillery, and rocket launchers.

There were labor shortages in the munitions industry throughout the war because of low wages and the constant danger of working with explosives. The munitions industry was plagued with mishaps resulting in death and severe injuries. . . .

Additionally, munitions work was often done below ground as a way of protecting the plants against possible enemy aerial attacks. Working all day underground, away from sunlight and fresh air, served to discourage many women from volunteering for the munitions industry.

Many munitions workers . . . were housed in company dormitories located inside the company grounds. The housing facilities served as an incentive for both men and women to work two shifts for extra money, since the workers did not have to worry about the time traveling to and from home. . . .

A small percentage of Mexican American women found employment in the forty-one steel mills operating in the major producing areas of Chicago, East Chicago, Detroit, Lorain, Gary, and Bethlehem. These women were employed by the American Steel Corporation, Northwestern Steel and Wire Company, Inland Steel, Cast Armor, Youngstown Steel Company, Great Lakes Steel, Bethlehem Steel Corporation, and United States Steel Corporation. Only ten percent of all steelworkers were women, compared to forty percent in the aircraft and munitions industries. A number of former Mexican American steel workers remembered the unbearable noise level inside the mills.

> What I remember the most after all the years was the noise. It was absolutely terrible working in that type of surrounding where you heard and felt the pounding and grinding of steel being rolled out for the war. It's hard to describe the feeling of your body shaking and your ears hurting because of the vibrations inside the plant. In addition, it was extremely hot because of the ovens melting down the steel.

Despite such hardships, women in the steel industry were still required to do the same type of work as men. Mexican American women . . . worked in the rolling mills, the blast furnaces, and the open hearths, operated fifteen-ton cranes, operated punch presses, and served as painters, loaders, welders, riveters and car dumpers. They assisted in the production of iron and steel for tanks, concertina wire, bullets, shells, jeeps, trucks, and steel beams for military housing.

The railroad system was vital to the war effort because trains transported nearly ninety percent of all military freight and seventy percent of all military personnel. Although women comprised only eight percent of all railroad workers, . . . a significant number were Mexican American women. . . . Many Mexican American women worked for the Burlington, the Santa Fe, and the Fruit Growers Express, while others were hired to maintain the privately owned railroads of the steel companies, including Inland Steel, and Northwestern Steel and Wire Company. Mexican American women labored as section workers, roundhouse mechanics, drawbridge tenders, train dispatchers, loaders, and as waitresses and tellers in the railroad lunchrooms and ticket offices. One important responsibility of railroad workers was to help clear the tracks during the winter months:

The wintertime was awful. We worked in freezing weather to clear the snow from the tracks in order for the troop and supply trains to travel to their final destinations. We also replaced ties and rails, loaded and unloaded war materials into the boxcars, and loaded heavy chunks of ice for the air-conditioning system for the soldiers during the hot humid summers. . . .

Finally, . . . the meat companies, including Armour, Morrell, Wilson, Swift, and Cudahay, employed a large number of Mexican American women during the war as pork and beef trimmers, butchers and packers. They also helped produce "C" and "K" rations.

One woman recalled the unfavorable conditions inside the packinghouses:

The slaughterhouses were the worst places to work during the war because of the coldness and terrible smell of dead animals everywhere. Many women were constantly suffering from colds and flu as a result of working all day in the freezers and loading refrigeration cars. We also had to be extra careful not to hurt ourselves with the butchering knives and the meat-cutting machines. . . .

After a hard day of work, the women workers would shower in company facilities before heading home to care for their families and to write letters to their loved ones overseas. One Mexican American woman outlined a typical day in her life during the war:

I woke up early and prepared both breakfast and lunch for my two boys, who were of school age. I walked them to school before returning home to do my domestic chores, including grocery shopping, purchasing ice for the icebox, washing dishes, ironing, and washing clothes by hand, because we could not afford a washing machine. I would take a nap in the afternoon before going after my children in school, and have their dinner ready. I tried to help them with their school work before leaving for work on the night shift. My neighbor took care of my children while I was working at the machine shops for the Santa Fe.

The problem of child care for female workers was never resolved by the government during World War II. . . . As one Mexican American defense worker remembered:

Our child care service was our own families. Our mothers, aunts, and even our younger sisters helped with the children while we were busy working. We could not afford private child care and none of the companies offered child care to their female workers. . . .

Mexican American women confronted a host of other problems, including budgeting their ration stamps for large families and overcoming the loneliness that came with their men away at war. Nevertheless, these economic and social difficulties were always overshadowed by the grim possibility that, at any time, they could be notified that a loved one had been killed in action:

I remember a few times during the war when I was working and all of a sudden (there would be) a loud scream followed by uncontrollable crying of a woman who had learned that her husband or son was dead. We all feared that moment when we, too, could be requested to go to the front office and find a representative of the military with an attache case tucked under his arm with a letter for the next of kin. . . .

Several other women recalled the fear of reading the casualty list in the local newspapers and of seeing the Western Union messenger riding his bicycle through their neighborhood, praying that he was not coming to their door with an official notification from the War Department. . . .

All of the Mexican American women interviewed vividly remembered where they were and what they were doing when they heard the news that the war had finally ended. . . . One woman recalled:

> I was welding some material together for a part of a tank when all of a sudden I noticed lots of commotion on the work floor as women were hugging and crying. I turned off my torch gun and heard the company whistle tooting and tooting. One of my friends ran up to me and told me that the war was over. I remember sitting down on a workbench, placing my hands over my face, and crying. All of the emotion which had been locked up for all these four years was released. All I could think of was that our boys would be finally coming home to be reunited with their families.

During the next several days, Mexicans throughout the Midwest streamed into their local churches to . . . thank God for sparing the lives of their loved ones. Ironically, some of these . . . churches still maintained segregated sections for Mexican Americans. The segregation . . . was the initial clue that the wartime contributions of the entire Mexican community had not helped . . . erase public discrimination. Both men and women . . . became increasingly indignant with the continuation of . . . social and economic discrimination. . . . They strongly felt that they had earned the right to be treated as first-class citizens, since they had fought and worked on the battlefield and in the defense plants. . . .

A former defense worker noted:

> During the war, there was a lessening of discrimination by some public places only because they needed our money, with so many Anglos in the service. After the war, some restaurants, stores and taverns again refused to serve us on an equal basis with whites. We knew this was totally unfair because we had worked hard to win the war. My generation realized then that we had to do something to change this condition, not only for ourselves, but for the next generation. . . .

The war years unquestionably modified the social and political attitudes and behavior of many Mexican American defense workers regarding their roles in the home and the community. . . . The war served as a social and economic apprenticeship for these women at a time when most of the men were in the service. Many women believed the war was an historical turning point in their lives . . . because it provided them with a rare opportunity to develop political awareness, social independence, grass-roots leadership, and economic self-reliance . . . :

> All of us were definitely changed by the four years of defense work. Prior to the war, we were naive young women with few social and job skills. But the war altered these conditions very quickly. By the end of the war, we had been transformed into young mature women with new job skills, self-confidence, and a sense of worth as a result of our contributions to the war effort. Just as the war had changed boys to men, the same thing happened to us girls.

Another defense worker . . . drew a parallel with the men:

When our young men came home from the war, they didn't want to be treated as second-class citizens anymore. Deep in their hearts, they firmly believed their wartime contributions had entitled them to better social opportunities. We women didn't want to turn the clock back either regarding the social positions of women before the war. The war had provided us the unique chance to be socially and economically independent, and we didn't want to give up this experience simply because the war ended. We, too, wanted to be first-class citizens in our communities.

Social independence had different meanings among Mexican American women in the post-war period. For the majority of single women, personal freedom was primarily limited to the newfound liberties. . . . Married women, on the other hand, defined social independence in a much broader perspective, including an equal voice in the decision-making at home, the right to pursue educational goals, and the freedom to . . . seek outside employment:

> . . . My working and traveling experiences during the war exposed me to a whole new world of opportunities that I didn't know existed before in my life. My point of view is that my family responsibilities are important, but at the same time I feel that I have the right to achieve my goals as well. . . .

Mexican American women . . . had mixed feelings about post-war employment. . . . A woman's decision to continue working was strongly determined by both her wartime occupation and marital status. Many women in the munitions and railroad industries were laid-off, while a significant number of women in the meat, steel, and aircraft industries were asked to continue working as these companies began . . . converting their wartime operations to peacetime production. . . . Many Mexican American women who were married or engaged looked forward to raising a family on a full-time basis. Women who continued to work or to seek employment after the war were generally single, divorced, or widowed. There were, nevertheless, some married women who were employed outside the home after 1945. . . .

The war served as a training ground for women regarding leadership and organizational development. As a consequence of these wartime experiences, women were very active with political campaigns on behalf of Mexican American candidates after the war. They walked precincts, helped with fund-raising, encouraged voter registration, and mailed campaign materials.

The political and economic forces in the immediate post-war period enhanced the status of women in the labor force and community affairs. . . . Some of the traditional male attitudes about the roles of women in the Mexican American community took a backseat to these economic and political realities after the war.

❧ F U R T H E R   R E A D I N G

Elizabeth Broadbent, "Mexican Population in the Southwestern United States," *Texas Geographic Magazine* 5 (1941), 16–24

Kitty Calavita, *Inside the State* (1992)

Albert Camarillo, "The G.I. Generation," *Aztlán* 2 (Fall 1971), 145–150

Hugh Carter and Bernice Doster, "Social Characteristics of Aliens from the Southwest Registered for Selective Service During World War II," *U.S. Immigration and Naturalization Service Monthly Review* 8 (January 1951), 88–94

Irene Castañeda, "Personal Chronicle of Crystal City," in Magdalena Mora and Adelaida R. Del Castillo, eds., *Mexican Women in the United States* (1980)

Rex W. Crawford, "The Latin American in Wartime United States," *Annals of the American Academy of Political and Social Science* (September 1942), 121–131

Cletus E. Daniel, *Chicano Workers and the Politics of Fairness* (1991)

Mark R. Day, "The Pertinence of the 'Sleepy Lagoon' Case," *Journal of Mexican American History* (1974), 71–98

Erasmo Gamboa, *Mexican Labor and World War II* (1990)

Beatrice Griffith, *American Me* (1977)

"Investigation of the Spanish-Speaking Congress," in U.S. Special Committee on Un-American Activities, House of Representatives, 78th Cong., 2nd sess. (1944)

Charles P. Loomis, "Wartime Migration from the Rural Spanish Speaking Villages of New Mexico," *Rural Sociology* 7 (December 1942), 384–395

Christine Marín, "La Asociación Hispano-Americana de Madres y Esposas: Tucson's Mexican American Women in World War II," *Renato Rosaldo Lecture Series Monograph* 1 (Summer 1985), 5–18

Mauricio Mazón, *The Zoot-Suit Riots* (1984)

Carey McWilliams, *Brothers Under the Skin* (1943)

Gerald D. Nash, "Spanish-Speaking Americans in Wartime," in Gerald D. Nash, *The American West Transformed* (1985)

National Catholic Welfare Conference, *The Spanish Speaking of the Southwest and West* (1944)

Guy Nunn, *White Shadows* (1947)

Alonso S. Perales, *Are We Good Neighbors?* (1974)

Robin F. Scott, "Wartime Labor Problems and Mexican-Americans in the War," in Manuel P. Servín, ed., *The Mexican Americans* (1974)

Coke R. Stevenson, *The Good Neighbor Policy and Mexicans in Texas* (1943)

CHAPTER 11

Mexican Americans in the Cold War Years, 1945–1960

By the end of World War II, large numbers of Chicanos were living in cities, where they suffered from poor housing, lack of employment and educational opportunities, and other consequences of discrimination. These Mexican Americans nonetheless began to demand changes in their communities and soon took up the civil rights issue. They fought against the rampant discrimination in employment and aimed for greater participation in postwar American society by working to bring about change within civic and religious organizations such as the Civic Unity Leagues, the Community Service Organization (CSO), and the Catholic Youth Organization. What effect would the era's anticommunism have on Chicano community and labor leaders?

Thousands of Chicanos joined the armed forces, which offered them the opportunity for economic and social advancement denied by the larger society. During World War II Chicanos had seen action in Africa, Europe, and the Pacific. The Korean conflict found them once again overrepresented in combat units; however, like African Americans, Chicano soldiers were often denied recognition for their bravery.

Over the next two decades about 5 million Mexican nationals were brought into the United States as contract labor (braceros) for seasonal employment in agriculture, with the majority working in the Southwest. The bounty of cheap Mexican labor increased during the postwar years through the influx of undocumented workers, pejoratively called "wetbacks." To counter this massive flow of Mexicans entering the United States illegally at a time of economic recession in which American unemployment doubled, on June 9, 1954, the Department of Labor initiated a roundup of undocumented Mexican workers code-named "Operation Wetback." Through a massive deportation drive organized by the Immigration and Naturalization Service, the United States apprehended over 1 million undocumented Mexican workers. What was the role of the U.S. government in the operation of Bracero Program?

The Asociación Nacional México-Americana (ANMA), led by longtime trade union organizer Alfredo Montoya, actively campaigned against the mass deportation raids. Veteran labor activist Ernesto Galarza organized Mexican undocumented workers as part of the effort by the American Federation of Labor (AFL) to establish unions among farmworkers. Through the CSO, ANMA, the American G.I. Forum (a World War II veterans' organization), and the Spanish-Speaking People's Council, Mexican Americans played prominent roles in the struggle for their civil rights in the Southwest and Midwest. What was the extent of this early civil rights activism by Mexican Americans?

❥ D O C U M E N T S

After World War II de facto segregation remained a problem for Mexican Americans. In many school districts throughout the Southwest, Mexican American school children were segregated into separate classrooms. Document 1 is an excerpt from *Méndez et al.* v. *Westminister School District,* the class action suit against school segregation brought by Mexican Americans in 1946, several years before the more well known case of *Brown* v. *The Board of Education* (1954). In Document 2 Isabel González, Executive Secretary of the Committee to Organize the Mexican People, notes that, in addition to facing social and economic discrimination, thousands of Mexicans in the 1940s had difficulty obtaining U.S. citizenship.

After 1881, no Mexican American was elected to the Los Angeles City Council until 1948, when Eduardo Roybal took office as councilman from the Ninth District. Document 3 captures the spirit of the efforts to elect Roybal, who represented the political ferment among Mexicans Americans during the post–World War II years. Despite the inauguration of the Bracero Program, which brought Mexican contract labor to the United States, tens of thousands of Mexicans crossed the border illegally to obtain work. Undocumented Mexican workers in Texas are the subject of Documents 4 and 5. In Document 4, dated 1949, the Texas author Hart Stilwell argues that the United States did not make any effort to control the numbers of Mexicans illegally entering the country. A 1953 report co-authored by the American G.I. Forum and organized labor in Texas, which is presented as Document 5, blames the undocumented Mexican workers for causing depressed wages as well as agricultural job displacement for Mexican Americans in Texas.

1. *Méndez et al.* v. *Westminister School District* Addresses School Segregation, 1946

McCORMICK, District Judge.

Gonzalo Méndez, William Guzman, Frank Palomino, Thomas Estrada and Lorenzo Ramirez, as citizens of the United States, and on behalf of their minor children, and as they allege in the petition, on behalf of "some 5000" persons similarly affected, all of Mexican or Latin descent, have filed a class suit . . . against the Westminister, Garden Grove and El Modeno School Districts, and the Santa Ana City Schools, all of Orange County, California, and the respective trustees and superintendents of said school districts.

Méndez et al. v. *Westminster School Dist. of Orange County et al.,* Civil Action No. 4292. District Court, San Diego, Calif., Central Division, Feb. 18, 1946. In *Federal Supplements,* Vol. 64, 1946, pp. 544–551.

The complaint, grounded upon the Fourteenth Amendment to the Constitution of the United States . . . , alleges a concerted policy and design of class discrimination against "persons of Mexican or Latin descent or extraction" of elementary school age by the defendant school agencies in the conduct and operation of public schools of said districts, resulting in the denial of the equal protection of the laws to such class of persons among which are the petitioning school children.

Specifically, plaintiffs allege:

. . . That all children or persons of Mexican or Latin descent or extraction, though Citizens of the United States of America, shall be, have been and are now excluded from attending, using, enjoying and receiving the benefits of the education, health and recreation facilities of certain schools within their respective Districts and Systems but that said children are now and have been segregated and required to and must attend and use certain schools in said Districts and Systems reserved for and attended solely and exclusively by children and persons of Mexican and Latin descent, while such other schools are maintained, attended and used exclusively by and for persons and children purportedly known as White or Anglo-Saxon children. . . .

. . . It is . . . admitted that segregation per se is practiced in the above-mentioned school districts as the Spanish-speaking children enter school life and as they advance through the grades in the respective school districts. It is also admitted by the defendants that the petitioning children are qualified to attend the public schools in the respective districts of their residences.

In the Westminister, Garden Grove and El Modeno school districts the respective boards of trustees had taken official action, declaring that there be no segregation of pupils on a racial basis but that non-English-speaking children (which group, excepting as to a small number of pupils, was made up entirely of children of Mexican ancestry or descent), be required to attend schools designated by the boards separate and apart from English-speaking pupils; that such group should attend such schools until they had acquired some proficiency in the English language.

The petitioners contend that such official action evinces a covert attempt by the school authorities in such school districts to produce an arbitrary discrimination against school children of Mexican extraction or descent and that such illegal result has been established in such school districts respectively. . . .

The concrete acts complained of are those of the various school district officials in directing which schools the petitioning children and others of the same class or group must attend. The segregation exists in the elementary schools to and including the sixth grade in two of the defendant districts, and in the two other defendant districts through the eighth grade. . . .

The ultimate question for decision may be thus stated: Does such official action of defendant district school agencies and the usages and practices pursued by the respective school authorities as shown by the evidence operate to deny or deprive the so-called non-English-speaking school children of Mexican ancestry or descent within such school districts of the equal protection of the laws?

The defendants at the outset challenge the jurisdiction of this court under the record as it exists at this time. We have already denied the defendants' motion to dismiss the action upon the "face" of the complaint. . . .

Are the actions of public school authorities of a rural or city school in the State of California, as alleged and established in this case, to be considered actions of the State within the meaning of the Fourteenth Amendment so as to confer jurisdiction on this court to hear and decide this case under the authority of Section 24, Subdivision 14 of the Judicial Code, supra? We think they are. . . .

When the basis and composition of the public school system is considered, there can be no doubt of the oneness of the system in the State of California, or of the restricted powers of the elementary school authorities in the political subdivisions of the State. . . .

. . . Upon an appraisal of the factual situation before this court as illumined by the laws of the State of California relating to the public school system, it is clear that the respondents should be classified as representatives of the State to such an extent and in such a sense that the great restraints of the Constitution set limits to their action. . . .

We therefore turn to consider whether under the record before us the school boards and administrative authorities in the respective defendant districts have by their segregation policies and practices transgressed applicable law and Constitutional safeguards and limitations and thus have invaded the personal right which every public school pupil has to the equal protection provision of the Fourteenth Amendment to obtain the means of education.

We think the pattern of public education promulgated in the Constitution of California and effectuated by provisions of the Education Code of the State prohibits segregation of the pupils of Mexican ancestry in the elementary schools from the rest of the school children.

. . . The common segregation attitudes and practices of the school authorities in the defendant school districts in Orange County pertain solely to children of Mexican ancestry and parentage. They are singled out as a class for segregation. Not only is such method of public school administration contrary to the general requirements of the school laws of the State, but we think it indicates an official school policy that is antagonistic in principle to . . . the Education Code of the State.

Obviously, the children referred to in these laws are those of Mexican ancestry. And it is noteworthy that the educational advantages of their commingling with other pupils is regarded as being so important to the school system of the State that it is provided for even regardless of the citizenship of the parents. We perceive in the laws relating to the public educational system in the State of California a clear purpose to avoid and forbid distinctions among pupils based upon race or ancestry except in specific situations not pertinent to this action. Distinctions of that kind have recently been declared by the highest judicial authority of the United States "by their very nature odious to a free people whose institutions are founded upon the doctrine of equality." They are said to be "utterly inconsistent with American traditions and ideals." . . .

Our conclusions in this action, however, do not rest solely upon what we conceive to be the utter irreconcilability of the segregation practices in the defendant school districts with the public educational system authorized and sanctioned by the laws of the State of California. We think such practices clearly and unmistakably disregard rights secured by the supreme law of the land. . . .

[6, 7] "The equal protection of the laws" pertaining to the public school system in California is not provided by furnishing in separate schools the same technical facilities, text books and courses of instruction to children of Mexican ancestry that are available to the other public school children regardless of their ancestry. A paramount requisite in the American system of public education is social equality. It must be open to all children by unified school association regardless of lineage.

[8] We think that under the record before us the only tenable ground upon which segregation practices in the defendant school districts can be defended lies in the English language deficiencies of some of the children of Mexican ancestry as they enter elementary public school life as beginners. But even such situations do not justify the general and continuous segregation in separate schools of the children of Mexican ancestry from the rest of the elementary school population as has been shown to be the practice in the defendant school districts—in all of them to the sixth grade, and in two of them through the eighth grade.

The evidence clearly shows that Spanish-speaking children are retarded in learning English by lack of exposure to its use because of segregation, and that commingling of the entire student body instills and develops a common cultural attitude among the school children which is imperative for the perpetuation of American institutions and ideals. It is also established by the record that the methods of segregation prevalent in the defendant school districts foster antagonisms in the children and suggest inferiority among them where none exists. One of the flagrant examples of the discriminatory results of segregation in two of the schools involved in this case is shown by the record. In the district under consideration there are two schools, the Lincoln and the Roosevelt, located approximately 120 yards apart on the same school grounds, hours of opening and closing, as well as recess periods, are not uniform. No credible language test is given to the children of Mexican ancestry upon entering the first grade in Lincoln School. This school has an enrollment of 249 so-called Spanish-speaking pupils, and no so-called English-speaking pupils; while the Roosevelt, (the other) school, has 83 so-called English-speaking pupils and 25 so-called Spanish-speaking pupils. Standardized tests as to mental ability are given to the respective classes in the two schools and the same curricula are pursued in both schools and, of course, in the English language as required by State law. . . . In the last school year the students in the seventh grade of the Lincoln were superior scholarly to the same grade in the Roosevelt School and to any group in the seventh grade in either of the schools in the past. It further appears that not only did the class as a group have such mental superiority but that certain pupils in the group were also outstanding in the class itself. Notwithstanding this showing, the pupils of such excellence were kept in the Lincoln School. It is true that there is no evidence in the record before us that shows that any of the members of this exemplary class requested transfer to the other so-called intermingled school, but the record does show without contradiction that another class had protested against the segregation policies and practices in the schools of this El Modeno district without avail.

While the pattern or ideal of segregating the school children of Mexican ancestry from the rest of the school attendance permeates and is practiced in all of the four defendant districts, there are procedural deviations among the school administrative agencies in effectuating the general plan.

In Garden Grove Elementary School District the segregation extends only through the fifth grade. . . .

This arrangement conclusively refutes the reasonableness or advisability of any segregation of children of Mexican ancestry beyond the fifth grade in any of the defendant school districts in view of the standardized and uniform curricular requirements in the elementary schools of Orange County.

But the admitted practice and long established custom in this school district whereby all elementary public school children of Mexican descent are required to attend one specified school (the Hoover) until they attain the sixth grade, while all other pupils of the same grade are permitted to and do attend two other elementary schools of this district, notwithstanding that some of such pupils live within the Hoover School division of the district, clearly establishes an unfair and arbitrary class distinction in the system of public education operative in the Garden Grove Elementary School District.

The long-standing discriminatory custom prevalent in this district is aggravated by the fact shown by the record that although there are approximately 25 children of Mexican descent living in the vicinity of the Lincoln School, none of them attend that school, but all are peremptorily assigned by the school authorities to the Hoover School, although the evidence shows that there are no school zones territorially established in the district.

The record before us shows a paradoxical situation concerning the segregation attitude of the school authorities in the Westminister School District. There are two elementary schools in this undivided area. Instruction is given pupils in each school from kindergarten to the eighth grade, inclusive. Westminister School has 642 pupils, of which 628 are so-called English-speaking children, and 14 so-called Spanish-speaking pupils. The Hoover School is attended solely by 152 children of Mexican descent. Segregation of these from the rest of the school population precipitated such vigorous protests by residents of the district that the school board in January, 1944, recognizing the discriminatory results of segregation, resolved to unite the two schools and thus abolish the objectionable practices which had been operative in the schools of the district for a considerable period. A bond issue was submitted to the electors to raise funds to defray the cost of contemplated expenditures in the school consolidation. The bonds were not voted and the record before us in this action reflects no execution or carrying out of the official action of the board of trustees taken on or about the 16th of January, 1944. It thus appears that there has been no abolishment of the traditional segregation practices in this district pertaining to pupils of Mexican ancestry through the gamut of elementary school life. . . .

Before considering the specific factual situation in the Santa Ana City Schools it should be noted that the omnibus segregation of children of Mexican ancestry from the rest of the student body in the elementary grades in the schools involved in this case because of language handicaps is not warranted by the record before us. The tests applied to the beginners are shown to have been generally hasty, superficial and not reliable. In some instances separate classification was determined largely by the Latinized or Mexican name of the child. . . .

It has been held that public school authorities may differentiate in the exercise of their reasonable discretion as to the pedagogical methods of instruction to be pursued with different pupils. And foreign language handicaps may be to such a degree in the pupils in elementary schools as to require special treatment in separate classrooms. Such separate allocations, however, can be lawfully made only after credible examination by the appropriate school authority of each child whose capacity to learn is under consideration and the determination of such segregation must be based wholly upon indiscriminate foreign language impediments in the individual child, regardless of his ethnic traits or ancestry.

[9–11] The defendant Santa Ana School District maintains fourteen elementary schools which furnish instruction from kindergarten to the sixth grade, inclusive.

About the year 1920 the Board of Education, for the purpose of allocating pupils to the several schools of the district in proportion to the facilities available at such schools, divided the district into fourteen zones and assigned to the school established in each zone all pupils residing within such zone.

There is no evidence that any discriminatory or other objectionable motive or purpose actuated the School Board in locating or defining such zones.

Subsequently the influx of people of Mexican ancestry in large numbers and their voluntary settlement in certain of the fourteen zones resulted in three of the zones becoming occupied almost entirely by such group of people.

Two zones, that in which the Fremont School is located, and another contiguous area in which the Franklin School is situated, present the only flagrant discriminatory situation shown by the evidence in this case in the Santa Ana City Schools. The Fremont School has 325 so-called Spanish-speaking pupils and no so-called English-speaking pupils. The Franklin School has 237 pupils of which 161 are so-called English-speaking children, and 76 so-called Spanish-speaking children.

The evidence shows that approximately 26 pupils of Mexican descent who reside within the Fremont zone are permitted by the School Board to attend the Franklin School because their families had always gone there. It also appears that there are approximately 35 other pupils not of Mexican descent who live within the Fremont zone who are not required to attend the Fremont School but who are also permitted by the Board of Education to attend the Franklin School.

Sometime in the fall of the year 1944 there arose dissatisfaction by the parents of some of the so-called Spanish-speaking pupils in the Fremont School zone who were not granted the privilege that approximately 26 children also of Mexican descent, enjoyed in attending the Franklin School. Protest was made en masse by such dissatisfied group of parents, which resulted in the Board of Education directing its secretary to send a letter to the parents of all of the so-called Spanish-speaking pupils living in the Fremont zone and attending the Franklin School that beginning September, 1945, the permit to attend Franklin School would be withdrawn and the children would be required to attend the school of the zone in which they were living, viz., the Fremont School.

There could have been no arbitrary discrimination claimed by plaintiffs by the action of the school authorities if the same official course had been applied to the 35 other so-called English-speaking pupils exactly situated as were the approximate 26 children of Mexican lineage, but the record is clear that the requirement of the Board of Education was intended for and directed exclusively to the specified pupils of Mexican ancestry and if carried out becomes operative solely against such group of children. . . .

The natural operation and effect of the Board's official action manifests a clear purpose to arbitrarily discriminate against the pupils of Mexican ancestry and to deny to them the equal protection of the laws. . . .

We conclude by holding that the allegations of the complaint (petition) have been established sufficiently to justify injunctive relief against all defendants, restraining further discriminatory practices against the pupils of Mexican descent in the public schools of defendant school districts.

2. Isabel González Offers a Dismal Report on Mexican Americans, 1947

There are approximately five million people of Mexican origin in the United States. Of these some three and one-half million are American citizens who live principally in the West and Southwest. The other million and a half are non-citizens, and constitute the largest group of non-citizens in the country. These are also concentrated in the Southwest and the West. . . .

Why is it that so many Mexicans in the United States have failed to become citizens? Is it because they do not wish to enjoy the privileges of citizenship; or is it because they do not feel a loyalty to the United States; or is it because, as some say, the Mexican people are too ignorant to meet the qualifications for citizenship?

Could it be . . . that obstacles are placed in the way of Mexicans who seek citizenship; or could it be because the depressed status of the Mexican people as non-citizens bears profits for certain economic interests? Could it be also that the U.S. Government has helped some economic interests in their search for cheap labor to lure Mexicans into this country only to suppress and terrorize them once they are here?

The answer to the first series of questions as to why the Mexicans have failed to become American citizens is an emphatic "*no.*" The Mexicans, like any other group, prefer equality. As to their loyalty, the first World War, as well as the last one provide ample evidence. . . .

There might be more validity to the question of ignorance, since the Mexican people, whether citizen or non-citizen, . . . have remained the "step-children of a nation," especially insofar as educational facilities and opportunities are concerned. . . .

Poverty, segregation, poorly paid teachers and inferior educational facilities are conditions which have not been conducive to the acquiring of an education by the Mexican people, or to even afford them the opportunity to learn a minimum amount of English. . . .

Health

Tuberculosis is the first cause of death among Mexicans precisely because of the economic conditions under which they live. In Los Angeles, a report given by a representative of the Tuberculosis Association in 1945 stated that, of the total number of deaths from this disease, 17 per cent were Mexicans; from diphtheria 33 per cent. . . . In Texas, the Mexican death rate from tuberculosis is seven times that of

As found in Isabel González, *Step-Children of a Nation: The Status of Mexican Americans* (New York: American Committee for the Protection of the Foreign Born, 1947), pp. 3–14.

the Anglo population. . . . This same ratio of T.B. deaths also applies to New Mexico and Arizona. In 1939 the Saginaw Tuberculosis Hospital in Michigan reported that of 100 beds, 25 were occupied by Mexican sugar beet workers. . . .

The statistical picture of infant deaths among the Mexican people from poverty and filth-borne diseases, such as diarrhea and enteritis, is just as appalling. . . . According to statistics furnished by Dr. Lewis C. Robbins, of the San Antonio Health Department, the number of live births among the Mexican and Anglo populations during the five-year period from 1940 to 1944 were about equally divided. . . . However, the number of infant deaths were far from equally divided. The total number of Anglo infant deaths for the five-year period was 781, while the total Mexican infant deaths was 2,295. In Denver, Colorado, the infant death rate in 1940 among Mexican-Americans . . . was three times as high as that of the Anglos.

Housing

Since health and housing are intimately related, it is only natural that we take a look at the housing conditions of the Mexican people. . . .

. . . It is the usual pattern for the Mexicans to live in one section of town . . . because they are not permitted to rent or own property anywhere except in the "Mexican districts". . . . As a rule, the "Mexican district" is devoid of paved streets, sewer lines, and frequently even electric power, gas mains, garbage disposal service and public transportation. . . .

. . . The Mexicans . . . also live in slums in the rural areas. . . . Consider the 70,000 workers, most of them Mexicans . . . , required to harvest the sugar beet and potato crops in Colorado, Montana and Wyoming. From sample studies made of the living conditions, a Government specialist in the field worked out the following conclusions: 60,000 live in houses that have no sanitary sewage disposal; 67,000 have no garbage disposal facilities; 10,000 use ditch water for drinking; 34,000 have a questionable water supply; 33,000 have no bathing facilities. . . . The average "house" consists of two and a half rooms and the average-size family consists of five persons. . . .

Studies conducted by the Children's Bureau in the agricultural areas of Texas give the same picture of squalor, shacks, overcrowding and disease. These are the conditions under which, generally speaking, the Mexican population . . . has to live throughout the Southwest. . . .

Let me repeat that no distinction is made between citizen and non-citizen when it comes to the treatment accorded to the Mexican people. . . . The word "Mexican" is often . . . applied as a term of opprobrium. . . .

Economic Exploitation

History has made economic exploitation by American interests the lot of the Mexican people. . . . Powerful interests . . . have succeeded in keeping the Mexican the most underpaid and most oppressed worker so that they will always have a surplus of cheap labor. This is amply demonstrated by the constant demand for importation of Mexican nationals by the sugar industries and the railways, supported by the powerful lobbies maintained by these interests in Washington.

The demand for importation of Mexican labor is based on the theory that the native American worker would not "work for the wages paid to the Mexicans.". . .

. . . A very small portion of Mexicans are employed in industry, and . . . no matter what field of employment you choose, you still find them in the lowest paid jobs with little or no chance of promotion or up-grading. . . . The wage pattern for Mexicans is the same everywhere, even in the states of Michigan, Wisconsin and Minnesota. . . .

Immigration from Mexico

. . . Most of the Mexicans living in this country entered from 1910 to 1930. . . . For most of these Mexicans, even though they have lived in this country many years, it is very difficult to establish proof of legal residence. Either they have lost their papers or are incapable of wading through all the red tape necessary because of their inadequate command of the English language. . . . For the Mexican immigrant who entered the U.S. prior to 1924, the process . . . is complicated, expensive and loaded with potential danger. . . . It is a recurring nightmare for him every time he has to fill out an application for public assistance, a job, as well as for citizenship. . . . For persons who have been excessively migrant, as most of the agricultural workers have been of necessity, or for those who were brought to the U. S. at an early age . . . , proof may be simply impossible. . . .

Naturalization Difficulties

. . . A large number of quasi-immigrants who remain unnaturalized, even though they have spent their lives in the U. S., and speak perfect English, quite frankly admit that they remain aliens because they have neither the finances nor the courage to tackle the job of proving that they entered legally. Even the older immigrant . . . is likely to settle on the difficulty of proving entry as the main deterrent. . . .

. . . Even the inducement of old age pensions . . . [is] insufficient to entice them into the perilous and costly business of applying for citizenship. Besides, as a number of them rightfully ask, "What added status or privileges can citizenship confer on me, as long as the tenet is held by the dominant group that 'once a Mexican, always a Mexican'?" He knows that the position of the naturalized citizen is little different from that of his alien neighbor.

3. Beatrice W. Griffith Analyzes Eduardo Roybal's Election to the Los Angeles City Council, 1949

The returned serviceman more than anyone else knows that the absence of a political life has seriously retarded the Spanish-speaking population in America. When these American sons of Mexican immigrants returned from a war overseas, they

From Beatrice Griffith, "Viva Roybal—Viva America," *Common Ground* 10, no. 1 (Autumn 1949): 61–70.

came with a new conception of what it means to be American. This became a living dream . . . to get political representation. . . . The lack of voting power among the Spanish-speaking throughout the Southwest, with the exception of New Mexico, has resulted in almost no representation in local communities and states, as well as in Washington. In turn, this has meant the continuation of miserable living conditions, unemployment, social discrimination.

. . . For the first time in their history in Southern California, the Mexican Americans are becoming a potential threat to the electoral status quo and Anglo American leadership in the communities in which they live.

But it is not only the returned veterans who have become aware of the value of the vote. The political apathy was being gradually disturbed before—because of Franklin D. Roosevelt. His name was the spark that started thousands of Spanish-speaking persons to the polls. . . . Political lassitude was overcome by benefits specifically associated with the election of Roosevelt. . . .

Southern California now boasts of four councilmen of Mexican ancestry. The electoral ferment is slowly bringing changes in municipal governments, and the politicians are becoming aware of the social currents penetrating the . . . streets of the Mexican communities. They know that in California the estimated Mexican American voting potential is over a hundred thousand votes—quite a substantial block, especially since it is largely concentrated in the southern part of the state. . . .

II

The story of Ed Roybal's election is a fine example of the new spirit that pervades some Mexican communities. In order to understand what happened in this election, it is necessary to know something about the man Roybal and his vote-getting power—and about the amazing growth of the Community Service Organization that was behind him and helped put him into office.

"Eddie" Roybal has long been a leader. He was a leader in school activities in Roosevelt High School in Los Angeles and also a track star; he knew what the CCC meant to Mexican families, for he attended a CCC camp; he knew the problems the returned veterans face when going to college, for he is a veteran, and he had helped support himself in UCLA . . . ; he knew first-hand the economic problems of many Mexicans in his community. As educational director for the Los Angeles Tuberculosis Association, he knew their health problems. He knew the ugly face of discrimination in employment, for doors had been slammed in his face, too. He knew the value of a democracy; he fought and his brother died to preserve it while fighting overseas. He has the reputation of being scrupulously honest and sincere. . . .

"Eddie" Roybal first ran for councilman from the 9th district, in which approximately 38,000 Spanish-speaking persons live, in 1946. Although he was defeated in that race, which had four other candidates, he polled approximately 3,400 votes, the largest number of votes ever received by a Mexican American in California up to that time. . . .

After his defeat in the first election, Roybal and several energetic leaders of his election committee banded themselves together into the Community Service

Organization (CSO), with about 15 keenly interested Mexican American men and women as a membership nucleus. For, as Roybal later said, "We realized that Americans of Mexican ancestry would achieve representation in public office only with voter education and organization." This was in September 1947.

In the beginning, the group met once a week to plan their program of education and civic activity. . . . The group first met at a public playground, then grew too big and moved to the YMCA; outgrew that and moved into a public school where it holds bi-monthly meetings. The membership now numbers over 800 persons. The interesting thing about the growth of this group is the manner in which they put on a membership drive. Each of the 15 original members went out one day a week to talk to another person about the CSO. . . . The first committees were for Housing, Health, Registration and Membership. . . . Later, other committees, such as Veterans', Civil Rights, Education, Labor Relations, Social Welfare, as well as Social, were set up and became active.

Traffic lights were set up where their absence was a hazard for children in the neighborhood; discrimination in housing was investigated, housing legislation was studied and reported upon, and occasionally evicted families were housed; delinquency of children was studied; money was raised for summer camps . . . ; health drives were put on for immunization and for x-rays to detect tuberculosis; meetings were held to try to promote understanding between labor unions and the community; where citizenship rights were infringed upon, as by police injustice or segregation in public institutions, a committee served . . . to secure legal assistance where warranted; and last, but of utmost importance, people were registered to vote and informed of the issues coming up in the 1948 national elections.

The CSO realized that to bring up the bargaining power of the Mexican community, there must be a "get-out-the-vote" drive. In October 1947 a campaign was started to secure volunteers for deputy registrars. Sixty-three persons volunteered. But classes for registrars were held only during the daytime, effectively eliminating working men and women who could not afford to lose a day's work. After considerable discussion, aided by the Central Labor Council of the AFL, the local office agreed to hold an unprecedented evening class during which the 63 Mexican American registrars, mostly young men and women, were sworn in.

. . . Each of the 63 worked his own precinct. . . . Teams of 2 and 3 members went out every night but Saturday; teams of 8 to 10 would cover a whole precinct; sometimes they would set up tables near churches on Sundays, . . .

Never did they forget that if Los Angeles had a Mexican American councilman there would be voter representation—a strong voice to speak for over a quarter of a million people who were now silent.

When the campaign ended, over 15,000 new Mexican American voters had been registered. They had assumed civic responsibility. . . .

For the most part money came in for Roybal's campaign in small amounts—nickels, dimes, and quarters—from the poor families in the area. The Committee for Roybal grew in size. Dances were given to raise money. . . . Small merchants gave perfumes, shaving sets, and cakes for raffles. The dream grew.

And how the Committee worked, a committee that grew from 20 to about 300. They worked long hours on their jobs during the day, stayed longer hours at night, some going home at four o'clock in the morning after having been out to tack up posters, address or stuff envelopes, or make out precinct lists. . . .

In the primaries there were four candidates from the 9th district. Two Spanish-speaking men had been advised to run by outsiders (with expenses paid) in order to split the Mexican vote, but they were fortunately talked out of it and they in turn backed Roybal. Roybal came in first in the primaries, receiving 12,000 votes—3,000 more than the incumbent councilman. . . . Roybal thus had a plurality of votes but not a majority.

In the final run-off election there were about 300 men and women, boys and girls working day and night for Roybal. . . . The campaign headquarters . . . were set up in a photographic studio next door to a singing teacher over a small department store. Then the Mexican American owner of Paramount Hall . . . donated his place for the larger meetings which frequently had more than a hundred persons gathered for work on the campaign.

For the first time in Los Angeles history, various nationality groups combined their forces to work unanimously for a councilmanic election. . . . Persons of Negro, Jewish, as well as Japanese, Chinese, Italian, Filipino, and Russian ancestry went into their own neighborhoods and plugged Roybal. Their various language newspapers often gave free space to the campaign. . . .

Aside from the election work in the predominantly Mexican American areas of the 9th district, two successful campaigns were made in Anglo neighborhoods. Campaign workers went into Bunker Hill. . . . In this area, . . . Mexican American college students with books under their arms went from door to door. They sat down to tell the tired men and women . . . of the plans . . . they held if Ed Roybal were elected . . . : "We want to improve our conditions; won't you please vote for him?". . .

The other Anglo neighborhood that backed Roybal was Wynverwood Homes, . . . also in the 9th district, but across the river from Bunker Hill. It is a restricted private housing project of about 5,000 persons, to which Roybal as a Mexican American would not be eligible. . . . Two committees were set up for Roybal from this project, and in the May election he carried all five precincts in the area. When he ran for councilman two years ago, he received exactly 14 votes.

Despite the fact that the Central Labor Council, AFL, backed . . . Roybal's opponent, other labor unions supported Roybal; and the national CIO Political Action Committee, the ILGWU [International Ladies' Garment Workers' Union]. . . , as well as several AFL locals made financial contributions. The Steel Workers of the CIO contributed time, personnel, equipment, and money. . . .

Probably no recent councilman has been elected in Los Angeles on a war chest of $5,500, as was Roybal. Usually it costs about $15,000. But Roybal had the cooperation of several hundred people who wanted to see him elected, including a hundred college youngsters of all nationalities who knew what he represented to them. . . .

The careful work of the Community Service Organization in conducting the campaign to get new voters registered and, later, to get out the vote had borne healthy new fruit. The fruit did not grow without hard work, however. . . . Fred Ross was in charge of the precinct organization in the Spanish-speaking areas. One hundred fifty persons were involved in this part of the campaign. . . . One hundred block workers went from door to door to talk and leave literature. Teams of precinct workers went out six nights a week to talk to the voters. . . .

The block work was supplemented by enthusiastic telephone teams of about 85 people spread out all over Los Angeles. . . .

The car pool was a very necessary part of the campaign, too, . . . for a reason singularly "Mexican"—that is, the location of polling places so far away from homes . . . that the great bulk of the voting population would be discouraged from voting. Now "Mexican" voters were . . . brought to the polls. . . .

Election night, after the votes were counted, Roybal had 20,581 votes to Parley Christianson's 12,015.

. . . Spanish-speaking people in Los Angeles had taken their first big step forward, a step forward from discrimination and injustice. . . .

III

. . . There is real and lively interest in Roybal, as well as curiosity about this representative of a people who have hitherto spoken only through their work and songs but who now speak through the vote. In a state where the votes in the electoral college number 25, this election cannot but be significant for the whole nation, for it is an indication of the political interest that has come alive among California's Spanish-speaking Americans—of whom there are nearly a million. It is not impossible that in the not too distant future they will determine state elections by being the balance of power, as they have proved they could be in small communities throughout the southern part of this changing state.

4. Hart Stilwell Warns of the Problem of Undocumented Mexican Immigration, 1949

II

Wetback is a term used in Texas to designate illegally entered Mexicans. Nobody knows how many wetbacks there are in Texas today. Estimates range from 100,000 to 400,000. . . .

. . . According to the statutes it is a crime for a Mexican laborer to enter illegally. Actually, it is not.

. . . The . . . two groups who want the wetbacks in this nation are the men who employ them and the state and federal officials who represent the employer group. . . .

The present flood of immigrants, starting in 1942 and 1943, has been steadily pushing the Texas-Mexican population northward in the state, and on to other states. Even some of the wetbacks who came several years ago . . . have been moving northward. Newly arrived wetbacks replace them just as *they* replaced the resident Texas-Mexicans, those legally entered. . . .

Hart Stilwell, "The Wetback Tide," *Common Ground* 9, no. 4 (Summer 1949): 3–14.

In some parts of Texas, particularly in the rich Lower Rio Grande Valley . . . , wetbacks make up almost all the unskilled labor and a part of the skilled. . . .

. . . The results of this northward movement are noticeable in many parts of Texas, in such cities as Houston, Dallas, Austin, and Fort Worth. In those areas it is the Negro who is beginning to feel the economic pressure. Mexicans are taking his job. . . .

. . . An almost limitless supply of manpower, willing to work at any wage offered, is pushing against this nation's southern border. . . .

. . . The wetback is here illegally and he is frightened. He is afraid he will be deported. . . . The immigrant virtually lives in hiding. He may live in some little hut, or in a corner of a barn, or under some trees. . . .

If the wetback is ill, he seldom makes any effort to get a doctor. The doctor . . . might report him to the officers and the wetback might be deported. . . .

Since he has no legal status, the wetback has no rights. If he is not paid, or if he is short-changed, he makes no complaint. . . . He is the ideal victim for those desiring to victimize him—there are plenty of them.

The lot of the wetbacks who work under contract . . . is perhaps a little better. . . .

The wetback follows the crop across Texas, from south to north. Then he may even move on into another state. Then, with his carefully hoarded savings . . . he may start back to his homeland. And the climax of a situation that . . . comes all too often when this wetback crosses the Rio Grande with his money. For along the south bank of the river a pack of human wolves has assembled to prey on these unfortunates.

Bodies float down the Rio Grande at frequent intervals—always "unidentified" bodies. . . . Few . . . give the incident a second thought. There's another wetback where he came from.

III

. . . Employers along the border, and particularly in the tremendously rich Lower Rio Grande Valley of Texas, set out to force a change in immigration regulations so that Mexican laborers could cross. . . .

. . . They had the staunch backing of their congressmen and senators. . . . The Valley convinced officials in Washington that it could not survive without such labor. It did this in spite of repeated reports of the U.S. Employment Service bureaus in the area to the effect that labor was available. . . . What these Valley employers wanted was what the employer always wants—an expendable surplus of labor. They wanted to be able to set a "prevailing wage," not have it set for them by labor.

The employer group won.

Word went down the line to immigration patrolmen that they were to ignore wetbacks actually at work on farms. They were to pick up only those they encountered on highways, or those who were formally reported to them. . . .

Mexico tried to check the flow, at least insofar as Texas was concerned. Texas was placed on the blacklist for contract labor from Mexico because of discrimination in Texas against Mexicans. In order to have this ban removed, the governor of Texas . . . formed what he called the Good Neighbor Commission. . . .

Many of the gains made by Texas-Mexicans during the war have been lost as a result of the recent influx of wetbacks. And these people have brought new problems. . . . There is little prospect that the Mexican in Texas will ever achieve anything approximating economic and social equality . . . so long as low-priced Mexican labor is desired in this nation. . . .

IV

The problems presented to those sincerely interested in helping these people are tremendous. In the first place, most of the wetbacks are illiterate. In the second place, they . . . accept exploitation and denial of simple rights. . . . Then, . . . they are likely to . . . keep sickness and disease secret to avoid contacts with doctors. . . .

Then these newcomers are quite dark in color. . . .

The Texan . . . is inclined to lump the Mexican Indian with the Negro. This intensifies his race prejudice. . . .

. . . Here are a people who are theoretically free, yet they are definitely not so, and in the opinion of the Anglo-Texan they are incapable of existing as free people. . . .

V

. . . For the present, there seems little hope for them.

5. The American G.I. Forum and the Texas State Federation of Labor Condemn Undocumented Mexican Immigration, 1953

Recommendations on the Bracero Program

First of all, we want to emphasize that we are opposed to the Bracero Program whenever the *braceros* brought into the United States displace American citizen workers. We believe that U. S. citizens, if offered comparable wages to those paid *braceros,* together with the other contract guarantees, will supply a much greater proportion of the agricultural labor needed than at present. But we agree, that where a genuine labor shortage does exist, *braceros* may be used rather than lose the crop.

But we, the public, must learn not to become infected with the panic that grips the farmer the moment his product is ready to harvest. When his cotton is open, it is almost impossible for him to have too many pickers available. He would like to have it picked immediately, and . . . it costs no more to pick it with one thousand workers than it does with twenty. Until his harvest is out of the field, he is apt to consider that he has a labor shortage, regardless of the number of

As found in the American GI Forum of Texas and Texas State Federation of Labor (AFL), *What Price Wetbacks?* Austin, Texas, 1953, pp. 1–59.

hands already in his fields. The same holds true in crops other than cotton. . . . We must remember that his "critical labor shortage" does not necessarily mean that there are not enough laborers to harvest his crop but may only mean that there are not enough to harvest it as cheaply or as quickly as he would like. Even Mexico is concerned with the inaccuracy of our labor requirement estimates. Too many *braceros* are contracted, then left idle after their arrival because the farmer shoved his requirement date up so as to be doubly sure he would have plenty of labor when he wanted it.

We must devise a more accurate method of determining labor requirements, taking into consideration the wages and conditions of employment offered citizen workers. Any employer who offers American citizens only 25 cents an hour is going to be faced with a labor shortage. Farmers should not be permitted to evade the clear intent of the . . . [Bracero Program]with this subterfuge. The *bracero* contract specifies a minimum wage below which the farmer cannot go, but it never was intended that this "minimum wage" should become the "prevailing wage." Unfortunately, that is the way it has worked. And now even this "minimum wage" is under attack by farm groups as being too high. The method of determining the prevailing wage must be strengthened with a firm guarantee that employees will be represented at the hearings where they are determined.

The letter of the law should be enforced. Labor shortages must not be certified unless domestic labor has been given a genuine offer of employment under terms, wages and conditions of employment at least equal to those offered foreign workers. If the offer concerns wages only, then the wage should be increased a reasonable amount to compensate for the additional guarantees in the *bracero* contract.

A primary factor in a successful Bracero Program is the personnel and facilities available to enforce compliance with contract provisions. . . . At the time of the survey the United States Employment Service was sadly understaffed with regard to the number of compliance officers it had in the field. In the Eagle Pass area, for example, John James had 40 counties to cover the year round with the help only of an office secretary and another fieldman who was available to him only during the peak harvest period. Since that time, the limited staff of compliance men has been further reduced . . . and the offices at San Benito and Laredo have been closed.

. . . It is recognized that, in certain areas, a genuine labor shortage may exist and that it may be necessary to continue to contract alien labor in limited numbers to fill these shortages. If as much effort and money were expended to attract domestic labor as has been devoted to obtaining alien labor, we feel sure that our farm labor requirements would be filled—or nearly so, at any rate—by American citizens. The American people, with a great stake in both the economic and physical health of the nation, should demand that the national policy work toward that end.

The Migrant Worker

Thousands of words have been written and spoken and thousands of dollars have been spent in spreading the myth that the American citizens who migrate in search of work do so because they are by nature nomads, gypsies with itching feet who travel for the sheer love of traveling. With a patronizing air, many a self-styled expert on American citizens of Mexican extraction (and many who may have just finished paying off a wetback crew at the rate of 25 cents an hour) has explained that "these Mexicans (meaning American citizens of Mexican extraction) are too lazy to do field work" or that "all they want to do is travel" or that "you can't trust them to do a job right."

What he really means is that American citizens—living in the U.S., paying taxes in the U.S., raising their families in the U.S.—can't work for 25 cents an hour and manage to survive. The wetbacks can—and do. So the wetbacks move in, and the American citizens are forced to look elsewhere for a living. They take to the road, following the cotton crop through Texas or going to the better paying jobs in farm or industrial work in northern and western states.

Does it stand to reason that Juan Garcia, a property-owning, tax-paying citizen of Hidalgo County, Texas, prefers to pack his family into a truck each year and travel from 1000 to 1500 miles in order to work for 70 or 80 cents an hour if work at comparable wages were available in Hidalgo County?

Is it wanderlust that sends the same worker back to the same area and the same farm in California or Colorado or Wyoming or Illinois each year? Is it a desire to see the country which results in workers following the same route up and back year after year?

Is it laziness that forces these workers to do the same type of work picking or chopping cotton in the Gulf Coast Area, Central Texas, Lubbock, the Panhandle or the same exhausting work in the beet fields of the Midwest—the same work at the same long hours which the Lower Valley farmer says the same workers will not do in the Valley because they are "lazy"? This myth which has been fabricated in the Valley and which the press . . . promulgates and promotes in its editorials is an unmitigated lie and a shameful defamation of a large group of American citizens of Mexican descent who built the railroads, laid the basis for our agricultural development, and have done every other type of backbreaking toil in the history of Texas and the Southwest.

The answer to all these questions is a flat "no." The records show that most of the 100,000 or more Texas citizens who migrate each year for agricultural work return year after year to the same jobs for the same employers. They are searching for a form of temporary seasonal security, and the relatively higher wages to be found in the other areas justify their departure from the 25-cent wage area along the border.

The Texan of Mexican descent no more enjoys the numerous difficulties and domestic problems entailed in the annual migration than would any other American citizen. The children must be withdrawn from school weeks before the school year ends. The house must be boarded up with the windows and doors nailed tight. . . . Domestic animals must be sold or pastured out with some neighbor. . . . Clothing, personal items and equipment to be carried must be carefully rationed— just enough clothes to get by with, enough kitchen utensils to handle the cooking, as little of everything as is possible. After all, the two-ton-stake-body truck has to carry 25 passengers as well as the equipment.

Utilities have to be disconnected. The post office must be notified either to hold mail or to forward it to the temporary address in the north. Milk deliveries must be discontinued. The health of the women and children must be watched carefully for fear that illness in the family at the time scheduled for departure might upset plans.

Then, at the end of the season, the same petty details must be attended to for the return trip to Texas where the children will enter school several weeks or months late.

Nobody knows how many Texas citizens migrate each year, following the seasonal crops. Official records of the Texas Bureau of Labor Statistics and the Texas Employment Commission show that at least 59,033 farm workers were recruited for out-of-state work in 1950, while 65,666 followed the out-of-state crop trails in 1951 and 51,329 in 1952. But those reports cover only workers legally recruited for out-of-state work and do not include the thousands of workers traveling only within Texas or who go out of the state on their own. Conservative estimates place the number of farm workers moving within the state at not less than 100,000 and probably considerably higher.

It is not the intention of this report to cover in detail the lives, the problems, the difficulties, the plight of the migrant American citizen. It is our intention to point up the simple fact that these migrant citizens of Mexican descent are in the fullest sense of the word "displaced persons"—displaced by the hordes of illegal aliens pouring in from across the Rio Grande to work at starvation wages.

The plight and the problem of the migrant citizen have been fully covered—by the Report of the President's Commission on Migratory Labor in 1951, by innumerable magazine articles and other reports. . . . In the light of the great volume of information, statistics and opinion contained in these numerous reports, there is no disputing the fact that the migrants are a national problem or the fact that they are a problem almost solely as a result of the wetback invasion.

Over 80 per cent of the present-day national migratory farm labor force is made up of American citizens of Mexican descent. . . . Many are third and fourth generation Americans. . . . Generally they are residents of agricultural communities and are skilled agricultural workers. Most are property-owners, either owning their homes or small acreages. . . . Most own cars or trucks. In their home communities, they are considered solvent citizens, devout, interested in community projects—first-class citizens in every respect.

Is it logical to adopt the reasoning of the wetback employers that these first-class citizens, of their own choice and desire, lower themselves to the second-class rank they are given as migrant workers? . . .

These migrant workers are the immediate victims of the wetback invasion. They felt the effects first when they were displaced from their jobs and their homes. But the effects in the long run, will go far beyond this group, hitting all levels of the population in the border country first, then spreading the virus to other sections—unless the wetback tide is halted.

The displaced persons of South Texas are the first victims—but not the last.

ESSAYS

The various civil rights organizations Mexican Americans established in the Southwest and Midwest reflected their growing political participation in order to achieve economic, social, and civic improvements. Organizations such as the American G.I.

Forum, the Mexican American Political Association (MAPA), and the Political Association of Spanish-Speaking Organizations (PASSO) aided the cause by launching intensive voter registration drives and placing pressure at the party level to get Mexican Americans into political office as either appointed or elected officials. The Mexican Americans' politics for social change had a radical dimension, according to Mario T. García, professor of history at the University of California, Santa Barbara. In his essay, he outlines the origins of ANMA and the organization's numerous activities on the behalf of Mexican Americans.

Postwar *Braceros* and undocumented Mexican laborers rapidly increased in numbers, peaking in the middle 1950s. These workers proved a bonanza for employers, who preferred them over local labor. This widespread practice produced underemployment, unemployment, and low wages for Mexican American farmworkers. In her essay, Kitty Calavita, associate professor of sociology at the University of California, Irvine, traces the intricate process by which documented and undocumented workers were brought from Mexico to the United States and then sent back again under the auspices of Operation Wetback. She argues that this was done through the collusion of government officials and the cooperation of farmer-growers.

The Asociación Nacional México-Americana (ANMA)

MARIO T. GARCÍA

Despite the onset of the cold war and the beginning of McCarthyism by the late 1940s, Mexican-American radicals . . . did not remain dormant. . . . Mexican-American labor leaders in progressive unions . . . successfully continued to organize among Mexican-American workers . . . during the 1940s and 1950s. Yet trade-union organization was not sufficient to deal with the varied problems and issues relevant to the majority of Mexican-American working people. A political movement . . . was likewise needed. Consequently, the late 1940s and early 1950s . . . witnessed the emergence of a second major Mexican-American left leadership and organization: the Asociación Nacional México-Americana (ANMA). . . . ANMA stressed Popular Front strategies and a multi-issue program on such issues as the peace movement, workers' struggles, the plight of Mexican undocumented workers, housing needs in the Southwest, education, Mexican-American political representation, youth work, the promotion of Mexican-American culture, and police brutality.

The Formation of ANMA

ANMA was mostly organized by [the militant union] Mine Mill through the union's national headquarters in Denver. . . . In New Mexico, Arizona, as well as in El Paso, Mine Mill consisted almost exclusively of Mexican Americans and Mexi-

From Mario T. García, "Mexican American Radicals and the Cold War: The Asociación Nacional México-Americana (ANMA)," in *Mexican Americans: Leadership, Ideology and Identity, 1930–1960,* Yale University Press, Copyright © 1989, pp. 199–227. Reprinted by permission of Yale University Press.

can nationals. By the early 1950s the three El Paso locals contained more than 2,000 workers, almost all of Mexican descent and led by Mexican-American officers. With such an important Mexican-American membership, the union believed that ANMA could function as its political arm in the Mexican-American communities of the Southwest.

The call for the establishment of ANMA initially originated from Mine Mill members along with other Mexican-American CIO leaders who had participated in the campaign of the Independent Progressive Party (IPP) to elect former Vice President Henry Wallace as president of the United States in 1948. . . . At a regional conference of these chapters in El Paso during the fall of 1948, the participating delegates agreed to meet again in a second conference with the intent of forming "a permanent national organization to defend the rights of the Mexican-American people." The delegates further stressed: "The time has come when the Mexican people *must* and *can* form a strong, militant national organization . . . through which the entire Mexican population and its friends and allies can fight for first-class citizenship."

About fifty delegates answered the call and organized ANMA at a two-day meeting in Phoenix on February 12 and 13, 1949. They came . . . from the sugar-beet fields of Colorado, from the factories of Los Angeles, from the mines of New Mexico, and from the cotton fields of Arizona and Texas. . . . Most of the delegates . . . came from southwestern locals of Mine Mill although some represented other militant CIO unions such as the furniture workers and the electrical workers. . . . Any person or organization interested in the progress of "el pueblo mexicano" could join ANMA regardless of citizenship, nationality, color, religion, or political affiliation. . . . ANMA did not insist on U.S. citizenship for membership. . . . ANMA projected itself as a broad civil rights organization that could be accepted in the barrios as a Mexican-American entity. . . .

The objective conditions for the founding of ANMA centered on the particular plight of Mexican Americans and Mexican nationals during the postwar period. Despite certain economic improvements during the war and gains in political and civil rights, Mexicans in the United States still represented, according to ANMA, second-class citizens. ANMA recognized that racial minorities such as Mexicans and blacks received "special treatment" in the form of greater economic insecurities, lower wages, inferior education, and suffered more than whites from recent rollbacks of New Deal welfare services. "What is even worse," ANMA proclaimed, the "Mexican people are objects of an accelerated program of discrimination, deportations, physical assaults, police brutality, and, at times, murder." In addition, Mexicans in the United States continued to suffer cultural discrimination and the stereotyping of Mexicans. . . . With such conditions plus the ascendance of political right-wing reaction in the country, ANMA concluded that the time was ripe for organizing all Mexicans into a national organization for ethnic self-defense. . . .

From Phoenix, ANMA state conventions were held in Colorado, New Mexico, Arizona, and California. . . .

Local chapters of ANMA sprang up throughout the Southwest. . . . Total membership in ANMA is difficult to gauge. In 1950 it reported a membership of 4,000 with more than thirty locals. . . .

Having organized at the state and local levels, the first national convention of ANMA took place on October 14 and 15, 1950, in Los Angeles with eighty delegates and observers representing thirty-five locals in six states. . . . In its General Principles, ANMA committed itself to five basic goals: (1) the political unification of Mexicans in the United States, (2) the achievement of basic democratic rights for all Americans, (3) the development of ethnic and political awareness, (4) the renewal of familiar ties with Mexicans south of the border, and (5) the operation of ANMA on the basis of democratic practices. Resolutions adopted at the national convention reflected the persistent problems facing Mexican Americans. . . . They included those on public housing, civil rights, mass deportations, constitutional rights, women, and cooperation with trade unions.

. . . Mexican-American members or sympathizers of the CP [Communist party] or those who had gravitated to a more radical position did play a role in the organization and guidance of ANMA. These individuals . . . were Mexican Americans who had inherited an organic Mexican-American radical tradition and who . . . had found in the Communist party a militant and supportive ally in the struggle to achieve democratic rights. . . .

Class, Race, and Culture

Ideologically, ANMA . . . voiced radical views within the context of Mexican-American politics. Its interpretation of Mexican-American history . . . for example, had a different emphasis. . . . Whereas LULAC . . . concentrated on the Hispanic foundation of the Southwest to convince Anglos of the integral role played by people of Spanish-Mexican descent in U.S. history, ANMA . . . focused on the conquest of northern Mexico by the United States in the mid-nineteenth century. For ANMA, Mexican-American history had commenced in violence, conquest, and the subjugation of the resident Mexican population. . . . Because Mexicans had been annexed through force rather than voluntarily entering the United States, in the Southwest they possessed a culture and tradition quite different from the rest of the country. These differences had been recognized by the Treaty of Guadalupe Hidalgo, which ended the Mexican War in 1848 and had promised to protect the Mexican's distinct culture and heritage. These guarantees, however, had not been fulfilled and arriving Anglos had abused the Mexican's culture, language, political rights, and economic holdings. Consequently, since 1848 Mexican Americans . . . had been treated as an underclass of American citizens. Such a legacy . . . continued into the twentieth century, when southwestern economic concerns imported and exploited thousands of Mexican immigrant workers. Important as cheap labor during boom times, Mexicans also served as surplus labor and hence . . . faced unemployment, deportations, and forced repatriations. This historical experience . . . had created much adversity for Mexicans in the United States.

. . . ANMA also emphasized unity through the fundamental working class nature of the Mexican population in the United States. Ninety-five percent of Mexicans north of the border were workers, and ANMA believed this condition to be not only objective grounds for organization but proof of the inescapable bonds between Mexican Americans and the union movement. . . . If the unions had recognized that unorganized Mexicans only weakened the labor movement, so too had

Mexican workers come to realize that if the unions were destroyed they would also suffer and lose their hard-fought gains. Noting that the aspirations and needs of Mexicans in the United States were fundamentally identical with those of the trade unions and stressing the basic working-class character of Mexican Americans, the first ANMA national convention resolved: "That . . . all members and leaders of ANMA not . . . lose a single opportunity to cement relations with the trade unions on the basis of mutual respect and solidarity." ANMA did not proclaim . . . a revolutionary class position calling on Mexican workers to overthrow capitalism and erect a socialist society. One could have been indicted and sent to prison for holding such views during the McCarthy period. Yet ANMA did bring attention to the working-class condition of most Mexicans, their class interests with other workers, and the exploitative nature of the class system in the Southwest. . . .

. . . ANMA . . . also paid attention to the realities of race and culture. Mexicans were exploited as cheap labor, but they were also oppressed as a distinct ethnic racial community. ANMA . . . did make it clear that Mexicans along with blacks faced double oppression. In a 1952 editorial, *Progreso,* ANMA's newspaper, commented that the Mexicans' participation in the class struggle had to directly contend with ethnic/racial segregation and discrimination. Such conditions aided in reducing the Mexicans' standard of living and forced them to accept hard, dirty, and cheap jobs. Besides suffering abuse in employment, Mexicans likewise faced discrimination in housing, education, political representation, public services, and other areas. Racism, according to ANMA, had become so pervasive and destructive that some Mexican Americans believed themselves inferior to Anglos and attempted to pass as "Spanish Americans.". . . However, ANMA observed that few Mexicans, regardless of skin pigmentation and class background, successfully escaped prejudice. . . . An exploitative class structure fueled racial/ethnic prejudice and discrimination. ANMA saw racism directly linked to a white ruling class and did not associate all whites, especially workers, with the perpetuation of such a system. ANMA would struggle alongside Anglo workers who also desired to eliminate racism. All workers would benefit from the elimination of an underclass of cheap labor. To ANMA both class and race had to be considered in developing a strategy for the liberation of Mexicans in the United States.

ANMA complemented its views on race and class by its discussion of culture. Although Mexicans in the Southwest had been deprived of an autonomous cultural development, they still possessed a distinct culture which . . . could also be an objective basis for political organization. . . . It acknowledged the Mexicans' distinct cultural heritage in the Southwest and praised efforts at cultural resistance. "This struggle is a cultural struggle," read a resolution on cultural freedom adopted by ANMA's second national convention in El Paso in 1952, "not only on behalf of Mexican-American people but on behalf of building a cultural democracy, our culture and our customs." Yet Mexican-American culture had come under a more aggressive attack in the early 1950s. The cold war, McCarthyism, and the "Great Fear" had resulted not only in violations of civil liberties and constitutional protections, unjust arrests, and deportations of so-called subversives, but also in an irrational apprehension over anything considered un-American. Consequently, Mexican Americans and Mexican nationals faced heightened cultural prejudice.

ANMA countered this cultural attack on Mexicans in the United States by calling on Mexican Americans to rediscover their cultural roots both in the Southwest and in Mexico. . . . Only by being proud of their culture and by promoting it could Mexican Americans enrich the cultural life of the United States and achieve mutual respect with other ethnic groups. . . .

. . . While ANMA endorsed ethnic and cultural nationalism, it insisted . . . that its basic aims were reformist in nature and consisted of the full attainment by Mexican Americans of democratic rights as provided in the U.S. Constitution. The goal was integration, although along pluralist rather than melting pot lines. . . .

In fighting for the rights of Mexican Americans, ANMA also believed it important to encourage an internationalist consciousness. This was of particularly keen concern with respect to Mexico and the rest of Latin America. . . . Discounting specific differences, ANMA proposed the interrelationship between Mexican Americans and Latin Americans to be crucial and that the struggle for Mexican-American liberation was linked with that of Latin America. . . . Calling on Mexican Americans to shun the idea of a frontier between themselves and Mexico, ANMA proclaimed its defense of the rights of Mexican nationals in the United States and promised to maintain and develop ties of solidarity with Mexicans south of the Rio Grande in their struggles and in adherence to a common history, culture, and tradition. . . .

ANMA advocated a domestic united front in addition to international solidarity. It . . . called for alliance with other Mexican-American organizations subscribing to similar general principles and goals. . . . ANMA . . . aspired to a united front with other oppressed peoples within the country, in particular blacks and Jews. Mexican Americans represented only one of several minorities, who in some cases were worse off than Mexicans. The struggle and gains of one aided those of the rest. . . . ANMA believed such a coalition . . . indispensable to the Mexican-American cause.

Political Praxis: The Peace Movement

. . . Responding to the cold war and U.S. military intervention in Korea, ANMA placed a high priority on supporting the peace movement in the country and throughout the world. This was no easy task due to the hostile and accusatory attitude of McCarthyism. . . . Despite these intimidations, ANMA encouraged other Mexican Americans to stand up for peace in Korea and for the easing of tensions between the United States and the Soviet Union. In 1950, for example, ANMA along with other organizations in Los Angeles participated in a two-day weekend mobilization to circulate the Stockholm Peace Appeal calling for an end to the cold war. . . .

. . . ANMA tied domestic reforms for Mexican Americans with the issue of world peace. "Progress cannot be made in a state of war," it declared. "For the well-being and progress of the people we must have peace." Encouraged by the community's response to the peace movement, . . . in 1950 . . . more than 20,000 Mexican Americans had signed the Stockholm petition. In addition, various ANMA locals invited peace advocates to address the membership. One speaker who had participated in the 1951 Warsaw Peace Conference further encouraged

ANMA's involvement in the peace movement. . . . Peace also included disarmament and an end to the production of atomic bombs. "They forget to tell you that an Atomic Bomb is not a national catastrophe like an earthquake," Professor Philip Morrison told an ANMA sponsored meeting on the nuclear threat. "Its fall can be predicted. It can be stopped, and furtherance of the peace movement is the rational system for defense of the A-Bomb." And in San Francisco the ANMA local held a fund-raiser to assist one of its members . . . to attend the Hemispheric Peace Conference in Mexico City.

The U.S. intervention in the Korean conflict in 1950 only accelerated ANMA's commitment to the peace process. . . . ANMA members questioned the necessity for U.S. involvement in Korea and protested the loss of Mexican-American lives. . . . At the second national convention in El Paso, the delegates approved a resolution urging the United Nations and President Truman to exert their influence for a quick settlement of the Korean conflict and for the calling of a conference of the major world powers "for the purpose of settling their basic differences through negotiations and reconciliations, thus laying the foundations for a lasting peace throughout the world." ANMA's Denver local also organized a Peace Committee. . . . Besides attending national peace conferences such as the Chicago Peace Congress in 1951, the Peace Committee publicized the human losses being sustained by the Mexican-American communities in Korea. . . . The Peace Committee . . . observed that in Colorado Mexican Americans represented 10% of the state's population but 28% of the casualties in Korea from that state. In Arizona Mexican Americans were 20% of the population and 44% of the casualties. In New Mexico the ratio of population to casualties was 49 to 56% and in Texas it was 17 to 30%. The Peace Committee urged Mexican Americans to protest such an unfair burden carried by Mexican Americans in the war by writing to President Truman. "Tell him that the Mexican-American people of the United States want peace. We want our boys home."

Not only was the war costing the lives of hundreds of Mexican Americans, but it was also affecting the well-being and rights of the Mexican-American community. . . . Attacks on Mexicans had increased since the commencement of the war in the form of police brutality, racial discrimination, the victimization of Mexicans through the application of the so-called anti-subversive Smith and McCarran acts, the loss of economic benefits through the use of the antilabor Taft-Hartley Act, and the loss of social services for the poor, the aged, and the young. . . . Consequently, ANMA believed that the war had to receive priority attention since it affected and magnified so many other issues. . . .

Labor, Undocumented Workers, and McCarthyism

With its emphasis on working-class solidarity, ANMA supported the particular struggles of Mexican-American workers in the Southwest. It endorsed and publicized the gallant efforts of Local 890 of the Mine Mill workers at Bayard, New Mexico, in its fifteen-month strike for improved wages and working conditions. The Bayard strike . . . would be immortalized in the classic film *Salt of the Earth*. The ANMA local in Denver provided money and donations of clothes to the strikers and their families and especially lauded the courageous role of the Mexican-

American women who walked the picket lines after their husbands had been barred from doing so. . . .

ANMA also brought attention to the plight of migrant workers in southwestern fields and supported a $1 an hour minimum wage for agricultural workers as well as a guaranteed annual wage. At the El Paso national convention ANMA endorsed support for migrant agricultural workers and their right to join unions. ANMA observed the magnitude of the migrant labor problem by declaring that it affected millions of workers on both sides of the border. . . . As part of its reaction to migrant labor, ANMA protested the Bracero Program under which Mexico supplied field hands to U.S. agriculture. ANMA considered the program to be a boom to agribusiness at the expense of both braceros and domestic farm workers. . . . ANMA advocated a suspension of the program and the involvement of both Mexican and U.S. labor unions in the drafting of an alternative solution to the need for agricultural labor in the Southwest. In addition, ANMA worked to secure better jobs and wages for other Mexican-American workers to protect them from employment discrimination and to secure assistance for them in time of need. . . . Finally, as part of its labor program, ANMA through its association with CIO unions encouraged unionism among Mexican Americans.

. . . ANMA protested the mass deportation of Mexican immigrant workers, especially the undocumented, that climaxed in Operation Wetback in 1954, when over a million were deported. Between 1951 and 1954 more than 3 million Mexicans were expelled from the United States. Moreover, with the passage of new and harsher antialien and antisubversive laws such as McCarran-Walter all Mexicans, whether Mexican national or U.S. citizen, became subject to harassment by the FBI or Immigration Service for their political views and activities. . . . Praising migrant labor from Mexico for extracting the wealth of the Southwest, ANMA contrasted their contribution with the continued poverty, irregular employment, and discrimination faced by these workers. . . . To bring attention to the maltreatment of Mexican immigrant workers, ANMA in 1951 unsuccessfully appealed to the United Nations Commission on Human Rights to investigate the status of Mexican agricultural workers in the United States. . . .

At the local level, ANMA chapters carried out actions designed to protect individual Mexican nationals apprehended for deportation. In Los Angeles in 1951 ANMA opposed deportation orders pending against certain Mexican nationals. In San Jose, ANMA Local 25 collected contributions for Mexican nationals ordered deported from California, and in San Francisco the ANMA chapter committed its program of action to protesting mass deportations. ANMA locals likewise organized mass meetings such as one . . . on March 13, 1952, in Los Angeles that featured Abner Green of the American Committee for the Protection of the Foreign Born and at which ANMA hosted as guests of honor sixteen Mexican nationals threatened with deportation.

ANMA linked its protest against mass deportations with its denunciation of intimidating antialien and antisubversive laws passed during the hysteria of the cold war and McCarthyism. Such legislation under the guise of controlling "subversives" in fact aimed to destroy legitimate organizations such as labor unions working for people's rights. Anyone who protested discrimination, police brutality, or injustice on the part of governmental agencies could now be accused of being a

Communist and prosecuted and even deported under the McCarran Act, passed by Congress in 1950, and the 1952 McCarran-Walter Act. ANMA declared both laws to be direct violations of the Bill of Rights. It further objected to the enactment of local red-baiting legislation that violated constitutional rights. . . .

ANMA's vehement reaction to McCarthyism also resulted from the political harassment experienced by its own members or supporters. . . . In early 1952 J. Edgar Hoover requested his special agent in charge in Los Angeles to determine whether ANMA members were native-born U.S. citizens, naturalized citizens, resident aliens, or undocumented aliens. At the same time, the Immigration and Naturalization Service requested from Hoover information that the FBI might possess on ANMA. . . . Investigation at times led to arrests. Immigration officials apprehended and held for deportation Adolfo Hernández, an ANMA member in San Jose, and accused him of belonging to a Communist organization through his membership in ANMA. . . . A few months later ANMA again protested, this time in Chicago the arrest and deportation of Refugio Ramón Martínez, an ANMA supporter and leader in the United Packinghouse Workers. . . . ANMA accused the Immigration Service of deporting Martínez because he had joined the Communist party for a brief period in the 1930s and more important[ly] because he had helped organize other Mexican workers.

What all this meant—the deportations and harassment of Mexican Americans—ANMA concluded, was that both employers and their government supporters would not tolerate efforts by Mexicans in the United States to improve their conditions. . . . Only unity could prevent such injustices and ANMA proposed itself as the basis for that unity and protection.

Cultural Politics

Culturally, ANMA pursued a twofold strategy. On the one hand, it attacked prevalent stereotypes of Mexicans especially in the mass media. . . . In its 1952 platform, ANMA specifically announced a national campaign against the perversions of Mexican culture through the press, literature, radio, and television and called particular attention to the Judy Canova radio show, which depicted Mexicans through the character of "Pedro" as lazy and stupid. . . .

To protest comedy at the expense of Mexicans, ANMA along with certain allied labor unions initiated a national economic boycott of the Colgate Palmolive Peet Company, the sponsor of Canova. . . . To ensure a successful boycott, ANMA pledged several additional steps. A nationwide petition addressed to the Colgate Palmolive Peet Company would demand the immediate removal of all slanderous references to Mexicans on the Canova show. . . . Appeals for assistance on the boycott would be made to unions, black organizations, and any other groups which would provide financial and moral support. ANMA chapters would be in charge of local boycott activities. Two months later, *Progreso* reported that owing to the boycott and protests, the Colgate Company had dropped its sponsorship of the Canova show and that NBC had canceled the program. . . . To prevent such future stereotyping in the media, ANMA adopted a resolution urging the employment of Mexican Americans in motion pictures, radio, and television. . . .

... ANMA actively promoted Mexican-American cultural traditions. ...
ANMA stressed the importance of culture in building a political movement for the
liberation of Mexican Americans. Yet ... ANMA leaders favored cultural and ethnic pluralism within the United States. "ANMA works to keep our rich Mexican
culture and language and history and seeks to bring before other American groups
a knowledge of our heritage" ANMA proclaimed in its constitution. "By bringing a
knowledge of each other's culture and problems we build a mutual respect so essential for building a strong democratic America." The flowering of Mexican-
American culture would enrich the cultural life of the country. ...

And to present a more positive image of Mexicans and to promote ethnic
pride, ANMA sponsored a variety of cultural programs. Through its national director of culture it encouraged locals to organize functions which would tap the talents of Mexican Americans. ...

As part of its program of cultural presentation and cultural revitalization,
ANMA stressed the maintenance of the Spanish language. Spanish expressed the
culture of Mexican Americans and ANMA believed that no Mexican should be denied the use of his or her native language whether in school, on the job, or in any
public institution. ... ANMA also encouraged more Spanish-language newspapers
in the United States. At the same time, ANMA acknowledged that bilingualism and
biculturalism should also be fostered to accommodate the heterogeneity of the
Mexican population in the United States, which resulted from cultural erosion and
language discrimination faced by Mexican Americans. ... In addition, certain
ANMA local provided language classes in both languages, as did the ANMA-
operated Lázaro Cárdenas School in Chicago.

Women in ANMA

... ANMA ... supported leadership roles for women. At the founding convention
of the Southern California regional of ANMA in 1949 the delegates accepted a resolution on women which stressed that ... because they were natural and courageous organizers, because history had proved that no "righteous causes can be won
without full support of women," and because women had played a tremendous role
already in the Mexican-American struggle for full democracy, ANMA resolved
to integrate women at all levels in addition to establishing a specific women's
committee. ...

... At the level of leadership, despite some opposition, women visibly exerted
themselves. Isabel Gonzáles, for example, was elected the first vice president. ...
Other women in national offices included Xochitl Ruiz, selected as first secretary-
general of ANMA, and Florencia Luna as the first secretary treasurer, and Celia
Rodríguez elected as vice president of ANMA in 1952. At the local level, women
served in a variety of positions. In 1951 the Los Angeles board of directors of
ANMA included Grace Monteñez as vice president, Mary Jasso as building committee chair, Amelia Camacho as public relations chair, and Virginia Montoya as
social chair. Julia Luna Mount, in addition, contributed as secretary-treasurer of
the Southern California regional. Finally, at least two women served as presidents
of local ANMA chapters: Carmen Contreras, an officer in the Longshoremen's
Union in San Francisco, and Dolores Heredia in Chicago. ...

Police Brutality

A final but critical aspect of ANMA's reform-oriented program concerned the sensitive issue of police brutality against Mexican Americans. The dislocating pressures of the postwar period only exacerbated a history of poor police-community relations in the Southwest. At the founding convention of the Los Angeles chapter of ANMA, delegates called attention to this problem. One resolution that was adopted pledged ANMA "to seek discipline of police responsible for acts of brutality." . . . Some ANMA locals originated as a reaction to cases of police brutality. . . . In the Rock Hill community of Los Angeles County, a group of youths established an ANMA youth club as a result of police threats. . . .

In a number of cases, ANMA objected to police overreaction in dealing with Mexican Americans. This seemed to be particularly true in the Los Angeles area. In October 1949, ANMA supported nine Mexican-American youngsters arrested for first degree murder in Santa Ana. . . . ANMA further accused the police of brutality in making the arrests and charged officials including the presiding judge with denying the suspects their civil rights. . . .

Building a United Front

. . . ANMA favored a united front not only with labor unions but with other liberal and left forces as well. Both Alfredo Montoya as president of ANMA along with Mauricio Terrazas representing Southern California participated in the short-lived American Council of Spanish-Speaking People headed by Dr. George I. Sánchez of the University of Texas. ANMA also had some ties with the Community Service Organization (CSO) in the Los Angeles area, which concentrated on voter registration and civil rights. . . . While ANMA's united front with such Mexican-American civic organizations was limited, its contacts with left-oriented non-Mexican-American groups was not. Progressive . . . associations supporting ANMA included the Independent Progressive Party, the Los Angeles Committee for the Protection of the Foreign Born, the Civil Rights Congress, and the Jewish Fraternal Order of the International Workers Order. Finally, ANMA in its bid for a united front placed major emphasis on unity with progressive Afro Americans. "The Mexican People in their struggles for first-class citizenship," ANMA officer Virginia Ruiz observed in 1951, "are becoming more and more aware that the only way to win this fight is to have the closest unity with our strongest ally, the Negro people." Ruiz pledged that ANMA would jointly struggle with Afro Americans against job discrimination as well as segregation in housing and education. Political unity with blacks, however, could be fostered by cultural relations as well. Hence in Los Angeles ANMA sponsored the first Mexican-American observance of Negro History Week in February 1950. One year later, *Progreso* affirmed that it was important for Mexican Americans to participate in Negro History Week "because it affords an opportunity to become more conscious of the contributions that the Negro people have made in the fight against oppression of all minorities throughout our history." Yet ANMA further recognized that race alone did not constitute the key foundation for a progressive united front. That foundation had to be based on a full commitment to democracy and social justice regardless of one's racial or ethnic background. To ANMA, one's politics in the end was more important than one's race.

The Cold War and Political Persecution

. . . ANMA faced much harassment and political persecution as a so-called red-front group.

. . . ANMA faced investigation and harassment by the FBI. . . . The agency . . . believed ANMA to be linked with if not controlled by the Communist party. . . . Available FBI documents reveal a number of agency informants within ANMA. . . . "I have joined an organization called the ANMA," one Mexican American wrote to the FBI in 1949, "which is taking a very strong hold in New Mexico, Colorado, California and Texas, and all it is, is a Communist organization, which is operating out of Mexico. It might be a good idea for you to investigate. I will be more than glad to help you in any way that I can." Another ANMA member appeared at the FBI office in San Francisco and agreed to become an informant because ANMA had gained the reputation of being Communist controlled. Besides reporting on ANMA activities, the informants provided the FBI with membership lists and background information on officers and members.

The FBI carried out an extensive surveillance of ANMA with the intent of making a case that ANMA possessed a direct link to the Communist party and hence should be declared a subversive organization. FBI agents charged . . . that many of ANMA's members had either been recruited to the CP or were Communist sympathizers. . . . If not card-carrying Communists, some ANMA members were tagged as "fellow-travellers.". . . Other ANMA members were charged with being Communist sympathizers if they spoke at rallies that included CP participants or were sponsored by the Communist party or if they associated with other groups declared to be "subversive" by the attorney general.

. . . The FBI additionally claimed that ideologically ANMA and the CP were one. After the founding of ANMA in 1949, the FBI reported: "Formation of this organization and its activities implement the Communist Party line as set forth in resolutions adopted at the National Convention of the CP 8-3-48 concerning work among the Mexican people." In particular, the FBI compared the CP resolutions on Mexicans in the United States with those of ANMA and concluded that owing to similarities ANMA had to be a Communist organization. . . . Hence it examined the two organizations' policies on police brutality and because both advocated greater community protection and an end to police violence against Mexicans, the FBI suggested a direct tie between the CP and ANMA. Guilt by ideological association was likewise extracted from comparison of stands on other issues such as racial discrimination, mass deportations, Mexican culture, the peace movement, the labor movement, the history of the Southwest, and black-Mexican unity. . . . On these as well as other issues the FBI in its extensive surveillance defined ANMA as a Communist front.

Convinced of this relationship, J. Edgar Hoover in 1952 instructed his agents in the Southwest to prepare evidence to list ANMA as a security threat under the Internal Security Act (McCarran Act) of 1950. ANMA would join other organizations also declared subversive. . . . One year later Warren Olney, the assistant attorney general, notified ANMA headquarters that the U.S. attorney general had decided to designate ANMA as a subversive organization due to its ties with the Communist party.

. . . Moreover, the attorney general aimed to intimidate ANMA members and potential members from political action. The attorney general, however, underestimated ANMA's determination. . . . The political persecution of ANMA also intended to divorce it from the labor movement and the black community. But rather than divide ANMA from other movements, the FBI harassment would actually strengthen these contacts. . . .

Despite ANMA's appeal, the attorney general listed it as a subversive organization in 1954. . . .

FBI harassment plus the political effects of the Immigration Service's deportation drives and local police intimidation tactics . . . eventually took their toll on ANMA. Although it pursued essentially a reformist program and declared its loyalty to the democratic principles of the U.S. Constitution, ANMA along with other radical and even liberal groups including the NAACP posed a perceived threat to a paranoid ruling circle during the cold war and could not be allowed to function peacefully. . . .

Conclusion

ANMA did not survive the cold war. By 1954 the FBI reported no ANMA activity in cities such as Albuquerque, Los Angeles, Phoenix, and San Francisco. Yet despite its demise, ANMA represents . . . one of the most important manifestations of a Mexican-American radical tradition in the United States. Concerned over the problems of working-class Mexican Americans and their communities, ANMA . . . articulated a particular Mexican-American radical or left political perspective. Yet although apparently influenced by the Communist party, ANMA . . . concentrated more on activism than on ideology, and . . . it was strongly shaped by its belief and commitment to the democratic principles of the Declaration of Independence and the U.S. Constitution. . . . Out of conviction and restrained by the political temper and culture of its time, ANMA developed a program and a praxis centered on democratic reformism. . . . ANMA correctly stressed the working-class conditions of most Mexicans in the United States and the exploitative class character of the American system in the mid-twentieth century. . . . ANMA's efforts to link class, race, and culture in integrating the Mexican-American experience constitutes one of the first significant intellectual efforts by Mexican Americans to explore these themes.

The U.S. Government's Unofficial Role in the Bracero Program

KITTY CALAVITA

Direct employer recruitment, the contracting of illegal immigrants, and lax enforcement by the INS [Immigration and Naturalization Service] and other federal agencies further consolidated growers' power over their workers—bracero as well

From Kitty Calavita, "Formalization and Informal Control: The Bracero Program Comes of Age," in *Inside the State: The Bracero Program, Immigration and the I.N.S.* (New York: Routledge, 1992). Copyright © 1992. Reproduced by permission of Routledge, Inc.

as domestic. In fact, the 1948–1951 Bracero Program was "tailor-made to the demands of growers." Convenient as the system was for employers, it was far from perfect. . . .

The direct recruitment system not only created confusion at the border, but it ultimately contributed to unpredictability of the contract itself. With no effective enforcement of bracero wages and working conditions, and no meaningful possibility for collective bargaining, desertion was one of the few recourses open to dissatisfied braceros. Braceros complained to Mexican Consuls in the United States of insufficient and substandard food and housing, inadequate wages, deplorable working conditions, and insufficient work during the contract period. Growers sometimes kept braceros unemployed for several hours a day or for weeks at a time due to weather conditions, a late harvest, or over-contracting. In some cases, braceros were charged for room and board during these slack periods, which they had to pay off out of their future wages, creating a system that some have likened to debt bondage. Under the circumstances, it should not be surprising that employers began to register complaints of increasing bracero "skips," or desertions. The President's Commission on Migratory Labor estimated that the desertion rate in some areas approached 50%. . . .

. . . The diplomatic fallout of the appalling conditions that underlay this discontent threatened to undermine the contract system altogether. Mexican policymakers had never approved of the direct contract arrangement and had for years lobbied for a return to a government-sponsored program, which they were convinced yielded them more leverage in limiting employer abuses. With the entry of the United States into the Korean War in 1950, and growers' rising calls for more farm labor to meet wartime needs, Mexican negotiators upped the ante. When U.S. officials met with their Mexican counterparts in Mexico City in the winter of 1951, they were given an ultimatum. Unless a bill was introduced in Congress to reestablish government sponsorship of the bracero system, Mexico would terminate the bilateral agreement. . . . At the conclusion of the Mexico City conference—which was attended by Senator Allen Ellender (D-Louisiana) and Representative W. R. Poage (D-Texas), Chairs of the respective Congressional Committees on Agriculture—the U.S. agreed to reestablish the government-to-government program.

Expansion and Institutionalization

Within days of their return to Washington, Congressman Poage and Senator Ellender introduced legislation that would formalize and stabilize the bracero system. Hearings on the bill began in March, and by June, Congress had passed the measure that became PL 78. . . . PL 78 for the first time explicitly authorized the importation of contract labor for agriculture. . . . In response to Mexican pressures . . . the U.S. government itself was to be the official contractor of Mexican labor, and hence technically the guarantor of the terms of the contracts. The law placed some restrictions on the administrative transformation of illegal workers into braceros. . . . It further required that before braceros could be imported, the Secretary of Labor must certify (1) that a labor shortage in agriculture existed; (2) that the importation would have no "adverse effect" on local farm workers; and (3) that the employer requesting braceros had made an effort to recruit domestic labor at comparable wages. In addition, braceros were to be paid the "prevailing wage" of the area, and employers of illegal aliens were to be ineligible to receive braceros.

Noticeably absent from the legislation were the recommendations of the President's Commission on Migratory Labor. . . . Specifically, the statute provided no guidelines for the determination of what constituted a "labor shortage" or how "prevailing wages" were to be set. Nor did it include any fines or criminal penalties against employers of illegal immigrants, a provision that the President's Commission had insisted was critical not only to the reduction of illegal migration, but to the elimination of substandard wages and working conditions.

The American Federation of Labor (AFL), its fledgling National Farm Labor Union, and the Congress of Industrial Organizations (CIO) were vehemently opposed to this institutionalization of the program that had originally been designed to fill temporary labor needs during World War II. . . . Labor representatives protested bitterly that in the absence of more specific protections the new program would recreate the abuses of the past. . . . The large growers of the powerful American Farm Bureau not only lobbied for the law, but took the opportunity to make a pitch for "opening doors so that farmers and their organizations can do the job for themselves." Just as the outbreak of World War II had justified Congressional legislation officially validating the Bracero Program a decade earlier, Senator Ellender warned that the emergency labor need precipitated by the Korean War left no time for further deliberation or footdragging. In the end, PL 78 passed with little opposition and in near-record time.

The law was extended four times through 1959, each time with relative ease and very little debate. . . . The program's congressional sponsors were clever in introducing the legislation as an amendment to the Agriculture Act. This ensured that it was routed through the Agriculture Committees, whose Chairs (Senator Ellender and Representative Poage) were known to be aggressive allies of agribusiness, and where the program was likely to receive a favorable response. . . . Periodic attempts were made to transfer jurisdiction over the Bracero Program to the Labor Committees in Congress, but they were met with strong opposition from the powerful Agriculture Committees and their farm block constituents.

. . . With only minor changes, the Migrant Labor Agreement of 1951, together with PL 78, set the official parameters for the Bracero Program until its termination in 1964. The agreement stipulated that the U.S. government, not individual employers, was the guarantor of bracero contracts. It provided for recruitment centers in the interior of Mexico as before, but supplemented them with border "reception centers" where braceros were distributed to their U.S. employers. Contracting illegal workers already in the U.S. was not permitted under the bilateral agreement, at the insistence of Mexican negotiators who were . . . convinced that such legislation encouraged illegal immigration. Braceros were to be paid the prevailing wage for given crops in specific regions or a piece rate equivalent of that wage. As in the past, if braceros were unemployed for more than 25% of the contracted period . . . , the grower was to provide them with a subsistence wage. Housing and meals for a nominal price were to be provided. Finally, no state was to be blacklisted or barred from importing bracero labor. This last provision was in clear reference to Texas which, in all previous agreements, had been excluded from bracero eligibility.

In response to the demands of Mexican negotiators, braceros were not to be used to break strikes, or to replace striking workers. Furthermore, they were to have the right to elect candidates of their choice to represent them in disputes with their employers. This by no means meant that braceros were free to negotiate wages and working conditions. . . . Neither did the provision imply the right to unionize. . . .

PL 78 and subsequent international agreements reestablished the role of the state as farm labor contractor par excellence. . . . PL 78 . . . injected increased predictability and control into the contract labor system that had begun a decade earlier as a wartime emergency measure.

Operation Wetback and the Expansion of Control

. . . Stability of the Bracero Program was enhanced by the government's official role as labor contractor, yet . . . uncontrolled illegal immigration . . . threatened to undermine that stability in the long run.

The President's Commission on Migratory Labor sounded an alarm over the rise in illegal immigration . . . , "The magnitude of the wetback traffic has reached entirely new levels in the past 7 years. . . . It is virtually an invasion." It concluded, "The wetback traffic had reached such proportions in volume and in consequent chaos, it should not be neglected any longer." The commission documented the effect of illegal workers on wage rates in Texas, New Mexico, Arizona, and California, and argued, "That the wetback traffic has severely depressed farm wages is unquestionable." It drew similar conclusions on the subject of "labor competition and displacement," reporting that illegal entrants pushed legal resident farm workers northward since they could not compete with the desperate newcomers. Finally, it presented data on infant mortality, disease, and housing conditions in areas where illegal immigrants were concentrated. . . .

Growers and their allies in Congress attacked the report as "ridiculous," biased by union sympathies and driven by a reformist agenda. . . . Despite its powerful detractors, the commission had opened a debate that quickly gathered momentum and ultimately transformed U.S. policy toward illegal immigration for the duration of the Bracero Program.

Immediately after the release of the commission's report, the *New York Times* ran a five-part series on illegal aliens blaming the employment of undocumented workers in southwestern agriculture—which it compared to "peonage"—for depressing wages and contributing to crime. The series triggered an onslaught of media attention to the subject. . . .

Organized labor stepped up its attacks on illegal immigration, as a particularly severe recession in 1953 brought renewed warnings that uncontrolled immigration depressed wages and increased unemployment. . . .

Increasingly, government officials added their voices to this chorus of concern. A State Department representative told Congress in 1952 that the illegal traffic constituted "one of the most difficult problems . . . that the agencies of this Government have ever been up against.". . . Newly appointed Attorney General Brownell made a tour of the Southwest border to view the situation for himself in the summer of 1953, meeting with local police, mayors, and health and employment officials, all of whom complained loudly of the costs of illegal immigration. Brownell concluded his tour with the proclamation that the magnitude of illegal immigration was "shocking" and constituted "one of the nation's gravest law-enforcement problems.". . .

In addition, policymakers pointed to the penetration of illegal immigrants . . . into the interior of the United States and industrial jobs. . . . Assistant Secretary of Labor Rocco Siciliano was also disturbed by the movement of illegal aliens into industrial employment: ". . . the wetback influx is no longer limited to farm employment. In the first eleven months of the 1954 fiscal year, we have been informed that the Immigration and Naturalization Service apprehended 40,860 illegal entrants in the industries and trades.". . .

Last, but certainly not least, was the impact of the Cold War and McCarthyism on attitudes towards illegal immigration. . . . Senator Pat McCarran, Chair of the Senate Subcommittee on Internal Security and noted cold warrior, alarmed his congressional colleagues in 1951 with his committee's estimate that as many as five million aliens were in the U.S. illegally, including "vast numbers of 'militant Communists, Sicilian bandits and other criminals' " that could "provide an enemy nation with 'a ready-made fifth column.' ". . .

By 1953, Cold War rhetoric permeated the debate. The Acting Immigration Commissioner told a subcommittee of the House Committee on Appropriations, "A harvest of dangerous byproducts from the seemingly harmless invasion by illegal aliens is now in the making. Who can say that Communists and subversives do not cross the Rio Grande?". . . Other immigration officials reiterated the warning, calling the situation "worse than ever before."

The following year, Senator Hubert Humphrey told the Senate that Mexico was "in almost a death struggle to keep out of Communist control," and that the U.S. might be infiltrated by Communist agents crossing the border. . . . Edmund G. Brown, Attorney General of California, agreed, "The comparatively easy influx that wetbacks now have . . . indicates that the door also is open for potential saboteurs and fifth columnists." Senator Pat McCarran, cosponsor of the comprehensive 1952 legislation that overhauled immigration policy for Eastern Hemisphere entrants, was more specific in his charges, claiming that communists and spies actually posed as farm workers and went back and forth across the border at will. . . .

. . . In March 1954, Brownell and his Deputy Attorney General met privately in the Attorney General's office with representatives of organized labor to discuss possible solutions to what was now known simply as "the wetback problem."

The next month, General Joseph Swing, a West Point classmate and friend of President Eisenhower, was appointed INS Commissioner. During his trip to the border, Brownell had met with General Swing. . . . According to later Congressional testimony by Commissioner Swing, Brownell told him at that meeting to begin preparations to take 4000 troops to the Mexican border "to stop this horde of invaders.". . . When Swing retired from the army in February 1954 and was appointed Immigration Commissioner, regaining control of the border was to be his first order of business. . . .

Commissioner Swing inherited an agency that was the target of increasing criticism and ridicule. . . .

Swing feared for the survival of his bureaucracy, given the continuing allegations of incompetence and the periodic recommendations to use the army rather than the Border Patrol to bring illegal immigration under control. . . .

As the agency responsible for controlling the borders, the INS bears the brunt of the contradictions surrounding illegal immigration. With the perceived costs of the illegal movement escalating, these contradictions were brought into sharp focus. A *New York Times* reporter summed up the policy dilemma, "The administration's expressed desire to minimize the illegal traffic, involving evils from slave wages to the spreading of diseases, has clashed head-on with the partial reliance of some segments of southwestern agriculture upon cheap Mexican labor. . . .

One symptom of this dilemma was the indecision and inconsistency of policymakers on the issue of border control. . . . A front-page *New York Times* article headlined "California Seeks More 'Wetbacks' " informed readers that Vice President Nixon was scheduled to meet with Department of Justice officials to discuss the allegation by California Congressmen that Border Patrol enforcement was "over-zealous." The principal item on the agenda was "the possible tempering of the stepped-up campaign against illegal immigration from Mexico, in the interests of assuring Southern California farmers of a supply of labor.

The Attorney General himself wavered in his position on border control. . . . In December 1953, after having declared to the House Appropriations Subcommittee that the "wetback problem" had never been so bad, Brownell recommended no increase in the Border Patrol budget and asked that the overall INS budget be *reduced* by over $3 million (out of a total budget of approximately $40 million). Citing the need for Mexican farm workers to harvest crops and noting that a new migrant labor agreement with Mexico was in process, Brownell cautioned that the elimination of illegal workers might be premature. . . .

The Attorney General's ambivalence was evident in the legislative arena as well. Despite his call for legislation to halt the illegal influx in 1953, and his subsequent promise to organized labor to back such legislation, Brownell's support was at best lukewarm. . . .

. . . The bulk of the fallout . . . was reserved for the Immigration Service itself, in the form of widespread charges of incompetence and complacency. Commissioner Swing was sworn in to an agency that was caught in the middle of a catch-22, and was under attack for the resulting paralysis. With his professional reputation on the line and the survival of his agency at stake, Swing approached Operation Wetback [as his notorious enforcement drive came to be called] with . . . determination. . . . Swing understood . . . that to win this battle would require careful planning. . . . Most important, he realized that he needed to enlist the cooperation of the very growers and ranchers whose illegal work force he intended to round up and deport.

Commissioner Swing set the cooperative tone through intensive communication with employers . . . early in the spring and summer of 1954. At these meetings, he assured his audience that he was aware of the importance of Mexican farm labor and promised growers that their undocumented workers would be replaced with legal workers, both Mexican and domestic. Reporting to Congress just before launching Operation Wetback, Swing made it clear that the purpose of his ten-day trip to the border was to spread the message that "*if there is any employer who can-*

not get legal labor all he has to do is let either the Department of Labor or Immigration know and we will see that he gets it.". . . .

On June 9, 1954, the Attorney General officially initiated the enforcement drive codenamed "Operation Wetback." The next day, the governors and police chiefs in California and Arizona received notices from the INS soliciting their cooperation in the campaign. The officials enthusiastically agreed to participate, and Operation Wetback quickly gathered momentum. The local Border Patrol, reinforced by units from around the country, set up road blocks, boarded trains, and cordoned off neighborhoods for inspection. Police in the area were instructed to detain suspected illegal aliens on vagrancy charges and then turn them over to Border Patrol agents. The Service launched a buslift, returning apprehended aliens to the interior of Mexico, in order to make reentry more difficult and to encourage aliens to depart on their own to avoid being deported to the interior.

On June 17, Swing assembled a "Special Mobile Force" of 800 Border Patrol officers and conducted a massive roundup in California and Arizona agricultural areas. Two days later, the special force was reportedly making over one thousand apprehensions a day. The drive soon spread to Northern California, and then the rest of the Southwest. By the end of July, the Border Patrol was doing "mop-up operations" of illegal workers in industrial jobs in the interior of the United States. According to the *Annual Report* of the INS, over one million apprehensions were made in fiscal year 1954, most of them during Operation Wetback.

The effectiveness of the drive depended on an intensive publicity campaign designed to convince immigrants of the inevitability of their apprehension and to scare them into "voluntary" departure. Well aware of the limitations of his resources, Swing capitalized on the sensationalism of the media coverage and a few well-placed and highly visible shows of force to create the illusion of a far greater presence than the Border Patrol could actually muster. The tactic seems to have worked, particularly in Texas where . . . more than 60,000 Mexican immigrants departed on their own in the first thirty days of the drive. . . .

Operation Wetback was declared an unqualified success by Commissioner Swing. There were widespread reports of abuses by the Border Patrol and charges that legal residents and in some cases American citizens had been deported, harassed and/or beaten. . . . Nevertheless, policymakers lauded the "efficiency" of the Immigration Service in regaining control of the border. Congress even increased the agency's budget in recognition of the job it was doing. The following year, Commissioner Swing was able to announce . . . , "The so-called 'wetback' problem no longer exists. . . . The border has been secured."

The roundup and deportation of illegal aliens during Operation Wetback ushered in a new era. . . . The drive had the effect of buttressing and entrenching a system of contract labor that was uniquely suited to agricultural production. . . . Commissioner Swing was true to his promise to supply growers with a substitute labor source. . . . Illegal aliens were replaced with legal braceros. While in 1953, only 201,380 Mexican contract laborers were admitted, by 1955 the number of braceros had risen to 398,650, reaching a peak of 445,197 in 1956.

The increase in braceros was particularly apparent in the lower Rio Grande Valley where illegal immigrants had for years constituted the bulk of the agricultural work force. At the height of the 1953 harvest, growers in the Valley contracted only 700 braceros; one year later, the Reception Center at Hidalgo, Texas, had issued 50,326 bracero contracts to Valley farmers. . . .

While the virtually limitless supply of Mexican migrants—both illegal aliens and braceros—had for years provided growers with the surplus work force with which to enhance the profitability of agricultural production, the contract system was unusually suited in a number of ways to the exercise of *control*. . . .

The long hours, sporadic employment, and arduous working conditions of agricultural production made the retention of workers problematic. In this context, the captivity of the braceros was extremely valuable. Unlike domestic workers or illegal aliens, the bracero was *confined by law* to a given crop and employer. As the Chief of the Farm Placement Service of the Department of Labor put it in 1957, "These workers [braceros] are not free agents in the labor market. They do not have freedom to move about as they please and shop for the best job that the labor market could afford." . . .

The piece rate system of payment, in wide use in western agriculture, put an additional premium on captive labor. Piece rates maximized profitability in the face of unpredictable labor needs, but at the same time contributed to high turnover, at least among workers who had the freedom to migrate in search of a full day's wage. . . .

If the arduous nature of the production process, together with the piece rate system, made labor availability and dependability problematic, the urgency of that production process and the limits imposed by nature made a captive labor supply all the more valuable. . . .

. . . The bracero, operating outside of the free labor system, contracted for short periods of time, and delivered to the employer to do specific tasks as the need arose, provided an important element of predictability, stability, and—above all—control, in what was otherwise an unpredictable production process.

Another element of control was provided by the reduction of bracero desertions following Operation Wetback. . . . It was even reported that braceros who had "skipped" their contracts prior to the drive had returned to their employers because they could not find work as illegal immigrants.

If braceros could be counted on at the moment of need and could be coerced not to "skip," this highly regulated supply of labor had the additional advantage that once the need had subsided, the workers could be sent home. . . .

Finally, as Commissioner Swing put it, "Under the Bracero Program [growers] are free of the troubles inherent in bootleg labor." Specifically, "When using legal labor [growers] do not run the risk of having the laborers taken from them by arresting officers. They can feel confident that they will have legal laborers of a good quality when and where needed". . . . Using data from the lower Rio Grande Valley in Texas where cotton farmers had traditionally hired undocumented workers, the Labor Department pointed out that 318,219 bales of cotton had been picked by August 5, 1954, with an entirely legal work force, compared to 255,161 bales the year before. Furthermore, whereas in the past, a work force of 150,000 illegal workers—including children—was needed for the harvest, a far smaller number of "physically able, adult male" braceros was sufficient.

While earlier episodes of Border Patrol enforcement elicited outrage from employers, Operation Wetback was generally applauded. . . . Indeed, it was understood by government officials that the operation could not have succeeded without the active cooperation and support of agricultural employers. . . .

Fundamental to employers' receptivity to Operation Wetback was the understanding that the enforcement campaign would uniformly remove illegal farm workers, and hence eliminate competition from growers who used the sometimes cheaper, but less predictable and stable, illegal labor supply. As long as the Border Patrol crackdown was uniform, consistent, and effective, it had the potential to stabilize an otherwise chaotic and competitive labor market, allowing growers collectively to reap the benefits of the more dependable bracero supply. . . .

Operation Wetback, and the expansion of the bracero system that it triggered, had a long-term impact that went well beyond the profitability of individual farms and ranches. Because it was more convenient and cost-effective to contract workers collectively, Operation Wetback precipitated a dramatic increase in the size of growers' associations and in the percentage of employers belonging to these associations. . . . This trend was particularly pervasive in California, where by 1959 over 99% of the 11,629 employers of braceros were members of growers' associations and contracted their braceros through those associations. . . .

If the successes of Operation Wetback and the expansion of the labor importation system had beneficial effects for growers, the Immigration Service reaped benefits as well. In the kind of self-conscious concern with their image that is typical of bureaucracies plagued by public criticism, the INS public opinion survey was conducted for the purpose of gauging the public relations impact of Operation Wetback. According to the regional officers who were responsible for carrying out the survey, the drive was a public relations coup. . . .

PL 78 and Operation Wetback together institutionalized and stabilized the Bracero Program and injected increased control in a farm labor system that had been largely informal and haphazard. Institutionalization did not make the system rigid, however, nor did it reduce administrative discretion. Rather, INS implementation ensured that the newly entrenched program would retain the flexibility that had always been a central feature of its utility to growers.

Another "Walk Around the Statute"

As institutionalized by PL 78 and the bilateral agreements with Mexico, the Bracero Program in the mid-1950s operated in the following way. Once the Department of Labor had certified a particular grower's (or grower association's) need for labor, Mexico was given a thirty-day notice as to how many workers would be required. Aspiring braceros had to obtain a permit from municipal Mexican officials, for which they often had to pay a "mordida" [bribe]. Those who obtained these permits were sent to central recruiting centers, where there were sometimes ten workers for each bracero vacancy. At the recruiting centers, workers frequently had to pay another bribe in order to be considered. It was from this pool that Department of Labor officials selected braceros to be sent to the border reception centers. . . . After security screening and medical examinations, the braceros were dispatched to border reception centers where they signed contracts (which were countersigned by the two governments) with employers' representatives. Workers technically had some freedom of choice in this contracting process. . . .

The "freedom of contract" provision, lauded in Congress, remained largely an abstraction. Those who turned down their first offer of employment for whatever reason were often blacklisted by subsequent employers and sent home empty-handed. Those who were "lucky" enough to secure employment after the degradation and bureaucratic delays at the recruiting stations and reception centers, risked physical injury as well. A Border Patrol memo from Yuma, Arizona, told of braceros being "fumigated prior to their departure to the United States . . . by spraying them by use of airplanes, much in the same manner as agricultural fields are sprayed." Working conditions were often so strenuous and the braceros' hands so "badly scratched" that efforts to obtain the fingerprints required for FBI clearance frequently failed. . . .

Once the contract was signed and the braceros admitted, the implementation of the program guaranteed that it would remain accommodating to the needs of growers. Until the late 1950s, the "prevailing wage" was determined by growers themselves, much as it was before the enactment of PL 78. While the Bureau of Employment Security . . . in the Department of Labor was in theory responsible for certifying that domestic labor had been sought at "prevailing wages," growers took the lead in establishing what that wage was. . . . Having offered employment to domestic workers at a given wage rate and finding a "shortage of labor" at that rate, growers were then free to contract braceros at the same wage that had been unacceptable to domestic workers. A 1955 amendment to PL 78 required that domestic workers be consulted in determining prevailing wages. However, employers and the Department of Labor were free to ignore the workers' recommendations. . . . In addition to the issue of wages, the determination of a "shortage of labor" was complicated by the fact that there was no provision for the transportation of domestic labor, as there was for braceros. So that a "shortage of labor" meant that domestic workers were not available *on the spot,* or could not get there on their own. The result was that braceros were transported from Mexico even when there were unemployed farm workers elsewhere in the United States, or even in the same state.

. . . While it was the duty of the Department of Labor to oversee contract compliance, the Immigration Service was responsible for removing braceros from employers who violated the terms of their contracts, and for reporting employers who used illegal aliens. In both activities, the agency was notoriously lenient. The international agreements of the late 1940s, PL 78, and all subsequent accords with Mexico, specified that employers of illegal workers were ineligible to receive braceros. Since it was generally the INS that apprehended undocumented workers in the course of its border patrol and investigations activities, enforcement of this provision depended on the agency reporting the aliens' employers. . . .

The immigration agency was even more accommodating with violators of the wage and working conditions provisions of bracero contracts. The *INS Information Bulletin* . . . announced that the District Director had instituted a system to deal with the violators without depriving them of their braceros. Employers under this system were permitted to retain their braceros after signing "pledges" with the Border Patrol that they would comply with their contracts in the future. . . .

The bargaining edge that Mexico enjoyed during negotiation of the 1951 accord as the Korean War escalated was steadily eroded, precluding Mexican officials from pressing for more effective implementation of the provisions of the bilateral agreements. . . . In January 1954, U.S.–Mexico negotiations for a new bracero agreement broke down over the issues of border recruitment centers, which Mexico continued to resist; how the prevailing wage was to be determined; and the amount of subsistence payments to be provided to unemployed braceros. For several months, U.S. officials threatened to import braceros on a unilateral basis if Mexico did not give in to U.S. demands. By January 15, when the existing bilateral agreement expired, no new accord had been reached. . . . The following day, the Department of State, Labor, and Justice announced that Mexican farm workers would be unilaterally contracted at the border on a first-come, first-served basis.

The result was a kind of international hiring hall, as U.S. officials stood at the border and called out the number of workers needed each day. Aspiring braceros rushed the gates, where Immigration Service and Labor Department representatives selected and processed the workers. . . .

. . . The unilateral episode in the winter of 1954 lasted only a few weeks, but its impact endured. Mexico's ability to press its interests in international negotiations or to contest implementation policies was effectively curtailed for the rest of the Bracero Program.

The Texas Proviso: A Textbook Case of Administrative Lawmaking

. . . In the spring of 1951, Democratic Senators Paul Douglas of Illinois, Wayne Morse of Oregon, and Hubert Humphrey of Minnesota attempted to amend S.984 (later to become PL 78), in response both to Mexican demands to reduce illegal immigration and to the recommendations of the President's Commission on Migratory Labor. Most controversial was the amendment introduced by Senator Douglas that provided:

> Any person who shall employ any Mexican alien . . . when such person knows or has reasonable grounds to believe or suspect or by reasonable inquiry could have ascertained that such an alien is unlawfully within the United States . . . and shall fail to report such information promptly to an immigration officer, shall be guilty of a felony. . . .

The amendment passed the Senate by a narrow margin, but was deleted from the bill by the Conference Committee. . . . Having assured the success of PL 78 by channeling it through the Agriculture Committees and bypassing the less friendly Judiciary Committees, growers' allies now scuttled the Douglas Amendment by arguing that all immigration matters had to be routed through the Judiciary Committees.

Pressure from Mexico continued to mount. . . . Following enactment of PL 78 and rejection of the Douglas Amendment, they threatened to close down recruitment centers unless evidence was provided that "the subject of sanctions would not be dropped as a dead issue." State Department promises that employer sanctions legislation was under serious consideration, and President Truman's apparent support for the measure, momentarily sufficed to bring Mexico to the bargaining table to sign a new bilateral agreement.

Seven months later, with the expiration date of this Migrant Labor Agreement fast approaching, the Senate hastily addressed the "anti-wetback legislation" which Mexico required to extend the pact. But in place of the Douglas Amendment's explicit prohibition of illegal alien employment, the bill introduced by Senator Harley Kilgore of West Virginia (S.1851) made it illegal only to "harbor, transport, and conceal" illegal entrants. . . . As the debate proceeded, Senator Ellender lobbied hard for the measure and reminded his colleagues that "the enactment of this [bill] is necessary . . . because the Mexican Government refuses to enter into another contract . . . unless we strengthen our immigration laws."

Repeated warnings of this kind left little doubt about the motivation for the legislation. Less clear was its actual meaning. Central to the confusion was an amendment known as the Texas Proviso, named after the Texas growers who fought for it. The Texas Proviso stipulated that "for the purposes of this section, employment . . . shall not be deemed to constitute harboring." The amendment was . . . introduced as a way to protect employers who were *unaware* of their workers' illegal immigration status, from prosecution under the harboring clause. . . .

It was left ambiguous as to whether "*knowing* employment" would be considered harboring. When a few senators who were interested in a strict employment prohibition pressed their colleagues on this issue, sponsors of the Texas Proviso assured them, "Once he [the employer] finds out the real situation, he is knowingly and willfully harboring the man, and the authorities can go after him." . . .

Despite assurances by Texas Proviso advocates that it did not provide a loophole for knowing employment, they rejected by a margin of 69 to 12 an amendment proposed by Senator Douglas specifically stipulating that knowing employment would be penalized. . . . Within days, the Senate had passed the bill [S.1851] with the Texas Proviso intact. The House quickly followed suit, and the bill was signed into law in March, 1952. . . .

Broadly interpreted by the INS to mean that illegal alien employment was altogether excluded from the category of "harboring," the Texas Proviso served as a *carte blanche* for the continued use of undocumented workers. Despite the potentially controversial nature of this interpretation and the ambiguity of the Congressional debate, the Immigration Service acted quickly. . . . The agency established in practice a policy that Congress was unwilling or unable to make explicit, and ignored normal administrative procedures in the process.

Congressional passage of S.1851 was designed to satisfy Mexican demands for a law against the hiring of illegal aliens. Together, growers' demand for cheap immigrant labor and Mexican pressure to curtail illegal immigration required that legislative intent be left ambiguous. Revealing it for what it was . . . would have jeopardized its utility to State Department negotiators for a renewed Migrant Labor Agreement. To explicitly prohibit the employment of illegal aliens would have deprived southwestern growers of a continuing source of labor and was unacceptable to members of Congress who, in the years before Operation Wetback and the increased availability of legal braceros, called such measures "employer harassment."

A Grower's Dream

Growers initially feared that the regulations and red tape of the government program launched by PL 78 in 1951 might constitute an undue burden on their labor recruitment efforts. However, protections built into the Bracero Program came to naught in the absence of rigorous enforcement. In fact, during its peak years in the mid-1950s, the program could not have been better suited to growers' needs. . . .

Wherever braceros were concentrated, wages tended to stagnate or even fall. According to a Department of Agriculture report, farm wages as a whole increased 14% between 1953 and 1959, but remained the same in regions with braceros. In California domestic farm workers earned *less* per hour in 1955 than they had in 1950. . . . A study conducted by the California Reference Service, a research unit attached to the California legislature, reported that the Bracero Program was used deliberately to lower farm wages. While growers insisted that "stoop" labor was inherently unacceptable to domestic workers, researchers at the Institute of Industrial Relations at the University of California, Los Angeles, linked the inability of growers to find willing domestic workers to the low wage rates resulting from the influx of foreign labor. . . .

A handful of persistent and well-organized unionists, first in the National Farm Labor Union (NFLU) and then in its successor, the National Agricultural Workers Union (NAWU), made the Bracero Program their main focus of attack. Ernesto Galarza, researcher and union activist, . . . writes that, by 1952, "the problems of organization . . . centered on Public Law 78 and its multiple effects. Without opposition, the bracero system would have a drastic effect on the hiring of domestic agricultural laborers, except as needed as standbys for emergencies." Launching investigations, testifying to Congress, prodding the Department of Labor into enforcement, and organizing collective actions against abusive employers, during the 1950s these unionists fought a losing battle against the labor importation system. Despite the efforts of farm worker unions, the Bracero Program expanded and grew. Over 2 million braceros entered between 1952 and 1958, with more than 445,000 coming during the peak year 1956. . . . In California, braceros comprised approximately 34% of the seasonal agricultural workforce in 1957, and in some California counties they made up over 90% of the total farm work force.

The *INS Information Bulletin,* speaking of the Bracero Program in Imperial Valley, described the effects of the system: ". . . One of the most significant developments in the decade here since the war has been the steady building of the biggest and most stable farm labor program of its kind in the history of the U.S."

F U R T H E R   R E A D I N G

Vernon Carl Allsup, *The American G.I. Forum* (1982)

American Committee for Protection of the Foreign Born, *Our Badge of Infamy* (1959)

Kaye Briegel, "Alianza Hispano-Americana and Some Mexican American Civil Rights Cases in the 1950s," in Manuel P. Servín, ed., *The Mexican Americans* (1974)

Guy S. Endore, *Justice for Salcido* (1948)

Ernesto Galarza, *Merchants of Labor* (1965)

Juan R. García, *Operation Wetback* (1980)

Mario T. García, "Americans All: The Mexican American Generation and the Politics of Wartime Los Angeles, 1941–45," *Social Science Quarterly* 65 (June 1984), 278–289

——, *Mexican Americans* (1989)

Louise Año Nuevo Kerr, "Mexican Chicago: Chicano Assimilation Aborted, 1939–1954," in Melvin G. Holli, ed., *Ethnic Chicago* (1984)

Pauline R. Kibbe, *Latin Americans in Texas* (1946)

Gloria López-Stafford, *A Place in El Paso* (1996)

Américo Paredes, " 'Texas' Third Man: The Texas-Mexican," *Race* 3–4 (May 1963), 49–58

John Rechy, "Jim Crow Wears a Sombrero," *Nation* 11 (October 10, 1959), 210–213

Julian Samora, *Los Mojados* (1971)

George Isidore Sánchez, *Forgotten People* (1996)

Daniel L. Schorr, " 'Reconverting' Mexican Americans," *New Republic* 115 (September 30, 1946), 412–413

Ruth D. Tuck, *Not with the Fist* (1956)

Liliana Urrutia, "An Offspring of Discontent: The Asociación Nacional México-Americana, 1949–1954," *Aztlán* 15 (Spring 1984), 177–184

Edmund Villaseñor, *Macho* (1973)

Michael Wilson, *Salt of the Earth* (1978)

The Struggle for Chicano Power, 1965–1974

In the 1960s President Lyndon Johnson's Great Society programs considerably improved opportunities for Mexican Americans, and an unprecedented political mobilization of racial minorities took place as new conceptions of racial identity were explored and debated by people of color. Inspired by the Black Power movement and informed by a newly discovered history of resistance, Mexican Americans similarly forged a unique collective identity known as Chicanismo, whose various manifestations in pursuit of diverse goals were marked by boycotts, land seizures, the formation of the Brown Berets, and the growth of a student movement. In 1969 Corky González sponsored the Chicano Youth Liberation Conference in Denver and gave the Chicanos of the Southwest a renamed homeland—Aztlán. The concept of Aztlán spread throughout the barrios and reflected the new direction the Chicano movement took in the 1970s. Was the struggle by Chicanos against racism and poverty successful?

The fight for social justice by Chicano farm workers was an important aspect of the Chicano movement. In September 1965 César Chávez called a strike for higher wages for grape workers in Delano, California, taking on the state's huge and powerful agribusiness concerns. In 1968 the newly formed United Farm Workers (UFW) proclaimed a nationwide consumer boycott of table grapes, a strategy that was eventually successful when the grape growers recognized and negotiated contracts with the union in 1970.

The Chicano student movement also grew as dozens of organizations appeared on high school, college, and university campuses. The impact of Chicano activism was considerable. Protesting the Vietnam War was an impassioned cause because the U.S. escalation of the conflict had dire consequences for Chicanos. Compared with Anglos, they were drafted in disproportionately greater numbers, more often received combat assignments, and suffered higher casualty rates. Between the years 1961 and 1967, for example, over 19 percent of U.S. Army casualties and 23 percent of Marine Corps casualties had Spanish surnames. As Chicano deaths mounted in Vietnam, Chicanos took part in demonstrations calling for an end to the war. This mounting opposition culminated in the Chicano Anti-War Moratorium, when more than 30,000 Chicanos gathered in Los Angeles in August 1970.

The largest anti-war demonstration by a racial minority quickly turned into a riot when law enforcement officers attacked the marchers. Three people were killed, including prize-winning Chicano journalist Rubén Salazar. What were the political manifestations of the Chicano movement?

During the social upheaval of the 1960s and early 1970s, Chicanas began demanding recognition and equality. The growing strength of the mainstream women's movement was an important catalyst. Under the banner of herman-dad *(sisterhood), Chicanas aired grievances they felt the women's movement had neglected, such as racism and poverty. By the early 1970s Chicanas began demanding recognition within Chicano student, community, and labor organizations. Were Chicanas successful in gaining equal participation in the Chicano movement?*

DOCUMENTS

Chicano farmworkers endure the worst living and working conditions and are paid among the lowest wages of any American laborer. In Document 1, María Moreno, a Chicana farmworker who was an early organizer for what would become the United Farm Workers (UFW) union, describes the typical life of hardship for Chicano farmworkers. As tens of thousands of Chicanos were drafted or volunteered for military service in Vietnam, a growing number were refusing induction, which is the subject of Document 2, dated 1968. It is the statement of Denver Chicano Ernest Vigil in which he explains why he refused to serve in the military. Reies Lopez Tijerina was the founder and first director of New Mexico's Alianza de los Pueblos Libres (Alliance of Free City-States), which raised the question of Spanish and Mexican land grants. Tijerina's activities grew bolder and led to his arrest for his involvement in the raid on the Tierra Amarilla courthouse in 1967. Document 3, dated 1969, is an excerpt from an open letter Tijerina wrote his supporters while incarcerated on charges of destroying public property and assaulting two officials. In the letter, he justifies the actions of the Alliance on behalf of the New Mexicans struggling for their land. The Movimiento Estudiantil Chicano de Aztlán (MECHA) was one of the more important Chicano student organizations of the 1960s to address the issue of education. The philosophy, organization, and function of MECHA are explored in Document 4. In the late 1960s, the Mexican American Youth Organization (MAYO), one of the most successful Chicano political groups, assumed the leadership of the school board, the mayor's office, and the city council of Crystal City, Texas. In Document 5 the Chicano essayist Armando Rendon recounts MAYO's original plan, the 1969 Winter Garden Project, for achieving full-scale participatory democracy in South Texas. César Chávez, leader of the grape-pickers strike in Delano, California, launched the nationwide boycott of table grapes on behalf of the UFW in 1968. Document 6 is taken from the interview Chávez gave Bob Fitch for the *Christian Science Monitor* in 1970, in which the labor leader discusses the nonviolent philosophy of La Causa, as the struggle of the United Farmworkers of America was called. Casualties in Vietnam among Chicano military personnel remained disproportionately high into the 1970s, leading to Chicano mobilization against the war. The methods Chicanos could use to avoid going to Vietnam are outlined in Document 7, which is taken from a pamphlet that was distributed on college campuses and in Spanish-speaking neighborhoods at this time.

1. María Moreno Remembers Farmworker Life, 1965

I am Maria Moreno, 40 years old, mother of 12 children. Born in Karnes City, Texas. Raised in Corpus Christi. Since 1928 I start working in agricultural work. I been a worker all my life. I know how to handle a man's job like a man and I'm not ashamed to say it. I'm American citizen, and I'm talking for justice. I'm asking for justice. Not only for me or for my family, but all the migrant workers. We been suffering for so long. . . .

We were working in Texas. Picking cotton, chopping cotton. 1932 we're picking cotton, 25 cents a hundred. We're chopping cotton, 10 cents a row. And have to support the children who in those days did never know what shoes were on their feet. . . . Our children drink milk once a week. Our children eat meat once a week. Why? We can't afford it. That is the reason we are . . . trying to get the agricultural workers organized.

. . . It is time to ask for justice. We're demanding $1.25 [an hour], which is, I think, not very much for a grower to give us. We're asking, we're waiting and we're hoping for get this $1.25.

1940, we came to California. Waiting and hoping to find a better living, a better living condition for ourselves and for our family. The braceros came in. We had to move on from the Imperial Valley. We hit Salinas. Here come the braceros. Well, we're tickled anyway when we work a little. We can earn a little money. We can feed our children. Half eat. . . . The road is our home. The ground is our table.

I've got a 23-year-old son. When he was 19 years old he was blind because he was without eat. 1958 . . . it start raining and raining. And kept on raining a month. We couldn't go to work. All our food was gone. All our money was gone. No hope held.

One day I decided to go to the welfare and ask for something to eat. They refused to help out. . . . They help them when they want to and when they like. If they help them the food they give we have to work for. They don't give it to us. We have to work and pay for it.

. . . We already had when I went to the welfare no hope and no place to get money or food or anything. . . . We had three weeks without eating more than once a day. Three weeks. I had my baby, three month. I was feeding him water and sugar. The days sped on.

The investigator came home and I told her that she might as well come in the home and search and see what she can find. . . . There was not a thing to eat in that place. . . .

Three days, my son got blind. He got so weak, he lost all his strength. He was blind for three days. The day that he was blind, my heart was broken in pieces. When I see a strong American. I see how richest America will live. And the real miserable life that we're living. I'm not ashamed to say this in front of nobody because it's truth. . . .

María Moreno, "I'm Talking for Justice," *Regeneración* 1, no. 10 (1971): 12–13.

. . . The days pass on, then the door was opened.

Said, "Mrs. Moreno, we didn't know that you really need the food." They did know because I went and knock the doors but got no answer because the agricultural workers been ignored, been forgotten for so many long years.

People been forgotten. They don't care about us. Our home is under the tree. That's the way that we have been treated. . . . We never had a word until now. Like I said, I'm mother of 12 children and I'm working for discovering the things that been hiding for so long—that people must know what we been suffering, what we been through.

People think that because somebody else have something to eat, they think that the whole world have some. . . . The only hope we have is God. We call for Him because we been calling to the people. They don't hear. They don't care. . . .

But the thing that really hurts me is this: that we are living in a rich America, that the people been sending food, the clothing overseas. And then forgotten us. That we are citizens, and we're living in America. That's what really hurts me, but like I said, I hope that you people help us do something for this situation. You won't have to go very far. . . . All places around here. You can find out. People sleeping on the floor for so long.

This is the way the agricultural worker lives. This is the way that we have been treated. This is the way that we have been keeping on going.

We're asking for a little different wages. And I hope we'll get it. Growers said that we don't need the $1.25, that we got enough. . . . The ranchers say they don't make any money, but one thing I know for sure: they're lying. I never heard about a rancher go and knock at the welfare doors and ask for something to eat like the agricultural workers do.

What I say it's truth, and I'm not afraid to say it. For too long the agricultural workers been afraid. When somebody hollers, we jump. We never answer back. Well, I'm not afraid no more. These are the things I have to say and I'm hope that you understand the things that I say.

2. Ernest Vigil Opposes Induction to Fight in Vietnam, 1968

On May 7, 1968, I reported to the New Customs House in downtown Denver to take an induction physical for the Armed Forces. I passed the physical examination but refused to go through with the induction ceremony. I was ordered for immediate induction as a "delinquent"; there is no reason for my being classified delinquent, and therefore there is no reason for being called for immediate induction as such. For refusing to cooperate I face a felony charge that can bring a minimum of 5 years, $10,000, or both.

As found in *El Gallo,* June 1, 1968.

I was fully aware of the consequences; I did not do this for kicks. . . .

The Selective Serve-Us System *is* inadequate and discriminatory and should be opposed until it is changed, so that the Spanish-surnamed, the Black, and the general poor do not have to bear the brunt of this undeclared war. I oppose the war on grounds of personal conscience and I oppose the war as a Mexican-American, a Chicano.

I look at the discrepancy between what our country says and what it does; between what it is and what it should be; and I arrive at the decision that it is beneath my dignity as an intelligent, well-meaning human being to quietly submit or blindly conform to a system that attacks noble meaning (if not meaning altogether) and whose values and practices will not and do not serve the ends of truth, peace, and justice.

Therefore, I hereby submit my draft-card as a gesture of my dissatisfaction and disaffection for the social, governmental, and political system of this nation.

My country is not my God; I will (and must) first serve the dictates of my mind, heart and conscience. There are laws and values that are higher than those of this nation's government and sometimes these come from the conscience of one lone individual; they cannot be legislated by politicians nor enforced by policemen and soldiers.

In this belief I now state that I will not fight the war of a power and system that I feel is unjust, hypocritical, deceitful, inadequate, and detrimental to peaceful, legal social revolution. . . . This forces people to prepare for what has been called "the fire next time." . . .

All this, while America says "I'm sorry" for the death of Dr. King and "We sympathize with the poor." Then during riots they say "Shoot to kill!" During demonstrations they say "Arrest those people." All of this in a country that has a gross national product of 800 billion dollars and 20% of its people in poverty. All this, while America says "Might does not make right." Yet look what happens to anyone who gets in the way of the American Establishment. Look at what happens to [Reies Lopez; see Document 3] Tijerina. All this, while Uncle Sam preaches democracy and then supports every dictator in South America with money, equipment and "military advisors."

All this, in a nation that condemns racism and genocide—but what has happened to the first Americans, the Indians? In South America they comprise anywhere from 1/3 to 95% of the total population. In America it is 1/10 of one percent. . . . And when Mexican-Americans are only 3 to 5% of the total population and 19 to 20% of the Vietnam casualties, it is obvious to me, as it should be to everyone, that something is happening that has to be stopped.

I'm specifically making reference to the Selective Service System and the Vietnam war, but my concerns are far greater than this. Every major institution in this nation is directly or indirectly responsible for the great inequities that exist between the elite, white, middle-class power structure and the disenfranchised minority groups whether Mexican-American, Afro-American, American Indian or Puerto Rican.

What we need as much as the changes to be made, is for the people to make the changes. NOW!

3. Reies Lopez Tijerina Writes an Open Letter from Santa Fe Jail, 1969

From my cell block in this jail I am writing these reflections. I write them to my people, the Indo-Hispanos, to my friends among the Anglos, to the agents of the federal government, the state of New Mexico, the Southwest, and the entire Indo-Hispano world—"Latin America."

I write to you as one of the clearest victims of the madness and racism in the hearts of our present-day politicians and rulers.

At this time, August 17, I have been in jail for 65 days—since June 11, 1969. . . . I am here today because I resisted an assassination attempt led by an agent of the federal government—an agent of all those who do not want anybody to speak out for the poor, all those who do not want Reies Lopez Tijerina to stand in their way as they continue to rob the poor people, all those many rich people from outside the state with their summer homes and ranches here whose pursuit of happiness depends on thievery, all those who have robbed the people of their land and culture for 120 years. . . .

What is my real crime? As I and the poor people see it, especially the Indo-Hispanos, my only crime is UPHOLDING OUR RIGHTS AS PROTECTED BY THE TREATY OF GUADALUPE-HIDALGO which ended the so-called Mexican-American War of 1846–48. My only crime is demanding the respect and protection of our property, which has been confiscated illegally by the federal government. Ever since the treaty was signed in 1848, our people have been asking every elected president of the United States for a redress of grievances. Like the Black people, we too have been criminally ignored. Our right to the Spanish land grant pueblos is the real reason why I am in prison at this moment.

Our cause and our claim and our methods are legitimate. . . .

This truth is denied by the conspirators against the poor and by the press which they control. There are also the Silent Contributors. The Jewish people accused the Pope of Rome for keeping silent while Hitler and his machine persecuted the Jews in Germany and other countries. I support the Jews in their right to accuse those who contributed to Hitler's acts by their SILENCE. By the same token, I denounce those in New Mexico who have never opened their mouths at any time to defend or support the thousands who have been killed, robbed, raped of their culture. I don't know of any church or Establishment organization or group of elite intellectuals that has stood up for the Treaty of Guadalupe-Hidalgo. We condemn the silence of these groups and individuals and I am sure that, like the Jewish people, the poor of New Mexico are keeping a record of the Silence which contributes to the criminal conspiracy against the Indo-Hispano in New Mexico.

As I sit in my jail cell in Santa Fe, capital of New Mexico, I pray that all the poor people will unite to bring justice to New Mexico. My cell block has no day light, no ventilation of any kind, no light of any kind. After 9 P.M., we are left in a dungeon of total darkness. Visiting rules allow only 15 minutes per week on Thursdays from 1 to 4 P.M. so that parents who work cannot visit their sons in jail. . . . My cell is dirty and there is nothing to clean it with. The whole cell block is hot and suffocating. All my prison mates complain and show a daily state of anger. But these uncomfortable conditions do not bother me, for I have a divine dream to give me strength: the happiness of my people.

I pray to God that all the Indo-Hispano people will awake to the need for unity, and to our heavenly and constitutional responsibility for fighting peacefully to win our rights. Already the rest of the Indo-Hispano world—Latin America—knows of our struggle. It is too late to keep the story of our land struggle from reaching the ears of the Indo-Hispano world. All the universities of Latin America knew about our problems when [Nelson] Rockefeller went there last summer. Will Latin America ignore our cry from here in New Mexico and the Southwest? Times have changed and the spirit of the blood is no longer limited by national or continental boundaries.

The Indo-Hispano world will never trust the United States as long as this government occupies our land illegally. The honest policy of the United States will have to begin at home, before Rockefeller can go to Latin America again to sell good relations and friendship. Our property, freedom and culture must be respected in New Mexico, in the whole Southwest, before the Anglo can expect to be trusted in South America, Mexico and Canada.

This government must show its good faith to the Indo-Hispano in respect to the Treaty of Guadalupe-Hidalgo and the land question by forming a presidential committee to investigate and hold open hearings on the land question in the northern part of New Mexico. We challenge our own government to bring forth and put all the facts on the conference table. We have the evidence to prove our claims to property as well as to the cultural rights of which we have been deprived. WE ARE RIGHT—and therefore ready and willing to discuss our problems and rights under the Treaty with the Anglo federal government in New Mexico or Washington, D.C., directly or through agents. . . .

Because I know WE ARE RIGHT, I have no regrets as I sit in my jail cell. I feel very, very proud and happy to be in jail for the reason that I am. . . . I am sure that not one of my prison days is lost. Not one day has been in vain. While others are free, building their personal empires, I am in jail for defending and fighting for the rights of my people. Only my Indo-Hispano people have influenced me to be what I am. I am what I am, for my brothers.

4. The Chicano Coordinating Council on Higher Education Discusses the Movimiento Estudiantil Chicano de Aztlán (MECHA), 1969

MECHA is a first step toward tying the student groups throughout the Southwest into a vibrant and responsive network of activists that will respond as a unit to

From *El Plan de Santa Barbara: A Chicano Plan for Higher Education* (Oakland: La Causa Publications, Inc., 1970).

oppression and racism and that will work in harmony when initiating and carrying out campaigns of liberation for our people.

. . . It is the function of MECHA to further socialization and politicization for liberation on all campuses. The student movement is to a large degree a political movement and as such must not elicit from our people the negative responses that we have experienced so often in the past in relation to politics. . . . To this end, then, we must redefine politics for our people for it to be a means of liberation. The political sophistication of our Raza [Race] must be raised. . . . In addition, the student movement is cultural and social as well. The spirit of MECHA must be one of *hermandad* and cultural awareness. . . . MECHA must bring to the mind of every young Chicano that the liberation of his people from prejudice and oppression is in his hands and that this responsibility is greater than personal achievement and more meaningful than degrees, especially if they are earned at the expense of his identity and cultural integrity.

MECHA, then, is more than a name, it is a spirit of unity, of brotherhood, and a resolve to undertake a struggle for liberation in a society where justice is but a word. MECHA is a means to an end. . . .

Other students can be important to MECHA in supportive roles; hence the question of coalitions. . . . Some guidelines might be kept in mind. . . . Is it beneficial to tie oneself to another group in coalition which will carry oneself into conflicts for which one is ill prepared or into issues on which one is ill advised? Can one safely go into a coalition where one group is markedly stronger than another? Are the interests of MECHA and of the community being served? . . . All of these and many more questions must be asked and answered before one can . . . say that he will benefit and contribute to a strong coalition effort.

Supportive groups. When moving on campus, it is often . . . advised to have groups . . . willing to act in supportive roles. For example, there are . . . faculty members who are sympathetic. . . . These faculty members often serve on academic councils and senates and can . . . provide another channel to the academic power structure and can be used as leverage in negotiation. However, these groups are only as responsive as the ties with them are nurtured. . . . It . . . means laying good groundwork before an issue is brought up, touching bases with your allies beforehand.

Sympathetic administrators. . . . Administrators are most interested in not jeopardizing their positions and often will try to act as buffers or liaison between the administration and the student group. In the case of Chicano administrators, it should not a priori be assumed that because he is Raza he is to be . . . trusted. If he is not known to the membership, he must be given a chance to prove his allegiance to *la Causa*. . . . It is from the administrator that information can be obtained as to the actual feasibility of demands or programs to go beyond the platitudes and pleas of unreasonableness with which the administration usually answers proposals and demands. The words of the administrator should never be the deciding factor in students' actions. The students must at all times make their own decisions. . . . Students must constantly remind the Chicano administrators and faculty where their loyalty and allegiance lie. . . .

In short, it is the students who must keep after Chicano and non-Chicano administrators and faculty to see that they do not compromise the position of the student and the community. By the same token, it is the student who must come to the support of these individuals if they are threatened for their support of the students. . . .

It is a fact that the Chicano has not often enough written his own history, his own anthropology, his own sociology, his own literature. He must do this if he is to survive as a cultural entity in this melting-pot society which seeks to dilute varied cultures into a gray-upon-gray pseudo-culture of technology and materialism. The Chicano student is doing most of the work in the establishment of study programs, centers, curriculum development, entrance programs to get more Chicanos into college. . . . Students must be careful not to be coopted in their fervor for establishing relevance on the campus. . . . MECHA must not compromise programs and curriculum . . . essential for the total education of the Chicano for the sake of expediency. The students must not become so engrossed in programs and centers . . . that they forget the needs of the people whom these institutions are meant to serve. To this end, barrio input must always be given full and open hearing when designing these programs, when creating them, and when running them. The jobs created by these projects must be filled by competent Chicanos. . . . Therefore, students must demand a say in the recruitment and selection of all directors and assistant directors of student-initiated programs. . . . All advisory and steering committees should have both student and community components as well as sympathetic Chicano faculty as members.

Tying the campus to the barrio. The colleges and universities in the past have existed in an aura of omnipotence and infallibility. It is time that they be made responsible and responsive to the communities in which they are located or whose members they serve. . . . Community members should serve on all programs related to Chicano interests. . . . All attempts must be made to take the college and university to the barrio. . . . Also, the barrio must be brought to the campus, whether it be for special programs or ongoing services which the school provides for the people of the barrio. The idea must be made . . . to the people of the barrio that they own the schools, and the schools . . . are at their disposal. The student group must utilize the resources . . . for the benefit of the barrio at every opportunity. This can be done by hiring more Chicanos to work as academic and non-academic personnel on the campus. . . . This applies to hiring Chicano contractors to build on campus, etc. . . . Many other things could be considered in using the resources of the school in the barrio. . . .

Most colleges in the Southwest are located near or in the same town as a barrio. Therefore, it is the responsibility of MECHA . . . to establish . . . working relationships with organizations in that barrio. . . . However, MECHA must be careful not to overstep its authority or duplicate the efforts of another organization already in the barrio. . . .

. . . MECHA . . . must determine with the help of those in the barrio where they can be most effective. There are, however, some general areas in which MECHA can involve itself . . . : (1) policing social and governmental agencies to make them more responsive . . . to the people of the barrio; (2) carrying out research on the economic and credit policies of merchants in the barrio and exposing fraudulent and exorbitant establishments; (3) speaking and communicating with junior-high and high-school students, helping with their projects, teaching them organizational techniques, supporting their actions; (4) spreading the message of the movement by . . . speaking, radio, television, local newspapers, underground papers, posters, art, theaters, in short spreading propaganda of the movement; (5) exposing discrimination in hiring and renting practices and many other areas. . . . It may mean . . . having to work in conjunction with other organizations. . . . Realize that MECHA . . . should accept the direction of the group involved. Do not let loyalty to an organization cloud responsibility to a greater force—*la Causa.*

Working in the barrio is an honor, but it is also a right, because we come from these people. . . . Mutual respect between the barrio and the college group should be the rule. Understand . . . that there will initially be mistrust . . . on the part of some in the barrio for the college student. This mistrust must be broken down by a demonstration of affection for the barrio and La Raza through hard work and dedication. If the approach is one of a dilettante . . . , the people will know it and react accordingly. If it is merely a cathartic experience to work among the unfortunate in the barrio—stay out.

Of the community, for the community. *Por la Raza habla el espíritu* ["The spirit speaks for the Race"].

5. Armando Rendon Recalls the Winter Garden Project of the Mexican American Youth Organization (MAYO), 1969

At a MAYO conference in Mission, Texas, in December 1969, MAYO unveiled the Winter Garden Project, a plan to redeem a ten-county area in South Texas for Chicanos. MAYO's purpose was twofold: first, to politicize as many young Chicanos as possible within a regulated format of social contact, with workshops on a variety of subjects and activities geared to impress the young people with tangible problems and objectives through symbolic means. . . .

Secondly, MAYO democratized the Winter Garden Project by involving the conference students in deliberating the kinds and extent of efforts to be made this year and establishing priorities. [José] Gutiérrez [a founder of Mexican American Youth Movement (MAYO)] envisions a number of projects such as Crystal City, but in the economic, political, and social arenas as well, which can serve as models for action elsewhere in Texas or the Southwest. Whether a strategy that is successful in Texas, given the political and social make-up of the region, can be exported to another region is questionable; but already through the Crystal City schools' victory and the more recent election triumphs, MAYO has proved that the . . . system can be beaten. Particularly where Chicanos predominate, there is no reason for Anglos to have the balance of power and influence. Chicanos can have their share of control, or all of it if need be, and that would just kill the gringo.

As found in Armando Rendon, "No Future Without the Young," in Armando Rendon, *Chicano Manifesto* (New York: Avon Books, 1971), pp. 203–204.

6. César Chávez Speaks with Bob Fitch About La Causa, 1970

FITCH: The first question I'd like to ask is "Why [table grape] boycott?"

CHAVEZ: You know, when you consider everything, we don't have any options. Most of the other things that would have been options depended entirely on the good will of the government and we know enough to know that they're not going to move. Especially, they're not going to move in a conflict situation like ours. Personally, the big reason was this: I thought the American public would respond affirmatively. . . .

F: What's the realistic basis for optimism about a public response to the boycott?

C: Well, first of all, I contend that not only the American public but people in general throughout the world will respond to a cause that involves injustice. It's just natural to want to be with the underdog. . . . In this struggle it's . . . a contest between a lot of people who are poor and others who are wealthy.

F: What happened to the other options? Such as legislation?

C: . . . Once you get into legislation then it's the whole question of compromise. The only reason growers are seeking legislation now, after 35 years, is because they are under pressure. They want to use legislation to take away that new-found right the workers have found through the boycott.

F: What do you mean?

C: Legislation that's being proposed permits unions but takes the boycott . . . away from the workers, and doesn't permit them to strike during harvest time. Of course that's the only time we work. The proposal comes not out of a spirit of giving the workers civil rights, but as a gimmick to further restrict their rights.

F: Why can't you stop the importing of Mexican labor?

C: It's a long history of the government and the employers working together. . . . In fact, it's part of the system. Even under the most liberal administrations we wouldn't get them to enforce border controls. The immigration service and the border patrol always worked on the assumption that it is not really illegal for these people to be here provided they are working, are being useful to the growers. The moment they stop being useful—either because they strike or because they don't work any more since the crops are finished—then of course it becomes very illegal and they are thrown out. It's a very corrupt system.

F: "Corrupt" implies collusion to break the law, which is a very heavy charge. Do you want to make that charge?

C: Sure, sure, except that I'm not saying that money crosses hands. What I'm saying is that the guy before me did it, the guy before him did it, so I can't change it. It's that kind of setup.

F: That takes any connotation of deliberate action away from the growers.

Bob Fitch, "Tilting the System: An Interview with Cesar Chavez," pp. 204–207. Copyright © 1970 Christian Century Foundation. Reprinted from the February 18, 1970, issue of the *Christian Century*.

C: No, it's a deliberate attempt, it's very deliberate, most deliberate! What I'm trying to explain is that it is more sinister than if they were paying money. This way the immigration service people are as much servants as we are. They're not getting paid off. They do it because of the power that the industry represents. So it's worse than if they were actually being paid money.

F: What happened to the strike?

C: To strike in any rural setting in any state today—and I don't care what state it is, California, Texas, Florida, Arizona—you're fighting the growers . . . in their own setting, so they are able to bring the tremendous powers from the police and the courts and all the structures against you on the picket line to break it totally. . . . The injunction is just a manifestation of the power they have. There isn't enough money or time or energy to be appealing all those things that they keep throwing at you. The boycott gets them out of the setting. They can't reach us in the boycott. The farther away from Delano, the more diffuse their power is.

F: Has the boycott worked?

C: We figure that we are cutting back the sales now by about 33 per cent. But all that means is that we are forcing them to cold-storage the grape. The grape hasn't been lost yet. And in order to be 33 per cent effective we would have to keep up the same kind of pressure or increase it in the coming weeks.

F: What is the main issue of the strike?

C: The central issue is the whole question of recognition. Do, or will, workers have the right to have a union and have it recognized by their employers?

F: How do the growers respond?

C: Mostly they say that workers don't want a union, that if workers wanted a union they would give them a union. . . . The employers are still at the point where industrial employers were 50 years ago. They say, "If you want a union come and get it." In other words, "Force me to give you a union."

F: And what evidence is there that the workers want a union?

C: Well, I think that the only kind of evidence we have . . . is the experience we've had in eight different cases where they've given workers a right to vote on whether they want unions or not. They have overwhelmingly voted that they want a union.

F: So you're ready to put it to a vote?

C: Oh sure. See, when the employers say that we don't recognize the workers or that workers don't want a union, we say give the workers the right to make this self-determination by giving them the right to an election, with the understanding on our part that if the workers vote against the union we'll call the thing off. But if the workers vote for the union, then the employers are duty bound to bargain collectively and to sign a contract with the union.

F: Who supports you?

C: Number one, the public. They were given something to respond with. That's important. Then labor, for money and technical assistance—and from just being around them you learn a hell of a lot. . . . I think the church brings the other kind of power. The moral power and the kind of assurance that what you're doing is really an important task. That fortifies you in your spirit. It legitimates the movement at least against the reckless attacks from the right. . . .

F: Why are you an advocate of nonviolence?

C: . . . I have been asked this question many times and I have really had to dig back and find out. I think it goes back to my family, particularly my mother. She's a . . . pacifist. She never learned how to read or write, never learned English, never went to school for a day. . . . In the old days, . . . there were occasions when she would gather us around her and she would call it *consejo*. "Consejo" means to council, to advise. . . . I remember that she would talk constantly about nonviolence—constantly. She used many *dichos*. "Dichos" are sayings, parables—for instance, things like "It takes two to fight; one guy can't fight by himself," or "Flies can't come into a closed mouth; keep your mouth shut."

F: So nonviolence was your nursery.

C: I would think so. . . .

F: Does the United Farm Workers Organizing Committee want to be more than a union, a force for social reform?

C: I think that if the union loses the social force it has now it's going to become pretty meaningless. The most important thing is to provide an instrument with which workers, by their own actions and their own desires, can work themselves out of poverty.

F: It's an instrument or tool for poor people in this nation?

C: Yeah, for poor people. This is always the first order of business. But once that's attained and once they are well on their way to attaining the first contracts, to having the union recognized—along with that comes responsibility. If the workers keep that social consciousness and use it as an instrument, not only will they help themselves, but they will also help others less fortunate, and they will be a voice in society against those ills that are part of our life.

F: . . . Why do you think you can succeed whereas that union wasn't able to?

C: Well, let's say we hope that it will be different; that remains to be seen. . . .

C: . . . We have such a big job, an overwhelming job, in building the union. That job hasn't been done yet. We're just now beginning to do it.

7. Lea Ybarra and Nina Genera Report on Chicano Mobilization Against the Vietnam War, 1972

The Vietnam war is far from being over. Since Nixon took office we've dropped more bombs in this war than both sides used in all of World War II. Nixon has expanded the war into Cambodia and Laos. And now, he has started bombing North Vietnam again. . . .

We know something about what the war cost us—**55,000 American dead, over 300,000 wounded**—many of them disabled for life. And the war has cost us two hundred billion dollars. Nixon will spend seven billion dollars more on this war this year alone. **That is money we needed here, for new schools and hospitals, better medical aid for our people, better education for our children. . . .** While our bombers tear apart Vietnam, this war also tears apart our own nation—

Lea Ybarra and Nina Genera, *La batalla esta aqui: Chicanos and the War,* El Cerrito, California; distributed by Chicano Draft Help, 197[?], pp. 1–6.

because there is not enough money to . . . deal with drugs, slums, medical care, housing. The poor and unemployed, the blacks and Puerto Ricans—these have paid the price of this war. Our veterans are coming back to find there are no jobs. . . .

In addition to the realization that this war is a direct imperialistic intervention by the United States and has caused an overwhelming amount of suffering and death, what does this war specifically mean to the Chicano?

The Chicano & the War

It has meant, up to the present, **death for more than 11,000 Chicanos.** In other words, Chicanos have accounted for more than 20% of this country's casualties while they make up only 10% of this country's population. . . .

Aside from being drafted in great numbers, Chicanos have also voluntarily joined the military for many reasons. Since they are considered a "foreign minority" they have been under great pressure to prove loyalty to the United States. Chicanos proclaim the sizeable military contributions of the Chicano soldier as proof of loyalty. They point to impressive records of heroism in time of war. There is also the desire for social status that military life offers. Another reason is economic, since many Chicanos help their families with service allotments. And, of course, there is also the fact that only a relatively small number of Chicanos have avoided obligatory military service by attending college, so they have volunteered rather than wait to be drafted.

One positive change to this is that more Chicanos, because of their political involvement, are becoming less willing to submit to induction into the armed forces. . . .

One need only remember the Chicano moratorium throughout California and the Southwest and especially the Chicano Moratorium in Los Angeles in August of 1970, when thousands of Chicanos marched to protest the Vietnam war, to realize that there is a growing awareness among Chicanos concerning the war. Unfortunately, . . . the majority of young Chicanos are still being drafted or are enlisting because they think that they will eventually get drafted anyway, and that there is nothing they can do about it. The point is, something **can** be done. The Chicano can use the Selective Service regulations to his own advantage by learning the legal procedures necessary to apply for and receive deferments. Realizing, of course, that any type of legal justice is always more difficult and sometimes impossible for the Chicano to obtain, in comparison to the Anglo, in the case of the Selective Service System, Chicanos have received deferments when they have obtained proper counseling as to their legal rights.

. . . We encourage the entire Chicano community, both young and old, male and female, to familiarize themselves with what is happening with the draft today and what alternatives are available to their sons, husbands, boyfriends, nephews, cousins, grandsons and so on.

Historically, Chicanos have played major heroic roles, particularly during World War II and the Korean War. . . . But for every Chicano hero that made it home alive, there were a great many more Chicanos who died in battle. . . . And today, with the Viet Nam war, our Chicanos are still fighting and dying to become war heroes, many because of the influence and pressures put upon them by their own families to continue the tradition that their own father's and uncles initiated 20 and 30 years ago. It is time that Chicanos begin to realize that our own sons, and brothers, husbands and boyfriends, cousins and nephews are the ones being used to fight a war from which La Raza gains nothing. We only lose—our men and our own honor and our pride by participating or promoting the killing of millions of innocent children, women, and men in Indochina. They are an oppressed people in the very same fashion that we, as Chicanos in the United States, are an oppressed people—oppressed by the same imperialist system. The U.S. mass media portrays North Vietnamese . . . as "the enemy" simply because they want freedom to choose their own form of government. Chicanos in the U.S. are equally portrayed when we make it known that we will attain our equal rights and justice through self-determination in all aspects of our life. . . .

. . . The main point is that thousands of Chicano men are the ones being sent . . . to kill the Vietnamese people and in the process, for every 100 Chicanos sent to Viet Nam, 20 Chicanos return dead and many more wounded or maimed for life. It is time to begin to use our potential here at home in constructive ways which will help our Raza. It is time to seek ways of keeping our Chicanos here at home with their families instead of encouraging them to prove their manhood ("machismo") by fighting and dying in a war we have no business in. Social status and patriotism must become secondary to the many lives being lost among our Chicanos today.

❤ *E S S A Y S*

Organizing the Chicano community politically was a main goal of the Chicano movement. To help achieve this end Chicanos developed student organizations throughout the Southwest and Midwest whose focus was not only engendering ethnic self-pride but also advocating for Chicano concerns. The Mexican American Youth Organization (MAYO), a Texas student organization, was founded in 1967 by José Angel Gutiérrez, who became its first president. MAYO's structure, goals, ideology, strategy, leadership, and membership base, as well as the role of women in the organization, are the subject of the essay by Armando Navarro, director of the Ernesto Galarza Public Policy and Humanities Research Institute at the University of California, Riverside. Navarro emphasizes that MAYO's aim was to effect social change through political empowerment developed by focusing on self-identity in the fight against discrimination.

Chicanas were active participants and leaders in many of the organizations of the 1960s and early 1970s, including the United Farm Workers of America. However, the failure of scholars to recognize the significance of the family in the farmworkers' struggle in turn has obscured the role of women in the movement, according to Margaret Rose, the author of the second essay. The co-director of the Central California Social Science History Project at the University of California, Santa Barbara, she considers the centrality of women to the UFW boycott strategy, focusing on their domestic roles and union activism by examining the protests of UFW Chicana and Mexican women in the Washington, D.C., boycott. According to Rose, the use of a family model for the organization of the boycott had the effect of bringing women to the forefront of the struggle, although in an less visible role than that of the men. By confining women to traditionally female-defined activities, the UFW helped create an awareness of gender issues among the women.

The Mexican American Youth Organization

ARMANDO NAVARRO

By 1967 a climate for change permeated the Chicano community. The growth of the Chicano Youth Movement (CYM) was given tremendous impetus by the formation of the Mexican American Youth Organization (MAYO). MAYO became the avant-garde of both the Chicano movement (CM) and the CYM in Texas from 1967 to 1972. No other CYM-oriented organization in Texas came close to matching its activism, militancy, and espousal of Chicanismo. . . .

MAYO: Creation of Antagonisms

In 1967 the CM was gaining momentum throughout Aztlan. The Chicano organizational renaissance gave rise to numerous advocacy-oriented entities; one such organization was MAYO, which epitomized the militantization of the incipient CM. It was organized in San Antonio in March 1967 by five young Chicanos, Jose Angel Gutierrez, Mario Compean, Willie Velasquez, Ignacio Perez, and Juan Patlan [Los Cinco], who were graduate and undergraduate students at Saint Mary's University, a small Catholic liberal arts college. . . .

The issue that catalyzed the meeting of Los Cinco was their common interest in supporting the Texas farm worker movement. In addition, their discussions were permeated by a profound sense of urgency, frustration, and anger over the powerlessness and poverty of Chicanos in Texas. They realized that they had compatible interests and ideas and agreed that they needed to do more than just support the Texas farm worker movement. With this in mind, they held discussions covering a range of topics and concerns. . . .

Of major concern was the inefficiency of Chicano organizations in Texas. Although Los Cinco were cognizant of the contributions made by Chicano organizations such as the League of United Latin American Citizens (LULAC), the GI Forum, and the Political Association of Spanish-speaking Organizations (PASO), they were critical of their conservatism and saw them as not doing enough for Chicanos. Moreover, Los Cinco saw these organizations as being incapable of resolving the manifold problems confronting Chicanos in Texas. . . . The more Los Cinco discussed, the more they realized that the main problem with traditional Chicano organizations was that their programs were not oriented toward helping or changing the barrios. They felt that these organizations were neither committed to nor capable of providing advocacy for the Chicanos in the barrios.

Their discussions also focused on other concerns emanating from the deplorable and impoverished condition of the barrios. They felt that something needed to be done to improve the people's quality of life. Moreover, they were concerned about the educational status of Chicanos and the extermination of Chicano culture that they felt the Texas educational system was perpetuating. . . . An-

From *Mexican American Youth Organization: Avante-Garde of the Chicano Movement in Texas* by Aramando Navarro, pp. 80–114, Copyright © 1995. By permission of the University of Texas Press.

other major concern was the Chicano's lack of job opportunities. They felt that Chicanos were relegated to low-paying jobs and that few Chicanos were professionals.

Their discussions brought them to the realization that they did not want to be part of the existing Chicano organizations. Instead, they wanted to create their own organization, which would be youth-oriented and committed to effecting social change for Chicanos. To deal with these concerns, they felt that Chicanos needed a new direction and a new approach to organizing. . . .

. . . The five young Chicano activists felt that their backgrounds and experience provided the talent and leadership necessary to form a unique organization that would benefit La Raza. Gutierrez . . . became the group's spokesperson. . . . Gutierrez's activism began in 1963 with PASO's electoral revolt in Crystal City, which led to the election of five Chicano city councilmen. In 1967, after attending Southwest Junior College and Texas A & I University, Gutierrez enrolled at St. Mary's University in the graduate program in political science.

Friendship among Los Cinco helped them to divide the labor among themselves. Initially the rap sessions started with Gutierrez, Patlan, Velasquez, and Perez. Compean, whom Gutierrez recruited, was the last to join Los Cinco; with his involvement the leadership chemistry of Los Cinco jelled. Compean, who was well known for his activism in the barrios of San Antonio, became a field organizer and second in command to Gutierrez. Velasquez was a community activist from San Antonio who worked for the Catholic Bishops' Committee on the Spanish Speaking. His role became that of an administrator. . . . Perez, who had been working for the Texas chapter of the United Farm Workers Organizing Committee (UF-WOC), became a field organizer. And Patlan, who was well known in South Texas for his activism, took on the role of recruiting talented youths. Regardless of their specializations, Los Cinco were organizers above all, and . . . they built MAYO on the premise that it was an "organization of organizers."

Few activists within the CYM were as methodical and deliberate in building their organizations as were Los Cinco. MAYO was not built on spontaneity, nor was it formed as a response to a specific crisis. The planning sessions focused on developing a youth organization that would be different from Chicano student groups that were based exclusively in the university or Chicano barrio youth organizations that were anchored in the barrio. . . . The civil rights and Black Power movements significantly affected the thinking of Los Cinco. . . . Because of the Chicano community's initial strong support for U.S. involvement in the Vietnam War, the antiwar movement did not affect MAYO's Los Cinco until 1968. . . .

During the spring months of 1967, . . . Los Cinco developed a programmatic approach toward building MAYO. . . . They read voraciously on a variety of topics they felt were important to building the organization, such as electoral politics, revolutionary movements, biographies of political leaders, community organizing, and parliamentary procedures. Gutierrez explains the kind of organization they wanted to build: "We wanted to be a group of active crusaders for social justice— Chicano style. . . ." . . . They decided that the new organization was not to be based on mass membership. They opted for an organization composed of talented, young Chicano organizers who would be able to move into areas where they were needed. They wanted a cadre organization of organizers.

To form an organization of well-versed organizers, Los Cinco read and studied various topics but concentrated specifically on four: (1) power structures; (2) for-profit corporations; (3) methods of organizing; and (4) existing Chicano and black organizations. The Anglo power structure and business corporations were studied meticulously and with a definite purpose in mind. Los Cinco felt that . . . knowing how the Anglo power structure makes its decisions and how it governs would facilitate their organizing efforts. Power as a concept was also studied. . . . Discussions often focused on the importance of understanding the intricacies of power relations for the simple purpose of learning how to manipulate power and direct it against the Anglo power structure.

Complementing their study of the power structure was their desire to learn how corporations were tied into the power structure and how they functioned. . . . In essence Los Cinco sought to ascertain who the power holders were and what made them tick. The principle of "know your enemy" thus guided their power structure research.

In their study and discussion sessions they also spent time on *Robert's Rules of Order* to learn the art of parliamentary procedure. This helped them to learn how the power structure operated and how it conducted its meetings and business. . . . Los Cinco felt that a thorough knowledge of parliamentary procedure could help them when confronting school boards and agencies or when participating in formal meetings with power holders by enabling MAYO organizers to use points of order, motions of sorts, and so on to disrupt meetings and beat the opposition with its own rules of the game.

Their sessions also dealt with various strategies and tactics of community organizing. Los Cinco read and discussed Saul Alinsky's *Reveille for Radicals.* Alinsky's use of issues as a means of organizing was studied and discussed thoroughly. During those spring months of 1967 they succeeded in bringing Alinsky to a symposium at Saint Mary's University. After the symposium Los Cinco had an opportunity to meet with him informally and discuss various aspects of community organizing. The influence of Alinsky's method of organizing subsequently became evident in MAYO's involvement in a multiplicity of issues.

Los Cinco rejected what they referred to as the "lone wolf approach" of the Mexican American old guard—writing letters, calling press conferences, using diplomacy, and raising substantive issues in an accommodating way. . . . Los Cinco chose a more unconventional, eclectic strategy of protest influenced by Alinskyism, the Black Power movement, and the civil rights movement. . . . In developing their eclectic approach, they based their integration of ideas, structures, and schemes on what worked. Emphasis was placed on pragmatism of application. . . .

Furthermore, African American organizations from both the civil rights and Black Power movements were studied meticulously. Of special interest to Los Cinco were the Black Panther party and the Student Non-Violent Coordinating Committee (SNCC), which had evolved from a civil rights organization into a Black Power advocate. Los Cinco traveled, sometimes together, sometimes alone, into the southern part of the United States to talk to [Stokely] Carmichael and the organizers of Martin Luther King, Jr.'s, Southern Christian Leadership Conference, both of which influenced the organizational design being developed by Los Cinco.

Los Cinco's pragmatic eclectic approach was also influenced by . . . antagonisms within the emerging CM. They spent a considerable amount of time analyzing the strengths and weaknesses of CM entities and leaders. They read, studied, and met with the three most prominent leaders of the CM: Reies Lopez Tijerina [see Document 3], who headed the Alianza Federal de Mercedes (Federal Alliance of Land Grants) in New Mexico; Cesar Chavez [see Document 6], founder of the United Farm Workers Organizing Committee in California; and Rodolfo "Corky" Ganzales, founder and leader of the Crusade for Justice in Colorado. . . .

Tijerina was the CM leader who most influenced Los Cinco. . . .

Los Cinco admired Tijerina's courage, audacity, and fiery rhetoric in attacking the Anglo establishment in New Mexico. . . .

One important issue during the incipient organizing stage . . . was what to call this organization of organizers. After some serious deliberating, Los Cinco named their new organization MAYO. . . . MAYO . . . was a safe name that did not conjure up any radical or revolutionary connotations. . . . They preferred the use of *Mexican American* because the majority of La Raza in Texas did not identify with the term *Chicano*. To some, *Chicano* had a pejorative connotation. . . . The word *Youth* in MAYO was believed to be important as an appeal to the Chicano youth of both the barrios and universities.

Los Cinco decided to target South Texas for MAYO's organizing activities after considering the monolithic size of Texas, the concentration of Chicanos in South Texas, the volume of issues plaguing that region, and their . . . limited resources. . . . After numerous study sessions and discussions, MAYO was activated during the summer of 1967, ready to do battle with its archenemy, the gringo.

The Gringo: Archenemy of La Raza

. . . MAYO felt that to address the plight of Chicanos, gringos had to be confronted and exposed. MAYO felt that gringos did not want to do anything to improve the lives of Chicanos in Texas. . . .

MAYO's organizing approach in part relied on attacking the gringo establishment with a degree of militancy unprecedented in Texas history. MAYO's rhetoric and action were directed at dispelling the gringo-perpetuated myth that the Chicano is apathetic, indolent, unsophisticated, and inferior to the European. MAYO sought to make Chicanos aware of the gringo's responsibility for their exploitation, oppression, and powerlessness. Furthermore, it wanted to prove that the gringo establishment was not omnipotent and could be beaten. Through its use of militant action and rhetoric, MAYO gave notice to the gringo that it was ready to defend the rights and interests of the Chicano community. . . . By identifying the gringo as the archenemy of the Chicano, MAYO resorted to an Alinsky rule of organizing: always foster a polarization.

MAYO's Purposes, Goals, and Views

MAYO's first step was to organize the barrios of Texas to improve the overall quality of life there. It attempted to mobilize Chicanos in the barrios to address problems and to develop indigenous leadership. . . . MAYO's constitution provided a

framework through which the group sought to become involved in such areas as
education, social welfare, and civil rights, as well as in lessening neighborhood
tensions, eliminating discrimination, combating juvenile delinquency, and foster-
ing political empowerment.

. . . Its activities were manifold—from politics to economics to social action
programs to advocacy on issues. It functioned very much as a zealous interest
group that was willing to use both conventional and unconventional methods to influence policies affecting Chicanos. . . . It propounded several goals in the areas of
politics, economics, and education. . . .

Of these three goals, education reform received MAYO's heaviest involvement, which resulted primarily from the decision Los Cinco made in 1967 during
their study and discussion sessions. They concurred that education was at that time
the paramount concern of most Chicanos throughout Texas. . . . Gutierrez . . . elab-
orates on how MAYO used education as a means of organizing: "people were concerned about education. . . . People think about education. . . . [Thus,] education
was simply an issue that was acceptable to the community. So we worked it."
MAYO's accentuation of education was evident in the thirty-nine walkouts it was
involved in between 1968 and 1970. . . .

MAYO's Pragmatist Quasi Ideology

MAYO as an organization did not have a definite ideology. . . . From MAYO's inception, it was oriented toward pragmatic action rather than a rigid ideological
framework. MAYO's pragmatism was predicated on the importance of getting the
job done and on being resilient, adaptable to shifting political circumstances, and
sensitive enough to the process of action and reaction to avoid being trapped by its
own tactics and forced into circumstances not of its own choosing. . . . Gutierrez,
when asked about MAYO's ideology, responded: "We . . . trained ourselves to be
organizers with no set ideology."

. . . MAYO organizers were also political relativists, persons who believe that
truth is relative and changing. Another idiosyncrasy of MAYO organizers was their
political realism in their pursuit of change. . . . MAYO's adherence to Alinsky's
political realism was evident in that it was more interested in being a cadre than in
being a mass-based youth organization. . . .

MAYO was more interested in solving problems through action than in philoso-
phizing on what had to be done. It confronted issues that were specific and immediate and proposed realizable solutions. Its propellant was action for the improvement
of the Chicano's quality of life. MAYO's end was to change the conditions of La
Raza through a variety of means. It understood well the needs for ends, but not at
the price of sacrificing its freedom of choice of action. MAYO sought to have a degree of control over the flow of events.

Even though MAYO did not have a well-defined ideology, it was extremely
critical of what it termed the gringo's institutions. During the late 1960s, pervasive
to its rhetoric and literature were its acrimonious attacks alleging that American institutions were racist, hypocritical, and undemocratic. . . .

Besides being critical of American institutions, MAYO was also critical of
capitalism, which it perceived as an exploitive and oppressive system that had

relegated the Chicano to an economically powerless and subordinate status within the confines of the gringo's economic order and perpetuated the Chicano's poverty. . . .

Nonetheless, although MAYO overtly criticized capitalism, it never committed itself to any one ideology. Tenets such as Chicano self-determination, the inherent goodness of the Chicano community, redistribution of wealth, cultural nationalism, free medical services, and an adequate welfare system, among others, were expounded by MAYO. Some of the principles adhered to by MAYO, such as redistribution of wealth and free medical services, are inherent to a collectivist type of political and economic system. Although it never openly advocated socialism, these views were popular and commonplace in MAYO's literature and rhetoric. . . .

MAYO's ideological eclecticism was covered by a thick veneer of Chicano cultural nationalism, or Chicanismo. Within the diverse student groups and barrio youth organizations that constituted the CYM, MAYO was the most zealous advocate of cultural nationalism. From the various discussion and planning sessions in 1967 to MAYO's demise in 1972, Chicanismo was a powerful force that energized its vehement rejection of assimilation. This was evident in the rhetoric of its leaders, literature, symbolism, and actions. . . .

. . . Unlike the individuals in some other Aztlan-based student groups, MAYO's leaders and members were "practicing" Chicanos or Mexicanos, bilingual and bicultural. They were articulate in both English and Spanish. This orientation was ascribable largely to the pervasive *Tejano* culture, which was grounded on its Mexicanness. Historically, the heavy concentration of Chicanos in South Texas and the border shared with Mexico helped to produce a culture that was much more Mexican than its counterparts in other states in Aztlan. . . . Within the CYM, MAYO stood out in its adherence to Chicano nationalism. . . .

At the core of MAYO's quasi-ideological approach, however, was its adherence to pragmatism. Few Chicano organizations during the epoch of protest were as practical as was MAYO. . . . MAYO's leadership was directed by Alinsky's principle of using "what works." . . .

MAYO's pragmatism was strongly influenced by the personality and leadership style of its main spokesperson, Jose Angel Gutierrez. . . .

MAYO's Protest Strategy and Tactics

MAYO's pragmatic orientation was particularly evident in the organization's use of direct action tactics. . . .

MAYO was a great aficionado of unconventional protest methods. . . . With its cadre-oriented membership, MAYO relied on verbal and written criticism, petitions, picketing, marches, nonviolent confrontations, sit-ins, and the use of obscene language to create a contagion that ultimately mobilized large numbers of people. Although it often alluded to the possible use of violence and self-defense, such rhetoric was part of its bravado strategy of showing no fear to gringos and demonstrating courage to Chicanos. For all its tough talk, it never used violence. MAYO in theory was committed to meeting violence with violence, but in practice it was nonviolent and worked within the framework of the system's institutions.

For several months in 1967 MAYO experimented with a variety of organizing techniques in San Antonio's west-side barrios. . . . MAYO did not organize simply to organize. In essence, it sought to assist the people in the barrios to organize themselves into effective groups to attain whatever change they deemed necessary. Concomitantly, it sought not to provide leadership but to develop the barrios' indigenous leadership by politicizing the people living there and providing leadership and encouragement via action.

Like its strategies, MAYO's organizing tactics were eclectic. MAYO was dramatically influenced by both Chicano and non-Chicano movement leaders and organizations. Concomitantly, it was the most "Alinskyist" of any of the CM entities to emerge during the epoch of protest. Attending to Alinsky's emphasis on issues as mediums for organizing, MAYO manipulated the issues that it felt would appeal to the self-interest of those segments of the Chicano community it was trying to organize. Because MAYO had limited resources, its tactics were often predicated on Alinsky's dictum that "tactics means doing what you can with what you have." MAYO's tactics were designed to rub salt into the community's sores of discontent. It relied on the people's pain and frustration to effect social change. . . .

. . . MAYO's tactics were essentially eclectic, amalgamating Alinsky's use of issues as a means of organizing with an unconventional protest approach that was common to a variety of organizations participating in the various movements during the epoch of protest. According to Compean MAYO's highest priority in 1967 was "to try to bring on the scene the tactics of the civil rights movement, which were picketing, demonstrating, and confrontation politics." MAYO felt that Chicanos had seldom resorted to such tactics and that circumstances rendered it expedient to do so. The use of such unorthodox tactics was seen as conducive to dispelling myths of Chicano docility and servility to the gringo. Overall, MAYO's tactics were designed to mobilize Chicanos, especially the youth, into social and political action.

Furthermore, the group's eclectic tactics were designed to differentiate MAYO from other, accommodationist Chicano organizations in Texas. Its vehement rhetoric coupled with its protest politics orientation was directed at the gringo power holders. In confronting them MAYO sought to demonstrate their vulnerability. The idea that the gringo could be beaten was accentuated throughout MAYO's existence. The principal objective was to find the tactics that would actuate and mobilize the Chicano community. Throughout its years of activism MAYO constantly sought to play a "war of nerves" against those it labeled the opposition. An element of surprise kept the opposition off balance and unaware of MAYO's next moves. Its tactics had strategic psychological underpinnings—to instill in the minds of La Raza that the gringo power holder in Texas was not omnipotent and could be beaten.

By 1969 MAYO leaders began expounding on the need for MAYO to alter its image and tactics. . . . Those who supported Gutierrez and Compean explained why it was important for MAYO to change its image. They argued that MAYO had to have an acceptable image that would not "turn off" the community but rather win its confidence. . . . Even though the opposition won the debate, there was general agreement among the board members that MAYO's tactics had to be changed.

MAYO's eclectic tactics were usually conceived in the planning sessions that were held prior to engaging any major issue. Planning was stressed from the beginning. It was used as a means not only for formulating strategy and tactics but also, and equally important, for engendering a collectivity of thought and action among the members. . . . Although planning was constantly stressed, MAYO was sometimes encumbered by its loose and decentralized structure.

MAYO's Decentralized Structure

MAYO's structure was designed to give flexibility to its operation. From its beginning MAYO opted for a decentralized structure that would give it the latitude needed to improvise and experiment with various tactics and programs. Creativity of thought and action were sought. . . . MAYO's decentralized structure called for a board of directors and individual chapters. There were no regional or district entities. Overall, its structure consisted of a board with little power and autonomous chapters with much power.

According to its bylaws, the governing board of directors was composed of Los Cinco and one representative from each chapter. Each chapter was also allowed to elect an alternate board member who would attend board meetings when its official elected delegate could not. The board met twice a year. . . . One meeting was devoted to planning; priorities and projects were selected for the year. The second meeting was usually held to evaluate the various programs and projects and to elect new officers. The board elected a chairman, a vice-chairman, a secretary, and a treasurer, each of whom held office for one year. All officers except the chairman were eligible for reelection. The chairman was allowed to appoint his own staff, which comprised two people, a secretary and an assistant. The chairman's primary responsibility was to ensure that the dictates or policies of the board were carried out. . . .

MAYO's voting procedures were based on majority rule. Decisions on resolutions, motions, elections, or any other business were decided by simple majority. A two-thirds majority among members present, however, was required for any amendment to the bylaws. Also, an amendment to the bylaws required fifteen days' written notification to the membership. A voting quorum was simply the board members present. The voting and meetings were conducted utilizing parliamentary procedures as established in *Robert's Rules of Order.*

In reality, however, MAYO's state structure, while always decentralized, changed over time. . . .

MAYO's state structure was buttressed by a small administrative staff that operated out of San Antonio. . . . MAYO's state officers would at times operate out of the San Antonio office, which was located in the barrios of San Antonio's west side. Because of the group's extremely limited resources, MAYO's small staff varied in size and was largely voluntary. . . . In comparison to other Chicano student groups, MAYO was unique in that it was able to maintain a statewide office and staff. At its administrative apogee, MAYO's staff numbered nine.

MAYO's Collective State Leadership

MAYO's leadership orientation was essentially collectivist. . . . Power struggles were commonplace among both Chicano student groups and barrio youth organizations during the epoch of protest, but unlike many other Chicano organizations, MAYO was not plagued by power struggles within its leadership. At the state meetings emphasis was placed on reaching a high degree of consensus before making policy decisions. There was a sense of democratic centralism practiced in decision making. Policy issues were often hotly debated, but the leaders closed ranks once the decision was made. Personalism was mitigated through a no reelection clause for the chairman. The structure allowed for a circulation of leaders, which in turn permitted leadership mobility. Consequently, there existed an aura of trust and solidarity and a commonality of purpose and goals. . . .

MAYO's Membership Base

MAYO's chapters were composed of youths from the barrios and colleges and its membership thrust was to bridge both segments. In the barrios it sought to transform gangs . . . into chapters and activists. Initially, in 1967, MAYO first focused on organizing barrio-based MAYO chapters. However, by 1968 MAYO chapters were also organized in the universities, colleges, and even high schools. The barrio chapters, however, remained the most numerous. They were composed predominantly of poor young men from the ages of thirteen to their early twenties. . . . At the university or college level, some members were poor, but in general they were middle-class.

Membership in MAYO was subject to the limitations set by the board of directors. MAYO's membership criteria were based on twelve requirements for new members. . . . Those wishing to join had to adhere categorically to all twelve requisites, which were oriented toward sacrifice, dedication, knowledge, sincerity, courage, and discipline. . . . MAYO sought to recruit individuals who were compatible with its philosophy and goals. It sought those individuals who had the qualities of good organizers.

The actual size of MAYO's membership was never known. . . . To safeguard MAYO from infiltration, each MAYO chapter was responsible for maintaining records of its membership. To MAYO's leadership, the number of members was not important. What was important, however, was the quality and commitment of its members. Because of MAYO's emphasis on networking and involving others in the struggle, a few members properly organized and motivated could easily multiply themselves tenfold. Intrinsic to MAYO's cadre orientation was the notion that change is always made by the few in the name of the many.

MAYO's chapter membership fluctuated as a function of the issues it confronted between 1967 and 1970, the years of its advocacy-oriented agenda. New members were recruited generally through two means, the use of issues and the dissemination of information. MAYO's membership ranks increased with every issue the group confronted. The issue was utilized both as a means of organizing the barrios and as a medium for recruiting. Members were recruited also through the dissemination of information—speaking engagements and rap sessions in the barrios and the distribution of MAYO newspapers and pamphlets, buttons, and posters. . . .

Even though each individual chapter was initially permitted one and later two board members, individuals had to go through MAYO's three levels of membership before becoming part of the core group . . . :

Level One: Those people interested in MAYO superficially, i.e., workers recruited through activity or issues, but did not believe or understand all of MAYO's position;

Level Two: After a time of being observed and of learning, people competent enough to make policy and provide leadership assistance—now they are MAYO; and

Level Three: People that are hard core to provide leadership, see direction; people with years of experience. . . .

Each chapter was sovereign in determining its own local priorities and agenda, providing these did not conflict with the board's general policies (the board seldom had a maverick chapter go against its policies and decisions). Consequently, the programs of action varied from chapter to chapter. Moreover, the level of organization also varied. Some were well organized, while others were loosely structured. . . . At the state level MAYO tended to be very deliberate in its organizing actions; some MAYO chapters, however, were the opposite, spontaneous and crisis-oriented. This sometimes violated MAYO's adherence to a theory of organization . . . of having a cadre of professional organizers ready for deployment when an emergency arose, ready to manipulate the issue or crisis to advance its own revolutionary agenda.

Not all MAYO chapters were hotbeds of activism. Because of MAYO's barrio and university base, they sometimes differed in size, style of activism, age of members, and commitment to action. In general the university-based chapters were better organized and had more older members. . . . Barrio chapter members were younger but stronger in their commitment to dealing with controversial issues. While *MAYOistas* in the universities were more cautious because of concerns about their careers, *MAYOistas* in the barrio had "no salida" (no way out). They were willing to take a risk.

At its peak MAYO had a minimum of forty chapters. Like the total number of members, this number fluctuated according to the issues and personalities at center stage. Although the bylaws did not mandate the creation of regional structures, MAYO's chapters were concentrated in four main geographic areas. . . . South Texas by far had the most MAYO chapters, reflecting MAYO's early decision to concentrate its organizing activities in South Texas, where Chicanos were the majority in many counties. . . . In some communities no chapters were formed, but ad hoc MAYO support entities existed that were not required to follow MAYO's prescribed bylaws, structure, or policies. One obvious idiosyncrasy of MAYO's state and local structure stands out: while women were involved as members they were generally absent as leaders of the organization.

MAYO and the Gender Factor

MAYO's leadership was essentially male. All the interviewees attested to the involvement of women in MAYO's membership ranks; they also pointed out, however, that no women served in an official state leadership capacity. Among the remaining four of Los Cinco and other MAYO leaders interviewed there were differences of opinion as to the level and scope of the Chicana leadership involvement.

Perez recalled that at the beginning of MAYO women were not directly involved. In contrast, Gutierrez explained that women were always involved in MAYO's development.... Patlan echoed Gutierrez's comments by saying that Chicanas played a very strong role. They were always present and were always a part of MAYO's chapter-level activities and brainstorming. While acknowledging that in MAYO's formative organizing stage there was not a focus on the role of Chicanas, Compean said, "Large numbers of women were involved, especially at the local level, in MAYO's activities. There was no formal definition of roles."

Although agreeing with the founders of MAYO that women were involved with MAYO, other MAYO leaders disagreed with them as to their role. Carlos Guerra illustrates this point: "Actually, we are going through a very serious rewriting of history in dealing with the role of women in the movement. We would like to think that in the old days we were progressive about it, but we were not. We were pretty sexist. They were essentially second-class participants by and large." Alberto Luera said that most of MAYO's leaders and spokespersons "were guys." Other MAYO leaders interviewed . . . concurred with Guerra and Luera. [Rudy] Rodriguez commented that "in the beginning women had no role at all with MAYO. It was male dominated. . . . We really didn't go out and recruit women. It just happened that way."

Chicanas were involved with MAYO and did play a significant role in its development, but they never occupied major positions of leadership. All the women interviewed on the gender issue agreed that women were involved, but not in major leadership positions. Luz Gutierrez explained, "Women were not necessarily in a leadership capacity because at the time we really didn't demand to be recognized as leaders as we do now. We were just partners in the whole development of MAYO." Choco Meza, who was active with MAYO, explained the Chicanas' lack of power within MAYO by saying, "There were no women in leadership roles in MAYO . . . because the male gender has always built a very strong network among themselves and have limited themselves to being in control. . . . I think males generally see themselves as ones who can out-strategize and out-think females . . . able to gain respect for their ideas better than females . . . unfortunately that's not true." Other Chicanas . . . were generally in agreement with Luz Gutierrez's and Choco Meza's analysis of the gender factor.

In essence, Chicanas played a vital supportive role in MAYO. Juanita Bustamante explained, "We were involved in different roles. We were in the picket lines. We provided support for the publication of MAYO's newspaper, either writing articles, typing, mailing, among other things." Viviana Santiago describes her work as "supporting," doing a lot of the legwork. Rosie Castro commented that it wasn't until Raza Unida that they saw a lot of leadership by women. Unlike Raza Unida, MAYO didn't have visible female leadership. Luz Gutierrez concluded, "As always the women are the ones that do most of the work and the men get all the credit."

The reasons for the absence of women in leadership roles are manifold. First, MAYO initially sought to organize the barrio youth who were members of gangs. . . . Second, the prevalence of a strong Chicano/Mexicano culture in Texas rendered the leadership involvement of women problematic. . . . Because MAYO's image was extremely radical, parents were concerned about their daughters getting involved with MAYO. Third, *machismo* was a factor. . . . Finally, there was a sense of partnership among MAYO women members. Luz explains why the Chicanas involved never really pushed the issue of leadership inclusion: "We tended to feel that we didn't want the feminist issue to divide us. So we tended to want to be united for *la causa* as a family and not divided. We wanted to go forward together."

The pervasiveness of the Mexican culture in Texas coupled with MAYO's strong adherence to cultural nationalism was the paramount obstacle to women playing a major role in MAYO. Rosie Castro reaffirmed this position: "Even in my own development when I would go out to the barrios and try to get women to register to vote they wouldn't without the men's permission. . . . It was told to women do not get involved in politics. That was a carryover from the Mexican [culture]." Viviana Santiago also agreed. The emphasis on cultural nationalism was evident in her response. She said, "From my point of view, our unified goal was to keep the family intact. By doing that we had to also boost the Chicano man, who had been emasculated by the system." Even the males interviewed agreed that the Chicanos' conservative culture in Texas was a major factor impeding the inclusion of women in MAYO's leadership ranks.

It was not until the transition from MAYO to the RUP [Raza Unida Party] that women began to play a leadership role. Even prior to the transition in 1971, Chicanas, particularly in the universities, were beginning to exercise leadership. All the women interviewed graduated from college. Armed with increased knowledge and somewhat free from their parents' direct influence, these Chicanas became MAYO spokespersons for various issues and were involved in various activities. Rosie Castro, for example, was an active member of the Young Democrats prior to working with MAYO. Juanita Bustamante, while attending Morehead State College in Minnesota in 1968, assisted in organizing a MAYO chapter there. In 1971 Choco Meza was a major spokesperson for a MAYO-sponsored school walkout at Eagle Pass High School. And Viviana Santiago played a major organizing role in 1971 and 1972 as a staff person in the transition from MAYO to the RUP.

At the local level there were numerous other women who played significant spokesperson roles in MAYO. There was Severita Lara, who led the Crystal City walkout in San Antonio; Evi Chapa in Fort Worth; Rebecca Flores in West Texas; Yolanda Birdwell in Houston; Alma Canales, who in 1972 ran for lieutenant governor under the RUP; and others. These women were indicative of how some women did take on a spokesperson leadership role. . . .

Newspapers: Vehicles of Organizing

Starting in 1968 MAYO began developing its own newspapers, which . . . were used for communication, propaganda, agitation, recruiting, and organizing. As propaganda vehicles they articulated MAYO's programs and views. They were used to agitate chapters, supporters, and communities into action. By encouraging action they also enhanced MAYO's overall recruitment and organizing efforts. Their paramount role was to influence the unorganized Chicano population of Texas and engender unity and action among MAYO's chapters. . . . MAYO's leaders, cognizant of the role of newspapers sought to use them to enhance MAYO's status throughout the Chicano-populated areas of Texas.

By 1969 MAYO had four newspapers operating in Texas: *El Degüello,* from San Antonio; *Hoy,* published in the Rio Grande Valley; *El Azteca,* printed in Kingsville; and *La Revolución,* from Uvalde. In general, the four newspapers served to promote MAYO's pro-CM orientation. . . . In another editorial, *Hoy* dedicated itself to the unity of the Chicano and to the downfall of all the forces that exploit the Chicano community. . . . Because of their content they increasingly came under political attack. . . . The tone of the articles in the four newspapers paralleled that of the antigringo statements made in public by Gutierrez and other MAYO leaders.

. . . The four newspapers were usually published on a monthly basis. Their audience was primarily the young segment of the Chicano community. Funds for printing the papers came from a variety of sources, from donations to ad sales. Their circulation was limited because of their limited finances; they were always plentiful, however, whenever MAYO was involved with issues.

Without the required resources, the four newspapers proved to be transitory and by 1969 began to go out of circulation. Other sources of financial and labor support . . . began to dry up. . . . Therefore, in the absence of its newspapers, MAYO relied on the periodic distribution of newsletters to its chapters and communities.

In addition, MAYO relied on manipulating the traditional electronic and print media for disseminating its views and advancing its *causa*. Often its tactic was to whet the media's appetite by using strategies and tactics that were controversial, polarizing, and loaded with the potential for conflict. MAYO understood well what was newsworthy.

The Significant Role of Chicanas
in the United Farm Workers' Boycott

MARGARET ROSE

This work examines the protest of a selected group of Chicanas and Mexicanas in the UFW—married women with children, particularly in the Washington, DC, boycott—who made the difficult transformation "from the fields to the picket lines" during the struggle for union recognition and collective bargaining rights.

In the early years, Anglo volunteers dominated the boycott operations across the nation. Farm worker participation was minimal. . . . Originally, few Mexican or Mexican-American women and even fewer entire families went to boycott; the family pattern evolved gradually as the UFW experimented, through trial and error, with the most effective response to grower tactics and as union attitudes towards women began to change. Over the years, as the boycott strategy was refined, women were increasingly recognized as important players. . . .

Changes in farm worker organization began during the intensified boycott in 1968 against Giumarra, the largest producer of table grapes (and later extended

Margaret Rose, "From the Fields to the Picket Line: Huelga Women and the Boycott, 1965–1975," *Labor History* 31, no. 3 (1990). Reprinted by permission of Labor History.

against the entire industry). This long term effort which lasted two years required a greater financial commitment and a much larger staff in major cities all over North America. . . .

In 1968 under pressure from her husband, Hijinio, and with urgent pleas from the union, María Luisa Rangel, a farm worker wife from Dinuba, a small agricultural town outside of Fresno, California, reluctantly agreed to transplant her family of eight children to Detroit to work on the Giumarra campaign. . . . Nevertheless, María Luisa provided essential stability for family life and the boycott as she worked alongside her husband and children until the historic grape contracts were secured in 1970. Soon after the announcement of the agreements the Rangels returned to California. From her Detroit experience, María Luisa emerged a strong advocate of the union's cause. . . .

However, convincing farm worker women to leave their homes and communities during these early years proved difficult for union officials.

With the strike and boycott against lettuce growers in 1970, new personnel were needed. This time recruitment of farm worker families was facilitated by changing attitudes towards and more recognition of Chicanas and Mexicanas in the UFW. . . . And also by the early 1970s, the union leadership and the permanent boycott staff had more experience in preparing for, accommodating, and utilizing farm worker families to maximum effect in the boycott.

During this period, the Juanita and Merced Valdez family and their seven children left the lettuce and strawberry fields in the Salinas Valley in northern California and moved to Cincinnati to help with the lettuce campaign. The parents tended to the day-to-day chores of the boycott. The children . . . devoted their summers, weekends, and after-school hours to picket lines. . . . During the week the parents and older children appeared before community meetings to talk about their work in the fields, their strike experiences, and to appeal for help for their union. Their activities generated publicity for the boycott in the local press and on television news and public affairs programs. . . .

By 1973, when the UFW had intensified its lettuce campaign, renewed its boycott against table grapes, and initiated its drive against Gallo wines, the family pattern of boycott participation was firmly entrenched. Some single Chicano and Mexican men and women participated in boycotts, but married men were discouraged from doing so unless accompanied by their wives and children. "This time," observed Dolores Huerta in 1973, "no married man went out on the boycott unless he took his wife." The family pattern exposed farm workers—husbands, wives, and children—to a new world of social activism and political protest. . . . In the family, in the fields, and in the boycott, responsibilities for men and women were divided along gender lines. A patriarchal order characterized the organizational structure and personal relations from the leadership down to the rank-and-file level.

Gilbert Padilla coordinated the union's effort in the nation's capital from 1973 to 1975. . . .

As director of the Washington, DC, boycott, Gilbert was the chief spokesman and strategist for the union in the federal district and the surrounding area. . . .

Gilbert was joined by his . . . wife, Esther, . . . and their baby daughter, Adelita. The 29 year-old Esther Negrete de Padilla, a California-born Chicana, brought sensitivity, educational training, and administrative experience to the Washington, DC, enterprise. . . .

While Gilbert oversaw the entire boycott operation, he received valuable help from Esther in gender-specific areas. This service . . . did not attract wide notice because of its traditional nature and because it often occurred behind the scenes. A conventional female concern in the home was the care and management of the family. Esther not only met these responsibilities, but also managed the domestic side of the boycott. The two-story frame house in Takoma Park, a suburb of Washington, DC, that served as headquarters for the boycott, . . . was home to the Padillas and to the families and individual organizers who came and went in the course of the two-year campaign.

Esther dealt with the problems that inevitably arose from the interaction of many people. Using her knowledge of the welfare system, she obtained food stamps and medical benefits for the transplanted farm workers. When one farm worker woman required emergency care upon arrival in the city, Esther arranged for her hospitalization. Children required visits to the doctor and glasses. . . .

. . . For the new boycott recruits from the fields, Esther sought medical attention and acted as a counselor and morale booster. As such she served as a liaison between the boycott leadership and the farm worker families scattered around the metropolitan area.

Esther's contribution was not limited to personal and domestic details. Because of her educational and work experience, she was a valuable asset in the formal administration of the boycott. Her public duties ranged from dealing with produce managers and political representatives to office work. Esther's day began with early morning visits to the central produce market. Along with staff members . . . she harangued uncooperative fruit and vegetable dealers who continued to purchase boycotted grapes and lettuce. . . .

After these 5:30–7:30 am daily encounters, she devoted the bulk of her time to political lobbying on Capitol Hill. After Gilbert arranged formal introductions to elected officials, Esther directed this effort. She intervened with influential Senators . . . on labor legislation of interest to the union. She prevailed on long-time supporters . . . to help. . . . Through her lobbying, other members of the California congressional delegation lent their important backing. . . . Public officials who were not sufficiently supportive of the union became the target of UFW campaigns. Esther organized a sit-in at the Washington, DC, office of California Senator John Tunney in response to his failure to support UFW boycotts and his advocacy of labor legislation opposed by the union.

In addition to personal contacts with legislators and their staffs, Esther testified before congressional committees. . . .

When she was not on Capitol Hill, Esther helped in the day-to-day operations of the enterprise. Working out of the boycott house in Takoma Park, she handled correspondence, issued press releases, supervised . . . supporters who volunteered to help in the office, attended staff meetings, and kept minutes for important regional boycott conferences. With her expertise on congressional matters, her knowledge of the Washington, DC, office, and her dealings with farm worker personnel, she also served as a confidante and advisor to her husband. . . . Within this formal patriarchal arrangement, there was a great degree of mutuality, cooperation, and female autonomy.

This family model of union activism also characterized the Washington, DC, boycott venture at the rank-and-file level. . . . With the announcements of the grape and Gallo boycotts and number of personnel increased rapidly. By 1974 there was a staff of 23, supplemented from time to time by temporary non-Hispanic and non-paid volunteers. This figure did not take into account the younger children who often participated in the boycott. The majority of the staff consisted of five farm worker families. . . .

The family of Herminia and Conrado Rodríguez resided in the Arvin-Lamont area, south of Bakersfield, before their move to Washington, DC. Their background and experiences were typical of the families who left their homes to work in the boycott during the 1973–1975 campaign. . . .

Like many other families, the Rodríguezes' politicization became a family affair. During the summer of 1973, the family participated in the widespread protests against local grape growers who balked at renewing the UFW contracts negotiated three years before. . . . As talks between grape producers and the union stalled, demonstrations intensified. When local grape industry representatives hastily concluded contracts with the Teamsters Union, protests heightened. While picketing against local growers, Conrado and his eldest teenage daughter, Lupe, were arrested along with other union supporters and transported to the county jail in Bakersfield. Herminia and the remaining children, together with other detainees' families, went into the city and denounced the incarcerations. . . .

The calamitous confrontations between agribusiness and the union in the summer of 1973 that resulted in the mass arrests of farm workers (men, women, and children) and their supporters politicized many families. When the UFW suspended picketing after the deaths of two union supporters in August, the activism of the Rodríguez family did not diminish. Packing up their personal belongings, they joined the caravans of farm worker families who left in the late summer and early fall 1973 to launch a renewed boycott campaign against corporate agriculture on a distant urban front, far away from the recent turmoil in the fields.

As with the Padillas, the Rodríguezes followed the family model of boycott participation with activities divided along gender lines. Herminia Rodríguez oversaw the domestic needs of her family and participated in traditionally female-defined boycott work. Like Esther Padilla, Herminia received much less attention than her husband and refrained from public speaking [*sic*] with the result that her actions, like those of most other Chicanas and Mexicanas, seemed "invisible." . . .

The traditional responsibility of making her family comfortable was not an easy task for Herminia Rodríguez given the disruptions in family life caused by the boycott. The Rodríguez family, like others, had to adjust to a strange environment, new people, different climate, an unfamiliar culture, and difficult living conditions. An entirely new system of survival and domestic decisions had to be adopted. . . .

As boycott wives and mothers learned quickly, domestic stability became secondary to the demands of the boycott. When organizing needs shifted, the family relocated. Herminia moved her family four times during their two-year stay in Washington, DC. . . . Frequent residential changes necessitated different arrangements for the entire family. Herminia's patient acceptance of this instability contributed to the smooth functioning of the boycott. Furthermore, her sacrifices of domestic tranquility were directed towards political ends. Herminia and other wives endured these dislocations to advance the goals of better wages, decent living conditions, and the opportunity for a better future in California. . . . In the boycott the thin line between personal family concerns and political action blurred in the lives of Chicanas and Mexicanas. Personal discomforts and domestic duties translated into a strong female political statement.

In addition to managing difficult living conditions and family affairs, Chicanas and Mexicanas also participated in public boycott activities, short of public speaking which was left to the men. . . . The most tedious, but most essential, task was picketing. Chicanas and Mexicanas spent hours on picket duty, particularly during the summers when the objective was to maintain daily picket lines. At grocery stores . . . and at local liquor stores . . . , Esther Padilla carried her two-year-old daughter . . . and Herminia Rodríguez took her five children. . . . At times picket lines were composed of women and children. . . . Becoming active participants in the boycott propelled Mexicanas and Chicanas out of the private sphere and into the public domain in ways they were unaccustomed to in rural California. . . . But while these pursuits expanded the public role of Mexican and Mexican-American women, it did not fundamentally alter gender roles. To the contrary, boycott women relied on a shared domestic culture and female reciprocity to relieve the hardships of their new urban lifestyle.

Farm worker women engaged in supportive jobs in the office, depending on their skill level, but did not participate in the formal decision-making process which was reserved for men. . . . Herminia and other Mexicanas answered phones, stuffed envelopes, or ran office equipment. María Castillo, Herminia's friend, assumed the task of selling union bumper stickers, buttons, key chains, and other items at union-sponsored events. . . . Possessing a fine singing voice, María also provided entertainment performing Mexican folk songs and *corridos* (ballads), such as "De Colores," a union favorite, accompanied by guitar-playing Conrado Rodríguez.

The domestic skills of Herminia, María, and other boycott wives also served the boycott. Herminia shopped, cooked, and cleaned so that other women could perform office duties. While Esther lobbied on Capitol Hill, Herminia babysat her daughter. . . . Farm worker women contributed their domestic talents in other ways at the UFW-sponsored fundraising dinners attended by the Democratic political establishment. . . . At these events, some attended by as many as 2000 guests, and at smaller gatherings, Herminia, María, and other farm worker women collected tickets at the door or assisted in the preparation and serving of food similar to the vital work of the women who ran the strike kitchens in California. In this context, the economically essential work of cooking was converted into a political act.

In contrast to Chicanas and Mexicanas at the rank-and-file level, their husbands exerted a more public and readily recognized presence in the boycott. The family model of social activism gave the male head of household more prominence, authority, and responsibility. . . .

While both men and women walked picket lines, the men were photographed more frequently for union publications and were often jailed—a very public event—for their activities. Whereas in rural California mass arrests of both men and women occurred, . . . in the cities men were more frequently arrested than women. If both husband and wife underwent arrest there was no extended family to care for the children; thus the less public responsibility to stay out of jail usually fell to the wife. . . .

For children, the boycott became a novel and exciting experience, offering a dramatic exposure to a different style of life. . . . But gender divisions prevailed here also. In the Cincinnati boycott, for example, sons Sergio (18) and Rego (15) Valdez often took charge of speaking duties and other responsibilities from their father while their sister Mary (17) performed a more auxiliary and less public, though no less vital, role in the office. Thus while teenage boys often served as spokespersons for their families, their sisters were expected to assume a supportive and behind-the-scenes presence, like their mothers.

The progress of the Washington, DC boycott accelerated after the arrival of farm worker families in the city. The immediate attention of the boycott focused on pressuring supermarkets to remove non-union products and to create strong grass-roots support for UFW collective bargaining demands. Farm worker families . . . were essential in the picketing strategy. Within the first three months of their arrival in the nation's capital, they had succeeded in gaining the cooperation of 137 independent and "Mom and Pop" stores. Local co-ops . . . joined the boycott. After the arrests of three farm workers, another small independent . . . agreed to remove grapes from its shelves. The California boycotters also achieved success in their campaign to pressure 275 liquor stores to stop selling Gallo wine products. . . . But as the local boycott leadership and farm worker families soon realized, the most difficult targets were the large supermarkets. . . . Farm workers and their supporters began picketing Giant Foods, a chain of 100 stores in the Washington area. The largest, and most intransigent chain was Safeway with 234 stores in the vicinity. Despite almost constant picketing at their stores and warehouses, and despite financial losses, both chains resisted demands of farm worker families to honor the boycott.

To create the necessary pressure to make the UFW campaign effective, the boycott leadership turned to the development of long-term community and regional support. Through the sustained cooperation of farm worker families, local organizers, and with the backing of labor, religious, political, consumer, and student groups, the Washington, DC UFW office mounted a viable boycott effort. After organizing the nation's capital, the boycott spread to other areas. Using the experience they had gained in Washington, DC, farm worker families moved to other cities [in the area]. . . .

In this region, the most successful campaign was directed against Gallo wine. . . . Overall, the nationally-coordinated campaign finally convinced agribusiness in California to endorse legislation, the Agricultural Labor Relations Act (ALRA), which guaranteed secret-ballot elections—an historic step in the state.

With the passage of the ALRA in summer 1975, a major shift occurred in the boycott structure. As a member of the UFW Executive Board, director Gilbert Padilla and his family returned to California. . . . A challenging and difficult job awaited the two in California—confronting growers who continued to resist attempts at unionization. Farm worker families also returned to California in anticipation of participating in field election campaigns. Herminia and Conrado Rodríguez moved their family back to the Arvin-Lamont area to cast votes for UFW representation at their struck ranches. In Washington, DC boycott operations were transferred to the local Anglo staff. . . .

The ultimate success of the two-year struggle, from 1973 to 1975, against the agricultural industry depended on a remarkable cooperation between Mexican and

Chicano activists and field workers, Anglo organizers, and middle-class supporters in cities across the U.S. and Canada. Farm worker commitment to the boycott was intricately tied to the family approach to organization that preserved gender designated forms of labor activism. . . .

. . . The family model of boycott organization reinforced the general expectation that Chicanas and Mexicanas would exert a crucial, but less visible, role in the boycott. Female cooperation and community prevailed over individual ambition. A familiar domestic culture eased the transition from the fields to the cities. . . .

While the UFW provided an outlet for class solidarity and a means for expressing ethnic pride for an exploited minority, it reinforced traditional gender relations by confining women to traditionally female-defined work and social activism. However, by raising the ethnic and class consciousness of its female membership and by exposing them to novel situations, new ideas, and different cultural expectations, the UFW may have inadvertently laid the foundation for the emergence of a greater awareness of gender issues among Mexicanas and Chicanas.

❤ *F U R T H E R   R E A D I N G*

Oscar Zeta Acosta, *The Autobiography of a Brown Buffalo* (1989)
————, *The Revolt of the Cockroach People* (1989)
Lucha Corpi, *Delia's Song* (1989)
José Angel de la Vara, "1970 Chicano Moratorium and the Death of Rubén Salazar," in Manuel P. Servín, ed., *An Awakened Minority* (1974)
"El Plan Espiritual de Aztlán," in Luis Valdez and Stan Steiner, eds., *Aztlán* (1972)
Richard Griswold del Castillo and Richard A. García, *Cesar Chávez* (1995)
David G. Gutíerrez, "Sin Fronteras?: Chicanos, Mexican Americans, and the Emergence of the Contemporary Mexican Immigration Debate, 1968–1978," *Journal of American Ethnic History* 10 (Summer 1991), 5–37
John C. Hammerback, Richard J. Jensen, and José Angel Gutiérrez, *A War of Words* (1985)
Patricia Hernández, "Lives of Chicana Activists: The Chicano Student Movement (A Case Study)," in Magdalena Mora and Adelaida R. Del Castillo, eds., *Mexican Women in the United States* (1980)
Juan Goméz-Quiñones, *Mexican Students por la Raza* (1978)
Clark Knowlton, "Guerrillos of Río Arriba: The New Mexico Land Wars," *The Nation* 206 (June 17, 1968), 792–796
Douglas Martínez and Manuel Goméz, "Chicanos and Vietnam," in Walter H. Capps, ed., *The Vietnam Reader* (1991)
Armando Morales, *Ando Sangrando—I am Bleeding* (1972)
Carlos Muñoz, *Youth, Identity, Power* (1989)
Peter Nabokov, *Tijerina and the Courthouse Raid* (1969)
Adaljiza Sosa Riddell, "Chicanas and el Movimiento," *Aztlán* 5 (Spring 1974), 155–165
Francisco A. Rosales, *Chicano* (1996)
Rubén Salazar, *Border Correspondent* (1995)
Charley Trujillo, ed., *Soldados: Chicanos in Viet Nam* (1990)
U.S. Commission on Civil Rights, *Stranger in One's Land* (1970)

CHAPTER
13

The Gaining of Power: Chicano

Political Empowerment,

1964–1980

By the late 1960s the political role of Chicanos had changed dramatically, as the U.S. government and the larger American society had begun to pay attention to their problems. The spirit of Chicano ethnic pride and solidarity was kindled by the noble struggles of César Chávez and La Causa, which began to have a national dimension through the grape boycott. Meanwhile, in South Texas Chicanos took over school administrations, the judicial system, and the county government of Zavala County. Also in Texas, José Angel Gutiérrez formed a political party based on race, language, and culture—La Raza Unida Party (LRUP). In Denver, Corky González, becoming disillusioned and frustrated by the failure of the U.S. government to end oppression of Chicanos, organized the Crusade for Justice. For many Chicanos, participation in these activities earned them valuable experience that they would put to use in their membership in the major political parties and in their election or appointment to public office. How did involvement in La Raza Unida Party represent change in the Chicano community? Why did Chicanos in Texas request federal intervention to achieve full political equality?

By the late 1970s Chicanos remained optimistic that American society could not continue to ignore them—the fastest-growing minority group in the nation. Working through the Southwest Voter Registration Education Project (SVREP), they went into the communities to increase and strengthen Chicano voting power. Chicanos believed that by such organizing, they could challenge Anglo political supremacy throughout the Southwest. The SVREP would be largely responsible for the growth of political power among Chicanos through voter registration, field research, coalition building, and on-sight training of volunteers; involvement in litigation on racial gerrymandering; and improved communication about their concerns. In such activities as conducting opinion polls and surveys, trying to influence public policy, working at the community level, and fighting discriminatory election structures, SVREP would remain an important example of citizen participation. Likewise, the expansion of the Voting Rights Act to the Southwest in the

411

mid-1970s benefited Chicanos, opening to them new opportunities for political participation at all levels. At this time both the Democratic and Republican parties began to express an interest in Chicanos; no longer would either party ignore them. How did the Nixon administration and the Republican party court the Chicanos and bring them into their state and national organizations?

❦ D O C U M E N T S

The strike by California grape workers for higher wages began in Delano, California, in 1965. As the strike continued, the workers called for a nationwide consumer boycott of table grapes to help their cause. Document 1 is the Boycott Day Proclamation grape workers issued in spring 1969. The organizing of an independent Chicano political party was one of the major developments in the Chicano movement in the early 1970s. La Raza Unida Party (LRUP) in Texas was quite successful, as it was the first such party to achieve electoral victories. Document 2 is an excerpt from a speech made by the party's leader, José Angel Gutiérrez, in San Antonio in May 1970, after the LRUP won the school board and city council elections in Crystal City, Texas. Document 3 lists the priorities adopted by the delegates to the LRUP's 1972 national convention that would be expanded into the party's platform. These points reflect the LRUP's emphasis on community control by Chicanos and embrace national as well as international issues of concern to Chicanos. By the early 1970s both the Democratic and the Republican party were acknowledging the importance of the Chicano vote in national politics. In Document 4, Dolores Huerta, vice-president of the United Farm Workers of America, discusses the responses by these two major political parties to the issues and needs of Chicanos during the 1972 presidential campaign.

The Mexican American Legal Defense and Educational Fund (MALDEF) advocated for the legal rights of Mexican Americans. Selections from the testimony that Vilma S. Martínez, president and general counsel of MALDEF, delivered before the U.S. Commission on Civil Rights in 1975, are reproduced in Document 5. Martínez asks the Justice Department to intervene to end the discrimination faced by Mexican Americans. A major voter registration drive by the Southwest Voter Registration Education Project resulted in nearly 300,000 new Chicano voters. In Document 6, dated 1979, journalist Juan Vásquez describes the numerous obstacles faced by Willie Velásquez, director of the SVREP, in his struggle to achieve electoral recognition for Chicanos.

1. Grape Workers Issue the Boycott Day Proclamation, 1969

We, the striking grape workers of California, join on this International Boycott Day with the consumers across the continent in planning the steps that lie ahead on the road to our liberation. As we plan, we recall the footsteps that brought us to this day and the events of this day. The historic road of our pilgrimage to Sacramento later branched out, spreading like the unpruned vines in struck fields, until it led us to willing exile in cities across this land. There, far from the earth we tilled for gen-

"Proclamation of the Delano Grape Workers for International Boycott Day, May 10, 1969," *El Malcriado,* April 15–30, 1969, as found in Wayne Moquin, ed., *A Documentary History of the Mexican Americans* (New York: Praeger, 1971), pp. 363–365.

erations, we have cultivated the strange soil of public understanding, sowing the seed of our truth and our cause in the minds and hearts of men.

We have been farm workers for hundreds of years and pioneers for seven. Mexican, Filipinos, Africans and others, our ancestors were among those who founded this land and tamed its natural wilderness. But we are still pilgrims on this land, and we are pioneers who blaze a trail out of the wilderness of hunger and deprivation that we have suffered even as our ancestors did. We are conscious today of the significance of our present quest. If this road we chart leads to the rights and reforms we demand, if it leads to just wages, humane working conditions, protection from the misuse of pesticides, and to the fundamental right of collective bargaining, if it changes the social order that relegates us to the bottom reaches of society, then in our wake will follow thousands of American farm workers. Our example will make them free. But if our road does not bring us to victory and social change, it will not be because our direction is mistaken or our resolve too weak, but only because our bodies are mortal and our journey hard. For we are in the midst of a great social movement, and we will not stop struggling 'til we die, or win!

We have been farm workers for hundreds of years and strikers for four. It was four years ago that we threw down our plowshares and pruning hooks. These Biblical symbols of peace and tranquility to us represent too many lifetimes of unprotesting submission to a degrading social system that allows us no dignity, no comfort, no peace. We mean to have our peace, and to win it without violence, for it is violence we would overcome—the subtle spiritual and mental violence of oppression, the violence subhuman toil does to the human body. So we went and stood tall outside the vineyards where we had stooped for years. But the tailors of national labor legislation had left us naked. Thus exposed, our picket lines were crippled by injunctions and harassed by growers; our strike was broken by imported scabs; our overtures to our employers were ignored. Yet we knew the day must come when they would talk to us, *as equals.*

We have been farm workers for hundreds of years and boycotters for two. We did not choose the grape boycott, but we *had* chosen to leave our peonage, poverty and despair behind. Though our first bid for freedom, the strike, was weakened, we would not turn back. The boycott was the only way forward the growers left to us. We called upon our fellow men and were answered by consumers who said—as all men of conscience must—that they would no longer allow their tables to be subsidized by our sweat and our sorrow: They shunned the grapes, fruit of our affliction.

We marched alone at the beginning, but today we count men of all creeds, nationalities, and occupations in our number. Between us and the justice we seek now stand the large and powerful grocers who, in continuing to buy table grapes, betray the boycott their own customers have built. These stores treat their patrons' demands to remove the grapes the same way the growers treat our demands for union recognition—by ignoring them. The consumers who rally behind our cause are responding as we do to such treatment—with a boycott! They pledge to withhold their patronage from stores that handle grapes during the boycott, just as we withhold our labor from the growers until our dispute is resolved.

Grapes must remain an unenjoyed luxury for all as long as the barest human needs and basic human rights are still luxuries for farm workers. The grapes grow sweet and heavy on the vines, but they will have to wait while we reach out first for our freedom. The time is ripe for our liberation.

2. José Angel Gutiérrez Calls for Political Action, 1970

As you know, there is a new political party in Southwest Texas. It's called La Raza Unida Party. The history of this party is rather interesting.

For years the Chicano farmworker has made up the majority of the population in the South Texas counties. But he goes trucking across this country . . . and so he's never there to vote. Yet this is precisely the time the primaries are held—in May. . . . So, you see, we are in fact not even able to vote.

We have had other problems which we have known about for a long time. . . .

Supposedly in this kind of a democratic society the citizenry is encouraged to participate in the political process—but not so in South Texas.

Someone asked me recently whether I thought any type of system other than the American political system could work in South Texas. I thought about it for a minute and suggested that the question be reworded because we ought to try the American system first. . . .

They accuse me and mexicanos in Cristal [Crystal City], in Cotulla and Carrizo Springs, of being unfair. One gringo lady put it very well. She was . . . interviewed . . . right after the school board elections and before the city council elections. . . . *Newsweek* asked her to explain the strange phenomena that were occurring in these counties: a tremendous voter turnout and a tremendous amount of bloc voting. She said, "Well, this is just terrible! Horrible! A few days ago we elected a bunch of bum Mexicans to the city council." And the reporter said, "Well, they are 85 percent of this county." And she replied, "That's what I mean! They think they ought to run this place!"

By all these little things you can begin to understand how to define the word "gringo," which seems to be such a problem all the time. It's funny, because the mexicano knows what a gringo is. . . . Let me elaborate on it. . . .

The word itself describes an attitude of supremacy, of xenophobia—that means you're afraid of strangers. . . . This attitude is also found in institutions, such as the Democratic Party. It's in policies like the one that says you can't speak spanish in school because it's un-American. It's in the values of people. . . .

The formation of this party came about because of the critical need for the people to experience justice. It's just like being hungry. . . .

We were Chicanos who were starved for any kind of meaningful participation in decision making, policy making and leadership positions. For a long time we have not been satisfied with the type of leadership that has been picked for us. And this is what a political party does, particularly the ones we have here. I shouldn't use the plural because we only have one. . . .

These parties, or party, have traditionally picked our leadership. They have transformed this leadership into a kind of broker . . . who deals in the number of votes or precincts he can deliver or the geographical areas he can control. . . .

A beautiful example of this is Ralph Yarborough [Democratic senator from Texas]. The only thing he does for Chicanos is hire one every six years. He's per-

José Angel Guitiérrez, "Mexicanos Need to Control Their Own Destinies," in *La Raza Unida Party in Texas,* Copyright © 1970 by Pathfinder Press. Reprinted by permission.

fectly content with the bigoted sheriff and Captain Allee [Texas Rangers] and the guys that break the strikes in El Rio Grande City and . . . all these other people.

Four years ago, when the guy who is now running for commissioner in La Salle County in La Raza Unida Party ran in the Democratic primaries, it cost him one-third of his annual income! That's how much it costs a Chicano with a median income of $1,574 per family per year. With the third party it didn't cost him a cent.

On top of the excessive filing fees, they have set fixed dates for political activity, knowing that we have to migrate to make a living. We are simply not here for the May primaries. Did you know that in Cotulla, Erasmo Andrade [running in the Democratic primary for state senator in opposition to Wayne Connally] lost by over 300 votes because the migrants weren't there? . . .

So you see that what's happening is not any big miracle. It's just common sense. The trouble is that everybody was always bothered and said, "We can't get out of the Democratic Party. Why bite the hand that feeds you?" . . . Others say, "Well, why don't you switch over and join the Republican Party?" Well, let's not even touch on that one.

Why can't you begin to think very selfishly as a Chicano? I still haven't found a good argument from anyone as to why we should not have a Chicano party. Particularly when you are the majority. If you want to implement and see democracy in action—the will of the majority—you are not going to do it in the Democratic Party. You can only do it through a Chicano party. . . .

But you see there is another, more important, reason, and that is that mexicanos need to be in control of their destiny. They need to make their own decisions. . . . We have been complacent for too long. . . .

You've got a median educational level among mexicanos in Zavala County of 2.3 grades. In La Salle it's just a little worse—about 1.5 grades.

The median family income in La Salle is $1,574 a year. In Zavala it's about $1,754. The ratio of doctors, the number of newspapers, the health, housing, hunger, malnutrition, illiteracy, poverty, lack of political representation—all these things put together spell one word: colonialism. You've got a handful of gringos controlling the lives of muchos mexicanos. And it's been that way for a long time.

Do you think things are going to get better by putting faith in the Democratic Party . . . ? Or that things are going to get better because you've got a few more Chicanos elected to office now within the traditional parties? Do you think that things are going to get better now that the U.S. Commission on Civil Rights has officially claimed that there is discrimination against mexicanos? . . .

No, it's not going to get better. We are going to have to devise some pretty ingenious ways of eliminating these gringos. Yet they don't really have to be too ingenious. All you have to do is . . . have a little common sense. . . .

In 1960 there were 26 Texas counties in which Chicanos were a majority, yet not one of those counties was in the control of Chicanos. If you want to stand there and take that you can. You can be perfectly content just like your father and your grandfather were, *con el sombrero en el mano* [with hat in hand].

That's why most of our traditional organizations will sit there and pass resolutions and mouth off at conventions, but they'll never take on the gringo. They'll never stand up to him and say, " . . . We've had it long enough!"

This is what we've got to start doing. If you don't go third party, then you've got to go the independent route, because there is no other way you are going to get on the November ballot. And don't try to put in a write-in candidate. That never works. . . .

The recent elections here in April for school board and city council demonstrated something that many people knew was a fact. . . . We won in an off year in the nonpartisan races, which means that we were able to elect a minority to these positions. . . .

. . . We've all got to work together. That means that all of us have to pitch in. And this is why in Crystal City you no longer hear "Viva La Raza" and "Chicano Power" and "La Raza Unida" all over the place. We don't talk about it anymore because it's a reality. . . .

Our actions have made "La Raza Unida" more than just a slogan. . . . We began organizing and moving in to counterattack every time the gringo tried to put pressure on the mexicano. . . .

So don't let anybody kid you. We . . . are the majority. We can stop anything and we can make anything in South Texas if we stick together and begin using common sense.

This third party is a very viable kind of alternative. It's a solution. For once you can sit in your own courthouse and you don't have to talk about community control because you are the community. . . .

We are talking about bringing some very basic elements into the lives of mexicanos—like education and like making urban renewal work for mexicanos instead of being the new way of stealing land. . . .

You can be as imaginative as you want and do almost anything you want once you run units of government. . . .

. . . The response that we've had to this third party in all sections of our communities has been overwhelming. You saw the results. You can count votes just as I did.

The third party is not going to get smaller. It's going to get bigger.

You have three choices. First, you can be very active in this thing. For once we are not talking about being anti-Democratic or pro-Republican or pro-Democrat and anti-Republican. We are talking about being for La Raza, the majority of the people in South Texas. . . .

If you don't choose that route, you can stay home . . . and just come out and vote. But otherwise stay home. Don't get in the way.

The third thing you can do is lend your support, your general agreement. . . .

So, you've got these three roles that you can play. Or you can get . . . defensive and say, "This is wrong, this is un-American because you're bloc voting." But don't forget that the Democrats do it too. You can say that this is racism in reverse, but don't forget that we are the majority. And you can say that this is going to upset the whole situation in the state of Texas . . . because we're segregating ourselves . . . and that this is not what we should be trying to do, that we should be trying to integrate, etc., etc. Well, . . . come down and tell that to my sheriff. Tell him how much you like him. Or, better yet, . . . tell it to Ranger Allee himself.

Build your constituency, build your community—that's how we will be electing three and possibly four congressmen in the very near future. There's going to be another congressman in Bexar County. . . . So we have some very interesting developments coming up.

3. La Raza Unida Convention Announces Its Priorities, 1972

LABOR: Support the right to strike and support the farmworkers' Union.
    Parity in employment opportunities and wages for Chicanos in the Federal government, public service companies and agencies, unions, etc.
    The end to exploitation of illegal aliens.
    Adequate minimum wage law.
    Guaranteed minimum annual income and benefits.
    Government subsidies shared with laborers who work for subsidized farmers.
    End of "right to work laws."
BUSINESS: Redistribution of wealth and the breakup of monopolies.
EDUCATION: Bilingual, bicultural education throughout entire educational system.
    Increased opportunities for Chicanos in higher education to have greater representation in the professions.
HOUSING: Adequate housing insured for Chicanos.
HEALTH: Free Clinics.
    Stop drug traffic in Chicano communities.
    National Health Insurance to insure adequate health care to Chicanos.
    Increase recruitment of Chicanos into medical schools.
INDOCHINA: Immediate withdrawal of American troops from VietNam and Indo-China.
PENAL SYSTEM: Prison Reform.
LATIN AMERICA: Elimination of U.S. economic and military intervention in L.A.
    Puerto Rican Independence.
LAW ENFORCEMENT: End to Police Brutality.
    Chicano community control of law enforcement agencies.
JUSTICE: Chicanos to serve in judgeship and juries at all levels.
    Free legal aid to insure adequate legal representation for Chicanos.
    Enforcement of the treaty of Guadalupe Hidalgo.
    Complete political independence.
    Support none of the two major candidates for President of the United States.
    Support of Ramsy Muniz for governor of Texas.
LAND: Honor original Mexican and Spanish Land grants.
    Cease taxation of land.
MUJER CHICANA: Pledge responsible support of Latina women in their struggle for equal rights in all spheres of life.
GENERAL: Community control of social, economic and political and educational institutions—Chicano self-determination.

"Raza Unida Convention," *El Grito del Norte* 5, no. 8 (October 1972).

4. Dolores Huerta Recalls Democratic and Republican Response to the Farmworker Issue, 1972

Introduction

The name César Chávez and the struggle to unionize farm labor have become virtually synonymous. . . . But Dolores Huerta, the union's fiery vice-president, doesn't seem to mind being overshadowed by Chávez. . . . She thinks of herself as a "common soldier" in the union's army of workers and volunteers. . . .

But her leadership ability is undeniable. Huerta went to the Democratic Convention as a delegate from California and turned this meeting of a political party into . . . a gathering of lettuce boycotters. As one of the union's chief negotiators, she matches the opposition's highly trained and highly paid lawyers with her own self-taught negotiating skills. . . .

Dolores Huerta Talks

It's hard when you learn how to do something but you have to do something else. But they've kept us on the run. . . . They got the bright idea in the Nixon administration to try to take the boycott away from us in the federal courts. . . .

We went to Washington and started putting heat on the Republican party all over the country. We picketed people like Bañuelos [U.S. Treasurer Romana Bañuelos]. . . . I was in Washington talking to the Republicans and the Democrats trying to stop this thing. . . .

We've been working more and more with the Democratic party, because it's been the more liberal of the two parties. We depended on the Democrats to pass all those bills. . . . You hardly ever get Republicans to vote for you. . . .

It's not true that both parties are just as bad for Chicanos, because the few benefits that we have gotten have come through the Democratic party. The only thing I have to say to people who attack the Democrats is that they should attack the Republicans. They should be going after Nixon, after Secretary of Agriculture Butz, after Reagan and all of these Republicans . . . who vote against us every single time. That's who they should be going after, not after the guys who are trying to help us. . . .

I think that if people are dissatisfied with the Democratic party they should get involved and take it over. I've told Assemblyman Moretti that he can make a decision either for or against the poor people, and that if he's against us we're going to fight him. But you can't go saying this to Reagan. He won't even meet with us.

There were some problems at the Democratic Convention. It was really unfortunate because there was a little clique that was trying to put down McGovern. The rumor was going around that McGovern wouldn't talk to Chicanos. Well, this was ridiculous because in East Los Angeles McGovern would go to every . . . place Chicanos wanted him to go, and speak to them. But there were people who were spreading this rumor around. I think they were part of the Nixon sabotage squad! . . .

"Dolores Huerta Talks About Republicans, César, Children, and Her Home Town," in *La Voz del Pueblo*, November–December 1972.

I know that the farm worker issue is not the only Chicano issue. But in terms of the visibility of the Chicano issues, . . . there wasn't an agreement among the Chicanos. . . . Some people talked about bilingual education, other people talked about something else. . . . There just wasn't . . . consensus on what we wanted to make public. So, I talked to Senator McGovern's staff, . . . and I told them that Chicanos wanted more visibility there. Naturally, they turned to me and said they wanted me to make a seconding speech for Eagleton. . . . And I told them that I didn't want to be in the limelight. . . .

. . . The Chicanos . . . had a platform with a lot of Chicano issues which they wanted to submit. But it was put together kind of fast, I think. . . .

Understanding that Chicanos have to come from all walks of life, from different experiences and different communities, you're not always going to get everybody to think the same. . . .

We're just now reaching a level where we can get mature political participation. We're going to get it as people get more interested in politics. . . . If we would have had fifteen Chicanos in California who were really involved in politics, . . . the whole McGovern campaign would have been run by Chicanos. . . .

It would seem that with the Republicans in for another four years, . . . we'll have a lot of obstacles. Their strategy was to get Chicanos into the Republican party. But we refuse to meet with . . . Henry Ramírez [chairman of the President's Cabinet Committee on Opportunities for the Spanish-Speaking]. He went around and said a lot of terrible things about us . . . back east. He thought that we didn't have any friends back there. But we do, and they . . . told us that he was saying that the farm workers didn't want the union, that César was a Communist, and . . . a lot of stupid things. This is supposed to be a responsible man.

Then there is Philip Sánchez [National director of the Office of Economic Opportunity]. I went to his home in Fresno once when a labor contractor shot this farm worker. I was trying to get the D.A.'s office to file a complaint against the labor contractor. So I went to see Philip Sánchez to see if he could help me. But the guy wouldn't help me. Later when the growers got this group of labor contractors together to form a company union against us, Sánchez went and spoke to their meeting. It came out in the paper that he was supporting their organization. As far as I'm concerned, Philip Sánchez has already come out against the farm workers.

5. Vilma S. Martínez Testifies Before the U.S. Commission on Civil Rights About the Mexican American Legal Defense and Educational Fund (MALDEF), 1975

I am Vilma S. Martinez, President and General Counsel of the Mexican American Legal Defense and Educational Fund, Inc. MALDEF is a non-profit organization which works to redress the grievances and vindicate the legal and constitutional rights of over six million United States citizens of Mexican ancestry. Our community

Testimony of Vilma S. Martinez (San Francisco, California: Mexican American Legal Defense and Educational Fund, 1975), pp. 1–14.

constitutes the second-largest minority in America today. . . . Its needs . . . are enormous; the barriers it faces are legion; the discrimination it has endured and continues to endure is pervasive. But I should like to believe that its hope and its ultimate faith in this country are abiding and deep-sprung. Today we call upon this committee and this Congress to vindicate that hope and faith.

At the core of that hope and faith necessarily must lie a belief that our voices are heard, our impact felt, and the society at large is willing to respond as best it can to the legitimate needs of our people. But too often in the American Southwest, we find our voices subtly but effectively silenced and our efforts cancelled. . . . This committee can help change that.

. . . Throughout the Southwest, Mexican Americans have not been able adequately to make their weight felt at any level of government. In Texas, where Mexican Americans comprise 18% of the population only 6.2% of the 4,770 elective offices—298 of them—are held by Chicanos. California is worse. There, Mexican Americans comprise 18.8% of the total population. Yet, in 1970, of the 15,650 major elected and appointed positions at all levels of government—federal, state and local—only 310 or 1.98% were held by Mexican Americans.

This result is no mere coincidence. It is the result of manifold discriminatory practices which have the design or effect of excluding Mexican Americans from participation in their own government and maintaining the status quo.

Now, Mr. Chairman, the United States Commission on Civil Rights is charged with informing the congress and the nation about such discriminatory practices on the part of state and local officials. I would like to review with the Committee what the Commission found in Uvalde County, Texas. What the Commission found in Uvalde, Mr. Chairman, exists all across the State of Texas. The pattern of abuse in Uvalde County is strikingly reminiscent of the Deep South of the early 1960's. The Civil Rights Commission study documents that duly registered Chicano voters are not being placed on the voting lists; that election judges are selectively and deliberately invalidating ballots cast by minority voters; that election judges are refusing to aid minority voters who are illiterate in English; that the Tax Assessor-Collector of Uvalde County . . . refuses to name members of minority groups as deputy registrars; . . . "runs out" of registration application cards when minority voter applicants ask for them; . . . refuses to register voter applicants based on the technicality that the application was filed on a printed card bearing a previous year's date.

Other abuses were uncovered . . . [:] widespread gerrymandering with the purpose of diluting minority voting strength; systematic drawing of at-large electoral districts with this same purpose and design; maintenance of polling places exclusively in areas inaccessible to minority voters; excessive filing fees required in order to run for political office; numbered paper ballots which need to be signed by the voter, thus making it possible to discover for whom an individual cast his ballot. . . .

This, then, is the situation in at least one of the 254 Texas counties. As the Civil Rights Commission found, the processes by which this country conducts its elections are riddled with subtle—and not so subtle—discriminatory devices which have the effect of excluding minorities. The atmosphere in which those elections are conducted is heavy with the clouds of discrimination and coercive control. . . . They exist all across the great swath of Texas where Chicanos are attempting to share in decisions affecting their county, their city, and their schools, decisions which are crucial to their daily lives. It is thus crucial that the constitutional rights of these citizens be enforced.

But, gentlemen, it is simply not possible to guarantee to these people a meaningful right to vote with private litigation alone. It would be like attempting to empty the sea with a sand pail.

There is, however, an alternative remedy: Sections 4, 5, 6 and 8 of the Voting Rights Act [of 1965]. Under Section 5, for instance, no change in a voting practice or procedure, however slight, could be enforced without the acquiescence of the Attorney General. . . . Practices that range from the most flagrant gerrymander to the most subtle transfer of a polling place . . . would all be objectionable under Section 5. . . . The presence of federal registration examiners under Section 6, and federal election observers under Section 8, both would . . . dampen the abuse of raw economic power and coercion directed against Mexican Americans.

These remedies are swift. They are efficient. They are effective. They are in great measure responsible for the extraordinary gains marked by minorities in the Deep South over the past decade. They are relevant to the problems faced by Mexican Americans in the Southwest today. The Congress should apply these remedies and safeguards to the Southwest. . . .

Mr. Chairman, this committee should clarify for the Justice Department its responsibilities under the Voting Rights Act of 1965. . . . The Congress should pass amendatory language which would afford Mexican Americans in Texas and elsewhere in the Southwest the powerful protections of Section 5 of the Voting Rights Act.

In all this, Mr. Chairman, there lies only the fervent desire to be heard, to participate in our own government and to ensure that electoral rules and procedures foster—not foreclose—our opportunity for self-expression at the polls. And ultimately, if this legislation is passed by the Congress and enforced by the Justice Department, it will mean better local government. . . . It will mean the beginnings of a fair share for Mexican Americans. I sincerely hope this committee will help us make that new beginning. Thank you.

6. Juan Vásquez Discusses Willie Velásquez and the Southwest Voter Registration Project (SVREP), 1979

West Texas has long been . . . a throwback to simpler, uglier times. In rural communities like . . . Ozona, Mexicans are still "Meskins," and the rest of the folks are "white people." The authority of the federal government and its courts is recognized only resentfully. West Texas is consequently a place of political powerlessness for Latinos, a place where gerrymandered districts are common and where the "Meskin" vote often goes into a ballot box that is really a trash can. Nonetheless,

Juan Vásquez, "Watch Out for Willie Velasquez," *Nuestro Magazine* 3, no. 2 (March 1979): 20–24. Reprinted by permission of the author.

Chicanos today are venturing into this political terra incognita, and . . . they are beginning to win elections.

This surge forward is being mapped mainly by one man. . . . He is a soft-spoken ex-activist who likes to invoke Jefferson, Franklin and Lincoln to disarm his critics. . . . William C. "Willie" Velásquez . . . runs . . . the most significant Latino political group in the U.S.—the Southwest Voter Registration Education Project—and his work is just starting to be recognized.

. . . He is the man the Anglo establishment hates to see. When he shows up, it almost surely means trouble for the old order that all too often still gives Anglos absolute political power over sizeable, sometimes majority, Chicano populations. Consider the progress that Velásquez and the SVREP have made since 1974:

•   Nearly a third of a million Mexican American, Native American and Black voters have been registered in six Southwestern states in the last two years alone.

•   Countless reports and analyses have been made, outlining minority voting strength and electoral contributions to date. . . .

•   Dozens of minority members have been elected to office in places like Conejos County, Colo., and Pecos, Tex. . . .

The biggest gain is, paradoxically, the least tangible. For there has been a definite change in Chicano attitudes—the change that comes from the discovery that they could actually win elections. And to understand just how big a shift that has been, one has only to recall the years and years of trying for elective office, and failing at every try. . . . Then there was a related question: How could Chicanos establish their political power across broad areas if they could not win even when they were in the majority?

The answers came with the founding of the voter registration project. . . . Using as a model the successful Voter Education Project launched by Southern Blacks in the mid-'60s, the project . . . got off the ground in 1975, with Willie Velásquez at the helm. Right away, SVREP began analyzing elections from a minority standpoint, conducting voter registration surveys and seminars and, perhaps most important, pointing out target areas that were ripe for political and legal action.

"What we found in a lot of these places is what the staff calls 'induced apathy,' " Velásquez explains. "The people kept losing and losing, and the more you lose, the more inclined you are to think you can never win. You tend to give up." . . .

The process begins with a visit to the courthouse of the target county to ask for the public records pertaining to voter registration and census. . . . "We're always extra polite when we go in because there's no point in antagonizing anyone," says Velásquez. "They've got to give it to you because it's a matter of public record, and they know it; so if they get a little hostile, you just endure it." . . .

A case in point is Sutton County, [Texas,] a sheep- and goat-raising area . . . where Chicanos . . . constitute 55% of the population. As in most Texas counties, the Latinos had been gerrymandered into political impotence. In spite of years of vigorous efforts, no Chicanos had ever been elected to an important office. "Induced apathy" was rife.

. . . Confronted with proof that the Chicano vote had been diluted, the county decided to redistrict rather than face the prospect of being sued in federal court for gerrymandering—and almost surely losing. Result: A Mexican American today sits . . . on the five-member commissioner's court. . . .

The Sutton County script has been replayed in dozens of counties and small cities. . . .

Currently, the project is filing suit against or negotiating with 21 Texas counties or municipalities over voting irregularities. . . . Further, Velásquez and the staff of SVREP have compiled a . . . list of 13 Texas cities and counties where future action is possible.

But if the prospect of gaining strength at the local level is encouraging, the prospect statewide—and across the Southwest as a whole—is something else. . . .

As for why the Latino voter—and the voter registration project, by implication—is having so little effect at the statewide level, Velásquez says that the project is geared to influence local elections. It does not fund registration drives designed to have impact on . . . gubernatorial or senatorial races because (1) it does not have enough money and (2) most of the complaints from voters who want to take part in a registration drive are focused on such local problems as drainage, streets and parks.

Velásquez knows the value of thinking small, keeping election goals concrete and specific. The project has even conducted 200-vote campaigns throughout the six states of the Southwest, and it has been generally welcomed with open arms by the minority community and its supporters. . . .

Velásquez grew up in San Antonio's West Side barrio of Edgewood but graduated from Central Catholic High School, just a few blocks from downtown. He then attended St. Mary's University. . . . Armed with a degree in economics, he entered graduate school but dropped out in 1966 to become involved full time in the grape boycott of the United Farm Workers' Organizing Committee. . . . Later, Velásquez went to work for the Bishops' Committee on the Spanish-Speaking, where . . . he was fired for running up huge long-distance phone bills that were unrelated to his job. . . .

. . . As for his firing, he says, "What we were really doing was putting together the first Raza Unida convention."

The convention, held in January of 1968 at a San Antonio high school, was a watershed event in the history of Chicano politics. It marked the first time so many Chicanos and their allies. . . . had come together to try to create a powerful faction aimed at capturing power. And Willie Velásquez was right in the middle of it.

. . . He was elected the first coordinator of what was then called El Movimiento Social de la Raza Unida. But if the meeting was a milestone, the aftermath was something else. No one seemed to know how to use the potential power assembled at the convention. When a separate political party called La Raza Unida was formed later that year under the aegis of . . . José Angel Gutiérrez . . . [,] Velásquez either quit or was read out of the party, depending on whom one talks to. . . .

Velásquez became the first executive director of the Mexican American Unity Council [MAUC], which . . . is an extremely successful organization, providing economic self-help programs for Chicanos. . . . After a year at MAUC and a stint with the National Council of La Raza, Velásquez became involved with the voter registration project. . . .

Significantly, the project is just beginning to step up its activities in California. One report being studied by the staff of the voter registration project was prepared for the California State Assembly Committee on Elections and Reapportionment in 1977. It looked at 65 cities with substantial minority populations and concluded: "Of these 65 cities, minority groups were significantly underrepresented in 63. In 60 of the 63, the Mexican American populations were underrepresented by from one to four Chicano City Council members per city." . . .

. . . As he surveys the Latino political scene across the country, Velásquez finds substantial grounds for optimism. In the first place, the median age of Mexican Americans is 19.7 years, compared with the national average of nearly 30 years. That means that as Mexican Americans cross the age 25 threshold, where frequency of voting picks up, they should turn out more and more on election day. Secondly, groups like SVREP and MALDEF are eliminating the institutional obstacles that have kept Latinos out of the voting booth in the past. And third, the era of Chicano-supported strikes and boycotts has served to give the Chicano a sense of purpose that was missing before. . . .

Velásquez cautions that the 1980s might be a decade of frustration. ". . . It could turn out to be 10 long years of misery unless we get equitable voting districts." The key factor, he feels, is the 1980 census, which should provide political planners with better information on Latinos than previous counts. That is vital because it is on the basis of the census that all subsequent political strategies and decisions are based.

"The other thing we've got going for us is the immigrants," according to Velásquez. "Whether anyone likes it or not, those immigrants have not had justice and they are going to demand that this country live up to its laws and its constitution. They are vital to the health of American democracy. . . .

. . . In the city of Ozona in west Texas' Crockett County, . . . the project had to issue an emergency appeal for money to carry out its case against outrageous gerrymandering. . . . Its treasury was depleted . . . because SVREP had to fight . . . delaying tactics and recalcitrance on the part of the Anglo establishment determined not to share its long-held power.

. . . Anglo election officials had been responsible for some egregious violations of the electoral code—unusual even by Texas standards. Ballots were color coded so that election officials could know which belonged to Mexican Americans. The ballot box was opened repeatedly before the election was over. The county clerk set aside a box for "questioned ballots" when Mexican Americans came in to vote. . . .

. . . After years of contested, postponed and special elections, there are finally two Mexican Americans on the commissioner's court in Crockett County. This happened after the SVREP conducted a registration drive that enlisted the participation of 95% of the eligible Chicanos in the county. In the crucial election, 93% of them cast ballots. Still, the election of one of the Mexican Americans is being contested by the man he beat; it may never end. But instead of being cheated out of office and being forced to sue to win his seat, Sostenes de Hoyos is sitting in the courthouse and forcing his Anglo opponent to go through the trouble and expense of filing suit. In west Texas, that's real progress.

☙ *E S S A Y S*

The Chicanos' struggle for racial justice and equality in the 1960s, along with similar efforts by other racial minorities, dramatically transformed the United States socially, culturally, and politically. Chicanos' achievements included bilingual education, admission to higher education, assistance for migrant farmworkers, and political participation in third parties and eventually in the major parties. La Raza Unida Party satisfied a need for Chicanos to participate in politics. The subject of the first essay, by Ignacio M. García, assistant professor of history at Brigham Young University in Provo, Utah, is the 1972 campaign of Ramsey Muñiz for governor of Texas. The author explains how Muñiz emerged as the major LRUP candidate for governor as well as the party's leading spokesperson. Despite the nationalistic and revolutionary platform of the LRUP, Muñiz quickly proved to be a very popular and charismatic candidate. He gained widespread support in both the rural and urban areas of Texas among Chicanos and Anglos alike. According to García, many Texas Anglo liberals, without a choice among the Democratic candidates for governor, opted to vote for Muñiz.

In the second essay Tony Castro, formerly a journalist with the *Houston Post,* offers a thorough description of the efforts of the Nixon administration and the Republican party to win the Chicano vote because of its growing potential to determine elections in California and Texas. The author argues that the Republicans began wooing the Chicano vote and shaping a so-called Chicano Strategy by appointing Mexican Americans to several key national offices, by increasing the number of Mexican American federal employees, and by distributing much-needed federal funds to Chicanos in the Southwest. Although such tactics were successful, Castro concludes that in the end the Republican Chicano Strategy became mired in the machinations of the Committee to Re-Elect the President.

The 1972 Campaign of Ramsey Muñiz
for Governor of Texas

IGNACIO M. GARCÍA

Ramsey Muñiz, by his own account, had been active in MAYO [Mexican American Youth Organization] since 1968 and had even served as an organizer for the group in northern Texas. Yet he was not well known in party circles. . . . Muñiz wrote in the area's Chicano newspaper but otherwise was not prominent in the movement before he became a [Texas] gubernatorial candidate. . . .

Once he became a candidate, Muñiz demonstrated a tenacity and a reservoir of energy and enthusiasm that astonished the party leaders. At twenty-nine, he still possessed the physical strength that had earned him . . . an honorable mention in the Southwest Conference's 1965 all-star selection for his play as a lineman for the Baylor University football team. . . .

After graduating from Baylor, Muñiz entered the law school there and paid his way by serving as an assistant student coach for the varsity team. When he

Ignacio M. García, "Ramsey Muñiz and the 1972 Campaign," from *United We Win: The Rise and Fall of La Raza Unida Party* (Tucson: University of Arizona, 1989), pp. 77–88. Reprinted by permission of Mexican American Studies and Research Center.

received his law degree, he served first as a law clerk for a local attorney, then as an administrative assistant, and finally as director of the Urban Community Development Corporation of Waco. . . .

When Muñiz filed to run for governor, there was no state campaign committee and no money, the platform was not complete, and no communications existed between him and the candidate for lieutenant governor, Alma Canales. . . . Despite being in the same party, they were a contrast in style and approach. Notwithstanding his militancy, Muñiz represented middle-class respectability with his law degree, nice clothing, and attractive spouse. Canales was the radical, poorly dressed, married to a MAYO activist, and a less articulate candidate. Her name on the ballot was a result of the women's strength in the party caucuses, and she remained on the ballot, despite efforts to remove her. . . .

On February 9 [1972] Muñiz was unveiled at a press conference in San Antonio along with Canales and a list of fifty-two other RUP candidates. Immediately, two questions arose in regard to the party's candidates and its ballot status. Reporters quickly pointed out that Canales, at twenty-four, could not legally take office if she won because the state constitution required a lieutenant governor to be at least thirty years old. Compean responded that the party would go to court if necessary to fight the age limitation. Reporters also asked Compean if he felt that raising the 22,358 signatures needed to get on the state ballot would be a problem. He answered that he saw no difficulty in getting them and warned the party's opponents that RUP stood ready to go through the long court process again to gain ballot status.

When it came her turn, Canales declared that the party had no interest in playing the same political "games" as the Democrats and the Republicans. "We're not going to replace a system that oppresses people with a brown system that oppresses people," she said. . . . For many, Canales proved to be a direct, gut-level candidate who expounded the MAYO and Raza Unida philosophy. Her candidacy signaled that women would play a major role in the party. Muñiz was more aggressive in his remarks. He challenged the reporters to compare his credentials to those of two of his Democratic opponents, Lieutenant Governor Ben Barnes, who at the time seemed the favorite of the Democratic Party leadership, and Dolph Briscoe, a South Texas millionaire rancher. . . .

Also present at the press conference were Flores Anaya, a lawyer, running for U.S. senator; Rubén Solis, candidate for state treasurer; Fred Garza, of the United Farm Workers Organizing Committee, running for state railroad commissioner; and Robert Gómez, candidate for land commissioner. Compean told reporters that the party also had candidates for such offices as state representative and county commissioner in nine counties. . . .

Shortly after the announcement Muñiz went on the road to rally support for the petition drive. . . . He toured the Rio Grande Valley, South Texas, West Texas, and cities such as Houston, Dallas, Austin, and his hometown of Corpus Christi. Everywhere he went he hammered away at both parties, although the Democrats, who controlled the state legislature and the governor's mansion, received the brunt of the criticism.

In a speech at Pan American University in Edinburg, deep in the Rio Grande Valley, Muñiz urged the audience of mostly Mexican American students not to vote in the primaries so they could sign the petitions to put the party on the state ballot. He also accused Preston Smith, the governor, of remembering the Mexican American only at election time. At Del Mar College in Corpus Christi he blasted both parties for making false promises.

> Mexican Americans have had it with the lies. *Ya basta* ["Enough"]. Raza Unida offers the people an alternative and the days of being led to the polls to vote straight ticket for these two other parties are over. . . . It is not a revolt of guns or violence, but by the vote. . . . If it's not done this year, it will come next year or the next. . . .

There and everywhere else he stopped he was greeted by chants of "Viva la Raza!"

In a short time Muñiz became comfortable as the lead man for the party. At first he felt nervous speaking in front of an audience and relied on prepared texts, but soon he discovered that his strength was in . . . drawing in his audience by asking them questions, leading the chants, and joking. His mingling with the crowds after his speeches proved particularly effective. Said one of the party leaders about him: "Ramsey had a likable personality . . . , so down to earth . . . straightforward, unpretentious. He was a perfect choice as a candidate. . . . He was sincere and he spoke from the heart." In a rhetoric-conscious community, he not only said many of the things people had been wanting to hear for a long time, but said them in Spanish and in a way that assured people he would not recant them even under Anglo pressure. Young Chicanos, students, and dropouts liked his direct style, his militancy. . . . The older Mexican Americans liked him because he carried good credentials . . . and could be the perfect gentleman. Wherever he went, Muñiz picked up the signatures.

It was a stroke of good luck for the party that Muñiz was so effective, because the signature gathering did not proceed as well as the leadership had hoped. There were not enough volunteers to carry the petitions, and too many of the registered voters were committed Democrats. Even when they were not, many of them felt uneasy about passing up the primaries, in which they could vote for a Mexican American . . . , to sign a petition for an unknown party. Despite the publicity that MAYO and the Crystal City takeover received, many Mexican American voters were uninformed.

The idea of a third party seemed to catch on faster among those who had not participated in electoral politics before. As Muñiz said at a rally: "The Mexican American and the black communities . . . don't vote because in the past they didn't have a real choice. . . . Our connection with the Democratic Party has been nothing more than a cheap marriage. . . . They have lied to us and betrayed [us]. . . . Now we are divorcing ourselves from the Democratic Party." Although many of these unparticipating Mexican Americans were enthusiastic about the new party, it became a big chore to qualify them to sign the petition. These people had to register to vote before they could sign, and the party did not have enough qualified registrars. The petition-gathering effort had been divided by region, and though the South and West Texas chapters had been able to pick up signatures at a fast pace, the big-city chapters in Houston, Dallas, Austin, and San Antonio were not keeping up with their quotas. By June 15, 1972, a month after the primaries, Muñiz told a crowd in San Antonio that the party had fifteen thousand of the twenty-three thousand signatures needed. . . .

Support began to increase rapidly, however, after the Democratic primaries when Briscoe won the nomination in a close race with Frances "Sissy" Farenthold, a maverick liberal from Corpus Christi who had attracted significant support from mainstream Mexican Americans. To many moderates and liberal Democrats, Briscoe recalled earlier times, when rural conservatives rode from out of their ranches to the state capital, where they maintained a status quo that excluded blacks, Mexican Americans and poor whites. . . .

Going into the state [RUP] convention on June 10, Muñiz saw a golden opportunity to recruit disenfranchised Democrats into the Raza Unida fold and move a little more toward the center, where he could attract many Mexican American Democrats. Shortly after the runoffs he called on the liberal Democrats to support his campaign, saying "we're talking about the same things. Liberals have always talked about helping minorities. How much more can they help than by voting for us. What we are saying to liberals is 'how liberal are you.' " . . .

At the convention Muñiz quickly established himself as one of the leaders of the party. He did it with his natural charm and through the number of people he attracted to the convention. In half a year Muñiz had traveled more, met more people, and been interviewed more than anyone else in the party except Gutiérrez and Compean. To many people outside the movement, Muñiz was the party. . . . Muñiz symbolized the state party, principally because he was its standard-bearer but also because he found himself a dynamic campaigner among a less-than-charismatic group of candidates.

While party activists were still defining the role of the party, its ideology and methodology, Muñiz already had a pattern to follow—that of a politician stumping the state for votes. Deeply conscious of La Raza Unida's premises, he brought to the campaign a militancy not seen since the days of the populist movements in Texas, but it was nevertheless a traditional campaign. He simply added a Chicano and personal twist to it. It was not hard, then, for him to come to the convention radiating confidence and feeling that momentum was on his side. . . .

At the convention Compean was elected state chairman. . . . Muñiz and the other candidates were also officially nominated, without opposition, although a few of the original candidates had dropped out by this time. After the formalities of nominations the party delegates debated and then approved a party platform.

> Contained in the various sections of this document are the hopes, ideals, and the future of many people. . . . Those who understand the full meaning of this document cannot deny that the course of history will be affected by the ideas contained herein. For the first time, a political party will exist which was started by Chicanos for Chicanos. The momentum that Raza Unida Party has started will continue, however, not only for Chicanos but for all who see the need for the people to once again have control of the government so . . . the voice of the people will be heard.

As might be expected from activists who concentrated so much time on educational issues and who gained their militancy through school boycotts and protests, the RUP platform committee made education its top priority. . . . After decrying the large dropout rates in Texas schools . . . and the unfair school financing system, the platform called for specific measures that at the time were radical. The party demanded that all school districts develop multilingual and multicultural programs at all levels from preschool to college; that state funds be distributed equally to all school districts; that school officials and school boards be proportionally representative of the community; that free early-childhood education, including daycare and preschool activities, be provided for all children; that schools without walls be created; and that standardized tests be eliminated as a measure of achievement until they accurately reflected the language usage and culture of those tested. And finally, the platform called for aid to private Chicano and black schools and colleges.

Aside from education, there were thirteen other sections dealing with politics, welfare, housing, justice, international affairs, natural resources, transportation, and health. In all areas the party platform followed a leftist-liberal line. It called for free education; lowering of the voting age to eighteen; giving the right to vote to foreigners; breaking up monopolies; fair distribution of wealth; implementation of equal minority representation in the judicial system; abolishment of capital punishment; passage of the Equal Rights Amendment; removal of trade embargoes and economic sanctions against Cuba; and the reduction of U.S. forces in Europe. The abolishment of the Texas Rangers was a popular resolution at the convention. The platform also called for the recognition of the new state of Bangladesh.

For a party representing the vanguard of Chicano separatism, its governing document was only mildly nationalistic. It reflected both an effort to attract liberal groups outside the Mexican American community and the influence of the antiwar movement. . . . It was evident in the document that party leaders recognized their own communities' conservatism in economic and social matters. They purposely avoided much of the socialist rhetoric fashionable at the time. . . .

After the convention, party leaders came out swinging, mostly at the Democrats. Briscoe was perceived to be vulnerable, and some party activists were angry because Farenthold had refused to support Muñiz, whose views were closer to hers. Muñiz avoided criticizing Farenthold, choosing instead to woo her supporters by pointing out some of the similarities of his campaign with that of the defeated liberal. He suggested to liberals that they initiate a "Democrats for Muñiz" movement. In the same vein he told black leaders in Austin that any demands they would make, he would sign. He also announced that in Houston and Dallas several black activists were organizing a "blacks for Muñiz" drive.

In seeking black support, Muñiz received two major boosts. The first came at the Democratic National Convention in Miami, where Briscoe, following the lead of numerous southern delegates, voted for George Wallace for the presidential nomination. After Wallace's apparent defeat Briscoe quickly shifted his vote to George McGovern, but most Texas liberal delegates left the convention sure that Briscoe was not going to do anything to help the Democrats carry the election in the state. Muñiz quickly announced that through his action Briscoe had . . . come out and shown his true colors. . . . He added that if Wallace's supporters launched another presidential campaign, as they had four years before, it would give the party a better chance of winning, because moderates and liberals who would vote against Wallace might also vote against Briscoe. . . .

The second major boost for the campaign came when the Reverend Ralph Abernathy, head of the Southern Christian Leadership Conference, the organization led at one time by Martin Luther King, Jr., endorsed Muñiz for governor. It was a major triumph for the RUP candidate. . . .

On August 8 the party was certified to appear on the state ballot. With the party legitimate, Muñiz, who up to this time had been without an official campaign manager, named [José Angel; see Document 2] Gutiérrez to direct his electoral effort. In announcing Gutiérrez, he criticized the Republicans and Democrats for hiring out-of-state, big-name public relations agencies to handle their campaigns. Briscoe had hired a Tennessee firm and Henry Grover a New York company. Said Muñiz: "I don't have to go to New York City and I'm not going to have to go to Tennessee to run my political campaign. All I'm going to do is go to Crystal City. There is a firm right there and it has a staff of 10,000 people . . . and José Angel is going to be my campaign manager." Muñiz rejected the reporters' notions that because of his reputation Gutiérrez would be a hindrance to the campaign. He added that already the organization was picking up support among conservative and older Mexican Americans.

The reference to Grover indicated that even La Raza Unida could see that the Republican candidate's campaign was picking up momentum. Grover had not been the choice of the Republican leadership, but he had won the primaries, had millions to spend, and excelled as a campaigner. Some political observers also believed that a McGovern-led Democratic Party meant a sure victory in Texas for Richard Nixon and a strong coat-tail effect. . . .

In Houston, a few days before naming Gutiérrez his manager, Muñiz lashed out at the Republicans, who had just concluded their national convention. He accused them of talking through both sides of their mouths because they promised to recruit minorities but had only one Mexican American in the Texas delegation and no blacks. Talking about both parties, he said, "We've put them in the state house, we've put them in the White House, but we stay in the dog house. We don't want to stay there anymore." Muñiz predicted that RUP and not the Republicans would be the second majority party in the state and added that he offered an alternative to the look-alike conservatism of Grover and Briscoe. He also denied that the party was trying to help elect a Republican to get back at the Democrats.

On August 28 some liberals who had remained silent, sulking after Farenthold's defeat, spoke cautiously about Muñiz and the RUP. In a cover story in *The Texas Observer* entitled *Ya basta!* they introduced Muñiz to their readers in this fashion: "If you can't stomach Dolph Briscoe and Henry Grover is unthinkable, the name of the Raza Unida candidate is Ramsey Muñiz." They went on to give some details of Muñiz's background, highlighting his assistance to Farenthold's legislative races. Then, in an almost melancholic reflection of their own party's failure to provide a better alternative, the editors wrote:

> Among many black, chicano and liberal Democratic leaders to whom the *Observer* has talked, it seems clear that as John Kennedy once said, "Sometimes party loyalty asks too much." For their own political sakes, they cannot support Muñiz against Briscoe. However, they are planning to telegraph to their supporters, in various ways, the equivalent of McGovern's great line from the Democratic convention, "Vote your conscience, folks, just vote your conscience."

Gaining the Mexican American Vote in the 1972 Presidential Election

TONY CASTRO

In historic San Antonio, the cradle of animosity between Mexican-Americans and Anglos, they joke that the Mexican-Americans in 1968 dealt Richard Nixon the worst defeat of a gringo since the Battle of the Alamo. That year, the San Antonio Mexican-Americans gave the Republicans 6 percent of their votes. . . .

It's clear that the Mexican-American vote cost Nixon the twenty-five Texas electoral votes in 1968. . . . GOP strategists conceded later that they were wrong to write off the Mexican-American vote, and their own figures showed that Nixon could have taken the state away from Hubert Humphrey if he had won only another 5 percent of the Chicano vote.

When the 1972 elections rolled around, President Nixon and the Republicans were determined not to make the same mistake in Texas and four other Southwestern states. Their plan was simple: . . . providing high administration positions and more government jobs to Mexican-Americans and . . . doling out a bigger share of federal dollars to programs aimed at Mexican-Americans. Observant GOP officials saw the potential bloc of voters, and the Mexican-Americans . . . had become disgruntled with the Democratic party.

Call it the Chicano Strategy. . . . It was a political move that aroused mixed feelings. On the one hand, Mexican-Americans were making unprecedented gains in the Nixon administration. Without a doubt, the GOP showed up the Democrats in getting things done for *la raza*. But on the other hand, there were strong, nagging doubts as to how long the trend would last. Indeed, the strategy came from the master of politicians, and one couldn't help but wonder whether the appointments, the jobs, and the federal money wouldn't suddenly develop a problem. . . .

When President Nixon came to office in 1969, . . . his administration inherited . . . the Inter-Agency Committee on Mexican-American affairs, created during the Johnson days to deal with complaints from Mexican-Americans in the Southwest. During Mr. Nixon's first year in office, Congress passed legislation changing the agency into the Cabinet Committee on Opportunities for Spanish-Speaking People—this was supposed to strengthen and broaden the scope of the agency. . . . The committee chairman had intended to meet with members of the President's cabinet to discuss problems, and an advisory council was supposed to be established. . . . Those parts of the law were not carried out.

. . . One of President Nixon's first high-ranking Mexican-American appointees, Martin Castillo, resigned as chairman of the committee along with committee executive director Henry Quevedo. Both resignations reportedly came under pressure from the White House, as a result of the Mexican-American's heavy Democratic vote in the California and Texas senatorial elections in 1970 in which the President and the Republican candidates were rebuffed. . . . Those

Tony Castro, "The Chicano Strategy," in *Chicano Power: The Emergence of Mexican America*, 1974, abridged from pages 198–214. Reprinted by permission of Tony Castro.

elections were tests for the GOP's Chicanos, and the White House quickly made known its displeasure with their performance. . . .

At this point, . . . the President suddenly decided to awaken the Cabinet Committee from its sleep. On August 5, 1971, President Nixon announced the appointment of Henry M. Ramirez, an educator from Mr. Nixon's hometown of Whittier, California, as the committee's new chairman. At the same time the President directed administration officials to step up the hiring of Spanish-speaking persons and to fund government programs for the country's Spanish-speaking population.

In the months that followed, Ramirez was joined by a flood of other Mexican-American appointees. Phillip V. Sanchez, an unsuccessful GOP candidate for congress in California, was named national director of the Office of Economic Opportunity [OEO], thus becoming the highest ranking Mexican-American official in the administration. Mrs. Romana A. Banuelos, a Los Angeles businesswoman, was appointed treasurer of the United States, the first Mexican-American woman ever named to such a high post. White House Counselor Robert H. Finch . . . was assigned to be the President's own liaison with the Cabinet Committee, and he was given responsibility for handling Mexican-American relations. The White House even directed a Spanish-speaking Japanese, staff assistant William H. Marumoto, to develop a government recruitment system for Spanish-speaking Americans. By election time in 1972, there were at least fifty high-ranking Mexican-American officials who owed their jobs to the administration's Chicano Strategy.

Why did the Mexican-American vote require a strategy all its own? . . . In mid-1971 . . . the President was going to need every vote he could get, and in several of the key states, it was the Mexican-Americans who made up the balance of power.

Texas and the 1968 election were one example of how the Chicano vote could mean the difference. . . . California was another state where the Chicano vote could mean the difference. . . . Indeed, the stakes were big. One study showed that a switch of only 6 percent of the Mexican-American vote could affect the elections not only in Texas and California but also in New Mexico and Illinois, four states with 101 electoral votes out of the 270 needed to elect a president.

By early 1972, the number of Mexican-Americans in the upper echelons of the administration left little doubt about the White House's intention of going after the Mexican-American vote. On the surface, the strategy appeared positive and well-meaning: first, there were the appointments, the jobs, and the money that would be going to Mexican-Americans and their programs. Second, and more important, there was the exposure of the administration's good deeds, to be accomplished by appointees acting as the President's Spanish-speaking surrogates.

But this was only a part of the story. . . . There were hints of questionable tactics woven into the Chicano Strategy.

The Committee to Re-Elect the President . . . included a division assigned to woo the Spanish-speaking voter. In charge of it was Alex Armendariz, . . . who prepared a memo recommending strategy for the Chicano . . . vote. The memo . . . went to Frederick Malek, deputy director of the committee. . . . The memo contained suggestions and recommendations that certainly were employed, then or later, to woo *la raza*.

The memo shows that Armendariz planned to use negative tactics in either attracting or neutralizing the Mexican-American vote. For example, he suggested that the GOP provide secret assistance to the fledgling La Raza Unida party in Texas as an effort to pull votes from the Democrats. . . . This is how Armendariz outlined the strategy:

> Any analysis of this area [Texas] would be incomplete without special mention of La Raza Unida. It is unique in that it is . . . an effective political party. The party is working on its own political organization, caucuses, slates, and the signatures necessary to present its own ballot. The rationale it presents is that if enough votes are siphoned away from the Democrats, there will be more of a power balance and La Raza could cast conclusive votes, or at least achieve bargaining power. *Republicans are in a good position to help to attract to La Raza as voters the 62.3 percent who already approve of that party.* La Raza's strategy usually is denouncement of old party politics. . . . McGovern could be exposed as an old-style party politician especially since his recent visit to [Alabama Governor George] Wallace, who is vastly unpopular among Mexican-Americans. Humphrey is easily attacked in this manner. Kennedy would present an enormous problem as his whole family is loved by Mexican-Americans. *Republicans would have to lay off him entirely and expend all negative efforts in the Spanish-speaking community helping La Raza.*
>
> On the other hand, the 19.4 percent who disapprove of La Raza may be the most conservative of the group, making them a natural Republican target. . . . Furthermore, *it will be our job to try to crystallize the remaining 33 percent of the Spanish-speaking who have never heard of La Raza, or who have no opinion of it, toward La Raza, the Republican party, or staying at home. . . .*
>
> Someone must come up with a slick advertising package showing the President doing, or having done, something about jobs and housing. . . . If he could be directly and personally identified with a push for bilingual education, we would have a strong positive issue. [Italics by T. Castro]

It is not particularly surprising, then, that George McGovern, during the last month of the campaign, accused the Republican party of bribing . . . La Raza Unida in Texas . . . to hold down the vote among Mexican-Americans. Through his Illinois coordinator, Gene Pokorny, Senator McGovern accused José Angel Gutiérrez of espousing neutrality in the presidential election in exchange for a $1 million health clinic for his hometown of Crystal City, Texas. Pokorny got his information from Dr. Jorge Prieto, a Chicano doctor who said he was offered a job at the new health clinic by Gutiérrez's wife. "She indicated that such funding had been made available because of an arrangement between La Raza Unida and Republican party officials," Pokorny said.

At its national convention in El Paso, La Raza Unida refused to endorse either Senator McGovern or President Nixon, and party leaders instead urged their followers to forego national politics and concentrate on races involving La Raza Unida candidates, such as Ramsey Muñiz, the party's gubernatorial nominee in Texas. This move came as a surprise and a disappointment to McGovern backers and other liberals, who counted on the support of Chicano activists. At the convention, Muñiz declared that the only way he would favor endorsing McGovern would be by securing a return endorsement of his own candidacy from the Democratic nominee.

McGovern's accusation against La Raza Unida evoked a rash of angry denials and denunciations. Muñiz charged that McGovern was "playing politics with the health needs of Chicanos." And Mario Compean, La Raza Unida's state chairman in Texas, replied: "We still maintain our position that there is no difference between George McGovern and Richard Nixon. It really doesn't make any difference to us who gets elected."

Meanwhile, the federal health grant to Crystal City ran into some red tape, and a group of Crystal City citizens wound up lobbying for the grant in Washington. At a press conference, Crystal City Mayor Francisco Benavides called McGovern a liar for alleging that "this grant was only a political arrangement between our city and the Republicans in return for the Chicano vote." And in a letter to Dr. Prieto, Gutiérrez's wife, Luz, wrote: " . . . since 1970, this community has been and continues to be demanding, threatening, and fighting to get not one million dollars for one clinic in Crystal, but $25 billion for clinics in Chicano communities throughout the Southwest. . . . Nothing is going to deter us from continuing our struggle for health care . . . so little political schemes designed to promote the presidential aspiration of a gringo will certainly not get in our way." . . .

But a Republican–Raza Unida "arrangement" was only one of the charges Democrats made against the GOP's Mexican-American ranks after the election. In the year leading up to the election, the Cabinet Committee and its chairman Henry Ramirez were extremely active in playing up the administration's pro-Spanish-speaking posture, and Democrats were quick to charge that both the Cabinet Committee and Ramirez had overstepped their boundaries by getting involved in the campaign. The Democrats also charged that the White House used some of the Mexican-American appointees, whom the Hatch Act prohibited from becoming active in politics, as spokesmen for the President's campaign.

In 1973, while Watergate and Senator Sam Ervin's investigating committee captured the national spotlight, Representatives Henry B. Gonzalez and Eligio (Kika) de la Garza, both from Texas, worked quietly to force changes in the Cabinet Committee or else curtail its funding by Congress. At the same time, the Cabinet Committee came under additional pressures at hearings conducted by the Government Operations and the Judiciary Committees of the House of Representatives. . . .

Ultimately, the House Judiciary Committee got the necessary weapons to use against Ramirez and the Cabinet Committee. For example, the Judiciary Committee learned that Ramirez had attended the GOP National Convention in Miami Beach on Cabinet Committee funds. . . . Using records belonging to the Cabinet Committee and to the Spanish-speaking division within the Committee to Re-elect the President, the Judiciary Committee staff uncovered more than 500 pages of memorandum, which told a good deal about the roles of Nixon's Mexican-Americans in the campaign.

Among the documents in question—which later fell into the hands of Senator Ervin's Watergate committee—was an intriguing hand-written letter from New Mexico's [Reies Lopez; see Chapter 12, Document 3] Tijerina to Ramirez: Tijerina was acknowledging he'd been offered an executive pardon for a federal . . . conviction in return for his support of President Nixon. Certainly, Tijerina had drastically toned down his rhetoric since being released on parole from a federal penitentiary. And the activists no longer looked up to him as a top movement leader, although Tijerina remained influential in New Mexico among the . . . Hispanos, . . . whose hopes he had once lifted with the possibility of some day regaining the ancestral Spanish land grants.

In his letter to Ramirez, dated August 14, 1972, Tijerina wrote: "I'm very glad that I got to know you. I also want to make it very clear that I am very thankful of what you mentioned to me in your office concerning . . . the possibility of a full executive pardon. As I said before while I was in your office, I want to repeat it in writing, most of the Spanish-speaking people in the United States would feel grateful if an executive pardon would be granted."

Ramirez forwarded Tijerina's letter to Armendariz along with a memorandum: " . . . Mr. Tijerina indicated that he would work for us in return for due consideration."

All through this controversy there were references to Henry Ramirez, Brown Middle America's answer to the likes of Tijerina, José Angel Gutiérrez, and Corky Gonzales. In 1972, Ramirez . . . established himself as the Nixon administration's leading Mexican-American spokesman, Ramirez claimed the administration moved him up to the Cabinet Committee chairmanship because he had credibility in the Mexican-American community. . . . The son of Mexican immigrants who began as migrant workers in California, Ramirez studied for the priesthood but instead wound up a language teacher in a high school in Whittier, the President's hometown. Later he worked for the Republican party on the precinct level in California. . . . Despite his political activities, Ramirez considered himself an educator, and he became director of the U.S. Civil Rights Commission's Mexican-American Studies Division where he headed up the commission's exhaustive study of Mexican-American education in the Southwest.

Then in August of 1971, the President elevated Ramirez to the chairmanship of the Cabinet Committee. By the end of the 1972 election campaign, the Cabinet Committee boasted that Ramirez had traveled more than 135,000 air miles in telling the story of the administration's good works. One of Ramirez's first trips was a two-day swing into Texas and the Lower Rio Grande Valley along with a host of other Mexican-American appointees. . . . Ramirez's rhetoric on that trip set the pace for the spiels by the administration's Spanish surrogates during the next few months. "No other administration has placed such a heavy emphasis on solutions to the problems of the Spanish-speaking," Ramirez told a press conference in Houston. "Next to the American Indian, Spanish-speaking rank lower than any other single group in such areas as educational attainment, housing conditions, employment, etc. Under the present administration, we have witnessed a new awareness of the problem and a willingness to take steps to alleviate these conditions within the Spanish-speaking community."

But by far the most revealing thing Ramirez said came at a press conference in Dallas during the last days of the campaign. Pressed by a reporter, Ramirez lashed back with a thinly veiled threat: If the GOP's presidential ticket failed to win at least 20 percent of the Chicano vote, President Nixon would cut off all "concessions" to the Spanish-speaking, meaning the end of federal appointments and the flow of federal funds into Mexican-American projects. But if the Chicanos did produce the required vote quota, "it will place us in a good negotiating position for further appointments and funds from the administration."

. . . Surely there was a cruel irony in the President's rejection of hiring quotas while on the other hand demanding a specific vote quota from Mexican-Americans. Possibly the incident reflected some late doubts about the Chicano Strategy . . . and also the impact of the administration's Chicanos. . . .

Besides Ramirez, Sanchez and Mrs. Banuelos were the other two Hispanos most visible in the campaign. Mrs. Banuelos, no doubt, strengthened the administration's support among Mexican-Americans who were offended by the Chicano activists' demonstrations against her. In San Antonio, for instance, Chicano activists and supporters of the farm labor movement, including Bishop Patricio Flores, picketed an appearance by Mrs. Banuelos. The next day, the *San Antonio Express News* carried the story and a front-page picture of Mrs. Banuelos . . . confronted by a young demonstrator pushing at her with a sign saying, "Go Back to Nixon." . . .

Meanwhile, Sanchez, as national director of OEO, represented the pinnacle of Mexican-American success within the executive branch. OEO, Lyndon Johnson's brainchild for administering the War on Poverty, is ranked just under cabinet level, and in 1972 Sanchez was the highest-ranking Mexican-American presidential appointee in the nation's history. Although overshadowed by Ramirez, Sanchez played the administration's . . . game well. But within three months of the election, Sanchez's lofty world came tumbling down.

In early 1973, the Nixon White House, which was never fully sympathetic with the Johnson dream of a war on poverty, announced its intention to dismantle OEO. The move, which caught Sanchez by surprise, no doubt cast a dark shadow over how he saw his role and influence within the administration in the previous year. . . .

Sanchez, Banuelos, Ramirez, and the other high-ranking Hispano appointees represented only a fraction of the Mexican-Americans who became government employees under the Nixon administration. In November of 1970, the White House announced what came to be known as the "Sixteen-Point Program" for assisting Spanish-speaking Americans in getting more lower- and middle-level federal jobs. But the president failed to set out any specific goals or timetables in the program, thereby creating a point of conflict between the administration and Mexican-American groups seeking a massive job-assistance effort.

In mid-1972, a year and a half after the President had launched the Sixteen-Point Program, five major Mexican-American organizations still saw it necessary to call for an "affirmative moral commitment" from the White House to step up federal employment of the Spanish-speaking. . . . The organizations, including LULAC [League of Latin American Citizens], the G.I. Forum, and the Mexican-American Political Association, asked the Equal Employment Opportunity Commission to set specific goals and timetables for employing the Spanish-speaking. The leaders of the organizations said that for almost two years they had sought unsuccessfully on ten separate occasions to meet with the President to discuss such goals and timetables. They claimed that Mr. Nixon's failure to ensure population parity in government employment to Spanish-speaking Americans cost Mexican-Americans 101 federal jobs and $950 million in 1971. According to statistics compiled by the organizations and their representative, the Mexican-American Legal Defense and Education Fund, Spanish-speaking Americans represented 7 percent of the nation's population but only 2.9 percent of the federal government's civilian full-time employees. . . .

One aspect of the Nixon Chicano Strategy that did stand out, though, was the amount of money the administration poured into Spanish-speaking projects. In the year preceding the election, an estimated $47 million was channeled into programs for the Spanish-speaking, many of them funded on a one-year-only basis. . . . An additional $24 million to $26 million was set aside through the Department of Housing and Urban Development for low-cost housing for Spanish-speaking groups.

The total amount spent in the Spanish-speaking communities was a figure the Nixon Hispanos hesitated to discuss. But there were indications that the $47 million figure was actually far below the total expenditure for the Chicano vote. Documents in the Cabinet Committee showed that at least $20 million was invested in Spanish-speaking projects in the Texas region and another $17 million in the California region, and these funds were in addition to what Mexican-Americans received through regular federal programs.

By the end of the campaign, the GOP's Chicano Strategy, despite its shortcomings, had the Democrats on the run. From the beginning, Democrats had taken the administration's wooing of the Chicanos lightly, and they appeared to disregard the discontent among Mexican-Americans even within their own ranks. Meanwhile, the Republican effort went beyond rhetoric, and it was hard for Democrats to argue with the Hispano appointments, the Spanish-speaking employment program, and the federal dollars flooding Mexican-American projects. . . .

By all indications, the strategy worked. Although the Republican ticket wound up winning with plenty of room to breathe, the President's Chicano Strategy succeeded in winning so many Mexican-American votes as to raise the question whether the Chicano vote would ever return to the Democratic fold in the one-sided proportions of past years. In Texas, where President Nixon had received only 10 percent of the vote in 1968, the Nixon-Agnew ticket made sweeping gains among Mexican-American voters, with predominantly Mexican-American counties in South Texas and the Lower Rio Grande Valley giving the President as much as 65 percent of the vote. . . . President Nixon carried 49 percent of the Spanish-speaking vote in Texas and Florida and 11 percent of the Spanish-speaking vote in California. . . .

The Committee to Re-Elect the President made its own check of Mexican-American voting trends, and in San Antonio it took a sampling of three predominantly Mexican-American precincts, which showed the relationship between income and voting tendencies. President Nixon received 20 percent of the vote in a low-income precinct, 49 percent in a middle-income precinct, and 68 percent in a high-income precinct. Similar precinct samplings in Los Angeles showed that the GOP ticket ran well, beating the Democrats in some places, and suggested a much stronger Nixon vote among Mexican-Americans in the state. . . .

On election night, Nixon's Hispanos celebrated along with everyone . . . , but the landslide victory and the success of the Chicano Strategy were both in for an abruptly short honeymoon. Just weeks after the inauguration, President Nixon and his administration found themselves entangled in the Watergate matter. And it was at about this same time that the Nixon Hispanos and others who had been wooed to the Nixon camp awakened to political reality.

The White House decision to dismantle OEO and the subsequent humiliation of Phillip Sanchez were representative of what some Mexican-American leaders felt was their betrayal by the administration. After the election, the number of high-ranking Spanish-speaking officials leveled off and actually dwindled. . . . Talk ended about stepped-up government hiring of the Spanish-speaking, and the President instead announced budget cutbacks in housing, manpower training, and health and education. . . .

The only rising brown star still in the administration in 1973 was Alex Armendariz, who was named director of the Office of Minority Business Enterprise within the Commerce Department. Suddenly there was a change in the rhetoric coming out of the mouths of the Nixon Hispanos. "This country is based upon the principle of private enterprise . . . and we will not be in the mainstream of American life until we, the Spanish-speaking, get into business on the same footing as everyone else," Ramirez . . . told the National Spanish-Speaking Business Development Conference in Chicago. . . .

But the rhetoric overlooked the major problem—the extremely high failure rate of small businesses. And, as much as the campaign strategy, the message was aimed at Brown Middle America rather than the masses in the *barrios* who were in much greater need of federal assistance. "Spanish-speaking voters gave the President a vote of confidence," observed Tony Gallegos, national chairman of the G.I. Forum, "and we've been left out in the cold."

The Mexican-Americans showed their participation in the mainstream of American life by joining other groups in expressing their discontent. In the year following his great victory, President Nixon, it would seem, stood in an enviable position. . . . Yet those were not reassuring times for the President. . . .

If the 1972 presidential election turned out to be a shattering experience for the country's faith in the political process, it was a stunning blow to the Mexican-American electorate for other reasons. The Chicano Strategy . . . became a political lesson not limited entirely to the Chicanos themselves. . . . The lesson is that the Chicano Strategy produced a remarkable transformation in the politics of Mexican-Americans from a predictable, homogeneous bloc into a fluid, ticket-splitting electorate that—much like the rest of America—has become disillusioned with politicians and the parties, weary of political promises and slogans, and eager to find a better way to solve its problems.

FURTHER READING

Tony Castro, *Chicano Power* (1974)

Alfredo Cuellar, "Perspectives on Politics, Part II," in Joan W. Moore, *Mexican Americans* (1976)

Alma A. García, "The Development of Chicana Feminist Discourse, 1970–1980," *Gender & Society* 3 (June 1989), 217–238

F. Chris García, *La Causa Politica* (1974)

———, ed., *Latinos and the Political System* (1988)

——— and Rudolph O. de La Garza, *The Chicano Political Experience* (1977)

Ignacio M. García, *United We Win* (1989)

Juan Goméz-Quiñones, *Chicano Politics* (1990)

Armando Gutiérrez and Herbert Hirsch, "Political Maturation and Political Awareness: The Case of the Crystal City Chicano," *Aztlán* 5 (Spring/Fall 1974), 295–312

José Angel Gutiérrez, "The Mexican American Youth Organization (MAYO)," in Antonio M. Stevens Arroyo, ed., *Prophets Denied Honor* (1980)

Ralph C. Guzmán, *The Political Socialization of the Mexican American People* (1970)

Benjamin Márquez, *LULAC* (1993)

———, *Power and Politics in a Chicano Barrio* (1985)

Vilma S. Martínez, *Testimony of Vilma S. Martínez* (1975)

Karen O'Connor and Lee Epstein, "A Legal Voice for the Chicano Community: The Activities of the Mexican American Legal Defense and Education Fund, 1968–82," in Rudolfo O. de la Garza et al., eds., *The Mexican American Experience* (1985)

Annette Oliveira, *MALDEF: Diez Años* (1978)

John Staples Shockley, *Chicano Revolt in a Texas Town* (1974)

U.S. Commission on Civil Rights, *Hearing Before the United States Commission on Civil Rights: Hearing Held in San Antonio, Texas, December 9–14, 1968* (1969)

Maurilio E. Vigil, *Chicano Politics* (1977)

———, *Hispanics in American Politics* (1987)

The Chicano Experience in
Contemporary America

Recent migration from Mexico and Central and South America has inaugurated a new era in the history of Chicanos, for it marks the beginning of the development of a truly Latino community in the United States. Chicanos, the country's fastest growing minority, comprise two-thirds of the more than 27 million Latinos in the United States. The 1986 Immigration Reform and Control Act, known as the Simpson-Mazzoli Act, attempted to deal with the problem of unlawful immigration to the United States, notably from Mexico, a country that has been gripped by a severe economic downturn. The bill proved controversial, however, since it did not punish American employers who continued to hire undocumented workers to fill the low-paying agricultural and service jobs refused by most American workers.

Despite the new legislation, hundreds of thousands of people continued to leave Mexico, fleeing severe poverty and unemployment. The North American Free Trade Agreement (NAFTA) of 1993 has not solved Mexico's high unemployment problem, and consequently Mexican immigration to the United States will continue. About half of all migrants from Mexico go to California, the nation's new Ellis Island, where by the next century more than a half-million Mexicans are expected to arrive.

The racial minority population of the United States grew dramatically in the 1980s. With the Latino population increasing by 50 percent as the Asian population doubled, people of color now account for one-fourth of the total American population.

In the 1980s, Reaganism exacerbated racial hostilities, which further eroded the gains made by minorities. The so-called white backlash and the rightward turn in national politics led to the suspension of affirmative action efforts. Racial minorities and women earned the attention and disfavor of New Right spokespersons whose charge of "reverse discrimination" became their main ideological weapon. Government programs were challenged in the courts as reverse discrimination, and many of the educational and income gains Chicanos had achieved through struggle and affirmative action programs were attacked. In California the passage of Proposition 187 in 1994, the passage of Proposition 209 in 1996, and the placement of the California Civil Rights Initiative on the ballot and the passage of the bill to abolish bilingual education, both in 1998, are recent examples of this sort of re-

trenchment, which has also launched a new phase of Chicano activism. How have Chicanos recently struggled to overcome inequality? What kind of impact will continued immigration from Mexico and Central and South America have on Chicano culture and identity? What are the concerns and issues of Chicana women?

D O C U M E N T S

The significant growth of the Latino population of the United States is raising questions about culture and identity. Los Angeles has one of the world's largest Spanish-speaking populations. In Document 1 Frank del Olmo of the *Los Angeles Times* explains the unique experiences of Latinos that distinguish them from other ethnic groups. Half of all immigration from Mexico to the United States is destined for California, principally the southern part of the state. In many instances, the journey north is a perilous one. In Document 2, an undocumented Mexican describes her sojourn from Mexico to California in a letter to relatives. Chicano political empowerment remains an important issue and is sociologist Marta López-Garza's topic in Document 3. Also noted is the increasing role of Chicanas in the political process. At the community level, they wield influence and power in their efforts to reclaim their neighborhoods. One of the most important community organizations to emerge is the Mothers of East Los Angeles, whose activities are examined in Document 4. Although the Los Angeles race riots of 1992 are still often viewed as involving only African Americans, many of its participants as well as victims were either Latino or Asian. In Document 5 two *Los Angeles Times* reporters discuss how the riots affected the Los Angeles Latino community, dividing both its leadership and its immigrant neighborhoods. In Document 6 Rubén Martínez details how Latino youth and community-based organizations throughout California demonstrated against the passage of Proposition 187, the California ballot initiative that called for denying benefits to undocumented workers and their families, and how the community groups are focusing on acquiring greater political empowerment. The passage of Propositions 187 and 209, the death of César Chávez, and the phenomenon of white backlash have all contributed to a resurgence in the Chicano movement. In Document 7 the potential impact of Proposition 209, which outlaws affirmative action in hiring, promotion, and college admissions, on California Latinos is explained by journalist Frank del Olmo.

1. Frank del Olmo Characterizes Southern California's Latinos as "A People Living on the Bridge Between Two Worlds," 1983

Now that The Times is concluding its three-week series of articles on Latinos in Southern California, about as detailed and thorough a look at that community as any newspaper has ever attempted, there can't be too many questions about Latinos left unanswered for either Latino or non-Latino readers—except one.

Why bother?

It may seem unusual in a city founded by Mexicans, in a state where thousands of place names are Spanish and where 4.5 million people—20% of the population—are of Latin-American extraction, but the question does get asked. And not just by Anglo newcomers. Many longtime residents, even a few with Spanish surnames, wonder why Latinos should be seen any differently than the dozens of other ethnic groups that preceded them into the proverbial American melting pot.

What sets Latinos apart from the other ethnic groups that have contributed to the United States, each in their own unique way and often despite discriminatory treatment, is the fact that for Latinos the language and culture of their Latin-American homeland has not faded away with the passage of time. And it will not fade away in the foreseeable future. The homeland is so close that migration to the United States continues virtually unabated to the present day.

Because of this unique situation, Latinos face a choice that no other ethnic group in this nation has had to deal with. How much of their home language and culture should they give up to blend into the Anglo-American mainstream? Or should they give up any at all? . . .

To one degree or another, this cultural and linguistic duality is at the root of many of the problems Latinos face in this society—the lack of economic opportunities, limited political representation, the high dropout rates among Latino students in school and colleges.

But as troublesome as it might be in social terms, the Latino's cultural duality is also logical. It is an outgrowth of the fact that the U.S.–Mexican borderlands are the meeting ground of two great cultures—the Anglo-American tradition of the United States and Canada to the north, and the Ibero-Indian tradition of Latin America to the south. And any people who have lived in such a region as long as Latinos have will serve as a bridge between two cultures and languages. . . .

Once this historic reality is accepted, some of the more controversial goals Latino activists are striving for can be better understood.

Almost everyone wants to reduce the high dropout rates among Latino students, for example. And few people would object to efforts aimed at getting more Latinos to become citizens and vote. But when Latinos push bilingual education or bilingual ballots as answers to these problems, they are also asking for something more profound—acceptance of the fact that the Spanish language is a common means of communication in this country.

Few people would seriously argue that farm workers don't deserve better pay and working conditions for harvesting this nation's agricultural bounty. And any humane person wants the exploitation of undocumented aliens in our urban industries to be prevented. But when Latinos suggest that these migrant workers could defend themselves more readily if they belonged to unions, and if those who are not citizens had their immigration status legalized, they are also asking for an acceptance of the fact that Latino labor has been important to this country in the past, and still is.

. . . They key word . . . is "acceptance." That summarizes what Latinos want of this society—acceptance not only as individuals, but of their cultural heritage. And by heritage I do not mean just food and music, but language and the cultural perspectives that come with it.

In the meantime, it will be difficult for Latinos to be fully accepted in any field of endeavor without limiting to a certain extent their role as Latino spokesmen. Politics is the one area where that is not necessarily all bad. For it is in the give-and-take of public life, and in debating public-policy issues, that Latinos will most clearly define their differences from other Americans, yet still find areas of agreement where compromise can be hammered out.

The diversity of the local Latino community was an important underlying theme in the Times series. But it would have been surprising if that community were not diverse, including as it does 3 million people living from Santa Barbara to San Diego, of different social classes, and with varied attitudes toward politics, the arts, religion, morality and even relations between the sexes.

Yet while conceding that this diversity makes generalizations difficult, I have concluded my work on this series convinced that there are notions and issues that unify most Latinos, even across class and political lines.

One is that cliche-burdened, but still viable concept Latinos call *el Sueno Americano* [the American Dream]. As the headline on one article in the Times series proclaimed, the American Dream is still very much alive in the *barrios*. And Latinos define that dream of success the same way most other Americans do—a productive career or job with decent pay, a nice home in a pleasant neighborhood, an enjoyable family life and a secure future for their children.

Latinos also want to retain whatever Spanish they know, and pass it along to their children. But they are also fully aware that English is the key to success in this country, and so they want to speak both languages.

Finally, we all revere our Latin-American heritage. And we look forward to a time when it gets the respect and understanding—the acceptance—it has always deserved from a nation whose rich past it helped build, and whose future it can make even richer.

2. Lety Martínez González Writes About Life as an Undocumented Mexican in California, 1990

Argelia, Jaime, Nancy, Grandma,

What's up? How are you all? I hope all's well at the house because I'm feeling very sad here, since never in my life did I come to think that I'd have to go through so many, many things in order to be here. Before anything, I want to tell you that I didn't cry very much when I said goodbye to all of you; well I made myself be brave since the stewardess informed us that we would be flying in the plane that transported Pope John Paul II, as you'll see, my plane was blessed and I felt very good knowing this. Thirty-five minutes later we arrived in Mexico City and we confirmed the flight and we waited for them to announce our flight. . . . When they announced it we boarded the plane; I got the window. . . . They gave Gaby another seat, since they don't allow there to be children near the window. Then they announced that they would give us headphones to listen to music or watch a movie, shortly after they passed them out they served the meal, really delicious by the way, and they ran the movie, likewise very entertaining.

We arrived in Tijuana. The airport's ugly, we had the luck to pass through without them inspecting our bags or anything. On the way out we bought a ticket for the bus that would take us to the Alaska motel. . . . Tijuana's horrible, it has nothing but pure slums at night. . . . When it struck 11 at night they directed us to a disguised diner. . . . From there we talked with the person who was going to take me across. But he told me to wait until the next day since everything was very rushed at that moment. . . . So we went back to the hotel, passing all the while through the so-called "Zona Roja," everything is corrupt. . . . There are many men in the street and women too, but you know which ones, don't you? We slept at the hotel and the next day the man called, telling us not to move from the hotel and that he'd arrive at 2 in the afternoon, he arrived and told us that at 9 at night he'd come by for us again to take us to the diner. In that time we ate something and slept, at 9 the man arrived, he took us and gave orders to his workers, we were waiting until 10 when the guys who would cross us over arrived, and they gave us orders that we all go out in pairs. . . . I'll make you a sketch below of the immense trip we took.

1. We left from here and walked these 5 blocks.
2. We crossed the Boulevard.
3. Wire Fence.
4. We travelled along the fence, walking.
5. We entered here. 1 block. Borde. This whole part of El Borde has lights and searchlights.
6. This is a bridge where we bought plastic bags to cross the *aguas negras* ["dark waters"].
7. This is a sandy area.
8. All this is like 6 blocks.
9. Here we crossed a large puddle of *aguas negras*.
10. This is the street where those of the *migra* [immigration] constantly pass by.
11. This that I mark over with the pen is a pit where you have to cross practically on all fours.
12. And these things like trees are pure shrubs.
13. Gaby fell in the *aguas negras*.
14. Police car.
15. Dirt road. Here we had to throw ourselves down so they wouldn't grab us. And when the car passed we were off to the races.
16. This was all running, to the point I couldn't bear my legs anymore.
17. Here we jumped into the gully because the *migra* saw us there and told us to stop.
18. When we jumped I fell because someone grabbed me. . . . I got myself up thanks to another guy who urged me on.
19. Here we left to enter this . . . country.
20. We walked up this street. Now we were supposedly on the other side.
21. This now is the U.S., one block.
22. Here they put us into some of their cars to go to San Diego.

I want to clarify that on the map where I put a Y we ran back and forth like 4 times since the guy . . . couldn't find the way out, until we ran into another *coyote* [labor contractor] who came up behind us, . . . and we passed through an immensity of bushes, we had to jump treetrunks, *aguas negras,* it was all very different from what I had seen, or what they had told me, Gaby says I was very brave. . . . Well don't believe it. If I'm here it's because I believe in God and because in those moments I asked the Virgin of Guadalupe, Juguila and the Virgin of Solitude, and above all my son counted a lot to me. But now I'm here, with pains and scratches, bruises. . . . But I'm here. I arrived yesterday in the early morning at like 5 in the morning. . . . Well though you won't believe this, I've never run so fast, now I laugh but in those moments. . . . Everything was worse than in the movies. I believe that we traveled like 7 to 10 kilometers, but in short I won't cross like this again, seriously, listen, follow the arrows that I put down here for you and read what I tell you in each one of them.

. . . Read it to everyone.

Anyway, . . . today Silvia arrives, I hope she arrives well. Tell me how my baby has been, you took him to the doctor yesterday, what did he tell you about his feet, his weight, his height, or what did he tell you in general, how is he? Tell me . . . if he's eaten well. I miss him very much. And Papa, how is he, what did he say? And Nancy, how did Nancy feel? And grandma, how is she? . . . Yesterday we went to the doctor because the boy's vomiting and he's super-pink, since I think the day he stayed with Rosa they didn't look after him very well. . . . Everardo now has a car, cassette recorder, television, not to mention the fact that yesterday Guicho himself bought a VW Caribe for 150 dollars. . . . Anyway now I say goodbye, tomorrow I'll begin my other letter. Answer me soon. Greetings to all, I'll keep you informed.

Kisses for my baby. Take care of him.

Warmly,

Lety

3. Marta López-Garza Chronicles the Chicano Quest for Power in Los Angeles, 1992

The first Mexicans in Los Angeles arrived in 1781 . . . , and a constant Mexican presence in Los Angeles has endured ever since. In the 1980s, the city acquired a critical mass of other Latino groups. The area now contains the largest concentration of Mexicans, Salvadorans, and Guatemalans outside the capital cities of their respective countries. Latinos comprise nearly 40% of Los Angeles County's residents. . . . Indicative of the rapid demographic change is the 62.2% increase in the Census category "Hispanic" between 1980 and 1990. By 2010, if the trend continues, more Latinos than Anglos will reside in this southland metropolis. . . .

NACLA Report on the Americas; Vol. 26:2, pp. 34–38. Copyright 1992 by the North American Congress on Latin America, 475 Riverside Dr., #454, New York, NY 10115-0122.

. . . Not until the post–World War II era did the Los Angeles Mexican community participate—as a community—in electoral politics. . . .

For nearly a quarter of a century after 1945, . . . middle-class Mexican-American political organizations such as the League of United Latin American Citizens (LULAC), the Mexican American Political Association (MAPA), and G.I. Forum attempted to facilitate assimilation into "American society," primarily through the ballot box. . . .

In 1960, LULAC, CSO [Community Service Organization], G.I. Forum and MAPA all worked toward the election of John F. Kennedy. . . .

In the mid-1960s, . . . the Chicano movement, brought class and race consciousness to Mexican-American politics. . . .

Despite the Chicano movement's loss of momentum in the mid-1970s, many reform programs and policies owe their existence to its . . . demands. Bilingual education, voting rights, [and] affirmative-action programs . . . all became reachable goals because of the efforts of the Chicano movement. . . .

Chicano organizations, such as Centro de Acción Autonoma (CASA) and Hermandad General de Trabajadores, also worked to defend Mexican immigrant rights throughout the 1970s. . . . When successive waves of Central Americans arrived in the 1980s, . . . Chicanos were well-positioned to extend their work, and struggle on behalf of Central American immigrants.

Nonetheless, conflicts between Chicanos and Latino immigrants do exist. An example is the schism during and after the recent uprising in Los Angeles. . . . Many members of these Latino immigrant communities took part in the disturbances. In East L.A., on the other hand, the Chicano residents did not participate at all. Chicano elected officials, with the exception of City Councilman Mike Hernández, . . . distanced themselves from the Latino immigrant communities, claiming they did not represent the immigrants, who don't vote.

Geographical dispersion and varying degrees of assimilation have also prompted the diverse political consciousness within the Latino community, which has created difficulties for political organizers. . . . In addition, gerrymandering, the use of at-large districting, and the constant harassment of Latinos in Los Angeles—including the periodic massive repatriation of undocumented immigrants—have all deterred political organizing.

Regardless of their motivation for migrating . . . and regardless of when their families arrived . . . , many Latinos stay in California. . . . Common motivations, along with a common language, have forged the beginnings of Latino unity. A more powerful source of unity are the common problems faced by the various Latino neighborhoods: police harassment, a shortage of affordable housing and overcrowded rentals, cutbacks in inner-city schools, unemployment and underemployment, and underrepresentation in the public-policy arena.

Of the key political struggles of the past 25 years, political representation has been one of the most important. Despite the substantial growth of the Latino population in the region, Latinos are just now attaining some access to political power. No elected officials were Latino in the Los Angeles city government until 1949, and again none were from 1962 to 1985. . . .

The historical lack of political representation has recently formed the basis of several lawsuits pressing for redistricting and voting rights on behalf of Los Angeles' Chicanos. Chicano activists and organizations, such as MALDEF [Mexican American Legal Defense and Educational Fund] and East L.A.'s Center for Law and Justice, along with the Department of Justice, . . . participated in federal lawsuits against the City of Los Angeles in 1985, and the County of Los Angeles in 1988.

Chicano plaintiffs successfully charged that the redistricting of the city council and the county board of supervisor district boundaries had deliberately diluted Chicano voting strength and illegally inhibited their complete and equal participation in the political process. The case against the city (*U.S. v. City of Los Angeles*) was eventually settled out of court and resulted in the creation of a second "Latino dominant" district which was filled by Gloria Molina in 1987. The present incumbent, City Councilman Mike Hernández, was elected after Molina moved up to a seat on the County Board of Supervisors in 1991.

In their lawsuit against the county (*Garza v. County of Los Angeles*), MALDEF presented a strong argument revealing the historical pattern of discrimination against Chicanos. . . . The lengthy legal struggle, which cost taxpayers $12 million, resulted in 1990 in the creation of the First County District, which Gloria Molina presently represents. . . .

. . . Latina women have become some of the most active political players. . . . They are among the most powerful and highly motivated of the politicians on the scene. Led by County Supervisor Gloria Molina, a group of Chicano Democrats has broken with the traditional Democratic Latino power structure, led by Los Angeles City Councilman Richard Alatorre and state Assemblyman Art Torres. Molina and her allies . . . are in the insurgent position, but have begun to muster the type of machine support usually at the disposal of their adversaries. . . .

. . . The increasing visibility of Chicanas was highlighted by the five women who ran for the State Assembly during last June's Democratic primary, four of whom won: Diane Martínez (49th District), Grace Napolitano (58th), Martha Escutia (50th), and Hilda Solis (57th).

. . . It was during the Reagan/Bush era that the Republican Party began to seriously court the "Hispanic vote." Of the registered Chicano voters in California, 20% on average vote Republican, with the highest percentage—25%—turning out in the 1984 presidential elections. Nevertheless, the Republican Party has made few overtures to California's Chicano voters this year. . . .

The Democratic Party may want Chicano votes, but the party does not appear to take Latino/Chicano issues seriously. Latino issues have been addressed only indirectly, through Clinton's economic message which is meant to pull together voters from diverse racial and economic backgrounds. The Democrats and Clinton are courting Chicano voters by handing the campaign over to powerful surrogates within the Chicano community. Clinton has won public endorsement of popular Chicano politicians like Gloria Molina and Henry Cisneros, former mayor of San Antonio. Now Molina is a vice chair of Clinton's national campaign. Clinton also has a National Latino Leadership Committee made up of prominent Latinos, which speaks of Latino issues in an effort to drum up Latino votes.

The race is on to see who can deliver California's Chicano voters. . . . Can "the leadership" deliver the Chicano community to Clinton in exchange for . . . the opportunity to fulfill political aspirations? Will the Republicans mount a

California-Chicano campaign? Who is looking out for the true interests of Latinos—voters and non-voters—in the Southwest?

4. Nina Schuyler Reports on the Mothers of East Los Angeles and Their Struggle for Their Community, 1992

When the pastor of the Church of the Resurrection parish [in East Los Angeles] told his congregation that the state was planning to crowd an eighth penal institution into their neighborhood, a group of women in the parish got mad. The Mothers of East Los Angeles began meeting regularly . . . in 1984 to talk about what was happening to their community. Soon they were making pilgrimages to Sacramento to pound on the doors of elected officials.

The elderly women . . . became a familiar sight to legislators and attorneys in downtown Sacramento. After a long series of appointments and hearings, the Mothers managed to tie up the prison plan indefinitely in the courts.

But their struggle had only begun.

Without telling East L.A. residents, the state started planning in 1985 to build the first large-scale hazardous waste incinerator in a metropolitan area—in the middle of East L.A.

The Mothers discovered a report commissioned by the California Waste Management Board outlining strategies for building incinerators in communities like theirs. According to the report, opposition is likely in liberal, college-educated, or middle- and upper-income communities. So when the state plans to build an incinerator, "communities that conform to some kind of economic-need criteria should be given high priority," the report said.

"So there it was, plain and clear," says Aurora Castillo, one of the founders of the Mothers. "Dump it in our backyard."

The fight against the incinerator lasted six years. The Mothers held midnight candle vigils, raised money for more flights to Sacramento, and organized protest marches.

"By the time the Mothers got involved, the corporation had received all the necessary permits," says Joel Reynolds, an attorney with the Western Center on Law and Poverty who helped the Mothers reopen the permit process. "It is truly amazing that the state regulatory agencies and the Federal Environmental Protection Agency did not require an environmental impact report or statement."

A study of autopsies of East L.A. kids confirmed the Mothers' worst fears. According to . . . the physician who conducted the study, eight out of ten Latino and black children who died by accident or street violence had lung abnormalities caused by breathing polluted air. More than one-quarter had severe lung lesions. The community buzzed with the results of a Greenpeace survey that showed 70 per cent of L.A.'s blacks and 50 per cent of Latinos live in the most polluted parts of the city.

"L. A. Moms Fight Back," by Nina Schuyler in *Progressive*, Vol. 56, no. 8 (August 1992), p. 13. Reprinted by permission from *The Progressive*, 409 E. Main Street, Madison, WI 53703.

The Mothers defeated the new incinerator, and a subsequent plan by one of the largest chemical companies in the nation, Chem Clear, to construct a waste and sludge cleaning plant in East L.A. . . . The latest battle is a lawsuit against a company that wants to build a terminal for hazardous-waste trucks in the area.

"We fight for the children," says Castillo, who grew up in East L.A. when alfalfa fields blanketed the then-visible hills. Her mother's family has lived in California since before the Anglos discovered it. . . . "We fight . . . not just for our children, but for everyone's children."

After the Rodney King verdict, the Mothers met and strategized to prevent violence in the neighborhood. With the schools closed, they kept their children inside. When the weekend passed, they joined an effort to distribute food to South Central L.A.

"We took care of each other," says Castillo, looking back on her family's long history in California. "We are trying to take care of each other now."

5. George Ramos and Tracy Wilkinson Analyze the Los Angeles Riots, 1992

Devastating riots that swept Los Angeles last week have driven a wedge in the city's diverse Latino community, widening the gap between hard-hit immigrant neighborhoods and traditional Latino leaders who were slow to respond to the crisis.

Though largely portrayed in the national media as a black uprising, the riots in fact involved many Latinos, both as victims and vandals. One-third of those killed and at least as many arrested for looting and other crimes were Latino; Latino-owned businesses were destroyed and many Latinos were left homeless by arson.

Elected Latino officials were quick to congratulate their Eastside constituency for restraint shown during the violence; very little looting was reported east of the Los Angeles River.

They appeared equally eager however, to distance themselves from what some officials called the less stable Latino enclaves of Pico-Union and South Los Angeles, which are populated by more recent immigrants, and which were caught in the eye of the firestorm.

The early exception was City Councilman Mike Hernandez, who traveled to the Pico-Union district that he represents hours after the violence erupted and set up an assistance network. He was the first elected official to do so. During the subsequent 24 hours, he went on Spanish-language television and radio to urge calm among Latinos.

But he conceded that Latino officials . . . were tentative and overly cautious. . . .

Most elected Latino officials . . . have little connection with newer, Spanish-speaking immigrant communities, many of whom come from Central America. And those immigrants show little faith in these leaders.

George Ramos and Tracy Wilkinson, "Unrest Widens Rifts in Diverse Latino Population," *Los Angeles Times,* May 8, 1992, Section A, p. 4. Copyright © 1992 Los Angeles Times. Reprinted by permission.

Their agendas and interests diverge, and because many newer immigrants are not citizens or came to the United States illegally, they do not vote. . . .

Consequently, say immigrant advocates, the more recent arrivals from Latin America have been ignored in these days of painful post-riot recovery. Or, worse, they are shouldering the bulk of the blame for the chaos that ruled the city's streets for three days.

"There are many Latino leaders who say they represent Latinos, but they do not represent all Latinos," said Carlos Vaquerano, an official with the Central American Refugee Center.

Madeline Janis, executive director of the center, which is headquartered in the Pico-Union district, urged that all Latino leaders unite to support new immigrants in the wake of the riots.

"There's going to be a big backlash now because immigrants are an easy target, and if we don't have the established Latino leadership defending the rights of the newer immigrants, then we are going to be in an even more desperate situation that we are," she said.

Janis experienced the backlash when she appeared on a live radio talk show Thursday. The seven or eight calls from listeners that she fielded advocated sending immigrants back to where they came from, she said. . . .

"It did not happen in East L.A., Wilmington . . . areas that are just as poor but which have a different, stronger sense of community, a stronger attachment to their neighborhood," UCLA demographer Leo Estrada said.

"These people are more likely to own their own homes. . . . Everybody said, 'How can they destroy their neighborhoods, their jobs . . . ?' Well, my answer is that they did not consider it to be their own.". . .

Latino-owned businesses in South Los Angeles and in Pico-Union were heavily damaged. . . . State officials believe at least 30% of the estimated 4,000 businesses destroyed belong to Latinos. . . .

In addition, 19 of 58 people killed in riot violence were Latino, and hundreds more were injured and left homeless. . . .

In contrast, the Eastside was largely quiet. Only 10 businesses were looted in a 15 1/2-square-mile area. . . . No fires or other acts of violence were reported, and only 70 National Guards troops were deployed there.

There were signs Thursday that some effort is being made to bridge the gap between the newer and more established communities. The Mexican American Legal Defense and Educational Fund (MALDEF) sponsored a meeting Wednesday night—a week after the riots erupted—with Los Angeles County Supervisor Gloria Molina and representatives of the Central American community, among others, who discussed emergency aid.

"There's a realization we have to strengthen our ties with the newer immigrant community," said Antonia Hernandez, president and general counsel of MALDEF. . . .

The immigrant community has also been alarmed over actions by the police this week. In violation of longstanding policy, Los Angeles police officers who arrest illegal aliens on suspicion of looting or other riot-related crimes are turning suspects over to the U.S. Immigration and Naturalization Service for probable deportation.

According to the INS, illegal aliens accounted for more than 1,200 of the nearly 15,000 people arrested in the riots. . . .

According to many accounts provided during the riots and in their aftermath, Latinos did more looting than burning. In interviews, Latino looters said they acted out of anger at the system and at years of discrimination. More than a response to verdicts in the trial of officers charged in the King beating, many said they were taking advantage of the anarchy to share in the wealth.

6. Rubén Martínez Describes the Fight Against Proposition 187, 1995

Political passions are inflamed . . . at the Peace and Justice Center, a quasi-underground youth hangout just west of downtown Los Angeles. In the August heat, as skateboarding daredevils go airborne in the parking lot outside, about 20 activists in their late teens and early twenties plot pyromaniacal political theater in a meeting room decorated with posters of revolutionaries including Malcolm, Martin, Che and Marcos. . . .

The young activists are planning a demonstration set to take place at the federal courthouse where the fate of Proposition 187 will be determined by Judge Mariana Pfaelzer on September 10. "We have to be there so that they will feel a serious presence," says César Cruz, a Chicano student at the University of California at Irvine. . . .

Nods around the room. "Yeah, I think we should . . . take the streets!" says a blond, blue-eyed . . . Chicana who goes by the name of "Lucha" (in Spanish, "Struggle").

"Logistics!" César cries out, furiously scribbling notes on loose-leaf yellow sheets that lie on the floor next to his copy of *The Diary of Che Guevara.* "Who's going to bring the bullhorn?" . . .

November, 1995 marks the first anniversary of the California election that placed the issue of immigration on the national agenda with the re-election of Gov. Pete Wilson and his all-out crusade for Proposition 187. It also marks the anniversary of the biggest student mobilization in Los Angeles since the late 1960s. . . .

Most of the activists at the Peace and Justice Center are veterans of last year's protests—high school and college students who led walkouts, organized teach-ins, and volunteered for get-out-the-vote efforts. Many were present at the pre-election October 16 march in Los Angeles which drew over 100,000 people onto the streets, one of the largest demonstrations in modern California history.

"Proposition 187 affects me in every way," says Ana Vásquez, a 20-year-old student at the University of Southern California. "My family is half documented and half undocumented. My mother's a citizen, my *tíos* came across the river."

Most of the advocates for the undocumented are young Chicano and Central American citizens like Ana who feel that 187 paints all Latinos, regardless of

NACLA Report on the Americas, Vol. 29:3, pp. 29–34. Copyright © 1995 by the North American Congress on Latin America, 475 Riverside Dr., #454, New York, NY 10115-0122.

immigration status, as welfare freeloaders, criminals, and the cause of the worst economic downturn in California since the Depression. In this, the activists of the 1990s differ from their 1960s forerunners. . . .

These activists want to reach out beyond the Latino community. "We're trying to break down the image that this is the 'Chicano movement' of the nineties," says Angel Cervantes, a founding member of the Four Winds Student Movement. . . . A lot of organizers are moving away from race and ethnicity towards issues of class."

This post-nationalist rhetoric has yet to translate into political reality, however. . . . The turnout at last year's marches was practically 99% Latino. And the election results once again confirmed California's political and cultural fragmentation. . . . White Californians voted nearly three-to-one in favor of 187, while Latinos voted nearly four-to-one against. Asians and African-Americans wound up in the middle, nearly splitting even. . . .

. . . Had Latinos voted proportionate to their population numbers (approximately one-third statewide), 187 may well have been defeated. But low voter-registration and turn-out rates—along with the fact that a substantial number of Latinos, both documented and undocumented, are not citizens—have historically held back not only a possible swing vote, but a bloc that could, theoretically, become the dominant force in California politics.

. . . Many Latino institutions—energized by 187, like the students—are focusing on political empowerment through more traditional channels.

Last year, community-based organizations such as the Central American Resource Center, One Stop Immigration, and the Catholic Church-based United Neighborhoods Organization recruited people for marches, conducted letter-writing campaigns, and coordinated media-outreach efforts. Latino newspapers, TV, and radio stations went on an unabashed crusade. . . .

Many community-based organizations are focusing on increasing the ranks of eligible Latino voters. The Southwest Voter Research and Education Project projects that some 100,000 people will apply for citizenship in California in 1995 alone. Nationally, applications for citizenship rose 250% from 1992 to 1995. . . .

The Catholic Church is active in the citizenship drive as well. There are 187 . . . Latino-majority parishes out of a total of 290 in the most populous archdiocese in the country. According to Assistant Director of Hispanic Ministry Louis Velásquez, half of these parishes are helping the immigrant faithful naturalize. . . .

Interestingly, the Protestant evangelical churches are equally involved in a grassroots effort to, at the very least, keep their brethren from being deported. . . .

Some evangelical churches have taken a more radical stance on the issue of immigration. . . . When undocumented brethren are deported, an elaborate network of contacts are often able to return the deportees to the flock in a kind of Pentecostal sanctuary movement. . . .

Nonetheless, the citizenship drive is seen as the principal vehicle for Latino empowerment. "We expect to have 2.1 million people registered by next year," says Antonio González, director of the Southwest Voter Research and Education Project. . . .

Absent from the discourse of most mainstream institutions (and elected officials) is word on the fate of the undocumented, who are, at least ostensibly, the direct target of 187. While most community organizations speak sympathetically of the undocumented, the practical and political upshot of this solidarity is conspicuous in its lack of definition. . . .

. . . Many activists . . . think that mainstream institutions have all but abandoned the undocumented. . . . The undocumented have begun advocating on their own behalf—forming, for instance, street-vending cooperatives and independent day-laborer unions.

Despite the recent high-profile crackdown at the border, the incessant sweeps of *la migra* in the cities, and the increasingly ill political winds blowing . . . in California . . . , many of the undocumented appear unfazed by the political storm. A visit to a day-laborer site on the corner of Sunset and Alvarado reveals the eternal hope of the immigrant. . . .

Ricardo Martínez, a 21-year-old man from rural Jalisco, still believes in the promise of California. "I'm hopeful that all this will change," he says, "and that one day the politicians here are 100% Latino, so that we can be treated better in California. Why do they put us down so much when they're practically living off of the work we do for them?" . . .

Still, the psychological impact of 187 politics has taken its toll on the undocumented. Whether children in classrooms distracted by fears that their families may be torn apart by *la migra* or working mothers nervous about sending their children to school or to public hospitals when they are ill, a climate of fear has dampened some of the immigrants' stubborn optimism. . . .

. . . Whatever the decision in court about Prop 187's constitutionality, the battle over the referendum will answer many questions about California's, and by extension the country's, future. The immigration debate, after all, includes issues of race relations, class disparity and the global economy. Three decades after the civil rights movement brought us both fire on the streets and major change to our public lives, a new and perhaps just as momentous struggle is upon us. At the center of the controversy are the newest Americans—and their blood relatives who have been here for generations.

7. Frank del Olmo Explains What Latinos Have to Lose by Proposition 209, 1996

The Times' last poll before Tuesday's election found that Latino voters in California are narrowly opposed to Proposition 209, the initiative that would abolish affirmative action in state hiring and contracting. All told, 42% of Latino respondents said they would vote against 209, with 38% leaning in favor of it and 20% undecided.

That more Latinos oppose Proposition 209 than favor it is no surprise. The initiative would force state and local government entities—most notably the University of California [UC] and the California State University system—to abolish the few programs to get more Latino students into higher education and to give more

Frank del Olmo, "Latinos Have a Lot to Lose," *Los Angeles Times,* Vol. 115 (Sunday, November 3, 1996), M5, Column. Copyright © 1996 Los Angeles Times. Reprinted by permission.

Latino business people a crack at government contracts. But to my mind, the most significant number in that poll is the 20% undecided. That means one in five Latino voters is not sure how he or she feels about a measure that could have a negative effect on them and their children.

This is a sadly accurate indication of how conflicted many Latinos are about affirmative action, both in theory and in practice. . . .

In its most benign form, this indifference toward affirmative action once was expressed to me by a Latina who works with recent immigrants from Latin America.

"Most of the Latinos I know don't need it," she said simply.

Indeed, it has occurred to me on more than one occasion that the Latino community would be better off if more U.S.-born Latinos shared the work ethic, confidence in the future and just plain gumption of their immigrant brethren.

Other Latinos take the pragmatic view of the successful Latino businessman who once told me he considered affirmative action "a program for the blacks." He was not angry about this, I hasten to add, merely stating what he considered a fact: that affirmative action is intended to help African Americans overcome the effects of centuries of slavery and racial segregation.

My position on affirmative action falls somewhat in between those two. I don't spend much time worrying about Latino businesses getting government contracts. Most of the Latino entrepreneurs I know figured out a long time ago that the public sector of the California economy (indeed, the national economy) is shrinking, and the place to pursue one's fortune is in the private sector.

But in order to compete in the private sector, one must be at least minimally prepared through a decent education. And that leads me to the reason I will vote against Proposition 209: the effect it would have on public higher education in California.

Thirty years ago, when I was an undergraduate at UCLA, there were just 25 Latinos in a student body that numbered about 25,000. I remember the number because we few "Chicano Bruins" got to know each other pretty well.

Each one of us came from working-class families and none of us could have afforded to attend college anywhere but at a public university. . . .

Even the most stubborn supporter of Proposition 209 must admit that Latino representation of 1 in 1,000 at the biggest public university in Los Angeles was pretty pathetic.

Well, things are a little better at UCLA these days—but not that much better. Last year's freshman class had 3,523 students, including 790 Latinos. . . . Even that minimal improvement would not have happened without the active recruitment of Latino students by UCLA.

Most Latino kids still come from working-class homes and would be hard-pressed to attend college, even community college, without some assistance. Faced with family financial needs, far too many opt to go right to work rather than pursue a college education. That costs California greatly, both in terms of future leaders and future high-wage taxpayers.

That is why UC and Cal State . . . must be allowed to recruit Latinos and other underrepresented minorities as aggressively as possible. Proposition 209 would not just stop that, but would also lock its prohibition against all such affirmative action programs into the California Constitution.

Proposition 209 must be defeated. And whether they realize it or not, Latino voters have a bigger stake than most other Californians in making sure it is.

❧ E S S A Y S

The 1980s brought major changes to Chicanos. While they continued their struggle to achieve equality, focusing on issues such as bilingual education and immigration reform, many of their gains were wiped out by the policies of Ronald Reagan. Poverty rates, joblessness, and segregation increased. These conditions set the stage for Chicanos in the 1990s: Three-fourths of the Latinos in the United States are concentrated in cities in Texas and California. Los Angeles remains home to the second largest population of Mexicans in the world. Because of the protracted recession, Governor Pete Wilson of California cut billions of dollars from school and other public programs.

The grassroots mobilization and activism of Mexican American women in East Los Angeles against a proposed state prison is the focus of the first essay, by Mary S. Prado, professor of Chicana/o studies at California State University, Northridge. Prado analyzes the process by which the women of Boyle Heights, organized as the Madres del Este de Los Angeles (Mothers of East Los Angeles), empowered themselves. Prado notes that the women later linked up with environmental groups to defeat an oil pipeline project, a hazardous waste incinerator, and other undesirable projects planned for their community. In the second essay, Rodolfo F. Acuña, professor of Chicano studies at California State University, Northridge, describes how the anger and frustration of Anglos in California's San Fernando Valley over the growing number of undocumented Mexicans and the cultural changes the Chicano presence created produced a white backlash.

Chicana scholar Elizabeth Martínez has written extensively on contemporary Latina issues. In the third essay, she states that although Latina identity is comprised of diverse backgrounds and experiences, their larger history of colonization unites them all. Latinas have resisted exploitation and experienced the growth of a new consciousness based on their unique experience of racial oppression, even though their feminism often was not well received by Chicano males. The growing Latina feminization is threatened by white backlash, yet young Chicanas and Latina working women have continued to express this new form of feminism. Martínez emphasizes that Latinas need to redefine their feminism and link their cause to that of other women of color, thus corroborating the sentiments of other Chicanas who have explored the importance of Latina identity.

Mexican American Women's Activism in East Los Angeles

MARY S. PRADO

During the summer months of 1986 and 1987, between five hundred and three thousand people marched every Monday evening on the Olympic Boulevard

Mary S. Prado, *Mexican American Women Activists: Identity and Resistance in Two Los Angeles Communities* (Philadelphia: Temple University Press, 1998), pp. 105–141. Reprinted by permission.

bridge that links downtown Los Angeles with Eastside Los Angeles. They carried bilingual placards proclaiming "No Prison in ELA" and "No Cárcel on Este L.A." A broad-based community group, the Coalition against the Prison, eventually defeated the first state prison planned for construction in a densely populated urban area. The prison proposal symbolized the legacy of "dumping" unwanted projects on the Eastside. The community victory in 1992 marked the end of an eight-year struggle and illustrated the potential power of grassroots activism in working class communities.

. . . Gender, class, and ethnicity became visible dimensions of Eastside politics when Fifty-sixth District Assemblywoman Gloria Molina voiced opposition to the project planned for her district. Many viewed the residents of the Fifty-sixth—predominantly working class, with significant numbers of Mexican immigrants and noncitizens—as politically powerless and unlikely to raise organized opposition.

. . . Editorials began appearing on a regular basis, with the influential *Los Angeles Times* initially backing the prison. One radio editorial stated, "Gloria Molina likens herself to a drum major in a march against the East L.A. Prison. Few have fallen in line behind her." The *Los Angeles Herald* questioned the fairness of the site selection, and *La Opinión* and local Eastside neighborhood papers opposed it. When Molina met with *Los Angeles Times* editors in 1986, she convinced them that the Eastside deserved a public hearing, although they continued to support the site selection. Within a year after the community mobilization gathered momentum and wider support, the *Los Angeles Times* began changing its position.

In 1987, as the prison controversy continued, Eastside residents in conjunction with Lucille Roybal-Allard, now representing the Fifty-sixth Assembly District, challenged another large detrimental project: one of the first toxic-waste incinerators planned for California. Through a maze of complex political maneuvers, Eastside residents contested both projects in the legislature, in the courts, in hearings at the state and federal level, and at the grassroots. . . . As women became activists, they reflected on their experiences as mothers and working-class Mexican Americans, converting long-established social networks into political networks. . . .

Mobilizing the Community: "Whatever It Takes!"

The mobilization began by involving existing community networks. Different segments of the community contributed their resources, among them merchants, business people, and extended family members, including the grown children of Boyle Heights residents. Widening the opposition to the prison meant continuing to spread the news and appealing to ethnic and class solidarity. East Los Angeles, historically the first neighborhood with a large concentration of Mexican Americans in the city, is a symbol of an "ethnic heartland," so Mexican Americans from outside the community joined the struggle in solidarity. These outside supporters included individuals as well as representatives of Chicano student groups, such as MECHA (Movimento Estudiantil Chicano de Aztlán), and the chapters of state and national Latino organizations, such as the Mexican American Political Association, the League of United Latin American Citizens and the Mexican American Education Commission.

Merchants and Business People.   Shortly before the massive 1986–87 community demonstrations, merchants and professionals from three Eastside Chambers of Commerce unsuccessfully promoted the creation of an enterprise zone in the area. An enterprise zone is an area specially zoned and subsidized by public funds intended to attract light industry, small businesses, and jobs. The business leaders had been meeting regularly, and had already begun to take issue with proposals for the community that they deemed detrimental. In 1984, for example, they stopped the siting of a junkyard in Lincoln Heights, across the street from a school for the mentally retarded. In August 1985 they brought two hundred people to testify at hearings over a Rapid Transit District proposal to curtail bus service to East Los Angeles. When members of the group found out about the prison, they were already primed for a political confrontation with state officials.

Frank Villalobos and other men from the group made many trips to Sacramento to lobby legislators to vote against the prison bill. Finally, Gloria Molina asked Villalobos, who had invaluable knowledge regarding land-use regulations, why there were no women traveling to Sacramento to speak against the prison. As he explained it, "I was getting some heat from her because no women were going up there."

In response to Molina's pointed question, Villalobos invited Veronica Gutiérrez, a law student who lived in the community, to accompany him on the next trip to Sacramento. (Gutiérrez later became a field representative for Gloria Molina when she served on the city council.) Meanwhile, representatives of the business sector, particularly Steve Kasten, José Luis García, and Carmine Baffo, and the Fifty-sixth district office were continuing to compile arguments and supportive data against the Eastside prison site. Villalobos explained one of the pressing problems: "The Senators . . . didn't even acknowledge that we existed. They kept calling it the 'downtown' site, and they argued that there was no opposition in the community. So I told Father Moretta, what we have to do is demonstrate that there is a link [proximity] between the Boyle Heights community and the prison." Father John Moretta, the pastor at Resurrection Parish in Boyle Heights, and as many priests as he could persuade to join the effort announced the many hearings and demonstrations from the pulpit and mobilized hundreds of people. . . . Information also traveled by word of mouth among families and in neighborhood shopping areas.

Extended Family Networks.   Extended family networks greatly contributed to the mobilization efforts. When I asked Dolores Duarte how she went about encouraging more people to participate, she reminded me that she comes from a large family born and raised in Boyle Heights. "All my six sisters came to the marches with my mom and my brother. I have a sister who lives in Commerce, another one in Monterey Park, one in Hacienda Heights, and two sisters that live here in Eastside L.A. Then, my sisters started bringing their daughters to the marches."

. . . In fact, some news about the Department of Corrections came through Dolores's sister before Dolores heard it at the meetings: "My sister works for the employment office in the area. So whenever anything came in on the prison she would let me know. She told us when they were accepting applications for the prison. She read all the qualifications [a high school diploma] to me and if you are an immigrant [and not yet a U.S. citizen] it is not that easy [to get a position]." Another women added that some neighborhood people had believed the promise of jobs until she mentioned the qualifications they would not be able to meet.

Because East Los Angeles holds a powerful symbolic meaning for the larger Mexican American community, Chicano student groups began joining the marches. *La Gente,* a UCLA-sponsored Chicano student newspaper, ran an extensive article on the issue. In turn the women in MELA came to the UCLA campus in West Los Angeles, a substantial distance through congested traffic, to join a student demonstration against campus discrimination. MELA and Chicano student groups developed a relationship of mutual support. . . . Several of the women in MELA had children or grandchildren attending UCLA. So it was a combination of family and ethnic ties that formed the social networks for political action.

The Parish Networks. Another woman, Juana Gutiérrez, active in the neighborhood for many years, found out about the prison issue when she received a call from Assemblywoman Gloria Molina's deputy field representative, Martha Molina. Juana stated, "You know, nobody knew about the plan to build a prison in this community until Assemblywoman Gloria Molina told me. Martha Molina called me and said, 'You know what is happening in your area? The governor wants to put a prison in Boyle Heights!' So I called a Neighborhood Watch meeting at my house, and we got five people together. Then Father Moretta started informing his people at the church, and that is when the group of two to three hundred started showing up for every march on the bridge."

Juana had an established information network in the community that ranged from local political offices to the Neighborhood Watch group to the parish; she commenced to link up these networks. Her husband, Ricardo, and a group of five women collected nine hundred signatures on petitions that Gloria Molina took to Sacramento to illustrate community opposition to the prison.

While capitalizing on her extended family networks, Dolores Duarte also used her work site as a place to disseminate information. She has been an employee for fifteen years in a large Boyle Heights pharmacy. Once the demonstrations began, she came to know her customers in a different way: "I have lived in this parish all my life and I have gotten to know so many people through my work in the pharmacy. But it was nothing until this prison march. . . ."

Father Moretta requested that priests in other parishes announce the marches after mass. In addition, the women would visit other parishes and make the announcements. Dolores did some of that work: "I met people from other parishes, like San Antonio de Padua, that I never knew. At Assumption, we would go out there on Sunday to invite them. Different people would go to other parishes every week."

Preexisting networks formed the core of the first groups of people who participated in the marches. After that, they took the marches through the Estrada Courts housing project, chanting "No Prison in East L.A." as they made their way through the small walkways separating the hundreds of housing units. Dolores tells how they called people to join them: "We would march past the houses and invite the people to join us. We used to yell come and give us your *apoyo* [support] in English and in Spanish." . . . They gained some people as they marched through the housing projects. . . .

Politicizing Motherhood: Mothers of East Los Angeles (MELA)

The women's activities and stories illustrated how they crafted oppositional strategies from gender, ethnic, class, and community identity. Feminist analysis often speaks about the "intersection" of race, class, and gender, but the term fails to capture the fluid dynamism of the women's interpretations and actions. Social identity may be interpreted and used in innumerable fashions; . . . the women creatively crafted their expressions of identity and used them to confront the state's agenda. . . .

"You Don't Have to Have Children to Belong." . . . One Sunday after mass, Father Moretta decided to ask all the women parishioners to meet with him. He told them about the prison site and asked for their support. . . .

> I felt so strongly about the issue, and I knew in my heart what a terrible offense this was to the people. So I was afraid that once we got into a demonstration situation we had to be very careful. I thought the women would be cooler and calmer and easier to control than the men. The bottom line is that the men came anyway. The first times out the majority were women. Then they began to invite their husbands and their children, but originally it was just women.

Father Moretta met with the women and named the group. He also selected a woman to be president and spokesperson for MELA. Thus bolstered by the authority of the church and by a mother's responsibility to protect her children, the women coalesced into a group. The name of the organization, "Mothers of East Los Angeles," clearly communicates gender identity and the metaphor of mother as protector of the community. Not all of the core activists, however, came to the issue as mothers or directly through the church. . . .

One of the core founders of MELA, a self-described senior citizen, is unmarried and has no children. She discussed the pastor's appeal to the group of women who stayed after mass:

> He wanted the mothers to get involved. You know if the safety of one of her children is jeopardized, she turns into a lioness. That's why Father John got the mothers. We have to have a well-organized, strong group of mothers to protect the community and oppose things that are detrimental to us. You know the governor is in the wrong and the mothers are in the right. After all, the mothers have to be right. Mothers are for the children's interest, not for self-interest; the governor is for his own political interest. Father Moretta told us on a Sunday. Lo and behold, on Monday following we were on the bridge.

Her statement . . . also modified my emphasis on the predominance of women: "Of course, the fathers work. We also have many, many grandmothers. And all this is with support of the fathers. They make the placards and the posters; they do the security and carry the signs; and they come to the marches when they can."

When the women explained their activism, most of them linked family and community as one entity. . . . Juana Gutiérrez identified family, community, and ethnic identity as the impetus for her involvement: "digo 'mi comunidad' porque me siento parte de ella, quiero a mi raza como parte de mi familia" (I say "my community" because I am part of it. I love my *raza,* my people, as part of my family). She clearly uses motherhood and family as a metaphor for civic responsibility and action. She has expanded her responsibilities and legitimized militant opposition to projects she assesses as detrimental to the community. . . .

Angie Flores, a senior citizen and mother of two sons in their thirties, read about the prison in the local free newspaper, the *Belvedere Citizen.* She recalls her first reaction to an article about the demonstrations on the Olympic Boulevard bridge. The article was accompanied by a picture of Mexican American women. . . .

> I saw a picture of the women. . . . Then I read that they wanted help in the demonstrations on the bridge. When I went, I told them that I want to help in any way I can because some of them [other residents, primarily recent immigrants] don't know how to be heard, and I want them to learn how to defend themselves and not get this prison. . . .

Some women found out about the issue through various family networks. Several have sons and daughters who attend college and participate in ethnic student groups, and thus knew of MELA's activities. Several of MELA's core activists have sons and daughters who work as lawyers, teachers, or community organizers in Los Angeles and continued to take a political interest in the community. The women also had strong preexisting associations and a civic consciousness that is historically rooted in Boyle Heights. . . .

Ethnic Identity and Language: Tools of Protest

Ethnic identity and language can be viewed as bases for discrimination or for solidarity. Some view the inability to speak English as a barrier to active citizenship; others see ways to include those with limited ability to speak English. . . . At each community meeting, women had to work with the varied language facility of the Eastside residents. At public forums they also advocated for interpreters so that Spanish-speaking residents could follow the proceedings and participate in them. In order to mobilize the community, women had to communicate with immigrants who are predominantly Spanish-speaking and with the English- and Spanish-language media. . . .

Language. . . . From the onset of the community mobilization, the local newspaper, the *Belvedere Citizen,* the Spanish-language newspaper, *La Opinión,* and the now-defunct *Herald Examiner* covered the marches and demonstrations when the group called them. Channel 7 (ABC) and the *Los Angeles Times* also covered the controversy, generally orienting their coverage toward the need to build new prisons and address inmate overcrowding.

Spanish-language media, both print and electronic, provided crucial information for the community. *La Opinión* covered the prison issue on a regular basis, featuring not only the legislative news but extensive coverage of community sentiment. The *Los Angeles Times,* in comparison, focused on legislative decisions and seldom noted the sentiments of community residents. . . .

For some core activists, speaking out was not a novel experience. For instance, Angie Flores noted, "I am not afraid to speak because I had my club meetings and senior citizen meetings." All the core activists are bilingual to varying degrees, but only a few were born and raised in Mexico. When one of the latter is available for the Spanish-language interviews, she is called on to act as the group's spokesperson. The women used bilingual skills to mobilize others by phone and to communicate with both Spanish-language and English-language media.

In public hearings held to allow community input and participation, language turned into a focus of protest, an act of resistance, and a critique of the city's disregard for the often cited but seldom respected multicultural and multilingual population. One example was a hearing held in the state office building auditorium, which was filled beyond capacity by Eastside community members. Councilwoman Gloria Molina approached the podium to speak against the prison project. She looked from side to side, seeking an interpreter. There was none. Facing the audience, she asked, "Who needs a Spanish translation of the hearing proceedings?" The audience was silent for a moment; no one responded. Then someone called out, "Ask that question in Spanish!" She did. About three-fourths of the audience raised their hands. She read her entire statement in Spanish and then again in English, dismaying the hearing panel with the extra time that was required to deliver her comments twice. . . .

Ethnic Identity.   One rainy morning, about 150 women demonstrated at a recreation center in East Los Angeles where the Department of Corrections was holding a job fair for people interested in working in the proposed state prison. Rectangular tables lined the walls of the large recreation room. Several DOC representatives staffed the tables, which contained information leaflets and job announcements neatly arranged in stacks. The women filed in. . . .

Juana Gutiérrez held a small bullhorn and led the women in a march, chanting, "No Prison in E.L.A.! No Prison in E.L.A.!" A woman from the DOC stood up and, seemingly oblivious to the protesters, began speaking to the crowd about job opportunities. Other protesters began calling out as the DOC representatives attempted to quell the demonstration: "¡Pues, yo no quiero trabajar en prisión! ¡Mejor mándeme hacer pan!" (Well, I don't want to work in prison! Better have me bake bread!) Another woman called out, "¡Yo quiero hacer pan dulce o tortillas!" (I want to make sweet bread or tortillas!) The other women began to laugh. Juana picked up the bullhorn and in Spanish told the crowd to pick up the pamphlets and take them out and throw them away. They followed her directions.

Dolores Duarte approached the only Latino Department of Corrections representative and began scolding him: "You know you are on the wrong side of town. You have nerve to sit here in a Hispanic area and let them do that to YOUR people. You say you want to give jobs to people who don't want the prison here—your

OWN people. And you support these gringos. You go along with them after the way we have been treated. You want to dump everything on us!" The representative made a feeble attempt to explain that he was from San Diego, where the community had willingly accepted a large prison. As she walked away, two women who had been listening to the exchange cheered, "Give it to him, Dolores!" Dolores expressed satisfaction that her efforts deterred the man from attending meetings because she never saw him again. The job fair ended in chaos, the intention of the demonstration achieved.

Continuity and Change: New Activities in the Public Sphere

. . . The summer of 1986 was one of great legislative and community activity around Senate Bill 904, which would authorize $31 million for the initial costs of the 1,750-inmate prison. The bill was expected to pass the Senate easily. The first week of July 1986, MELA members traveled to Sacramento on chartered buses. Hundreds of women marched with signs reading, "Our children need schools, not prisons—MELA." They also lobbied representatives.

As the issue was debated, about two hundred members of MELA . . . converged on the capital. It was clear that the strong show of community opposition to the prison had a major impact on the Senate debate. The governor's administrative aides tried to delay the vote until the following week, hoping the Eastside residents would have left Sacramento by then. But Democratic senator David Roberti convinced Republican senator Robert Presley to bring the bill to a vote. Partly at issue was the environmental impact report; Senator Presley assured the legislators that the EIR would be completed once the land for the prison had been purchased. MELA held up signs chiding Senator Richard Polanco, the newly elected Eastside representative, for casting the vote that released the bill from the assembly committee. Passage had been all but assumed, but that day the Senate reversed itself and rejected the plan to build the prison in East Los Angeles by a four-vote margin. The Senate now rejected the bill that it had passed 35–0 and then sent to a Senate-Assembly conference committee in 1985. Surprised by the Senate's vote, Deukmejian offered a compromise to sway the senators, agreeing to a limited environmental impact report to be completed before the purchase of land for the prison. The Senate voted down the bill a second time in as many weeks. Democrats cast all the opposing votes, with Republicans providing all the votes in favor. The governor was stunned by the rejection. According to news sources, he had underestimated the effect of strong lobbying efforts by Latino organizations. Several senators were up for reelection, and they feared antagonizing the Mexican American community and had voted against the bill. In 1987 the legislature reached a compromise and passed a bill authorizing two prisons to be built, but challenges to the environmental impact report and legislative debates over the funds for prison construction further stalled the start of construction. . . .

. . . Core activists are recognized as grassroots community leaders. They have acquired public visibility; they are the focus of many newspaper interviews and popular magazine articles. Now they are sought out by other organizations—parent education projects, such as the one sponsored by the Mexican American Legal

Defense and Education Fund (MALDEF, a national organization established to pursue civil rights litigation and focused on the Latino community), and environmental groups such as Greenpeace—and by local political representatives. . . .

New Community Issues: Environmental Justice

As thousands of residents became politicized in the process of organizing against the prison, they learned about other undesirable projects planned for their community. . . . When Lucille Roybal-Allard informed them of a proposed toxic waste incinerator to be built in the industrial city of Vernon, MELA decided they should fight it. . . .

While the fight against the prison engaged other Latino groups on the basis of ethnic and class identity, few if any groups of other ethnic backgrounds joined the grassroots battle. But when the women decided to oppose an oil pipeline and a toxic waste incinerator, they began linking up with other environmental groups, particularly those calling for environmental justice. The environmental-justice movement exposed the racism inherent in the pattern of placing toxic waste sites in low-income minority communities. The pattern holds throughout the state and country: three out of five African Americans and Latinos live near toxic waste sites, and three of the five largest hazardous waste landfills are in communities with at least 80 percent minority populations. Greenpeace joined in at some of the meetings and provided testimony at the hearings.

The Oil Pipeline.   MELA joined with another local group, the Coalition against the Pipeline, when oil companies proposed a pipeline to carry oil from offshore rigs at Santa Barbara, a wealthy coastal resort ninety miles north of Los Angeles, to the port of Long Beach, forty-five miles south of Los Angeles. The pipeline, to be located only three feet underground, would be routed close to many schools, presenting a safety problem in the event of a gas leak. Further upsetting residents, the proposed route detoured into East Los Angeles, bypassing affluent white coastal cities such as Pacific Palisades.

MELA noted that the detour around the Westside presumed the political vulnerability of the Eastside. At one community meeting, for example, representatives of several oil companies sought support for running the oil pipeline through the center of East Los Angeles. The exchange between the women in the audience and the company representative was heated, as women asked questions about the chosen route for the pipeline.

"Is it going through Cielito Lindo" (President Reagan's ranch)? The oil representative answered, "No." Another woman stood and asked, "Why not place it along the coastline?" Without thinking, the representative responded, "Oh, no! If it burst, it would endanger the marine life." The woman retorted, "You value the marine life more than human beings?" The man's face reddened with anger, and the hearing disintegrated into angry chanting. The proposal was quickly defeated. But one of the women acknowledged that it was not solely their opposition that brought about the defeat: "We won because the Westside was opposed to it, so we united with them. . . . "

As they took on other issues, the women of MELA began meeting community activists from other sectors of Los Angeles. . . .

The Toxic Waste Incinerator.   Soon after the defeat of the pipeline, Lucille Roybal-Allard, assisted by her field representative, Miguel Mendívil, notified MELA that the small industrial city of Vernon, three miles south of downtown and on the border of Boyle Heights, had granted permits to one of the first entirely commercial hazardous waste incinerators proposed for California. While the city of Vernon, with a population up from ninety in 1980 to 150 in 1990, constituted the smallest city in the county, 51,000 people work there daily. The smaller residential population and the dominance of industry result in city council decisions that favor industrial development. The incinerator would operate twenty-four hours a day and burn 125,000 pounds of waste daily. As with the prison site selection, no environmental impact report had been completed. Regulatory agencies at each level—the Southern California Air Quality and Management District (SCAQMD) at the regional level, and the California Department of Health Services (DHS) at the state level, and the Environmental Protection Agency (EPA) at the national level—had granted permits for the incinerator without requiring an environmental impact report.

Governor Deukmejian and the DHS argued that any health effects would be minimal because no residential communities were close enough to the incinerator to be at risk. The company argued that conducting an EIR would increase their costs and delay construction. Opponents of the incinerator, including the *Los Angeles Times,* emphasized the dangers of locating the incinerator within blocks of dozens of food processing plants, including the Leslie Salt Company, across the street, and the Oscar Meyer and Farmer John meat companies, a few blocks away. Residents emphasized that the incinerator would worsen the already compromised air quality of the entire county and set a dangerous precedent throughout California.

After opponents had collected more than four thousand petition signatures and staged marches and rallies at the Vernon site, the city of Los Angeles, MELA, and Assemblywoman Roybal-Allard filed suit against the DHS for approving the project. Further investigation revealed that the operator had a poor safety record and a long history of safety violations at its other facilities. Environmental groups such as Greenpeace supported the demonstrations and invited MELA to support other working class communities confronting environmental threats. In 1988 MELA members traveled to Casmalia, 150 miles north of Los Angeles, to join in a demonstration for the closing of a toxic dump site. They also visited Kettleman City, which was also fighting a toxic waste incinerator. Later that same year, grassroots groups from small northern California cities with large minority populations—Kettleman, McFarland, Casmalia, Richmond—joined the march led by MELA in opposition to the toxic waste incinerator.

In 1991 the company abandoned the incinerator project, stating that the process had proceeded smoothly until the community was alerted. Company representatives charged that political pressure had unraveled the six-year-old deal and that "interminable law suits led to their decision." As a result of the community struggle, Assembly Bill 58 (Roybal-Allard), which provides all Californians with the minimum protection of an environmental impact report before the construction of hazardous waste incinerators, was signed into law. . . .

Juana Gutiérrez, along with some of the other women who formed the core group of activists, has taken the lead as a spokesperson on Eastside community issues. She is now invited to speak at conferences, demonstrations, and community meetings. While she does not see herself as political, she expresses herself forcefully as an advocate for social justice and the rights of the Latino community. She once commented, "I don't consider myself political. I'm just someone looking out for the community, for the youth . . . on the side of justice." In August 1990, as a representative of the Mothers of East Los Angeles, Santa Isabel (MELA-SI), Juana spoke at the twenty-year commemoration of the Chicano Moratorium march against the war in Viet Nam.

Madres del Este de Los Angeles, Santa Isabel (MELA-SI)

In 1990, after establishing considerable community presence and a reputation for championing community causes, the Mothers of East Los Angeles split into two separate groups, generally along parish lines. . . . The separation occurred when women and some men began questioning who could decide which community issues to address, who was entitled to speak for the group, and the relationship of the pastor to the group. One group continued to work with Resurrection parish and Father John Moretta. Juana Gutiérrez, a core member of MELA, established the second group at the adjacent parish of Santa Isabel. . . .

After 1990 the newly formed Madres del Este de Los Angeles, Santa Isabel (MELA-SI) continued to attend community hearings on urban development issues that affected the Eastside. . . . Juana Gutiérrez continues to act as the spokesperson for MELA-SI. In 1992 she and other members developed the collaborative Water Conservation Project with the Metropolitan Water District, the Los Angeles Department of Water and Power, and Corporate Technologies Service International (CTSI). They offered free low-flush toilets and recycled old ones. The old toilets are crushed into a material that is mixed into the asphalt used to pave the streets. The joint effort allowed MELA-SI to generate funding to develop several community betterment programs.

In just one year the Water Conservation Project created twenty-seven employment opportunities, with medical coverage and salaries well beyond the poverty levels of many inner-city employment projects. The jobs were created during a national and (even more acute) state economic crisis, without any additional taxpayer foundation or government monies. MELA-SI's partnership with the Water Conservation Project also made possible other community endeavors, including a graffiti clean-up project run entirely by Eastside youth and a scholarship program for high school and college students.

During this period, Los Angeles County budget cutbacks led to drastic reductions in funding to clinics offering infant immunization and basic health care. Well aware of the dangers of the budget cuts, given that 75 percent of Eastside residents are uninsured, MELA-SI developed the Child Immunization Project in conjunction with the nearby White Memorial Hospital. MELA-SI coordinated a program that sent high school volunteers door to door to inform Eastside residents about the importance and availability of vaccinations and tuberculosis testing; they also offered free transportation to the hospital.

. . . The mid-1980s marked a turning point when Eastside residents developed a harmonious working relationship with their local elected representatives. The strong show of unity among residents complemented the efforts of elected officials who kept the residents informed of legislative developments. Women's success at community mobilization emanated from the daily face-to-face interactions that occur as they meet their social obligations to their families and construct the social networks that bind a community.

. . . The women also redefined mother to mean anyone who "does for" children. Family became a metaphor for community, and community identity was closely tied to ethnic identity or *la raza*. The women reinterpreted their identity within existing power relationships, including the church and the family. . . .

. . . The victories over the proposed prison and the toxic waste incinerator now represent much more than success on isolated issues; they symbolize the Eastsiders' pride and willingness to struggle and successfully defend the quality of life in their community.

The Struggle for Control of Los Angeles Government

RODOLFO F. ACUÑA

The citadel of L.A. nativism and anti-immigrant hysteria is the San Fernando Valley, located almost entirely in the city of Los Angeles. . . . The Valley was the home of Bus-Stop, a movement of white middle-class activists who, during the 1970s, fought the busing of white children from the Valley to inner-city schools. During the 1980s, however, the inner city seemed to move to the Valley as the number of its Latino residents doubled. . . . By the 1990s, 38 percent of the Valley's adults were foreign-born, and 30 percent spoke a language other than English at home. . . .

In fact, by 1990 Brown people could be found everywhere in the Valley—even in upscale neighborhoods like Northridge, where hundreds of Mexicans lined the intersection of Parthenia and Reseda boulevards waiting for day-labor work. . . . Reseda, Canoga Park, Granada Hills and Chatsworth all had enclaves of working-class Mexicans and Central Americans. Within the white areas were also sizeable numbers of middle-class Latino professionals and business people. . . . Yet working-class Mexicans and Central Americans for the most part remained outside the life of the Valley. . . . Few middle-class Chicanos sat on the boards of homeowners associations or the Chamber of Commerce outside areas where they formed the vast majority. . . .

It is therefore no wonder that recent anti-immigrant campaigns have derived much of their strength from the San Fernando Valley. According to *Los Angeles Times* reporter Alan C. Miller, "The Valley has been in the vanguard of a rising backlash throughout California and elsewhere against the tide of newcomers, *particularly those crossing the Mexican border.*" . . .

Rodolfo Acuna, "The Politicization of the 'Other,'" from *Anything But Mexican: Chicanos in Contemporary Los Angeles* (New York: Verso Books, 1996), pp. 139–164. Reprinted by permission.

. . . Local sentiment was summed up by signs seen at Los Angeles Valley College when President Bill Clinton visited the campus: "L.A. Is a Third World Cesspool," and "Deport Illegal Aliens Now."

Valley Schools: The Fight for Equality

Valleyites had long resented the large number of minority students bused into its schools. . . . Residents saw this busing as an invasion of their neighborhood schools and blamed the incoming children for crime, the delinquency of their own children, and the urbanization of what was once thought to be a suburban community.

Many Valley residents were also upset with the ruling of retired Superior Court Judge Ralph Nutter in *Rodriguez* v. *LAUSD [Los Angeles Unified School District]*, which mandated that the district equalize its funding of individual schools. The suit, brought by the Mexican American Legal Defense and Education Fund (MALDEF), called for the district to factor teacher salaries into the budgets of individual schools. For years Valley schools had employed more educated and experienced teachers whose salary totals were much higher than those of teachers at inner-city schools. Its therefore cost the LAUSD more money to run Valley schools than their inner-city counterparts.

The redistricting of the Los Angeles Board of Education, which also resulted from the 1990 Census, fell to City Council members. . . . They approved creation of a second Latino Board of Education district. . . . This district . . . was 80 percent Latino. . . .

Valley leaders charged that additional Latino representation was at their expense. . . .

. . . Valley forces immediately sponsored a state initiative to change the outcome and formed The Coalition Against Unfair School Elections (CAUSE), calling for the breakup of the LAUSD.

By October 1992 CAUSE and the breakup movement were well under way. . . .

. . . By July the breakup movement was on the fast track. . . .

The breakup would have undermined the Supreme Court's historic decision in *Brown* v. *Board of Education,* which prohibited segregation of students by race. It would have meant increased segregation in Los Angeles schools. A Valley district would have 190,000 students, with close to 27 percent . . . of them white. The total number of students would include the 18,000 already bused. In the remaining system of 460,000 students, the white proportion would decline from 13 percent to 7.4 percent. . . . Most would be concentrated on the Westside. . . .

After losing the breakup fight, Valleyites turned to Proposition 174, which provided for vouchers—a logical extension of the politics of the breakup movement. . . .

. . . The initiative proposed giving a $2,600 voucher to all parents, who could then use it for private education if they wished. . . . In the end, Proposition 174 went down in defeat. However, the idea was not dead, and extremism had gained respectability during the Prop. 174 campaign. . . .

The 1993 Mayoral Race and the San Fernando Valley

The San Fernando Valley School breakup movement and anti-immigrant hysteria played important roles in Los Angeles' 1993 mayoral election. In large part Republican and Democratic Party leaders were intimidated by the San Fernando Valley, whose power went well beyond the number of its voters. They knew that like the Westside and the Downtown corporate community, much of the Valley's clout rested on the size of its financial contributions. The 1993 election campaign also marked the end of the Tom Bradley era. Even if it could be said that Bradley served corporate interests more than those of his own Black community, symbolically the end of his era meant the end of Black power within the city.

Whether a Latino candidate would emerge was unclear. [Los Angeles City Councilwoman] Gloria Molina declared that she would not be a candidate. . . . Molina wisely concluded that she had been in office only twenty months and that Latinos had fought too hard for her seat, which Governor Pete Wilson would fill with his own choice in the event that Molina ran for mayor. When asked whether she would support Richard Alatorre, Molina scoffed: "We need an assertive, hands-on leader. We don't need anyone who enjoys the political game." Despite Molina's sarcasm, Alatorre would have been a formidable candidate. Although only 11 percent of voters citywide were Latino, Alatorre had a base beyond the community. He . . . had accumulated a considerable number of chips with other politicians and with developers; he surely could have amassed a considerable election warchest.

Ultimately, the only Chicano candidates were Julian Nava, former LAUSD Board member (1967–79) and ambassador to Mexico under Jimmy Carter; and Linda Griego, a deputy mayor under Bradley. . . . Nava had not been active in electoral politics since 1979 and did not have a base of support. . . . Within the political community the most frequently mentioned reason for not supporting Nava was that he had not been in politics for over fourteen years. . . . Some Chicano elected officials supported Linda Griego, who, although intelligent and capable, did not have a long history of political activism. In general the mayoral candidates avoided Latino enclaves and many did not even bother to attend candidate forums in heavily Latino neighborhoods.

Los Angeles Times writers Frank Clifford and John Schawada reported in January 1993, "With an emotional power reminiscent of the 1970s furor over school busing, the movement to break up the Los Angeles Unified School District is muscling its way into the 1993 mayor's race." Nearly 40 percent of the city's voters lived in the San Fernando Valley; they were mostly white and anti-inner city. It mattered little to them what the mayor could or could not do about the schools. Indeed, most of the candidates supported the breakup, including Councilman Nate Holden, a Black, and Julian Nava. Even Michael Woo, the Asian American candidate preferred by many liberals, had refused to dismiss the idea.

Dovetailing with the breakup movement was anti-immigrant hysteria. . . . Meanwhile, the mayoral candidates exploited L.A.'s fear of violence as the Rodney King verdict and the uprising that followed it still hung over the city. . . .

On election day [Richard] Riordan received 144,690 votes (32.88 percent) to Woo's 106,596 (24.22 percent). Poorer Angelenos were more likely to vote for someone other than Riordan, while homeowners tended to favor him. Riordan supporters were also more likely to be white. As in no other election, the power of the

San Fernando Valley hung over the city like a pall. Council Districts [CDs] 2, 3, 7 and 12, all located in the Valley and containing 75 percent of the Valley's residents, gave Riordan 42.4 percent of their vote. In the heavily Latino 1st and 14th CDs, 26.6 percent voted for him, not far behind Woo's 29.5 percent. . . .

Since neither Riordan nor Woo received a majority, a runoff election was scheduled for 8 June 1993. . . . During the runoff campaign Riordan emphasized crime and the economy, while Woo portrayed himself as a reformer and the heir apparent to Bradley's coalition of minority activists and liberals, with added support from gay activists and feminists.

Riordan had strong business ties in Los Angeles, not only in the white community but also with Latinos, Blacks and Asians. . . . Riordan received the support of Richard Alatorre, whom he had backed in the struggle over Olvera Street.* Alatorre, in turn, banked his continued position on the board of the Metropolitan Transit Authority [MTA] on Riordan's winning the election. In the political game, that position was important because it gave the major players major access to money through contracts the MTA granted. . . . The agency had a budget of $3.7 billion at a time when other agencies were severely cutting back. . . . Riordan was also expected to be much friendlier than Woo to Alatorre. . . .

Woo, an upper-middle-class Chinese American businessman, had represented the Hollywood area since the mid 1980s; his father was an owner of the Cathay Bank. Considered a liberal, Woo had earned his reputation as a reformer by confronting the LAPD. During the campaign, however, he vacillated and seemed to believe that he could win by wearing the Bradley mantle and appealing to a coalition of minority groups and Bradley supporters. Supervisor Gloria Molina and Assemblyman Richard Polanco supported him. . . .

In the runoff, however, the Valley voted for Riordan and turned the tide in his favor. When it came down to the wire, Angeleno voters were simply tired of Bradley, and they viewed Woo as his surrogate. It also didn't help Woo that, as a member of a minority group, he was associated with the inner city. Finally, Woo alienated many of his supporters by vacillating during the campaign on key issues like immigrant rights and police oversight. This contributed to a low turnout by Blacks and other voters who tended to be generally sympathetic to him. Riordan defeated Woo by a margin of almost 2 to 1 in the Valley. In an article entitled, "Politicians Who Ignore Valley Voters Pay the Price," *Los Angeles Times* reporter Dan Brennan cited taxation, illegal immigration and an ineffective LAUSD as the Valley's main political concerns—Riordan passed the Valley's litmus test: Woo did not.

The Los Angeles mayoral election satisfied no one outside the white Valley and the business community. . . .

Black–Brown Relations and the Appointment of Hermosillo

. . . Mayor Richard Riordan lost his first major battle with the City Council when he nominated as fire commissioner a Latino [Xavier Hermosillo] who was viewed by leaders of the Black community (as well as some Chicanos) as racist and divisive. . . .

---

*Olvera Street, in the Old Mexico section of Los Angeles, is a tourist attraction. In the early 1990s Olvera Street was scheduled for gentrification. *Ed.*

African Americans had built their political power in council districts south of the central city, and they had voting strength well beyond their numbers. Proud of their political achievements, they were 13 percent of the population and cast 18 percent of the vote in the 1989 mayoral election. In contrast, Latinos constituted just under 40 percent of the city but cast only 8 percent of the vote. During the 1980s Los Angeles had grown by more than 17 percent and much of this growth was among the Latino (and Asian) populations. Nevertheless, Latinos were grossly underrepresented, . . . and they held only two seats on the City Council.

For Chicano leaders, getting more seats on the City Council signified respect and not being taken for granted. Pouring over the 1990 Census maps, they found the possibility that a Chicano could be elected in the 7th CD in the San Fernando Valley and another by shifting the boundaries of Rita Walters's 9th CD. The 9th CD had declined from 56 percent to 36 percent Black during the 1980s, and its Latino population had increased from 36 percent to 61 percent. . . .

The African American community had slowly lost political ground. During the 1980s, some 75,000 African Americans had left South Central for the Inland Empire [San Bernadino County]. . . . Economic restructuring was the reason for the 20 percent drop in the Black population in South Central: plant shutdowns and the resulting loss of blue-collar jobs in the areas just east of South Central. Moreover, African Americans also paid higher mortgage interest rates in South Central, suffered police repression, and had lower-quality schools. With a loosening of housing segregation elsewhere, much of South Central's Black middle-class population moved out. Meanwhile, thousands of Latinos moved into the abandoned areas, further unsettling Blacks, who depended on South Central as a political power base. More was at stake than just electoral representation: Blacks had learned that political power and jobs go hand and hand.

At the same time, Latinos resented the fact that they had made few political gains under Mayor Tom Bradley. . . . Less than 30 of the 217 city commissioners were Latinos. Some 45 percent of the elected and appointed positions in L.A. were held by Anglos, who formed 37.2 percent of the population. African Americans held 22 percent of the elected and appointed positions, although they made up less than 14 percent of the population, while Latinos held 20 percent of the jobs, but were 39.8 percent of the population.

The city had 44,157 employees, 6,700 of them Latinos. Of the jobs with decision-making power, Anglo-Americans held 62 percent and Latinos less than 10 percent. . . . The push for political representation meant that Latinos wanted a greater piece of the public job pie, as well as more respect and recognition.

. . . In this climate, all talk of carving out an additional Latino City Council district went nowhere. Indeed, contrary to the national trend, many Black politicos had second thoughts about using redistricting as a method for correcting imbalances in political representation. . . .

. . . In the end, Bradley approved the redistricting plan, which denied Latinos the potential for a fourth seat on the City Council and increased resentment among Latinos and especially among Chicanos. . . .

Meanwhile, the City Council did little to ameliorate tensions. Los Angeles trailed major Southwest cities in reforming the political structure during the 1970s. It remained a city whose political process had changed minimally since the days of

Calvin Coolidge in the 1920s, when the local elites devised a system that allowed the city's "finest" to rule. The city was controlled by a commission government that was vulnerable to the influence of the "right" people.

It was against this backdrop of recent tension and resentment between African Americans and Latinos in local politics that Mayor Riordan nominated Xavier Hermosillo, a former reporter turned public relations consultant to the Los Angeles Fire Commission. Hermosillo . . . allegedly rejected the notion that Latinos should form coalitions with other groups. . . .

Riordan's nomination of Hermosillo to the Fire Commission drew an angry outcry from African Americans, progressive whites, some Latinos, reactionaries and anti-immigrant forces. . . .

In criticizing the nomination of Hermosillo, Councilwoman Rita Walters said, "There is a difference between being outspoken and being divisive. Martin Luther King was outspoken but he was always inclusive. Mr. Hermosillo has been outspoken and always divisive." Joe Hicks, the respected executive director of the Southern Leadership Conference of Greater Los Angeles, called on the council to reject Hermosillo because of "his documented insensitivity to other groups." Councilman Mark Ridley Thomas told a columnist that Riordan "behaved irresponsibly and created unnecessary conflict between African Americans and Latino members in the council.". . .

Ultimately Hermosillo was rejected by a nine-to-five vote. What he should have been criticized for was swept under the rug. Hermosillo interpreted Chicano Power to mean, basically, Mexican or Chicano capitalists getting their share of the economic and political pie. In this pursuit, he erroneously used Blacks as the standard for judging Latino successes and failures, instead of the system itself. On the positive side, he stood against his party on anti-immigrant legislation, criticizing both parties for supporting populist racism. And there was a popular perception that he defended Latino workers. . . . The Hermosillo case showed the need for all groups—white, Brown, Black and Asian—to explore the limits of group advocacy and the need to judge everyone by the same standard.

Immigration and the 1994 State Elections

"Valley fever" dominated the 1994 state elections. Anti-immigrant hysteria had reached moblike proportions by then, allowing Pete Wilson to make the greatest comeback in recent political history. Constantly in the news, his job rating hit 15 percent in May but rose to 22 percent in August as the result of immigrant bashing. . . . Democrats were partly responsible for his success in that they themselves engaged in immigrant bashing, including, to one degree or another, Senators Dianne Feinstein and Barbara Boxer and Congressman Anthony Beilenson, along with Attorney-General Janet Reno and the Democratic contender for governor, State Treasurer Kathleen Brown. Brown even proposed tying a prisoner-transfer pact to the North American Free Trade Agreement, and called for a tamper-proof Social Security card, employer sanctions and military troops on the Mexican border. . . .

Wilson's strategy was to highlight the proposition that "We Americans" have lost control of our borders and to blame undocumented residents for the state's fiscal problems. He continually distorted the November 1992 Los Angeles County study that alleged that the county spend $946 million . . . on services to recent immigrants. . . . He distorted or ignored such evidence as a July 1993 report by the state Senate Office of Research . . . : "The unfortunate backlash against immigrants, exploited by too many politicians in the past year or so, tends to belittle newcomers to the country as a drag on the economy and an imposition on residents of longer standing. This dismissal of the immensely varied ranks of new and future Americans is unjust to the great majority, and is simply mistaken." The bottom line was that "blaming the immigrants won't solve economic woes."

Simultaneously, the Federation for American Immigration Reform (FAIR) carried on a war of propaganda and misinformation using "illegal immigration as a convenient excuse to urge drastic cuts in legal immigration, from the current 800,000 a year to nearly 200,000." Nationally, Pat Buchanan argued that the Republican Party should go further in exploiting the issue of immigration. . . .

While many Latinos supported a tougher policy toward illegal immigrants, the intensity of Wilson's attacks began to frighten them. . . . Fifteen Latino organizations, led by MALDEF in San Francisco, announced a new coalition called the Latino Civil Rights Coalition to combat anti-immigrant hysteria. In Southern California, Latino leaders including US Rep. Xavier Becerra, Richard Alatorre and Assemblywoman Hilda Solis sent a letter accusing Wilson of stirring up racial tensions. . . .

In February 1994 Latino leaders and politicos formed Proponents for Responsible Immigration Debate in Education (PRIDE) in order to put some sanity into the debate on illegal immigration. PRIDE wanted candidates to support the right of immigrants to medical care, education and citizenship if born in the United States, and to support keeping the INS [Immigration and Naturalization Service] under civilian control. . . .

Proposition 187

By May 1994 the campaign to place the draconian SOS (Save Our State) initiative on the ballot had 600,000 signatures, 200,000 more than needed to qualify for the November election. As expected, Governor Wilson endorsed SOS, which became Proposition 187, and stepped up his inflammatory rhetoric about an "invasion." "California simply can't wait any longer. Our borders are a sieve that makes a mockery of our laws and cripples our ability to shape our own identity." He also filed a suit against the federal government for reimbursement of state costs of providing services to immigrants. . . .

In reality, an INS survey showed that of those legalized under the Immigration Reform and Control Act of 1986 (IRCA), only 1 percent had received any government assistance. A San Francisco study showed that of the 23 percent of undocumented mothers eligible for welfare because they had US-born children, only 5 percent took advantage of their eligibility. Pro-immigrant studies had little impact on politicians such as Wilson: they had their minds made up, based on their calculation of political advantage. The immigrant was a convenient and politically safe scapegoat, and the only thing they cared about was getting elected.

At the heart of the tension between Latinos and the white community was numbers. By the year 2020, the Latino population in California would increase from 27.3 percent to 36.5 percent, while the Euroamerican population would fall from 52 percent . . . to 34 percent. Prop. 187 was based on the color of Latino and Asian skins. . . .

In other words, Prop. 187 went far beyond scapegoating immigrants for the state's economic woes. It signified a profound resurgence of legalized racism in response to a historic national upheaval. There was a convergence of interests in Prop. 187, bringing together supporters of the school breakup movement in the Valley, the school voucher campaign, the "Three Strikes and you're out" proposition and homeowner associations of the San Fernando Valley. Although SOS backers maintained that the initiative was not race specific, . . . polls suggested otherwise. Prop. 187 was favored 59 percent to 32 percent, with 64 percent of whites supporting the measure while 60 percent of Latinos and a narrow majority of African Americans disapproved. . . .

The Mobilization Against Proposition 187

As the campaign continued, the racism of Prop. 187 galvanized opposition. . . . A coalition of Chicano groups against Prop. 187 mobilized in February 1994. A march in Los Angeles drew 6,000, followed by another march on 28 May when about 18,000 trekked up Broadway to City Hall. On 16 October, over 100,000 protestors marched down Avenida César Chávez to City Hall. . . .

The National Coordinating Committee for Citizenship and Civic Participation, also known as *la cordinadora,* played a central role in planning the march. . . . Separate from *la cordinadora* was the Los Angeles Organizing Committee, which included Local 660, the International Garment Workers Union, Justice for Janitors and the California Immigrant Workers Association, among others. . . . Within this network, but not part of the governing committee for the march, was a contingent of activists . . . who did effective outreach. A list of 7,000 volunteers signed up on the day of the march for the No on 187 campaign. . . .

. . . Opponents of Prop. 187 were heartened during the last days of the campaign as polls showed that support for the proposition had declined, and they seemed afraid that demonstrations might upset this momentum.

There is no doubt that the 16 October march had a profound impact on . . . students. . . .

. . . Altogether, it is estimated that 10,000 . . . walked out of thirty-nine schools. District officials cooperated with Chicano activists, and teach-ins were held at those schools where the students did not walk out. Authorities were shaken and the National Guard was put on alert for possible violence at these events.

The dramatic participation of students from the San Fernando Valley shocked many Angelenos. Although Latinos were a majority of the school population there—60 percent of Valley students were Latino—they had been taken for granted. . . . Often alienated from other students, they heard the anti-immigrant remarks, and their teachers were more outspoken about their own biases. Moreover, the Valley's Latino population had grown so rapidly that a sense of place had never really developed. . . .

. . . On 8 November California overwhelming passed Prop. 187. Only the San Francisco Bay Area voted against the measure, by 70 percent to 30 percent. Angelenos voted for Prop. 187 by a 12-point margin; the Valley voted 61 percent for

Prop. 187. Exit polls showed Latinos opposing the proposition 77 percent to 23 percent statewide. Some 53 percent of Asians voted against Prop. 187, as did a like proportion of African Americans. . . . Republicans voted 78 percent in favor, versus 36 percent of the Democrats. . . . Middle-class white Americans had spoken; 80 percent of those who voted were white. . . .

As expected, legal challenges were filed the day after the election. Initially many municipalities joined the suit, but local officials were intimidated by threats of recall. Vigilantes calling themselves "loyal citizens" asked Mexican-looking people for their green cards. CHIRLA [Coalition for Humane Rights of Los Angeles] was flooded with complaints, as were other social service agencies. The pro-Prop. 187 forces pushed forward.

As a result of the passage of Prop. 187, many in the immigrant community feared to seek health care. One of Governor Wilson's first acts after his reelection was to order health clinics not to give prenatal care to undocumented mothers. . . .

Where will the struggle against Prop. 187 and the whole assault on immigrant rights go from here? The students are the key to this. They were morally outraged at the injustice of Prop. 187, and they acted. . . . Moreover, the vast majority of the protestors are documented residents who will be able to vote soon. What direction their militancy takes will in great part depend on their future political education. . . . In another response to Prop. 187, Chicano and Latino organizations have begun the work of speeding up the naturalization of noncitizens. . . .

A Balance Sheet

As many observers have noted the 1994 California elections reflected the national trend toward meaner . . . politics that pointed to a grim future for people of color and all poor or working-class residents. In California, the reason for the right-wing sweep would certainly include the massive financial support for Republican candidates and causes; the rampant white racism that scapegoated immigrants, welfare recipients, youth in the barrios and ghettoes, and other vulnerable groups; and the fact that Democrats did not address Latino issues or campaign seriously in Latino areas.

Rather than recognizing the power of these forces, the media attempted to portray an apathetic Latino community that did not care enough even to come out against Prop. 187. . . . The Southwest Voter Research Institute corrected this claim, reporting that its exit polls showed that Latinos turned out 10.2 to 11.4 percent of the vote. . . . That number takes on more meaning when we recall that white voters turned out in unusually high numbers, and that two-thirds of California's Latinos were noncitizens or not old enough to vote. Poverty and lack of education also had an adverse impact on voting patterns. . . .

Statewide, 72 percent of Latinos voted for Brown and 23 percent for Wilson. . . . Wilson's making illegal immigration the cornerstone of his political resurrection thus seems to have alienated many Latinos who might otherwise have voted for him. . . .

In other races, Chicanos suffered both losses and gains. The defeat of state Senator Art Torres for insurance commissioner dealt a vital blow to Chicano interests. He would have been the first Latino to hold statewide office since 1876. . . .

At the same time, Latinos had their victories. In the state Senate, Richard G. Polanco won in the 22nd District, Hilda Solis in the 24th, Charles Calderón in the 30th, and Rubén Ayala in the 32nd. In the state Assembly, Antonio Villaraigosa won in the 45th, Louis Caldera in the 46th, Diane Martínez in the 49th, Martha Escutía in the 50th, Martin Gallegos in the 57th, Grace Napolitano in the 58th and Joe Baca in the 62nd. . . .

What really went wrong? It is evident that Kathleen Brown's campaign was thrown together hastily and filled with internal dissension. . . . Registration, the key to political success, was expensive and reactive. The Democratic Party was stingy with its money. According to Bob Mulholland, adviser to the Democratic Party, it cost the party $3 to $5 for every new registered voter, and up to $12 to send the voter to the polls. . . . The Latino Vote Project, aimed at registering Latinos in East Los Angeles and the Central Valley, fell far short.

Then there was the strategy for defeating Prop. 187. . . . This strategy recognized that the Latino community could not by itself change the outcome—so it simply ignored Latinos. Hence, with no planning at higher levels the campaign was caught off balance when . . . the governor pounded out last-minute ads for Prop. 187, wrapping himself around the issue. The Democrats just did not have the money or the will to counter these ads or to entice Latinos to vote. . . .

After the election, the Chicano/Latino community was left to regroup and reconstruct. Claremont political scientist Harry Pachon of the Tomás Rivera Center estimated that there were at least 2 million Latinos in California who could qualify for citizenship. The process of gaining citizenship, however, is an arduous one that takes resources. . . . Meanwhile, the Democratic Party had lost much of its moral authority among Chicano and Latino communities, where it had become overwhelmingly evident that immigrant bashing was not just insensitive, but a deadly threat.

In 1995 Republicans gained control of the California legislature, which then enacted legislation that would facilitate passage of an initiative to break up the Los Angeles Unified School District. . . . The splintering of the LAUSD will undoubtedly have a profound impact on Latinos. Smaller districts will not only produce white rule in areas outside the inner city, but also intensify Latino–African American tensions. . . . that were somewhat ameliorated by the need for Blacks and Latinos to form coalitions within the mammoth LAUSD.

Latina Liberation

ELIZABETH MARTÍNEZ

Who and what is a Latina? Ignorance, confusion, and often impassioned controversy make it necessary to begin this commentary with such basic questions. Latinas, like Latinos, are in general a *mestizo* or mixed people. They combine, in varying degrees, indigenous (from pre-Columbian times), European (from Spain's invasion of the Americas), and African roots (from the millions of slaves brought to the Americas, including at least two hundred thousand to Mexico alone). Today

Elizabeth Martínez, "In Pursuit of Latina Liberation," *Signs* 20, no. 4 (Summer 1995): 1019–1028. Reprinted by permission of the University of Chicago Press and the author.

in the United States, Latinas include women whose background links them to some twenty countries and going back one, two, or ten generations.

The term "Latina," used here, is problematic for many people but preferable to the totally Eurocentric label "Hispanic" with its obliteration of our indigenous heritage. "Hispanic" also carries the disadvantage of being a term that did not emerge from the community itself but has been imposed by the dominant society, in particular by its census bureau and other bureaucracies, during the 1970s. (People from Brazil, of course, reject the term "Hispanic" because it replaces Portugal with Spain in their history; this is just one example of the many existing complexities and problems related to terminology. Such distinctions concern not only scholars but also organizers and activists like myself.)

To many of us in the United States, *La Raza* or simply *Raza,* meaning the People, is a better name than either Hispanic or Latina/o; it dates back many years in the community. In the end, the least controversial and most common form of identification is by specific nationality: Mexican, Guatemalan, Colombian, and so forth. "Chicana/o," a term for Mexican Americans, became popular during the 1960s and 1970s movement years for its strong message of pride in one's peoplehood. In essence a political term of affirmation, it continues to be widely used, especially among youth.

Whatever the terminology, Latino peoples in this country have in their historical background a deep experience with colonization, direct or indirect, and mainly by two countries: first, Spain (or Portugal), and later the United States. Among Latina/os, it is Mexicans in what we now call the Southwest who have experienced U.S. colonialism the longest and most directly, with Puerto Ricans not far behind. Almost one-third of today's United States was the home of Mexicans as far back as the 1500s, until Anglos seized it by war in 1848 and treated its population as conquered subjects. (The Mexicans, of course, themselves occupied lands that had been seized by Spain from Native Americans.) This treatment occurred despite the Treaty of Guadalupe Hidalgo, which ended the 1846–48 war and promised respect for the civil and property rights of Mexicans remaining in the Southwest.

The imposition of U.S. rule included taking over millions of acres of Mexican-held land by trickery and violence. Colonization also brought the imposition of Anglo values and institutions at the expense of Mexican culture, including use of the Spanish language. Anglos lynched many Mexicans in ways similar to the lynching of Southern blacks.

In the early 1900s, even as the process of colonization continued, the original Mexican population of the Southwest was greatly increased by an immigration that continues today. This combination of centuries-old roots with relatively recent ones gives the Mexican American people a rich and varied cultural heritage. At the same time, the institutionalized racism imposed by U.S. colonization confronts the entire population to one degree or another, regardless of when any sector arrived.

But we cannot understand all that history simply in terms of victimization: popular resistance is its other face. Resistance, which took the form of organized armed struggle in the Southwest during the last century, continues today in many ways. These include resistance to what we can call the colonized mentality: that process of internalizing belief in the master's superiority and our inferiority. (As a resident of California and a Chicana, I am drawing primarily on the experience of

Mexican/Chicana and Central American women, who predominate among Latinas here.)

Advances by Women

Without attempting to review the history of Latina feminist struggle in these few pages, it should be noted that such a tradition does exist despite the stereotype of the passive Latin woman. The historical landmarks in Mexico are numerous, from the seventeenth-century feminist thinker Sor Juana Inés de La Cruz, a nun, to the first feminist congress of 1911 and the suffrage movement of the 1930s. Cultural mainstays like the powerful pre-Columbian queens and goddesses who ruled alongside male deities and the timeless *curandera* or healer demonstrate the power of women's historical presence. The many women who participated in the Mexican war of independence from Spain (1810–21) and the Mexican Revolution may or may not have been consciously feminist, yet their collective image resonates with strength and courage.

We also note a growing feminism and advances over sexism by Mexican and Chicana women in recent years. During the Chicano liberation movement of 1965–75, open challenges to male supremacy began to be heard from Chicana participants. As sociologist Alma García tells us in "The Development of Chicana Feminist Discourse, 1970–1980" (1990) and as confirmed by my personal experience, the contradiction of encountering male supremacist practices within a movement supposedly fighting for social justice spurred many Chicanas to new consciousness. In the process they made minimal feminist demands. (Women in the African American and Asian American movements of the 1960s and early 1970s were similarly encouraged in a feminist direction by experiencing sexism inside their movements.)

In response, male supremacy hurled two weapons at such Chicanas. The first was the accusation that "you're acting like a white woman" [*agringada*]. In other words, you're a traitor to your people, your culture. This could be devastating to Chicana activists, given that a central goal of the *movimiento* was liberation for brown people from Anglo-imposed domination and its values. In effect, the charge accused women of undermining ethnicity as a unifying force.

The second counterinsurgent weapon was the accusation, "You're being divisive." It could be equally devastating, because unity and the sense of *Raza* as family were so important to the movement. What could be worse, in a hostile society, than to be divisive among your own people? That charge also resonated with certain realities about the women's liberation movement as Chicanas saw it then, including many strong activists. As a participant in New York Radical Women in 1968 (the only Latina member, I believe), I shared the powerful sense of feminist discovery that illuminated those years yet also came to understand why so many Chicanas in the Southwest saw the women's movement then as irrelevant because it was overwhelmingly Anglo and middle-class. Again, like many African American and Native American women, Chicana activists believed that the women's movement saw men as the enemy, a view they could not accept because *Raza* were fighting racism and oppression as a people; men suffered from those same forces. To focus on women's oppression alone and to discount racial and class oppression, as the national women's movement often did, contradicted our perception. This sense of clashing worldviews, which resulted from having such different historical experiences, became a major reason why only a few Chicanas looked for lessons that could be learned or alliances that could be forged with Euramerican feminists.

In the next twenty years a self-defined Chicana feminism flowered, mainly in academia and most visibly among young faculty and graduate students. Under pressure, the National Association for Chicano Studies (NACS) established a women's caucus at its 1985 meeting in Sacramento, California. A lesbian caucus was formalized at its 1992 meeting in Albuquerque, New Mexico, which established an active rejection of homophobia in NACS toward lesbians. Another organization, Murjeres Activas en Letras y Cambio Social (MALCS), emerged in the 1980s as the locus of Latina feminist academics' work for social change that prioritizes mentoring young Chicanas in their scholarly development. Its initial leadership came from Adaljiza Sosa Riddell at the University of California, Davis, and the University of California, Berkeley's Mujeres en Marcha, a graduate student women's group.

At the undergraduate level, signs of growing feminism exist alongside visible hesitation about being labeled "feminist." As elsewhere, symbols and terminology often define the debate; changing the name "Chicano Studies" to "Chicano and Chicana Studies" (or some similarly inclusive phrase, necessitated by a gendered language) has become common on California campuses. At the same time, when I speak about feminism as such to Latina and Latino undergraduate students, I frequently encounter a telling combination of reactions from mixed audiences. Few Chicanas in the audience support my ideas publicly or declare themselves feminist; few if any men are sympathetic, and many air sexist attitudes or make such statements as, "I believe in equal rights for women but not in feminism"; and several Chicanas express agreement after the event, in private. As might be expected, feminist expression intensifies in any all-women's gathering, where Chicana students analyze and grapple with issues of patriarchy and sexist practice.

These developments suggest two realities. First, the women's movement of the 1960s has had positive effects, despite its racial and class biases. The idea of separate women's organizing, once anathema to *Raza* activists and energetically opposed by the men, has become widely accepted. Latina lesbians would have stayed in the closet longer without the national women's movement to encourage them out, I believe. The articulation of concerns common to almost all women, such as health, child care, and reproductive rights, is much more frequent than it was two decades ago.

Our second reality is that Latina feminism, like other forms of feminism, has been sabotaged by backlash forces that rage everywhere. We can thank those forces for making the term "feminist" so unpopular, for making so many Chicanas and Chicanos buy today's bra-burning, man-hating images. In the case of Chicanas, another political trend sometimes strengthens the general assault on feminism: a nationalism that has intensified in direct relation to the racist backlash of the last twenty years and especially since President Reagan's election in 1980. That nationalism, for all its other positive effects, is often accompanied by sexist forms of pride in one's peoplehood that leave women in stereotyped and inferior places. . . .

The present picture, then, can seem almost surreal in its contradictions. One can observe young Chicanas who will unequivocally distance themselves from the word "feminist" but who act in ways that objectively are so very feminist.

Who Says Teenagers Aren't Feminist?

Portents of change can often be found. For example, the California division of the Chicano student organization Movimiento Estudiantil Chicano de Aztlan (MEChA) declined a few years ago to establish a Chicana caucus, despite urging from a women's workshop I attended. It now has such a caucus. More than a few MEChA chapters in California are formally headed by women, which rarely happened ten or fifteen years ago (although women may well have been the real leaders in practice).

In the 1993 hunger strike to win departmental status for Chicana/o studies at the University of California, Los Angeles, half of the strikers were women students. In 1994 women also formed a major part of the hunger strikes for similar causes at the University of California, Santa Barbara, and the University of Colorado in Boulder. In the May 1994 Stanford University hunger strike for Chicana/o studies classes and other demands, the fasters were four Chicanas. Through such experiences, women have often developed new attitudes toward themselves—perhaps the most subversive change of all. . . .

As for the reactions of Latino men on California campuses, contradiction is often written across their faces. The same Chicano student who articulates extremely backward ideas about women may also recognize that change is blowing in the wind and that he cannot oppose it in obvious ways. A day or week devoted to "La Chicana" or Latinas in general is institutionalized on many campuses. Unfortunately, this is less true with respect to gays and lesbians; among Latino college students, homophobia still runs more freely than sexism toward women.

At the level of secondary school in California, one can find an even stronger current of self-conscious feminism (without the word being used) than at the college level. Last year I spoke before six hundred Latina/o high school seniors who had come for "Raza Day" at the University of California, Berkeley, when students visit Cal as a college they might want to attend. My talk was about Latina women's history. I began by describing how, at marches and other demonstrations, you could hear cheers for this man or that—"Viva Zapata! Viva César Chávez!"—by name. "And them," I said, "we hear 'Viva la mujer'—Long live women!" I was going to make the point that it is rare to hear a woman's actual name cheered and to ask why women, unlike men, were celebrated anonymously. But this audience upstaged me with thunderous applause and cheers shaking the auditorium: "Viva la mujer!" Dozens of young women were jumping in their seats.

More examples have accumulated since then, during various encounters with junior high and high school girls. In an era when we are told that feminism does not appeal to young women, the opposite seems true, at least for working-class or lower-middle-class Chicanas in the San Francisco Bay Area, and again if the "F word" is not used. Last April 22, Latina/o and other students from thirty-eight schools in eleven Bay Area towns held walkouts—called blowouts—or similar protests. They demanded educational reforms: more bilingual counselors, more retention programs, no more cutbacks, a relevant multicultural curriculum. At the staging-area rally, during the march downtown, and at the main rally facing City Hall, a good half of the speakers were female. That would have been unthinkable during the 1960s movement years.

During the San Francisco walkouts, it was the women who called loudest and most clearly for unity and peace among their peers rather than gang warfare over "colors." One moment that vividly demonstrated this concern came when the marching crowd was shouting a chant against Governor Pete Wilson's educational cutbacks: "Wilson, Wilson, *a la chingada!* Viva, viva Che Guevara!" I overheard one young woman say to another, "We have to change that chant—the kids from Wilson High will think it's about them." So they started shouting, "Pete Wilson, *a la chingada . . .*" to make sure listeners knew they were trashing the governor and not their peers.

The April 22 blowouts, which formed the third wave of such actions in less than a year, involved five to six hundred high school students in San Francisco and environs plus another thousand in nearby Hayward (just to mention two areas). They had been organized by different groups. Several have a fifty-fifty rule on male-female participation in leadership, handling the press, and so forth. During the summer of 1994 I saw key organizers meet weekly to develop a structure, program, and outreach for ongoing work in 1994–95; they took the fifty-fifty rule seriously.

All this anecdotal evidence leaves many questions, such as how deep the teenage women's feminism runs—for example, does it operate at home in the form of resistance when mothers tell daughters, "Make your brother's bed," as tradition demands? Perhaps, perhaps not. Two Latinas aged thirteen and fourteen who had participated in the blowouts told me that "in this protest we do not feel put down"; "boys have not put down girls for being leaders." On the personal relations level, however, "We get called 'ho' if we have sex but for a boy, it makes him a man." Despite these and other contradictions, the evidence of a Latina feminist consciousness evolving among young women has been too constant, too strong, for me to doubt its existence.

In the provocation and shaping of that consciousness, Chicana artists and writers have had great influence. We would not be as far along as we are today without the beautifully bold writing of lesbian authors Cherríe Moraga, Gloria Anzaldúa, and others or the performance art of lesbian comedians like Marga Gómez and Monica Palacios. We would not be as far along as we are today without the heretical work of painters Yolanda López and Ester Hernández, whose feminist transformations of the Virgin of Guadalupe offer a liberation never before available. We would not be this far along without some biting poems from Sandra Cisneros, the multifaceted work of feminist writer Ana Castillo, and painter Juana Alicia's images of Latina women as strong survivors all. So many more names could be set down; all have nurtured the feminist impulse of young Chicanas, especially those in their upper teens and/or college students.

Working Women Speak Feminist Tongues

Chicana workers and other community women who do not define themselves as feminists but lead objectively feminist lives have been among us since the United States took half of Mexico by war in 1848. Often this feminist practice resulted from their becoming involved in labor organizing and other forms of collective struggle. They have provided the backbone of male-dominated groups but also formed all-women's groups. Today various Latina labor organizations offer shining examples of such activism.

Look at Fuerza Unida (United Force, or Strength), formed in San Antonio, Texas, when Levi Straus laid off eleven hundred garment workers there in 1990 and moved the plant to Costa Rica for cheaper labor. Angered by their experience of lies, broken promises, inadequate compensation, pathetic retraining, and no special aid to workers crippled with carpal tunnel syndrome, the former Chicana and Mexican employees have still not given up five years later. From often being shy or nervous because of their lack of formal, higher education, Fuerza Unida women have become administrators and amateur labor lawyers, steadily developing as leaders. In 1994 they opened an office in San Francisco, home to Levi's international headquarters, and held a three-week "fast for justice" in Levi's face. Fuerza Unida has become an inspiration for women workers everywhere. So has Mujer Obrera (Working Woman), founded in El Paso by garment workers who demanded thousands of dollars in back pay and won some of it with such bold tactics as chaining themselves to their sewing machines.

The garment industry is one arena in which Latinas are superexploited; another is the *maquiladoras,* plants in the U.S.–Mexico border zone where workers assemble everything from bikinis to transistors. Thousands of *maquila* women have been organizing steadily for a decade. The plants' deliberate employment of very young, preferably teenage, Latinas reeks of cynical exploitation. The corporate goal: hire them young, suck out the best of their energy, exploit their inexperience as workers and their fear of angering the boss—then toss them aside like so many rag dolls when they become pregnant, injured, or "troublemakers." But these women are fighting back, often with a clear sense of being a class unto themselves as *maquila* women.

Then look at the first statewide gathering of Latina farmworkers in August 1993 at Fresno, California, where a hundred women came together from all over the state as part of the new Farmworker Women's Leadership Development Project. They discussed not only labor issues like wages, pesticide poisoning, and contracts but also sexual harassment, domestic violence, and sexual discrimination. In those workshops you could sense the women's desire to talk, to tell their stories, along with their feelings of awkwardness and perhaps fear.

At the beginning I was concerned that only the workshop facilitators and other prepared participants would feel able to talk. Wrong: as one spoke, another gathered strength to open up on painful subjects, and then another. Very few outsiders like myself had been allowed in the room, and we were wisely assigned to sit on the outer edges. Millie Treviño is director of the project and a former farmworker herself; a second statewide conference took place in 1994 at Irvine, California, with ongoing discussion of those thorny topics.

Indeed, across this state our moon is rising!

Back to the Word "Feminism"

Like other women of color, most Latinas have rejected any feminism shaped by an exclusively white middle-class perspective that denies the racist, classist oppression of Latino men alongside the women. Such a feminism does not understand how, for a colonized racial/ethnic people, cultural integrity is profoundly interwoven with survival. Or how the family can be seen primarily as a key weapon of self-defense in a hostile world rather than as an oppressive institution. Thus we had to define our own Chicana feminism in the 1970s.

The problem continues today. We still find some Anglo leaders of the pro-choice movement, for example, who defensively refuse to yield control of the agenda or to prioritize the women-of-color perspective that demands reproductive choice in every sense of the term, including adequate prenatal care and freedom from forced sterilization. In a white supremacist world where so many women are of color and poor, it should be obvious that any true feminist must be constantly and passionately antiracist and anticlassist. The times cry out for work by Anglo women that combines resistance to oppression based on race and class as well as on gender.

Today the need to build bridges among all women could not be greater. Xeno-phobic immigrant bashing reaches new and frightening heights as the corporate elite scapegoats working-class people of color—primarily Latina/os and Asians—for the ongoing economic crisis. We would all do well to remember: there is no more exploited, vulnerable person in the United States today than the undocu-mented woman worker of color. Her lack of papers means she can almost never fight back, no matter how vilely she has been abused.

Evidence of that exploitation and abuse has come to public attention sharply in recent years. In March 1993, Latinas presented a full day of testimony in San Fran-cisco about how they had been recruited from their home countries to serve as housekeepers or in similar positions for professional families in the Bay Area. They gave chilling, detailed accounts of being raped on their first day at work; of being kept on duty around the clock as housekeeper, nursemaid, cook, laundress, cleaning woman, baby-sitter, and personal maid; of not being paid for months at a time; of being locked up in their employers' homes; and of being kept ignorant about how to seek help in a strange land, or being too terrorized to try. Their treat-ment in the United States of the late twentieth century is simply barbarous.

Yet even these Latinas are no longer silent, no longer invisible. The moon is rising even as the sky fills with new storm clouds. Time for sharp eyes, open minds, and the tenacity that has stamped our historic Latina heritage.

FURTHER READING

Rodolfo Acuña, *Anything but Mexican* (1996)

Gloria Anzaldúa, *Borderlands/La Frontera* (1987)

T. Coraghessan Boyle, *The Tortilla Curtain* (1995)

Sandra Cisneros, *The House on Mango Street* (1994)

Ted Conover, *Coyotes* (1987)

Rodolfo O. de la Garza et al., *Latino Voices* (1992)

Alma A. García, "The Development of Chicana Feminist Discourse, 1970–1980," *Gender & Society* 3 (June 1989), 217–238

David G. Gutiérrez, *Walls and Mirrors* (1995)

Ramón A. Gutiérrez, "Unraveling America's Hispanic Past: Internal Stratification and Class Boundaries," *Aztlán* 17 (Spring 1986), 79–101.

David E. Hayes-Bautista, Werner O. Schink, and María Hayes-Bautista, "Latinos and the 1992 Los Angeles Riots: A Behavioral Sciences Perspective," *Hispanic Journal of Behavioral Sciences* 15 (November 1993), 427–448

Rubén Martínez, *The Other Side* (1992)

Debbie Nathan, *Women and Other Aliens* (1991)

Alejandro Portes and Robert L. Bach, *Latin Journey* (1985)

Armando Rendon, "Latinos: Breaking the Cycle of Survival to Tackle Global Affairs," in A. Aziz Said, ed., *Ethnicity and U.S. Foreign Policy* (1981)

Luis J. Rodríguez, *Always Running* (1994)

Richard Rodríguez, "Prophets Without Papers," *Harper's* 20 (April 1995), 23

Larry Siems, *Between the Lines* (1992)

Luis A. Urrea, *By the Lake of Sleeping Children* (1996)

———, *Across the Wire* (1993)

Raúl Yzaguirre, "Keys to Hispanic Empowerment," in Roberto E. Villareal and Norma G. Hernández, eds., *Latinos and Political Coalitions* (1991)

Major Problems in American History Series

Titles Currently Available

Boris/Lichtenstein, *Major Problems in the History of American Workers,* 1991 (ISBN 0-669-19925-7)

Brown, *Major Problems in the Era of the American Revolution, 1760–1791,* 1992 (ISBN 0-669-19755-6)

Chambers/Piehler, *Major Problems in American Military History,* 1999 (ISBN 0-669-33538-X)

Chan/Olin, *Major Problems in California History,* 1997 (ISBN 0-669-27588-3)

Chudacoff, *Major Problems in American Urban History,* 1994 (ISBN 0-669-24376-0)

Escott/Goldfield/McMillen/Turner, *Major Problems in the History of the American South,* 2nd ed., 1999
  Volume I: *The Old South* (ISBN 0-395-87139-5)
  Volume II: *The New South* (ISBN 0-395-87140-9)

Fink, *Major Problems in the Gilded Age and the Progressive Era,* 1993 (ISBN 0-669-21680-1)

Gjerde, *Major Problems in American Immigration and Ethnic History,* 1998 (ISBN 0-395-81532-0)

Gordon, *Major Problems in American History, 1920–1945,* 1999 (ISBN 0-395-87074-7)

Griffith, *Major Problems in American History Since 1945,* 2nd ed., 1999 (ISBN 0-395-86850-5)

Hall, *Major Problems in American Constitutional History,* 1992
  Volume I: *From the Colonial Era Through Reconstruction* (ISBN 0-669-21209-1)
  Volume II: *From 1870 to the Present* (ISBN 0-669-21210-5)

Hurtado/Iverson, *Major Problems in American Indian History,* 1994 (ISBN 0-669-27049-0)

Kupperman, *Major Problems in American Colonial History,* 1993 (ISBN 0-669-19922-2)

McMahon, *Major Problems in the History of the Vietnam War,* 2nd ed., 1995 (ISBN 0-669-35252-7)

Merchant, *Major Problems in American Environmental History,* 1993 (ISBN 0-669-24993-9)

Milner/Butler/Lewis, *Major Problems in the History of the American West,* 2nd ed., 1997 (ISBN 0-669-41580-4)

Norton/Alexander, *Major Problems in American Women's History,* 2nd ed., 1996 (ISBN 0-669-35390-6)

Paterson/Merrill, *Major Problems in American Foreign Relations,* 4th ed., 1995
  Volume I: *To 1920* (ISBN 0-669-35077-X)
  Volume II: *Since 1914* (ISBN 0-669-35078-8)

Perman, *Major Problems in the Civil War and Reconstruction,* 2nd ed., 1998 (ISBN 0-395-86849-1)

Riess, *Major Problems in American Sport History,* 1997 (ISBN 0-669-35380-9)

Smith/Clancey, *Major Problems in the History of American Technology,* 1998 (ISBN 0-669-35472-4)

Vargas, *Major Problems in Mexican American History,* 1999 (ISBN 0-395-84555-6)

Wilentz, *Major Problems in the Early Republic, 1787–1848,* 1992 (ISBN 0-669-24332-9)

CPSIA information can be obtained
at www.ICGtesting.com
Printed in the USA
FFOW03n1653190115
10410FF